What users of the TEN WEEKS program are saying:

"This is deep important work. The TEN WEEKS process approaches money from a place that honors the whole person and appreciates our individual uniqueness. It gives us permission to discover who we are and to lead lives that are consistent with our deepest values, hopes and dreams." —*Jeff, California*

"My wife and I are very inspired by this book. It is thought provoking and soul searching. We find ourselves reflecting on the important things the author brings to our attention such as living authentically by being in touch with our creative imagination, and our children!"

"The technical process side (engaging Quicken) is of significant value but the worksheets and resulting discussions are the key for us."

"The flow of the book is a very personal journal by the author—what has influenced, inspired, disappointed and motivated him. I'm a 'doer'—I find myself wanting to get on with the transactions—but am brought to my senses by the worksheets. I then sit and reflect on what the author has shared of his personal journey, then on mine. That naturally leads me to what I am inspired to do now. Very powerful." —*Brian, Colorado*

"I felt very relieved to read that Week Three, Worksheet A was to identify who has the loudest voice in my head over money—the Critic, Child, or Adult. Until I read that, I wasn't aware of the tension I was holding for all the 'shoulds' that I have concerning money. It relieved a lot of guilt and shame…The challenge is to hear the still, small voice with all that noise going on."

"Grounding gives me the space for those creative moments to come into my life. It is the space where no 'critic' is allowed."

"Doing the detailed budget helps us to see 'reality as it is'. Authenticity is living in reality. Seeing our finances in this detail, I realize that we are in a financial state of grace in which we can live our values and fulfill our real needs and do our soul work." —*Katherine, Colorado*

"It takes some time and effort to organize and collect all the documents for the 'My Documents' notebook, but there is a great sense of relief and accomplishment upon completing the task. It puts all your important documents in one place, which gives me peace of mind knowing my wife and son would have an easy reference if something were to happen to me."

"Answering the personal questions about my ideas on money, finance, and goals was revealing and somewhat painful. It is never easy to face ones shortcomings. I felt that this exercise was constructive rather than destructive." —*Ken, Colorado*

Ten Weeks to Financial Awakening

A Guidebook to the Creation of Your Own Financial Plan using Quicken® Software

BY
Paul Lemon, CPA, CFP™

Beaver's Pond Press, Inc.
Edina Minnesota

Quicken 2004 Deluxe screen shots © 2003 Intuit, Inc. All rights reserved. Used by permission. Quicken is a registered trademark of Intuit, Inc.

ISBN 1-59298-025-2

Library of Congress Catalog Number: 2003111546

Printed in the United States of America

First Printing: September 2003

06 05 04 03   6 5 4 3 2 1

Beaver's Pond Press, Inc.

7104 Ohms Lane, Suite 216
Edina, MN 55439
(952) 829-8818
www.beaverspondpress.com

to order, visit *www.tenweeks.com* or *www.BookHouseFulfillment.com* or call 1-800-901-3480. Reseller discounts available.

Cover art © Chase Swift / Corbis.

To my Mom, Laura ('Lollie') Lemon,
who taught me how to work
and honor my Spirit nature.

TABLE OF CONTENTS

Ten Weeks to Financial Awakening

Computer System Requirements

This book includes video instruction CDs that will guide you through the use of Quicken® Deluxe in implementing the Ten Weeks Program on a step-by-step basis. These CDs were developed using this version of Quicken®, running under Microsoft Windows. Minimum System requirements for viewing these CDs on your computer are:

➤ Pentium II 200 MHz or higher recommended

➤ Windows 95, 98, ME, NT4, 2000, or XP

➤ 32 MB or more of installed RAM

TEN WEEKS TO FINANCIAL AWAKENING

Book and CD Set
Statement as to Liability

Because use of this PRODUCT (including information contained in this publication and the related software) is beyond the control of the distributor, Integrated Financial Planning, PC ("IFP"), the user assumes all responsibility for results of the use of the product, and it is sold subject to the following conditions:

Disclaimer. To the extent allowed by local law, the PRODUCT is provided "AS IS" without warranties or conditions of any kind, whether oral or written, express or implied. IFP specifically disclaims any implied warranties or conditions including, but not limited to, merchantability, satisfactory quality, noninfringement and fitness for a particular purpose. Some jurisdictions do not allow exclusions of implied warranties or conditions, so the above exclusion may not apply in some specific circumstances.

Limitation of liability. Except to the extent prohibited by local law, in no event will IFP or its subsidiaries, affiliates, or suppliers be liable for direct, special, incidental, consequential, or other damages (including lost profit, lost data, or downtime costs), arising out of the use, inability to use, or the results of use of the PRODUCT, even if advised of the possibility of such damages. Use of the PRODUCT is entirely at the user's own risk. Should any portion of the PRODUCT prove defective, user assumes the entire cost of all service, repair, or correction. Some jurisdictions do not allow the exclusion or limitation of liability for incidental or consequential damages, so the above limitation may not apply in some specific circumstances. Any liability, consequential or otherwise, will be limited to replacement of the PRODUCT or to an amount equal to that paid for the PRODUCT.

Please remember that different types of investments involve varying degrees of risk. Therefore, there can be no assurance that the future performance of any type of investment, investment strategy, style, system, or product made reference to in this book will be profitable or equal historical or anticipated performance level(s), or be appropriate for your personal situation. Moreover, you should not assume that any discussion or information contained in this book serves as the receipt of, or as a substitute for, personalized investment advice from Paul Lemon, CPA, CFP or IFP. To the extent that a reader has any questions regarding the applicability of any specific issue discussed in this book to his/her individual situation, he/she is encouraged to consult with the professional advisor of his/her choosing.

FOREWORD

If you think that life is guided only by numbers, then Paul Lemon's financial life planning guidebook, TEN WEEKS TO FINANCIAL AWAKENING, is not for you. My thirty-five years of working with clients has proven that it is the qualitative part of life that transcends the enormous anxieties that surround money. If those unresolved anxieties persist, then you never achieve a higher level of freedom and independence in your life.

Too many people end up being a slave to their money. Money needs to be subordinated to more meaningful values in life. It takes commitment to keep money in its place. Time and again clients have proven that when money is treated as a means and not an end, their lives are more fulfilling.

To do effective financial planning you simply need to consistently apply the Socratic principle "Know Thyself". While you may have to neutralize Wall Street's cry for immediate gratification by doing Paul's ten-week program, you will illuminate the dark corners of your financial life. His process helps you to successfully integrate financial planning issues into your entire life.

We often talk about the whole being the sum of the parts and miss the most important point. It is the interaction between these parts that brings true meaning to the whole. It isn't just paying the bills or making investments or getting the right amount of insurance that completes the questions of your financial life. Paul helps you answer the "How" questions and then he raises some of the "Why" questions only you can answer. When you answer them, money will begin taking it's rightful place as your life continues to unfold with greater understanding.

I encourage you to not be intimidated by the amount of work this process will take. Think about the times of your life when you had the biggest payoffs. Maybe you were lucky once or twice but chances are you put in a lot of hard work for that big payoff.

Committing to ten weeks with Paul's process will result in a big payoff. You'll not only find answers to the financial puzzle, but you will find it provides a roadmap to peace, understanding and success in the 'wholeness' of your life.

—Vern C. Hayden, CFP™

President, Hayden Financial Group, LLC

Author of *Getting An Investing Game Plan: Creating It…Working It…Winning It* (John Wiley & Sons, Inc., March, 2003)

Current Member of the Board of Directors, College for Financial Planning

Founding Chairman, National Endowment for Financial Education

What You Will Need to Complete
Ten Weeks to Financial Awakening

A sense of need

If you were satisfied with your life and the way you interact with money, then you wouldn't have purchased a book like this in the first place!

The Introduction and Sections One and Two will help clarify some of the goals of the Program and how they relate to the suffering most of us experience when it comes to money and personal finance.

A realistic set of expectations

Section Two clarifies what will be involved in completing the Program. It provides you with the opportunity to schedule the 60–120 hours you will need for a genuine transformation with money.

If you are completing the Program with a spouse or partner, please refer to *Weeks One & Two Appendix B* and read the "Partner Work" section. This will help alleviate fears you may have about one of you not being able to commit to more than just reading the book and completing the worksheets.

If you choose to use this Program to complete your personalized financial plan (Your Authentic Money Guide), as opposed to just reading the book to consider its philosophy about money, you will need patience to follow carefully the book's instructions. It will be several weeks before you can begin using Quicken® to manage your finances—it takes time to set up downloads and input your financial information.

Careful attention to the Program is essential in avoiding serious financial errors. The reason for the detailed and thorough financial explanations and screen-by-screen TEN WEEKS CD is to prevent you from making input errors into Quicken® that could result in misleading financial projections.

BY FOLLOWING THE "TEN WEEKS" PROGRAM, EACH USER ACCEPTS FULL RESPONSIBILITY FOR THE FINANCIAL RAMIFICATIONS OF USING THE PROGRAM.

Financially, you will be investing approximately $190 by the time you purchase the TEN WEEKS book, Quicken® program, office supplies, and file organization system. That may seem like a lot until you realize an unbiased financial plan would cost you ten to thirty times that much and not provide you with a day-to-day financial management system!

Current Version of Quicken® Deluxe for Windows

Order the version of Quicken® Deluxe printed on the CDs with your book if you do not already have it. The price for the program should vary between $40 and $60, depending on the rebates offered by various vendors. The following sites are listed here for your convenience:

➤ *www.officedepot.com*

➤ *www.amazon.com*

➤ *www.intuit.com*

Note: This version of TEN WEEKS TO FINANCIAL AWAKENING is compatible only with Windows operating systems.

The Ten Weeks to Financial Awakening Worksheet Workbook

If you are completing the Program with a spouse/partner, it is important that each of you completes the worksheets. To avoid making copies of all those pages, you can simply purchase the companion Worksheet Workbook for $7.95 + shipping and handling. Order from *www.tenweeks.com*

Office supplies

You will need some office supplies to help keep your financial journey organized. Since it will take a few days to get to the point in the book where you'll need these items, may I suggest that you go to *www.officedepot.com* and order the items listed in this section. Scan the list for items you may already own and cross them out.

A file organization system

Order the Financial Planning Organizer Kit described below unless you already have a meticulous filing system in place that works for you.

A sense of optimism that this Program can work

The TEN WEEKS TO FINANCIAL AWAKENING PROGRAM is based on the premise that we all long to live authentically. That capability is within each one of us. I believe giving money our careful attention is the best tool to establish a whole new way of living in accordance with our Authentic Self.

OFFICE SUPPLY SHOPPING CART

- ❑ Three—two-inch three-ring binders (item # 492942, $8.39 each)
- ❑ Two—packets of eight extra-wide big tab insertable dividers (item # 349341, $1.89 each)
- ❑ One—packet of 12 binder dividers—monthly tabs (item # 313395, $3.89)
- ❑ Three—packets of five extra wide big tab insertable dividers (item # 349350, $1.49)
- ❑ One—multi-page capacity sheet protectors—25-pack (item # 500587, $5.49)
- ❑ One—three-hole paper punch (item # 427151, $7.49 each)
- ❑ One—Perma heavy-duty storage box (item # 403840, $9.99/set of three boxes)
- ❑ One—hanging file folders, letter size (item # 810994, $4.29/each)
- ❑ One—box of Smead manilla files, letter size (item # 300251, $11.29 for box of 100 files)

Reclaiming your Authenticity is worth so much more than the 60–120 hours this Program asks of you. You are worth this investment!

The total cost of the above items (as of June 28, 2003), before shipping and sales tax, at *www.officedepot.com* is $75.86. The easiest way to place your order is under "Shopping Tools." Select "Order by Item Number."

This investment will benefit you for years to come in the hundreds of hours you will save in unnecessary paperwork.

There is one other item you will need to order now:

Order the Homefile *Financial Planning Organizer Kit* from Homefile Fulfillment Center, *www.homefile.net*. Don't be frustrated if it takes time to arrive.

The Financial Planning Organizer Kit is the system I recommend as a *must have*. It includes 24 preprinted file divider cards (which list what to save and how long to save it) and a Quick-File index with over 200 items. There is also a handbook that gives you a place to record critical personal information, as well as explains all the ins and outs of filing and record-retention. Item #204

Cost: $24.95 + $5.46 S&H = $30.41

I have arranged for a $5.00 mail-in rebate with the publishers of the *Financial Planning Organizer Kit*. Order the kit at full price from *www.homefile.net* and then mail in the attached coupon for your rebate.

You have taken a courageous first step toward starting this Program!

Remember that nothing in your financial past or future matters. Each day you receive a new opportunity to take one more step toward Awakening—and each of those individual steps is how you will progress on this journey for which you were born!

Give yourself what may be the greatest gift you will ever receive—the chance to live in alignment with your Authentic Self, using money as your ally. Begin this exciting journey now—order your supplies and start reading!

Be Sure to Register for Program Support & the Ten Weeks Newsletter

Get the most out of your TEN WEEKS financial planning investment—Register on the **TEN WEEKS TO FINANCIAL PLANNING website (*www.tenweeks.com*, or send in this card)** and receive:

Information on valuable product updates

Our Monthly Newsletter filled with:

➤ Free Financial Planning Assistance

➤ Program Questions Answered

➤ TEN WEEKS Events Calendar

Just complete your personal information to the right.

Obtain a $5 rebate on your purchase of the HOME-FILE *Financial Planning Organizer Kit!*

➤ Enclose a copy of your proof of purchase, and mail this and the card to the address on the back of the card.

(An original rebate request card is required for this rebate request to be processed, so please don't send in a copy of this card.)

Just complete your personal information to the right.

REGISTER FOR TEN WEEKS PROGRAM SUPPORT & NEWSLETTER

Please fill-in this form to join the TEN WEEKS TO FINANCIAL AWAKENING support community. We will keep you posted via our monthly Email newsletter on advances in the TEN WEEKS **Program**, events in your area, and personal financial planning and Soul Journey comments from Paul Lemon.

_____
Name

_____
Address

_____   _____   _____
City,   State   ZIP

_____   _____
Country   email address

_____   _____
Date/Location of Ten Weeks Purchase   Current Version of Quicken® Used

Your information will not be shared with other parties for any reason.
You may remove yourself from the Newsletter list at any time.

OBTAIN A $5 REBATE ON YOUR PURCHASE OF THE HOMEFILE *Financial Planning Organizer Kit!*

Please fill-in this form to receive your *TEN WEEKS User Rebate* from HOMEFILE PUBLISHING, Inc.

(An original rebate request card is required for this rebate request to be processed, so please don't send in a copy of this card.)

_____
Name

_____
Address

_____   _____   _____
City   State   ZIP

_____   _____
Country   Daytime Phone Number

_____   _____
Date/Location of Ten Weeks Purchase   Current Version of Quicken® Used

Your information will not be shared with other parties for any reason.

Ten Weeks Support
269 North Road
Durango, CO 81303

HOMEFILE Publishing, Inc.
1290 Bay Dale Drive, Suite 355
Arnold, MD 21012

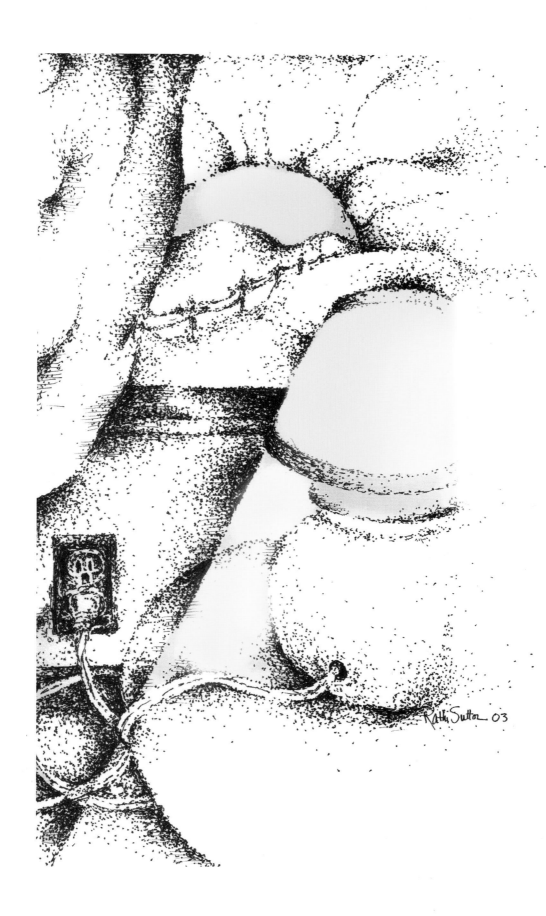

INTRODUCTION

I am a lucky man. I love my life, my family, the work I do, and the clients I serve.

Life is not perfect in the sense that I experience no suffering or have no problems. I hold the challenges and specific details of my life as opportunities for Awakening.

My mother's suicide and the ensuing turmoil led me into the desert on a vision quest. After days alone in intense quiet, I heard something deep and vital within me speak. A passage from David Whyte's poem, **All the True Vows** captures that moment:

ALL THE TRUE VOWS

Remember,
in this place
no one can hear you

and out of the silence
you can make a promise
it will kill you to break,

that way you'll find
what is real and what is not.

I know what I am saying.
Time almost forsook me
and I looked again.

Seeing my reflection
I broke a promise
and spoke
for the first time
after all these years

in my own voice,

before it was too late
to turn my face again.

After my vision quest, I realized that there was a longing in me for something different from that which I had been working hard all my life to attain. Beneath all my desperate strivings for security, success, and significance was "my own voice." Even though I had abandoned it long ago, that voice was still capable of speaking.

When I honored my life as something more than all the hats I wore, I saw how money—rather than an end unto itself—was simply a means to help me see when I was or was not living in alignment with my Authentic Voice.

I had served thousands of clients as a tax and financial advisor up to that point. I had done my best to solve their financial problems. Despite my good intentions and technically competent advice, I was frustrated that so many of my clients were trapped in money habits that kept them in bondage to ongoing uneasiness, worry, and suffering in their lives. I knew there had to be something I was missing. I constantly refined the system I used to guide my clients through a comprehensive financial planning process. I knew that there had to be a way that I could help my clients find more happiness and less suffering in their financial lives.

I wanted to help my clients discover that increasing their happiness and reducing their stress would not be achieved by merely acquiring more money or solving a concern they had about their finances. I wanted to help them understand that, regardless of where they were on their own journeys in life, that their relationship with money bore a critical impact on their living in a manner true to themselves.

I appreciate how author Bo Lozoff expresses the basic reason for our unhappiness:

"The gap between our sincere values and our actual behavior is the source of all self-hatred. And self-hatred is the antithesis of personal happiness... We will not find happiness while we are divided between the two."

—It's A Meaningful Life: It Just Takes Practice

After the two-week vision quest, I knew how I had to change my financial planning practice. What I didn't know, though, was if these changes might scare away all 150 of my clients and force me back into the desert to live!

I was apprehensive when I handed out poetry at my next client meetings! But by their responses, and the responses of many others who followed, it became obvious to me that, deep down, most of us

"Money is God in action."
—Raymond Charles Barker

"It is neither wealth nor splendor, but tranquility and occupation, which give happiness."
—Thomas Jefferson

are seeking the same thing—a connection to our own Authentic Voice and the happiness of expressing it in our lives.

Real happiness begins with real honesty. An honest assessment of the role we have assigned to money can reveal so much to us about what we most genuinely desire, and that which we most fear. Such an assessment can have a transformative impact on our misperception that more money will solve all our worries. Coming to consciousness about our relationship to money can help us bring our actual behaviors into a natural, easy alignment with our deepest values.

TEN WEEKS TO FINANCIAL AWAKENING offers a down-to-earth guide that will gently lead you, step by step, through such an assessment, and help you transform your money behaviors from frustrating, fear-based habits into conscious acts of embodiment of your unique self. Most of us are sick and tired of our dance of suffering with money and are ready for a transformation.

During my initial meeting with prospective clients, I warn them that the simple creation of a financial plan cannot provide them with a guarantee of financial security. Most people, though a bit uneasy, will express surface agreement with this until I go on to a second warning. I disclose that they may be challenged to surrender the idea that there is such a concept as financial security at all! Upon hitting my prospective clients with such a disclosure, a few of the braver souls blurt it out, "Well, why in the world would we pay you $5,000 to remind us that there's no point in planning responsibly for our future?!"

"Because," I usually respond, "it's only when you give money the attention it deserves that you can actually see what money can and cannot do. It's only then that you experience some peace of mind and begin to stop resisting the inherent uncertainty of life. You feel a sense of relief that you have done what you can, and that's as good as it gets—money no longer needs to consume your precious life energy."

Oftentimes I'll pull out Jacob Needleman's classic, "Money and the Meaning of Life," and read my unsuspecting prospective clients these words:

> In order to obtain the most serious good of life it is necessary to give exactly the right amount of attention to the aspect of life represented by money. For, if we do not give sufficient attention to what is secondary in life, then, sooner or later, what is secondary will take all our attention and leave us no energy or time to pursue what is most essential.

"I bow to the ancestors. They came for their lessons; I've come for mine."

—Sy Safransky

Deep down we all want to "obtain the most serious good of life." We forget what that really means to us, when so many voices tell us that we need what they have in order to be happy. It is time to change all that by slowing down to notice what money shows us about ourselves and how it can actually help us pursue what we believe is most essential.

To my surprise, most prospective clients decide to engage with me in this exciting journey, despite all my efforts to shatter the standard reasons to embark upon a financial plan. I hope that you, too, will give yourself the gift of that choice through the pages of this book over the next 10 weeks.

My intent is that these pages beckon you to speak "in your own voice." Your relationship with money holds a critical key to that Voice, of all your treasures, the most precious.

—Paul Lemon

"Life shrinks or expands in proportion to one's courage."

—*Anaïs Nin,*

SECTION ONE

The Lesson from Electricity: Wally's Electrical Diagram

Section One introduces you to the principle of "grounding." You will also experience the benefits of "staying" rather than "leaving" when things get uncomfortable. These attitudes will serve as a foundation for an entirely new relationship with money and the financial details of your life!

PREFACE

This book is about your relationship with money. If you have the courage to admit that there is more suffering and worry than joy and peace in your "money life," and if you want straight answers to your financial concerns, then you are in the right place.

TEN WEEKS TO FINANCIAL AWAKENING will show you how to cultivate financial awakening through the process of "money groundedness." Hang on, you're standing at the threshold of a whole new way of living, and the ride won't be what you might expect!

You will be shown how to slow down and notice what is actually happening right now in your money life. In the process, you will discover what need(s) you are trying to meet with money. It is time that

> *"The real voyage of discovery consists not in seeking new lands but in seeing with new eyes."*
>
> —*Marcel Proust*

you are supported with a new approach to money rather than influenced by the predominant wisdom of our society that says you must go faster and work harder to make more money and that more money gives you the freedom to ensure your happiness.

FEELINGS FIRST—THEN THE "FACTS"

TEN WEEKS TO FINANCIAL AWAKENING takes a different approach to money and finances than what you may be used to. The "number crunching" comes in the TEN WEEKS CD and Money Attention Page (MAP) section of the book, while the body of each chapter explores what lies beneath the surface of a particular money concern with which you may be dealing. The attention you give to the insights you garner from this material will infuse the weekly Quicken® exercises with a sense of purpose and anticipation that you have yet to equate with financial management.

Each of you can experience genuine freedom and happiness, using money as a valuable teacher. May the following pages serve as a companion and encouragement to you in this exciting journey of giving money your attention rather than your energy; leading to an Awakening of your slumbering Authenticity.

> *"The breeze at dawn*
> *Has secrets to tell you.*
> *Don't go back to sleep."*
>
> —*Rumi*

WALLY'S ELECTRICAL DIAGRAM

A Broken Fan

Six years ago on a hot summer day, I was in my basement workshop trying to sort through the accumulation of abandoned projects piled on my workbench. I was determined to reclaim my workbench for work. Before I could get serious about tackling this new project, however, I had to do something about the unbearable heat in the room! Amongst the clutter, I noticed a small room fan. I plugged in the fan, but no cooling breeze blew on my sweaty brow.

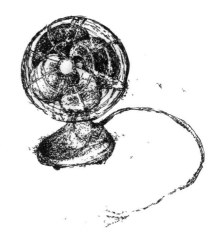

I smiled at the broken fan. On this blistering hot summer day, the fan had rescued me from my stalwart resolution to clean up the mess in my shop. Ah procrastination, my first love. I did, albeit briefly, entertain the notion of tearing the fan apart and attempting to fix it myself, but then I noticed the remnants of my old bread machine. I remembered that the bread machine, now permanently disabled, had been a project I knew I could fix in a jiffy. So, rather than fixing the fan and cleaning up the mess, I decided to take the fan to my neighbor, a handy man, and tackle the workbench another day.

I picked up the fan and resolutely started down the driveway. My wife, Katherine, watched me emerge from the shop with her long lost fan in hand. She stood up from her gardening, and said, "Oh, did you finally fix that old fan?"

"No, I'm taking it over to Wally's. See you later."

My neighbor, Wally, a retired construction engineer, had recently opened up the Mend-it Man, a small home repair shop in his garage. Since the opening of his business, I had beat a dusty path to Wally's shop with things that needed his attention. Katherine and Wally's wife, Jane, enjoyed collaborating on how to get their flower gardens to survive in our high desert climate.

"No need to knock; come on in," was the familiar response to a knock on the shop door. "It's me again, Wally. Do you have a minute to take a look at this worthless old fan?"

"It's darn hot. In fact, I was just thinking about getting a cold one. Care to join me?" Wally replied.

We walked into the house and Wally popped open a frosty beer for each of us. After catching up on some of the neighborhood gossip, we headed to Wally's shop. Wally plugged in the fan and flipped the switch, and then he started to poke at a wire with some probes from an electrical meter. He quickly unplugged the fan. "Sure is a good thing you didn't leave this thing plugged in. It could have caused quite a fire!"

"The breaker would flip before that happened—wouldn't it?"

"When there's an overload or 'short circuit,' the breakers will stop what could be a dangerous flow of electricity. But most folks don't realize that breakers don't work when there's some small escape of power from either the 'hot' or the 'ground' wire. Here, feel how hot this section of cord is!"

I was shocked to feel how warm the fan cord had become in just a few seconds. "This really could have set my shop and our whole house on fire!"

"Exactly." Wally showed me a small bite mark on the cord. Gracey, a springer spaniel puppy, had joined our family about the same time the fan went on the fritz.

Wally stripped the wires and wrapped them with new insulating tape. He then hooked up a voltage meter to the repaired cord to make sure everything was working. He flipped the switch and a cool breeze filled the muggy shop.

I was about ready to head back up the driveway to show Katherine how I had turned over a new leaf and was no longer the world's greatest procrastinator. A brief flashback to my messy workshop, however, prompted a question to Wally that would grant me a brief reprieve. It was too much to expect a complete recovery from this postponement affliction in just one day!

> *"Give light, and the darkness will disappear of itself."*
>
> —Desiderius Erasmus

"I always thought that the ground wire was neutral. I guess I'd understand the severity of Gracey's bite if it had exposed the hot wire. My way of thinking is that 'neutral' is synonymous with 'nothing.' Why did the ground wire damage result in such an electrical hazard?" I asked him.

"That's a valid question and makes a lot of common sense," explained Wally. "A better name for this neutral wire would actually be the positive wire. In reality, the ground wire does carry an electrical charge that is essential for electricity to function properly. When Gracey nicked the ground wire with her teeth, she created what is technically known as an 'arc fault'—a low-level short, or an electrical 'leak.' Think of it like the hole in my sprinkler hose that I discovered last month after getting my water bill.

"If you don't have to get right back, I could draw you a simple little diagram that may help explain some of this."

"Why not," I replied. "It's clear that there are a few 'shorts' in my understanding of electricity!"

The Diagram

Wally began to sketch on a pad of drafting paper with a mechanical pen. The diagram seemed to come to life as his pencil skimmed the paper. As he sketched, he explained what each piece of the electrical system meant. When he finished, he slid the diagram toward me.

Before I looked at it, I glanced at my watch. I had been with Wally for over an hour. I had completely lost track of time.

WALLY'S ELECTRICAL DIAGRAM

LEGEND
1. Sun
2. Solar Panel
3. Transformers
4. Transmission lines ("Positive" and "Negative")
5. Circuit Breaker
6a. 12A wire size
6b. 5A wire size
7. Switch Boxes
8. Ground Wire
9. Outlets or "Load"

(−) Ground Wire

(+) Positive Wire

Ground Wire Switch

WC Birza

"So," Wally continued, "when you combine all those pieces, you end up with a safe and reliable electrical system that serves its users' needs. Does that help you see how critical that ground wire is in getting your fan to work and in keeping electricity safe?"

"It sure does," I said. "I just noticed what time it is. I better get on home or Katherine'll have my hide. Do you mind if I take this diagram as proof that we didn't just sit around and drink beer?"

"With one caveat…you are not allowed to rewire your house tonight, OK?"

"No worries there! If you hadn't moved in next door, there's a good chance we'd be looking at this fan as fire fighters' Exhibit One! Thanks a million!"

I picked up my fan and the electrical diagram and was headed out the door when Wally said: ***Paul, don't underestimate the importance of being grounded!***

Wally's Parting Words

I plugged in the fan and stood there soaking in the cool breeze. Wally's last words, "Don't underestimate the importance of being grounded," seemed to mix with the cool air.

"Paul, dinner's ready. What took so long?" Katherine's voice interrupted my introspection, and I headed for the stairs.

"Oh, you know Wally. We got into a bit of a discussion."

As Katherine and I ate dinner, I tried to convey what had gone on that afternoon with Wally. I pulled out Wally's diagram and Katherine patiently listened to my version of that afternoon's Electricity 101 class.

When I finished my plate, I sat back and said, "As I left, Wally said something that I just can't seem to get out of my mind: 'Don't underestimate the importance of being grounded.' I know Gracey damaged the ground wire and that its short, I mean *arc fault*, prevented the fan from working. It's clear that little tiny problem could have burned down our whole house, but do you have any clue as to why he would emphasize the ground wire over tapping into the power source or turning on the switch or matching wire and breaker size? It seems like each of those things is critical in the safe delivery of power to its end use."

Katherine studied the electrical diagram.

"If the building of a bridge does not enrich the awareness of those who work on it, then that bridge ought not to be built."

—*Frantz Fanon*

"Wally's illustration routes the ground wire through this Ground Wire Switch," she said, matter-of-factly. "Isn't that what this *GW* means?"

"Yes, as far as I can remember."

"Well, nothing works unless the ground wire finishes the electrical loop. Correct me if I'm wrong, but didn't Wally say that the ground wire in a two-wire system is the neutral wire that actually communicates with the energy source about what's really going on throughout the system? The hot wire is full of electricity, but it can only flow if someone's turned on a switch and that usage is communicated via the ground wire."

Katherine paused for a second and then spoke as if a light had gone on in her understanding, "I think what Wally was getting at when he said, 'Don't underestimate the importance of being grounded' is that we need that *neutral place* where we can notice what is really happening and what *power is being used,* so to speak. It makes sense that Wally would emphasize this life lesson, since most of us are so busy and preoccupied. It seems we have trouble grounding."

"That's it!" I exclaimed. "When the lights are out I'm constantly looking for what's wrong with the power source. It's hard to remember how important it is to slow down long enough to notice that I've flipped the ground wire switch 'off'!"

"Don't mention it, Honey! It's just easier for women to understand these more advanced concepts!" Katherine laughed as she walked behind me, placing her hands over my eyes.

"Now you see it, now you don't," she said as she alternately covered then uncovered my eyes.

Her little game produced an accurate analogy for how my understanding had shifted in the course of the past several hours. Maybe this was one of those "Aha!" revelations that had potential to change the way I saw life. I began to feel a bit uneasy because I wasn't quite sure of the consequences this new discovery might have on my nice predictable world.

Turning out the light that night, I was still thinking about what Wally and Katherine had helped me see. What would it mean to be grounded in my life—to just be still and notice? It was such a foreign concept that I tossed and turned, struggling to reduce it to yet another "five-step process." I finally drifted off to sleep. In my dreams, the refreshing breeze of the repaired fan helped calm my busy mind.

"What a disappointment I am: When I'm working, because I think I could be working harder, and when I work so hard I ignore the beauty all around me; when I don't meditate, because I think I'm too busy, and when I do meditate, because I get lost in my busy mind. Today, before doing any of my practices, or not doing them, or agonizing over whether I should or shouldn't do them, can I just pause for a moment? Can I remember that I don't have to be perfect to experience a moment of perfect love?"

—*Sy Safransky*

Staying vs. Leaving

The next morning, rather than my usual routine of springing out of bed, I turned off the alarm and returned to my dreams. When I finally got up, it seemed as if something had shifted within me. I felt at ease, relaxed, and more importantly, below the surface of these uncommon feelings was a rare sense of permission that said I could stay relaxed rather than dive into my endless to-do list.

"It all comes back to this—just let it all be. Step over here where it is cool, out of the battle. Why not give it a try? Do you dare?"

—Achaan Chah

Katherine and I took Gracey on a leisurely walk and marveled at the beauty around our home. Why had it been so hard for me to appreciate what was right in front of me?!

I was down at the office, bright and early Monday morning, working on a financial plan for one of my clients. What wasn't typical was the constant background message rolling around in my head: *Don't underestimate the importance of being grounded!* My conversation with Katherine about those words Wally had spoken just two days earlier made it clear that quiet and reflection were necessary for the "lights to come on."

As I looked down at my spreadsheets, I realized that all the financial projections I created for my clients could simply be yet another desperate attempt to fix the uncertainty of life. I had never been one for writing poetry, but I paused and tried to capture my feelings around my compulsion to fix things. I smiled as I noticed that the title I had written was so similar to the name of Wally's business, The Mend-it Man!

THE FIX-IT MAN

What do I do
with this broken
chair that no longer
holds me up?

Maybe I'll smash
it to splinters
and throw it
in my dumpster.

I'll get another—
and sit in it.
Sitting will be better then—
an easy fix.

What do I do
with this problem
child that won't
keep the rules?

Maybe I'll make it
real clear—
"As long as you live here
you'll do it my way.

"And if you're good
and stop complicating my life
you can have that new car—
I'll fix your problem"—and mine, too.

What do I do
with this ache inside
that disrupts my sleep
almost every night?

Maybe I'll buy some
sleeping pills and
take a few right after
my nightcap.

I'll wake up refreshed
and go straight to work
to lay off 10 workers—
those faltering profits—easily fixed.

What do I do
with my nagging wife,
my pathetic portfolio,
my feeble old parents…?

Just give me
some time.
I'm the Fix-it Man.

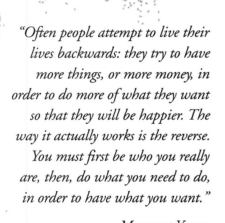

Could it be that I actually perpetuated my client's suffering by failing to examine the traditional "wisdom" that advocated fixing people's discomforts with good financial advice? This was a painful realization. Out of this regret, however, began to emerge some hope. It occurred to me that the financial planning process could also be used to help examine what we really longed for in life and ground us to the reality of our lives. The *solution* all of a sudden became less important than the *process*! Was it possible that the process of wandering the back roads of our experience with money could result in a state of happiness? If so, it meant a radical shift from the "interstate" approach of offering only logical money and financial analysis to my financially distressed clients. For me, was it possible to make a shift into a more contended relationship with money if I slowed down long enough to see what it was I was really asking it to do in my life?

I didn't want to miss what I was beginning to understand, so I wrote:

> **Groundedness is being still enough to notice what need I am longing to satisfy at this current moment. If I want happiness in my life, I need to learn to resist fixing things that call, not for a fix, but for a deeper look.**

I had to admit it wasn't just my clients who were ungrounded—disconnected—from a power source. "Money Mania" seemed a much better description of the way that I interacted with money in my life, rather than "Money Groundedness."

Just as the ungrounded fan threatened our entire home, my ignorance of the real lessons of money—quietly waiting beneath the layers of my years of financial training and ideas about what financial success looked like—threatened my ability to ever find the genuine happiness and contentment for which I searched.

Rather than noticing *what is* with my financial circumstances and the feelings that come up with that experience, I saw how I had been programmed to constantly *improve* my circumstances. I thought the things that frustrated me, and most of my clients, would vanish when I "saved a little more," "made a better investment return," "got the kids through college," or "retired and finally had time to rest."

"Often people attempt to live their lives backwards: they try to have more things, or more money, in order to do more of what they want so that they will be happier. The way it actually works is the reverse. You must first be who you really are, then, do what you need to do, in order to have what you want."

—Margaret Young

LOOK AROUND

If you try to comprehend air
before breathing it,
you will die.

If you try to understand love
before being held,
you will never feel compassion.

If you insist on bringing God to others
before opening your very small window of life,
you will never have honest friends.

If you try to teach before you learn
or leave before you stay,
you will lose your ability to try.

No matter what anyone promises—
to never feel compassion,
to never have honest friends,
to lose your ability to try—
these are desperate ways to die.

A dog loves the world through its nose.
A fish through its gills.
A bat through its deep sense of blindness.
An eagle through its glide.

And a human life
through its spirit.

—Mark Nepo

It seemed like I had been programmed to "leave" before I "stayed." In my constant attempts to improve my life with financial fixes, I had missed the lessons that were revealing that for which I genuinely longed.

I pondered the consequences of "leaving" before "staying." Mark Nepo's poem says that "leaving" would result in "losing your ability to try." Could it be that staying, or honestly facing what was happening beneath all the noise in life, was at the very core of what it meant to "try"? Was the most genuine expression of effort found in refusing to keep "moving on"? I was ready to try rather than accept my pattern of outcome-oriented choices that kept me on the surface of life.

It was then that I realized that I had been dangerously close to losing the awareness that there was something worth trying for with every ounce of energy I could muster. I had forgotten that it was only through "spirit" that I was able to enter fully into loving life! How miserable Gracey, my springer spaniel, would be if I muzzled her and deprived her of loving the world through her nose. Wouldn't my life be so much richer if I were grounded and noticed the myriad ways in which I fail to honor my need to live authentically, aligned with my spirit?

I caught a glimpse of money's valuable role in translating that very ethereal quest into reality as my eye lingered on a full-page ad in the *Wall Street Journal*. Was I beginning to notice how corporate marketers could easily influence me to purchase the products in their ads? Isn't it my discontent, insecurity, and focus on external fixes that reward their investment of hundreds of thousands of dollars in single-page ads like these? I had looked to those promises to give me a sense of well-being, without much success.

I pulled out Wally's Electrical Diagram for a clue to how I could reestablish the flow of power in my life by staying vs. leaving. Wally's parting words, "Don't forget the importance of being grounded," resonated in my mind as I scanned the components. I flashed back to Wally's explanation of the ground wire and the switch that activated it in his diagram.

The Ground Wire Switch (Diagram Component # 8) *** a flashback ***

"Gracey's sharp teeth caused an arc fault. The tear in the wire insulation allowed the electricity to bleed off and literally try to get to the nearest ground. When the fan was plugged in, you felt how warm this wire became, but it's unlikely the breaker would have flipped until after it got warm enough to ignite something lying close to the cord.

"Electricity only works safely when there is a closed loop of energy. Power from the electrical source can go nowhere unless there is a return or neutral wire returning to the source of power. The electrical flow of energy is impossible unless there is a return of at least some power to the source via the neutral wire."

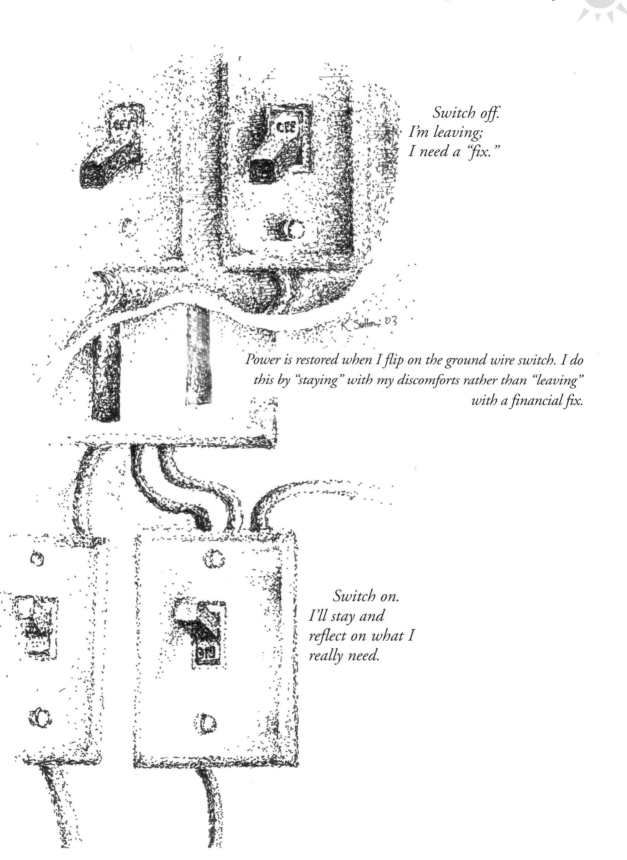

Switch off.
I'm leaving;
I need a "fix."

Power is restored when I flip on the ground wire switch. I do
this by "staying" with my discomforts rather than "leaving"
with a financial fix.

Switch on.
I'll stay and
reflect on what I
really need.

Wally pointed out the window to the power lines running along the road. "One of those lines is the hot, or positive, cable; the other is the ground, or neutral, cable. The hot wire carries power generated up in northern Colorado at a coal-fired plant. The ground or neutral wire carries a charge back to that power plant. The electrical charge of this ground wire informs the power source of how much load is on the system."

Wally paused for a moment as if to emphasize what he was about to say: "Without that ground wire reporting to the power plant, it would be impossible for additional electricity to flow out from that energy source into the 'hot' wire."

"So is the ground wire a messenger of sorts that communicates with the power source about what has been used, and, in a sense, asks for more?" I asked.

"Well, Paul, I never thought of it quite like that, but that's a pretty good way to describe it. Not only is the ground wire a critical messenger, electricians know that in a safe power delivery system, the ground wire has to have the same electrical carrying capacity as the hot wire. In other words, there has to be a big enough return—or 'ground'—to accommodate all the electricity that has been sent via the hot wire. Most of the time, the ground wire will only be 'asking' for a small percentage of the total power made available to the system in the hot wire.

"In my diagram, I wrote 'Ground Wire Switch' next to the largest switch. No matter if the circuit with the smaller wire [6a] or the one with the larger wire [6b] is being used to turn on the lights, if I turn off the Ground Wire Switch, absolutely no lights will work. There has to be an operational ground or neutral wire for any power to get through to the lights. Without the ground wire, there is no completion of the loop that allows the electricity to flow to where it is needed!"

Wally's Ground Wire Switch helped me see that I had a choice. I could choose to "stay" and notice what I really needed when uncomfortable feelings and situations presented themselves in my life, or I could "leave" by attempting to simply fix the discomfort in some way.

SECTION ONE
WORKSHEET A

Money Groundedness Practice:
Grounding with My Tendency to "Leave" Before I "Stay"

Take a few minutes to complete this first worksheet. Please deal with whatever you are feeling concerned or uneasy with right at this moment. If it is a money concern, fine. It may even be a level of frustration with this book and its approach to money. What matters is that you access your present discomfort.

? At this moment I'm feeling some discomfort about:

_____

_____

? My typical reaction to this kind of feeling is to:

_____

_____

? To "stay" with this uneasiness means that I will:

_____

_____

? The longer I stay with this feeling, the more clearly I see that I need:

_____

_____

? When I acknowledge this need, I feel:

_____

_____

? If I had left, I would have missed out on:

_____

_____

? By staying, I have learned or experienced:

_____

_____

As I worked with this exercise, I saw how little experience I had in paying attention to what was really going on. I had developed a hundred skills to "fix" or "leave" but felt totally disarmed by my sense of vulnerability when trying to access my feelings and true longings. The amazing thing, to my surprise, was the relief and sense of happiness that grew out of this place of "weakness"!

Looking back at my life from where I sat in my office that Monday morning, I couldn't help but see how I, and so many others, were like our home with a defective fan plugged into the outlet: on the verge of catching fire from the lack of any real grounding around money and its true purpose: i.e. what it could and could not do.

It was at that point that I made the resolution to revise my way of relating to money both within myself as well as with my clients. Since I started practicing "staying vs. leaving," with money as my teacher, I have seen some powerful changes take place.

When I stop to notice those changes, I feel so thankful for the day Wally fixed my fan and took the time to say, "Don't underestimate the importance of being grounded."

"Character cannot be developed in ease and quiet. Only through experience of trial and suffering can the soul be strengthened, vision cleared, ambition inspired and success achieved."

—Helen Keller

SECTION TWO

The Plan:
What to Expect—An Authentic Money Guide—and More!

This section provides hope that you can find genuine freedom and happiness and that money can actually serve as your ally rather than as an adversary in that process. It's important to make a commitment to this process, and Section Two provides each of you an opportunity to carve out specific time in your schedule for TEN WEEKS. You know it's time for a change with your money. Take heart! Happiness and money can co-exist in your life!

"On a hot day in the southern desert of Africa I had wanted to go and speak to one of my favorite Stone Age hunters. He was sitting in the middle of a thornbush…He was huddled in an attitude of the most intense concentration…but his friends would not let me get near him, saying, 'But don't you know, he is doing work of the utmost importance. He is making clouds.'"

—*Laurens Van der Post*

THE MONEY THORNBUSH

There must have been a desperate need for rain for this man to willingly subject himself to such discomfort and intense concentration. What hope do you have in "sitting in the middle" of this *money thornbush*?

So far in TEN WEEKS you have heard Wally remind me how important it was to be "grounded." You have also listened to language about "staying" vs. "leaving." <u>What does it really mean to slow down long enough to notice what needs you are longing</u> to satisfy? All that language means very little at this point.

What matters is that there is some reason to continue to sit "in the middle of a thornbush." If there is no real sense of hope that taking a long and painful look at money will lead to some genuine relief from all the suffering that most of us experience with it, then I would be the first to stand up and begin to pull "thorns" from my posterior!

There's a reason you bought this book. Maybe you're sick and tired of feeling like you always draw the "short straw" when it comes to finances and money—there's never enough, and the harder you try to manage it the worse your situation gets.

> *"He who refuses to embrace a unique opportunity loses the prize as surely as if he tried and failed."*
> —William James

Or you may feel completely overwhelmed and helpless when it comes to dealing with the money garbage that inundates your life. From piles of bills—to shattered investment dreams—to money fights with your partner/spouse—to the dread of facing it all over again the next day—the list goes on and on.

Or you might be "privileged." You have plenty of money and most of the things that go with it. But you still worry constantly about keeping what you have. You are suspicious of most everyone who approaches you for fear that they only are after your money. You would give most of it away to feel genuine love and acceptance rather than feeling as if you had to pay for people's affection.

Your pain is real and intense, whatever your brand of money suffering, or you would not have willingly sat down in the middle of this money thornbush—again!

So what relief do you expect from subjecting yourself to TEN WEEKS?

For Freedom You Are Here

The hope that TEN WEEKS TO FINANCIAL AWAKENING offers is that you will be free.

Free to cry and laugh with an intensity you have not known for years. Free to love the sunrise and the rain. Free to be yourself and say to others "It doesn't matter what you think" in a selfless and responsible way. Free to love what money was meant to help you love. Free to honestly look yourself in the mirror at day's end and feel good about the way you walked on the Earth. Free to love this amazing roller-coaster ride of life—complete with its heart-wrenching terror and passionate embrace. Free to face your weakness and, yes, even your own death with a depth of peace and calmness that you have rarely felt.

> *"You must learn one thing.*
> *The world was made to be free in.*
> *Give up all the other worlds*
> *except the one to which you belong."*
>
> —*David Whyte,* Sweet Darkness

If there is one thing we want in life, it is to experience the freedom of finding where we belong. So much of our suffering with money comes from desperately trying to create a world with it that will result in feeling that belonging. Can you remember the last time you felt completely at home with yourself and your life? If you are lucky enough to grab that memory, please hold on to it with a tight embrace—for that is the essence of what makes sitting in this thornbush worthwhile!

Mark Nepo reminded us in Section One:

> *"A dog loves the world through its nose.*
> *A fish through its gills.*
> *A bat through its deep sense of blindness.*
> *An eagle through its glide.*
>
> *And a human life*
> *through its spirit."*

TEN WEEKS TO FINANCIAL AWAKENING advocates finding our way back home the same way we got lost. We have all wandered far from the one world to which we really belong—from the spirit essence of our being—and it has been our preoccupation with the allure of money that led us astray. Now it's time for us to let money teach us how to find that home deep within our spirit.

"All I Want Is a Financial Plan!"

"Soul talk" may be as numbing to some of you as was the promise of "grounding" to others! If you're needing some reassurance that I'll ever get around to dealing with your financial questions, please take a moment and thumb through the Money Attention Page (MAP) Section of the book. All those financial solutions need a solid foundation if your new "money house" has any hope for improvement from your old one. Please continue reading Section Two to see what kind of time it will take to create that foundation.

> *"Is there anyone here who, planning to build a new house, doesn't first sit down and figure the cost so you'll know if you can complete it? If you only get the foundation laid and then run out of money, you're going to look pretty foolish. Everyone passing by will poke fun at you: 'He started something he couldn't finish.'"*
>
> —*Jesus, The Bible: Luke 14 ("The Message")*

There is a good chance what prompted your purchase of this book was its promise to help you create your own financial plan. You may also have been interested in how you could use Quicken® software to help you with this process rather than having to consult a financial professional or to work through the manual worksheets offered in most personal finance self-help books.

I have discovered that my clients have a wide range of expectations when it comes to what is involved in creating a financial plan. It is important for all involved to discuss these expectations at the outset of the planning process; otherwise, it is inevitable that frustrations will surface. No one wants to end up like the person Jesus described who wasn't able to finish what he/she started because of failing to figure the cost or align his/her expectations with reality.

The first opportunity for misunderstanding can arise when a client says he/she is seeking a *financial plan*. People mistake a *financial fix* for a *financial plan*. I try and explain financial planning with this little story:

"Why do you hasten to remove anything which hurts your eye, while if something affects your soul you postpone the cure until next year?"

—*Horace*

Suppose you live in a very old, run-down house. It has been years since you've done any maintenance on the place, and as a result, the roof has started to leak. You have tried to catch all the drips with buckets, but you know that you really need a new roof. You'll admit there are a few other problems with the house, but the annoying leaks are your focus at the moment.

When you call the contractor over to give you a bid on a new roof, he smiles and politely replies, "It'll be between a hundred and a hundred and a quarter." You can tell by the look in his eye that he didn't mean under $200—he was talking $100,000–$125,000!

"I only want a new roof!" you reply. "What are you planning to use for roofing material, gold-plated shingles?!"

"Mister, I have to attach the roof to a house. On this sweetheart, we need to start at the foundation!"

There are usually one or two pressing concerns that draw in most people for financial advice. Maybe it's that our retirement account investments have taken a beating, and we finally are willing to pay a professional for some investment advice rather than watching a television money channel or relying on the advice of a coworker. Perhaps we want to buy a bigger house or deal with the credit card balances that just keep on growing. The specific need is not nearly as important as the underlying incentive that got us to a financial advisor or prompted us to purchase a book about creating a financial plan.

"Thousands of people have talent. I might as well congratulate you for having eyes in your head. The one and only thing that counts is: Do you have staying power?"

—*Noël Coward*

There is no question that if our homeowner were able to track down a contractor that was willing to risk his life to crawl up on that shaky old "sweetheart" house and nail some new shingles to its rotten decking, there would be some temporary relief from the annoying leaks. It wouldn't be long, however, until the temporary fix had failed.

Deep down, we know a few "shingles" won't do—our financial "house" is built on a faulty foundation. The fact that the words *happy* and *money* do not usually occupy the same sentence in our vocabulary is a good indication of the extent of the damage. Getting the nerve to really take a look at our old "home, sweet home" reveals the need for some extensive work. Once the problems are identified, the necessary repairs can be performed in a way that relieves us from having to deal with ongoing crises.

My goal as a financial planner is to free my clients from being distracted from their Authentic Lives by money repair issues. Shifting into a new relationship with money involves leaving the crisis mode by agreeing to look at everything that needs to be done. A willingness to do this engages a client in the Comprehensive Financial Planning process.

I define a *Comprehensive Financial Plan* as a product that includes a thorough inspection of our financial house. Not every component will need extensive work, but enough work needs to be done to have the peace of mind of knowing that a good inspection has been conducted and that no critical problems have been ignored. Optimally, we would like to look forward to coming home to a house that provides the opportunity to relax, reflect, and think about more than the leaky roof. Because we have paid proper attention to the house, and are committed to doing so, we have energy left over for what really brings us happiness.

REASONS FOR THE ROT!

The shape of our money house is a product of some clear deficiencies. It's as if three *money termites* have all but destroyed our relationship with money and filled us with dread when faced with financial matters. It won't do us much good to build a new house if we don't deal with these three culprits!

VOID OF TRAINING

Lynn Patterson, a client, shares her experience with the "void of training" termite;

> *As a child, I lacked no material comfort and was so fortunate that my four-year college education was paid for by my father. Concepts of finance were never discussed with me…. [As a young adult] I sought advice from my father, who told me it was unimportant since I would ultimately marry and be supported by my husband. This clearly illustrates the level of mentoring I received from my family where finances were concerned.*

Paradoxically, our society places a very high value on money but very little practical guidance on how to manage it. As of October 2002, Americans were saving slightly more than 1 percent of their income. There's a big gap between what is set up as the ideal ("You should save at least 10 percent of your income.") and people's actual behavior, in large extent because of poor training.

> *"Whatever people in general do not understand, they are always prepared to dislike; the incomprehensible is always the obnoxious."*
>
> *—L.E. Landon*

Is there any question that Landon's words apply to our relationship with money?

"Money is a good servant but a bad master."

—Francis Bacon

BROKEN PROMISES

Even if the first money termite hadn't chewed your home to splinters, there is a second close behind! None of us likes to deal with disillusionment and the pain of broken promises.

Say you were one of the disciplined few who saved 10 percent of your income for retirement. You did all the right things but your retirement account balance at the end of 2002 was less than half of what it was three years ago. The promise that you would have "the good life" has been broken! The pain from that broken promise makes it unlikely that you are eager to poke the wound with a closer look at money!

PUT OUT THE FIRE ENERGY

And finally the most devastating money termite makes sure we are scrambling for cover as the walls of the house collapse! In our dealings with money, we have confused attention with energy. We deal with money when we are forced to, in as little time as is required. The remainder of the time, we spend indulging ("I deserve…"), ignoring ("It's not that bad…"), or insulting ("I'll never get my act together…") ourselves financially. We invest a lot of energy but no direct attention toward money.

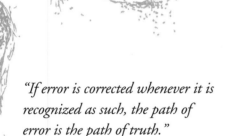

"If error is corrected whenever it is recognized as such, the path of error is the path of truth."

—Hans Reichenbach

The truth is that the financial planning process is not actually as painful as sitting in the middle of a thornbush. You may find that relief comes much more quickly than you ever thought possible because you had the courage to face up to your financial fears. Giving money your attention results in your using it as a tool to help you live your life in a rich and meaningful way.

TEN WEEKS TO FINANCIAL AWAKENING **will not insult you with quick financial fixes but will give you the opportunity to experience the freedom and belonging that come when you allow money to help you live in accordance with your Authentic Self.**

So what's the first step?

First you have to identify a need that will help you realize that "band-aid" treatments are insufficient to solve your problems. If you can relate to the responses about money described at the start of this Section, you are most likely ready to commit to an extensive remodel of your money house.

Second, you have to be realistic about your expectations, or "sit down to figure the cost," as Jesus said.

If you want to get a clearer idea of some of the specifics of what we'll be covering, turn to the *It's About Time for a Change with Money Schedule* at the end of this Section. There, you will find a description of the TEN WEEKS Program. If you are ready to commit to financial awakening and to living authentically with your finances, this Program will give you what you are looking for. You just need to decide how to schedule it into your life.

This book is an outgrowth of how I work with my own financial planning clients. Though the format of the book is modified for a self-directed planning experience, the process is basically the same. The core of the TEN WEEKS Program is the *Circuit Inspection Worksheets*. These worksheets assist you in understanding who you are, what you really want, and how money can assist, rather than hinder, how you actually express those realizations in your day-to-day life. Take a few minutes to thumb through the book and review the worksheets, or if you have purchased the *Worksheets Workbook*, pause to glance at some of the issues you will be facing. **Financial solutions that have no connection to your inner needs and feelings will only create more suffering in your life**; these Worksheets will help you avoid that result.

TEN WEEKS TO FINANCIAL AWAKENING empowers you to build an entirely new financial house from the ground up. What better time than now to start living where you belong!

If you go back to the *It's About Time for a Change with Money Schedule* and add up the time estimates for each of the segments of the TEN WEEKS Program, you will see that you are looking at about 60–120 hours. When you think about it, that's about the same amount of time most of you spend working in two to three weeks. Aren't you worth an investment of three weeks' work? **I can say with confidence that no other time investment will yield such long-term rewards as your whole-hearted attention to the TEN WEEKS Program!**

But life is full of commitments, and there is simply only so much time to complete a program like this—no matter how life-changing it is. All the material in the TEN WEEKS Program is essential, but there is a way of dividing the work into manageable pieces. What is important is that you commit to engaging with this Program now—otherwise the busyness of life will rob you of this opportunity for you to shift out of money suffering. Consider these options:

"There is no try. There is only do or do not do."

—*Yoda, "The Empire Strikes Back"*

Options for Engaging with TEN WEEKS

"Take your life in your own hands and what happens?
A terrible thing: no one to blame."

—*Erica Jong*

Option 1—TEN WEEKS for Me

➤ I know it's a big commitment, but I'm willing to carve out the time to finish it in the next 10 weeks.

Option 2—Two-Three Weeks Now: Eight Weeks Later

➤ I want to reorganize my paperwork and get all my finances set up in Quicken® for now. I'll commit to the 20–40 hours that this phase of the TEN WEEKS program will take and schedule that time now.

➤ I want to finish the entire program, however, so I will assign dates and times when I will complete each section, right now.

Option 3—TEN WEEKS: More Like Twenty?!

➤ I know I will not be able to commit to six to eight hours per week for the next two and one half months. I'd rather set aside _____ hrs. per week to work the program, which equates to _____ weeks if an average completion estimate is 100 hours. I'll use this guideline in completing the Time Schedule that follows.

Option 4—FOUR OR FIVE WEEKS NOW—WITHOUT QUICKEN® AND AN AUTHENTIC MONEY GUIDE

➤ I am not ready to tackle Quicken® and a Comprehensive Financial Plan (Authentic Money Guide). I am willing, however, to take an honest look at my relationship to money and what this book has to say about Financial Awakening.

➤ I'll use the reading and worksheet time estimates in the *It's About Time for a Change with Money Schedule,* to estimate how much time this should take.

➤ I realize that if at some future time I want to create my own Authentic Money Guide, I will need to follow the detailed TEN WEEKS CD instructions—otherwise, I could make mistakes that could distort the accuracy of my financial projections. If it's been more than one-year since I purchased TEN WEEKS, I realize I'll need to buy an updated version of Quicken®, TEN WEEKS CD, and the current MAP Section.

"You will never find time for anything. If you want time, then you must make it."

—*Charles Buxton*

YOU CAN DO HARD!

"You can do hard," Bo Lozoff says in his book, "It's a Meaningful Life: It Just Takes Practice." To elaborate, he says:

"…in our modern era, the words 'It's too hard' have become an anthem for giving up… Maybe we have become afraid to tackle anything that might be very hard…We can do hard. Really, we can… Because change usually requires sustained commitment, one of the best ways to get that commitment rolling is to take a vow in the presence of others… By giving up some minor freedoms of changing your mind, you give yourself major freedom to change your life. Try it and see."

Complete the TEN WEEKS TO FINANCIAL AWAKENING Time Schedule Worksheet. After setting specific dates and times, I recommend you make a vow to yourself and another person, who is willing to bear witness, to follow through with your intention.

If you are completing the TEN WEEKS Program with a partner or spouse, please read *Week One/Two Appendix B—"Partner Work."* Each partner should complete his/her own Time Schedule Worksheet, and you should expect the time each of you is willing to participate to be quite different. Reading "Partner Work" will help put to rest the normal resentment that such an arrangement is somehow unfair.

When you start to question your time commitment, pause to realize that you will be well compensated for your time.

The cost for the above process with a qualified CFP™ ranges between $3,000–$10,000.

By surrendering to the journey prescribed by TEN WEEKS, you will go on a financial adventure and end up with a life-transforming comprehensive financial plan, or what I call the ***Authentic Money Guide***. The careful attention you give to each step will be worth it; start by believing this to be true!

May I suggest you start each session of this Program with a simple mantra:

"I intend to open today by being wholly present with this material. I'll try and notice when I've shifted into my "fix-it' mode since this will prevent me from accessing the benefits of this Program and experiencing the happiness I want in my life."

"A tree growing out of the ground is as wonderful today as it ever was. It does not need to adopt new and startling methods."

—Robert Henri

But There's More!

Completing any comprehensive financial planning process is cause for celebration! As we have seen, the scope of such an undertaking is much more extensive than we originally thought. When you give each of these aspects of your financial affairs attention, you will experience a certain level of relief.

When you finish the TEN WEEKS program and end up with a "grounded" financial plan—an Authentic Money Guide—you will have accomplished something much more amazing.

You see, TEN WEEKS elevates a comprehensive financial plan to a point far above scrutinizing and pushing numbers. It leads you to the discovery of what those numbers tell you about yourself, your life, and your true longings. Any financial plan that fails to take into account these critical factors is doomed to perpetuate, rather than alleviate, suffering.

The reason for the recurrence of money suffering after engaging in a traditional financial planning process, which focuses mainly on financial solutions, can be summarized in three words—No Energy Shift.

We can't just give money attention. We have to practice redirecting the energy that used to be consumed by money. We have to practice grounding.

In my day-to-day dealings with people and money, as well as my own journey of discovery with money groundedness, I am convinced we all have trouble staying grounded.

Remember Wally's electrical diagram? When we flip the ground wire switch to ON, we shift out of old destructive patterns of postponing life, ignoring our deeper longings, covering over our sadness with addictions, and focusing on countless other futile efforts to protect ourselves from the inherent insecurity of life. When the ground wire switch is ON, we get the authentic feedback from our Interior that allows us to live the life of our deepest desires.

But flipping a ground wire switch that is disconnected from an overall electrical system would not do us any good. We have already established that a "financial fix" is not the same as a "grounded financial plan." If we take the time to build a new relationship with money, the lights will work when we flip the switch.

Let's take a sneak preview of what is in store.

➤ A close look at your finances helps you see the true nature of your life. Suddenly, you notice that being present with daily details allows you to experience the wonder of life.

➤ Money's true purpose is to remind you of your dependency—no amount of money can satisfy your longing for help outside yourself.

➤ There is such a thing as enough money. Real satisfaction comes not from more money but from knowing you are opening to a truer sense of Self.

➤ Consciousness of the emotions associated with money issues are at the base of finding groundedness.

➤ If you want honest feedback as to how aligned your actual behaviors are with your professed values, you must look closely at how you make, spend, share, and save money. This money mirror reveals the source of your discontent.

"Man's main task is to give birth to himself."

—*Erich Fromm*

I'm building a new, grounded relationship with money.
I know it means establishing an entirely new system,
but it's worth the effort.

➤ When you pay attention to your financial life and follow through with action around steps that need to be taken, you are less distracted by the money noise that calls you in a hundred different directions.

So, you can see that you are in for an exciting journey! An Authentic Money Guide and Financial Awakening are within reach.

It's time for money and happiness to co-exist in your life!

A REFLECTION

As I walked down the driveway just a few days ago to my little country office, I wondered about some new clients coming in for their first meeting. I thought about this journey that had caused me to ask my clients to use the financial planning process as an opportunity to examine their lives. I thought of this David Whyte poem as I put the key in the front door:

THE WELL OF GRIEF

Those who will not slip beneath
the still surface on the well of grief

turning downward through its black water
to the place we cannot breathe

will never know the source from which we drink,
the secret water, cold and clear,

nor find in the darkness glimmering
the small round coins
thrown by those who wished for something else.

—David Whyte, from Where Many Rivers Meet

It is terrifying not to be able to catch your breath. I wonder if these clients will have the courage at this point in their lives to open to their fears? I know oftentimes I choose to stay at the edge of the "well." I also know that I need encouragement and support to keep opening to this vulnerable place in my life. It seems that money brings up plenty of terror for most of us, helping us find this sacred place within.

A few minutes later, the clients arrived. As we spoke, I could see they longed to live a life that lay beyond simple financial solutions and growing financial net worth. Their courage to deal with their finances would help them dive below the still surface to find that "secret water—cold and clear—the source from which they drink."

How about you?

It's About Time
for a Change with Money
Schedule

My Intent to Complete the
TEN WEEKS TO FINANCIAL AWAKENING Program.

Book Section	Time Recomended	Date/Time To Complete	Completed

Ready...

Introduction & Section 1:

➤ Reading. 1 hr.   ❑

➤ Worksheet A . . . . 1/2 hr.   ❑

Get set...

Section Two: *What to Expect—and More!*

➤ Reading. 1 hr.   ❑

➤ Time Schedule. . . . . 1 hr.   ❑

GO!!!

Section Three:
Weeks One & Two—Money Inventory

➤ Reading. 1 hr.   ❑

➤ Money Reflection Inventory
Worksheet A . . . . 3/4 hr.   ❑

➤ Reflection Inventory—Pt. 2 . . . . . 3/4 hr.   ❑

➤ Data Collection—Appendix A . . . . 6 hrs.   ❑

➤ Quicken® Input—Pt. 1 . . . . 6 hrs.   ❑

➤ Quicken® Input—Pt. 2 . . . . 6 hrs.   ❑

Week Three—*What I Really Want*

➤ Reading . . . . 3/4 hr.   ❑

➤ What Is it I Really Want?
Worksheet A . . . . 2 hrs.   ❑

➤ Checkbook Checkup
Worksheet B . . . . 3/4 hr.   ❑

➤ Quicken® Budget Setup. . . . . 6 hrs.   ❑

BOOK SECTION	TIME RECOMENDED	DATE/TIME TO COMPLETE	COMPLETED
Week Four—*Work Woes*			
➤ Reading . . . . 3/4 hr.			❏
➤ Work & Identity CI* Worksheet A 3/4 hr.			❏
➤ Work & Identity CI Worksheet B . 3/4 hr.			❏
➤ Quicken® "What if" Analysis . . . . . 2 hrs.			❏
Week Five—*Credit and Loans: Friends or Foes*			
➤ Reading . . . . 3/4 hr.			❏
➤ Debt & Credit CI Worksheet, Pt. 1 & 2 . . . . 3/4 hr.			❏
➤ Debt & Credit CI Worksheet, Pt. 3 . . . . 2 hrs.			❏
➤ Debt Management Principles, Appendix A. . . . . 2 hrs.			❏
➤ All Those Other Debts Appendix B . . . . 1 hr.			❏
➤ Quicken® Debt Reduction Planner, Appendix C . . . . 2 hrs.			❏
Week Six—*Investments: Money Working You or Working for You*			
➤ Reading . . . . 3 hrs.			❏
➤ Investment CI Worksheet A . . . . . . 1 hr.			❏
➤ Investment CI Worksheet B . . . . . . 1 hr.			❏
➤ Investment CI Worksheet C . . . . . . 1 hr.			❏
➤ Investment CI Worksheet D . . . . . . 1 hr.			❏
➤ Investment CI Worksheet E . . . . . . 1 hr.			❏
➤ Investment CI Worksheet F . . . . . . 1 hr.			❏

CI = Circuit Inspection

*"Time brings out today's special. Every day it's the same routine. 'You call this a meal?'
I scowl. Time looks me in the eye. 'Twenty-four hours,' he says. 'That's it.'"*

—*Sy Safransky*

BOOK SECTION	TIME RECOMENDED	DATE/TIME TO COMPLETE	COMPLETED
Week Seven—*Insurance: Risky Business*			
➤ Reading	3/4 hr.		❏
➤ Insurance CI Worksheet A	3/4 hr.		❏
➤ Insurance CI Worksheet B	3/4 hr.		❏
➤ My Insurance Deductibles Worksheet B-1	1/2 hr.		❏
➤ My Home Insurance Summary Worksheet B-2	1/2 hr.		❏
➤ Do I Need a New Health Insurance Policy? Worksheet B-3	1/2 hr.		❏
➤ My Health Insurance Options Summary Worksheet B-4	1/2 hr.		❏
➤ Liability Insurance Worksheet B-5	1/2 hr.		❏
➤ Property Insurance Worksheet B-6	1/2 hr.		❏
➤ My Insurance Philosophy and My Life Worksheet C	1 hr.		❏
Week Eight—*Tax Liabilities: More than Paying Uncle Sam*			
➤ Reading	1 1/2 hrs.		❏
➤ Citizen Awareness & Involvement CI* Worksheet A	3/4 hr.		❏
➤ My Community Connection CI Worksheet B	1 hr.		❏
➤ College Funding Philosophy Worksheet C	1/2 hr.		❏
➤ My House...My Home Worksheet D	1 hr.		❏
➤ Mind Your Own Business Worksheet E	1 hr.		❏
➤ Quicken® Tax Analysis	2 hrs.		❏

CI = Circuit Inspection

Book Section	Time Recomended	Date/Time To Complete	Completed
Week Nine—*Retirement:* *Is the Grass Really Greener?*			
➤ Reading . . . . 2 hrs.			❑
➤ Retirement Anticipation/Appreciation CI Worksheet A . . . . 1 hr.			❑
➤ "I'll Trade This for That" Worksheet B . . . . 3 hrs.			❑
➤ True Retirement Worksheet C . . . . 1/2 hr.			❑
➤ Facing the Loss CI Worksheet D . . . 1 hr.			❑
➤ Top Ten Ways to Prepare for Retirement Worksheet E. . . . . 1 hr.			❑
➤ Retirement Phase Worksheet F . . . 1/2 hr.			❑
Week Ten—*Estate Planning:* *Will I or Will I Not?*			
➤ Reading. 2 hr.			❑
➤ The State of My Affairs CI Worksheet A . . . . 2 hrs.			❑
➤ Where to Find What Worksheet B . . . . 2 hrs.			❑
➤ "I'll Leave it All Behind" Worksheet C . . . . 3/4hr.			❑
Section Four: *Keep the Energy Flowing!* *Moving to Groundlessness*			
➤ Reading . . . . 2 hrs.			❑
➤ Completion of Your Authentic Money Guide . . . . 3 hrs.			❑
➤ Monitoring and Updating Your Authentic Money Guide. . . . . 1 hr.			❑
➤ When Do I Need Help and Whom Do I Ask?. . . . . 1/2hr.			❑

Estimated Range of Time to
Complete TEN WEEKS . . . . 60–120 hrs.

CI = Circuit Inspection

SECTION THREE

The Program:
Weeks One & Two

Your Money Inventory: Notice and Get Involved

> *By the end of the second week, you will have documented two critical inventories: a "Money Reflection Inventory" that clarifies how you currently feel about money and a "Financial Snapshot Inventory" represented by your financial Net Worth and Cash Flow reports. You will experience a powerful shift into the present with money, sustainable through ongoing use of Quicken® to give your finances proper attention rather than precious energy.*

"Don't underestimate the importance of being grounded," Wally said to me.

Katherine clearly summarized Wally's exhortation: "We need a neutral place where we can notice what is really happening… since most of us are so busy and preoccupied. It seems we have trouble grounding."

Most of my clients struggle with finding a "ground switch" or *neutral* in their financial lives. They are swamped in advice about what they should be doing with their investments, insurance, college savings, and retirement planning that they feel totally lost. Although advice on those topics has a place, groundedness is about noticing what is really going on before hastily acting to fix things. The financial choice may be the same, whether we pause or not, but if we act because of a clear understanding of our emotions and longings, then we experience freedom from the suffering that accompanies unexamined solutions.

Consider this illustration: You may have $50,000 sitting in an investment account earning less than 1 percent interest. You know you need to make a decision and get the money invested because inflation and taxes are putting you 2.5 percent a year in the hole. The solution is to choose an investment vehicle, "fix" the problem, and reverse negative earnings.

"The best way to make your dreams come true is to wake up."

—*Paul Veléry*

The concept of money groundedness advocates pausing to notice what is going on. Why are you hesitant to take action? Why are you so reluctant to even open this investment statement each month? What do you hope this money will provide? You finally acknowledge your fear of making another poor investment decision. You cringe at facing the uncertainty that what you had been looking forward to may no longer be realistic—retiring at 60, adding on to the house, paying for your children's college, etc. To admit that this money, accumulated through hours of hard work, has failed to flood your life with happiness leaves you angry, scared, and confused as to where to turn for some hope.

On the advice of a friend, you decide to buy the *Pimco Total Return Bond Fund*. With no grounding, you'll constantly be looking to its performance for some piece of your happiness. You know such a path leads to more money suffering. Failure to ground keeps your basis for well-being outwardly focused. Only from within can you find true contentment.

Taking the time to ground around your fears and aspirations helps you refocus your longing for happiness away from the investment and back to your mindfulness at this very moment. In that place, you can accept rather than resist the inherent uncertainty of life. You are finally able to smile at your illusion that money could actually guarantee you safety, security, and significance.

LOST

Stand still. The trees ahead and
the bushes beside you
are not lost.
What do I do when I'm lost in the forest?
Stand still. The trees ahead and
the bushes beside you
are not lost.
Wherever you are is called here,
and you must treat it as a powerful stranger.
You must ask permission to know it and be known.
Listen. Listen. The forest breathes.
I have made this place around you.
If you leave it, you may come back again saying here.
No two trees are the same to raven.
No two branches are the same to wren.
If what a tree or a branch does is lost on you,
then you are surely lost.
Stand still.
The forest knows where you are.
You must let it find you.

—David Wagoner

It is easy to feel lost in the money forest! The best thing we can do to regain our grounding and direction is to "stand still." When we stop long enough to notice where *here* is, we are less panicked and can begin to make decisions that lead us toward home. One step at a time, we journey toward our Authenticity.

From the very first day I met Wally, I knew that he was able to be in the *here* and *now*.

MOVING DAY

Katherine and I were unloading our rental moving van. On one of the many trips, I noticed "Wally & Jane" painted neatly on an old mailbox at the end of a rocky driveway next to ours. I caught a glimpse of a log cabin nestled in the trees.

As I carried a box of books up our driveway, a strong male voice greeted me. "Hello! I'm your neighbor, Wallace Smith. My friends call me Wally!"

Startled, I lost hold of the box. It hit the ground and burst.

"Didn't mean to scare you there."

"It's OK. My mind was somewhere else." I crouched to pick up the books.

"I'll have to say, you must be in pretty good shape," I said to my new neighbor. "If I had tried to walk up that hill, you would have heard me huffing and puffing a hundred yards off!"

In my nervous reaction I managed to make eye contact with Wally. In that brief moment I felt his calming presence. I relaxed.

"Can I lend you a hand?—looks as if you have your work cut out for you!"

"Oh, that's quite alright. We're making pretty good progress…"

At the very sound of my words I laughed, stopped resisting, stood up, and extended my hand.

"I'm Paul. I wasn't expecting that anyone would voluntarily walk into this hornet's nest!"

Wally knelt down and began gathering books and placing them back in the tattered box. "I don't mean to intrude," he said, "but the old saying goes 'Many hands make light work.' I remember what a chore it was when we moved in a couple years ago. So much stuff.

"Yeah, I wish I would have figured out the simple life *before* we moved!"

Wally, already on his way up the stairs with the books, turned and said to me, "Oh, but then you might have refused my offer!"

We sat down that evening for a cold lemonade. I couldn't help but be overwhelmed with gratitude for this new neighbor. Not only did Wally help carry a good many boxes, his calm and kind voice always seemed to have a story or a word to take my mind off the heavy lifting. "Wally, I can't remember the last time I asked for, or for that matter, gave, any neighborly help. What prompted you to come over here and help us like you did today?

"I just try and notice what's going on and get involved with it."

Later, as I thought about the events of the day, I wondered why I was so resistant to accepting Wally's help when he first walked up the driveway. I could easily have refused Wally's offer to "get involved" with our lives and, as a result, missed the experience of developing what I sensed would be a close friendship. Maybe it was

"Most of the shadows of life are caused by standing in one's own sunshine."

—Ralph Waldo Emerson

that old stubborn self-reliance that is so deeply ingrained in my Western psyche. It could also have been my reluctance to admit how big the task was that confronted Katherine and me.

Notice What's Going On

Wally's comment that day on the deck summarizes a powerful principle in TEN WEEKS: "Notice what's going on and get involved with it."

It's common to avoid taking a look at the details of our finances. It's hard enough for most of us to get our annual tax returns filed before April 15, much less really track where all the money goes.

The only way to begin this process of shifting into a new relationship with money is to focus attention on your money life and "get involved with it." If you actually take a look at the details of your life, as reflected in your money transactions, you can begin to admit, as I did that day Wally offered his help, your need for energy or power outside of yourself.

The 12-step programs talk about taking a "fearless moral inventory." Such an inventory starts with an admission to being "powerless." Those working this program then have faith that "a power greater than ourselves could restore our lives to sanity." Such an inventory takes a lot of courage and is usually prompted by suffering that the addicted ultimately find unbearable. Most of us postpone an honest look at our finances as long as possible. Could it be because we're addicted to thinking that we really can depend on money and our own power to survive in this world?

> ### The whole system depended on an energy source: The Sun (Diagram Component #1) ** a flashback **

Wally picked up his pencil, pointed to the smiley-faced sun in the diagram and began our lesson.

"You'll note that I drew the sun as the source of energy in my diagram. Except for nuclear power, all energy comes from the sun.

Each year, the sun shines down the energy equivalent of 1,000 trillion barrels of oil—500 times more than the energy currently being used worldwide."

"Many times a day I realize how much my own outer and inner life is built upon the labors of my fellow men, both living and dead, and how earnestly I must exert myself in order to give in return as much as I have received."

—Albert Einstein

An honest inventory, admitting my need, connects me to an abundant energy source.

As I pondered Wally's diagram and his explanation about the source of energy, I had to smile. I thought about how my own resistance to pay attention and to "get involved" with the details of my finances drained my energy.

I resist committing to a schedule of updating Quicken® with my personal transactions that are scattered throughout my financial records. For instance, sometimes I use a business check to pay for a personal bill because I only have my business checkbook with me. Even though the transaction is properly accounted for in my business records as a personal draw, our personal Quicken file fails to record that expenditure until I make an entry.

> *I wonder what is beneath this resistance? Is it just plain laziness—I just don't want to go to the trouble? That may be some of it, but I know there's more to it than just procrastination or sloth. I think that it's the awareness that when I do these final little steps, I have to face the reality of my spending. In some ways, I'd rather not have to look because it's easier to convince myself I'm living out my stated values with a vague awareness of how I manage my money. Facing the truth is a hard pill to swallow, especially when it exposes a problem I can't fix right away by myself.*

What would happen if I paid proper attention to this pattern? I would notice that I'm not getting much happiness from my denial. I'd also notice that I invest a lot of time in my finances, only to have those benefits minimized by this pattern. I find that money still robs me of energy in the form of dread, guilt, and confusion. I would notice that I fear thorough financial attention because it may reveal that I'm not that concerned about the world's problems. Maybe I'd notice that money is neutral and carries no judgment and that all my fears and self-doubt are coming from somewhere else. I'd have an opportunity to explore my compulsion to prove my "worthiness" to be alive.

Attention vs. Energy

I believe that giving money our attention creates happiness, whereas giving money our energy creates suffering. Let's pause briefly to explore what it means to follow Jacob Needleman's advice and "give exactly the right amount of attention to the aspect of life represented by money."

Don't we give money attention in our society? We spend hour after hour accumulating money, investing money, protecting money, wanting more money, so isn't that giving it our attention?

"The greatest of faults, I should say, is to be conscious of none."

—*Thomas Carlyle*

No, it is actually giving it our energy. It may be necessary for us to define what it means to give something our energy before we explore the true nature of giving money our attention.

To give money, or any object, energy is to acknowledge our dependence on it. Our energy is our very life force, best symbolized by the breath that sustains us moment by moment. When we allow our minds to trick us into thinking our well-being is dependent upon a certain person or a desired outcome (financial or otherwise) rather than some deep connection to the essence of life, we have misplaced our energy. We have taken our essence and sought to nourish it with our preconceived conceptions of what we like (vs. dislike) and what we see as good (vs. bad). Most of us in modern civilization have been convinced for quite some time that possessing more money is a necessary ingredient for personal well-being.

> *"Those who set out to serve both God and Mammon [Money] soon discover that there is no God."*
>
> —*Logan Pearsall Smith*

We are called to give Spirit our energy. In doing so, we reconnect with the life sustaining energy that only Spirit can give. In an electrical system, the power source replenishes the system with energy when a completed circuit is functioning. But money does not have the power to replenish our energy. The simple fact that we think money can replenish our energy does not mean that it will. So, we give it our energy, we look to it to sustain us, we bestow upon it power which it does not possess, and in so doing lose our vital energy, lose our ability to reconnect to the true energy source that can actually revitalize us, moment by moment.

We know we've given energy rather than attention when we become upset when things don't turn out a certain way. In my example about my reluctance to finish my Quicken® entries, I see my energy loss packaged as guilt, confusion, and dread. I never have those feelings when I direct my energy toward the essence of my being or when I actually finish taking a thorough look at my finances.

But what about giving money our attention, you may ask. When someone says, "I just wish you'd pay attention to me," what does he/she really mean? We know "attention" to this person means

"If our life lacks a constant magic, it is because we choose to observe our acts and lose ourselves in consideration of their imagined form instead of being impelled by their force."

—*Antonin Artaud*

he/she simply wants us to be completely present and hear what is being said. What if money were to speak and ask us this question? Is it not the same request? "Be present; stop thinking about what your money work will get you. Notice what is happening, right here, right now, and as Wally would say, 'get involved with it.'" This is the essence of giving money proper attention.

But how is attention linked with acceptance of my dependency? Wally said that the sun provided plenty of power to satisfy our needs. But the sun is the furthest thing from my mind when I pay my electric bill each month. I am thinking about how I'm glad to have enough money in my checking account to keep the lights burning!

ADMITTING DEPENDENCE

Uncomfortable as it was at first, I accepted Wally's help. I was so glad I did, not just for how it spared my back weeks of recovery, but for how it facilitated the opportunity to develop a fulfilling relationship with him.

To give money real attention allows us to see the extent of our dependency and the fallacy of our self-sufficient attitudes. Or, as described by Jacob Needleman in his book, "Money and the Meaning of Life":

> All by itself, as a thing, a substance, it [money] was useless. It was meant only for helping people directly to live in the material world, while at the same time recognizing their dependence, first upon God and then upon each other.
>
> The exchange of money could serve as a constant reminder of this mutual interdependence.

I thought about the change that took place financially in my own life several years after my mom's death. I was in the position of having what I considered "enough" money. Extra money enabled me to insulate myself from people. Rather than asking my neighbor for help to clear brush from my land, I could afford to hire someone to do the work. My self-sufficiency fostered reluctance in me to ask for help.

The additional money also contributed to my "tunnel-vision efficiency." It just made good economic sense to spend my time making more money than what I was paying people to work for me. I could maximize my financial efficiency and delegate less lucrative tasks to others. Nevermind how my focus on efficiency left me inept at anything other than my work.

"We plow the fields and scatter the good seed on the land,
But it is fed and watered by God's almighty hand;
He sends the snow in winter, the warmth to swell the grain;
The breezes and the sunshine, and soft refreshing rain."

—Matthais Claudius

Fortunately, I began to realize how more money and efficiency did not automatically bring me more happiness. Maybe this walling off of myself in my self-reliance from others and preoccupation with my schedule, my recreation, my pursuit of pleasure was a more abusive use of money than greed or overconsumption. What kind of life was I creating wherein working my land was now deemed *inefficient?*

When I pause long enough to look at my life, as it really is, by examining what my financial records reveal, I begin to understand yet another benefit of "getting involved" with the details of my finances:

Money's true purpose is to remind us of dependency. No amount of money is enough to satisfy my longing for help from beyond myself.

WHEN I LOST MY FAITH

When I lost my faith in people
I put my trust in things
To avoid the disappointment
Trusting people brings.

What trust in people brings
What I've brought myself
What I've brought to others
When they hoped for someone else.

I tried to do it all myself then
Surrounded by my stuff
All I found were limitations
I could not rise above.

There are gadgets and contraptions
Immaculate machines
There's a program you can download now
That will even dream your dreams.

It'll even dream your dreams
For a monthly fee
Clear up your complexion
You get a hundred hours free.

Possessions cannot save you
The way somebody can
When I learned to care for others
Then the boy became a man.

When I lost my faith in people
I lost everything
Though I lose my independence
I will have my faith again.

I will have my faith again
I will get it back again
Though I lose my independence
I am a freer man.

—*John Gorka, songwriter*

THE IMPORTANCE OF COMPLETING THE WORKSHEETS AND EXERCISES

The Money Reflection Inventory, a worksheet with three parts, is a useful tool to integrate money attentiveness into our experience. Looking for a "quick fix" will not uncover the source of suffering in our lives with money.

Taking the Money Reflection Inventory is critically important in the TEN WEEKS program. But, if you're like me, you avoid the suggested exercises in the books you read like they were some form of electro-shock therapy! You will also most likely be tempted to scan the next few pages to see how involved they get and then decide whether or not you will just skip to the next chapter. Please resist that temptation.

> *"Man can learn nothing except by going from the known to the unknown."*
>
> —*Claude Bernard*

When you notice that this form does not ask for numerical information but for an introspective view of your life around money, you may also be tempted to skip over it. Again, resist that temptation.

It is common for people who skip over a section of a book to never return to it. To skip over the Money Reflection Inventory is to forego the placement of an important building block in the TEN WEEK program. Without the proper foundation, actual money groundedness will be difficult, if not impossible, to grasp in your day-to-day experience.

This first two parts of Worksheet A will take about 30-45 minutes, each, to complete. Don't rush! Honor the pace that has delivered you to this important step in your financial life—one step at a time. By taking one step at a time, you will shift into a happier, more peaceful relationship with money.

If you do not have the time for this right now, please put the book down. Pick it back up when you have the time, place, and frame of mind to explore this practical application of money groundedness.

What can you expect to gain from doing the Money Reflection Inventory?

➤ **Practice staying vs. leaving.** As uncomfortable as it is at first, being quiet and listening results in a longing for more of the same.

➤ **Gain clarity about what you really need, right now.** You may find a few needs are trying to get your attention through a multitude of money concerns. Continued inattention to those needs has resulted in your feelings of exasperation and helplessness in relation to your money and finances.

➤ **Notice your expectations of life and money.** Rarely does life "go according to plan," and the way we deal with those disappointments has a drastic effect on our well-being.

➤ **Clarify the events at the *top of the hill.*** Most of us are waiting for some future event that will give us the life for which we long.

➤ **Face your time/money balance.** What would it look like if you seriously questioned the exchange of your time for money?

➤ **Notice how money is affecting your relationships.** Money is a powerful tool to build or destroy relationships with our family, friends, and people we encounter at work.

Your openness to this conversation will facilitate a genuine transformation in how you relate with money. Your new money house will sit securely on this foundation you are building.

"If we are suffering illness, poverty, or misfortune, we think we shall be satisfied on the day it ceases. But there, too, we know it is false; so soon as one has got used to not suffering one wants something else."

—*Simone Weil*

Week One
Worksheet A

Money Reflection Inventory

When we stand on the ground, we are connected to one place in one moment of time. Reflect back on a passage from the poem, *Lost:*

> *Wherever you are is called here*
> *and you must treat it as a powerful stranger.*
> *You must ask permission to know it and be known.*

> —David Wagoner

Most of us are on the move and find it difficult to stop long enough to notice where we are right now. We think it is our constant striving that will finally provide us with happiness and the "good life."

This worksheet is intended as a tool to help you notice the ground on which you stand. Don't worry about writing down everything that comes to mind. Jot down key words or maybe a brief glimpse of an image or memory. These can serve as guideposts for you to consult later to help summarize your experience.

Transition for Busy Minds

Please begin each session in quietness. Sitting quietly as described below is equivalent to flipping the ground switch to the "on" position.

Sit quietly—Close your eyes—Be still for at least five minutes.

Focus on your breathing rather than thinking.

Send a message to your body/Spirit that you want to listen.

"The degree to which we are able to see honestly who we are, what we need to do, and how we relate to the world, is the degree to which our minds are … quiet."

—Bo Lozoff

PART I

Here vs. There

? Ask yourself, "What am I feeling right now? Am I restless and discontented or peaceful and at ease?" (Try and follow those feelings to your underlying needs or intentions. Don't worry if you don't come up with anything specific or concrete.)

discontented

? Think back on a specific incident that you thought—before it happened—would improve the quality of your life. Did things turn out like you expected?

living in Bot – no

? What do you love about your life? What do you regret about your life?

I am healthy. I don't have the time to do all the things I would like: reading, studying languages, learning new music

? Imagine that you are on a hike. You work hard to reach the top of the hill only to arrive and realize that it is a "false summit." Your destination, the true summit, remains far off, over yet another ridge looming in the distance!
What is at the "top of the hill" in your life? What is it that you feel will give you the permission to rest and finally enjoy your life?

financial security

? What word would those who know you best use to describe your attitude toward money? Can you think of a recent occurrence that would confirm their assessment?

insecure

"I have people go back to their childhood and look and see what happened that resulted in their making a decision about money that holds them back from everything that's possible for them in their lives. I call that our 'money baggage.'"

(Karen Ramsey, Money Matters Radio Interview)

? What advice did your parents or caregivers impart to you? Has that advice negatively influenced the way you deal with money? As Karen Ramsey would say; "What is your 'money baggage'?"

no advice, but a good example of living within their means, (which I have always had to do) My father's example was that he was always working, as if driven by an insecurity about not having enough money (my interpretation)

PART 2

"My Money and Me" Reflection Inventory

? What word comes to mind that best describes your actual experience with money or financial matters?

inadequate

? If you could change one thing about your finances, what would it be?

make more money

? If enough money were not an issue (i.e. you had plenty), what would you change in your current life?

ye

? What is it you most deeply believe in, or what is it you value most as a human being?

intellectual exploration

? What behavior 'proves' its importance in your life?
(Example: "I value time with my family. I spend Saturdays at home with my kids.")

I buy books on topics of interest

Complete the following question using the following endings:

? How is this value reflected in how you currently...
...make or earn your money? (Example: "I refuse to work on Saturdays.")

not

...spend your money?
(Example: "We live in an older home so we can afford to live on a single income and have one parent at home with the kids.")

I buy cheap books

...share your money? (Example: "We encourage the kids to invite their friends over and we consistently have two to three extra mouths to feed at dinner time.")

I give to charities and enjoy doing so

? If your employer pays you $70,000/year ($35/hour) and asks you what combination of money and time-off would be ideal to you, how would you answer his/her question? (Example: "I'd work 25 percent less (30 hrs. per week) and accept $52,500 in salary.")

choose working less

? What concerns you most right now financially?

having enough to cover expenses ' retirement

MONEY REFLECTION INVENTORY SUMMARY—PART III

You may have uncovered some tender, sensitive spots in the process of taking this inventory. Let's pause and notice what lessons may be surfacing?

One of the fallacies of our Western mindset is that there has to be a clear answer for our questions. We may be more willing to forego an immediate answer if we at least can see that the process is going to get us somewhere! Even though we have to gradually wean ourselves from this "outcome orientation" if we are to be more grounded in our day-to-day lives, there are, nonetheless, tremendous benefits of taking such a deep look into our actual lives.

Staying vs. Leaving:

? Were you able to identify something in the here and now that you would rather avoid?

possibility of leaving music

? Are there money habits you have developed that perpetuate that avoidance?

The Top of the Hill

? Do you believe that there is happiness to be found in the day-to-day journey of life and that you can experience it?

yes

? What do you see as the biggest obstacle to this possibility?

insecurity in earning a living through music — Bob's refusal to let me teach our home.

? What "conditions" have you placed on granting yourself permission to experience such happiness?

the necessity to work many hours to try to stay in music.

? What part of your life do you truly enjoy right now?

reading · cooking · entertaining on occasion

Money vs. Time

Wayne Muller, in his book, *Sabbath—Restoring the Sacred Rhythm of Rest*, says:

"What if we were to expand our definition of wealth to include those things that grow only in time—time to walk in the park, time to take a nap, time to play with children, to read a good book, to dance, to put our hands in the garden, to cook playful meals with friends, to paint, to sing, to meditate, to keep a journal? What if we were to live, for even a few hours, without spending money, cultivating time instead as our most precious resource?… The truth must be told: With all the money in the world, and no time, we have nothing at all."

—Wayne Muller

? If your job were downsized from 50 to 40 hours a week, what would you do with that extra 10 hours a week?

read
_____

_____

? What would you be willing to "exchange" for that time?

_____

_____

 For Love or Money

"The only reason that we don't open our hearts and minds to other people is that they trigger confusion in us that we don't feel brave enough or sane enough to deal with. To the degree that we look clearly and compassionately at ourselves, we feel confident and fearless about looking into someone else's eyes."

—Pema Chodron

? How has your current relationship with money affected one of your personal relationships?

_yu_

_____

_____

_____

_____

ONE WORD

This Money Reflection Inventory has opened up Pandora's Box for many of you. You may be awash with feelings of sadness, despair, anger, and frustration. Honor these feelings. It is impossible to ground with money if you refuse to feel this pain. Such pain opens the doorway to your Authentic Self.

TEN WEEKS TO FINANCIAL AWAKENING offers each of us an opportunity to stay with rather than leave the fear that money has triggered for so long. It's as if you have the opportunity to experience a whole new world, but you must be willing to honor the resistances that have cut you off from that expansive and liberating way of living in this world. There is a part of geography that precedes this paradise; it is known as the wilderness. Each great spiritual tradition has shown us that passage through such territory is necessary and that it rarely kills us! We have to go into this wilderness to recover our hearts and discover true paradise.

Only as we stay with our feelings long enough to let their tumultuous cry subside will we have the presence and serenity to hear our Own Voice. Then, and only then, will we discover what it is we really want and need.

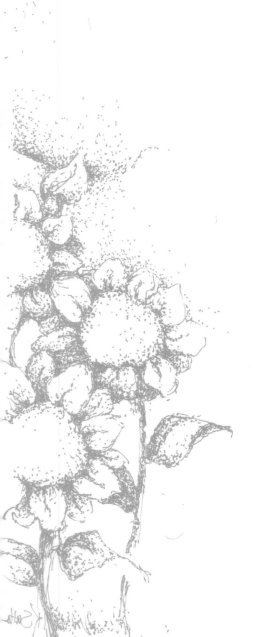

IT IS NOT ENOUGH

It is not enough to know.
It is not enough to follow
the inward road conversing in secret.

It is not enough to see straight ahead,
to gaze at the unborn
thinking the silence belongs to you.

It is not enough to hear
even the tiniest edge of rain.

You must go to the place
where everything waits,
there, when you finally rest,
even one word will do,
one word or the palm of your hand
turning outward
in the gesture of gift.

And now we are truly afraid
to find the great silence
asking so little.

One word, one word only.

—David Whyte

You have courageously entered a wilderness where money has been given powers it was never intended to possess. Out of that silence and confrontation, what is the Word that summarizes your deepest *lament* or suffering around money? Read over your Money Reflection Inventory, or just sit quietly. Hidden behind each of your reflections is that one Word.

This is the Word that must be honored as you deal with money.

This is the Word that will ground you like no other.

This is the Word that will preserve your True Life.

This is the Word that captures your gift to the family of the Earth.

Embracing this Word will finally bring you the freedom you have sought for so long.

? What is that Word for you?

fear

THE FINANCIAL INVENTORY PROCESS AND PRODUCT

In my early days as a Certified Public Accountant (CPA), I had to assist clients with year-end inventory counts. When I reflect back on those auditing days, there was a lot of work that went into preparing for the year-end inventory. These days were like no other workday when staff could expect to leave promptly at 5 p.m.

To end up with an accurate inventory, great care had to be taken to avoid duplicate counts and omissions. Assets at different locations had to be accounted for, including materials at numerous job sites, for commercial construction contractors. Obsolete inventory had to be identified and factored into the final inventory valuation. Current pricing of materials that had changed in value since their original purchase also had to be considered.

"It's not that I'm so smart, it's just that I stay with my problems longer."

—*Albert Einstein*

A sloppy, "good enough" year-end count often resulted in months of extra work in which actual inventory balances had to be extrapolated from inventory changes on account of ongoing operations. To avoid this nightmare, our job as auditors was to emphasize that the details mattered, and careful attention and diligence was a necessity if the inventory were to be effective and the count accepted. Weeks of preparation, scheduling, pricing research, and intense days of counting and tabulation went into accurate inventory accounting!

"This comes up all the time in mechanical work. A hang-up. You just sit and stare and think, and search randomly for new information, and go away and come back again, and after a while the unseen factors start to emerge."

—Robert M. Pirsig

While your financial affairs are probably less complicated than that of a typical business, you will still need to do some preparation in order to avoid a surplus of frustration and confusion to see where you are financially. In order to compile an accurate financial inventory, you will need to gather some documents and information.

As you gather these documents notice the physical process:

➤ Are your records disorganized or meticulously filed?

➤ Have you found a way to manage the inordinate amount of paperwork that stresses most of us on a daily basis?

➤ Do you see any hope of reclaiming some precious time by being able to put your hand on things when you need to?

After considering these questions, consult Step Two of Weeks One & Two Appendix A—"Ways to Take Charge of the Clutter."

A step-by-step approach to taking your financial inventory is outlined in Appendix A to this chapter. Each and every document you will need to arrive at an accurate financial picture of your current life is listed. Once your documents are located and you have identified what information you will need at some point during the program, you will be carefully guided through Quicken® data entry. Once your initial data entry has been done, you will print out two financial reports.

NET WORTH STATEMENT

The first report is a Financial Net Worth Statement that summarizes the difference between what we own (assets) vs. what we owe (liabilities). This report is a *snapshot* of our financial life at a particular point in time. If I had $1,000 in the bank and owed $500 on a credit card as of the end of last month, my financial net worth was $500 at that time.

The following month, if I earned $100 more than I spent and was able to deposit that into my checking account plus pay $50 on my credit card balance, then my Net Worth will have grown by $150 to $650. (Bank balance of $1,100 less credit card of $450 = $650).

The TEN WEEKS CD explains, screen by screen, how to enter all your financial records in Quicken® and how to understand the reports that result from such input.

A sample family—Greg, Ginger, and Gil Grounded—will illustrate each of the steps of this process, giving you a model that can easily be followed.

CASH FLOW STATEMENT

The other financial statement is the Cash Flow or Net Income Statement. It shows the difference between cash inflows and cash expenditures—usually on a monthly basis. The excess of income over expenditures results in an increase to the Net Worth statement, while expenditures in excess of income causes financial Net Worth to decrease. As opposed to the Financial Net Worth Statement, which captures our financial status on a certain day, the Cash Flow Statement gives us a picture of activity over a period of time.

Think of these two financial statements as taking a different picture of your financial life. The Net Worth Statement is like a camera snapshot at one moment in time, and the Cash Flow Statement is like a video camera of your activity for a period of time. The videos tell the story behind the snapshot. We need both to gain a realistic picture of our financial lives.

The process of compiling these two financial statements helps you ground your financial life. It feels good to give money proper attention, and it's much easier because your records are organized. Your financial reports clearly help you see the choices you are making with your money. This level of awareness allows you to pause long enough to activate your ground wire switch. It is in these details of your financial life that you can notice what is really taking place—and begin to ground.

Unfortunately, this new way of approaching money will create a bit of a ruckus! Simply preparing a set of financial statements does not ensure that you have entered into a new liberating relationship with money. As soon as you declare your intention to tap into the deeper lessons, resistance will emerge.

When you start to threaten the status quo, Ego (what might be thought of as the "Social Self"—the part of our psyche that seeks to relate to our social environment) understands the threat and defends accordingly. "Ego's Last Stand" might be a good way to describe what takes place. You have adopted coping skills in order to survive in this world. Even though you admit that those patterns often interfere with your Authentic dreams and aspirations, these *tools* are known and familiar. Beginning anew with key landmarks of your life rearranged is, to put it mildly, disruptive.

Despite the disruption, you will learn ways to honor the Ego and make the transition to financial awakening as pleasant as possible.

"Deepening my awareness is a challenge. It isn't a challenge because my parents didn't love me enough. It's a challenge because it's a challenge; I don't need to take it personally. I've spent years excavating my past, sorting and cataloging the wreckage. But who I really am, the essential truth of my being, can't be grasped by the mind, no matter how acute my insights. I've confused introspection with awareness, but they're not the same. Becoming the world's leading expert on myself has nothing to do with being fully present."

— *Sy Safransky*

"Awakening is not possible so long as the mind is constantly distracted from Truth by remaining habitually egocentric, by instinctively seeking personal gratification. Divine Grace, the healing and illuminating energy that rains down ceaselessly upon the human mind, heart, and soul, cannot be absorbed or assimilated by the high, rocky hill of personal interest and personal importance. This precious, life-giving water runs off the high ground of ego, without ever penetrating its hard, barren soil."

—Ramakrishna

Just don't be discouraged if you hear a lot of background noise questioning your ability to change old patterns.

Wally said that he tried to "notice and get involved" with what showed up in his life. That intent brought him into the middle of our personal lives. Since taking some of Wally's wisdom into my daily life and work habits, I have noticed that participating in, rather than avoiding, the details of life can be quite satisfying.

In this chapter, you open wide the door to Wally's approach. From your Money Reflection Inventory to the gathering of documents and data that show you just where you are right now financially, to actually printing up a black-and-white summary of your existing financial net worth and current cash flow, you are about to take a big step toward money groundedness.

Watch out, the current is flowing—the lights are flickering on!

"Nothing contributes so much to tranquilize the mind as a steady purpose—a point on which the soul may fix its intellectual eye."

—Mary Shelley

Weeks One and Two

APPENDIX A
Data Gathering and Organizational System Setup

THE FINANCIAL INVENTORY PROCESS

Even though taking a physical inventory can be overwhelming if viewed in its entirety, the process is less intimidating if it is broken down into smaller steps. The same is true with taking your financial inventory.

Right now, please find the first CD in your TEN WEEKS book and watch the introductory video. This video will help you understand the relationship of these CDs with Quicken® and the manual worksheets included in this Appendix.

To give you an overview of what is ahead, the following steps will enable you to take a thorough and accurate financial inventory and organize your records:

1. Gather all the financial information and documents you need to accomplish your Quicken® input. These documents will be placed in two three-ring binders—a "My Documents" binder and a "My Authentic Money Guide" binder. The ability to easily find accurate financial information is essential to your success with the TEN WEEKS program.

   You will also set up a "My Financial Education" binder, where you can organize the financial analysis work you do each Week and insert helpful articles and resources about a particular aspect of your personal finances.

2 Take charge of the clutter!

3. Install Quicken® and enter your financial information—Part A.

4. Enter your financial information in Quicken®—Part B.

5. Print your current Personal Net Worth and Cash Flow Statements.

6. Spend some time understanding your Statements.

STEP ONE—PART 1

If you haven't already done so, purchase the following items at a local office supply store or go online to *www.officedepot.com* and order them now.

OFFICE SUPPLY SHOPPING CART

❑ Three—two-inch three-ring binders (item # 492942, $8.39 each)

❑ Two—packets of eight extra wide big tab insertabler dividers (item # 349341, $1.89 each)

❑ One—packet of 12 binder dividers—monthly tabs (item # 313395, $3.89)

❑ Three—packets of five extra wide big tab insertable dividers (item # 349350, $1.49)

❑ One—multipage capacity sheet protectors—25 pack (item # 500587, $5.49)

❑ One—three-hole paper punch (item # 427151, $7.49 each)

❑ One—Perma heavy duty storage box (item # 403840, $9.99/set of three boxes)

❑ One—hanging file folder, letter size (item # 810994, $4.29/each)

❑ One—box of Smead manilla files, letter size (item # 300251, $11.29 for box of 100 files)

The total cost of the above items (as of June 28, 2003), before shipping and sales tax, at *www.officedepot.com* is $75.86. The easiest way to place your order is under "Shopping Tools." Select "Order by Item Number."

There is one other item you will need to order now:

Order the Homefile *Financial Planning Organizer Kit* from Homefile Fulfillment Center, *www.homefile.net* (1-800-695-3453).

The Financial Planning Organizer Kit is the system I recommend as a *must have*. It includes 24 preprinted file divider cards (which list what to save and how long to save it) and a Quick-File index with over 200 items. There is also a handbook that gives you a place to record critical personal information, as well as explains all the ins and outs of filing and record-retention. Item #204

Cost: $24.95 + $5.46 S&H = $30.41

Refer to the "What You Will Need to Complete the Program" section of this book for a $5.00 mail in coupon, if you have not done so already.

Binder Setup

The first three-ring binder should be labeled "**My Documents.**" The two extra-wide big tab eight-divider packets should be inserted and labeled as follows:

Tab #	Tab Title/Contents
1	Prior Year Tax Returns
2	Income
3	Expenses
4	Investments Information
5	Checking and Savings Accounts
6	Retirement Plan Benefits
7	Credit Cards
8	Mortgages and Loans
9	Home, Real Estate, Timeshares
10	Cars and Personal Property
11	Insurance Policies—Property
12	Insurance Policies—Life
13	Insurance Policies—Health
14	Insurance Policies—Other
15	Copies of Wills, Trusts, Estate Documents
16	Business Information

The second three-ring binder should be labeled **"My Authentic Money Guide"** and the following extra-wide divider tabs inserted (please label the dividers according to your personal life situation—as a single person or couple):

Tab #	Tab Title/Contents
1	What I/We Really Want
2	Where I/We Started
3	What Are My/Our Options?
4	My/Our Authentic Money Guide
5	AMG Action Items What I/We Want to Do

After these five dividers, insert the 12 monthly dividers in your My Authentic Money Guide binder. Each month's documents and reports will be organized in the following order, from back to front (i.e. #1 goes at the back of the monthly divider):

My Authentic Money Guide—Monthly Divider Contents
Financial Documents and Reports:

1. Pay Stubs
2. Income Receipts—Rents, Royalties, Gifts, etc.
3. Business Income Summaries
4. Investment Account Statements/IRAs/401(k)s
5. Credit Card Statements
6. Mortgage Statements
7. Other Loan Statements
8. Savings Account Statements
9. Checking Account Statements

Quicken® Reports:

1. Bank Reconciliation Reports
2. Transaction Report
3. Budget Report
4. Cash Flow Comparison Report
5. Cash Flow Report
6. Net Worth Report

Don't worry right now about what these reports mean. Before you complete the TEN WEEKS program you will discover what reports are most useful to you—these are just samples of ones I have found helpful.

The last three-ring binder should be labeled "**My Financial Education.**" Insert two of the five binder divider packets—10 dividers—that have extra-wide tabs. Use this notebook to file the financial analysis reports you print from Quicken®, the Internet or obtain from other sources. Organize this notebook in any way that best allows you to find these reports when you need them. My recommendation is to use the TEN WEEK Topical Format as follows:

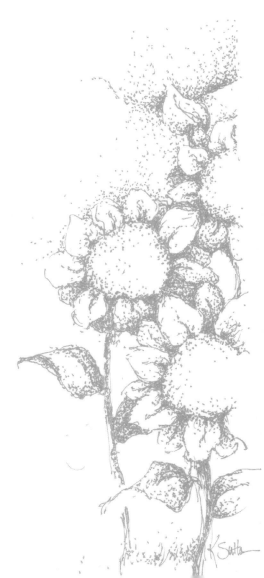

Tab #	Tab Title/Contents
1	Week One and Introduction—Organizational Resources
2	Week Two—"Big Picture" Resources
3	Week Three—Budget and Cash Flow Resources
4	Week Four—Work/Life Balance Resources
5	Week Five—Credit and Debt Management Resources
6	Week Six—Investment Resources
7	Week Seven—Insurance Resources
8	Week Eight—Tax Planning Resources
9	Week Nine—Retirement Planning Resources
10	Week Ten—Estate Planning Resources

The time you take to set up your **My Documents**, **My Authentic Money Guide**, and **My Financial Education** binders will simplify the creation of your Authentic Money Guide and help you keep your finances organized. You will be able to easily find the information you need to use money as that ally we have mentioned before—reminding you of your Authentic desires.

STEP ONE—PART 2

The next step is to unpack your Homefile *Financial Planning Organizer Kit* and Turn to Chapter 2 of the handbook—Setting Up Your HomeFile System. If this kit has yet to arrive, move on to Step 3 for now.

DO NOT ATTEMPT TO DUPLICATE WHAT YOU HAVE ALREADY DONE WITH YOUR THREE NOTEBOOKS. THE HOMEFILE SYSTEM IS SIMPLY A PLACE TO FILE OTHER PAPERS THAT DON'T ALREADY HAVE A HOME IN ONE OF THOSE BINDERS.

Having said that, follow the process on page 6 of the handbook in order to set up this filing system, either using your existing filing cabinet, or using the boxes and hanging files you obtained from your local office supply store or ordered from *www.officedepot.com*

Use the following recommendations as to what to file in your binders rather than in the Homefile system.

Use the HomefileProfile Dividers for guidance as to filing other papers for each of the following categories.

HOMEFILE FILE CATEGORY	FILE IN *AMG* OR *MY DOCUMENTS* BINDERS
Automobiles/Vehicles	Copy of Registrations and Service Contracts (#6)**
Bank Accounts	Monthly Statements
Charities	None (#2)**
Credit	Monthly Statements
Employment	Employment Contracts and Paystubs (#4)**
Expenses	None (#1)*
Insurance—Autos, etc.	Policy Summary Sheet
Insurance—Health and Disability	Policy Summary Sheet
Insurance—Home and Property	Policy Summary Sheet
Insurance—Life and Annuity	Policy Summary Sheet
Investments	Monthly or Quarterly Statements
Medical Records	None (3)**
Personal	None
Real Estate	Settlement Statements
Residence	Settlement Statements and Form 2119 (#6)**
Retirement Savings	Monthly or Quarterly Statements
Schools and Childcare	None
Self-Employed	None (#5)**
Social Security	Statement of Projected Social Security Benefits
Taxes—Income	Last Year's Tax Return
Warranties and Receipts	None
Wills and Trusts	Copies of All Estate Documents

Other Filing Recomendations

➤ *I recommend you set up a file called (#1) "Current Bills to Be Paid." File your bills here and, once or twice a month, sit down and pay them. I also recommend you create a separate file for each month of the year, entitled "(Month) Paid Bills." These files can be inserted in this section of the Homefile filing system.

➤ **The only paid bills that don't go into these monthly "paid bills" files are:

(#2) charitable donation receipts, (#3) medical receipts,

(#4) employee business expenses, (#5) small business receipts, and (#6) real estate tax and car license receipts.

By creating a manila file for these other tax return-related receipts, you won't need to re-sort your filing at the end of the year (as outlined in the Homefile Handbook).

All your financial records now have a home. (The "My Financial Education" binder will contain a printed financial analysis and educational material, not financial documents). One of the biggest reasons you have given money so much energy and so little attention is the overwhelming amount of financial paperwork under which you are buried. In order to be free to ground, you need to establish a system that organizes these papers.

STEP ONE—PART 3

Compile Your Financial Documents and Place Them in Your "My Documents" Binder

Gather the most recent copies you have of the following documents—for tax returns and other bulky documents, use the Multipage capacity sheet protectors rather than having to three-hole punch original documents.

❑ Federal and State Tax Return (Tab 1)

Insert a copy of your latest tax returns in this section, using one of the pocket-dividers.

If you and your partner do not file a joint tax return, consider entering your financial information into Quicken® separately. (This means you would each set up a separate data file to record your individual finances.) This will help minimize errors that can come from differing tax brackets, as well as maintain the identity of your respective financial affairs.

❑ Income (Tab 2)

Insert any employment contracts or agreements that indicate the terms of how you are compensated at work.

If you receive a salary and a year-end bonus, complete an estimate of the bonus information in terms of when you expect to

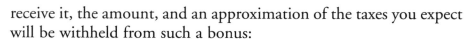

receive it, the amount, and an approximation of the taxes you expect will be withheld from such a bonus:

Date of bonus ____/____

$ _____ Bonus amount

$ _____ Taxes

$ _____ Take-home from bonus

If you do not receive a regular salary but are either paid hourly or your income fluctuates on a seasonal basis, locate your prior year W-2 form that will summarize your earnings and withholdings. Calculate how you expect your income to change from the prior year and staple this information to your W-2.

$ _____ Prior-year earnings

$ _____ Estimated change

$ _____ Current-year estimated earnings

☐ **Expenses—Summary of Prior Year's Spending or Check Registers and Credit Card Statements for that Year. (Tab 3)**

In order to prepare an accurate Cash Flow Statement, we need to know what your historical spending has been. Don't worry if you have no idea of what that is—much less any desire whatsoever to find out. If you are one of the few who has a summary of spending for a recent 12-month period, then locate a copy of that report and you have completed this step!

For the rest of us, there are two options available to determine our historical spending.

Option 1 for Summarizing Historical Expenses

Online Download of Financial Transactions.

The first option is to use Quicken® to help you determine what you have spent over the past 90 days. There are distinct advantages, as well as disadvantages, of setting your checking accounts up for online downloads.

The main advantage is that you can capture historical transactions quickly—even though you still need to categorize each individual transaction. You must determine what your actual spending has been in order to accurately prepare a budget, as well as review future planning scenarios.

The main disadvantage of online banking transaction downloads is the confusion they can create in keeping your Quicken® accounts reconciled with your actual checkbook register.

My recommendation is to summarize your historical expenses manually and not set up your bank accounts for downloads. I would, however, recommend setting up your credit cards for downloads, as well as enrolling in an online bill-pay service, which will be explained in more detail in the TEN WEEKS CD.

If you choose to use the online download method, please wait to insert your spending summaries into this Tab until you have completed these online account setups and downloads.

Option 2 for Summarizing Historical Expenses:

I recommend you complete your expense documentation by manually summarizing your historical expenses. You will need to summarize at least three months of historical information, though it is best if you do a year-to-date summary.

To summarize historical expenses, you can enter those item by item in Quicken®, or you can do a manual summary from your charge cards and check registers. Once you have a total for each expense category, you can enter this into Quicken®.

To summarize your expenses manually, you can simply list your check amounts or credit card charges under their proper category, using the expense summary in this section. I have highlighted the minimum categories you will need. I recommend you complete this summary by following these steps;

1. Locate a pad of paper. Turn it so it is wider rather than longer—landscape vs. portrait.

2. Title the page _____ (month) Expense Summary.

3. Copy the expense categories across the top of your pages (use several sheets for one month if you need to.) Use the categories from the chart on page 70.

4. Locate your check registers and credit card statements. Copy the individual purchases from those source documents onto your summary form. Do not enter the total credit card bill you pay from your check register in your summary— enter the individual charges, even if you haven't paid your credit card bill in full at the time you do this summary.

5. It is unnecessary to enter details such as the actual vendor, check number, or credit card date.

By summarizing spending by month, you create a basis for creating a current monthly spending budget.

HOUSING	Month	Year
Mortgage(s)		
Property taxes		
Rent		
Condo/assn fees		
Other		
UTILITIES		
Gas, electric		
Water and sewer		
Telephone/Internet		
Trash collection		
Cable TV		
TRANSPORTATION		
Gas, oil, repairs		
Parking/other		
License/taxes for autos		
Bus/train/taxi/limo		
RECREATION		
Vacations		
Entertainment		
Books and subscriptions		
Sports/Hobbies		
Health club		
Membership fees		
Other		
INSURANCE		
Homeowners		
Auto		
Life		
Medical/dental		
Disability		
Long-term care		
Excess liability		
Other		
PERSONAL ITEMS		
Gifts		
Charitable contributions		
Education/classes (self)		
Personal care		
Pet care		
Other		
Sub Total column 1		

PROFESSIONAL	Month	Year
Lawyer		
Other		
HOUSEHOLD		
Maintenance/repair		
Furnishings (purchases)		
Services (cleaning, lawn)		
Home Security		
FOOD		
Groceries		
Meals out		
CLOTHING		
Purchases		
Cleaning/tailoring		
HEALTH CARE		
Prescriptions		
Medical out-of-pocket		
Dental		
Other		
OTHER FIXED		
Alimony		
Child support		
Child care		
Elder care		
Other		
DEBT		
Vehicle loans		
Credit cards		
Education loans		
Investment loans		
Other		
EDUCATION		
Private school(s)		
College(s)		
Other		
Sub Total column 2		
Sub Total column 1		
TOTAL		

❏ Investments (Tab 4)

Insert your actual investment statements in your My Authentic Money Guide binder's monthly divider.

In this tab, enter account registration and indicate you have posted online access information to the Quicken® password vault. Instructions for using this vault are located on the TEN WEEKS CD, Week One, *Password Vault Usage*. I do not recommend you write those access codes here. Simply place a check mark under the "vault" column when you have entered your PIN and password information into the Quicken® vault.

Investment Name/Owner:	Account Number:	PIN & Password Posted to Vault:	Date/Balance:

❏ Current Cash (Checking and Savings Accounts) (Tab 5)

As your savings account and checking statements arrive each month, insert them in the My Authentic Money Guide binder.

Complete the following information as it pertains to your checking and savings accounts for this section:

Bank/Owner:	Account Number:	PIN & Password Posted to Vault:	Date/Balance:

❑ Company Retirement Plan Statement of Benefits (Tab 6)

In general, there are two types of company retirement plans. One is funded (paid for) completely by the employer, and the other is funded either entirely by the employee via elective contributions (payroll deductions) from his/her pay, or partially by the employer and the employee.

The Plans that are funded entirely by the employer do not always send out monthly or quarterly statements. These plans, however, should provide you with a statement at least annually of your "vested," or nonforfeitable share of the pension plan assets. These reports are commonly called an "Employee Benefits Statement." If you have misplaced your copy, your employer will provide you with another. Insert this statement here.

The plans that have a mixture of employee and employer monies usually send monthly or quarterly investment reports. Please locate the most recent statement and circle the account owner information, date of the statement, and the current account valuation and insert it in your Authentic Money Guide monthly divider.

Record the following information in your "My Documents" Binder:

Pension Plan Description:	Owner:	Date of Last Statement:	Vested Balance:

❏ Statement of Projected Social Security Benefits (SSA-7004) (Tab 6)

The Social Security Administration (SSA) sends out an annual statement that estimates your retirement benefit from Social Security based on a continuation of your present income levels, as well as differing retirement date assumptions. File your most recent statements here.

If you have failed to receive this statement, you can request one by calling your local Social Security office and asking that they send you form *SSA-7004: Request for Earnings and Benefits Estimate Statement.* If you would prefer to request this information online, go to *www.ssa.gov—"Understanding Social Security"—"Request a Social Security Statement."* You will need your Social Security number, date and place of birth, mother's maiden name, telephone number, and current address.

If you do not have this information now—don't worry. It is just important to request the information now so that it will be available when we are ready for this input later on.

❏ Credit Cards (Tab 7)

As your credit card statements arrive, insert them in the monthly section of your Authentic Money Guide binder.

Complete the following information for this section: (Remember, just place a check mark under the "vault" column to indicate that you have entered that information to the Quicken® vault.)

Card Name:	Account Number:	PIN & Password Posted to Vault:	Date/Balance:	Interest Rate:

❏ **Mortgage Information (Tab 8)**

If you have refinanced your original home mortgage, please ignore this section and proceed to the next item.

Each month, you should receive a statement showing your current payment due, along with a breakdown of principal, interest, and escrow (i.e. money set aside monthly for payment later on for taxes and insurance). Please insert that statement in your Authentic Money Guide binder.

Please complete the following information for this section:

You will find this information on the Promissory Note you received at closing when you purchased your home. Locate that note and insert it in a sheet protector in this section. Since the original document has been recorded at your local County Clerk's office, you can keep your copy of the note here.

Lender:	Date of Loan:	Amount Borrowed:	Interest Rate:	Loan Length:

❏ **Loan Refinance Documents if Your House Loan Has Changed Since Purchasing Your Home (Tab 8)**

Another "big, fat file" that probably hasn't seen the light of day since you refinanced your mortgage now comes in handy. The *Settlement Sheet* and *Consumer Disclosure Statements* are both helpful in determining the amount of money you originally borrowed, period for repayment, interest rate, and initial escrow deposit requirements. Please locate these two statements and insert them here.

Complete the same information requested in the prior section for your refinanced loan:

Lender:	Date of Loan:	Amount Borrowed:	Interest Rate:	Loan Length:

❑ Other Liability Statements—Car Loans, etc. (Tab 8)

Locate your most recent loan statements for all debts and circle the current balance, interest rate, and monthly payment amount. Insert them in your Authentic Money Guide binder under the appropriate month.

Complete the following information for these other loans for this Tab.

Lender:	Account Number:	Current Balance:	Interest Rate:	Monthly Payment:

❑ Loans Made to Others (Tab 8)

Many times, loans that are made to family members or friends have no specific repayment terms. Please evaluate whether or not you really expect to be repaid for these types of loans.

Note: It is usually best to categorize these transactions as "gifts" and to pause and ground around how that leaves you feeling. This may be a good opportunity to consider a discussion about these feelings with your partner and possibly the person who received this money.

For other loans that were made in a more business-like manner, please locate the promissory note that summarizes the terms of your loan. Most likely, there will be an amortization schedule (which shows how the loan should be repaid on a payment-by-payment basis) attached to the promissory note. Insert a copy of those documents here. (The originals should be kept in a safe place.)

Complete the following information for these loans:

Loan #1

Payor (whom I/we loaned the money to): _____

Amount of Loan: _____

Regular Payment Amount: _____

Frequency of Payment: _____

When Loan Is to Be Repaid: _____

Current Balance: _____

Loan #2

Payor (whom I/we loaned the money to): _____

Amount of Loan: _____

Regular Payment Amount: _____

Frequency of Payment: _____

When Loan Is to Be Repaid: _____

Current Balance: _____

❏ Purchase Documents for Your Home (Tab 9)

First of all, we need to determine the cost of your home because there may be tax due when you sell it in the future.

Remember that big, fat folder you were handed when you bought your dream home? Please find it. Look for a two-page legal paper that has the words "Settlement Statement" or "Buyer's Statement" on the heading. This will tell you exactly what you paid for your home, as well as the original amount of the mortgage. Insert those papers here.

What if you can't find these documents? Please try and remember what you paid for your home and when you purchased it. Write that information in this section.

Since you purchased your home, you have most likely made improvements. I recommend that a big-picture approach be taken here rather than going back and trying to document every expenditure. The reason for this is that, under current tax law, you are entitled to exclude up to $250,000 of gain from the sale of a residence in which you have lived at least two of the last five years prior to sale. If you are married and own the house together, that exclusion is raised to $500,000. Unless the potential gain on your home exceeds those amounts, establishing the exact cost of your home for tax purposes is not critically important. Please refer to MAP 21 for a worksheet that will help calculate this gain.

What is critically important, however, is that you do not underestimate any potential tax exposure from the sale of your home. Even with the $500,000 gain exclusion that applies to a couple who have owned and lived in their home at least two years preceding its sale, large real estate appreciation, coupled with a low tax cost from their prior homes, can trigger tax. There are tax consequences as well if you have converted your residence to a rental. Please see "Purchase

Documents for Any Real Estate You Own" at Tab 9 if this applies to your situation. Let me illustrate the impact of errors in estimating the tax cost of your residence:

Let's say you estimated your house tax basis was $100,000. Since you plan to sell your home for $350,000 and you have owned and lived in your home for more than two years, you think you will be fine and owe no tax. What if you forgot about the gain on prior homes on which you didn't pay any taxes? What if that gain reduced your tax cost in your current home to only $10,000. In that case, when you sell your home, you end up with a capital gain of $340,000, of which $250,000 is exempt from tax (assuming you don't qualify for the joint exclusion). The remaining $90,000 could end up costing you about $18,000 in tax, assuming you have a 5 percent state income tax rate and that the lower capital gains tax rates passed in 2003 will not be repealed in the future.

Failure to pause and determine "real numbers" would cause you to overstate your assets by this amount once we get around to entering values in Quicken®. Even though this may not seem like a large error now, just look at what happens later on.

If you are 40 now and need this money at age 70, this error would result in an overstatement of assets of $137,026, if you were able to make 7 percent per year with that original money. **This could end up reducing your monthly income after age 70 by approximately $1,062/month**, *assuming that same 7 percent return.*

Determining your home cost is important not only for tax filing requirements, but also for making sure that you are aware of your actual investment in your home when you try to determine your selling price. Follow the steps outlined below to accurately calculate your home's tax cost;

? **Step One: Did you sell your prior residence before May, 1997? If so, please complete the following; if not, please proceed to Step Two.**

Date Sold:	Unreported Prior House Sale Gains from Form 2119*

*Prior to current tax rules—re: the exclusion of gain from a sale of a residence—gain was not recognized on the sale of a home as long as a more expensive replacement home was acquired within a certain amount of time. In determining whether your gain is in excess of the current $250,000 ($500,000 if married) exclusion, the amount of gain on all prior residences that was never subject to tax must be subtracted from your current home's purchase price.

Rather than spending hours trying to recalculate how much gain on prior home sales needs to be subtracted from the cost of your current home, find your tax return that reports your last home sale prior to May of 1997.

Enter these prior gains in the worksheet above as they are on the "unreported gain from Form 2119" line.

? Step Two: Calculate the initial cost of your current home.

(This information comes from the Settlement Statement you found at the first of this Tab's section or from your best recollection.)

Initial Purchase:

Date of Purchase	Purchase Price	Settlement Charges*

*Loan costs, taxes, utilities, and homeowner fees are not allowed as items that increase the tax cost of your home. Enter other items than these listed from your settlement statement here.

? Step Three: Calculate the improvements you made to your home after its purchase.

Subsequent improvements:

Date of Improvement	Improvement	Estimated Cost of Improvement

? Step Four: Summarize the above information to arrive at the actual tax cost of your current home.

Please add the initial cost and improvement costs to total:

Total Actual Cost of Current Home:

See Steps 2 & 3 $ _____ *

    Less: Unreported Gain from Form

    2119—See Step One $ _____

Total Tax Cost of Current Home: $ _____

(When Quicken® asks for the cost of your home, enter the "Tax Cost.")

*You may want to use this cost when you consider what the sales price of your home should be. Many times, market value will be far greater or less than your actual investment, and other times it can be close. In this latter case, documenting your cost can help you or your Realtor convince a purchaser that your asking price is reasonable.

❏ Purchase Documents for Any Real Estate You Own (Tab 9)

If you happen to own a rental unit, a lot, or other real estate, the process of establishing your investment in that property is more important than what we have just described for your residence. The reason for this is that all of the gain is subject to tax upon you receiving money from a sale. The information you will need is the same as was outlined for your home. Rather than "estimated" cost of improvements, though, you should provide "actual" costs of improvements.

A good place to look for this information is the Depreciation Schedule (IRS Form 4562) attached to your tax return. This schedule should be supported by a detailed listing of your real estate investment, which shows your original cost and any subsequent improvements you made to the property that were not taken as current repair items.

The only item that may not be included in your detailed listing is the portion of the purchase price that was allocated to land. Since land doesn't theoretically drop in value, it is not eligible for depreciation allowances. You may need to call your accountant if the land portion of your investment seems to be missing.

Don't forget to outline current year improvements you have made to the property on a plain paper summary sheet titled "Real Estate Cost and Improvements."

If you sell your residence that you converted to a rental, you will owe tax based on the difference between that property's tax basis (cost less any prior gains you never paid tax on plus improvement costs) and net sales price (after selling expenses). Unless you choose to reinvest all the cash from the sale in another piece of real estate (as an Internal Revenue Code Sec. 1031 "like kind exchange"), you will owe tax at a rate of 5 percent–20 percent on that gain. See MAP 8-23 for more information on "Like Kind Exchanges."

Property	Initial Cost	Improvements	Depr. Claimed	Tax Basis

❏ **Cars and Other Personal Property (Tab 10)**

Make a copy of your vehicles' registration cards and insert them in this section. Also include any extended service contracts or warranty information that apply to these vehicles.

Other *personal property* (as compared to *real property*, which is land and buildings) includes an estimate of the value of the following items:

	Replacement Value	Liquidation Value
1) Furniture and Household Effects:		
2) Antiques		
3) Recreational Vehicles		
4) Art		
5) Jewelry		
6) Other		

(When estimating the replacement value, write down what it would cost to replace the items currently. Next to this value, write down what you think you could sell the item for with only 30 days notice, the 'Liquidation Value'.)

❏ **Property Insurance (Auto and Home) Statement (Tab 11)**

Depending on whether you pay your insurance on a monthly, quarterly, or annual basis, the frequency of the statements you receive will vary. In order to determine what your premiums are for your cars vs. your house, you may need to find the annual billing summary even if you receive monthly statements. (In most cases, home casualty insurance premiums are paid by the mortgage company from an escrow account to ensure that coverage is maintained).

Please circle the following information from your latest property insurance policy or summarize it below.

Property Description	Premium	Term of Coverage	Annual Deductible	Expiration

Insert your policy's annual premium sheet in this section. Please review the summary to ensure that no property changes have occurred since it was issued.

☐ Life Insurance Statement (Tab 12)

Locate the latest billing statement you received for any life insurance policies you own, as well as the actual policies themselves. On another blank piece of paper, write: "Life Insurance Coverage Summary" and fill in the following information.

Company/Owner	Beneficiary (1)	Death Benefit (2)	CSV (3)	Loan (4)	Premium (5)

The following explanation may be helpful in completing this summary sheet:

1. "Beneficiary" refers to the person(s) who would receive the death benefit if you were to die. Many times, the actual beneficiary is no longer whom the policy owner prefers.

2. "Death Benefit" is the amount of life insurance proceeds your beneficiaries would receive upon your death.

3. "CSV" refers to cash surrender value. This is the amount of money you could receive today if you were to request the policy be terminated in exchange for cash. This type of feature only applies to Variable or Whole Life insurance policies.

4. "Loan" refers to monies you have borrowed against the cash surrender value in the policy. If you have outstanding loan balances, they are repaid upon surrender.

5. Please note if the premium is fixed for a certain period of time after the policy was issued. Fixed-term insurance is common and guarantees you a certain premium until a certain age as long as the policy is maintained in force.

❏ Health Insurance Statement if You Pay Your Own Health Insurance (Tab 13)

Many families and individuals have health insurance coverage through their employment. If this is true for you, please locate the packet that describes your health benefits and insert it in one of the sheet protectors in this section. Each time you receive a new packet, discard the old one and insert the new one.

For those of you who pay for private coverage, it is important you summarize this current coverage and cost history. In order to accomplish this, locate your latest billing statement, as well as the packet that summarized your coverage when you purchased the insurance. From those documents, complete the following:

Company	Policy Number	Current Premium	Last Year's Premium	Total Out-of-Pocket*

*List the total "out-of-pocket" medical cost your family is required to pay as part of your health insurance policy in the last column of the worksheet.

From the current premium and last year's premium column, subtract last year's premium from this year's and take the result and divide it by the prior year's premium to determine the annual increase as a percentage.

For example: If I paid $500/month last year and now pay $600/month for health insurance, my premiums increased $100/month—$100/$500 is 20 percent. My health insurance increased 20 percent this year. This is critical information when we come to working on cost projections!

_____ percent increase in health insurance premiums

❏ Other Insurance Statements (Tab 14)

Other types of insurance you may have include: disability, long-term care, business overhead, umbrella, and professional liability. If you have any of these coverages, locate the latest billing statement, as well as the most recent policies and summarize coverage on another sheet entitled, "Other Insurance Coverages."

Disability Insurance:

Disability Insurance	Insured	Waiting Period (1)	Term (2)	Monthly Benefit (3)	Monthly Premium

Some explanation:

1. "Waiting Period" refers to the time after being disabled that you must wait for coverage to begin. Ninety-day waiting periods are common.

2. "Term" refers to the length of time that disability coverage will last.

3. "Monthly Benefit" is the dollar benefit to be paid.

Other critical features to be reviewed are integration with Social Security and "own occupation." These will be discussed in more detail in Week Seven.

Long-Term Care Insurance:

Insured	Elimination Period (1)	Daily Benefit (2)	Term (3)	Inflation Protection (4)	Premium

Some Explanation:

1. "Elimination Period" is similar to the "Waiting Period" for disability insurance. It is the period of time that the insurance company will not pay benefits after you are using nursing home or home care.

2. "Daily Benefit" is the daily benefit that will be paid for nursing facility care. It is important to note if the same benefit will be paid for home care.

3. "Term" refers to the maximum amount of time that the benefits will be payable. "Unlimited" means that the daily

benefit will be paid as long as qualifying costs are incurred. "Three years" would provide only that period of coverage.

4. "Inflation Protection" covers the increase in costs at a certain rate. It is important to note if the protection is "compounded" or "simple." Over time, there is a big difference between coverage increasing on a compounded or a flat percentage basis from the original coverage amount.

Much more detailed information about Long-Term Care Insurance will be presented in Week Seven, so don't worry if some of these terms are difficult to understand now.

Other Insurance:

Insured	Type	Coverage	Deductible	Premium

This section is a place to summarize other aforementioned insurance coverages you own.

Locate your other insurance policies. Place them in a sheet protector and insert them under this Tab.

❑ Estate Documents (Tab 15)

Make copies of documents listed on page 402 and insert them here.

❑ Business Information (Tab 16)

Identify the type of business entities you own. Gather the related documents for that particular entity, and insert them in a sheet protector under this Tab:

❑ Sole Proprietorship

➤ Schedule C from Form 1040 for past two years

➤ Most recent tax depreciation schedule or listing of property with depreciation claimed

➤ Most recent year-to-date Income Statement and Balance Sheet, if available

❑ Limited Liability Company (LLC)

➤ If you own the LLC as a single member and file a Schedule C, locate the same documents as requested for the Sole Proprietorship.

- ➤ If you own the LLC with other members:
  - ➢ Copy of Form 1065—Partnership Tax Returns (for the past two years)
  - ➢ Most recent tax depreciation schedule or listing of property with depreciation claimed
  - ➢ Most recent year-to-date Income Statement and Balance Sheet, if available

❑ **Corporation or S Corporation**

- ➤ Form 1120 or 1120S Corporate Tax Returns (for the past two years)

- ➤ Most recent tax depreciation schedule or listing of property with depreciation claimed

- ➤ Most recent year-to-date Income Statement and Balance Sheet, if available

In order to integrate your business interest(s) into Quicken®, you will need to compile the following information for each entity you own:

1) **Income Information**—Most recent tax return profit or Form W-2;

Entity	Salary (1)	Distibution (2)	Dividend (3)	Other (4)

1) Salary from a Corporation or S Corporation will be entered in Quicken® as a Paycheck.

2) Distributions are cash payments made to owners from a Sole Proprietorship or LLC or Partnership. These will be reported in Quicken® as Deposits and coded to an income category that relates to this particular business. For example, "Nurse Network Income" for Ginger's business in our Quicken® example.

3) Dividends are payments to a corporate shareholder in excess of his/her salary. In most instances, these dividends will be paid from an S Corporation. They will

be entered in Quicken® as a deposit to one of your checking accounts and categorized as "Dividends from (name of business)." These payments are not subject to Social Security (self-employment) taxes.

4) In some instances, a business will make a temporary cash loan to its owner. In this instance, the deposit in Quicken® will be coded to a liability account, "Note Payable to (name of business)."

2) Valuation Information

Entity	Liquidation Value	Going Concern Value

The valuation of an entity can be illustrated using an example. The value of Nurse Network, Ginger's business, can be determined by Ginger asking the following questions: (If you own a business, please take out several blank pieces of paper and answer the questions as well. When finished, please three-hole punch those pages and insert them under this Tab.)

? Does this business make a profit in excess of what I could earn working for someone else doing the same type of work?

If Ginger works an average of 10 hours per week at Nurse Network and makes a profit (after expenses) of $250 per week, her average net profit is $25/hour. If she could only make $15/hour doing similar work for someone else, assuming her employer-paid benefits amounted to 15 percent of her pay, then her "opportunity cost" (what she could make elsewhere without buying a business) is $17.25/hour. This leaves Ginger with a premium for owning her business of $7.75/hour. Assuming Ginger works 500 hours per year, then her Nurse Network Premium income is $3,875.

If the above calculation results in a negative number, then the only value of the business would be the liquidation value of the business assets. This would be determined by subtracting any debts from the assets of the business. Ginger's liquidation value would be what she could sell her office equipment for plus any amounts she was owed (accounts receivable) that were actually collectible, less any bills she owed and less any loans she needed to pay off. The "liquidation value" of Ginger's business is $5,000.

Ginger's business may be worth more than the $5,000 because she has a "business income premium" from our first step. This means that her business may have a "Going Concern" value, in that it generates profits in excess of a fair salary to the owner.

? Are there items of income and expense in my current profit calculation that do not properly reflect my economic cash flow from this business?

The following items should be **subtracted** from the business income premium, should they apply:

➤ Nonrecurring income items—such as income from the sale of equipment

The following items are **added** to the business income premium, should they apply:

➤ Tax depreciation expense in excess of actual wear/tear on equipment

➤ Interest expense related to business loans

➤ Vehicle mileage rate reimbursements that exceed actual operating expenses

➤ Nonrecurring expense items—such as losses from the sale of business equipment

The above items convert tax-return profit to "economic" profit. The key here is to remember that it is only true economic profit for which a buyer is interested in paying.

Ginger's only adjustment item was a $1,000 addition to business income premium for tax depreciation in excess of actual economic wear and tear on her equipment.

Adding this $1,000 results in the adjusted business income premium of $4,875.

Is this the business value we should add to Quicken®?

No, this is the cash flow that the purchaser of Ginger's business might expect to receive, in addition to a salary for his/her time in the amount of $8,625 (500 hours at $17.25/hour). Depending on how dependable this income stream has been for Ginger over the past few years, the multiplier that would be applied to the adjusted business income premium could vary from two to four. (See worksheet below for an explanation.) This leads us to our third and final question.

? What income multiplier is applicable to this business' earnings?

If Ginger's business has shown a reliable track record over the past three to five years and there's no reason to think that business would decline because Ginger is leaving the business, then a potential purchaser might be willing to pay her $19,500—or four times her annual adjusted business income premium. This would result in a 25 percent annual return on the buyer's investment.

On the other hand, if Ginger had just been in business for two years and had yet to "prove" the reliability of her business profits, she may be able to receive only twice her adjusted business income premium, or $9,750, or 50 percent return for the buyer since the risk is larger.

We will assume that Ginger's business is worth $9,750 because she has only been in business a couple of years.

I have summarized this valuation process with the following worksheet:

BUSINESS VALUATION ROUGH ESTIMATE WORKSHEET *(See Page 90.)***
METHOD ONE
Capitalization of Earnings Method

STEP ONE

Is the profit shown on the tax return accurate? The first way the tax profit can distort economic profit is when the business owner's efforts have not been reflected in the tax statement or when payments made do not reflect the true economic benefit provided.

Most recent tax return profit   (a) $_____

+ Add: Salary to owner or his/her family
     shown in the above profit
                                 (b) $_____

- Less: Fair market wage to
  replace work provided by owner and family   (c) $\underline{\hspace{3cm}}$

= Equals unadjusted net premium income   (d) $\underline{\hspace{3cm}}$

(If the value determined on line d is negative, see the bottom of the worksheet for calculation of the business liquidation value.)

STEP TWO

Adjust "unadjusted net premium income" for other items which distort economic profit.

Unadjusted Net Premium Income   (d) $\underline{\hspace{3cm}}$

- Minus: Nonrecurring income*   (e) $\underline{\hspace{3cm}}$

  Office-in-home below market rent   (f) $\underline{\hspace{3cm}}$

  Other items inflating profit   (g) $\underline{\hspace{3cm}}$

+ Plus: Tax depreciation in excess of
  actual wear/tear on equipment   (h) $\underline{\hspace{3cm}}$

Interest expense on business debt   (i) $\underline{\hspace{3cm}}$

  Tax vehicle expense in excess of
actual vehicle costs   (j) $\underline{\hspace{3cm}}$

  Nonrecurring expense items, such as
losses from sale of business equipment   (k) $\underline{\hspace{3cm}}$

Other items deflating profit   (l) $\underline{\hspace{3cm}}$

= Equals: adjusted business
  income premium   (m) $\underline{\hspace{3cm}}$

* sale of assets or special income not usually received in the business

STEP THREE

Determine capitalization rate based on level of risk assumed with the business purchase.

Times: Capitalization rate multiplier (two to five times earnings with following guide):

2x—Short history of earnings—risky = 50 percent capitalization rate

3x—Stable earnings—moderate history = 33.3 percent capitalization rate

4x—Growing earnings—moderate history = 25 percent capitalization rate

5x—Growing earnings—lengthy history = 20 percent capitalization rate

(n) $\underline{\hspace{5cm}}$

= capitalization rate for my business

= **Equals: Capitalization of earnings**

Value of business (m times n) = (o) $_____

METHOD TWO
Liquidation Value of Business

Value of physical assets if sold within 30 days

$_____

Accounts receivable actually collectible within
90 days (what customers owe the business)

$_____

Cash and checking balances

$_____

- Less: Accounts payable due
(what the business owes vendors)

$_____

Business/equipment loans due

$_____

Final business closing costs

$_____

= **Equals: Business liquidation
estimate of value**

$_____

**This explanation of business valuation procedure is offered only as a means of increasing the accuracy of your Quicken® entry and should not be relied upon for determining the actual sale price of your business or an interest in a business.

Should you be faced with a potential business sale or purchase, you should always consult a qualified business valuation expert to determine the exact value of the subject property. See Section IV, Appendix D for additional information regarding finding such an advisor.

CONGRATULATIONS!!

You have organized your documents and created a record-keeping system that will allow you to stay abreast of changes in your financial life. This is essential to your grounding with money and developing attentiveness to what it is you really want.

In summary, each month, the following documents should be placed in the monthly My Authentic Money Guide dividers:

Authentic Money Guide Monthly Divider Contents
Financial Documents and Reports:

1. Pay Stubs
2. Income Receipts—rents, royalties, etc.
3. Business Income Summaries
4. Investment Account Statements
5. Credit Card Statements
6. Mortgage Statement
7. Other Loan Statements
8. Savings Account Statements
9. Checking Account Statements

Quicken® Reports:

1. Bank Reconciliation Reports
2. Transaction Report
3. Budget Report
4. Cash Flow Comparison Report
5. Cash Flow Report
6. Net Worth Report

My Documents Binder Contents

Documents that track changes in any of the 16 sections of the My Documents binder should replace those already there.

The Homefile *Financial Planning Organizer Kit* will provide a place to put the rest of the papers that don't belong in your other three binders.

Since your intention is to focus your attention on what money has to reveal to you, then it is time to take an inventory of how to reduce some of the clutter.

STEP TWO
Take Charge of the Clutter!

If you can save 10 minutes a day over the course of a year, you save 60 hours of dealing with junk mail. Here are some suggestions that can help eliminate some of the clutter:

➤ **Register on the National Do Not Call Registry**

Go to *www.donotcall.gov* and enter up to three phone numbers. You'll also need to enter an e-mail address so your registration can be verified. If you don't have an active e-mail address, you can call 1-888-382-1222 if you live in a state west of the Mississippi River (including Minnesota or Louisiana) from the phone number you want to protect.

This "free" Federal Trade Commission service will prevent telemarketers from calling these numbers.

➤ **Contact Organizations that will eliminate your name from lists that marketers buy:**

Direct Marketing Association Mail Preference Service (DMA)
PO Box 9008
Farmingdale, NY 11735-9008

DMA requires your name, address, and signature indicating your desire to be removed from all possible marketing lists. This should help reduce about 70 percent of the national direct marketing.

DMA's Telephone Preference Service
PO Box 9014
Farmingdale, NY 11735-9014

This DMA service will remove your phone numbers from telemarketing lists. Just provide your name, address, and phone number.

➤ **Call 888-567-8688 and ask that credit bureaus block your credit files from being screened for preapproved credit offers.**

➤ **Install software that screens out junk e-mail.** One good program is McAfee's SpamKiller—you can download it from *www.spamkiller.com*. This program costs $39.95, so consider the next option if you are willing to do a little more footwork.

➤ **Create a second e-mail account and use that ID when you buy products online.** All the junk e-mail associated with those purchases can then accumulate in this second e-mail, freeing you to focus your attention on e-mails that matter.

➤ **Automate financial transactions.** One of the steps of the TEN WEEKS program will be to assist in the setup of your paycheck and all regular payments for direct deposit or automatic debit from your checking account. If you regularly invest in a mutual fund, we will also automate this process. Think of the time this will give you to direct your energy to your imagination, wonder, and creativity.

For all the other paper bills, you can use Quicken® Bill Pay. Or, you can hire a service called Paytrust *(www.paytrust.com)* $12.95/month to receive all your paper bills and convert them into an electronic version you can pay with a click of your mouse! Go ahead and leave for months at a time without a worry of missing a payment deadline.

➤ **Eliminate multiple investments.** See how the paperwork changes once you establish online access to your investment accounts using the TEN WEEKS CD. If you are still overwhelmed with multiple investment statements, consider the following option:

If you're willing to use a discount broker like Schwab, Fidelity, or Vanguard, you can own your mutual funds and have them reported in one statement. With these accounts you can then request online electronic statements, thus eliminating the paper pile on your dining room counter every night. Built right into Quicken® is an investment brokerage that will also accomplish this consolidation step, as well as facilitate immediate online access and download of current valuations.

➤ **Be ruthless in trashing and recycling unnecessary paper.** Consolidate to no more than two credit cards—preferably those that will download your activity directly into Quicken®. Get rid of the multitude of department store and gas cards.

See your Homefile Handbook, Chapter 6, for categories of documents that you need to keep to verify your tax return in the event of an audit. Keep these documents for six years—preferably in a large envelope next to that particular year's tax return. Keep all your tax returns, even after the six-year period.

➤ **Touch the paper once.** As hard as it is initially, try and get into a routine with the leftover paper pile. Once a day, sort through the junk mail and throw what you can in the recycle bin and file any bills to be paid either the first or middle of the month in the "Bills to be Paid" file. Magazines should have a "home" so you can find the issue you want when you find time to read it. When it's time to pay the bills, use your filing system to save the necessary receipts (like medical records and charitable receipts); trash/recycle the rest or save them in a "Paid Bills (month)," file as we have already discussed.

STEPS THREE THROUGH SIX

You are ready to start entering your financial information into Quicken®! Start by reading Appendix B—"Recommendations for Using the TEN WEEKS CDs."

Appendix B
Recommendations for Using the TEN WEEKS CD's

Quicken® Deluxe—Windows Version is the tool that enables you to take what you have discovered about money and your Authentic Self and integrate those insights into your day-to-day life.

Because it is easy to get overwhelmed with Quicken® or any other money management software program, TEN WEEKS TO FINANCIAL AWAKENING comes with a set of instructional CDs that provide screen-by-screen guidance in using all the program's features. Throughout this book, these CDs will be referred to as the TEN WEEKS CDs and they will help you use the program to manage your finances and give money your attention rather than your energy.

The TEN WEEKS CDs are written for Quicken® Deluxe for Windows. Start by installing that program on your computer by simply inserting the Quicken® disc in your computer and following the installation instructions. This process will include setting up a new Quicken® file for your records. You can name this file whatever you like. If you have difficulty with this step, please call Quicken® Technical Support at 1-**520-618-7140.** Even though the customary charge for Technical Support is $1.95/minute, this fee is waived if you are (a) registering Quicken®, (b) Installing Quicken®, (c) converting data from a prior Quicken® version, or (d) resolving a Quicken® Bill Pay service issue. The hours for accessing this support number are 5 a.m. to 5 p.m., Pacific Time, Monday through Friday.

Once you arrive at the setup screen, remove the Quicken® CD and insert the TEN WEEKS CD #1.

The Quicken® screens that you see in the instructional CD will mirror what you will see in your Quicken® file. The TEN WEEKS CD Quicken® screen shots are not interactive; that is, you cannot enter financial information directly onto those screens. You have to return to your personal Quicken® file in order to enter your financial information.

The TEN WEEKS CD will guide you through each pertinent Quicken® screen. Once you receive instructions, simply pause the TEN WEEKS CD and click on the Quicken® icon at the bottom of the screen. When you've completed the task, return to the instructional

CD and click on the play button. By toggling back and forth between the two programs, you will see your financial picture taking shape.

Included with the TEN WEEKS CD are Helpful Hints that summarize key steps or important financial information for that section of Qucken®. You can print these Helpful Hints and place them in the appropriate section of your "My Financial Education" binder.

If you encounter a TEN WEEKS CD section that does not seem to pertain to you, I recommend you print out the Helpful Hints included in that section of the CD presentation anyway. Because many pieces of your financial education are integrated into these Helpful Hints, it is better that you determine their relevance to your particular financial situation after reading them.

The time you invest in setting up and familiarizing yourself with Quicken® will reap tremendous dividends for years to come. Once you complete the TEN WEEKS program, I anticipate you will spend no more than 30 minutes to one hour a week managing your finances, including paying bills, reconciling your cash and credit card accounts, and printing weekly budget reports and monthly financial statements!

Visit *www.tenweeks.com* for answers to Frequently Asked Questions—FAQ's—regarding the use of the TEN WEEKS CD.

Greg, Ginger, & Gil Grounded

A sample family will be used to illustrate the steps you will take in Quicken® in order to set up your finances and create your Authentic Money Guide. As a step is taken for the Grounded family, pause the instructional CD and perform the same action as it pertains to your situation. There may be screens that do not apply to you, in which case you can simply let the TEN WEEKS CD play until the next relevant screen appears.

The Process

TEN WEEKS emphasizes the importance of grounding, or pausing to notice what the details of our lives show us. The first step of learning to ground is to practice "staying" rather than "leaving" when it comes to those details. From the careful organization of documents to the precise entry of those details into Quicken®, you will practice what it means to ground and to give your money your full attention. The outcome of this process will be real-life insights into how you are aligning your true values with your actual behaviors, the foundation of true happiness.

This process is sacred and, I feel, should be honored as such. Each of you may have a symbol, routine, or practice that helps you remember this sacredness, whether it be the lighting of a candle or placing a small water fountain near your workplace. Please use whatever helps you honor the sacredness of this journey.

There will be times when you want to quit. Honor your limits and take a break. If possible, however, take a few moments to see what it is that lies beneath the surface of your frustration. Those insights will be as valuable as your continued perseverance with the program.

Partner Work

Many of you will be completing TEN WEEKS with a spouse or partner. This adds a depth to the program that can enhance its benefits to each of you, but it also brings some potential frustrations that should be addressed.

It is likely that one of you is more highly motivated to complete this program than the other. This difference in perspective can be honored as a blessing rather than resisted. There will come a time when your partner will ask you to support something he/she sees as an opportunity for growth, thus inviting you to grow in a way you may have easily avoided. I feel it is completely valid for one partner to complete all of the Quicken® work alone and share the benefits of that work with the other. If possible, I recommend that both partners at least read the materials and complete the worksheets that do not require Quicken® input.

It is important that each of you release your expectations of the other and how he/she should interact with the program. What may be extremely helpful to you may not speak to your partner at all, and visa versa. The best chance of completing the program as a team will come out of a commitment to focus on your own growth and development and not what the other person should be learning. Fostering this atmosphere of support and personal responsibility, without judgment, will not only produce an Authentic Money Guide that incorporates each of your longings but will deepen your relationship as well.

Should each of you desire to participate more thoroughly with the program, it is still important to realize that schedules will not always allow you both to be present when completing each phase of TEN WEEKS. If possible, read the book and complete the worksheets during the same Week of the Program. I also recommend that each of you answer the worksheet questions individually. To facili-

tate this, please consider purchasing the **TEN WEEKS TO FINANCIAL AWAKENING** *Worksheet Workbook.* (Available from *www.tenweeks.com*) If you want to avoid this extra cost, simply number the question and write down one partner's answers in a notebook. Whenever you are able to read the material and complete the written portion, try and take some time to share your discoveries before moving on to the next Week.

When you are able to input your financial transactions or prepare planning scenarios in Quicken® together, I recommend you take turns entering information into Quicken® every 15 minutes or so. The person not entering data can watch for a while or simply take a break. This trade-off allows each of you practice with Quicken®, as well as a chance to interact with the process in a more complete manner.

If a Quicken® input session is completed by only one of you, it is important that the details of that session be shared with the partner. Rather than be frustrated with scheduling conflicts, try and stick to the time schedule commitment you each individually committed to in Section Two.

Please be gentle with one another. In my 25-plus years of advising clients on financial matters, I have learned that the money attentiveness you are practicing will trigger reactivity and blaming. When that happens, please try and see what it is within yourself that is asking for your gentle attention. Money has separated and divided you for long enough—allow it to bring you closer together.

Don't expect to avoid all conflict in this process. When those conflicts arise, practice listening rather than judging. When you want so badly to respond defensively, practice repeating what you heard and asking the other person if what you heard was what he/she wanted to convey. This simple step can work wonders in fostering mutual support and understanding.

Staying Organized

It is important to follow the guidelines for organizing your Quicken® work, as well as your day-to-day financial records. Nothing will derail your completion of the TEN WEEKS program more quickly than paper scattered around your workspace.

To avoid this, make a point of identifying useful reports and using a three-hole punch to prepare them for placement in the appropriate section of your three binders. Throw out everything else

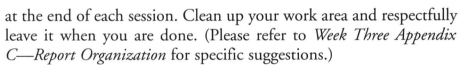

at the end of each session. Clean up your work area and respectfully leave it when you are done. (Please refer to *Week Three Appendix C—Report Organization* for specific suggestions.)

Also, take 10 minutes a day to sort your mail. Soon, you will have the option to set up certain bills in Quicken® Bill Pay as automatic payments. Any written invoices or statements for those automatic payments should be three-hole punched and filed in the current month section of your Authentic Money Guide binder if those documents fall into one of the nine categories listed. The remaining automatic payment invoices can be filed in the Current Month Paid Bills file. For other bills that require a Quicken® Bill Pay entry or a printed or manual check, place them in a file labeled "Current Month's Bills." Once or twice a month, take that file to your workspace and pay your bills, filing the documents after you are done.

Bank and investment statements should also be three-hole punched and filed immediately upon receipt in the current month divider of your Authentic Money Guide binder.

Make a commitment to keeping your My Documents binder current. For example, when you receive a new insurance policy, review the Homefile *Organizer Kit* to see if you need to retain the old document, and replace the old policy with the new one. Then take a minute to update your Authentic Money Guide with any new data provided in the new document. I find it helpful to place a check mark and date on the lower right-hand corner of the first page of the document, indicating you have integrated it into your Authentic Money Guide.

These suggestions may seem *nit-picky*, but trust me, these simple steps will help you regain the energy and freedom that we all lose so easily to the mountain of data that assaults us each day.

If you are already a Quicken® Deluxe user, please insert your first TEN WEEKS CD into your computer.

If this is your first time using Quicken®, please open Quicken® Deluxe and install the program. Once you reach the Setup section, remove the Quicken® CD from your computer and insert the first TEN WEEKS CD.

Now, let's start this exciting journey, together!

WEEK THREE

Your Spending and Budget: What Is It You Really Want?

After the third week, you will have taken a close look at your spending and what it reveals about your life. Using Quicken®, you will have crafted a budget that integrates into your daily life the priorities that honor what it is you really want.

THE UNCONSCIOUS/CONSCIOUS CONNECTION

It wasn't long after Wally had fixed my fan that another problem surfaced with our new home—the thermostat on our furnace. After banging around in the utility room for an hour with no resulting warm air, Katherine pleaded with me to "Just call Wally; he'll know what to do!" Swallowing my pride, I conceded, knowing that Mend It Man, Wally's business, would most likely become a frequent entry in our check register!

It was no surprise that just 10 minutes after Wally's arrival he had located the problem and ordered the part. Seeing Katherine's dismay that there would be no heat for 24 hours, he walked back to his truck and returned with a large space heater. As the kitchen warmed, we asked Wally to stay and join us for breakfast. He obliged.

It happened to be a Saturday morning, so we ended up sitting around the kitchen table for a couple of hours.

The conversation meandered back and forth comfortably, as we learned about how Wally and Jane had met and eventually decided to semiretire in Durango.

"It seems that you and your family have an ideal life, at least from our vantage point from this side of the valley. You've been successful enough in your careers to move to Durango from Denver in your early…50s?" Katherine had a way of getting to the pertinent facts.

Wally shook his head and smiled. "Fifty-five in my case, and I'm not at liberty to discuss my wife's age or dress size."

"I'll have to agree with Katherine, Wally. If the American Dream is to work hard and then retire at an age when your health is great

99

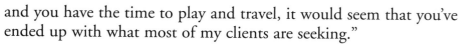

and you have the time to play and travel, it would seem that you've ended up with what most of my clients are seeking."

"Jane and I are very grateful to be living here in Durango. When we moved here five years ago, I think we both thought Durango would provide an escape from some of our problems. The concept of a simple life away from the hectic pace of Denver was appealing. I had always wanted to build a log cabin, and I think Jane felt that reducing our standard of living would help ease some of the financial tensions in our marriage."

"And Durango didn't solve all your problems?" Katherine said.

Wally smiled and responded, "The *geographical cure* didn't work. 'Wherever you go, there you still are' has turned out to be true in our experience."

I wasn't sure if I was overstepping, but I blurted out what was on my mind: "Did the move help to ease some of the financial tensions in your marriage?"

"Yes and no. The trouble wasn't a lack of money. The trouble was not knowing how to really discuss each of our hang-ups about money. Jane's first husband, Jerry, was killed in a small plane crash eight years ago. Jane and her son, John, got a sizeable settlement from Jerry's life insurance policy."

"I had no idea, Wally. I'm so sorry," Katherine responded, slightly shocked as all was not as it seemed for the "ideal neighbors in the rustic little cabin."

"It's definitely taken some time for us to finally realize that how we were dealing with money and our financial matters was a reflection of what we were afraid to look at in our lives. I'm not able to speak for Jane, but I can clarify what I mean, if you're interested."

"It sounds like there's something here for Paul and me. I'd be grateful if you'd be willing to give us some insight in how money could give us a clue as to some recurring conflicts we have—'minor' as they are!" Katherine glanced my way with a mischievous little grin as she finished her sentence.

"When Jane and I married, I felt like we could move to a small town somewhere and leave our pasts behind. Jane and I had spent quite a bit of time in counseling, trying to deal with my divorce and Jerry's death and all the 'baggage' that surrounded those events in our lives. We even did some sessions with John, and it seemed like we were making some real progress toward building a new life.

"What we hadn't been able to confront was the impact of the life insurance money on our relationships. It was the reminder that, no matter how hard we tried, there were wounds from the past that would never completely heal.

"I guess that I forgot to mention that I had some pretty significant money leftovers, too. I was married 16 years, and the court decided that Anne, my ex, was entitled to half of my retirement plan from work. So, Jane ends up bringing money that reminds us of Jerry, and I end up bringing a lack of money that reminds us of Anne.

"Whenever I wanted to sit down and see how we could better stay on top of our finances, Jane would just freak out. I should have had a clue that there was more going on than a resistance to abide by a budget, but I'm a slow learner! We'd always end up in this blaming contest and eventually decided that it was one area that we'd have to let go of if we wanted to stay married. The problem was that just because we didn't talk about the money didn't mean that our conflict vanished.

"It took the downturn of the economy and the offer of early retirement from the engineering firm where I worked, and our deep longing to move to Durango, to make us confront the money monster that lurked behind every corner. Thank goodness we found a financial planner who not only helped us see what some of the financial issues were in our lives, but who could listen to us talk long enough to help us begin to see what was really going on.

"We discovered that we both found it difficult to believe that we were acceptable, what with our baggage and wounds. We resisted dealing with our money problems because of its link to those fears.

"We just weren't able to deal with money in a very forthright and conscious manner until we could uncover the unconscious motivations that were operating beneath the surface.

"Once we started to accept ourselves and what had taken place in our lives, we found it easier to accept and support one another. This sensitivity to each other's wound left Jane and me with a deeper compassion for each another. We finally could accept that our regrets and past histories could enhance our current relationship, rather than drive us further apart.

"Understanding this dynamic of how we got triggered into our fears because of the powerful money association with those painful events in our lives, seemed to completely shift our ability to finally

pay attention to how money could be used to help us live the life we really wanted.

"It was then that we were able to make the decision to move to Durango and finally slow down from the hectic pace of our city life."

Wally paused for a moment, as if to ponder whether or not to continue opening up to neighbors he'd just recently met, but then confided, "It's just been recently that we've become more clear about what it is we really want, not only in our external but also internal worlds. Jane and I finally have surrendered to the fact that taking care of the financial details in our lives is critical in realizing our aspirations—it's as important as daily meditation or our other spiritual practices. I believe that some call this practice karma yoga. Every detail of life is sacred. A devotee honors each moment by being fully present and releasing the outcome of his/her actions."

Wally glanced at his watch. "I can't believe I went on and on like this! Here I barely know you and I've burdened you with all the dirty laundry of our lives. I'm sorry."

"It hasn't been a burden, Wally. It's really shed some light on why I feel a resistance to enter into a very conscious relationship with money," Katherine replied. "It really made sense when you said that unconscious motivations were in charge of your reactions until you took an honest look at them."

"I also appreciate your honesty, Wally," I said. It helped me to see how there are some strong emotions around my divorce that are most likely affecting my resistance to pay full attention to our financial affairs."

"You're welcome, Paul. Once again I have witnessed first-hand what you've told me about several times. Katherine sure does have a way of saying in one sentence what I was trying to communicate over the past half hour. I so enjoyed breakfast together and am glad that space heater finally seems to be taking the chill off this beautiful fall morning. I probably ought to see if there are any more crises waiting back at the shop."

Wally thanked Katherine again for the breakfast and commented to me as he walked by the space heater: "It's nice to have neighbors who take some time to talk. Let's not wait until there's a repair to continue this conversation. I know Jane would love to meet you both."

I walked Wally out to his truck and commented, "Wally, thanks for warming up the house and also sharing with Katherine and me about your life. I look forward to continuing our conversation."

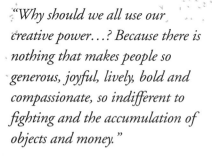

Wally agreed and rolled his car down the driveway, pausing to yell, "I'll call as soon as the part comes in!"

What Is It You Really Want?

In the first two weeks of the TEN WEEKS program, you completed the work to take a fearless inventory of your financial life. You have invested hours of time in organizing your financial records and entering them, one screen at a time, into Quicken® so you can actually see what is happening in your life, financially. You have also taken an emotional financial inventory and have been courageous enough to look at your hopes, disappointments, and fears around money and finances. All of this work has laid the foundation for the construction of a whole new "money house." Rather than constantly reacting to one financial crisis after another, you finally have the tool to use the money mirror to see what *actually is* in your life. Once you see where you really are, it's much easier to determine if there are things you'd like to change about your life. Change usually begins when we are willing to ask ourselves some important questions.

"Why should we all use our creative power…? Because there is nothing that makes people so generous, joyful, lively, bold and compassionate, so indifferent to fighting and the accumulation of objects and money."

—Brenda Ueland

The great German poet, Rainer Marie Rilke, addressed the importance of asking questions in a letter to a young friend:

> *You are so young, so before all beginning, and I want to beg you, as much as I can, to be patient toward all that is unsolved in your heart and try to love the questions themselves like locked rooms and like books that are written in a very foreign tongue. Do not now seek the answers, which cannot be given you because you would not be able to live them. And the point is, to live everything. Live the questions now. Perhaps you will then gradually, without noticing it, live along some distant day into the answer.*
>
> *—Rainer Rilke*

Now that you have taken a cold, hard look at your life by giving money your full attention, what is this "do not seek the answers" language all about? Haven't most of us lived for years "in the fog" and are finally sick and tired of wandering aimlessly?

I believe that until we gain clarity with our finances and our emotional dance with it, it is very difficult to open ourselves to meaningful questions about our lives. When the ground switch is in the "off" position, there is no energy flow that provides the insight or courage to consider the type of questioning process to which Rilke refers.

"All things are ready, if our minds be so."

—*William Shakespeare*

This week, we ask a Rilke-type question, "What is it you really want?" Another way to get to the same place is to ask, "What is my life really about?" The point of this exercise is not to arrive at a precise answer, rather to begin a process of attentiveness to your True Life.

Before beginning the questionnaire, take a few moments to sit quietly with this David Whyte poem:

THE OPENING OF EYES

The day I saw beneath dark clouds
the passing light over the water
and I heard the voice of the world speak out,

I knew then, as I had before
life is no passing memory of what has been
nor the remaining pages in a great book
waiting to be read.

It is the opening of eyes long closed.
It is the vision of far off things
seen for the silence they hold.
It is the heart after years
of secret conversing
speaking out loud in the clear air.

It is Moses in the desert
fallen to his knees before the lit bush.

It is the man throwing away his shoes
as if to enter heaven
and finding himself astonished,
opened at last,
fallen in love with solid ground.

—David Whyte

Week Three
Worksheet A

What Is It I Really Want?

Imagine you are entering an art gallery featuring your Current Life picture on display. As you gaze at your current life picture, what do you notice?

By answering the questionnaire below, compare your actual life picture to what you really want and complete the sentence for each category:

"When I compare my actual life picture with regard to _____ (area of my life), what I notice is _____ and I'd like to _____"

Examples:

Area of my life	what I notice is...	and I would like to...
Work	I come home exhausted at the end of each day with no energy for exercise or my family	leave work each day by 5:00 p.m. and leave work early two days a week so that I have time for family and/or exercise.
Things to Have	our house is too large for just the two of us to spend time maintaining it and cleaning it	free up my time for house care; consider a smaller house that is big enough for guests.
Work		
Soul/Spirit Work		
Creativity/Passion		
Play		

Area of my life	what I notice is…	and I'd like to…
Relationships (Family/Friends)		
Philanthropy/ Giving		
Things to Do (Travel, vacation, etc.)		
Things to Have		
Other Money Goals		

Please prioritize the "I would like to" statements below.

I Would Like (Priorities)	One Step Toward This Goal and Its Estimated $ Consequence
1.	
2.	
3.	
4.	
5.	

CHANGE—FROM THE INSIDE OUT

> *"No one has to change.*
> *You only have to enter into conversation."*
>
> —David Whyte

The *What Is It I Really Want?* questionnaire continues a conversation with your Authentic Self that has surfaced at different times in your life. Out of this dialogue flows a desire to change certain things in your life experience. Close attention to these desires will allow you the opportunity to embody them in your Authentic Money Guide, a document that assists you in respecting the vibrant fluidity of your life.

We've all experienced times in our lives when we "got it!"—when a new truth or realization made us feel alive again. Our daily routines, however, seemed to suck the life right out of our new-found vision, and soon we had forgotten what had quickened us so in the first place.

Is it really possible to change or to honor what we really want? How can taking such a detailed look at our money and finances help shift us into a place of fulfillment rather than disappointment with this journey of life?

Change Pitfall #1—Guilt and Deprivation

Personally, I am motivated to change because of my deep-seated belief that I am "bad" and need to try harder to be "good." I come by this honestly, after years of hearing that my true nature is sinful and prone to selfishness. Though I'm motivated, real change is both unpleasant and difficult to accomplish because I know that there will never be a place that I can rest. Even if I've made some "improvement," I'm sure that another failure will soon surface that will fuel my guilt and shame.

I have no problem relating to Sy Safransky's critical relationship with himself:

> *"This morning, I'll refrain from passing judgment. This morning, I'll be merciful to the man who drank too much and smoked too much and ate too much last night. I'll take off my black robe, step down from behind the bench, and sit beside him. This morning, he'll be amazed to find a sympathetic ear. I might even laugh at one of his jokes; he means no harm. How many*

times has he begged for forgiveness? How many times have I condemned him? Now it's just the two of us, the courtroom empty, the sun rising in the east."

—Sy Safransky, The Sun Magazine, February, 2002)

When you grow up trying to prove you're "good enough," you inevitably end up in a counselor's office! When I visit my counselor (on a regular basis) he often suggests I examine what aspect of myself is driving my behaviors and reactions. He tells me I have at least three internal voices telling me how I should best survive in this scary world: My *Critic, Child,* and *Adult.*

The vocal chords of my Critic are very well developed, drowning out the cries of my Child and Adult. Whenever my Child "acts out" and behaves impetuously or in an "irresponsible manner," he is immediately reprimanded by my Critic. Of course, the more my Child's needs are ignored, the more frantic and unreasonable his demands become. My Critic definitely has his hands full with this screaming Child. My Critic means well, after all, he's just looking out for my best interest by leaving no room for a real-life rejection that could end up with the whole Trio in exile!

"It's never too late to have had a good childhood."

—Jim Roi

I'm told that as I open up and live more Authentically, I can insist that when my Child is scared or has a complaint, my Critic allow my Adult to enter into the conversation. You can imagine the terror my Critic feels when he's asked to surrender control of this maniacal Child, even for a minute. He might acquiesce, but my Adult will not only need to be patient, but genuinely grateful for his unrelenting diligence to provide a safe place for this dysfunctional family.

Like a good parent, my Adult patiently and compassionately listens to the needs of both my Child and my Critic. Once they've voiced their needs and felt assured that he genuinely wants to honor their concerns in responding to the situation, they quiet down. When I "ground" long enough to identify my underlying needs, the reactive responses of my Child and Critic are tempered by the calming voice of my Adult. It is then that my behaviors become more aligned with my grown up Authentic Self.

I can change old patterns if I lend a sympathetic ear to what fears I've ignored for far too long.

After reading about Sy's courtroom encounter, I took another look at how I had answered the *What Is It I Really Want?* questionnaire. It finally made sense why these goal-based exercises had rarely worked for me. If my Critic were the one speaking as I tried to discern what I wanted, the focus would be on finding the right answers or filling out all five "I would like to" goals. He would be concerned about how my answers might threaten the place he'd worked so hard to secure. He, most definitely, would need to keep the Child's unreasonable demands from ever being heard.

If my Child were able to get a few words in edgewise, he would advocate for making up for lost time in expressing myself; like a sensory-deprived adolescent, no amount of stimulation would be in excess. There would definitely be a strong tone of defiance against authority and structure, as the Critic's use of these tools had kept the Child imprisoned all these years.

My Adult is capable of honestly facing my sadness over spending most of my life trying to be "good enough," as well as squelching my playful authenticity and creativity. Out of that honesty, a sense of calmness and clarity emerges, and I'm surprised at what it is I really want. In that quiet place, I am able to finally rest, knowing that there is nothing to prove or achieve. I see that there is no longer a need to react to external authority. My Child and Critic had reached a joint decision long ago that survival depended on sacrificing personal Authenticity. Problems arose when my Child wanted to break the covenant. My Critic responded harshly and the Child's resistance to his authority intensified each year.

I also see that money has no power to make me either good or bad, but it can facilitate a conversation with my Authentic Self. I can begin to look for ways in which my core goodness is surfacing in money decisions. There are plenty of indications that what I say I want is, in fact, finding expression in my life.

No longer do I have to try and force money into covering up my inherent failure and unworthiness to measure up to an unattainable ideal. No longer do I have to be trapped in the cycle of "deprivation to decadent indulgence to deprivation to…" that accompanies my guilt. By releasing the shame, I am able to live in a more balanced way, not only with my money, but also with all the other areas of my life identified in the *What Is It I Really Want?* questionnaire.

'Trust that still, small voice that says, "This might work and I'll try it."'

—*Diane Mariechild*

I now realize the most important aspect of integrating the specific monetary goals into my Authentic Money Guide is that they remind me that what had caused my suffering was not so much *what* I had done with my money as *why* I had been making those decisions.

Please take a few minutes and review your *What Is It I Really Want?* questionnaire. What aspect of yourself spoke loudest when you initially answered the questions? What voice emerges as you allow your Adult to calm the conflict between your Critic and Child? What is it you REALLY want?

Please don't read any further until you've identified *who* (i.e. your critic, child or adult) answered *what*.

Change Pitfall #2—Dread and Avoidance

Guilt and Deprivation is not the only deterrent we humans struggle with as we seek to change. Change is also stifled by a sense of fear. The faces of fear are innumerable, but the central character speaks to us in the language of dread and/or avoidance. Deep down, we cringe with the thought that one day all our efforts to be safe and secure in this world will fail, and we'll have to face the hollow shell of our lives. This fear manifests itself in two dialects: *dread* and/or *avoidance*.

Those speaking the dread dialect generally feel no guilt about improving their life situations. After all, they are reminded many times a day that a compulsion to get ahead is what will give them happiness and security. Money gives this group the power to plan for a brighter future, complete with increased leisure/comfort and the ability to savor the sweet nectars that are paraded as not only accessible but as necessary. Money is also critical in securing the three A's that are essential for happiness: Appearance, Affluence, and Achievement.

"It is a great obstacle to happiness to expect too much."

—*Bernard de Fontenelle*

Avoidance, on the other hand, manifests itself as inertia while dread surfaces as frantic busyness. If we ignore our fears long enough, they begin to rob us of our will to do much of anything to improve our lives. A "What's the use, anyway?" despondency settles in. This depression, combined with the confusing noise of the countless solutions proposed everywhere, justifies our path of avoidance.

While those in the shame and guilt camp gravitate toward introspection and solitude, those in the dread camp tend toward busyness and activity. Even when dread leads to inertia, the constant hum of background "money noise" helps to fill the uneasy silence we seek to avoid. Whatever the pitfall to change is for us individually, this noise deafens the small voice of our own wisdom that tells us the truth about our lives.

Money Noise

Money noise is advice that promises us the key to happiness and the good life through what money can buy.

"Noisy" is one word that can capture the essence of our 21st century American lives. We are bombarded with noise in our lives, from without—horns, planes, cars, garbage truck beepers, radio, TV's drone—and from within:

> *"I wonder if I should sell the mutual fund I bought last month—it sure isn't doing very well."*

> *"I know I don't have the money, but this could be the Lotto ticket that puts me on 'easy street'!"*

> *"I sure would like to go to Florida over spring break and show off a nice tan when I get back to the office."*

Over 15 years ago, the well-known *Washington Post* columnist Ellen Goodman summarized this state of affairs in a column entitled "Country Music":

> *"Without even knowing it, we are assaulted by a high note of urgency all the time. We end up pacing ourselves to the city rhythm whether or not it's our own. In time, we grow hard of hearing to the rest of the world. Like a violinist stuck next to the timpani, we may lose the ability to hear our own instrument.*

> *"...it seems to me that it is only when we leave behind the alarms and bells and buzzes and sirens, all these external demands, that the quietest sound of all comes into range: our inner voice....*

> *"George Eliot once wrote, 'If we had keen vision and feeling of all ordinary human life, it would be like hearing the grass grow and the squirrel's heart beat, and we should die of that roar which lies on the other side of silence.'*

> *"I think of that sometimes. How overwhelming to literally hear the life story of everyone we meet. But I think more often of*

"Go placidly amid the noise and haste, and remember what peace there may be in silence."

—*Max Ehrman*

the roar that keeps us from silence, the roar of daily life that makes it impossible to hear myself think."

Part of this noise is this frantic compulsion we feel to get ahead. We believe that if we pay our dues today, there will be a nice reward later. If we just work 50 hours per week now and save extra money, we can retire someday and really enjoy life. To deaden some of the pain of living in a state of "deferred fulfillment," we become addicted to all kinds of behaviors: excessive eating, drinking alcohol, taking prescription (or nonprescription) drugs, having sexual fantasies, using shopping as therapy, or even participating in high-thrill sports or gambling. There are many ways to avoid the awkward silence that reminds us that life is scary, and we are called to some deeper sense of self that is also unknown and uncertain.

Underneath the noise is a longing for something serene and restful. We long for contentment. Robert Johnson, in his book, *Contentment—A Way to True Happiness,* writes:

> *"Contentment grows out of a willingness to surrender preconceived ideas and affirm reality as it is…about the dance between what we want and what reality presents to us."*

The realities of our lives can become our best friends in helping us escape the trap of modern society. There are few teachers as powerful as money in showing us *what really is* if we are brave enough to really sit and learn what is presented.

> *"If you ask the Grail to give you happiness, that demand precludes happiness. But if you serve the Grail and the Grail King properly, you will find that what happens and happiness are the same thing. A play on words becomes the definition of enlightenment."*

> —*Robert A. Johnson*

We are looking for a way to rediscover the energy that empowers Authentic living. There's got to be more than, *I owe, I owe—it's off to work I go!* We want to be able to examine our lives in the light of silence and feel like we embody this prayer:

> *"Endow us with the wisdom to produce and share what each being needs to grow and flourish…."*

(Aramaic translation of "Give us this day our daily bread…")

We can reclaim that "inner voice." We can hear that "roar which lies on the other side of silence." We can tap into "the wisdom to produce and share what each being needs to grow and flourish." We do these things in simple steps of dealing with what presents itself right now.

For those who relate more to dread and avoidance than guilt and deprivation, the *What Is It I Really Want?* questionnaire responses and the related *I Would Like To* statements provide links to reframing those goals differently from when they were just another way to keep running from the fear. They serve as reminders of the capacity we all have for enjoying the wonderful gifts of life, but not getting too attached to the pleasures or too obsessed with avoiding the pains that are sure to come our way.

Help to Change

"It is easier to produce ten volumes of philosophical writings than to put one principle into practice."

—*Leo Tolstoy*

Remember the symbol we used during Weeks One and Two to capture the essence of taking an honest inventory and how that related to linking up with a functional and complete electrical system? It was the image of the Sun—we saw that when we finally had the courage to admit what was true in our lives, we were much more willing to receive help to deal with it. We saw that underneath our resistance to do our money homework, to take an honest inventory of our finances and emotions around money, was a reluctance to really admit our need and our inability to fix that need on our own.

I believe there is a powerful energy source available to each of us who ground and notice our real needs. I've discovered I suffer when I try desperately to meet those needs with my tried-and-true survival tools. My experience testifies that my close attention to my money behaviors gives me a much better chance of actually changing and feeling better about my life.

If I want to be a kinder and more compassionate husband by being fully present with my wife at dinner, how in the world can that aspiration be reflected in my finances?

First, giving money my attention, like my Adult finally paying attention to the rantings of my Child, resulted in a sense of calm that allowed me to hear what I really wanted in life. That "one word" (Week One) started to express itself. Second, I could do something about building a bridge between that deep longing and my actual life via a financial decision that reminded me of my intention on a daily or weekly basis.

My "one word" was *Wanted.* I felt unwanted from the moment of my birth. That deep wound became the unconscious master of my life, influencing how I lived and interpreted each interaction. It was only in the intense quiet of my solitude on the vision quest that this wound could surface and be held.

I finally was able to understand my fear of *Wanting,* of reaching out in loving vulnerability to those who could reject me—reinforcing my terror of being unwanted.

I knew that real happiness somehow was to be found in the integration of my longing to *Want* others and my daily money decisions. It wasn't enough to discover my wound and how it affected dinner with my Katherine. To deal with a well-entrenched pattern of avoiding future perceived rejections would take some help. Budgeting money for counseling, as well as buying (and reading) helpful books about compassionately relating to my survival tools would be an authentic use of money and a clear marker of my intention.

The inclusion of $900 in my annual budget becomes a powerful vehicle for actualizing what I want. It also serves as a marker that reminds me I am changing.

Money choices are not simply related to what we purchase, but also what we consciously choose not to purchase. For example, I may notice that my liquor purchases have exceeded a certain monetary level even though I would be reluctant to admit I drink too much. At that juncture, I may then choose to limit my consumption by establishing a financial limit on my "booze budget." My choice, in effect, is to apply my money to something more gratifying, in this case my overall health. My budget helps me embrace some temporary discomfort while I forego the ritual of drinking to "take the edge off" my discontent rather than stay with it and see what it is I really need.

This new lifestyle decision is merged into my experience by the intentional inclusion of that choice in how I have set my budget and monitor my actual spending in relation to it.

The Money Tail Wagging the Dog

In my years as a tax accountant, I had to constantly remind myself that sometimes it made sense to recommend paying a little more income tax rather than adopting a plan that was inconsistent with the client's overall goals, just to save taxes. I referred to this process as, "Don't let the *tax tail* wag the dog." It seems that we often let the *money tail* wag the dog.

One of the main reasons you have taken so much time to set up your finances in Quicken® is to reclaim the time you have to spend on managing your money and financial responsibilities. But if all we did in the TEN WEEKS program was increase your financial management efficiency, there would remain plenty of opportunity for money woes to persist.

Rather than recommending a compulsive tracking system for each of our expenditures simply for the sake of saving more money or facilitating a purchase of another possession, TEN WEEKS proposes an entirely new mindset around careful attention to the details of our financial lives. We can finally begin to see why we do what we do with money.

We can easily fall into a "sacred/secular" rut that is rooted in dualistic thinking, generically expressed as follows:

> *Matter, money, and the physical life is a distraction from personal Authenticity.*

It's not about promoting some guru's self-proclaimed ideas about what a simple or meaningful life should look like. It's not saying that the purchase of a movie ticket, a new suit, a nice car, is somehow superficial or meaningless.

We've all known advocates of the "simple lifestyle" who had squeezed every ounce of compassion out of their lives in their compulsion to achieve a certain level of material simplicity. The more adept they became at limiting their acquisition of possessions, the more difficult it became for them to live with empathy and compassionate understanding with those around them who had yet to embody their particular priorities.

Wally said, "Don't underestimate the importance of being grounded." Time and time again, we've talked about how pausing to "shift into neutral" unleashes power. Pausing to notice what need we try to meet through the purchase of a $14 bottle of wine may have

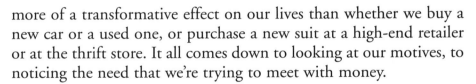

more of a transformative effect on our lives than whether we buy a new car or a used one, or purchase a new suit at a high-end retailer or at the thrift store. It all comes down to looking at our motives, to noticing the need that we're trying to meet with money.

"If I give everything I own to the poor and even go to the stake to be burned as a martyr, but I don't love, I've gotten nowhere. So, no matter what I say, what I believe, and what I do, I'm bankrupt without love."

(The Message, Bible translation—I Corinthians 13)

But you say, and rightfully so, "How can such introspective analysis—this deep soul-searching, over the tiniest details of our lives—be sustained? If every purchase in my budget leads me into a dark canyon of personal regret over my shallow life, what happiness is in that? I'd just as soon stay, 'fat, dumb, and happy' in my current relationship with money!"

Developing a new mindset based on personal and financial freedom is not about a guilt-based, introspective, psychoanalysis of each of our monetary transactions. It is, rather, a willingness to pay attention to our habits and attitudes and to notice whether they are consistent with the lives we really want. Awakening follows attention!

Cash Flow Confrontation

During the first two weeks of TEN WEEKS, you paid attention to the tiniest details of your financial life. You spent hours downloading, categorizing, and reconciling each of your individual bank and credit card accounts. You kept track of what you spent and maybe even had to own up to that box of chocolates no one else knew about!

You actually created a Cash Flow Statement. This report showed exactly what took place in your life over at least a three-month period in terms of money inflows and outflows. As you did this work, you slowly uncovered the reality of the life you live. The "small things" added together equal the whole of your life.

When my clients summarize their actual spending, they usually have one or more of the following responses:

1. "How could I have spent that much on *that*?"
2. "*You* spend too much!" (If a partner is involved)
3. "It's hopeless—there's no way we'll ever get ahead."
4. "We spend too much, we need to save more."

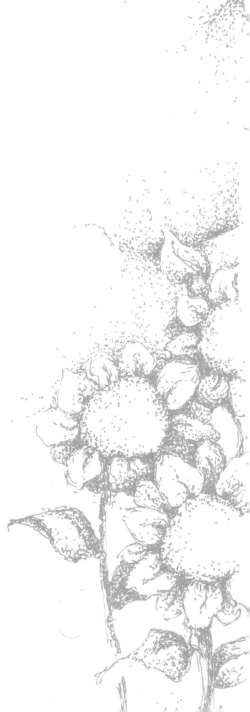

All of these responses reveal their frustration with how little they have to show for all that they spend, not only in terms of savings, but especially in terms of satisfaction and happiness.

Deborah Knuckey, author of *The Ms. Spent Money Guide*, is an advocate of "conscious spending"—taking the time to determine what types of spending brings us the most happiness and satisfaction and then aligning our financial choices with that realization.

Deborah and I talked about conscious spending on my radio program, "Money Matters." She offered these insights:

"Conscious spending is about getting more of what you want from what you already have. And it's about becoming a lot more aware of how you spend your money and aligning that with what you really value.

"Conscious spending is about, first of all, getting very clear about what it is you do value and then minimizing the money you spend on the things you enjoy less in order to free up money for the things you enjoy more.

"Unconscious spending involves having no plan, or even if you have a plan, not following it and kind of frittering money away.

"I need to choose how much of the money I earn today I'm going to spend on today vs. tomorrow, and if I'm in debt, on yesterday as well.

"Sit down, do the math and say, 'What's that all going to cost me? How much does it add up to? What do I need to do to earn that sort of money?'

"You may need to go without some things if you don't have the money for them. But in the long run, it's about saying, given the money I've got—how can I get as much of the life I want out of it?

"I took some figures from the Bureau of Labor Statistics on spending and realized that a couple of categories people spend an awful lot of their money on—almost two-thirds of every after-tax dollar they spend goes on one of two things—shelter and transportation. For most households that accounts for 50–65 percent of every dollar spent.

"We live in a society where we're not concerned about a roof over our head or a meal in our stomach—for most families that's pretty much handled. So I put security at the base of the model because it really is the foundation that we have to build our financial lives on. Security includes things such as retirement savings, disability insurance, life insurance, and a good cash cushion."

Deborah's message is clear: We don't get much satisfaction out of our spending because most of us are not clear what it is we really want, and we don't have a clue where our money goes.

There are several reasons why I believe it's hard for most of us to apply Deborah's great *conscious spending* mindset. One goes back to what Wally had to say about our unconscious fears controlling our conscious behaviors. Another is that the greatest benefit of becoming more conscious with our money is to see what it reveals about our lives. If we pause and notice—ground—with what we see, ("Why am I really buying this?") then we'll have a better chance of narrowing "the gap between our sincere values and actual behavior…the source of all self-hatred" (Bo Lozoff from the *Introduction*).

Before we look more carefully into these resistances to change, let's step back and notice a few things about our lives with the help of what we see in our financial statements.

Week Three
Worksheet B

Cash Flow Checkup

Grab a pencil and take 30 minutes to take a closer look at your spending. Retrieve the Budget Report you printed in Week One from your Authentic Money Guide binder (focus only on the middle column of this report):

Use this Budget Report to answer the following questions:

? What is the overall total at the bottom of your budget column?

_____

? Based on this cash flow surplus or shortfall, what immediate sense do you have about your overall spending?

_____

_____

? Turn the Budget Report over and close your eyes—think of life experiences that hold a high priority for you that you long to embody into your life. Write down your thoughts.

_____

_____

_____

_____

? Turn your Budget Report back over and circle the categories that are included in your list. Feel free to add some new expense categories with related spending amounts. Summarize here what you spent (or would like to have spent) in those categories:

_____

_____

_____

_____

_____

? Flip back to the "What Is It I Really Want?" Week Three Worksheet A and see if you would like to change your response to the prior question based on what you wrote in that worksheet. What expense categories reflect your true priorities? Summarize those items and the spending amounts below.

_____

_____

_____

_____

_____

_____

_____

Now file your Budget Report in your Authentic Money Guide binder—"Action Items—AMG" Section.

? Imagine that you are a newspaper reporter and the editor hands you the Budget Report you've been studying. He said the document was the only possession found on the body of a person (You!) at a crime scene. Your job is to write your obituary based on your financial statement. What would you write?

_____

_____

_____

_____

_____

_____

_____

? Now find your Net Worth Statement you filed last week in your AMG monthly divider section.

➤ Circle the categories on your Net Worth Statement that cause you the most concern. Also indicate what need you feel underlies your worry. List those categories and needs below:

_____

_____

_____

_____

_____

➤ Related to the above question, look at the "TO" categories at the bottom of the Budget Report, as well as the current balances of your assets and liabilities on your Net Worth Report.

If you had extra money from cash flow, how would your prioritize the use of that to following categories?

Increasing Cash Reserves	$_____
Decreasing Credit Card Balances	$_____
Increasing Retirement Savings	$_____
Paying off Loans	$_____
Giving It Away	$_____
Saving for College	$_____
Spending It on_____	$_____

Write a paragraph about what you have learned about your spending during this exercise and include the one thing you would like to integrate into your Authentic Money Guide because of this realization.

_____

_____

_____

_____

_____

_____

_____

THE BUDGET BUDDY

Financial Awakening is a process of paying attention to what genuine needs we are seeking to satisfy and evaluating how our financial choices and attitudes are facilitating or deterring our longings.

I believe one of the most powerful yet underutilized tools to help us reconnect to our personal authenticity and restore to us the happy, satisfied, and fulfilled life we long for is the budget.

In my 25-year professional advisory career of working with clients, I have seen the "B" word put sheer terror into the eyes of many people! We've all seen a budget as an Authority Figure of Deprivation, reminding us that we can't have what we really want. In fact, recalling the days of our adolescent rebellion, the budget makes what we're not supposed to have just that much more desirable!

If that weren't bad enough, the Budget Cop constantly reminds us that we're *bad.* If we were *good,* we could stay within our budget. About the only positive experience any of us have had with a budget is when we established one without really even knowing it. Remember a time when you wanted something so badly that you figured out you would have to go without something in order to get it? Maybe it was a special vacation or just a weekend away, but focusing more on what you wanted rather than what you were giving up was the key to the success of those unconscious budgets.

How is it, then, that the budget can become such a powerful tool in helping us find the lives that we long for? The first and most powerful way of transforming your attitude about a financial budget is to see it as a *buddy* rather than some sort of authority figure ruling your life. Most of us have had positive experiences with a buddy. Maybe it was in scouting, when our buddy kept us from getting lost in the forest. Maybe some of you have had experience with scuba diving when a buddy is absolutely essential to a safe and enjoyable diving experience. In these situations, a buddy provides companionship and helpful feedback—an outside perspective—to help us see when we've lost our way or are on the verge of danger. Such are the attributes of an Authentic or genuine financial budget.

In the first two weeks of TEN WEEKS TO FINANCIAL AWAKENING, each of you has accomplished something you have most likely never achieved before with your finances. You have captured a comprehensive view of what actually is taking place with your cash flows and the effect those cash flows are having on either the growth or decline of your financial net worth.

"In the midst of winter, I finally learned that there was in me an invincible summer."

—*Albert Camus*

It is not unusual that you may discover actual cash outflows exceed recurring cash inflows. Taking the time to summarize your financial information into Quicken® has confirmed your fears. You are going in the hole financially. There's a hole in the bottom of your *financial ship*—and you're sinking fast! The conversation you've entered into with money leaves the opportunity for significant changes to flow into your life. You are willing to surrender denial as a primary survival skill.

For others of you, your financial statements may not paint such a dire picture. Even though cash flows are sufficient to pay your bills, you're still concerned about the adequacy of your savings for retirement, your children's college education, or reserves for future "extra expenses" such as medical bills and car repairs.

What each of you brings to a conversation with a financial budget, as a result of your work so far in the TEN WEEKS program, are two very important factors. These factors can transform your budget from a *cop* to a *buddy*.

Help to Meet a Need

First, you can clearly identify, after seeing "what is" with your finances, at least one critical need. Whether that need is to control excess expenses over your income or to finally establish a savings program for one of your children's college fund or to determine if you are saving enough for retirement, you are willing and eager to see how you can apply your financial resources to the attainment of that objective.

In the TEN WEEKS CD, you will be shown how to integrate those specific needs into the creation of your Authentic Budget.

The *What Is It I Really Want?* questionnaire has revealed that the biggest need we all have is to start asking "Why?" and not just "What?" when thinking about our finances. This is critical as you create your Authentic Budget, your buddy, to guide you into the life that you want.

Timely Feedback

The second critical thing you have accessed as you develop an entirely new relationship with a financial budget, is an ease of implementing the budget—of knowing, before it's too late, how your actual finances align with your intentions.

What good is a budget if it serves as a constant reminder of your failures—nagging you, after the fact, of your inability to limit your spending or achieve your financial objectives? If the only words that come out of your budget's "mouth" are negative, critical, and full of condemnation, you'll be sure to sever your relationship with your budget.

On the other hand, if you develop an ongoing conversation with your budget buddy—noticing what is going on with your finances before you deviate from a plan that you have established as important in your life—you'll welcome the friendly reminder that alerts you to diverging values and behaviors.

The reason that TEN WEEKS encourages you to establish on-line access to your credit cards and investment accounts is to facilitate a friendly conversation with your budget buddy. If you take 5–15 minutes every evening, or possibly even 30–45 minutes once a week, you can categorize all your financial transactions, update your financial reports, and be fully aware of the categories that are close to exceeding your objectives for your Authentic Money Guide. With that knowledge, you can proceed, empowered to make choices that are aligned with the budget you established to reflect what it is that you really want.

You are finally empowered to take action before it's too late.

Discretionary and Nondiscretionary Expenses

This week, you will learn how to fine-tune your Cash Flow Statement. During that process, you will assign all your expenses to one of two categories, discretionary and nondiscretionary.

Nondiscretionary expenses are items you would have difficulty changing within six to 12 months. These are recurring bills and expenses to which you have made a commitment, e.g. house mortgage, loan payments. One of the largest components of your nondiscretionary expenses includes your income and payroll taxes. These tax obligations can consume as much as 30–50 percent of your overall income.

"Teach us to delight in simple things."

—*Rudyard Kipling*

As you establish your budget, focus mainly on your discretionary expenses.

Let's take a brief glimpse into a life that challenged the whole concept of discretionary and nondiscretionary expenses. Charles Gray took the approach that nearly all of our expenses were discretionary.

There are few within our society who take seriously the question, "How much is enough?" At the age of 52, Charles Gray, a successful college professor from Portland, Oregon, seriously asked himself what was enough. He asked himself what a "nonviolent" economy would look like.

"I thought a good and modest first step would be to neither own nor control nor consume more than my equal share of the world's wealth and to do my share of the world's work to produce that wealth…In October, of 1977, I began to live on my equal share, what I have now dubbed as the World Equity Budget (WEB)."

—*Charles Gray,* Toward A Nonviolent Economics

To do this, he liquidated his assets and gave away all but $1,200. He lived on an average of $99 per month from 1977–1993, less than the actual World Equity Budget, which was $160 per month in 1993.

From Mr. Gray's testimony, nondiscretionary expenses can be as low as $100 per month. What he really shows us, however, is the power of living an examined life around money. Do we realize that when we give money our attention, our lives cannot help but be transformed?

When asked whether or not it was worth it to sacrifice a simple meal in a restaurant, a beer with his friends, and his right to a place to call home, Mr. Gray responded,

"On balance, how do I feel about the path I have chosen, or the path that has chosen me? Most of the time I feel blessed and at peace."

—*Charles Gray,* Toward A Nonviolent Economics

How many of us, with all of our money and possessions, can say the same?

This is the reason Mr. Gray's story is included in TEN WEEKS— not to make us feel guilty that we spend more than our fair share of the world's resources. (Sadly, that goes without saying, and we will talk more about that in Week Five.) The point here is that in a relatively

short period of time, say within one to two years, we could drastically alter our nondiscretionary expenses if we were to choose to do so. In many instances, that choice is made for us when we lose our job or are faced with a similar financial crisis in our life.

Deborah Knuckey discussed this on my radio show:

"You just may assume there's a base level of costs that you face in terms of housing and a car and so forth, but at some point you've chosen what sort of neighborhood you live in, what sort of house you live in, what kind of car you drive. There are choices being made every day in every aspect of your life. And when it comes to the money choices, there are a lot of things that are really optional. I mean, you can choose to live in a nice home or you can choose to downscale your living a little to get more of something else that's important to you. So it's about getting really clear…the next time I get a car do I want to automatically upgrade my cost of living?"

Your involvement in the TEN WEEKS program indicates your willingness to take a good look at the financial assumptions you have adopted. You have summarized your financial affairs and can finally face the realities of your expenses. The Authentic Budget process gives you the opportunity to reevaluate everything, including your housing and transportation needs.

Having given money the attention it requires, you are now equipped to make wise financial decisions that flow from an awareness of your unconscious and conscious longings.

Remember Wally's Electrical Diagram? The part of his diagram labeled #9 referred to the "load" or "output." This is the component that transfers the electricity to the lamp, appliance, or whatever else was waiting to be plugged in to the outlet and receive energy it needed to function properly.

I recall the day in Wally's shop after he fixed my broken fan. This is what he said about that "load":

Output or Load
(Diagram Component #9)
** a flashback **

Wally turned off the fan and unplugged it. As he talked, he showed me the male plug on the end of the cord.

"The whole point of installing any electrical system is that it energizes something. Whether that be to light a dark room, run a fan like yours, or just percolate my morning coffee, each of these modes of output must allow for the flow of energy suited for its particular needs. Most appliances are fitted with a cord and plug that prevents them from being used in a noncompatible energy source. See how easy this plug fits into this outlet receptacle?"

Wally inserted the fan's plug into the wall outlet and flipped the switch. The fan's motor began to hum and its blade to stir the heavy air.

"Yes, I see that, but I doubt that a stove cord would fit in that receptacle."

"Even if you were stubborn enough to try and make it work, the stove is wired for 220V, and most household receptacles are wired for 110V. That's what I mean; there are different plugs for those 220 systems, so it's extremely difficult to make that mistake."

"I do remember one repair job," Wally grinned. "This determined do-it-yourselfer had managed to strip the wires on his microwave and plug them into his range receptacle. To say the least, he ended up with some kind of newfangled dual-phase oven for a few short seconds until the microwave literally exploded!"

"Now I understand why you carry that yellow hard hat in your pickup! Home repair is a dangerous occupation when you're dealing with experts like me!"

"Yeah, maybe if you excuse me for just a minute, I'll run out to the truck!"

As Wally explained it, the male end of the cord has to be suited to fit into the female receptacle in the wall outlet. Trying to force a 220-volt cord plug into a 110-volt receptacle ends up creating a lot of "suffering."

Your budget buddy helps you align your "cord"—the actual details of your life—with the "receptacle," the ever-expanding awareness of your Authentic Self.

It is that compatible connection that results in an abundant flow of power into your experience and a whole new relationship with money—a genuine Financial Awakening!

Insert the TEN WEEKS CD in your computer now and begin the creation of your Authentic Budget in Quicken®.

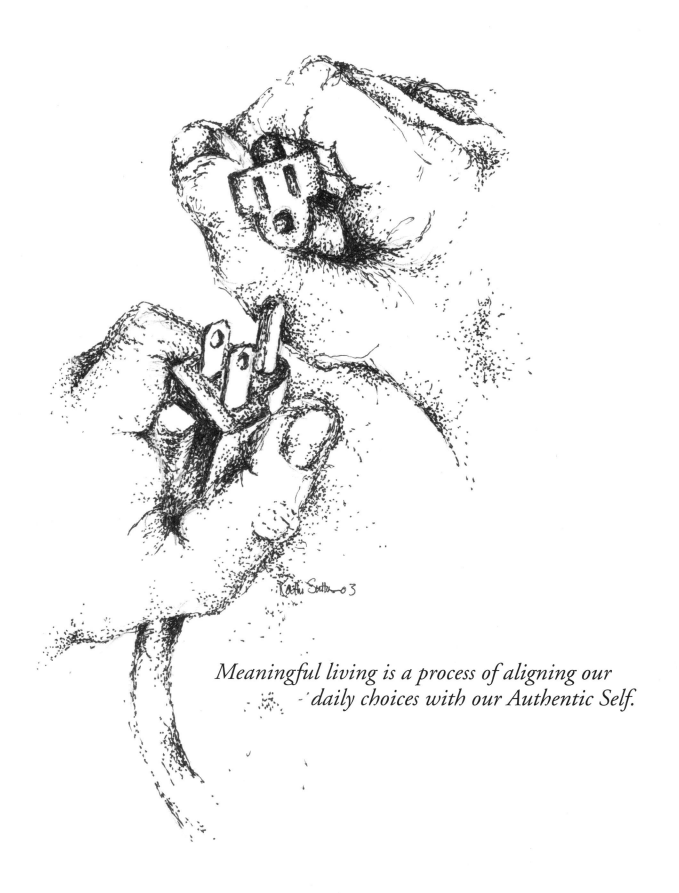

*Meaningful living is a process of aligning our
daily choices with our Authentic Self.*

Week Three
Appendix A
Your Spending and Your Budget—
What Is It You Really Want?

Carefully remove Appendix A from your TEN WEEKS book and place it in the "Action Items—AMG" section of your Authentic Money Guide Binder.

Sample

Authentic Money Guide Scenario Summary

Scenario #	Scenario Name	Date Created	Change from Prior Scenario	Action Items
1	As Is—Base Plan	07-20-03	Initial Plan—income/expense/asset/liability as is	None
2	Sell Rental 2013	07-21-03	Sell rental in 2013; Stop all related income/expense at that time	None until 2013.
3	Increase Investment Return	07-21-03	Increase returns from 5 percent to 6 percent and 6 percent to 7 percent	Review investments to see if new return rates are feasible.
4	AMG Trips	07-21-03	Add $2,000 for getaways and $2,000 for Canada.	Plan trips, monitor budget and adjust witholding.
5	Greg's Reduced Hours	07-25-03	Reduce income $12,000. Reduce expenses $6,500.	Cut five hrs./week from work and eight hrs./quarter. Update budget; monitor time.

Authentic Money Guide Scenario Summary

Scenario #	Scenario Name	Date Created	Change from Prior Scenario	Action Items

Authentic Money Guide Scenario Summary

Scenario #	Scenario Name	Date Created	Change from Prior Scenario	Action Items

Authentic Money Guide Scenario Summary

Scenario #	Scenario Name	Date Created	Change from Prior Scenario	Action Items

Week Three

APPENDIX B
Financial Transaction Integration
with Quicken®

Your financial transactions can be summarized in the following categories. With each of those categories is the most efficient manner of integration with Quicken®. The drawbacks to each method are also listed in terms of an accurate daily update to your Quicken® Budget Report, with the best solution in bold type.

Transaction Type	Quicken® Integration	Weakness in Integration/Solution
Cash Purchases	Cash Account Summaries	Weekly input delays accuracy. **Input cash summaries daily.**
Manual Checks	Quicken® Checks or Bill Pay	Computer checks are time-consuming. **Sign up for Quicken® Bill Pay and enter manual checks daily.**
Bank Debit Cards	Manual Entry	Tendency to neglect Quicken® entry. **Input debit payments daily.**
Automatic EFT*	Scheduled Transactions	Can result in overdrafts. **Monitor account balance in Quicken® after posting scheduled transactions. Arrange for overdraft protection at your bank.**
Computer Checks	Check payment In Quicken®	Manual process—takes time. **Convert to Online Bill Pay.**
Credit Cards	Credit Card Downloads	One- to two-day delay; ease of use can result in tendency to overspend. **Carefully monitor budget.**
Online Bill Pay	Quicken® Bill Pay	Minimal—manual entry of nonrecurring bills. Monthly fee. **Set up recurring transactions as scheduled online payments, requiring no action on your part.**

*Electronic Funds Transfer

Advantages of Quicken® Bill Pay:

1) Recurring bills can be paid automatically, even if the vendor does not provide for automatic electronic bank withdrawals. This eliminates the problem of late fees and the time it takes to repeat this process each month. You can even prompt Quicken® to send e-mail inquiries re: how these payments have been posted to your account.

2) New bills and payments, even to private parties, can all be paid with Quicken® Bill Pay. All that is required is that the payee has an address and phone number.

3) Unlike downloaded bank transactions, bills paid via the Bill Pay feature are precategorized, so there is no need to enter a category for each downloaded transaction. This helps immensely in staying current with actual and budgeted spending awareness and saves time as well.

4) You can use up to 10 different bank accounts from which to pay bills—at no extra charge. There's no need to do away with multiple accounts that serve particular purposes. Ginger's Nurse Network account can access the same bill payment features that she and Greg use for their personal checking accounts.

5) You can even set up many of your bills to be sent to you online and view and pay your bills from the Web in the event you are away from home and want to see the status of your bills.

6) The service is very affordable—$9.95/month for the first 20 transactions and $2.49/set for an additional five transactions. Twenty (20) stamps alone would cost $7.40/month!

Review the Week Three TEN WEEKS CD for guidelines as to how to sign up for this service.

Week Three
APPENDIX C
Report Organization

YOUR SPENDING AND BUDGET—WHAT IS IT YOU REALLY WANT?

PART 1
Planning Report Format

See Attached Reports with example of notations

PART 2
Report and Document Organization

1. **Historical financial documents and reports that tell us what has happened with our money for a period of time—usually on a monthly basis.**

   The following is the order of documents and Quicken® reports located in your Authentic Money Guide monthly dividers with the Quicken® reports highlighted.

Authentic Money Guide Monthly Divider Contents
Financial Documents and Reports:

1. Pay Stubs
2. Income Receipts—Rents, Royalties, Gifts, etc.
3. Business Income Summaries
4. Investment Account Statements
5. Credit Card Statements
6. Mortgage Statements
7. Other Loan Statements
8. Savings Account Statements
9. Checking Account Statements

Quicken® Reports:

1. Bank Reconciliation Reports
2. Transaction Report
3. Budget Report
4. Cash Flow Comparison Report
5. Cash Flow Report
6. Net Worth Report

2. **Budget and planning reports that reflect the changes that are flowing into our actual life experience through the Authentic Money Guide creation.**

These reports give us a target that represents our current commitments to align our money decisions with what we really want. Since the most recent budget is critical to our current course of action, it should be filed in the "Action Items—AMG" Tab of the Authentic Money Guide binder. The contents of the "Action Items—AMG" section of the binder includes the following items:

Budget Report—Year-to-date

Week Three Appendix A—Authentic Money Guide scenario summary

Most recent (highest #) Planning Scenario that has been chosen

3. **Planning Scenario Reports**

Using Quicken® Planner, we will summarize different scenarios and file them chronologically in the My Options section of the Authentic Money Guide binder. Each set of reports should be numbered, and the highest numbered analysis should be on top.

Each scenario should be entered on Appendix A so you can easily see the changes that have taken place since you started with your Base Plan.

Use the planning report format to clearly identify each scenario's change from the prior scenario as outlined in Part 1 of this Appendix.

#4—AMG Trips

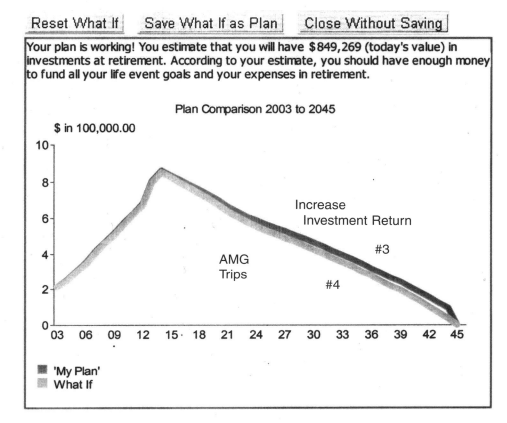

Choose a goal type

Special expense ▼

What if I:
- Change the timing?
- Change the amount?
- Remove the expense?
- Take out a loan?

Or, change any assumption:
- About you
- Salary
- Retirement benefits
- Other income
- Tax rate
- Inflation
- Savings
- Investments
- Rate of return
- Current homes & assets
- Future homes & assets
- Current loans
- Future loans
- Debt reduction
- Living expenses
- Adjustments
- College
- Special expenses

You can temporarily change any of your assumptions or goals (and even exclude goals) to see the effect. If you like the changes, you can save them.

Reset What If   Save What If as Plan   Close Without Saving

Your plan is working! You estimate that you will have $849,269 (today's value) in investments at retirement. According to your estimate, you should have enough money to fund all your life event goals and your expenses in retirement.

Plan Comparison 2003 to 2045

$ in 100,000.00

Increase Investment Return

AMG Trips   #3   #4

■ 'My Plan'
▨ What If

Detail of Changes

Assumption Change	Description	Amount
#1	2003 Canada Trip (2003 only)	$2,000
#2	Quarterly Getaways (2003 →)	$2,000/year

#4—AMG Trips

Your plan is working! You estimate that you will have $849,269 (today's value) in investments at retirement. According to your estimate, you should have enough money to fund all your life event goals and your expenses in retirement.

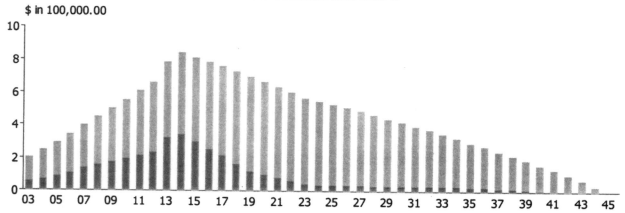

Account Balances 2003 to 2045

$ in 100,000.00

■ Taxable
■ Your Tax-deferred
■ Spouse Tax-deferred

Ev...			
2003	Regular Repairs	2003	Insurance
2003	College expense for Gil	2003	Greg's 2003 Tacoma
2003	Quarterly Get Aways	2004	Rental Repairs—extra
2007	Ginger's 2007 Car	2011	Greg's Car Purchase Fund
2013	Ginger's Car Purchase Fund	2014	Ginger retires
2015	Greg retires		

#4—AMG Trips

Plan Summary (2003)

(All amounts are reported in today's value.)

Income Summary

Income	
Salaries	
Greg's Salary	$36,000
Community Hospital	$25,000
Nurse Network Income	$5,400
Total Salaries	$66,400
Employer Contributions	
Greg's 401(k): Profit Sharing	$2,988
Total Employer Contributions	$2,988
Social Security Benefits	
Self	$0
Spouse	$0
Total Social Security Benefits	$0
Withdrawals	
Taxable	$10,535
Your Tax-deferred	$0
Total Withdrawals	$10,535
College Incomes	
Financial Aid for Gil	$2,400
Student Contribution for Gil	$4,400
Gifts Contribution for Gil	$1,000
Total College Incomes	$7,800
Special Income	
Interest Income -Jill & John's Loan	$75
Income from Serenity Rental	$9,000
Total Special Income	$9,075
Gross proceeds from asset/home sales	
Ginger's Prius	$0
Greg's Tacoma	$14,100
Nurse Network	$0
Serenity Rental	$0
Total Gross proceeds from asset/home sales	$14,100
Total Income	$110,898

Expenses Summary

Expenses	
Living Expenses	
Living Expenses	$24,570
Living Expenses	$0
Total Living Expenses	$24,570
Savings	
Taxable	
Total Taxable	$1,500
Your Tax-deferred	
Total Your Tax-deferred	$9,988
Total Savings	$11,488
Loan Payments	
Mortgage loan for Ginger & Greg's House	$4,046
First loan for Ginger's Prius	$1,623
Balloon pmt from First loan for Greg's Boat	$0

#4—AMG Trips

Plan Summary (2003)

(All amounts are reported in today's value.)

First loan for Greg's Boat	$1,487
First loan for Greg's Tacoma	$609
First loan for Serenity Rental	$5,000
Loan for Greg's 2003 Tacoma	$1,268
Loan for Ginger's 2007 Car	$0
Total Loan Payments	$14,033
Special Expenses	
2003 Canada Trip	$2,000
Quarterly Get Aways	$500
Greg's Car Purchase Fund	$0
Ginger's Car Purchase Fund	$0
Greg & Ginger's House Insurance	$240
Taxes on Serenity Rental	$570
Regular Repairs	$300
Insurance	$300
Rental Repairs - extra	$0
Total Special Expenses	$3,910
College Expenses	
College Expense for Gil	$10,820
Total College Expenses	$10,820
Invest special income	
Interest Income -Jill & John's Loan	$64
Income from Serenity Rental	$7,650
Total Invest special income	$7,714
Invest proceeds from asset/home sales	
Ginger's Prius	$0
Greg's Tacoma	$14,100
Nurse Network	$0
Serenity Rental	$0
Total Invest proceeds from asset/home sales	$14,100
Down payment on assets/homes	
Greg's 2003 Tacoma	$7,000
Ginger's 2007 Car	$0
Total Down payment on assets/homes	$7,000
Taxes	
Social Security & Medicare Taxes	$5,493
Tax on Salaries and Benefits	$9,960
Tax on Special Income	$1,361
Property Tax	$450
Tax on sale of assets/homes	$0
Tax on Withdrawals	$0
Total Taxes	$17,264
Total Expenses	$110,899

Total Summary

Portfolio Value	
Taxable	
Plus: Deposits	$23,314
Plus: Gains	$1,836
Less: Tax on gains	-$275
Less: Withdrawals	-$10,535
Less: Inflation	$0
Total Taxable	$60,268

#4—AMG Trips

Plan Summary (2003)

(All amounts are reported in today's value.)   Page 3

Your Tax-deferred		
Plus: Deposits		$9,988
Plus: Gains		$4,896
Less: Withdrawals		$0
Less: Inflation		$0
Total Your Tax-deferred		$151,384
Spouse Tax-deferred		
Plus: Deposits		$0
Plus: Gains		$0
Less: Withdrawals		$0
Total Spouse Tax-deferred		$0
Total Portfolio Value	2045 = $32,000	$211,652

#4—AMG Trips

Budget *
7/1/2003 Through 7/31/2003 Using My Budget

Category Description	7/1/2003 Actual	Budget	7/31/2003 Difference
Telephone	0.00	75.00	75.00
Water	25.00	25.00	0.00
TOTAL Utilities	224.00	319.00	95.00
Vacation	1,400.00	2,400.00	1,000.00
2003 Canada Trip	0.00	2,000.00 *	2,000.00
Lodging	0.00	0.00	0.00
Quarterly Get Aways	0.00	166.66 *	166.66
TOTAL Vacation	1,400.00	4,566.66	3,166.66
TO Greg & Ginger's Savings	1,157.17	250.00	-907.17
TO Spouse's Flex Spending	100.00	100.00	0.00
TO Ginger & Greg's House Loan 1	173.74	153.00	-20.74
TO Ginger's Prius Loan	228.01	232.00	3.99
TO Greg's Tacoma Loan	292.40	250.00	-42.40
TO Serenity Rental Loan	122.48	123.00	0.52
TO Ginger's IRA	0.00	250.00	250.00
TO Greg's 401(k)	1,500.00	1,500.00	0.00
TOTAL EXPENSES	15,040.33	15,550.49	510.16
OVERALL TOTAL	-1,443.61	-2,300.49	856.88

* Sample Page from Budget Showing Scenario #4 Changes

WEEK FOUR
Your Work: Work Woes

When finished with Week Four, you will have taken a close look at your relationship with work and making money. The insights will open the door to finding fulfillment in your work and to seeing possibilities in life other than earning more money. You will have examined several work scenarios and clearly understood the financial impact of each one. You will have gained confidence that your Authentic Money Guide can actually help you live and work Authentically!

TOO CLOSE FOR COMFORT!

The thunderstorm rolled in over the rugged La Plata Mountains to the north. A deafening clap of thunder and simultaneous lightning strike lifted me out of my desk chair and sent me running out of the office to see which neighbor had been the victim of the storm's fury.

I was terrified by what I saw. Only 50 yards from where I stood was fire! I knew it would spread quickly. The grass and surrounding bushes and trees were tinder-box dry after two years of drought. I raced for the house. Katherine called out from the deck, "Did you hear that thunder!? That lightning had to be a close strike—all the windows in the house rattled when it hit!"

"It struck near the office!" I wheezed. "Call 911! Unroll a garden hose from the office as quickly as you can!" I grabbed a shovel out of the garage and raced back down the driveway. Katherine called out, but I couldn't stop. Every second mattered.

By the time I reached the site of the strike, the flames were three feet high and had created a 40-foot circle around the host ponderosa pine. Visions of our entire property going up in flames raced before my eyes. The flames were lapping their way up the tree toward its delicate crown. At any time a tiny spark could ignite the forest canopy. Then it would be too late. I felt helpless and frightened, yet adrenalin raced through my body demanding fight or flight.

As I tried desperately to dig a break around the ground fire, I heard a labored, yet calm voice: "We came as soon as we figured out where the strike hit. Looks like you've made a good ring around this. What can we do?" I should have known that Wally would show up when I really needed him. Jane and their teenage son, John, were right behind Wally who had a chain saw in one hand and a fire extinguisher in the other...ready for action.

"Jane and John," I barked. "Help Katherine get the hose set up. We've got to stop the flames from going up this tree!"

Wally ran to the fire's edge and emptied his small extinguisher on the tree trunk. The flames continued devouring the tree.

The scream of a chain saw startled me. Wally wasted no time in clearing oak brush at the fire's boundary and dragging it away from the flames. He knew how important it was to keep the heat level down by removing large fuel sources.

Just then John called to Jane and Katherine, "Turn it on!" A stream of water shot out of the garden hose, and John immediately directed it toward the flames advancing up the tree trunk, now dangerously close to the tinder-dry pine needles. I paused from my shoveling, my eyes riveted to the stream of water. Would there be enough pressure to reach the blaze, now at least 30 feet above us?

We all cheered as John skillfully extinguished the highest branch and doused the fire creeping up the trunk. Now we could focus on containing the ground fire.

Just then, a fire engine roared up the driveway. Dave, our neighbor, stepped from behind the wheel and jogged to where we were working. As his crew unrolled their hoses, he made a quick triage of the situation. "Looks like you didn't leave us much to do—nice job here."

"Thanks, Dave." I said. "I'm just glad Wally and his crew showed up when they did or this wind would have given you plenty to do."

With the arrival of the fire crew, we realized our usefulness had run its course, so our motley crew walked back and watched the professionals extinguish what remained of the fire. I put my arm around Katherine and felt exhaustion begin to settle in. We sat on the ground, numb with what had taken place in the last 15 minutes.

"Since they say lightning never strikes twice in the same place, why don't you come over to the house for some cookies and lemonade?" offered Wally. "We might get to practice this again over on our side of the gulch by the looks of these clouds." Wally's words somehow comforted me and gave me hope that with help we might find a way to make it through this fire season.

Firefighter Dave said, "You've earned a break. We'll clean up here and make sure there are no hot spots." Now that the water was rushing through the two-inch diameter fire hose snaking from the tanker, I sensed I had been given permission to join Wally, Katherine, Jane, and John as they headed down the driveway.

When I caught up with the group, my relief and exuberance spilled out, "I can't believe how fast you got those hoses linked up and unrolled, John. You really saved the day!" My gratitude was apparent.

"I'm just glad I could be of some help." I smiled as I caught a glimpse of the moving day when Wally had said the same thing to me! Like stepfather like son.

We took off our sooty shoes and plopped down at Jane's kitchen table. I was glad that John sat down with us instead of heading up to his room.

The conversation soon focused on how good it felt to have joined energies in putting out the fire.

"Now I understand why Dave is willing to volunteer so many hours with the fire department," I commented.

"It's not only an adrenaline rush, but a chance to make a very huge difference in someone's life," Jane added.

As the summer storm, complete with a few smatterings of rain, dispersed to the south, talk at the table focused on how different our experience that afternoon had been from most of our jobs. The feeling of camaraderie and mutual respect, nurtured by our common cause, seemed to reveal to us how work in its ideal form might appear.

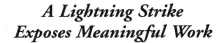

A Lightning Strike
Exposes Meaningful Work

THE JOURNEY

Above the mountains
the Geese turn into
the light again

painting their
black silhouettes
on an open sky.

Sometimes everything
has to be
enscribed across
the heavens

so you can find
the one line
already written
inside you.

Sometimes it takes
a great sky
to find that

small, bright
and indescribable
wedge of freedom
in your own heart.

Sometimes with
the bones of the black
sticks left when the fire
has gone out

someone has written
something new
in the ashes
of your life.

You are not leaving
You are arriving.

—David Whyte, *from* The House of Belonging

That day's experience and the evening conversation distilled for each of us what meaningful work, without the drama and danger, might look like.

Workers in the United States put in the longest hours on the job of any industrialized country. In 1980, the average annual hours at work per American worker was 1,883 hours; by 1997 that had increased to 1,996 hours. By contrast, workers in Canada worked 1,732 hours in 1996 (Steady rise in hours at work by U.S. workers). That's an average of almost seven weeks less time at work each year. This may be one of the most critical personal and financial issues calling out for our attention.

> *"Choose a job you love, and you will never have to work a day in your life."*
>
> —*Confucius*

Our shared fire-fighting experience gave our group an uncommon opportunity to discuss the elements of meaningful work. Many ideas sprang forth from our discussion, all of which contributed to our understanding of Authentic Work, but three elements stood out as most meaningful for each of us. What we realized, then, is that Authentic Work:

1. summons our core essence and destiny;
2. fosters belonging and an experience of contribution; and
3. provides meaning, not just money.

AUTHENTIC WORK
SUMMONS OUR CORE ESSENCE AND DESTINY

Each of us had his/her heart into fighting that fire. No one needed external prodding to give 100 percent because there were no doubts that the task demanded whole-hearted presence and effort. The fire served us well in reminding us of how little in life was under our control. We had to deal with the drama unfolding before us, or something terrible could have happened. Destiny placed us there together. Destiny bonded us, and we allowed it to shape us.

During the course of my radio show, "Money Matters," I was honored to interview David Whyte, poet and author of a captivat-

> *"In order that people may be happy in their work, these three things are needed: they must be fit for it; they must not do too much of it; and they must have a sense of success in it…a sure sense that so much work has been done well, and fruitfully done, whatever the world may say or think about it."*
>
> —*John Ruskin*

"A person works in a stable.
That person has a breakthrough.
What does she do?
She returns to the stable."

—*Meister Eckhart*

ing treatment of work, *Crossing the Unknown Sea—Work as a Pilgrimage of Identity*. David spoke with me about how critical it is to take our heart into the work we do:

> *"I do feel that you have to make work personal before you can really take any courageous steps because courage comes literally from the old French word coeur, meaning "heart." You have to be heartfelt about what you want and about what you feel— you intuit—you have to contribute. You don't even have to know exactly what it is, you just have to have a feeling for it and follow that gravitational field.*

> *"If working is an abstraction to you, if it's just a career, if it's something you're doing because your mother and father and career counselors told you to do it, because its what you've seen in the magazines, because the media would expect it to be a successful life, then you've abstracted it. It's a secondary life that you're swimming through treacle to get to. Make it personal. What the hell do you want to do?*

> *"You don't even have to take a step to begin with, you've just got to allow yourself to feel incredibly personal about your own life. You can sit alone and think about it; you can drive alone and think about it. In all of our great traditions, I think, especially the poetic tradition and many of our religious traditions, you don't do the willful work finding what your real vocation is in life.*

> *"Instead, you feed your longings and desires, and they do all the work for you. They put you at the frontier. Your desires, your longing, your passion, and your personal involvement get you into the conversations that transform your life."*

What does it mean to "feed your longings and desires, and they will do all the work for you"? How in the world can you do that as you sack groceries, clean houses, wait tables, or program a computer?

I believe you feed your desire by honoring the fact that you have a deep and powerful inner essence. You begin to bring Soul into whatever task you are called to do when you see yourself as giving a quality to that work that no one else can give. Each experience of life longs for your personal touch that is transmitted through such a belief.

"There is a vitality, a life force, an energy, a quickening, that is translated through you into action, and because there is only one of you in all time, this expression is unique. And if you block it, it will never exist through any other medium and will be lost."

—*Martha Graham*

Thinking back to the fire, maybe it was the adrenaline rush that got our hearts involved. There was no question that our contribution mattered. There wasn't time to pause and figure out what task we were properly trained to do or whether somebody else might be better at it. Our deep longing for physical survival shocked us into action. We tapped into something powerful within that enabled us to do what we needed to do.

That connection and related response to our deepest Authentic Nature is what we all want so very badly.

> *Hold to your own truth*
> *at the center of the image*
> *you were born with.*
>
> *Those who do not understand*
> *their destiny will never understand*
> *the friends they have made*
> *nor the work they have chosen*
>
> *nor the one life that waits*
> *beyond all others.*

—*David Whyte, from poem, "All the True Vows"*

Oftentimes, we think it all depends on our effort and talent, so we work harder to achieve some level of competence that will guarantee our success and happiness at work. We've become adept at willfulness and quite awkward with soulfulness. Is there such a thing as a "call" that transcends my choices and plans?

"No trumpets sound when the important decisions of our life are made. Destiny is made known silently."

—Agnes de Mille

"Destiny sets limits for us physically, psychologically, and culturally, and equips us with certain talents. Confronting these inborn limits and assets allows us to find satisfaction. Those persons who often seem the most capable of accepting the inevitable are also the most productive and the most capable of pleasure and joy."

—Rollo May, *as quoted in the article by Pythia Peay,* Who are you really? *in the* Utne Reader *(November-December, 2002)*

It is a challenge to understand our destiny. Most of us don't have the luxury to contemplate such deep issues. It seems there's another *treadmill* awaiting us a the end of each of our life thresholds; high school to college; college to career; career to family; careeer/family to saving for retirement…If we're miserable enough in our jobs to step off the *treadmill* and honestly see what our lives have become, it's common for a deep sense of loss and regret to surface over what we have lost. Buried beneath these true feelings, however, is something core to our happiness.

"We will discover the nature of our particular genius when we stop trying to conform to our own or to other peoples' models, learn to be ourselves, and allow our natural channel to open."

—Shakti Gawain

"…the original meaning of the word happiness stems from the Greek eudaimonia: *the deep satisfaction that comes from keeping faith with the soul's purpose."*

—James Hillman, *as quoted in the article by Pythia Peay,* "Who are you really?" *in the* Utne Reader

Pause and complete *Week Four Worksheet A—Work Awareness Circuit.* This worksheet is designed to help you discover what place work occupies in your overall life and what you are exchanging your life energy for. Remember, we all have a job, whether we actually receive a paycheck. Reflect on your current work now.

"Life shrinks or expands in proportion to one's courage."

—Anaïs Nin

WEEK FOUR
WORKSHEET A
Work and Identity Circuit Inspection Worksheet

Work Awareness Circuit

This worksheet provides you an opportunity to notice how work currently fits into your overall life. Make a conscious effort to complete the worksheet with no judgment regarding your current job and your relationship to it.

> ## *"Riches are chiefly good because they give us time."*
> ### —*Charles Lamb*

? How much time each week do you exchange for your paycheck?

_____

? What additional time is spent commuting and working on job-related projects at home?

_____

Total time working and commuting =_____(3)

Calculate your net hourly income by completing the following:

Category	My Job	Partner's Job	Total Jobs
Gross Income (1)			(a)
Total Taxes (2)			(b)
After-tax Income (a-b)			(c)
Total Hours/Week (3) Times (x) 50 Equals Annual Hours			(d)
Earnings per Hour (a divided by d)			(e)

1-   From Annual Budget Projection—"Actions Items—AMG" divider of Authentic Money Guide Notebook.

2-   From Annual Budget Projection—same as #1.

3-   See hourly estimate calculated in the previous paragraph.

? Does this net hourly income surprise you in any way?

_____

_____

_____

_____

The well-known book, *Your Money or Your Life*, by Joe Dominquez and Vicki Robin, encourages a thoughtful look at how much of our life energy we choose to exchange for the components of our lifestyle.

"The cost of a thing is the amount of what I call life which is required to be exchanged for it, immediately or in the long run."
—Henry David Thoreau

Take a minute to calculate the hours each month that are devoted to the following expenses by referring back to your Current Annual Budget:

Expense Category	Annual Cost	Hourly Net Income	# Hours
Housing			
Transportation			
Dining			
Groceries			
Other			

? Do you feel any desire to explore ways of rebalancing your income and expenses as you look at these results?

_____

_____

_____

_____

_____

AUTHENTIC WORK FOSTERS BELONGING AND CONTRIBUTION

Something happened that day we came together and fought the fire. I didn't think of myself as a financial planner. There was no thought of Wally as an engineer, Jane as a nurse, Katherine as a landscape designer, or John as a landscaper. We were stripped of individual work identity as we strove for a common objective. Each person's contribution was valued, and our common need took precedence over any individual aspiration or need for recognition. That common need reminded us, if only for a moment, of the superficiality of our individual labels and identities.

"Only a life lived for others is a life worthwhile."

—Albert Einstein

Our work goes to the very core of our existence and quest for meaning and significance. In our society, the "What do you do?" question is normal conversation within the first 10 minutes of meeting someone new. The response to those words is immediately converted into a salary estimate or societal prestige ranking with an associated estimation of value. Like it or not, we think that way, and so does most everyone we meet.

> *"Love is the measure of identity because in love is the timeless and untrammeled, the presence of things, the hours illuminated and celebrated like the steeple bell across the fields, filling the hollows and the hot afternoon to the brim. Death taps us on the shoulder and asks us to encapsulate a life by its loves. Death is not impressed by what we have done, unless what we have done leaves a legacy of life; death's tide washes over everything we have taken so long to write in the sand. What is remembered in all our work is what is still alive in the hearts and minds of others."*
>
> *—David Whyte,* Crossing the Unknown Sea

In my "Money Matters" interview, David offered insight to the above passage in his book:

> *"That image came from a common experience we have at a memorial service where when you hear the list of achievements there's no sense of movement in the room but as soon as you start hearing what the person loved in their life and who they loved, the home-made telescopes, the jokes around the office meeting table, the grandchildren, the visits to a well-loved place, then you know who you've lost. It's just as if everything else is blown away and what's left is*

what they actually held in their affections, and I think it is one of the great measures of identity. No one seems to be very impressed by achievements that are abstracted or that leave no loving legacy of life. I do think that we are trying to have that conversation. We're collectively tired of ourselves, of how far we have to drive and the kind of life that we've inherited in our glass and steel structures that we work in everyday..."

It takes a lot of energy to protect our external identity. We work long and hard to succeed in our careers. *What we do* is more important than *who we are* in our modern society. Deep down, we're tired because all that energy is lost—just like all the wasted energy we've given to money when we look to it to keep us safe, secure, and comfortable in the world.

How do we shift our obsession with work while it occupies the lion's share of our lives? If we never make time to nurture our lives outside of work, there's very little chance we'll have the courage or insight to shift into a more balanced, authentic relationship with our jobs.

Our fire-fighting experience stripped us of any titles and barriers. Rarely do we experience such transformative opportunities in the workplace; that is, unless we are handed a pink slip. Then we have to deal with the superficiality of Corporate America's loyalty to our well-being in exchange for the sacrifices we have made for our jobs.

"Money will come when you are doing the right thing."

—*Mike Phillips*

Work as Identity—"Status Quo," "Extraction," or "Displacement"?

How is it that we shift into a more holistic view of identity? Maybe the status quo works for you right now. You are good at what you do, you like the status and affirmation, and you feel it is a fair measure of personal worth. To clearly acknowledge such contentment with your work, I feel, is a powerful step of attentiveness.

At this point in my life, I am tired of proving my worth based on work performance. I have tried the "extraction method" in dealing with my unhealthy preoccupation with job identity—"What will they think of me if I don't have this job?"—"I am what I do for a living"—but that method was an exercise in futility. I equate that effort with trying to prevent the fire in my forest with some kind of *lightning fence* around my property.

I have, however, found the "displacement" method to work better in placing less stock in my work as a basis of personal identity. As our forest fire was "displaced" with water (via the garden hose) and oxygen deprivation (via the shovel and the fire extinguisher), so my preoccupation with work is displaced with a personal practice of honoring the whole of my life. I begin to see that how I engage with work from 8 a.m to 5 p.m. can be altered by what I cultivate in my life from 5 p.m. to 8 a.m.

In his book *Crossing the Unknown Sea*, David Whyte had written an intriguing line, "Stress means we have committed adultery with regard to our marriage with time."

I wondered about this "adultery" and its relationship to time. His response to my inquiry relates to the moment-by-moment presence we can enter into throughout the hours of the day:

> *"I think that most of our experience with time, especially in the stress of the workday, has to do with seeing it as a series of boxes into which we shoe-horn ourselves. We look at our calendar, and we're going to fit ourselves into that day and this hour and this holiday.*

> *"What human beings need in order to sustain themselves is an experience of the timeless of the eternal everyday, which is not an endless amount of time but a moment outside of time. Blake's book about all our great poets speaks to this; music speaks to this; a moment of joy with our children or our families or a loved one or a partner speaks to this. Time seems as if it is growing out of your own experience and you cannot tell how long you've been in the moment. You can have this even writing a memo at your desk if it's a really creative moment and a really creative memo. You don't know if you've been there five minutes or an hour because you're on some sort of frontier in which everything makes sense.*

> *"I have a whole chapter in the book,* Crossing the Unknown Sea, *in which I look at the hours of the day almost as you might if you were part of a monastery in medieval times, that there are actually cycles to the day. There are ways of being that are different in the morning than you would be in the afternoon. And just to be aware of your own cycles and the cycles of life around you and the cycles of the particular landscape in which you live. If you live in the desert, then the day has a very different adventure to it than it does if you are out in the mists of the Pacific Northwest in winter. Have a real conversation with the hours of the day.*

"When a father, absent during the day, returns home at six, his children receive only his temperament, not his teaching."

—Robert Bly

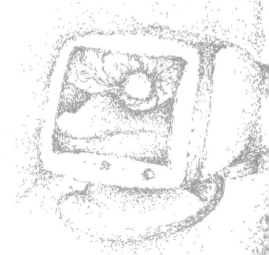

"When you wake in the morning, you have this whole cargo of revelations from your visitation to sleep. You've really undone all of your willfulness in the night. You've reimagined yourself, and your dreams are trying to make sense of the pattern which you've made of your life. The moment you wake up is an incredibly important threshold when you should take notice of everything that your subconscious imagination is trying to tell you about your life. But many of us just wake up into the great to do list of life. Which means, in a way, you've halted your personal evolution because what it means is you've got to be exactly the same person you were the day before. You're going to be exactly the same willful, busy person who never feels there's enough time in the world to do what is necessary and never has enough time to actually ask the great questions of life."

"Always leave enough time in your life to do something that makes you happy, satisfied, even joyous. That has more of an effect on economic well-being than any other single factor."

—Paul Hawken

With only 24 hours in each day, I have to pick and choose from an array of life experiences that can help me open to my core Authenticity. Gradually, I become less concerned with my status and security from work. Slowly, life becomes less stressful. It's as if those individual choices gradually displace my distorted view of work.

It's easy for me to follow David's advice since my life circumstances are pretty ideal. I live in a serene and tranquil rural setting. I can take a contemplative walk through the forest surrounding my house and office. There, I can listen to the birds and revel in Gracey's delight to, as the poet Mark Nepo so eloquently put it, "love the world through her nose." I am blessed with a healthy body that is nurtured through yoga practice. My spirit is refreshed each morning with the discipline of silent meditation. I delight in leisurely conversations with Katherine at the end of each day over a mindfully prepared dinner. I am filled with pride and fulfillment when I have the opportunity to connect with my three beautiful daughters.

I'm also beginning to see how important it is to actually be present with what I am doing. If I drive to town, I try and notice how the landscape has changed since the last trip rather than turn on the radio. When I am annoyed by the delays with phone messages or Internet connections, I try and notice my breathing and touch the essence of my life.

PRACTICING

As a man in his last breath
drops all he is carrying

each breath is a little death
that can set us free.

—Mark Nepo

What about you? You may be "stuck" in a work schedule that demands a minimum of 50 hours at your job and a weekly commute of 10 hours. After preparing for work, getting the kids off to school, doing laundry, grocery shopping, and cleaning house, if you're lucky, you can drop your exhausted body into bed for six or seven hours of sleep. Who am I kidding with this discussion about displacing destructive work habits through a practice of daily mindfulness and personal nurturance? You need to give yourself a pat on the back for making it this far in the TEN WEEKS program! I would ask that you do one thing, however.

Ask yourself one question: ***Do I sense my work and its related demands are good for me and for my family?***

If you are willing to honestly answer this question, you have "cracked the door" to seeing a new possibility for your life.

There is, however, a danger to dismissing completely any possibility for a shift in something you sense is destructive.

"Provision is necessary; sometimes a job is necessary, but if you spend too long in a work that is bad for you, it will actually shape away your character almost to nothing."

—David Whyte, "Money Matters" Radio Show

"There are certain things we should not do, certain people we should not work for, lines we should not cross, conversations to which we

"We must do what we conceive to be right and not bother our heads or burden our souls with whether we'll be successful. Because if we don't do the right thing, we'll do the wrong thing, and we'll be part of the disease and not part of the cure."

—E.F. Schumacher

should not descend, money we should not earn however easily it may come, things we should not allow ourselves to be called in public."

—David Whyte, Crossing the Unknown Sea

The Week Four TEN WEEKS CD will provide a forum for considering the possibility of shifting away from your current work patterns that you know are destructive, to whatever degree you sense is feasible. You finally can explore the ways that money can assist, rather than hinder, your desire to honor your longings for a more balanced, sane lifestyle.

AUTHENTIC WORK PROVIDES MEANING, NOT JUST MONEY

"I am still looking for the modern equivalent of those Quakers who ran successful businesses, made money because they offered honest products and treated their people decently, worked hard, spent honestly, saved honestly, gave honest value for money, put back more than they took out, and told no lies. This business creed, sadly, seems long forgotten."

—Anita Roddick

As Katherine and I got up to head home after dinner with Wally, Jane, and John, I pondered what these friends had done for us that day.

"We'll never be able to repay you for what you did, today," I said. "I hope you know how grateful we are."

John replied, "Well, in that case, I could sure use...." Jane promptly placed her hand over her son's mouth. We all had a good laugh. It made me realize that money and compensation were secondary in the type of work we had all been discussing the last several hours.

We have already seen how interlinked our career is with personal worth. It's like our work life could be compared to a three-legged stool. The "seat" of the stool is Personal Worth that is supported by these three feeble legs:

1. Five-Star Job Status

2. Flawless Security

3. Fat Salary

With something as precious as our personal self-worth at stake, there is no limit to what we expect from these three legs! The

"Status" leg needs a constant stream of commendation and job promotions. The "Security" leg feels inferior unless present and future lifestyle needs can be guaranteed. The "Salary" leg is the pivotal expression of significance and validation of our self-worth.

What if work became a vehicle for bringing one aspect (of many) of our Authentic Self into the world, as opposed to an icon of obtaining our sense of self-worth and identity? What if our work stool had as its seat our need to have an opportunity for Authentic Work—a job that was both good for the worker and world? Suddenly, the legs of the stool, similar to the first model as support, take on an entirely different role:

1. Fond Mutual Respect

2. Feasible Essential Benefits

3. Fair Salary

Individual status would no longer be so important as the focus of work became the common objective. A "fond mutual respect" would flow from honoring the integral importance of each worker in achieving the common goal. A conversation between the employer and employee would honor the whole of life and the powerful creativity sustained by a balanced, healthy lifestyle.

"Feasible essential benefits" would be a normal part of a compensation package in an Authentic Work setting. Mutual respect would foster a level of trust that would ensure the basic human needs for health care and retirement benefits were provided for each worker. The constant struggle for "flawless security" could be seen as unachievable and those energies redirected toward productive work.

Authentic Work results in a sense of meaning and fulfillment that tempers the unquenchable thirst for more money. A fair salary is one that is sustainable for both the worker and employer. Money is but one aspect of wealth, and work that honors this truth is what we long for. An employer who considers a 30-hour workweek for employees who are willing to simplify their lifestyles values the whole of his/her employees' lives—not just what they do at work.

Does such an authentic work environment exist? It exists for each of us individually, as we find the courage to arrange our lifestyle for it.

"The key to the door to your freedom and your belonging is usually some kind of radical simplification. Almost always when you're faced with what seems like a binding situation, 'I must stay in this job because I've got to make the car payments, put

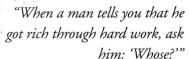

the kids through college,' you find that there is actually some way through, but it involves simplifying your life and arranging to get down to the core of what you're about.

"We spend so much time in secondary emanations of our existence with regards to insulation—third cars, second homes, things that take maintenance and that actually take us away from the core relationships: time with our children, time in the natural world, time keeping our friendships strong. Quite often we're so busy that we're living in the periphery rather than at the center of the wheel. And quite often a radical simplification of some kind or another will get you back to the point."

—David Whyte, "Money Matters" Radio Show Interview

"When a man tells you that he got rich through hard work, ask him: 'Whose?'"

—Don Marquis

Remember Wes and Lynn? One day, they came into my office feeling a need to get their investments and finances in order, having recently received a modest inheritance. The key words that they used to describe their relationship to money were "worry" and "stress." Wes saw the financial planning process as a way to alleviate these unhealthy emotions involving money.

During the course of our meetings, it became clear that both Wes and Lynn were less than fulfilled in their jobs. Wes had been struggling to justify his position in an industry that was shifting from outside contracts to internal operations. Lynn was an artist who worked at a job that helped pay the bills but allowed some time for her artistic passion.

What they didn't expect out of the financial planning process was that it would arouse their deeper longings as well as complicate things rather than make everything all neat and tidy.

Wes: *"I'm getting tired of this type of work. In fact, I've been tired of this type of work for a very long time. I've just been avoiding the reality. We need to make some changes. We need to decide what we need to do."*

Lynn: *"Twelve years ago, I recognized my desire to return to art. I began by fitting art in around employment and responsibilities. This meant working from after our child's bedtime until I retired for the night. I was working outside of the home about 32 hours a week at that time, caring for our young daughter, and running the household. It was not unusual for Wes to be at work 60 hours or more per week, and we depended greatly upon his income.*

"Over time, I began to establish myself in the art community, and I started to generate additional income through my art.

Four years later, I moved into a new 'day job,' working from 12 to 20 hours a week in order to spend more time in my studio. For the first several years, this worked: my part-time job allowed for 'taking the edge off' financially, and I was left with a significant amount of time to make art. As I continued to develop in the studio, I found that my other job was becoming disruptive to the continuity I was trying to establish in my studio work. At first, the job enabled me, and then it became a liability.

Fast forward to the spring of 2001 when we first met with Paul. Wes and I were both interested in getting off the treadmill we were on for so many years, working so hard, no longer feeling fulfilled in our work, and not being able to find a way out. During our goal-setting session with Paul, it became immediately clear that being a full-time artist was my desire. At the time, I didn't believe there was any way we could set ourselves up financially to allow for me to pull out for a while and spend time in research and development. I would not be contributing significant income for a time, if at all. Wes's employment was coming to an end, as we were informed that the company he worked for was closing their local office. Wes was ready to take a stab at freelancing. I was absolutely terrified by the prospect of no regular paychecks for either of us. Neither one of us had ever been self-employed.

"The decisions we were considering were completely outside of our experience and, for many months, my fear had the upper hand over the appeal of what could be. Part of the plan Paul created for us involved using some of the equity we had in our home, in the form of a sizable (in our opinion) mortgage. For many weeks, we worked towards this goal, but in the 11th hour, decided we were not ready for this big step. It took a solid year for us to ease into the various other aspects of the plan, along with leaving and losing our jobs. Finally, about 15 months after our first meeting with Paul, we both felt ready to borrow the funds we needed to help us move forward.

"It's been just over a year since I left my job to work in my own studio. I panicked intermittently for months over the reality of not being employed. I had to remind myself constantly that we had a reasonable plan in place, and that we would be able to provide for ourselves during this period of transition and growth. Emotionally, it was not easy, and yet I recognized that languishing in a job that no longer had meaning for me, in the name of security, was not an option I cared to consider.

"At the same time, my work in the studio was wonderful. I was focused, productive, unhurried, and able to pour myself into the work I love. After several months, the feeling of panic subsided but was replaced by concern over what kind of job I might find if my art career did not pan out. As I have become more and more comfortable with this new life, this concern has also lessened. And although life continues with its ups and downs, accomplishments and disappointments (as it does for us all) I recognize the underlying quality of contentment I now have. Some of the initial decisions we needed to make in order to find a new way of working and living made me feel as though we were jumping off a cliff. But now, in looking back over the past two years, I see an incredible transition that has taken place.

"I have no regrets."

Rather than focusing on what incomes Wes and Lynn had been making in their existing jobs, we determined what income levels would be necessary to pay for a lifestyle that allowed them to pursue their authentic work. It would involve some "radical simplifications," as well as a strong belief in their own capacity to grow their businesses over a six-year time period.

By giving finances their complete attention, they discovered there was a way they could honor their longings for meaningful work;

1. Over the years, they had diligently paid down their home mortgage. Their home had increased in value dramatically. The combination of these factors left them with over $200,000 in equity. Refinance mortgage rates also happened to be at 30-year lows. If they chose, they could refinance their current loan and take some cash that would allow them to pursue alternate careers.

2. Conservative investment of the loan proceeds would help offset the mortgage payment, as well as provide monthly cash flow.

All the financial analysis, however, only brought them to the threshold of this radical shift. It took six months to arrive at a financial plan that seemed to fit. It took another year before Wes and Lynn were actually ready to quit their jobs and refinance their home.

WEEK FOUR TEN WEEKS CD

The starting point in this process is the "conversation." Quicken® will provide a tool for the exploration of financial options that show what combination of financial decisions (income, spending, savings, investment return) will give you what you really want.

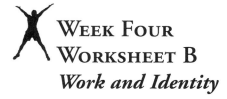

WEEK FOUR
WORKSHEET B
Work and Identity

Circuit Inspection

This worksheet explores the powerful link between our work and personal sense of identity and feelings of significance.

> *"One must not always think so much about what one should do, but rather what one should be. Our works do not enoble us: but we must enoble our works."*

> —*Meister Eckhart*

? Reflect on this quote while keeping in mind your feelings of work, personal sense of identity, and feelings of significance. Does the quote ring true in your own work experience?

_____

_____

_____

_____

? What is your basic philosophy of work?

_____

_____

_____

_____

? What do you feel your work is meant to provide in your life?

_____

_____

_____

? What is the difference between "work" and "career"? Do you feel your career has consumed more of your life than you would like?

_____

_____

_____

_____

? Do you feel that your work benefits the world (the Earth, the human family, your family, yourself)?

➤ How does your work make the world a better place?

➤ How is it harming the world?

_____

_____

_____

_____

? Are there specific changes you feel you want/need to make because of this realization?

_____

_____

_____

_____

? What parts of your work do you enjoy most?

_____

_____

_____

_____

➤ Are there ways you can engage even more fully with these aspects of your work and in so doing offer the world the gift of your unique, personalized "signature"?

_____

_____

_____

? What parts of your work do you enjoy least?

_____

_____

_____

_____

➤ Are you now being called to embrace and surrender to these difficulties and find a way to reframe them into more enjoyable work? How do you see this as possible?

_____

_____

_____

➤ Do you sense a need to relinquish this part of your job because you can see no way to do it and remain true to your Authentic Self? How do you see this as possible?

_____

_____

_____

? What frame of mind are you generally in at the end of a workday?

_____

_____

_____

_____

? Do you look forward to going back to work on Monday morning?

_____

_____

_____

_____

? Do you feel there are things about yourself that would cause you to be less than content after awhile even in your "ideal" work situation?

_____

_____

_____

_____

➤ What clues does your current life situation offer you in this regard?

_____

_____

_____

_____

? If you were able to do work you love, how long do you think you would continue working?

_____

_____

_____

_____

? If you did not need to make money from working, would you continue to do what you do?

_____

_____

_____

_____

➤ If you would make changes in your current job, or even start a whole new career, because of this financial freedom, what do you think you might change?

_____

_____

_____

_____

? If you had the option of not working at all, do you think any of the following would be difficult to deal with, and if so, how?

➤ Your loss of social interaction?

_____

_____

_____

➤ Your extra time?

_____

_____

_____

➤ Your lack of an identity or title?

_____

_____

_____

➤ Your purpose in life?

_____

_____

_____

➤ Your feelings of adequacy?

_____

_____

_____

? What, if anything, do you want to change about your work?

_____

_____

_____

_____

A MILK STOOL AND MEANINGFUL WORK

Growing up on a ranch afforded me the opportunity to master the art of balancing on a single-legged milk stool. The idea behind a single-legged milk stool was that the milker (also known as the "victim") needed only a single wooden leg beneath the seat while the victim's own legs and feet provided the other two "legs."

The loss of comfort and stability of a traditional three-legged stool was compensated for by the increased agility afforded by the single-legged stool. In the event the milk cow (aka the "perpetrator") decided that she had had enough of getting milked, rather than the victim risking a damaged or spilled milk bucket—and maybe a kick in the groin—he/she could grab the bucket handle, stand up quickly and swing the bucket over the top of the fallen stool, now lying flat on the barn floor.

My relationship with milk pail, perpetrator, and barn was less than pastoral and serene. The idyllic farm life scene of a warm, cozy barn on a cold, snowy night with the soft glow of light cast on the daily milking, complete with kittens happily lapping up fresh warm milk, did not mirror my actual experience. Mine was nothing less than a brutal battle between man and beast in which I was given an impossible task: fill a pail with enough milk to appease Mom and survive the fury of Black Lucifer, our possessed coal-black milk cow!

My milk-the-possessed-cow work experience had been anything but meaningful and enjoyable. Despite the positive side to the design, my stool was faulty. I was milking in a cold, dark barn. Had I not been in such a rush to do something else, the scene could have been transformed into a pleasant one for all creatures involved.

Thinking back to Wally's diagram and how it related to what I had learned about work that day of the fire, I remembered Wally describing the load or outlet:

Outlets or Load
(Diagram Component #9)
*** a flashback ***

"The whole point of installing any electrical system is that it energize something. Whether that be to light a dark room, run a fan like yours, or just percolate my morning coffee, each of these modes of output must allow for the flow of energy suited for its particular needs."

Work is one of the biggest outlets of our precious life energy.

Consider this Week's illustration as you open to a more balanced approach to your work outlet.

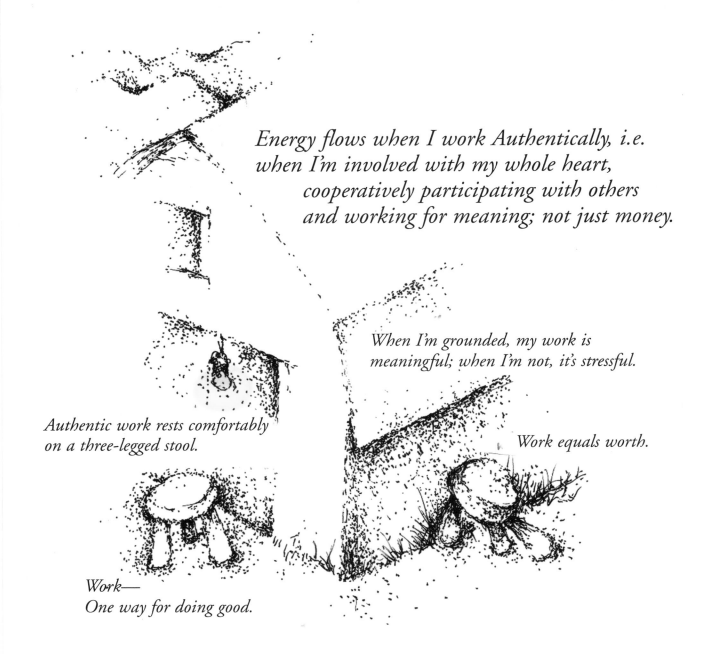

Energy flows when I work Authentically, i.e.
when I'm involved with my whole heart,
cooperatively participating with others
and working for meaning; not just money.

When I'm grounded, my work is
meaningful; when I'm not, it's stressful.

Authentic work rests comfortably
on a three-legged stool.

Work equals worth.

Work—
One way for doing good.

WEEK FIVE

Your Credit Cards and Loans: Friends or Foes?

> *Week Five brings you enhanced clarity about debt and credit, both emotionally and financially. Specific debt-related questions are answered using Quicken®, and your Authentic Money Guide is updated after different credit scenarios are examined. The fact that you finally take an honest look at your relationship to financial debt and credit provides you with a sense of relief and energy to face the most serious debt of all—your Soul Debt. How can such a teacher continue to be a foe?*

PROFESSOR CHARGE-IT

It wasn't long until Katherine and Jane had met and discussed how their husbands were spending a lot of time together in the workshop. Jane had noticed that Wally's fix-it projects were piling up and Katherine commented that the "to do" pile in my own workshop didn't seem to be getting any smaller. What did seem to be shrinking every Friday afternoon was our beer supply.

The girls decided that if Wally and I could philosophize on all matters great and small while savoring our favorite microbrew, they would indulge in what they enjoyed, shopping the specialty shops in downtown Durango. One afternoon, I overheard Jane comment to Katherine, "As long as we stay out of the hardware or office supply stores, we'll never have to worry about running into Wally or Paul!" It was a bit frightening to both Wally and me to witness the ongoing development of this alliance that, bit-by-bit, exposed our comfortable patterns.

The evidence of these shopping excursions surfaced about 30 days after each episode—when the monthly credit card statements arrived in our mailboxes. One day, after opening the mail, I walked over to Wally's and asked him if he and Jane had figured out a way to keep credit card purchases under control.

"One thing I have discovered about using credit cards is how easy it is to overspend. There is something kind of addictive about getting what you want, right now, and not having to count out hard-earned dollars to pay for it. When those individual 'immediate gratification' purchases are added up, it can cause a lot of stress at the end of the month. I will have to say that I have more of a problem with the credit cards than Jane does."

"I can sure agree with that," I said. "When I take a look at the things that I charged last month, I can usually see how I could have gone without about half of my purchases."

Later that night after dinner with Wally and Jane, Katherine opened the door to this sensitive topic. "Paul mentioned that he and Wally had discussed credit cards and that we may not be alone in the love/hate relationship that comes with the them."

"I was reading Ralph Waldo Emerson some time back," Wally said. "I don't often memorize quotes but this one stood out as having some real relevance:

> *Debt is a preceptor whose lessons are needed most by those who suffer from it most."*

Katherine thought for a minute and replied, "I guess I never thought of debt and credit cards as being a wise sage or advisor. From what we've discussed, it seems that Professor Charge-It's classroom should be standing room only."

Jane laughed at the thought of such a class and teacher, and said, "Unfortunately, Katherine, I can attest that even though there were times I needed to be in Professor Charge-It's class, I was down at the mall practicing retail therapy. I used to live by the mantra, 'When the going gets tough, the tough go shopping!' It seems that we're programmed to consume as the solution to all of our problems.

"I think we'd be kidding ourselves if we thought we weren't impacted by the media and the message that happiness awaits those who own the right things—the magazine ad cover with the beautiful couple, all dressed in their comfortable cotton clothes, sipping mixed drinks on the porch swing of their 5,000 square-foot summer cottage, for instance."

"Oh, don't forget the golden retriever fast asleep at the foot of Mr. Perfect," added Wally, "gloating at the performance of his stock portfolio as he scans the *Wall Street Journal.*"

"When I look back at some of the lessons I have learned from Professor Charge-It and the real-life pictures that I could have been taken of me," continued Jane, "I'll have to say they wouldn't have sold two copies.

> ## *"Eliminate something superfluous from your life. Break a habit. Do something that makes you feel insecure."*
> —*Piero Ferrucci*

"Once, I made myself lay out all the stuff I had purchased with my credit card during the month. I was so depressed to actually see how little I wanted or needed of what lay in front of me. If I could have, I would have gladly repackaged it all and taken it back for a refund. The only item that was returnable was the darn credit card statement that was due by the 10th. I was shocked at how much money I owed for so very little satisfaction and fulfillment."

"Jane, before you reveal to us how Professor Charge-It transformed your life, would anyone like some tea or coffee?" offered Katherine.

"Thanks, Katherine," Wally responded. "Just bring the pot over to the table. We might be here awhile."

A Surplus—of Debt

If there is one thing we are not short of in America it is opportunities for increasing our debt. There isn't a day that goes by without an enticing offer to apply for a new low-interest rate credit card or to wipe our slate clean by transferring all of our credit card balances to a tax-deductible home equity line of credit.

A recent newspaper article captures the cycle:

➤ "Low mortgage rates are feeding a boom in mortgage refinancing. Savings or extra cash coming out of refinancing deals is helping to support consumer spending…." *(Durango Herald)*

➤ "Today more than ever, a higher percentage of our earnings goes to pay debt. In 1989, this percentage was 11 percent. By 2002, this had increased to 17.6 percent. (*Newsweek*)

A few more interesting statistics from the *Journal of Financial Planning*:

➤ Americans charged $28.4 billion between Thanksgiving and Christmas in 1990. In 2000, during that same period, Americans were expected to charge $113.7 billion.

➤ A Southfield, Michigan, woman received 170 credit card solicitations during 2000.

➤ Fifty percent of American households carry credit card balances from one month to the next.

➤ National bankruptcy filings increased 14 percent from the 2001 fiscal year to the next year.

➤ American consumers were in debt more than ever at the end of September 2001—to the tune of $7.5 trillion dollars.

➤ In 1992, 65.5 percent of older American households reported having no debt. In 2002, that percentage had dropped to 41.2 percent.

➤ 80 percent of an online debt counselor's clients have incomes over $50,000/year.

One debtor describes her family's predicament: "We have more than $20,000 in credit card bills, and we haven't even used the cards in five years. The accounts are closed, the cards cut up, but we just keep paying...."

For many people, one unfortunate life episode follows another with increasing frequency because of the inability to pay for the "basics" of life. How do these expenses usually get paid? With loans and credit cards.

But What's Wrong in this Picture?

I remember how fun it was to play the game where you tried to count all the features of a picture that didn't quite fit. What seemed fine on the surface, under closer inspection, was incongruent.

The same holds true for many who would claim they have no problem with overspending because they pay their credit card balances each month in full. Many of my new clients are under the impression that they have no problem with overspending. It can often be a real shock to find that they have been spending *tomorrow's* money *today*.

Greg and Ginger Grounded, our sample Quicken® family, discovered that their current financial lifestyle would leave them eight years short of money when they ran their first retirement planning projection. In real life, the shortfall is usually much greater.

"Whatever you have, spend less."
—*Samuel Johnson*

To face the prospect that we spend more than we can afford based on our current income, resources, and future needs, seems painful enough. To strip away the illusion of how things will turn out all right in the end could be seen as downright cruel.

BLUE SKY CREDIT OPTIMISM

"Too many people spend money they haven't earned,
to buy things they don't want,
to impress people they don't like."

—*Will Rogers*

"My problem lies in reconciling my
gross habits
with my
net income."

—*Errol Flynn*

Our dinnertime conversation about debt revealed to me how comfortable I had become with buying things on credit—whether on a credit card or through a longer-term loan. I reflected on what might be driving this apathy toward growing levels of debt.

"Be not made a beggar by banqueting upon borrowing."

—*Ecclesiasticus*

The essence of credit is that we consume or spend before we pay. The simple fact is that we don't think of it that way.

When we pull out our credit card to pay for dinner and walk out of the restaurant, content, with a full belly, we don't give a second thought to the fact that somebody else paid for the meal and that we have incurred a debt.

"So, what's wrong with that?" you may ask. "It's not like I'm going to eat dinner and not pay my credit card bill at the end of the month. And even if I choose not to pay the whole thing, I'll compensate them well by paying their high interest rates. Those credit card companies wouldn't be hounding me to take out more credit cards if they weren't making out like bandits."

Our comfort with credit and consuming things before we have to pay is built on a premise: "Things will get better and better—there will always be more money to pay back what I've borrowed—Don't worry, be happy!"

DON'T WORRY, BE HAPPY

Here's a little song I wrote
You might want to sing it note for note
Don't worry—be happy

In every life we have some trouble
But when you worry you make it Double
Don't worry—be happy

Ain't got no place to lay your head,
Somebody came and took your bed
Don't worry—be happy

The landlord say your rent is late,
He may have to litigage
Don't worry—be happy
Look at me—I'm happy
Don't worry—be happy…

Ain't got no cash, ain't got no style,
Ain't got no gal to make you smile
Don't worry—be happy

'Cause when you worry your face will frown
and that will bring everybody down
Don't worry—be happy…

—Bobby McFerrin

The baby-boom generation has known little else than this message of optimism and prosperity—that is until the last three years when we've witnessed the stock market decline year after year. But we're still told, "Don't worry, it's just a matter of time; it'll all come back and be better than ever. Just hang on!"

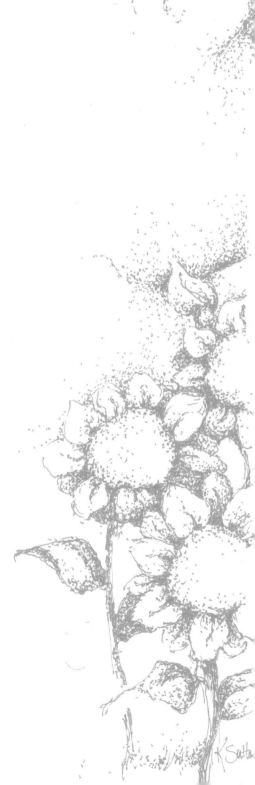

We are convinced in myriad ways that the proliferation of debt-based spending is good for the economy; that it's what keeps America, the economic powerhouse of the world, growing and robust. Our government backs this philosophy with its own deficit spending. Current budgets are formulated on projections of future income that continue to grow and grow and grow.

My own experience resonates with that catchy "Don't Worry—Be Happy" tune as it relates to my willingness to accumulate debt. Even though I tend toward a pessimistic outlook on life in general, I like my optimistic credit mindset that allows me to have what I want today because there will always be more money in the future. After all, haven't we learned that **Money Scarcity** is *out* and **Abundance** is *in*? We want to *attract* and not *repel* that abundance, especially as it relates to more money and material prosperity.

But the statistics are clear. This Blue Sky Credit Optimism can result in a lot of excessive debt and, yes, abundance; but it's an abundance of suffering.

I had the special honor of interviewing Jerrold Mundis, author of the best-selling book, *How to Get Out of Debt, Stay Out of Debt, and Live Prosperously,* for "Money Matters," a radio talk show I hosted in the summer of 2001. (Jerry's website is *www.mundis-money.com*) Jerrold's comments about the debt trap and the ways he had experienced liberation from its bondage seem relevant to those of us who can easily justify our inattention to credit:

> *"I began my own recovery, my personal recovery, from debt and indebtedness way back in 1984 and at that point, I woke up and found myself $50,000 in unsecured debt. About $85,000 in today's dollars. I had a guaranteed income then of only $350 a month and expenses of $3000 a month. So I know this problem very vividly.*
>
> *"Problems with debt in this country are epidemic at this point. More than 30 million people are overwhelmed by debt, meaning they're not going to get out of it without some radical alteration of their life; and another 30 million are living at some level of daily stress and discomfort because of it.*
>
> *"Debt engenders fear and hopelessness, despair, depression, and a sense of futility and frustration. It tears marriages apart, gets siblings not talking to one another, gets people waking in the morning the way I was in those days. I was getting up every morning with ground glass in my stomach. My first thought was, 'Oh no, there's another bill coming in, what am I going to do?'*

*"All the years of my own recovery from this condition and the books I've written on the subject, the workshops I've led for people around the country, and the people with whom I have worked personally as a counselor, have led me to understand first in myself and then in others that debt—**the major problem, the reason people get into it—results from distorted attitudes and perceptions about self, about money, and about self in relationship to money.***

*"People believe, for example, **I don't understand money**. And the idea that women can't handle money is still around to some degree today. Or, more commonly, it's contemporary variation: that **women were never taught about money**, 'So you can't expect me as a woman to be able to handle money.'*

*"**Entitlement**—'I sweated my tail off all day in graduate school for two years, day after day. I'm entitled to charge that vacation in Hawaii or that designer dress.'*

*"**Grandiosity**—'I'm the greatest, so like Muhammed Ali, I buy drinks for the house.'*

*"**Low self esteem**—'I'm not worth much more than I have or already make.'*

*"The idea that **money corrupts**, that people who have it have to be somehow thievish and unprincipled.*

"These are some of the distorted attitudes and perceptions that people, and great numbers of them, have about money, and self, and self in relationship to money.

"The way we begin to change and break free of the downward spiral is, first, to surrender. To give up the denial, the justification, the excuses. I need finally to recognize there's pain in my life, there's a problem around this area, I have increasing debt, something's wrong, I don't understand something, have been misperceiving something. I have to recognize that and then admit it to myself.

*"The most important thing we can do is, starting today, not to incur any more new unsecured debt. In any form—credit card debt, to not paying utility bills on time, to borrowing money from a relative. **We can't get out of debt by borrowing more money.** We have to stop the outflow first, stop the hemorrhaging; stop incurring any more new unsecured debt.*

"That's the threshold, the platform from which we begin recovery, the first step toward complete liberation and freedom from debt and going on to live with a kind of joyousness and peace that's nearly unimaginable to people who are still suffering from a downward spiral of debt."

Jerrold speaks from experience. His compassion and concern flow from a heart that has been broken by those misconceptions about self, money, and money in relation to self. We would be wise to heed his advice.

Dark Cloud Credit Pessimism

Bad Moon Rising

I've often wondered about the radical difference in attitude in my senior clients, those who experienced the Great Depression. I have heard stories of people who, owing just several thousand dollars, lost their homes to foreclosure. There was no money anywhere to make the payment. The reality of scarcity compelled the banks to take the action to which they were legally entitled, despite the horrific human consequences. Those experiences forged my *Depression Clients'* attitudes about money for the rest of their lives. They couldn't seem to save enough for the day it could happen again.

Many of my clients I served in the 15 years I owned my own tax practice were old-time ranchers and farmers. They knew what it was like to eat pinto beans meal after meal and to wonder how they would survive the next few months until their calves were ready for market. They were very reluctant to buy something they couldn't pay for with cash or spend down their ultraconservative bank CDs and savings accounts.

In contrast to the Blue Sky Credit Optimist who allows the illusion of better days to justify present gratification, the Dark Cloud Credit Pessimist lives each day chained to the memory of a painful past.

As it pertains to credit and debt, the words of rock legend Creedence Clearwater Revival's "Bad Moon Rising" resonate with the Dark Cloud Pessimist's outlook:

"To have just finished repaying all one's debts. Ah, is this not happiness?"

—Chin Shengt'an

BAD MOON RISING

I see a bad moon a'rising,
I see trouble on the way,
I see earthquakes and lightnin'.
I see bad times today.

Don't go around tonight,
Well, it's bound to take your life,
There's a bad moon on the rise.

I hear hurricane's a'blowing,
I know the end is coming soon.
I fear rivers overflowing,
I hear the voice of rage and ruin.

Hope you have got your things together,
Hope you are quite prepared to die.
Looks like we're in for nasty weather.
One eye is taken for an eye.

—*John C. Fogerty*

This latter philosophy is gaining popularity, however, as more and more experience disappointment with unfulfilled promises of financial prosperity.

We are all a bit less inclined to believe all the stock market analysts and their rosy economic forecasts. We've seen what happens when those projections don't materialize. Bitter realities overshadow the "It'll all turn out just fine" mantras, and hundreds of thousands of people are looking for work and wondering how they'll provide the essentials for their families. It's written all over the headlines. Consider these from the *Wall Street Journal*:

Layoffs at Janus Eliminate More Customer Relations Jobs

Stocks' Relentless Slide Begins to Touch Many Investors' Lives

Stock Prices Head Lower as Economic Concerns Grow

After the Pain Comes a Gain? Don't Bet on It.

And this headline from the April 6, 2003 edition of *USA Today;*

More Job Searchers Just Quit Looking

Is the antidote for this *Blue Sky Credit Optimism* and its attendant gravitation toward excessive accumulation of debt, *Dark Cloud Credit Pessimism*?

If the headlines about doom and gloom are all we have to look forward to, then making such a shift in attitude won't be difficult to achieve!

Dark Cloud Credit Pessimism may result in a fear-based debt curtailment, but its roots grow in the same soil as Blue Sky Credit Optimism. Let me explain.

When we are told how great life will be, we're lulled into inattentiveness to the present. When we dread the terrible things that might happen tomorrow, our minds constantly scheme to protect and avoid future pain, distracting us from present attentiveness as well. We forget that our pattern of focusing on "tomorrow" clouds our ability to be pay attention to what happens to us "today." When we aren't present with today's issues, they resurface at a later time— complete with "a sticky residue."

> *"But when our attention is scattered and distracted, this is like burning soft coal, which scatters soot all around. We keep making messes out of situations, and having to go back and clean up these messes. Being mindful, on the other hand, is like burning hard coal. When we attend to the details of each situation, our actions have no messy, sticky residues."*
>
> —Ordinary Magic, *by John Welwood*

The most valuable tool we possess for giving the present our attention is daily attentiveness to our financial affairs.

Did you know where you stood financially before you began the TEN WEEKS Program? Did you even have a budget? If you had a budget, were there categories of spending you were exceeding in your budget, even though it was two weeks to pay day? Had you paused long enough to gain clarity about what was important in your life and then link that to your financial budget? Did you have a way to know whether an individual purchase contributed or distracted you from the embodiment of the life you've chosen by its relation to your budget?

Things have definitely begun to change since you purchased TEN WEEKS only five or six weeks ago. You have made great progress in reducing that "sticky residue" that plagues us all.

Jerrold Mundis summarized it well during our interview:

*"I think facing the reality of our financial lives actually is the single most powerful step we could take in beginning truly to face ourselves. Today, money overarches every activity in society. When we begin to face the reality of our financial lives, we are brought of necessity into confrontation with ourselves. **Very little else we can do in life will force us into facing our deeper reality than beginning to face our financial reality, and in particular, beginning to deal with our debts.**"*

Freedom or Bondage?

The wisdom scriptures of the Jewish faith tell us that the debtor is slave to the creditor:

> *"The rich rule over the poor,*
> *And the borrower is*
> *Servant to the lender."*

—The Bible, *Proverbs 22:7*

Maybe that little bumper sticker that says, "I owe, I owe, it's off to work I go!" has BONDAGE written all over it. But we've been trained to think that we're really free when we can buy what we want, when we want it. The proof of our success is written on each of those credit card notices—"***Your credit limit has been increased.***"

There are two sides to the Debt Dysfunction Coin! Those clients of mine in their elder years have no debts or outstanding credit card balances, yet they are enslaved to fear—fear that economic woes could threaten their lives again and they will not have enough money to be safe and secure in this world. Does their refusal to accumulate any debt, to be a servant to the lending system, set them free?

Reluctance to spend is oftentimes linked to an unhealthy aversion to debt. It's not just those who have experienced the Great Depression who suffer from this affliction:

"I have no debts: no mortgage, no car loan, no student loans— nothing. I have accomplished this by living well below my means, but the roots of my thrift run much deeper than simple common sense.

"I learned the value of being debt-free from my family. We never bought anything we couldn't pay for up front, and, if we didn't

have the money, we either figured out how to make what we wanted or learned to do without. Thus, my family grew or raised fruit, vegetables, and livestock, and made furniture, clothes, bread, canned goods, and even soap. This was all commendable, except that it continued far beyond the point of necessity.

"What life inside my family had taught me was not to accept anything from anyone else, lest you find yourself beholden to that person. As a result, I was both as naïve and as untrusting as it was possible to be at the same time.

"I went on to make many bad choices in life: a distant marriage; jobs I took only for the money and the (false) sense of control; friends who weren't really friends. I finally went into therapy.

*"My parents are now at the end of their lives, and my siblings and I are well into middle age. Looking back, I can't help but think that a little indebtedness to others, a little neediness, would have been good for all of us. **A small amount of financial debt is a lot better than a life of emotional bankruptcy.**"*

—Rose Wild

Are we willing to acknowledge our particular bondage? Do we notice when we are not "paying attention to the details of each situation" and are being distracted from living our lives fully in the present?

No one captures this as well as Eckhart Tolle, in his book, *The Power of Now:*

> *"What you refer to as your 'life' should more accurately be called your 'life situation.' It is psychological time: past and future. Certain things in the past didn't go the way you wanted them to go. You are still resisting what happened in the past, and now you are resisting what is. Hope is what keeps you going, but hope keeps you focused on the future, and this continued focus perpetuates your denial of the Now and therefore your unhappiness."*

> …

> *"Forget about your life situation for a while and pay attention to your life."*

> …

> *"Your life situation exists in time. Your life is now. Your life situation is mind-stuff. Your life is real…Narrow your life down to this moment…Do you have a problem now?"*

"Pride does not like to owe, and self-love does not like to pay."

—François La Rochefoucauld

Our minds are constantly working, always scheming for ways to get ahead or relieve some of the anxiety we feel. Ancient Hindu teachings describe the mind as busy, chatting monkeys. The more clutter we have in our minds around money, the more we give the monkeys to play with!

I, a die-hard Blue Sky Credit Optimist, realize I am a master of denying that such bondage actually exists. What if I took the risk of noticing what might happen if things do not automatically get better and better? Would my credit card habits change if I noticed what was happening with the *bigger picture*? My pattern is to shift out of present awareness in favor of immediate personal gratification.

Would some of you Dark Cloud Credit Pessimists be willing to admit that there is no amount of money or worry about the past that can protect you in the future? Can you begin to notice when you fail to participate in the joy of the present because of this bondage to the past?

We no longer have to believe that all will flourish and grow to cater to our unlimited appetites or that our own diligent efforts can guarantee protection from pain. We can experience freedom, knowing that we are finally present to our life as it is right now by finally giving money our full, undivided attention. As a natural consequence of that process, we are living within our means, unfettered by excesses or deprivations.

WIRE SIZE

Wally's diagram might help us to integrate these insights about credit and debt into our lives by giving us a symbolic reminder from the functional electrical system. Wally had emphasized why there were so many wire sizes used in an electrical system.

Circuit Wire Size
(Diagram Component #6)
** a flashback **

"Some circuits only feed one output. An example would be the 30-amp circuit that feeds your electrical range. The power needed to operate that appliance will determine the size of the electrical wire on that circuit, as well as all the related breakers, switches, and receptacles. Here is a 30-amp cord to an electrical oven. So much power is required to burn that Thanksgiving turkey that it requires this one-inch diameter wire and a circuit all of its own!"

"Each day a bird would shelter in the withered branches of a tree that stood in the middle of a vast deserted plain. One day a whirlwind uprooted the tree, forcing the poor bird to fly a hundred miles in search of shelter—till finally it came to a forest of fruit-laden trees."

—Buddhist saying.

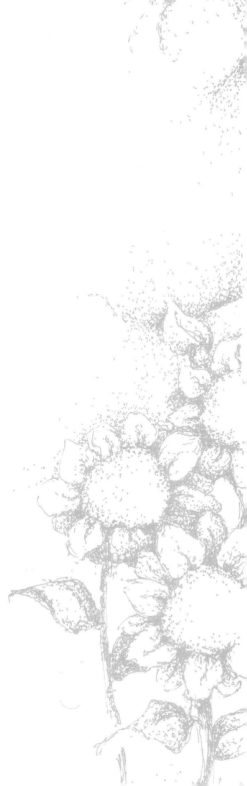

Wally handed me the cord.

"Other circuits may service lights in a whole section of a home, requiring much smaller sized wire," Wally continued, pausing only to pull out another roll of wire. "Here is some 15-amp wire that would be used to run a typical outlet/light circuit in a house. If I tried to use this to cook that turkey in the oven, we'd have to start cooking that bird on Labor Day!" As Wally pushed the roll of wire back underneath his workbench, I marveled at the attention to detail and knowledge he needed to do his job. His workbench sure looked a heck of a lot different than mine. At least my office was nice and orderly!

"In my diagram here I've drawn two sizes of wires coming out of the breaker box running to these lights. As I mentioned before, one I've labeled 6b on the top. This is a very small 5-amp wire and the one labeled 6a on the bottom is a much larger 12-amp wire.

"If I try and turn on all four lights on the 6b circuit, it won't be long before the breaker flips. The 6a circuit with the larger wire can easily handle those three 60-watt bulbs.

"It's important to match the wire size with the output or load. This prevents an imbalance and resulting loss of power flow."

To make sure I understood, I asked, "So is that why the breaker box is filled with so many breakers—each one matches a safe wire size with a certain electrical load from all the outlets on that circuit?"

"Exactly," said Wally, "and failure to do so would result in lots of trips to the breaker box!"

Wire size is a metaphor for acknowledging our limits or capacities. The motor on my little fan did not need very big wire. Small wire is suitable for the fan, whereas the heating elements in a range require much larger wire.

A mismatch of wire size and intended load or usage results in an imbalance that severs the continuous flow of power.

The same may hold true with credit. When I pause to ground and accept my limits, my life works much better than when I frantically seek to ease my discomfort with the acquisition of more than I can truly afford. I tend to exaggerate my wire size and try to conduct more flow than I can handle.

On the other hand, it may be that you're tendency is to limit the natural flow of energy by underestimating your wire size. In that instance, the challenge is to allow the flow rather than restrict it out of fear. I have a client that calls me on a regular basis: "I'm sending you more money today, Paul. It just keeps piling up in our checking account."

I often ask her if there is something that she could do with the money that would bring her real satisfaction. She often replies, "Oh, we'd love to take the kids and the grandkids on a trip" or "I guess we could see if all the grandkids have a college account set up—maybe we could use some of the money to do that."

There seems to be a relief in her voice as she feels some sort of permission to spend rather than hoard up a bigger and bigger pile of money. Freedom for this client is letting the money flow.

An honest review of our finances gives us the opportunity to notice the ways we tend toward bondage in relationship to credit and debt.

It is time to pause and see if there are some "shorts" in your Debt and Credit Circuit.

Find a quiet place and sit for five minutes to "ground." When you are grounded, use this worksheet to look deeper into what Professor Charge-It is teaching you right now.

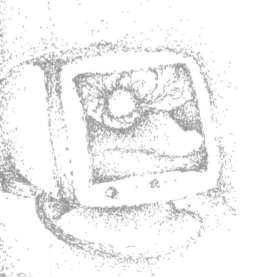

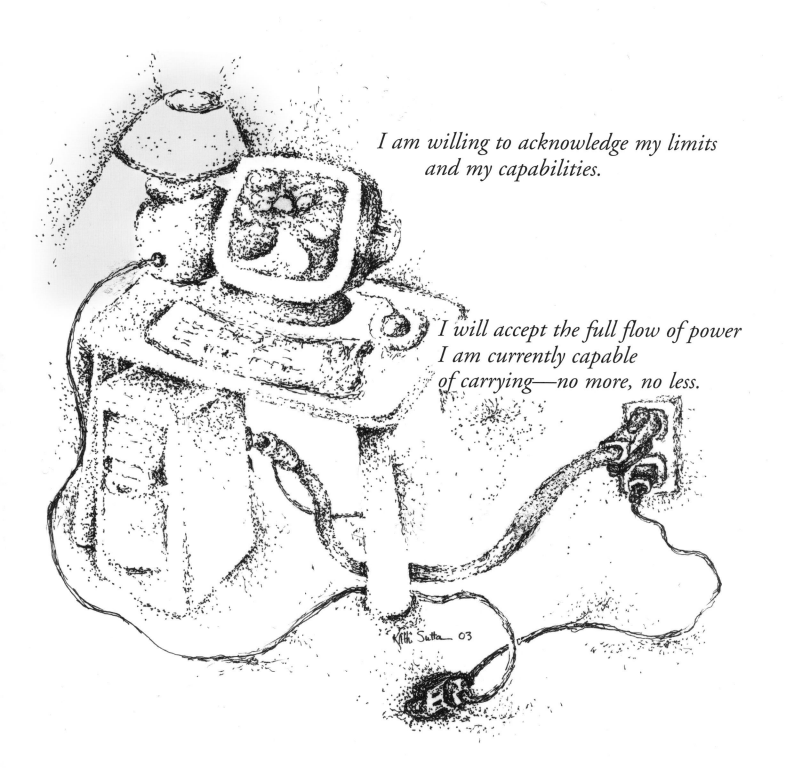

I am willing to acknowledge my limits and my capabilities.

I will accept the full flow of power I am currently capable of carrying—no more, no less.

187

WEEK FIVE
DEBT & CREDIT
Circuit Inspection Worksheet

PART I

"If you want the time to pass quickly, just give your note for 90 days."

—*R.B. Thomas*

Please take a minute to Summarize your Current Loan and Credit Card Balances and Related Information by starting Quicken® and following the instructions for "Week Five Worksheet Part I" on your Week Five TEN WEEKS CD.

Loan Due to/For*	Mo. Pmt.	Int. Rate	Current Balance/Date

*List the lending institution and what you borrowed the money for.

? What does the above debt summary reveal to you as it pertains to:

A. Your potential Debtor Type—

➤ *Blue Sky Credit Optimist*

_____

_____

_____

➤ *Dark Cloud Credit Pessimist*

_____

_____

_____

B. Jot down a recent experience that illustrates how this mindset around debt resulted in inattention to your present circumstance and the perpetuation of some imbalance in your life.

_____

_____

_____

_____

_____

C. How does your TEN WEEKS work assist you in responding differently to these debts and this recent experience?

_____

_____

_____

WEEK FIVE
DEBT & CREDIT
Circuit Inspection Worksheet

PART II

"We all know how the size of sums of money appears to vary in a remarkable way according as they are being paid in or paid out."

—*Julian Huxley*

? Which of the following best describes your relationship with your credit cards?

❑ *I have this love/hate relationship with my credit cards. I don't see how I could get along without them, but I spend way too much and I can't seem to figure out how to stop the cycle.*

❑ *I have sworn off them because of bad past experiences. I find that total abstinence is the only way I can deal with credit purchases.*

❑ *I don't use credit cards. I abide by past lessons that say that if I can't pay cash, I shouldn't be buying.*

❑ *I charge things or buy them on credit when it makes good financial sense. Maybe I can get some free air miles, or maybe there is a 0 percent interest rate offer that allows me to keep my savings earning interest, rather than pay cash for things immediately.*

❑ *None of the above begins to describe my relationship with my credit cards. Here's a better summary of my relationship and what I'd like to change or leave the same:*

_____

_____

_____

_____

Do you remember what Jerrold Mundis said?

"The major problem why people get into debt, results from distorted attitudes and perceptions about self, about money, and about self in relationship to money."

? Can you identify any distorted attitudes and perceptions in any of the three areas mentioned above?

A couple of examples may help:

I'm not happy having to deny myself a credit card because of my tendency to abuse it. I don't like to admit that I'm not able to control myself. I think my distorted perception is that freedom is being able to do what I desire at the moment rather than having the courage to stay with my discomfort and do something I won't regret tomorrow.

— *or* —

I can't seem to live with or without my credit cards. I'm not happy with the roller coaster ride of constantly beating myself up over this cycle of overspending and shame-based restraint. Underneath this conflict lies my difficulty in seeing that I am a good person, even when I overspend. I think it's hard for me to accept that I subconsciously make poor decisions to reinforce my bad self-esteem.

_____

_____

_____

_____

_____

_____

SOUL DEBT

Most of us have experienced a knot in our stomach when we couldn't pay a bill when it was due. There are other kinds of late payments, however, that society tends to overlook.

The exercise that Jerrold Mundis opens us to in paying attention to underlying distorted attitudes about ourselves and money may be trivialized by many people that we know. "Just do it!" "Get over it!" "Stop whining!" There are many more pieces of advice that encourage us to ignore what is really going on beneath our day-to-day choices involving money.

Remember the line from that Gary Snyder poem from the Week One Ten Weeks CD?

"You must first be on the path before you can turn and walk into the wild."

So far in TEN WEEKS we have been taking a machete to our overgrown pathways. We are finally able to walk on this path through this jungle of money, filled with amazement at the simplicity and ease of moving from place to place. Financial concerns that had tripped us up can now be attended to efficiently and precisely.

This cleared pathway provides us with yet another discovery. We now have the energy and perspective to see that life is much more than hacking back the jungle of money confusion. There is a genuine wilderness that calls us. This is the call to explore and rediscover our own uniqueness and ways of being in the world. Terrifying as it is, we are finally free to follow this call. Deep down, we long to know our ultimate purpose for living.

The essence of financial debt is that we have yet to make a full and complete payment for some product or service that we have received. But there is yet another element of debt that we all owe. I refer to this as **Soul Debt**.

Each of us has been bestowed with a unique essence. No other human being's purpose and manner of interacting with this world matches our own.

…
Sometimes reading
Kavanagh I look out
at everything
growing so wild
and faithfully beneath
the sky
and wonder
why we are the one
terrible
part of creation
privileged
to refuse our flowering.
…

—from the poem **The Sun**, *David Whyte*

To "refuse our flowering" is to remain in debt to our Soul. Our Soul is not only the channel by which we access our own longing for personal purpose and meaning, but it provides us the honor of offering up our special and unique gift to the world. Our flowering usually takes place after we've risked a "wilderness experience" like you're experiencing with TEN WEEKS. You finally have been given an opportunity to quiet down enough to hear your own voice.

For an example of paying the debt we each have to offer up our Unique and Authentic Selves as a gift to the world, may I offer the imagery that helped me process this journey—my own wilderness and fasting experience. The story I weave for you is not representative of any particular people or culture, but is intended only as a way of describing my own process of finally listening to my own voice.

My Vision Quest

A common theme in most every spiritual tradition is that a time of isolation and fasting in a wilderness setting is useful in reconnecting with a deeper sense of Self. In the fall following my mother's suicide, I sensed a need to face myself as honestly as I could. When I signed up for a 14-day vision quest I had no idea what was in store.

Because the journey is intensely personal and not meant to be shared in a detailed manner, I offer to you some broad strokes that describe my own journey.

If a civilization is to survive over time, it is essential that it cultivate a respectful and teachable relationship with the Wild. Each year, seekers longing for clarity of their individual purpose and place in the community would volunteer to engage in a wilderness fast. The Wild holds a message for each of us individually, as well as for our communities. Without this fresh voice, we all begin to wither and eventually relinquish our ability to "flower" in our own unique way.

> *"Dwell as near possible to the channel in which your life flows."*
>
> —*Henry David Thoreau*

This journey was referred to in some traditions as a Lament Quest, known as such because the elders knew that the seekers would only find their gift to the people beneath the experience of their own sadness or lament. Only out of their own woundedness would they discover the gift that could restore not only their own lives but bring a new and fresh vision to their community.

Who would be allowed to go on such a journey? Those who understood their own need as well as their responsibility to their community. They departed the village, usually one by one, but sometimes as a group, with the knowledge that some might not return. In some traditions, those leaving were clad only in a buffalo hide. Without food, they exposed themselves to both the care and the fury of Mother Earth. Armed only with their openness and utter vulnerability, they left the safety of the village and entered the world of the unknown.

The journey into the Wild may have begun as it did in my modern-day vision quest experience. Those allowed to go first stood solemnly in a circle with the village elders. One by one, they left the circle, metaphorically stepping down a symbolic hole into the underworld. The solitude and harshness of the wilderness seemed tranquil compared to the terror of stepping into the dark and mysterious inner world of soul. Once this threshold was crossed, those who had crossed were unapproachable to those remaining in the outer world.

How would these seekers find their deepest lament? The weakening of their ego through hunger, exposure to the elements, complete solitude, and vulnerability to the unknown were contributing factors.

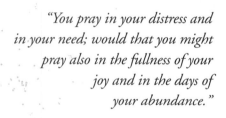

"Attending to the voice of the soul rather than the needs of the ego means learning to distinguish between the 'social self' and the 'essential self.' The 'social self' learns to adapt to the expectations of society. The 'essential self,' on the other hand, is made up of the core desires a person is born with."

—*Martha Beck,* Finding Your Own North Star*, as quoted by Pythia Peay in the* Utne Reader.

Out of that time of silence, the lament would surface. It would speak, not from the rational mind, but from the imagination, intuition, and "gut feeling" that had suddenly become essential for survival of the seekers. This woundedness would reveal itself as each individually sat with the unavoidable disappointments and losses of their own human existence. These losses had resulted from disowning their Essential Selves in order to find acceptance and survive in this frightful world.

It would soon become clear that this lament had set itself up as the way in which all life experience had been interpreted. Only after this realization could there be any way of receiving a message, a gift, that transcended this self-protective armor. Accessing this utter vulnerability prompted a genuine compassion for others and an understanding of their similar need to guard and protect their own "soft spot." (Pema Chödrön) This feeling of connectedness with the suffering of others gradually began to dissolve the need to be special or "better than." Now, fulfillment was found in joining the Circle of Life rather than in standing in isolation.

Like the birth of a baby after hours of intense labor, slowly the seeker's gift began to emerge and breathe its first breath. Its voice was strangely familiar yet its language indiscernible. Day after day, its message began to reveal itself, reminding the young person that his/her role was not to possess this calling but to be possessed by It. To offer this experience as a gift to others the seekers had to be willing to humble themselves and allow this voice to express itself as it would. As the invisible wind shifted the shape of the canyon wall, so the powerful and unpredictable Spirit would settle for nothing less than full surrender to how the gift would be formed and shared.

Often weeks would pass until the seekers slowly made their way back toward the village. Their weakened limbs strained to carry their precious cargo of Soul back to the circle. The entire village gathered to welcome them back, respectful and fearful of what changes had taken place in their lives.

"You pray in your distress and in your need; would that you might pray also in the fullness of your joy and in the days of your abundance."

—*Kahlil Gibran*

After taking nourishment, the young seekers entered the sacred Circle of the Elders. It was here that the elders questioned and discerned the true gift. This was the process by which the indiscernible language became understandable. Those who left had discovered the journey of Soul. Their intent had been accomplished in that they had experienced their essential nature and how they could cultivate an ongoing relationship to Soul. Eventually, they would have the honor of helping to discern the messages from the Wild that other young seekers would carry back to the village.

We can go through our entire life in Soul Debt. We can stay in debt by "refusing our flowering," as David Whyte says. The flower blooms only after the seed is buried in fertile soil. We can't flower until we experience a sort of dying and burial.

This dying and rebirth occurs as we surrender to feeling the disappointments of life and the depth of woundedness at the very core of our beings. Embracing that wound, we discover the gift we have to offer lies not only in our calling or life's work, but in how we go about living in the world. Because we have accessed our deepest lament, we finally feel compassion for everyone who naturally seeks to protect his/her own wound. We no longer have to journey through life as if it were a bumper car arena—my car bouncing off your car, one reaction after another. Feeling this frustration, I wrote the following poem:

"Freedom is what you do with what's been done to you."

—*Jean-Paul Sartre*

"The first step in the acquisition of wisdom is silence, the second listening, the third memory, the fourth practice, the fifth teaching others."

—*Ibn Gabrio*

MISUNDERSTOOD

*You throw me the ball
and I'm supposed to catch it—
then throw it back.*

*So simple, this childhood
game of catch.
So simple, yet I can't remember how.*

*You speak and your words
elude my catch.
I run in the direction of their
meaning to me.*

*What I finally retrieve
and throw back to you
is not what you
had thrown to me.*

*Like chasing a fumbled catch,
I rush to send my discomfort
back to you.*

*"Keep your eye on the ball"—
I know what I'm supposed to do,
and knowing only intensifies
my frustration.*

*Surrendering my plans, my response;
acknowledging the filter of my own woundedness,
I'm able to focus on this message from you—
"I caught It!"*

*Day after day
being so misunderstood,
I just want to understand—to be understood;
to experience that wonder if only for a moment.*

"Catch, anyone?"

WEEK FIVE
CREDIT AND DEBT
Circuit Inspection Worksheet

PART III

Take time to take an inventory of your Soul Debt. Start by reflecting on these words:

"What can I do to always remember who I really am?"

—*Juan Ramon Jiminiz*

"Most of our searching is looking for ways to discover who we already are..."
"So what can we do? Well, it is no secret that slowness remembers and hurry forgets; that softness remembers and hardness forgets; that surrender remembers and fear forgets."

—*Mark Nepo*

? TEN WEEKS has provided each of you with the opportunity to experience a lament quest! How has your Ego ("Social Self") been weakened by taking a thorough and attentive look into your finances?

_____

_____

_____

_____

_____

_____

_____

_____

_____

? What disappointments have you had to face?

_____

_____

_____

_____

_____

_____

_____

? At the very core of your being, what do you sense is your biggest fear or wound?

_____

_____

_____

_____

_____

_____

? How does this wound affect how you see almost every experience and interaction in life?

_____

_____

_____

_____

_____

_____

_____

? Experiencing this woundedness, do you hear the uttering of a voice that expresses how your "weakness" can help you offer your gift to the world?

_____

_____

_____

_____

_____

_____

? How can you cultivate a conversation with this voice? Remember, this process is more important than naming your gift. The gift will emerge as you journey in awareness of your voice.

_____

_____

_____

_____

_____

_____

_____

_____

_____

Week Five
Appendix and MAP* Material
Money Attention Page

Appendices:

There is more to say about debt and credit in a financial and nonfinancial sense. Each of these topics is addressed in the first two Week Five Appendices.

Appendix 5A—Debt Management Principles

- Six guidelines that steer you clear of the most common debt pitfalls.

Appendix 5B—All Those Other Debts

- What is the point of pretending we do not benefit at the expense of workers who fail to earn a livable wage?

- Are we finally willing to pay attention to the fact that we presently consume between five and ten times what the Earth can sustain and the devastating impacts that will have on our own children and grandchildren?

- How will paying attention to these debts affect your Authentic Money Guide?

Appendix 5C—Quicken® Debt Reduction Planner Summary

- Use this chart to summarize your debt reduction analysis, outlined in the Week Five TEN WEEKS CD.

Money Attention Pages (MAP):

MAP 5-1—Some Debt Management Techniques. Here are five practical suggestions for getting some control over your debts. Couple these with the insights you've gained this Week by completing the Debt and Credit Circuit Inspection worksheets.

MAP 5-2—Mortgage Planning Tips. This is a great resource for your questions about qualifying for a mortgage, deciding when to refinance, and the impact of paying extra on the principal of your loan. Test these ideas by running several loan "what if" scenarios in Quicken®.

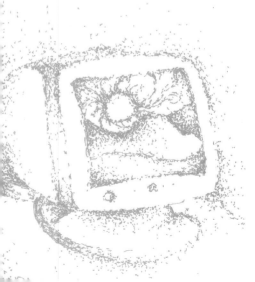

MAP 5-3—Types of Mortgages. As you can see from reviewing this MAP, there are a host of mortgages from which you can choose. (What a society values it proliferates.) Study these options before making a decision on which mortgage best meets your needs—and test those decisions with "what if" scenarios in your Authentic Money Guide.

MAP 5-4—The Bi-Weekly Mortgage. By paying your $100,000, 7 percent mortgage every two weeks, rather than every month, you can cut 6.1 years off your repayment term and save $34,141 in interest. See if your mortgage company offers such a plan. You will most likely need to convert to automatic withdrawals for your payments, which is also consistent with what the TEN WEEKS program encourages.

MAP 5-5—Mortgage Indebtedness—Tax Rules. Everything, and possibly a little more than you ever wanted to know about mortgage interest deductions. Note the limitations under the Home Equity Indebtedness section to see if you have a problem with deducting the interest on that loan.

MAP 5-6—Credit Cards. For the one or two credit cards you end up keeping, use this MAP to help you select those cards. Especially note how the cards calculate the "unpaid balance" as explained in this MAP.

MAP 5-7—How Can I Get a Copy of My Credit Report? What is unknown, that can be known, has more power over us than it needs to. Many of us lose sleep over how our credit report may be impacted by the events of our lives. Rather than worry and waste all that energy, why not just give that question our attention by following these procedures for seeing what our credit report actually is?

MAP 5-8—What Should I Do if I Find Mistakes in My Credit Report? Don't be surprised, after obtaining your credit report, to find some mistakes. There's no reason to be alarmed—just follow these steps in correcting the errors—and then go on about your Authentic Life!

MAP 5-9—Financing an Auto. Purchasing a car is a significant financial commitment. Remember the portion of our income that goes toward shelter and transportation?—between 50–65 percent. As you can see from the chart from the last section of this MAP, the cost differential is significant between paying cash, borrowing the money, or leasing. Test these options in your Authentic Money Guide by running the different automobile scenarios you are considering in the "what if" event section of Quicken®.

Week Five

APPENDIX A
*Your Credit Cards and Loans:
Friends or Foes?*

DEBT MANAGEMENT PRINCIPLES

In my personal and client financial dealings, over time, the following "markers" have emerged around dealing with credit and debt in a positive, friendly way rather than a fearful, adversarial manner. The practical application of these principles will be further illustrated in the TEN WEEKS Week Five CD, using Quicken®.

1. **Overspending is the real issue, not how many credit cards a person has.** Until a person understands that actual spending is sustainable and allows for future as well as present needs to be met with a reasonable degree of certainty, it is difficult to set meaningful goals around credit management.

   In your Quicken® work, you have been able to see whether your current level of expenses jeopardized the financial viability of your Authentic Money Guide. Greg and Ginger initially ran out of money eight years before their projected longevity.

   Review your Authentic Money Guide "Where I Started" Tab, and make a note of your shortfall.

Number of Years Short: _____

   Did you reduce future or existing spending levels in order to eliminate this shortfall, and if so, by how much?

Current Expense Reductions: _____

Future Living Adjustments: _____

2. **All debt is not created equal.** Taking out a mortgage to buy a house, or borrowing money to buy a car rather than leasing or paying cash is different than charging $500 on a VISA. The mortgage and car loans are "secured debt" which means that the creditor can take back the asset that is used as collateral (i.e. a promise that if you don't pay, the lender gets the house or car) if you don't abide by the terms of the loan. The worst-case

scenario is that you are out your down payment and the entire balance of the payments you have made. Once the asset is handed back to the lender, you owe nothing.

Refer to the Week Five Credit and Debt Circuit Inspection worksheet, Part I. Note those debts that are secured by an asset by writing the asset that you would lose if you could no longer make the payments.

For each of those loans, estimate the difference between the current loan balance and what that asset could be sold for within 30 days:

Secured Loan	Balance	Liquidation Value	Difference

The problem is that many secured loans do not let you off the hook that easily. These loans have **personal guarantee** provisions that give the lender the ability to continue to expect repayment from you if the asset wasn't sufficient to repay what you owed. (Avoid personal guarantee provisions on secured loans if possible.)

List any of the secured loans for which you have given a personal guarantee. Review your My Documents binder, Tab 8, to review your individual loan provisions, or call the lender and ask them to tell you if you have granted such a guarantee.

Secured Loan	Personal Guarantee?	Willing to Remove?

If your loan includes a personal guarantee, call the lender and ask these questions:

1) What do I need to do to remove the personal guarantee from this loan?

2) Will you be willing to drop this guarantee at a certain point?

If the lender refuses to drop the guarantee, shop around for another loan that does not insist on such an additional security feature. Be willing to pay a bit more interest (no more than one percent more) for such a loan.

3. Paying off debts with a home equity loan is not always wise.

➤ See the TEN WEEKS Week Five CD ("Home Equity or Credit Card Repayment?") for how to determine the true cost of a Home Equity Loan vs. a Credit Card Repayment Plan.

➤ Converting unsecured debt to secured debt doesn't eliminate the potential cause of the debt. Has spending been reduced to prevent the accumulation of new debt? Unless credit is no longer used to purchase goods or services, there will be a growing reduction in financial net worth and bondage to it.

➤ Jeopardizing your home by converting unsecured debt to secured debt is granting your creditors more collection power than they originally had.

➤ Tax laws regarding home equity indebtedness must be carefully examined. There are serious pitfalls to those

who assume that all debt secured by their primary and second homes is fully tax-deductible. (See MAP 5-5 for a detailed summary of tax rules relating to mortgage interest payments.)

Home equity debt interest is tax deductible as long as the home equity loan in addition to the "acquisition indebtedness" does not exceed the fair market value of the home. Another important restriction is that the total home equity indebtedness cannot exceed $100,000 for a primary and second home combined.

What is "acquisition indebtedness"? This is the loan that was originally used to purchase your home. If you refinanced that original loan and borrowed some extra money, the acquisition indebtedness is only the amount of the old loan that was paid off. In other words, as you pay down your mortgage, the amount of acquisition indebtedness is reduced.

An example may be helpful:

Joe and Shirley bought their first home in 1990. The home cost $200,000, and they took out a mortgage for $160,000. The interest rate on this loan was 8 percent and it was to be paid off (amortized) over 30 years. In 1995 their credit card debt had reached $25,000 and the couple was having difficulty making the minimum payments each month. Since the value of their home had increased to $250,000 they decided to borrow $200,000 in a new refinance with a lower interest rate of 7 percent.

The $156 per month increase in payment was a "drop in the bucket" to the minimum payments on all the credit card bills.

Joe and Shirley repeated this process three more times before they finally came in to my office. At this point they had borrowed 95 percent of the value of their home. Their current home value was $300,000. Their current mortgage carried a 9 percent interest rate because the lender had taken on more risk with only a 5 percent cushion between the value of the home and the loan balance. Joe commented: "Well, this loan really helps us reduce our taxes since all of the interest is tax deductible."

"I'm sorry, Joe," I responded. "Such is not the case. In fact, only the interest on $250,000 of your total debt of $285,000 is deductible. The 'acquisition indebtedness' has been reduced from $160,000 to $150,000 over your years of principal payments on the various loans. Your 'home equity indebtedness' is limited to

$100,000 in addition to this amount. It looks like you'll need to amend your last three years' tax returns and remove the interest deduction for this excess loan amount."

I explained the additional taxes and penalties amounted to $5,000. The saddest part of this story was not this extra tax and penalty. The underlying problem of overspending still had yet to be addressed.

4. **Real interest includes all the costs of refinancing, including the payment of points.**

   ➤ See the TEN WEEKS Week Five CD for how to run a Refinance Analysis and locate the best loan.

   ➤ The projected term of the new loan is critical in the decision to refinance. If a job relocation or other move is contemplated, the break-even point for the refinance must be determined to see if the refinance costs can be offset by the lower interest rate. Refer to MAP 5-2—Mortgage Planning Tips. This information will aid your understanding of the refinance analysis you perform using Quicken®. Also refer to the "Points" section of MAP 5-5.

5. **Secured Debt must be evaluated in terms of alternative risk-free investment return opportunities.**

   ➤ Using investments or savings to pay down a mortgage faster than required may make sense if alternative investment returns are paying less than the mortgage interest rate. Please refer to MAP 5-2, Section Three for additional information about opportunity costs.

   ➤ Be careful not to compare risky investment return rates with the mortgage rate. Paying down the mortgage principal guarantees you a savings of interest at the current mortgage rate. Investing in a growth mutual fund may return 10 percent one year and lose 10 percent the next. Investing in a 10 year Treasury Bill at 4–5 percent is a better basis of comparison. Paying extra on a 7 percent mortgage would make sense in this case.

   ➤ Future cash flow requirements must be evaluated before deciding to use investments to prepay a mortgage. Will there be adequate cash to implement your budget if you choose to pay down the mortgage or pay it off entirely?

➤ See the TEN WEEKS Week Five CD for an illustration of evaluating mortgage prepayments.

6. **Consider the Risks/Rewards of Leverage in Purchasing Assets.**

➤ Leverage, or using borrowed money to purchase an investment, has definite rewards but also serious risks that must be carefully considered. Consider the following example:

Ron came into my office for his annual review. I noticed a new loan statement as well as a summary of rental income and expenses in his paperwork. When I asked about the transaction he explained that he had purchased two small houses as rental investments. He said it was a great deal because he only had to put 25 percent down and the bank financed the rest.

Currently, the houses were rented and there was enough rental cash flow to pay the mortgage payments, property manager, and the ongoing operating expenses of the rental units. I explained to Ron the risk of leveraging so much of the investment purchase in the event of rental vacancies and encouraged him to establish a reserve account to provide for cash shortfalls that may exist in that event. Ron felt that was unnecessary since the real estate market was strong and he had good renters.

Six months later, Ron called and told me he wished he had followed my advice. One of the renters had moved out and the house had been empty for three months. Suddenly Ron was having difficulty making the mortgage payment and was afraid he might have to let the bank foreclose. Had Ron only borrowed 50 percent of the purchase price for one of the houses, instead of 75 percent for both pieces of real estate, he would have been able to weather this rent shortfall.

See the TEN WEEKS Week Five CD for an example of how to evaluate different leverage scenarios in the creation of your Authentic Money Guide.

Week Five

APPENDIX B
Your Credit Cards and Loans:
Friends or Foes?

WHAT ABOUT ALL THOSE "OTHER" DEBTS?

I. My Benefit at Another's Expense

My daughter works as a waitress. She works while going to college and is determined to pay her way with minimal financial help from her parents. Whenever we eat a meal together at a restaurant she often offers to leave the tip, usually a minimum of 25 percent of the ticket. I have come to appreciate her reasoning behind this—she knows how difficult it is to survive without patrons who tip above-average amounts.

In her book *Nickel and Dimed,* author Barbara Ehrenreich illustrates for us the woes of many restaurant workers:

> *"So begins my career at the Hearthside, where for two weeks I work from 2:00 till 10:00 p.p. for $2.43 an hour plus tips…as the tourist business slows in the summer heat, I sometimes leave work with only $20 in tips. With wages included, this amounts to about the minimum wage of $5.15 an hour. The sum in the drawer is piling up, but at the present rate of accumulation will be more that $100 short of my rent when the end of the month comes around. Nor can I see any expenses to cut…So unless I want to start using my car as a residence, I have to find a second or alternative job…."*

Ehrenreich set aside her privilege as a nationally respected author and journalist and discovered what it was like to live as 60 percent of Americans workers who earn less than $14 an hour, which is the minimum "living wage" for a family of one adult and two children (*Nickel and Dimed*).

Recounting her actual experiences, she writes:

> *"Guilt, you may be thinking warily. Isn't that what we're supposed to feel? But guilt doesn't go anywhere near far enough; the appropriate emotion is shame—shame at our own dependency, in this case, on the underpaid labor of others. When someone works for less pay than she can live on—when, for example, she goes*

hungry so that you can eat more cheaply and conveniently—then she has made a great sacrifice for you; she has made you a gift of some part of her abilities, her health, her life. The 'working poor,' as they are approvingly termed, are in fact the major philanthropists of our society. They neglect their own children so that the children of others will be cared for; they live in substandard housing so that others homes will be shiny and perfect; they endure privation so that inflation will be low and stock prices high."

—*Nickel and Dimed,* by Barbara Ehrenreich

What debt do I owe to the people who make my life so comfortable? Is it enough to leave a generous tip and do nothing to correct the social injustice? What happens to me over time as I ignore the decline in my *Ethical Net Worth*, even though my *Financial Net Worth* improves every day?

II. Consuming More Than My Fair Share

Limited Natural Resources—Consumption is the mother of all environmental problems! We are using more than our fair share of the Earth's limited natural resources at a pace that is set to leave behind too little for future generations. Our lifestyles are built on spending tomorrow's resources today, which we have seen is one of the indicators of bondage to debt.

> ➤ **Calculate your "Ecological Footprint"**
> Go to *www.lead.org/leadnet/footprint* to see how sustainable your lifestyle habits are with food, housing, and transportation. I was shocked to find out that my footprint is 87 percent as large as an average American. It would take four planet Earths to support each member of the present human population at my standard of living. If I wanted to leave just 50 percent of the biosphere's resources for other species of life, then we would need eight Earths to sustain my standard of living.

> ➤ **Consider the power of "grounding" in healing the Earth.** What would happen if the rest of the world thought like you do about living on the Earth? If you and I take practical steps, no matter how small, to live more simply, the consciousness of the world can shift as well. The change depends on doing what we can as an expression of a different way of thinking.

"We do not inherit the Earth from our fathers, we are borrowing it from our children."

—*David Brower,*
Let the Mountains Talk,
Let the Rivers Run

In June 2002, our community was ravaged by wildfire. More than 100 square miles of forest was burned and over 50 homes destroyed. Drought, year after year of it, had left the forests tinder dry. The neglect of properly thin undergrowth by homeowners compounded the dangers. I don't often make a public statement, but my conscience nagged at me to the point that compelled me to write this letter to the editor of our local paper:

> *The fires are raging out of control. We all sit and watch the smoke-filled sky and wonder how this will end. Nonetheless, I have my life to live, and until the fires displace me from my routine—life goes on.*
>
> *One of those people who were displaced last week said that even though it was sad to think that their family may lose their home, what was really sad was to lose the beauty of the forest that surrounded their home. Will the beauty we have taken so for granted be restored to us?*
>
> *Those of us who grew up here have noticed the decreasing snowfall and precipitation and change in climate. My father spoke of 15–20 foot snowfalls as commonplace less than 75 years ago. Now we're lucky to get 5 feet at Durango Mountain Resort. This trend isn't limited to our own backyards:*
>
> ➤ *This last winter in the U.S. was the warmest on the books—4.3 degrees warmer than the 1895–2001 average.*
>
> ➤ *The maximum amount of temperature increase to which ecosystems can adapt is 1.8 degrees F per century. "At current rates, half of the Earth's plant and animal species will cease to exist by the end of the century…"—Edward Wilson*
>
> ➤ *Each year, we add over 6 billion tons of carbon into the air (5 pounds for every gallon of gas we burn), which serves as a blanket—trapping the warmth from escaping back into space.*
>
> *It takes a lot to stir me from my slumber. The beautiful trees that are capable of absorbing a portion of the excess carbon I have dumped into the air are now burned stumps—their destruction accelerating my children's loss. These fires are a wake-up call for me. Will I realize I have to start thinking about more than my convenience?*
>
> *I would like to propose a weekly "Circle of Silence and Intention" at Fassbender Park on Wednesday evenings at 7 p.m.*

"There are two ways to live your life. One is as though nothing is a miracle. The other is as though everything is a miracle."

—Albert Einstein

If we could all come together and join hands and energies with the intent to do less harm in our lifestyles, I believe a miracle can happen. We desperately need each other, though, to shift into a new way of living.

If not me—Who?

If not now—When?

If not here—Where?

It has been 12 months from our first meeting of the "Circle." Each week, people have come and have joined hands in silence for five minutes, listening—opening to wisdom that is needed to heal the Earth. Each person can then share what his/her intention for practical action is for the following week. There is a feeling of hope and satisfaction when we leave. I am encouraged that there are others who also will be trying to take small steps toward reducing the debt we've all accumulated to the Earth and others who depend on her for life.

Why not start a "Circle of Silence and Intention" where you live?

- **Think about some statistics:**

  1. The United States comprises 5 percent of the world's population and consumes 25 percent of its resources. (Dinyar Godrej, *No Nonsense Guide to Climate Change*)

  2. The wealthiest fifth of the world's people consume 86 percent of all goods and services while the poorest fifth consume 1 percent. (*www.bread.org*)

  3. In the last 50 years, almost 400 million people have died from hunger and poor sanitation—3 times the number of people killed in all the wars of the 20th century. (Charles Gray, *Toward a Nonviolent Economics*)

  4. "At current rates, half of the Earth's plant and animal species will cease to exist by the end of the century, forever impoverishing the human experience, materially and spiritually." (Edward O. Wilson, *The Future of Life*)

  5. "People in industrialized countries generate 62 times more carbon dioxide pollution per person than

people in the least industrialized countries…The group of seven industrialized countries are actually $13 trillion in debt." (Dinyar Godrej, *No Nonsense Guide to Climate Change*)

6. "The news is that the heating of our atmosphere has propelled our climate into a new state of instability and that this new era of climate change could well be the most profound challenge ever facing humanity…As we continue to act like adolescents by denying our new-found power, we are putting our entire history at risk. I think it is time for us to honor our obligations to the future. It is time to honor our obligations to our children. It is time for all of us, all over the world, to finally grow up." (Ross Gelspan, speech: "Global Warming: The Heat Is On")

7. The financial costs to end hunger are slight. The United Nations Development Program estimates that the basic health and nutrition needs of the world's poorest people could be met for an additional $13 billion a year. (*www,bread.org*)

8. The 2004 Fiscal Budget allocates $804 billion to current and past military expenditures. (*www.warresisters.org*)

- **Focus on the three categories of consumption that account for the vast majority of all environmental damage.**

Consider the following action steps that could be taken to reduce your ecological "debt."

Transportation:

1. Choose a place to live that reduces the need to drive.

2. Think twice before purchasing another car.

3. Choose a fuel-efficient, low polluting car.

4. Set concrete goals for reducing your travel.

5. Whenever practical, walk, bicycle, or take public transportation.

Food:

1. Eat less meat.

2. Buy local whenever possible.

3. Eat less.

4. Buy only what you use—be mindful of how much is wasted.

Household Operations:

1. Choose your home carefully. Consider downsizing.

2. Reduce the environmental costs of heating and hot water. Buy "green power."

3. Install efficient lighting and appliances.

The above information was taken from *The Consumer's Guide to Effective Environmental Choices,* by Dr. Michael Brower and Dr. Warren Leon. Please consider this as an excellent resource in understanding the impact of our choices on the Earth.

MONEY'S ROLE—ASSIST US IN PAYING OUR DEBTS

Just as we need a clear plan for getting out of financial debt, we need to cultivate a mindset that will help us reduce other debts, whether they are Soul Debt, Natural Resource Debt, or Inequality Debt. There is no better tool than our financial budget to help us translate those intentions into reality.

You may want to revisit Week Three and look for areas in which you would like to adjust your Authentic Budget and Authentic Money Guide to integrate these *Other Debts* that are oftentimes overlooked.

See how different an Authentic Budget is from the budget to which you had grown accustomed.

Week Five

APPENDIX C
Quicken® Debt Reduction
*Planner Summary**

Plan Scenario Name & #	Loan Change Description	Total Int. Savings	Debts Retired In-Yr.

*If you like, remove this Summary and file it in your Actions Items—AMG Section or Your Authentic Money Guide binder.

WEEK SIX

Your Investments: Money Working You
or
Money Working For You?

> *After Week Six, you will understand the basics of investing and be empowered to make wiser investment choices. More importantly, you no longer will need to gauge your personal well-being on the fickle movement of the stock markets. Your investments will show you a great deal about yourself and the natural human gravitation toward desire, aversion, and denial. By acknowledging these "poisons," you are able to convert them to "medicine" that help you on your journey of Authenticity. Finally, you have a tool that allows you to examine all the other pieces of your financial life that are as important, or in most cases more important, than investment return. Your Authentic Money Guide provides the framework to integrate this new approach to your investments into your actual experience.*

A Call from Wally

"Integrated Financial Planning—this is Paul."

"Paul, this is Wally."

I was shocked to hear Wally's voice. In the two years I had known him, Wally had never called me at work.

"Is everything, alright?"

"Before we go any further I want you to promise me that you'll send me a bill for any time and expenses you incur on my behalf."

"I'll keep track of a few charges if it will make you feel more comfortable," I offered. "I know that you haven't made any profit on my account, especially when you count all the hours I spend chewing the fat with you once you've fixed whatever I bring to your shop."

"I just want this business relationship to be fair to you," said Wally. "What I need is some investment advice. I guess I thought that if I just 'hung in there' with my portfolio that it would eventually start to regain some of what I've lost. I'm embarrassed to admit that I've lost 30 percent of the value of my portfolio in the last three years. I should have done something long before now.

"To make matters worse, I've sat idly by and watched Jane and John's life insurance money dwindle by nearly the same amount. I feel like I've really let them down by not suggesting they come talk to you and get a second opinion from what their broker has been saying."

"I know it's no consolation, Wally," I said, "but I've had new clients who have lost almost 50 percent in that same time period before they finally determined they had to talk to someone. Don't be too hard on yourself. What's important is that you've decided to deal with these losses and make some informed decisions."

"The main thing I need to know is whether or not what is left will be enough to allow us to sustain our lifestyle," said Wally, adding, "I sure would prefer not having to return to the jungle of Engineer World."

"All of those questions can be explored as they relate to your investment decisions," I said. "Why not gather up your latest investment statements and last set of Quicken® reports and come on over to the office tomorrow morning?"

"That sounds great, Paul. Thanks for being willing to help us out with this mess." Wally paused and then continued, "I think at the root of all of my reluctance to face our investments is my greed. I just wanted to hold on to those profits that I once saw in the accounts. I know now that they were just paper gains generated by a host of falsehoods. Somehow I feel better just admitting this."

"It's tough facing these realities, Wally." I said. "I think you've gotten a lot further than most folks in looking below the surface of investment performance. I look forward to continuing our conversation tomorrow."

"Wealth is like a viper, which is harmless if a man knows how to take hold of it; but if he does not it will twine round his hand and bite him."

—St. Clement

After I hung up, I looked out my office window across our little valley to the Smith's cabin. It struck me how they, like everyone, encountered difficulties even though they had settled comfortably in so many aspects of their lives. Even Wally, as aware as anyone I had ever met, struggled with money issues. What a step to admit that he needed help. I was grateful that I might be able to return a favor to this family that Katherine and I had grown to respect and love.

Investment Insanity

LIFE IS JUST A BOWL OF CHERRIES

> *Life is just a bowl of cherries.*
> *Don't take it serious.*
> *Life's too mysterious.*
>
> *You work, you save,*
> *You worry so*
> *But you can't take the*
> *Dough when you*
> *Go, Go, Go...*
>
> *—Fosse*

No other area of personal finance seems to take us to the emotional extremes as the performance of our investment portfolio. When annual stock market returns were 10–20 percent everyone lived in euphoria. The recent years of negative returns has caused no small amount of anger, depression, and even fear. Like Wally, we wonder if we'll run out of money at a time in our lives when we're helpless to do anything about it.

(Please see the summary for MAP 6-10 later on in this section for an explanation of the difference between stock [equity] and bond [debt] investing, if you have trouble with those distinctions.)

A sampling of recent investment news can illustrate why we are feeling so helpless:

➤ The Standard and Poors 500 Index outperformed 75 percent of professional money managers from 1973–1992. (*Intelligent Asset Allocator*)

This statistic supports the argument that passive investing, which uses index funds that mimic stock and bond indexes, is a superior long-term strategy to active investment management. Actively managed mutual funds are run by individual managers or a management team that believe they can identify investments that will enhance performance of a portfolio over the stock indices.

Given that computer-driven index investing is more effective than active management—and at a much lower cost—why would millions not feel a sense of betrayal?

"He that trusteth in his riches shall fall."

—Proverbs

➤ "In an effort to exceed analysts' projected operating earnings of .73/share (10-15-02), Citigroup conveniently included gain from the sale of its headquarters on Park Avenue of $323 million. This accounted for .06/share and landed them at .74/share." (*MS Money*, Jubak's Journal)

This is a perfect example of an earnings distortion—as sales of assets are one-time gain items—not to be included in operating income. Investors have become increasingly wary of financial reporting practices in light of these developments.

There seems to be corruption at every level. Earnings reports seem to be manipulated to "prop up" stock prices, only to collapse when the distortions are discovered.

➤ "Every sector of the U.S. Equity market sustained damage in the third quarter of 2002. Not since the fourth quarter of 1987 has the market taken such a plunge." (First Affirmative Financial Network,1-800-422-7284, Market Commentary)

Three years of stock market losses resulted in the following annualized performance and standard deviation (risk) results as of December 31, 2002:

Index*	3 Yr. Return/Risk	10 Yr. Return/Risk
S&P 500(1)	-14.55%/15.1	9.34%/17
Wilshire 5000(2)	-14.37%/16.4	8.74%/17.1
Dow Jones Ind. Avg.(3)	-8.55%/16.9	12.01%17.9
NASDAQ Compos.(4)	-30.83%/28.4	7.62%/32
Wilshire Real Estate(5)	14.01%/15.1	9.97%/14
MSCI Eafe—Ndtr D(6)	-16.67%/12.8	6.26%/15.9
Lehman Bros. Aggr.(7)	10.10%/3.65	7.51%/3.95
1 Year Treasury Note	5.94%	5.31%

* Please Refer to MAP 6-3 for additional information about the indices.

1—500 Widely held U.S. stocks

2—5000 U.S. publicly traded common stocks

3—30 Industrial U.S. stocks

4—All issues of NASDAQ stock market

5—Comprised of companies whose charter is the equity ownership of commercial real estate.

6—Benchmark for international stock performance. An aggregate of 21 individual major country indexes.

7—Composed of the Lehman Brothers Govt./Credit Index, the Mortgage-Backed Securities Index, and the Asset-Backed Securities Index. Common benchmark for diversified bond portfolios.

This chart reveals the frustration that investors have felt. To translate the statistics into reality: an investor who purchased an S&P 500 Index Fund on January 1, 2000 would have lost three times the 14.55 percent annualized return listed, or 43.65 percent. The 15.1 volatility indicates that the 14.55 percent annual loss could have varied between + .55 percent and -29.65 percent!

We have to ask the question, "Is all that risk worth achieving the possibility of a .55 percent return?"

We have become a nation of investors over the past 20 years. The introduction of the IRA in the early '70s, along with the popularity of mutual funds, made investing an option for anyone with $25/month to save toward retirement. No longer was it necessary to have $5,000–$10,000 in order to see a stock broker and invest in stocks and bonds. Double-digit annual stock market returns made bank certificate of deposits and savings accounts as antiquated as a Model T. In 2001, it was estimated that half of all U.S. households owned mutual fund shares, up from 6 percent in 1980.

At the end of 2001, there were 8,321 mutual funds (triple from 1990) with almost $7 trillion dollars invested—a seven-fold increase from 1990.

This dramatic growth in stock market investing over the past 13 years has also inundated investors with investment information. Unfortunately, more information is not always what people need.

LOAVES AND FISHES

*This is not
the age of information.*

*This is not
the age of information.*

*Forget the news,
and the radio,
and the blurred screen.*

*This is the time
of loaves
and fishes.*

*People are hungry,
and one good word is bread
for a thousand.*

—*David Whyte, from* The House of Belonging

The one good word that begins to address our longing for an escape from having our *money working us* vs. our *money working for us* is "ground."

Before we jump in to fix our investment portfolios, we need to pause and notice what is really going on beneath the surface. Only then will we be able to honor the longing that is asking for our attention and to find some degree of peace and well-being. Only then can we begin to make wise investment decisions.

"Do not despise the world, for the world too is God."

—*Muhammad*

Hooked!

Wally had grounded around his investment dilemma by the time he called me to set up an appointment. The next day, as we continued our discussion, there were several matters about which I was curious.

"Wally," I began, "you said it was your greed that got you into what you perceive as a mess with your investments. I don't see you as a greedy type!"

"After hanging up yesterday," Wally responded, "I thought more about what I had said. Greed, to me, is wanting more than I need. It's grabbing for more, thinking that getting it will somehow make my life better. At the root of it seems to be a fear that I'll somehow suffer without that extra "cushion." As I finally took an honest look at why I was avoiding our investment losses, it became obvious that I didn't want to admit that the money I thought would ensure our comfort in retirement had been reduced 30 percent. I also realized that I didn't know what we needed to retire and that the broad spectrum of "comfort" carries with it a lot of trade-offs. I do know one thing: My denial and desire to recapture my losses sure hasn't resulted in much comfort!"

Wally reminded me that illusion of our ability to obtain safety and security brings with it a lot of suffering. His confession also resonated my own experience of easily getting hooked by my emotional reactions.

> *"In the Buddhist teachings, the messy emotional stuff is called klesha, which means poison. There are three main poisons: passion, aggression, and ignorance. We could talk about these in different ways—for example, we could also call them craving, aversion, and couldn't care less. Addictions of all kinds come under the category of craving, which is wanting, wanting, wanting—feeling that we have to have some kind of resolution. Aversion encompasses violence, rage, hatred, and negativity of all kinds, as well as garden-variety irritation. And ignorance? Nowadays, it's usually called denial… The pith instruction is, whatever you do, don't try and make the poisons go away. When you're trying to make them go away, you're losing your wealth along with your neurosis…These juicy emotional spots are where a warrior gains wisdom and compassion."*
>
> —*Pema Chödrön,* Comfortable with Uncertainty

Before we can shift into a relationship with money that serves our Authentic Self and helps us offer our gift to the world, we have

"Some of God's noblest sons, I think, will be selected from those that know how to take wealth, with all its temptations, and maintain godliness therewith. It is hard to be a saint standing in a golden niche."

—*Henry Ward Beecher*

to practice grounding with our human tendency toward desire, aversion, and denial. Each of these poisons provide a critical entry into feeling compassion for every other human who, at one time or another, suffers in these ways as well. As I refuse to identify with the emotion as the essence of my identity, I am able to drop down into the depth of my Authentic Self where I am capable of contentment even in the midst of uncertainty. This process actually transforms the poison into medicine.

Investments and portfolio decisions easily hook us. Let's examine a few specific ways.

"The larger the income, the harder it is to live within it."

—Richard Whately

Desire

The "More Money to Spend = Better Life" Hook

There is no doubt that poverty is not fun. When there's not enough money to pay for food, shelter, health care, and basic transportation, then it is an insult to state that more money will not help improve life.

Remember in Week Five Appendix B—all those *Other Debts*?

"The shocking thing is that the majority of American workers, about 60 percent, earn less than $14/hour."

—Barbara Ehrenreich, Nickel and Dimed

We all have to ask ourselves what we can do to narrow, rather than widen, this ever-expanding gap between the *have's* and *have not's*.

A first step in that process can be to take an honest, yet gentle, look at this first poison—desire.

When we receive a raise at work or some other increase in cash flow, our automatic response is to upgrade to a nicer car, take a more expensive trip, or buy a nicer piece of furniture for the living room. We are programmed to expand our consumption to match, even exceed, our incomes. Consider a few troubling statistics and quotes compiled from the book *Affluenza,* by John De Graaf, David Wann, and Thomas H. Naylor:

➤ The size of our homes; 1945—750 sq. ft., 1950s—950 sq. ft., 1960s 1,100 sq. ft., 1970s—1,350 sq. ft., Today—2,300 sq. ft.

➤ We spend more money on restaurant food than on food we cook ourselves.

- ➤ We drive twice as much per capita as we did half a century ago and fly 25 times as much.

- ➤ The savings rate in America in the eighties was 4 percent; half of the German rate and a quarter of Japan. Now it hovers at or below 0 percent.

- ➤ "Greed is good."—Ivan Boesky

- ➤ "Advertising's most important social function is to integrate the individual into our present-day American high speed consumption economy." (quote by Pierre Martineau, *Chicago Tribune,* 1957)

- ➤ The average American will spend nearly two years of his or her life watching TV commercials. A child may see a million of them before he or she reaches the age of 20.

"We've mutated from citizens to consumers in the last 60 years. The trouble with being consumers is that consumers have no duties or responsibilities or obligations to their fellow consumers. Citizens do. They have the obligation to care about their fellow citizens, and about the integrity of the town's environment and history."

—James Howard Kunstler, The Geography of Nowhere

"I make myself rich by making my wants few."

—Henry David Thoreau

"No wealth can satisfy the covetous desire of wealth."

—Jeremy Taylor

It's apparent. Desire for more is deeply ingrained in us—we come by it honestly. To sustain the "good life" we must expect high returns from our investments.

Say you have $500,000 in your IRA when you reach 60. If you want that money to last for 25 years and are given the following three options, which one would you choose?

- ➤ Spend $55,084 per year by earning 10 percent with a 100 percent stock allocation.

- ➤ Spend $46,839 per year by earning 8 percent with a 60 percent stock allocation.

- ➤ Spend $39,113 per year by earning 6 percent with a 10 percent stock allocation.

Why would anyone turn down almost $16,000 per year by choosing the 10 percent stock portfolio rather than the one with 100 percent stocks?

Traditional investing wisdom says that accepting more risk is necessary if we want to achieve "the good life." Of course "the good life" is dependent upon all the things that more money can buy. Unless you already have loads of money, there is really no better way to get from here to there than by taking more risk and making the money work harder.

> *"Make money your God*
> *and it will plague you like the devil."*
>
> —*Henry Fielding*

The following chart provides an example of the trade-off we take with possible return and loss of principal as the equity (stock) portion of our portfolio is adjusted.

Potential for Return and Associated Loss
Table #1

Long-term Average Return*	% Stocks	Downside Loss Probability**
9.6%	80%	-35%
9.1%	60%	-25%
8.7%	50%	-20%
7.5% (estimate.)	40%	-15%
6.9%	20%	-5%

*per AAII, "Portfolio Building," Table 3

** per "The Intelligent Asset Allocator," page 144

We know that the 80 percent stock portfolio is much riskier than the one with 20 percent stocks. Is the fear that we have seven times the chance of losing our investment strong enough to overcome our desire to have more money to spend? The answer may be *Yes* when the stock market is losing money, but what about when it starts to generate those double-digit annual returns? How firm will our resolve be then to stick with the lower-risk portfolio?

Desire—from Poison to Medicine

In order to free ourselves from the bondage of desire, we first have to admit the bondage exists. To pretend that we don't want more simply doubles the poison by coupling desire with denial. As we sit with our desire for more, we notice the tension in our bodies. We feel the agony of being chained to a treadmill that is constantly increasing in velocity. We admit, possibly for the first time, how very tired we are of chasing more money. In that moment we catch a glimpse of our deeper self. We know that our well-being no longer has to be linked to getting everything we want. We see that greed enslaves us by causing us to forget what is important and what it is we already possess. We begin to feel our sufficiency and temper our desires accordingly.

Author Wayne Muller was a guest on my radio show. In his book, *Sabbath: Restoring the Sacred Rhythm of Rest,* he addressed this tension between a desire for abundance and contentment with that which is sufficient:

> *"Lynn Twist is a friend who has dedicated her life to eliminating world hunger. She has traveled around the world, working on behalf of starving children. She tells me that our search for 'abundance'…is actually fed by a lingering belief in scarcity. If we are afraid there is not enough for us, we will grab for abundance— which is actually more than we need. Thus, even in abundance, there is great fear….*
>
> *"Lynn makes a crucial distinction between abundance—a fearful response to scarcity—and sufficiency—which invokes an experience of satisfaction and well-being. Sufficiency is that moment when we have enough…The instant we have enough, dissatisfaction and desire melt away."*
>
> —*Wayne Muller,* Sabbath: Restoring the Sacred Rhythm of Rest

What is "enough"? Remember the example of Charles Gray in Week Three, how he decided to live on the World Equity Budget, consuming no more than his fair share of the world's resources? Though very few have chosen to follow Mr. Gray's courageous example of living on $99/month, thousands have taken the "road less traveled" toward a simpler lifestyle.

"A man is rich in proportion to the number of things which he can afford to let alone."

—Henry David Thoreau

David Heitmiller and Jacqueline Blix, co-authors of *Getting a Life,* were living the good life back in 1990. They both had corporate jobs with great salaries and benefits and plenty of things that money could buy. One day shortly after his 45th birthday, David asked himself the question, "Is there something else I might want to do with the rest of my life?" rather than stay in a job that had become less and less fulfilling and meaningful.

Jacqueline had also discovered that "what I was doing didn't really have much relevance in the larger scheme of things." Those questions led them to ask themselves what was really enough.

"You start evaluating things and becoming aware of what you're doing. What we immediately realized was that the house we were living in was too big, and we were paying way too large of a percentage of our income to support this house. Eventually. we were able to sell it. We moved into a one-bedroom apartment and lived there for a couple of years, and that gave us time to evaluate living in a smaller space, as well as how much stuff we had. Finally, we ended up with a medium solution, in about a 1,300-square-foot townhome. In this process, we decided what our needs really were."

—Jacqueline Blix, Money Matters Radio Show

Pause to evaluate what underlies your current investment choices as it relates to your natural desire for more money. This next worksheet will help you.

WEEK SIX
WORKSHEET A
Investment Circuit Inspection

My Investments and the *"More Money to Spend"* Hook

Refer to the TEN WEEKS CD—"Week Six: Portfolio Analyzer" and follow the screen-by-screen instructions. Record the results of your analysis below:

Your portfolio's performance;

Year to Date   _____%

Last Year   _____%

Last Three Years   _____%

Last Five Years   _____%

? What kind of performance were you expecting? _____%

? What was the basis for your expectation?

_____ _____

_____

_____

_____

_____

? What kind of performance do you need to reach your goals?_____%

? Do you think you may have chosen different investments had you been clear about the last question before you invested?

_____

_____

_____

_____

_____

Your Portfolio's Risk:

From the Risk Profile section of your Portfolio Analyzer report:

? What is the Standard Deviation of your Portfolio?   _____%

Calculate the volatility (range of returns) for your portfolio:

Step 1—Your portfolio's five-year average annual return   _____%

Step 2—Add 1 times the standard deviation percentage   _____%

Step 3—Upper level of Return Range—67 percent of time   _____%

Step 4—Your portfolio's five-year average annual return   _____%

Step 5—Subtract 1 times the standard deviation percentage   _____%

Step 6—Bottom level of Return Range—67 percent of time   _____%

I would expect my portfolio's return to fall between Step 6   _____%
and Step 3 _____% 67 percent of the time.

I *was/was not* (circle one) aware that my portfolio had the potential to vary this much in return. I understand that the negative value means that I could lose more than that percentage of my principal, or original amount invested, once every six years.

Don't worry if this is confusing right now, we'll discuss standard deviation in more detail a bit later on in this section.

? What changes, if any, would you have made in selecting your investments after completing this analysis?

_____

_____

_____

_____

_____

_____

Your Portfolio's Revised Risk/Return:

? What percentage of your portfolio would you be willing to lose, referring back to Chart #1 in this section?   _____%

? What percentage of return could you expect given your willingness to risk that portion of your investment?   _____%

Please insert the TEN WEEKS CD, complete the Revised Return Analysis section, and then answer the following questions:

? What impact did this change of return have on your Authentic Money Guide scenario?

_____

_____

_____

_____

Now, let's determine what level of spending will result in a sustainable plan. Please complete the "New Spending" Analysis Section in the Week Six TEN WEEKS CD.

? Did you have to reduce expenses to offset your projected investment return? _____ If so, how much? $_____/year.

? Knowing the impact on your spending, what feelings come up about your decision to take less risk?

_____

_____

_____

_____

_____

? Do you want to change your allocation to stocks, knowing what you know now?

_____

_____

_____

_____

_____

? What specific accounts would you adjust in order to facilitate this expense reduction should you select it as part of your final Authentic Money Guide?

_____

_____

_____

_____

If you choose to adopt these changes, please checkmark (✔) the Budget Updated column to verify that the reductions have been included in your actual budget.

Category	Expense Reduction Amount	Budget Updated

? How does it feel to adjust your spending levels rather than your rate-of-return assumptions in an effort to create a realistic and sustainable Authentic Money Guide?

_____

_____

_____

_____

? Do you feel a sense of relief or freedom in knowing how much you can really afford to spend?

_____

_____

_____

_____

AVERSION
The "It's All Their Fault" Hook

Investment Irritations

Investments, especially in the last three years, provide plenty of ammunition for "violence, rage, hatred, and negativity of all kinds, as well as garden-variety irritation." (Pema Chödrön) Another *klesha,* or emotional poison, is our tendency to avoid the painful, unpleasant parts of life. There is plenty of news about our investments that we would rather avoid!

> *"The saddest thing I can imagine is to get used to luxury."*
>
> —*Charlie Chaplin*

It seems like the floundering economy is the least of our worries when it comes to investment performance. Financial reporting of company earnings has fallen into disrepute amidst allegations of massive conflict of interest between auditors and their corporate clients—many of whom paid millions of dollars in consulting fees to the same accounting firms performing their "independent audit." When the basis of all investment decisions relates to company profitability and no one really has any confidence in financial reports, it is easy to get angry and upset. Consider a few headlines:

WorldCom accounting scandal.
"WorldCom, the once high-flying telecom giant, appears to be headed for more trouble, according to an exclusive report by CNBC's David Faber. The Company appears to have greatly inflated its operating earnings over the past five quarters…" (CNBC Market Dispatches)

Roots of accounting scandals lie in incentive structure, not ethics.
"Andersen's senior management seems to have revised its partners' compensation and performance evaluation to encourage them to behave more like salesmen and less like auditors, resulting in a lot of sloppy audits." (Professor Ronald A Dye, Kellogg World Alumni Magazine, *Winter 2002)*

Coupled with questionable financial statements came one news story after another about an epidemic of CEO compensation abuse schemes.

We're all paying for CEOs' greed.
"Spring proxy statements have investors seeing red. They show that greedy CEOs took home tens of millions last year while the stocks of the companies they ran tanked. This isn't the case of a few bad apples, either—it's a fundamental reason the stock market is struggling." (MSN Money, Jubak's Journal)

And if that weren't enough, May 2003 brought news of widespread conflicts of interests among the largest brokerage firms.

Your broker misled you.
"There wasn't a wet eye in any boardroom after the news that 10 large brokerage houses will pay, collectively, $1.4 billion in fines for dishonest, double-dealing, fraudulent, counterfeit, sham, yes sham, research reports that bilked investors of billions... The fines were insignificant enough that the day following the news, Standard and Poor's reported that it was not likely to change its ratings on any of the companies charged. (www.motleyfool.com—Jeff Fischer, May 1, 2003)

These headlines contribute to our general irritability regarding our investments. A common response these days from new clients whom I ask to gather recent investment statements is, "I haven't opened those for months. I got tired of feeling depressed for days after seeing the account value drop even further."

Beneath all these headlines lies a fundamental dilemma. It is you and I, as individual shareholders, who own these companies. It is up to us to take the responsibility to either change how the company conducts itself or sell our shares.

"Shareholders should start acting like the owners they are. They must make the most of the voting power that they have today while they mobilize to strengthen their rights to have a meaningful say in the companies they own."

—The Power of the Purse: How Investors Can Restore Integrity to our Financial Markets *(White Paper State of California Treasurer's Office, 2002)*

The anger and frustration we feel with our investments lies in part with our natural tendency to ignore our responsibilities. We want to participate in the benefits of corporate profitability, but we turn a deaf ear to the abhorrent corporate ethical void and the social cost many of our investments ignore. All of those decisions end up coming back to haunt us—not only economically, but also emotionally.

To ground thoroughly involves taking an honest look at what we actively support with our investment portfolio. Once this inventory is conducted, we can evaluate which investments are consistent with our Authentic Core and which are not. After an honest assessment, our decision may be to radically shift the process by which we select investments. Maybe there really is a way we can turn this poison into medicine.

AVERSION: POISON TO MEDICINE
Investing with Heart

As we take notice of our judgment, irritability, and anger, we begin to realize how much energy we lose each day to our investments. The negative energy does nothing to improve matters. Rather, it clouds our ability to see our own failure to invest responsibly. Only when we finally face ourselves can we begin to tap into the healing power of changing our old patterns of avoiding personal responsibility.

FACE YOURSELF

Now or never
Face yourself
No one else will do.
Face your weakness
Face your past
Let your scars show through.

—Michael Hedges, excerpted from the song *"Face Yourself"* from the album *"Watching My Life Go By"*

Socially responsible investing seeks to integrate our values with our need for investment return. A specialist of "socially responsible investing" (SRI), Jack Brill, co-author of *Investing with Your Values,* appeared on "Money Matters" in 2001 to talk about SRI, or what he also refers to as "natural investing." Jack shared his belief that most people want to be philanthropic and kind and to leave the world a better place for their children and future generations. These "natural" longings, he said, can be honored in each aspect of human life, including investment decision-making.

Jack reminded me that each major faith tradition emphasizes the importance of cultivating behavior that aligns with our value to "do no harm." The Golden Rule is truly a universal teaching, as illustrated in faith teachings around the world:

Christianity—*As you wish that men would do to you, do so unto them.*

Islam—*No one of you is a believer until he desires for his brother that which he desires for himself.*

Buddhism—*Hurt not others in ways that you yourself would find hurtful.*

Judaism—*What is hateful to you, do not do to your neighbor; That is the whole Torah; the rest is commentary; go, study.*

Hinduism—*Do naught unto others which would cause you pain if done to you.*

Given these spiritual directives and our "natural" tendency to want to do good rather than harm, the growth of SRI has been phenomenal. Consider these statistics from *Socially Responsible Investing*, by Amy Domini:

➤ In 1995, $165 billion of investments were socially screened. By 2001, that had grown to $2.343 trillion (an increase of 1,153 percent in six years).

➤ The growth in professionally managed assets from 1995–2001 was 184 percent—SRI managed growth for that same period was 266 percent.

➤ In 1999, there were 168 mutual funds for socially aware investors. By late 2001, that had grown to 230.

But what does *Socially Responsible Investing* really mean?

According to *Investing With Your Values*, by Hal Brill, Jack A. Brill, and Cliff Feigenbaum, there are four spokes on the Socially Responsible Investing Wheel:

1. *Affirmative Screening—Identify companies whose products and business policies are important to you and good for their employees, consumers, and the environment.*

2. *Avoidance Screening—Identify companies whose behaviors and products are inconsistent with your values. If you own them, sell them—if you don't own them, don't buy them.*

3. *Shareholder Activism—Encourage shareholders to take an active role as owners of their companies and actively influence corporate behavior for the good.*

4. *Community Investing—Provide financial capital to people in low-income communities at either a market or below-market rate of return. A current initiative within the SRI community has as its goal that 2 percent of all funds invested in socially screened investments be invested in Community Development Financial Institutions.*

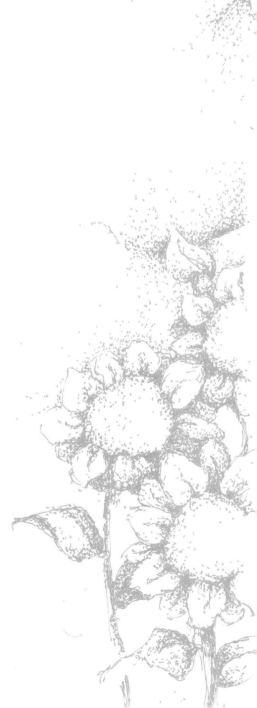

Many advocates of SRI agree with the following comment that Jack Brill made in a reference to a "double bottom line":

"Screening actually eliminates potential economic disasters…the companies that are good to their employees and environmentally sensitive are actually more profitable. By taking this extra step of screening your investments, you are actually enhancing your possibilities of profit and attaining your goals—the first part of the double bottom line is economic—the second is social."

—*Jack Brill,* "Money Matters" Radio Show Interview

A mature industry has developed to honor this deep longing to integrate our values with our need for a reasonable investment return. The questions we all have about evaluating the values of our existing portfolio, as well as how to begin the process of evaluating socially screened investments, are addressed in our next Circuit Inspection worksheet. Before you begin Worksheet B, take a moment to review the following Appendix material for Week Six:

MAP 6-1, The Natural Investment Services, Inc. (NIS) Social Rating. This is the perfect place to begin to see which of the mutual funds you already own apply social screens to their stock and bond selection process. NIS, the financial consulting firm of Jack and Hal Brill, updates this analysis of current mutual funds and the extent of their screening process periodically through their webpage *www.naturalinvesting.com*. This webpage is a tremendous resource for locating specific socially responsible issues that may interest you. With over 200 web links, carefully organized under broad categories, you can use this as "home base" in learning more about SRI.

To research a specific company in which you own stock, go to *www.corpwatch.org* and enter that company's name in the "Search Corpwatch" dialog box on the home page. You can also see if your company is listed as passing the social screens of both the Calvert and Domini Socially Responsible Indexes found at *www.naturalinvesting.com*.

MAP 6-2, Socially Responsible Investing Resources provides links to SRI resources that can facilitate the implementation of a socially screened portfolio, as well as help evaluate the social impact of your current investments.

WEEK SIX
WORKSHEET B

INVESTMENT CIRCUIT INSPECTION
My Investments and the Aversion—"It's All Their Fault" Hook

? What phrase best describes your attitude about investing right now?

_____

_____

_____

_____

_____

? Do you sense a need for any kind of change in the way you relate to your investments? If so, what kind of change?

_____

_____

_____

_____

_____

? Are any of the mutual funds you currently own listed in MAP 6-1? If so, which ones:

_____

_____

_____

_____

_____

Consider the following quotation:

"We seem to have surrendered community excellence and community values in the mere accumulation of material things. The Gross National Product (GNP) counts air pollution, and ambulances to clear our highways of carnage, the destruction of the redwoods, and the death of Lake Superior. It grows with the production of napalm and missiles with nuclear warheads. Yet the GNP does not allow for the health of our children, the quality of their education, or the joy of their play. It measures neither our wit nor our courage; neither our wisdom nor our learning; neither our compassion nor our devotion to our country; it measures everything, in short, except that which makes life worthwhile; and it can tell us everything about America—except whether we are proud to be Americans."

—*Robert F. Kennedy, as quoted in* Investing With Your Values

? Do you sense that your current investment choices put more emphasis on GNP than other, less quantifiable, measures of wealth?

_____

_____

_____

_____

Insert the TEN WEEKS CD, "Investment Research" and complete the following:

Click on your web browser and type in *www.corpwatch.org*.

? In the "Search Corpwatch" dialog box, enter the name of one of the corporations your mutual fund owns. Did anything come up in the search? If so, what did you discover?

_____

_____

_____

_____

Select one of the funds you currently own.

Follow the screen-by-screen instructions for Week Six "Morningstar Profile" from the TEN WEEKS CD and complete the following:

Print out all four reports and answer the following questions:

Return vs. Risk—

? What does the Sharpe Ratio tell you about its risk-adjusted return?

_____

_____

_____

_____

_____

? What does Beta tell you about its volatility given the return it earned?

_____

_____

_____

_____

Fund Holdings—

? How expensive is the stock compared to the earnings it is producing (see "Price/Earnings" ratio)?

_____

_____

_____

_____

Cost of Ownership—

? Is the annual expense ratio for this fund higher or lower than its category average?

_____

_____

_____

_____

? What is the three-, five-, or 10-year expense projection for your fund compared to the category average?

_____

_____

_____

_____

_____

Summary

? What are the fund's two biggest strengths?

_____

_____

_____

_____

_____

? What are the fund's two biggest weaknesses?

_____

_____

_____

_____

? Overall, how did this fund compare to its category?

_____

_____

_____

_____

_____

Take a minute to visit *www.calvertgroup.com* and run their "Know What You Own" analyzer on this mutual fund. Refer to Week Six/Appendix B/Section 2 for detailed instructions.

Print out your analysis and place it in your My Financial Education binder under Week Six—Investment Resources.

After completing this analysis, answer the following questions:

? Have you ever analyzed a mutual fund in this detail?

_____

_____

? What did you discover about your investment and yourself in the process?

_____

_____

_____

_____

_____

_____

? Based on the companies and investments you own, what causes are you supporting?

_____

_____

_____

_____

_____

? Have you ever received a voting proxy from a company or mutual fund you own? _____ If yes, did you vote?

_____

_____

_____

_____

? Do you feel any differently about investing after having completed this analysis?

_____

_____

_____

_____

_____

_____

? Are you interested in considering Socially Responsible Investing options after what you have read and experienced?

_____

_____

_____

_____

_____

_____

Three-hole punch your mutual fund analysis and place it in the Week Six—Investment Resources section of your My Financial Education binder.

IGNORANCE AND DENIAL

"I Don't Understand Investing" Hook

I cannot remember a client ever saying, "I love investing—it's something I understand and find very satisfying." When the topic of investing comes up, it's usually more like, "I haven't a clue as to what I'm doing. I'm happy when my investments grow and depressed when they lose value. It's an emotional roller-coaster ride that I'd just as soon live without."

If ignorance is a poison that threatens our ability to experience our Authenticity and Awaken, then we must first admit that we have taken this poison, thinking it to be medicine. We have interpreted the investing mantras, "Buy and Hold" and "Invest for the Long-term" as reasons for our denial and refusal to face what is really going on with our portfolios. Such wisdom has its place when coupled with awareness but when married to denial it can be devastating. Millions of investors routinely leave their investment statements unopened, thinking:

"Portion of U.S. Stock owned by the wealthiest 10 percent of Americans—90 percent."

—Harper's Index Book

"Those who have not found their true wealth, which is the radiant joy of Being and the deep, unshakable peace that comes with it, are beggars, even if they have great material wealth. They are looking outside for scraps of pleasure or fulfillment, for validation, security, or love, while they have a treasure within that not only includes all those things but is infinitely greater than anything the world can offer."

—Eckhart Tolle, "The Greatest Obstacle To Enlightenment", The Sun, *July 2002.*

"Why bother opening the statements, anyway? I don't understand anything on the statement other than the 'Current Account Value' line. It seems to always be less than the prior month's balance. To be reminded of my ignorance and poor investment choices just feeds my sense of inferiority as it pertains to the investing world. To spend any more time with these statements than is absolutely necessary is like rubbing salt in my wound."

Pema Chödrön reminded us at the beginning of this section, "Whatever you do, don't try to make the poisons go away." Underneath the denial and ignorance is something powerful. It takes a lot of courage—a warrior's heart—to notice when we are pretending life isn't scary and volatile. It's difficult to admit that things do not always go our way, especially when it comes to accumulating the money we anticipated would ensure our happiness.

When we access the disappointment and fear beneath the denial, we allow ourselves to feel genuine compassion for millions of others who suffer in the same way. We also find the freedom to wake up and pay attention to the issues at hand. Rather than create another form of suffering that accompanies our compulsion to fix our portfolios once and for all, we accept the reality that no perfect solution exists. Ignorance and denial begin to fade into awareness and surrender—poison to medicine once again.

If we remove all equity or stock risk from our investment portfolios by investing only in U.S. Treasury Bills and Notes, we end up with negative returns after the effect of inflation and taxes are considered. We just traded a potential risk for a certain risk!

On the other hand, if we invest 80 percent in a diversified stock portfolio, we could lose 35 percent of our original investment in an effort to obtain an investment return sufficient to pay for the lifestyle we want.

Paying close attention to our investments helps us accept this normal tension in our human experience—this give and take between our need for safety as well as sufficient provision. We experience more peace and happiness in life when we're not constantly insisting there be equilibrium.

Investing—Just Use the Map!

"Learning how to invest successfully on your own is much like getting from one city to another..."

—Bill Bernstein, Intelligent Asset Allocator

Some studies suggest that most drivers, especially women, find it much easier to buy a road map when traveling in unfamiliar territory. Of course, there are many of us who think that is way too much work—it is easier to head off in the general direction and trust our instincts. When we do stop to ask directions, oftentimes we discover the person didn't really understand where we were trying to go.

Contrary to popular belief, investing is not impossible to understand. If we started with some basic principles in junior high, by the time our children graduated from high school they would know more about investing than many stockbrokers and investment professionals. I believe that, equipped with a few basic principles, you can make wise, confident investment decisions that respect your core values and personal propensity for, or aversion to, risk. The financial marketplace has a vested interest in keeping the average investor confused. In this state of affairs, you are more likely to purchase products or services that may not be in your best interest. A couple of examples illustrate the impact education of investors can have on the status quo.

> *"If you should put even a little on a little, and should do this often, soon this too would become big."*
>
> *—Hesiod*

During the Quicken® setup process, we encountered a screen that asked about investment fees. There were questions about "front- and back-end loads," as well as asset-based fees. If you were aware of the different fees that can be imposed by a mutual fund, you might be more inclined to research low-cost "no load" alternatives rather than purchase a fund from a commission-based broker. The investment industry wants you to be informed—just not too informed.

As an example, consider two U.S. Mid-cap Mutual Funds, Calvert Capital Accumulation Fund (CCAFX) and Vanguard Extended Market Index (VEXMX). The TEN WEEKS CD will walk you through how to perform an analysis of two funds in the Week Six—"Comparing Two Funds" section.

The Calvert Fund A shares have a front-end load of 4.75 percent of the purchase price. Thereafter, its annual expense ratio is 1.67 percent. These two expense categories result in an estimated three-

year expense of $1,003 for a $10,000 investment. Compare that with Vanguard's three-year expense projection of $80 and $701 for the category (Mid-cap Growth) average. If all other comparisons were equal, knowing this dramatic difference in fees would influence an investor's decision.

Let's consider another situation wherein your investment knowledge could make a difference in what investment options are presented to you.

What about your 401(k) investment options? Let's assume you have three domestic large-cap funds, a domestic mid-cap fund, a domestic small-cap fund, two international funds, a corporate bond fund, a government bond fund, and a high-yield bond fund as your investment options. If you chose to split your money into four equal baskets between U.S. large companies, small companies, international companies, and the high-yield bond fund, selecting the fund in each category that had generated the highest 10-year annualized return, you might feel that you had a pretty well-diversified portfolio.

If you take a closer look at your portfolio, however, you may realize that the combination of your funds leaves you with a large concentration of U.S. large-cap stocks, a smaller than expected allocation to overseas companies, and a higher than anticipated level of risk due to the risky high-yield bond choice. By paying proper attention, you discovered weaknesses that could have increased your overall risk and lessened your potential for return.

Your awareness could also serve as a platform to request suggested portfolio allocations from your 401(k) provider—for investors with varying degrees of risk tolerance. The fund sponsor is finally expected to assume a higher level of responsibility than they had prior to your informed discovery. Your "squeaky wheel" could result in a change that will make it much easier for you to keep your investment 401(k) accounts properly allocated, as well as protect your co-workers who have yet to learn the importance of proper asset allocation.

So, how does an individual investor navigate the maze of investment decisions and restore some awareness and sanity to this aspect of their financial lives? The acronym *SANE* helps me remember the essentials of investing:

S **Slow** Down and Understand Investing

A **Appreciate** the Risk/Reward Relationship

N **Notice** the Whole Is Greater than the Sum of Its Parts

E **Examine** the Cash Flow Needs of your Authentic Money Guide and Invest Accordingly

SANE Investing—There Is a Different Way!

Life is Just a Bowl of Cherries

…so keep repeating

It's the berries,

The strongest folk must fall

The sweet things in life

To you were just loaned.

So how can you lose

What you never owned…

—Fosse

I was honored to have Dr. William "Bill" Bernstein as a guest on my radio show. Dr. Bernstein wrote, *The Intelligent Asset Allocator—How to Build Your Portfolio to Maximize Returns and Minimize Risk* as well as *The Four Pillars of Investing*. The essence of Dr. Bernstein's investment wisdom can be captured in those two words: "Sane Investing." Let's examine each of the four components to his investment approach.

SLOW DOWN *and Understand Investing*

"The very first thing that you want to do, the very first signpost on the road that you want to pass, is simply to do nothing. You want to take a deep breath and don't do anything because the worse thing that you could possibly do is to radically alter your finances without doing a proper amount of study and work…the time you take to learn and plan is going to be well spent."

—Dr. Bill Bernstein, "Money Matters" Radio Show Interview

We get better at things when we practice. So far in TEN WEEKS, you have set up your investment accounts for online updates so you will know where you stand every day. You have done some preliminary analysis of your existing portfolio, as well as practiced some mutual fund analysis skills. These hands-on exercises, coupled with some basic understanding, will prepare you for specific action with your investments—but first it is critical to take the time to understand the basics of investing.

When you feel a compulsion to leave before you stay and bypass the wisdom that can only come through "grounding," remember Dr. Bernstein's wise words: "take a deep breath." You work hard for the money you invest. Until you understand investing, it is better to leave your money under the mattress. So slow down and give some attention to investing. Ask questions.

One question immediately comes to mind: What makes investing so different from saving?

Saving might be illustrated by the purchase of a Certificate of Deposit (C.D.) from a bank. You enter into a contract with the bank that says you provide $10,000, and in five years the bank will pay you $11,593, assuming a 3 percent reinvested interest rate.

If the bank gets into trouble, most likely you will get your $10,000 back, since the Federal Deposit Insurance Corporation promises to return your money. The essence of saving is that there is very little risk that you won't get back your original investment.

It is important to notice that saving involves taking risk. In an inflationary environment, your $10,000 will be worth less in three years than it was when you gave it to the banker. After paying tax on the interest earned, you'll have even that much less to offset the effects of inflation.

Investing, on the other hand, makes no guarantee that your original investment will be returned to you. In simple terms, it's like your friend Joe asking you to become an investor in Joe's Bar and Grill, his new enterprise. He pulls out some grease-stained financial projections that indicate your share of the profits should amount to $2,500 per year—all on an original investment of $10,000. There's no guarantee, however, of getting back your money, much less the 25 percent projected return.

But you believe in Joe and his idea. Sure enough, the restaurant is a hit. Five years later, you want to evaluate your investment. Joe has a little extra cash and is willing to buy back your shares.

Investing, you realize, means that you have to be able to evaluate what happened both financially and emotionally with you and your money.

Going back through your records, you write down the checks you received the first of each March. You make note of what emotions you experienced when the checks arrived (or failed to arrive) each year:

Joe's Bar and Grill $10,000 Investment Ledger

Year	$ Received <Invested>	What I Felt
1998	<$10,000>	This is great—where else can I get a 25 percent return!
1998	$1,200	What about the $2500?
1999	$0	Oh no, it's all gone!
2000	$1,800	Now I'm only $4,500 behind where I was supposed to be!
2001	$3,000	Finally, a bit more than I was promised but still $4,000 behind
2002	$2,000	Not out of the hole yet!
2002	$10,000	If I decide to 'cash out'
Total	**$8,000**	A lot of worry and lost energy!

You can see that life got quite a bit more complicated with Joe than with the bank C.D.—but you also made more money. Was the extra money worth "investing" rather than just "saving"? That leads us into the next phase of SANE investing.

APPRECIATE the Risk/Reward Relationship

"The second thing you do is you have to acquire an appreciation of the fundamental relationship between risk and return in the capital markets…if you want high returns you're going to have to take a lot of risks."

—*Dr. Bill Bernstein,* "Money Matters" *Radio Show Interview*

If the second aspect of restoring some sanity to our investment responsibilities is to understand the interplay between risk and reward, another question immediately pops up: How do we calculate *return?*

Investment Return

Going back to Joe and the cash flow stream from his business, your average return would be 16 percent, calculated by taking the total cash payments divided by the number of years the money was invested. This average annual return would then be divided by the original investment to arrive at the average return percentage.

As you can see, *average annual return* can be misleading. You didn't receive $1,600 per year ($10,000 x the average annual return of 16 percent)—it was paid to you in differing amounts and times, thus affecting the true annualized rate of return.

To calculate the more accurate *annualized rate of return*, which is the return rate you earned considering the timing of your dividends and final payback of your loan, you would need a financial calculator, like the Texas Instruments BA-35. Look up the annuity calculation instructions, and within no time you will know how your investments are really performing. If you decided to take your $10,000 back in 2002, the overall annualized rate of return would amount to 14.75 percent. That's a far cry from the 25 percent that Joe promised initially—but a lot better than losing your whole $10,000!

Investment Risk

Now you have a clear picture of the "return" side of your investment with Joe. But what about the other side—"risk"? The variability of returns can be analyzed and a statistic, referred to as "standard deviation," can be calculated. Standard deviation comes from the concept of "scatter." The more scattered or varied the returns are for a particular investment, the higher the standard deviation and the greater the risk. Using the same financial calculator, we entered each annual cash flow's return as follows:

Year	% Return for that Year
1998	12%
1999	0%
2000	18%
2001	30%
2002	20%

The average of those returns (added up and divided by 5) = 16 percent.

The calculator tells us that the standard deviation for this investment was 11 percent.

In his book, *The Intelligent Asset Allocator,* Dr. Bernstein illustrates this rather difficult concept:

"What does the standard deviation number really mean? It means that two-thirds of the time the annual return of the asset will lie between one standard deviation above and one standard deviation below the mean (average) value...Let's assume you are considering a Latin American stock fund with an expected return of 15 percent and a very high standard deviation of 35 percent. This tells you to expect a loss of 20 percent (15 percent–35 percent) or worse every six years(*), a loss of worse than 55 percent (15 percent-70 percent) every 44 years(**), and a loss of 90 percent(15 percent–105 percent) every 740 years(***). (Reprinted with permission of The McGraw-Hill Companies. William J. Bernstein, The Intelligent Asset Allocator, *© 2001 The McGraw-Hill Companies, Inc.)*

* Out of a six-year period, one year we might achieve more than a 50 percent return and one year more than a 20 percent loss. The remaining four out of six yearly returns (66 percent of the time) should fall between those two extremes.

** Out of a 44-year period, one year we might achieve more than an 85 percent return and one year a loss of 55 percent or more. The remaining 42 out of 44 yearly returns (95 percent of the time) should fall between those extremes.

*** Out of a 740-year period, one year we might achieve more than a 120 percent return and one year a loss of 90 percent or more. The remaining 738 out of 740 yearly returns (99 percent of the time) should fall between those extremes.

Can you begin to see how critical it is to evaluate investments in light of their volatility and not just their performance?

Now, with these two performance numbers—Return of 14.75 percent and Standard Deviation of 11 percent—you have what you need to shop around and see if you want to leave your money with Joe or take it and invest it elsewhere. Take a minute to compare your investment with alternatives listed below. These returns are reflective of performance from 1926–1998 (*The Intelligent Asset Allocator*).

Table 2

Investment	Return	Risk = Std. Deviation
30-day T Bills	3.77%	3.22%
Five-Year Treasuries	5.31%	5.71%
20-Year Treasuries	5.34%	9.21%
Large Stocks	11.22%	20.26%
Small Stocks	12.18%	38.09%

After comparing your investment with Table 2, it seems like you did pretty well. You achieved a higher return than had you invested in small stocks at less than one-third of the risk for that asset class. Before you get too excited and run out and invest another $10,000 with Joe, consider two more issues: liquidity and stability/reliability of long-term returns.

Investment History

How were the payments you received from Joe determined? Did he take a large salary or draw from the business that prevented him from paying you the 25 percent he originally promised. Privately held companies, like Joe's Bar and Grill, that do not sell their shares to the general public over a stock exchange, are different than publicly traded ones. Publicly traded companies are supposed to abide by a host of security laws that help protect the individual investor. This helps you and me make informed decisions about companies in which we might invest. Had you been the shareholder of a publicly held company, you could have determined what management decisions affected your dividend. You could also analyze audited financial statements (or run a *Morningstar* analysis) to see how the company's financial position has changed over a longer period of time. It's doubtful that Joe has a set of audited financial statements that allows you to see how secure your investment is, and the fact that he has been in business only five years adds another level of risk as well.

Investment Liquidity

The other feature of owning a publicly traded security is your ability to liquidate, or sell it, in a very short period of time. Even though you may get only a portion of your money back, you still have the freedom to cash it in. We all know, however, that even publicly traded companies can go bankrupt and then your ability to sell your shares in the open market is of no help. When you think about it, Joe's willingness to pay you back now may not be replicated anytime soon. Your investment is liquid only to the extent that you act now.

As compared to investing in a stock of a publicly traded company, how much extra return should you expect for assuming these extra risks? A conservative estimate would be at least 20–40 percent. All of a sudden the 14.7 percent annualized return looks pretty marginal considering what risks are involved.

Given all this information, you decide it's time to take your $10,000 and find an investment that has a better risk/return balance.

Let's take a minute to return to Quicken® and evaluate the risk/return mix of your existing portfolio.

WEEK SIX
WORKSHEET C
Investment Circuit Inspection

Appreciating My Own Risk/Return Mix

Please insert your Week Six TEN WEEKS CD, "Asset Allocation Guide" and complete the following information:

Return _____%

Std. Deviation _____%

Write down one of your investment accounts ("Ginger's Investment AC"), or a category of investments ("Ginger's Retirement Accounts"):

_____

Find the model portfolio which best fits your time horizon* for the above account or category. _____ yrs.

*Time horizon simply asks the question: How long will it be before you need some or all of this money?

Refer to Table 3 below and complete the following:

The largest loss I can tolerate for this account is _____%

The portfolio associated with this loss has _____% invested in stocks.

The time horizon associated with this loss, per Table 3, is _____years, which is/is not (circle one) consistent with the time horizon noted above.

If the time horizon is not consistent, then I choose to select a portfolio with a _____% loss potential and a _____% stock allocation.

(Use your historical experience with the 2000–2003 bear "loss" market to honestly evaluate your tolerance for loss. If you weren't comfortable losing 37 percent in actuality, don't select the 83 percent stock allocation portfolio now, even though you have more than nine years to invest.)

Table 3 is derived from Quicken®'s 2003 Deluxe's model portfolio ranges (available at press time). My professional recommendation is to ratchet down the expected return by 1 percent for each line and adjust the time horizon years. I have adjusted the chart accordingly.

Table 3

Exp. Return	Time Horizon	Std. Dev.	Stock/bond	% Portfolio	Loss *
6%-1%=5%	3 yrs.	2.5%	16%–84%	A	5%
7%-1%=6%	3 yrs. +1=4	4.7%	32%–68%	B	10%
8%-1%=7%	3 yrs. +2=5	6.9%	47%–53%	C	20%
9%-1%=8%	5 yrs.+2=7	9.4%	64%–36%	D	27%
10%-1%=9%	7 yrs.+2=9	11.8%	83%–17%	E	37%

*Estimated loss exposure for stock allocation per Table 1.

Consider Dr. Bernstein's recommendations in selecting the portion of your portfolio invested in stocks (*Intelligent Asset Allocator*):

1. Start by referring to Table 1. Select the largest annual portfolio loss you are willing to tolerate. The above table includes similar percentages in the last column.

2. Adjust your stock allocation downward from the first step if your time horizon multiplied by 10 is lower. For example, if you need the money under consideration in five years, your maximum stock allocation should be no greater than 50 percent (five years x 10 percent/year stock allocation).

3. **Circle the portfolio from Table 3 that satisfies both your tolerance for loss as well as your investment time horizon.**

   Return to Week Six, **Worksheet A—My Investments and the *More Money to Spend Hook.***

? What was your Revised Rate of Return? _____%

? How did that affect your lifestyle expenses?

_____

_____

? Does your rate of return answer in Worksheet A differ from the portfolio you circled above?_____

? If there is a difference, what do you feel changed in your decision-making process?

_____

_____

_____

Before you finalize how much you'll invest in stocks and bonds, let's discuss Asset Allocation.

NOTICE *the Whole Is Greater Than the Sum of Its Parts*

"The fourth thing you have to do is to appreciate that a diversified portfolio of many different asset classes (many different kinds of stocks, many different kinds of bonds) behaves in a way that is very counter-intuitive (i.e., sometimes adding a volatile investment class can actually lower the risk of the entire portfolio).

"It's as if you make a cake with shortening, flour, butter, and sugar— none of those things taste very good at all on their own—but together they taste quite wonderful. So the behavior of the whole is very, very different than that of the ingredients. And this is called Portfolio Theory, and it's absolutely critical to your success as an investor."

—Dr. Bill Bernstein, "Money Matters" Radio Show Interview

Not only do we like cake a lot better than any of its separate ingredients alone, we like what happens when we invest using the principles of asset allocation.

Lack of Correlation is the Key

The magic of asset allocation lies not only in the principle of diversification—"Don't put all your eggs in one basket"—but especially in the power of "negative correlation," or what I refer to as "chicks and calves."

If I were a farmer, I'd just as soon not have my entire livelihood depend on the power staying on all winter and the warming lights hatching my new chicks. It would be nice if I also had a few cows that were ready to calve naturally. These two birthing processes are unrelated, or negatively correlated. A diversified farmer might raise cows and sheep because the birthing processes are similar, or related. An uncorrelated farmer then would raise cows and chickens. It may not have been until the power went out that the "chicks and calves" farmer appreciated the benefits of linking negative correlation with diversification.

When one of my asset class investments behave differently from another of my asset classes (when one is profitable, the other is not) it actually helps to increase my overall return and reduce my overall risk. A particular investment's correlation to the Standard and Poors' 500 stock index is quantified by a statistic, R2 (R squared), the correlation coefficient. A value of 1 means that this particular investment vehicle behaves exactly like the S&P 500—perfectly correlated. A value of –1 indicates the opposite—they move in exact opposition. (We know when a number is squared, its result is always positive, so the correlation coefficient is always a positive number between 0 and 1.) It makes sense to combine asset classes that have a low correlation coefficient.

Asset Allocation and Investment Attention

Studies have shown that asset allocation accounts for the majority of an investment portfolio's return. Once you have chosen a portfolio that honors your investment time horizon, tolerance for loss, and social parameters, you don't have to worry about finding the perfect mix of asset classes. What is most important is sticking to the allocations, with minor adjustments, over time.

There are several benefits of using asset allocation as a vehicle for giving your investments your attention rather than your energy.

➤ First, you don't have to worry about picking the right stocks and then buying and selling them at the right time. That would be as absurd as pulling the cake out of the oven every five minutes and adding something to the mix. Once you combine the ingredients, the best thing you can do is let the cake bake. We have learned that the financial markets are much smarter than even the most adept money managers. It's a lot of wasted effort to pretend differently.

➤ Second, you don't need to agonize over how to invest new money or keep your portfolio balanced. It's as easy as following the instructions in the cookbook for that cake. There are even cake mixes for those of us who have trouble measuring ingredients.

You can also use a "box mix" for your portfolio by following predetermined asset allocations, or "model portfolios," suggested by Quicken®, *The Four Pillars of Investing*—the book by William J. Bernstein, and various Socially Responsible Investment companies.

At least once each year, the portfolio is rebalanced by adjusting the holdings in each asset class to its targeted allocation. We will illustrate this in the next Worksheet and TEN WEEKS CD lesson.

It's a Rebalancing Act

"To get back to equal weighting, what you've got to do is sell the best ones, sell the best performing ones, and use the proceeds from those sales, to buy the ones that have performed the worst. It's a way of forcing yourself to sell high and buy low."

—Dr. Bill Bernstein, "Money Matters" Radio Show Interview

The reason rebalancing works is it keeps our overall allocation percentages in line, rather than letting our emotions dictate our investment decisions. If I have set my international stock percentage at 10 percent and it now only occupies 5 percent of my portfolio, then I am forced to buy more of it when its price is lower than when I would normally buy it.

Index Funds—You Only Need a Few

Investment choices are simplified dramatically through the use of index funds that track each chosen asset class. Consider the following chart that lists Vanguard Index funds that cover the major asset classes:

Table 4

Vanguard Fund	Index	Asset Class	Expense Ratio	Taxable or Retirement
500 Index	S&P 500	U.S. Large Co.	.18%	Both
Value Index	Barra Value	Lg.-cap Value	.22%	Retirement
Growth Index	Barra Growth	Lg.-cap Growth	.22%	Both
Extended Mkt.	Wilshire 4500	U.S. Mid/Small Co.	.25%	Retirement
Small-cap Value	S&P600SC	Small-cap Val.	.27%	Retirement
Small-cap Growth	SP 600 SC	Small-cap Grth	.27%	Retirement
REIT Index	Morg. St. REIT	Real Estate	.33%	Retirement
Emerging Mkts.	MSCI-EAFE Emg. Mkt.	Em Mkt. Intl.	.58%	Both
Developed Mkts.	MSCI-EAFE	Europe/Pacific	.32%	Taxable
Infl. Prot. Secur.	NA	Govt. Bonds	.25%	Retirement
GNMA	NA	Govt. Mortgage	.27%	Retirement
Total Bond	Lehman Agg.	Total Bond	.22%	Retirement

"Consider the little mouse, how wise an animal it is which never entrusts its life to one hole only."

—*Plautus*

Narrowing the field from almost 9,000 funds to 12 makes it easier to tackle this task of choosing funds to build your portfolio.

Expenses and Taxes—More Important Than You Think!

Last, reduction of annual expense fees and unnecessary income tax consequences can be easily accomplished through index funds.

The annual expense ratio for the majority of the index funds just listed is .25 percent. (On a $10,000 investment account, $250 would be paid annually for investment fees. The typical mutual fund averages between 1–1.5 percent annual expenses. The difference in fees alone can account for a 10-15 percent increase in annualized return on a 7 percent portfolio.

The chart on the previous page indicates which funds are best suited for "taxable accounts." All funds are candidates for retirement accounts since there are no immediate tax consequences for such transactions as dividends and purchases and sales of stocks within the fund (turnover). On the other hand, when one of the listed funds is held in a "taxable" or nonretirement account, these transactions trigger a tax bill. Let me explain:

All current tax consequences are tax-sheltered in a retirement account—no taxes are due on any income or gains until monies are withdrawn from the account. At the time of withdrawal, all distributions are taxable.

The unwary investor has most likely been "bitten" by the mutual fund "tax snake." It is not uncommon for a mutual fund shareholder to feel ill when he/she receives a 1099 at the end of the year from his/her mutual fund company that results in thousands of dollars of income tax—all in a year in which the value of their mutual fund dropped! It is important that mutual funds with high turnover (lots of purchases and sales) be placed in retirement accounts, as well as those that pay out larger dividends. Table 4 indicates how to avoid this problem by selecting which funds go in taxable and retirement accounts.

Now it is time to go take some of this theory and apply it to your investments! Insert your TEN WEEKS CD and complete the next Worksheet.

Week Six
Worksheet D
Investment Circuit Inspection

Asset Allocation—Giving My Portfolio My Attention

Insert the TEN WEEKS CD, find the section entitled Week Six—"Be Smart About Your Target," open up each of the dialogue boxes, and then print the list as well as the Helpful Hints listed on the TEN WEEKS CD. File these reports in your My Financial Education binder under the Week Six Investment Tab.

EXAMINE The Cash Flow Needs of Your Authentic Money Guide and Invest Accordingly

Cash Flow—The Key to a Cohesive Portfolio and Financial Plan

The last step from darkness (or at least dusk) into some light with our investments is to test some of the initial asset allocations we have selected in Quicken®. We will do that by making sure the investment time horizon, or period of time we can leave the money alone before beginning distributions, is consistent with our most recent Authentic Money scenario.

This process of linking the myriad financial details together in one cohesive plan lies at the core of the power of comprehensive financial planning. A certain portfolio composition may seem very reasonable when it is considered separate from other important financial considerations and yet quite unsuitable when looked at as just one "room" in the financial "house."

Even though the focus of our attention will now turn to how the cash flows of your investments align with your Authentic Money Guide, remember that the real challenge is to integrate and honor your core Authenticity with the choices that we have outlined thus far in Week Six:

➤ Spending (and the level of return you need)

➤ Shareholder participation (and the types of investments you support)

➤ Informed decision-making (and the ability to know why you invest as you do)

WEEK SIX
WORKSHEET E
Investment Circuit Inspection

Investments Integrated with the Rest of My Life

Please insert the TEN WEEKS CD and learn how to integrate your portfolio with your Authentic Money Guide. Start with Week Six, "Plan Cash Flow."

In the Portfolio Value Section, circle the withdrawals from either the Taxable or Tax-deferred accounts and make a note of it. This is the first year that the investments will be relied upon to meet the cash flow requirements of your Authentic Money Guide.

Plan Scenario #	Year	Account Withdrawals	Retirement or Taxable

? What is the length of time between your current plan date and this first year of withdrawals? _____ years.

For Greg and Ginger, the length of time is 12 years (2015–2003).

Since the 12-year investment time horizon is much greater than the seven years that we used to design their investment portfolio, we know that the portfolio is consistent with the needs of their Authentic Money Guide.

IT IS CRITICALLY IMPORTANT THAT THIS TEST BE RUN EACH TIME THERE IS A SIGNIFICANT CHANGE IN EITHER THE PLAN ASSUMPTIONS OR THE DESIGN OF THE INVESTMENT PORTFOLIO.

FAILURE TO TIE THE INVESTMENT PORTFOLIO TO CASH FLOW NEEDS CAN RESULT IN EXPERIENCING SEVERE LOSSES AND PENALTIES FROM HAVING TO LIQUIDATE OR SELL INVESTMENTS TO MEET LIFESTYLE CASH FLOW REQUIREMENTS.

Now, pause to think a few minutes about what you have done.

? What changed in your Authentic Money Guide as you completed this section?

Investment Return: From_____% to_____%.

Living Expenses: From $_____ per year to $_____ per year.

Income: From $_____ per year to $_____ per year.

Other:

_____

_____

_____

_____

? Do you notice any patterns in your choices?

_____

_____

_____

_____

? Are those patterns leading you closer to or further away from your Authenticity? How?

_____

_____

_____

_____

Now is a good time to go back and make any changes to your most recent Authentic Money Guide scenario that honor what you just paused to notice.

Investment Implementation

I recommend you wait to finalize the selection of actual investments and finish the rebalancing of each of your individual investment accounts.

Until you finish the TEN WEEKS program, you will have gaps in your Authentic Money Guide that can distort your cash flows. For example, in Week Seven, you will analyze your insurance needs and may discover your cash flow needs change. This change may affect which investment portfolio is suitable for you.

At this point, our discussion will help prepare you for the time when your Authentic Money Guide accurately reflects the cash flow ramifications of all the decisions you have made and you are ready to choose the actual investments to be held in your new portfolios.

Before beginning this Week's final worksheet on Investment Implementation, consider the MAP materials outlined below.

As an alternative to these resources, set aside one hour to read "Investing Basics" at *www.Quicken.com*. To get to this section:

➤ Go to *www.Quicken.com*

➤ Select "Quicken® Brokerage"

➤ Click on the "Planning and Tax" Tab

➤ Select "Investing Basics" from the "Investing Education" section.

➤ Print out the "Introduction to Investing" report. After reading it, file this report in your "My Financial Education" binder under your "Investment Resources" Tab.

Take a moment to review the following MAP (Money Attention Pages) documents:

MAP 6-3—Index of the Indexes explains five common stock indexes and which companies are represented. A basic understanding of these common standards of comparison (benchmarks) for different asset classes (large, medium-sized, and small) of U.S. stocks is essential in purchasing suitable index funds for a diversified portfolio of investments. Please see Week Six Table 4 for other index categories.

MAP 6-4—Many Faces of Risk outlines nine different kinds of risk an investor must consider when selecting investments. One measure of risk is how variable an asset class' returns are over different period of times. The Compound Annual Rates of Return by Decade chart reflects the greater risk in Small Company stocks (<4.5 percent> to 20.7 percent) as compared to Large Company stocks (<.1 percent> to 19.4 percent) as well as Treasury Bills (.4 percent to 8.9 percent).

MAP 6-5—Mutual Fund Investing. This document explains the various categories of mutual funds available to investors. "Share price appreciation" refers to an increase in the value of the fund's stock investments over time, whereas "income and price stability" refers to a fund's bond holdings.

Please read carefully the "Factors to Consider Before Investing" section. The TEN WEEKS CD provides instruction as to how to evaluate a fund using these criteria.

Note also the warning about purchasing a mutual fund before it makes its annual capital gains distribution in November/December of each year. The negative tax consequences would only apply to investment accounts that are not tax sheltered (nonretirement accounts.)

MAP 6-6—Types of Bonds. Bonds are essentially an IOU. The issuer owes the money to the holder of the bond and promises to pay the money borrowed in addition to a certain rate of interest. Bonds vary dramatically in terms of safety, with Treasury Notes and Bonds being the safest and unsecured, high-yield Corporate bonds being the most risky. Refer to MAP 6-4 for an explanation of risk. Also read the following explanation of the difference in risk to an investor in purchasing bonds directly or through a mutual fund.

The value of a mutual fund will vary every business day. For all funds except the most liquid, such as money market funds, there will be a potential for some gain or loss depending on market conditions.

Consider the U.S. Savings Bond Considerations section of MAP 6-6. If you hold U.S. Savings Bonds, I strongly recommend you order an analysis of those bonds from the Savings Bond Informer (800-927-1901). If you own fewer than 10 U.S. Savings Bonds, the report will cost only $15 and will tell you when to sell the bonds you own as interest rates fluctuate.

If you want to avoid any analysis fees, you can go to *www.app.ny.frb.org/sbr*, type in the face value and issue date of your bond, and the current redemption value will be computed. This will not provide, however, an analysis of when interest rates may change on your bond, as does the Savings Bond Informer report.

MAP 6-7—Treasury Inflation Protection Securities (TIPS). TIPS provide an valuable addition to portfolios because of their inflation-protection feature. If an investor purchases a TIPS with a 2 percent real return, and inflation is 3 percent, the nominal return is 5 percent. Should inflation rise to 5 percent, the nominal return increases to 7 percent. Since the underlying bond is issued by the U.S. Treasury, and they have the authority to print more money, technically there is no safer investment.

TIPS can be purchased either directly or through a mutual fund. The Vanguard TIPS fund (VIPSX) offers investors the option of being paid both the interest and inflation-adjusted principal amount as a cash distribution. Direct TIPS purchases have restrictions about cash payouts.

MAP 6-8—Bonds 101. Read this material for a concise explanation of how bonds can change in value. Also consider the following example;

Say Greg wants to buy $10,000 of five-year U.S. Treasury Notes, and he is able to purchase them at that face value. As long as he holds those bills until they mature five years later, he can be reasonably certain he will get his $10,000 back, as well as the stated interest rate for that period of time.

Alternatively, Greg could have taken the $10,000 and purchased a mutual fund that invests in short–intermediate-term Treasuries. If Greg sells all the shares of this fund five years from now, he may get more or less than his $10,000 and accumulated interest, depending on the market price for the shares of the fund on the day he sold. In general, Greg takes the risk that increasing interest rates will cause the value of his shares to drop. The shorter the duration (average maturities of the bonds held in the fund) of the bond fund, the less risk he takes that the value of his shares will fall significantly.

On the other hand, a bond fund is able to buy in quantities that result in higher yields for their shareholders. Certain bond funds can reduce risk by investing in hundreds of issues, whereas an individual bond holder takes greater risk of default. For this reason, it is important to understand that a bond mutual fund purchase and an individual bond purchase each have unique risks that must be considered.

MAP 6-9—Bond Maturity and Duration. How can two bonds that mature on the same day (and issued on the same day) have a different duration? Read this resource to find out and prevent yourself from making common mistakes with bond purchases.

MAP 6-10—Categories of Equity Investments Helps to Differentiate Between Stocks. Remember, a stock represents your ownership interest in a company, whereas a bond indicates that the company has simply borrowed money from you. Stocks historically have rewarded investors for the extra risk they have taken with higher returns than bonds, but the excess earnings over bonds, referred to as the equity risk premium is shrinking. Just keep in mind that common-stock shareholders in a company are the last to get paid when financial difficulties beset a company.

MAP 6-11—Advantages and Disadvantages of Investing in Real Estate. Many clients ask about investing in real estate instead of the stock market. Recent real-estate returns have enticed many investors to direct their investments into this asset-class.

This Money Attention Page reminds us that there are definite advantages and disadvantages to real estate investing. The comment about "opportunities for investments highly leverged with nonrecourse debt because of real estate's value as security for loans" simply means that you can purchase real estate with 20–30 percent cash downpayment and use the value of the property to borrow the rest of the money—hopefully without having to pledge your personal assets. Over a 15–30 year period, income from the real estate investment pays off the bank loan and you end up with an asset that pays you a nice monthly income.

When evaluating a real estate investment opportunity, I have found a "1 percent of purchase price per month" rule of thumb to be useful. This rule is applied as follows:

A residential rental property is for sale in my hometown for $95,000. It is currently rented for $950/month and is in excellent condition. The vacancy history for this property is excellent (it has always stayed rented) and a property manager charges only 5 percent of gross rents as a management fee. My rule of thumb test is met in that the $950/month rent is 1 percent of the purchase price.

Even though I would be responsible for property taxes, insurance, repairs, and management fees, the net cash flows result in a 9 percent return. If the property appreciates at 2–3 percent per year, the overall return of 11–12 percent is attractive, despite some of the disadvantages of investing in real estate outlined in MAP 6-10.

MAP 6-12—Real Estate Investment Trust. An excellent way to invest in real estate without all of the hassles and risks of direct ownership is to purchase shares in a Real Estate Investment Trust. Read this Money Attention Page for additional information and consider the Vanguard REIT Index outlined in Week Six

MAP 6-13—The Key to Investing—Invest! We all know how powerful compounding is in accumulating money. This page illustrates this truth.

The last chart illustrates the growth of various levels of monthly savings for a seventh grader. What other advantages are there to a seventh grader of saving $50/month besides accumulating $509,157 by the time he/she is 65? What a wonderful gift to help our youth turn investment poison into medicine early in life by sharing the "rest of the story" (Paul Harvey) about Authentic Investing!

MAP 6-14—What Are Mutual Fund Sales Charges and Loads?
The Ten Weeks CD covers some of this material. When a mutual fund name is followed by an A, B, or C, it indicates that there is a sales fee imposed on the purchase of the fund.

Exercise caution when a broker tells you that a B-Share fund has no up-front sales charge. Technically this is true, but ask the broker to explain the difference in the annual expense ratio between an A-Share and the B-share. Also ask how long you have to own the fund before you are no longer obligated to pay a "deferred sales charge"?

MAP 6-15—What Are Mutual Fund Annual Operating Expenses?
Even mutual funds that invest according to a specific index without trying to select specific stocks or bonds have small annual expenses. For example, most Vanguard index funds have annual expense ratios of approximately .25 percent. Be aware that a mutual fund with a 1.5 percent annual expense ratio consumes 21 percent of an investors return, assuming an annual return of 7 percent. The index fund would consume only 3.5 percent of that same return.

MAP 6-16—Comparing Index Funds and Actively Managed Funds.
For a concise explanation of passive vs. active investing, read this Money Attention Page. You will remember earlier in the chapter that the S&P 500 Index outperformed 75 percent of professional money managers from 1973–1992.

MAP 6-17—Comparing Variable Annuities and Mutual Funds.
Annuities are a popular investment vehicle with much of the investment community because they pay hefty commissions. These commissions result in higher annual expenses, however, and lower returns for the same level of risk with a mutual fund investment. Review Bill Bernstein's comments about Variable

Annuities earlier in this chapter. I recommend you seriously consider consulting a TEN WEEKS financial advisor if you own annuities.

MAP 6-18—Dollar-Cost Averaging and Dividend Reinvestment Plans. Since it is impossible to time the stock and bond markets (i.e., purchase when values are low and sell when values are high on a consistent basis), it makes sense to invest on a regular time-schedule. This page illustrates the power of this discipline in enhancing returns without increasing risk.

Dividend Reinvestment Plans work not only with direct stock ownership but also with mutual fund shares. Take a few minutes to verify with your mutual fund company that you have chosen to reinvest all dividends and capital gains distributions.

MAP 6-19—Glossary of Investment Terms. This is an excellent resource to help you demystify investing. Take back your ability to understand investing by referring to these definitions when you are confused by the terminology.

WEEK SIX
WORKSHEET F
Investment Circuit Inspection

Investments—Intent to Action

> **Insert the TEN WEEKS CD and follow the Investment Implementation Steps.**

Use this outline to summarize your implementation decisions.

STEP 1

Check to See that Actual Spending Aligns with Current Authentic Money Guide Assumptions.

➤ Compare actual income and expenses to those budgeted. Is there significant excess in actual expenses over the budget? If so, please calculate the following estimated annual adjustment as follows:

➤ Total expenses over budget* $_____

*Overall Total at bottom of page 2 "Difference" column.

➤ Annual variance = Total variance divided by the # months reported on the budget report = monthly variance x 12 months = annualized variance $_____

In order to reconcile this difference in budget to actual cash flows, specifically how do you plan to adjust one, or both, of the following?

Adjustment to Plan Expense Assumptions_____

and/or

Adjustment to Budget_____

STEP 2:

Calculate targeted emergency cash funds and required monthly savings.

A. Determine Your "Rainy Day" or Emergency Cash Reserve Fund:

Total Expenses per *Plan Summary* $ _____

Subtract Taxes   _____

Add: RE Taxes   _____

Less: Investment Proceeds included in
Both income and expense section   _____

Less: College expenses covered by
Sources listed in Income Section   _____

Adjusted Annual Expenses* $ _____

Divide above result by 12

Average Monthly Expenses $ _____

Low Range: three times Avg. Mo. Exp. $ _____

➤ Appropriate for couples or singles with less possibility for extra expenses than for families.

High Range: five–seven (choose)_____ times

Avg. Mo. Expense = $ _____

➤ Appropriate for families.

Step A Total: $ _____

B. Determine Anticipated Special Purchases:

Special Expense Item	Planned Expense Date	Amount

➤ In Quicken®, review *Planning Assumptions—Special Expenses* for special purchases over the next three to five years. List those items, starting with next year:

➤ Total liquid cash required for these expenses:

One-time purchases after current year: $_____

Annual purchases after current year: $_____

Total future years' purchases for _____# of years

Step B Total: $_____

C. Compare Liquid Investments with Short-Term Cash Reserve Need

Step A total $ _____

+ Add: Step B total $ _____

        - Subtract: Short Term Cash* $_____

        = Equals: Additional Needed $_____

        - Subtract: Investments** $_____

    = Equals: Cash Reserve Shortfall $_____

*From most recent Quicken® *Net Worth Report*—Total Cash and Bank Accounts"

**Review Investments section of *Net Worth Report*. Include only nonretirement accounts that hold cash or other investments that could be liquidated in an emergency without incurring a significant loss.

D. Calculate Monthly Savings Needed to Save Emergency Funds.

Monthly savings required to cover shortfall within *_____months.

*If future cash expenses are significant, the period of time you take to build your emergency fund balance can be longer than if most of the reserves are needed to cover living expenses over the next three–eight months.

To calculate the monthly savings required to meet this objective, follow the directions provided on your TEN WEEKS CD in the Week Six "Savings Calculator."

Greg and Ginger determined they needed to set aside an additional $23,180 to current savings. This addition would leave them with five months of living expenses, as well as provide for special cash needs for five years.

Using the Savings Calculator, they determined they would need to set aside $700/month into a savings account earning 2.5 percent to reach this goal. They realize as soon as they accumulate $64,720, they can stop funding this monthly transfer to savings.

STEP THREE:

Honestly Evaluate Your Current Investment Complexity

Over the years, it is easy to accumulate a multitude of investment accounts. Not only does the volume of accounts become overwhelming, but other issues can develop that may make obtaining outside advice the smartest thing you can do. The following questions will help you decide if such a course of action makes sense because of your investment complexity.

Please refer to your most recent *Net Worth Report*, found in your Authentic Money Guide notebook. Check the box if your answer is "yes"—

❏ Do you have more than five separate investment accounts?

❏ Do you participate in a 401(k) or other retirement plan that limits your investment choices to offerings within that plan?

❏ Do you own individual stocks and bonds and not just mutual funds?

❏ Do you have taxable investment accounts for which you don't know your "tax cost" for?

❏ Do you have a portfolio in excess of $250,000?

❏ Do you have the option of converting IRAs, 403(b)s, or 401(k)s into a public pension through the purchase of service credits?

❏ Do you own any fixed or variable annuities?

If you checked at least two of the above boxes, then consider the following options:

➤ Consider retaining a TEN WEEKS Advisor™ listed on the *www.tenweeks.com* website. These qualified advisors will assist you in the construction of a portfolio that matches your Authentic Money Guide. Each advisor is trained in the use of the TEN WEEKS TO FINANCIAL AWAKENING program and will be able to pick up where you left off with helping you implement your investment plan, as well as any other questions you have about your experience. Visit that website for more information about this option.

➤ Consider *www.financialengines.com* This web-based investment service offers unbiased investment recommendations for an annual fee. The fee for retirement accounts only is $149.95/year and for all investment accounts $300/year. Please consider the following items when considering this Internet advisory service:

1. Couples need to be aware that investment recommendations do not result in each individual having an independently balanced portfolio. I recommend both individuals submit his/her investment accounts separately.

2. The service does not provide detailed investment advice for variable annuities. If you own annuities, I recommend that you consult a fee-only financial advisor for advice on how to create your portfolio.

➤ Choose one of the following options for creating your investment portfolio and then have it reviewed by a TEN WEEKS Advisor™ or another advisor recommended in the Section Four Appendix D materials.

STEP FOUR
Create Your Own Portfolios

Option One: Bill Bernstein's Model Portfolios as Outlined Below:

In his book *The Four Pillars of Investing*, Dr. Bernstein describes four investor profiles. Take a few minutes to read the following information to see which profile best matches your own.

Taxable Ted:

Ted finally sold his business last year and has a pile of cash. He never had the time or inclination to set up an IRA or retirement plan, even though it would have saved him a fortune in taxes.

Investments Ted can use will need to fit into the "Taxable" or "Both" column of Table 4 that lists suitable Vanguard Index Funds.

In *The Four Pillars of Investing*, Dr. Bernstein makes one exception to this rule:

"There is one other option available to him, and that's to open a variable annuity (VA) so that he can invest in REITs. I didn't have many nice things to say about these vehicles a few chapters ago, but here I'd make an exception. Vanguard does make available a relatively low-cost VA…this will enable him to hold REITs in his portfolio without being punished by the taxes on their hefty dividend distributions since they would be sheltered inside the annuity account. The disadvantages are an extra .37 percent in insurance expense and not being able to withdraw funds before age 59½ without a penalty."

(Reprinted with permission of The McGraw-Hill Companies. William J. Bernstein, *The Four Pillars of Investing*, © 2002 The McGraw-Hill Companies, Inc.)

If your situation resembles Ted's, use the following table to choose the Vanguard Funds, based on the stock/bond allocation you used in Week Six Worksheet C.

"Taxable Ted's" Portfolios

Stock/Bond	100/0	90/10	80/20	70/30	60/40	50/50	40/60	30/70	20/80	10/90	0/100
Vanguard Total Stock Market Index	40%	36%	32%	28%	24%	20%	16%	12%	8%	4%	---
Vanguard Tax-Managed Small Cap	20%	18%	16%	14%	12%	10%	8%	6%	4%	2%	---
Vanguard Tax-Managed International	25%	22.5%	20%	17.5%	15%	12.5%	10%	7.5%	5%	2.5%	---
Vanguard REIT Index	15%	13.5%	12%	10.5%	9%	7.5%	6%	4.5%	3%	1.5%	---
Treasury Ladder	---	2.5%	5%	7.5%	10%	12.5%	15%	17.5%	20%	22.5%	25%
Vanguard Short-Term Corporate Bond	---	2.5%	5%	7.5%	10%	12.5%	15%	17.5%	20%	22.5%	25%
Vanguard Limited-Term Tax-Exempt	---	2.5%	5%	7.5%	10%	12.5%	15%	17.5%	20%	22.5%	25%
Vanguard California Intermediate-Term Tax-Exempt	---	2.5%	5%	7.5%	10%	12.5%	15%	17.5%	20%	22.5%	25%

Reprinted from *The Four Pillars of Investing* by William J. Bernstein, Published by McGraw Hill, 2002

Sheltered Sam:

Sam's investment portfolio is almost all in IRAs and other retirement accounts since, as a CPA, he knew how valuable tax-deferred compounding could be in meeting his retirement goals.

Since Sam is over 59½ and ready to retire, he doesn't have to worry about penalties for withdrawing his money too early. He does have to consider, however, the cash flow distributions he will need to live after retiring.

Sam's retirement accounts shelter any income tax until he chooses to take the money out, so he can utilize the entire range of investment options outlined in Table 4. He, unlike Ted, would not benefit by opening a variable annuity since his accounts are already tax-deferred (or tax-sheltered).

Use Sheltered Sam's investment options if most of your investments are in retirement accounts. Select the stock/bond mix that most closely resembles that on your Rebalancing Worksheets.

Sheltered Sam's Stock/Bond Mixes

Stock/Bond	100/0	90/10	80/20	70/30	60/40	50/50	40/60	30/70	20/80	10/90	0/100
Vanguard 500 Index	20%	18%	16%	14%	12%	10%	8%	6%	4%	2%	—
Vanguard Value Index	25%	22.5%	20%	17.5%	15%	12.5%	10%	7.5%	5%	2.5%	—
Vanguard Small-Cap Index	5%	4.5%	4%	3.5%	3%	2.5%	2%	1.5%	1%	0.5%	—
Vanguard Small-Cap Value Index	15%	13.5%	12%	10.5%	9%	7.5%	6%	4.5%	3%	1.5%	—
Vanguard REIT Index	10%	9%	8%	7%	6%	5%	4%	3%	2%	1%	—
Vanguard Precious Metals	3%	2.7%	2.4%	2.1%	1.8%	1.5%	1.2%	0.9%	0.6%	0.3%	—
Vanguard European Stock Index	5%	4.5%	4%	3.5%	3%	2.5%	2%	1.5%	1%	0.5%	—
Vanguard Pacific Stock Index	5%	4.5%	4%	3.5%	3%	2.5%	2%	1.5%	1%	0.5%	—
Vanguard Emerging Stock Markets Index	5%	4.5%	4%	3.5%	3%	2.5%	2%	1.5%	1%	0.5%	—
Vanguard International Value	7%	6.3%	5.6%	4.9%	4.2%	3.5%	2.8%	2.1%	1.4%	0.7%	—
Vanguard Short-Term Corporate		6%	12%	18%	24%	30%	36%	42%	48%	54%	60%
TIPS (3.375% of 2032)		4%	8%	12%	16%	20%	24%	28%	32%	36%	40%

Reprinted from *The Four Pillars of Investing* by William J. Bernstein, Published by McGraw Hill, 2002

In-Between Ida:

Ida, 57, just lost her husband and received some life insurance and her husband's $100,000 pension plan, which she rolled over into her IRA. Her total portfolio is $1 million, of which $900,000 is in taxable accounts.

Since Ida's portfolio is very similar to Ted's we can use that Table for selecting her investments. The only item that is different is to allocate 12.5 percent to an Ohio state bond fund rather than to a California fund. Since both Ted and Ida end up in a 31 percent federal tax bracket, it makes some sense to invest in these state bond funds that will be exempt from state and federal taxes.

Consider the following chart to determine if selecting a tax-exempt municipal bond fund really makes sense:

TE Yield	Tax Bracket Percentage (Federal Only) and Taxable Yield Equivalent				
	15%	27%	30%	35%	38.6%
4%	4.71%	5.48%	5.71%	6.15%	6.51%
5.5%	6.47%	7.53%	7.86%	8.46%	8.96%

A state income tax rate of 8 percent would enhance the taxable equivalent yield on the 5.5 percent tax exempt bond, assuming the owner was in the 27 percent tax bracket, from 7.53 percent to 8.19 percent. As you can see, in many instances the tax-free yields are so low that it makes sense to purchase taxable bond funds and just pay the tax.

Young Yvonne:

Yvonne, 26, has just finished law school and finally has a job that allows her to save about $5,000/year. She has no current investment accounts and wants to save for retirement with an IRA since her employer won't offer a retirement plan for several years.

The portfolio Dr. Bernstein recommends for a person in Yvonne's shoes deals with the following problems for small investors:

> ➤ Some of the $5,000 will need to be directed to the creation of a liquid Emergency Fund. Since Yvonne is entitled to contribute $3,000 to an IRA in 2003, she'll open up a good money market account with the other $2,000.

> ➤ To avoid small IRA account charges with Vanguard, $10 per fund with a balance of less than $5,000 in each fund, she will take a laddered approach in purchasing her investments. This means that she will buy one piece of her desired portfolio at a time. Though she will lack the diversification early on, as her money grows, she will be able to add the funds she needs, while avoiding unnecessary expenses.

"Young Yvonne's" Investment Path: Vanguard Funds.
Note: Funds are added from left to right, in $5,000 increments.

Total Amount	Money Market (Taxable)	500 Index	Total Int'l Index	REIT Index	Small Value Index	Value Index	Small Cap Index	Short Term Corporate	Prec. Met Fund	European Index	Pacific Index	Emg Mkt Index	Int'l Value Funds	Inflation Prot. Sec. (TIPS)
$5,000	$3,000	$2,000												
$10,000	$4,000	$4,500	$1,500											
$15,000	$6,000	$6,000	$2,000	$1,000										
$20,000	$8,000	$6,500	$2,500	$1,500	$1,500									
$25,000	$10,000	$3,500	** $3,000	$2,000	$2,000	$4,500								
$30,000	$10,000	$4,000	$3,500	$2,000	$2,500	$5,000	$1,000	$2,000						
$35,000	$10,000	$4,100	$4,600	$2,100	$3,100	$5,100	$1,000	$4,000	$1,000					
$40,000	$10,000	$4,800	$5,000	$2,400	$3,600	$6,000	$1,200	$6,000	$1,000					
$45,000	$10,000	$5,400	$5,800	$2,700	$4,000	$6,750	$1,350	$8,000	$1,000					
$50,000	$10,000	$6,000	***	$3,000	$4,400	$7,500	$1,500	$10,000	$1,000	$1,500	$1,500	$1,500	$2,100	
$55,000	$10,000	$6,600	***	$3,300	$4,950	$8,240	$1,650	$12,000	$1,000	$1,650	$1,650	$1,650	$2,310	
$60,000	$10,000	$7,200	***	$3,600	$5,400	$9,000	$1,800	$12,000	$1,080	$1,800	$1,800	$1,800	$2,520	$2,000
$65,000	$10,000	$7,800	***	$3,900	$5,850	$9,750	$1,950	$14,000	$1,170	$1,950	$1,950	$1,950	$2,730	$2,000
$70,000	$10,000	$8,400	***	$4,200	$6,300	$10,500	$2,100	$14,000	$1,260	$2,100	$2,100	$2,100	$2,940	$4,000
$75,000	$10,000	$9,000	***	$4,500	$6,750	$11,250	$2,250	$15,000	$1,350	$2,250	$2,250	$2,250	$3,150	$5,000
$80,000	$10,000	$9,600	***	$4,800	$7,200	$12,000	$2,400	$16,000	$1,440	$2,400	$2,400	$2,400	$3,360	$6,000
$85,000	$10,000	$10,200	***	$5,100	$7,650	$12,750	$2,550	$17,000	$1,530	$2,550	$2,550	$2,550	$3,570	$7,000
$90,000	$10,000	$10,800	***	$5,400	$8,100	$13,500	$2,700	$18,000	$1,620	$2,700	$2,700	$2,700	$3,780	$8,000
$95,000	$10,000	$11,400	***	$5,700	$8,550	$14,250	$2,850	$19,000	$1,710	$2,850	$2,850	$2,850	$3,990	$9,000
$100,000	$10,000	$12,000	***	$6,000	$9,000	$15,000	$3,000	$20,000	$1,800	$3,000	$3,000	$3,000	$4,200	$10,000

** When portfolio reaches $25,000 in size, approximately $3,000 is exchanged from the 500 Index Fund into the Value Index Fund.

*** When portfolio reaches $50,000 in size, the Total International Index Fund is exchanged into the International Value, European, Pacific, and Emerging Markets Index funds.

Reprinted from "The Four Pillars of Investing" by William J. Bernstein, Published by McGraw Hill, 2002.

Option Two—Use Quicken® to select a portfolio of mutual funds.

See the TEN WEEKS CD with Greg and Ginger using this approach. Guidance can be found in the Quicken® "Portfolio Implementation" section of the CD.

Option Three—Construct a socially-screened portfolio, using resources outlined earlier in this chapter.

➤ First, choose a Bernstein model portfolio and then pick socially-screened investments from those asset classes as follows.

▷ Consider the Asset Allocator at *www.calvertgroup.com* with specific recommendations of Calvert Funds. Please note that these funds do carry front-end and back-end loads unless purchased through a load-waived program such as that offered by *www.naturalinvesting.com*

▷ Another option for getting started with Socially Responsible Investing is the Vanguard Calvert Social Index that can be purchased at *www.vanguard.com*.

Option Four—No stock market approach

If you have problems accepting any risk associated with equity (stock) investing, or you philosophically don't feel that you can support the system it represents, then consider discussing these concerns with a TEN WEEKS Advisor™. These advisors assist other clients with the purchase of direct bond and alternative investments. They may also assist in the evaluation of a rental property in your geographical area that may meet your investment criteria.

To locate such a trained advisor, visit *www.tenweeks.com*.

STEP FIVE:

Monitor Your Investment Contributions and Rebalance Your Investments Once Each Year

Set up each of your investment accounts in Quicken® for online downloads. This will enhance the accuracy of your monthly financial reports and make tax preparation much less "taxing."

The most important aspect of investing is to invest. (See MAP 6-13.) If you spend your energy worrying about performance and fail to contribute regularly to your portfolio, you will find your investment balance falling short of your targets.

"Anyone who can live on welfare should be courted by Wall Street. He is a financial genius."

—*Joanna Clark*

Since you have taken the risk involved in investing very seriously, you can contribute new money to your accounts with the confidence that your concern about losses has been factored into the creation of your portfolio of investments.

The power of asset allocation can only be accessed if you follow the disciplines of rebalancing on an annual basis. By selling a portion of the funds that have performed well and purchasing those that have not, you increase the chances of enhancing your returns while lowering your risks over time.

The Solar Panels and My Investment Choices

We started this section on investing with a discussion about the three *kleshas,* or poisons, we humans deal with on a daily basis: desire, aversion, and denial. Rather than attempting to distance ourselves from these poisons, we have tried to cultivate our warrior's heart and begin to access their medicinal qualities as they relate to our money and how we seek to have it work for us, rather than have it work us into a frenzy. With each opportunity to "stay" before we "leave," we have used money to help us align our behavior with the power of our Authenticity.

> *"Adversity is something hard upon a man; but for one man who can stand prosperity, there are a hundred that will stand adversity."*
>
> —*Thomas Carlyle*

By facing our greed and desire, we saw how we could be less controlled by investment returns when we took the initiative to limit our lifestyle. There is such a thing as "enough." We can experience "sufficiency." There is more to life than squeezing the last ounce of performance from our investment portfolio and having it poison this precious life journey. Aligned living is much simpler than that of one excess after another.

There is a numbing dread and disillusionment that accompanies our taking of little or no responsibility for our investment choices. We did feel some relief from the numbness when we began to take our role of Citizen as seriously as that of Consumer. There is a way, with the development of the Socially Responsible Investment industry, to invest with our values rather than in opposition to our Authenticity.

Wally mentioned the importance of alignment when he explained his electrical diagram several years ago:

Conversion Method—The Solar Panels
(Diagram Component #2)
** a flashback **

"Since I've chosen the sun as our source of energy, we have to figure out a way to harness that energy. We'd be in the same predicament if we had chosen coal, oil, natural gas, or wind as the power source. If I had drawn the Hoover Dam, the conversion method would be turbine-driven generators. In my diagram I've used a photovoltaic cell, or solar panel, to illustrate this conversion. We now have electrical energy ready to move to the next step in our system, the transmission lines.

"The critical thing in the conversion of energy is proper alignment.

"The solar panels here in my diagram are useless if they aren't positioned properly to capture the sun's rays. In the same way, the

Hoover Dam wouldn't generate any power if Lake Powell suddenly dried up. Those generators have to be placed where the fall of water will turn the turbines."

Wally and the Path of "No Ecstasy"

"In some ways I think I just wanted you to tell me how to invest my money," recalled Wally. "I had no idea what was in store for me when I asked you for some investment advice. I didn't think you would actually make me understand investing as it related to comprehensive financial planning!"

That was three months after Wally had come to my office for our first meeting. Since that time, he and Jane had agonized over the creation of an investment portfolio that honored the life they valued.

"Did you really think that I was going to let you off that easily," I said, "after what you put me through with that electrical diagram?!"

"I sure should have seen that one coming," was Wally's light-hearted reply.

Just like Wally, you eventually tackled your reluctance to understand investing. Rather than blindly following advice, you experienced some freedom from the insanity of being blown every direction by the fierce winds of opinion and "expertise."

By Slowing down, Appreciating the risk/reward relationship, Noticing the whole as greater than the sum of its parts, and Examining the cash flow needs of your life and investing accordingly, you accessed SANE investing. This process of finally giving your investments your attention was by no means a walk in the park; it involved some serious realignment.

"With money in your pocket, you are wise and you are handsome and you sing well, too."

—*Yiddish saying*

Aligning my investments with my Authenticity results in powerful returns. I'm no longer satisfied with economic performance alone.

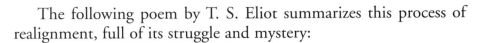
The following poem by T. S. Eliot summarizes this process of realignment, full of its struggle and mystery:

Shall I say it again? In order to arrive there,

To arrive where you are, to get from where you are not,

You must go by a way wherein there is no ecstasy.

In order to arrive at what you do not know

You must go by a way which is the way of ignorance.

In order to possess what you do not possess

You must go by the way of dispossession.

In order to arrive at what you are not

You must go through the way in which you are not.

And what you do not know is the only thing you know

And what you own is what you do not own

And where you are is where you are not.

—T. S. Eliot, excerpted from the poem "East Coker"
from Four Quartets

Come to think of it, I bet T.S. Elliot, Hermes, and maybe even Wally have been hanging around one another. I can hardly wait to see what else money has to show us about how to cultivate our comfort with all this uncertainty.

WEEK SEVEN
Your Insurance: Risky Business

> *By the end of this Week, you will have both a clear philosophy that guides you in your insurance decisions and a practical understanding of specific insurance products that fit your needs. Having dealt with your own human frailty and taken steps to act in acceptance rather than denial of that, you experience a sense of relief. Quicken® is utilized throughout this process and your Authentic Money Guide is updated with your insurance choices.*

"Even monkeys fall out of trees."

—*Japanese Proverb*

I couldn't believe it—they wanted an extra $1,500! I knew it was coming, but the life insurance premium increase still shocked me. I thought to myself, "I just turned 49 and everyone's telling me I'd better eat my dessert first—I might not get to the pie ala mode if I start with the main course."

"Humans—despite their artistic pretensions, their sophistication, and their many accomplishments— owe their existence to a six-inch layer of topsoil and the fact that it rains."

—*Source Unknown*

Within the last month, my doctor had warned me that my cholesterol readings were higher than they should be. Such news prompted a new-fangled gene test for my heart. The genomic results revealed that out of six genes that gave a clue about my heart's propen-

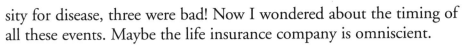

sity for disease, three were bad! Now I wondered about the timing of all these events. Maybe the life insurance company is omniscient.

I was grateful I had purchased an adequate term life insurance policy five years earlier. I definitely didn't want Katherine or my daughters to have to deal with financial headaches after my death. I wrote the check, as painful as it was, and then decided to take a walk and personally deposit it in the mailbox. I didn't want to take any chances, as it seemed I was already skating on thin ice.

"Where are you headed, Paul?" Wally was working on thinning some oak brush and thought it a bit strange to see me pensively walking, rather than jogging, up the road.

"Oh, Hi Wally. I'm sorry. I didn't see you. I guess I'm feeling a bit…vulnerable. It seems my life insurance company thinks I'm getting to the age where my death is more than a remote possibility. I wish they would have asked me—my opinion is quite to the contrary!"

By now Wally and I knew each other well enough to speak what was on our minds. Wally put down his axe and motioned me over to sit down on the grassy bank near his oak grove.

"From the looks of your long face, there must be more to it than the life insurance—anything else going on that you want to talk about?"

"Oh, just some news from the doctor about my heart. I didn't think about the consequences of knowing my future when I had a genomic gene study done. The test came back with some sobering results. I guess it didn't really matter that I've logged over 10,000 running miles over the past 25 years and have tried to live a moderately healthy life. I sure shouldn't complain. My woes are minor compared to Katherine, who literally faces death eye to eye each and every day with her Type I diabetes."

"I think I'd be a bit discouraged, too," comforted Wally, "if all that news had landed in my lap at once. Do you remember that little book you gave me after we worked on my investments? I think it was called *Comfortable with Uncertainty*. I just happened to finish it last night before bed. You'll have to go look it up when you get back to the office, but Pema Chödrön said something about 'leaning into the discomfort of life and seeing it clearly.' I think you might be on the verge of learning something very special. Most of the time, I just blow this stuff off and all those emotions usually come boiling to the surface at the most inopportune times—kind of like when the breaker flips and the power goes off in the middle of your shower."

"So does that mean that I shouldn't pay this god-awful premium?" I said. "Maybe I'm upset because I'm trying to protect myself from the inevitable."

Wally smiled and responded, "The last time I studied life insurance, it seemed there was very little in it for the owner."

I had to laugh at Wally's comment and at the same time cry inside at how hard it was to lean into this discomfort, as Wally had reminded me. "Thanks for the reminder, Wally. If I'm in the middle of class, it feels like it must be called *Frailty 101.*"

"If you want to run somewhere, don't forget I could use some help in cleaning up my shop." joked Wally.

I felt better when I got back to the office from dropping the check in the mail and after my visit with Wally. I decided that now was the best time to take a few minutes and find that section in the book *Comfortable with Uncertainty*. It didn't take long as the title of the short reading, which contained Wally's quote, was called "This Very Moment Is the Perfect Teacher"!

> "…no matter the size, color, or shape of the catastrophe, the point is to continue to lean into the discomfort of life and see it clearly rather than try to protect ourselves from it…'This very moment is the perfect teacher'…."
>
> —*Pema Chödrön*, Comfortable with Uncertainty

I knew this was a class that I had played hooky from for far too long. It was time to learn how to open rather than close to this fear of dying. Maybe that insurance bill was more of a blessing than I had realized.

Catastrophes— All Sizes, Colors, and Shapes

Recent events have given us all a dose of our inability to control things. War in Iraq, 9-11, an economic downturn, SARS… just getting on an airplane is reminder enough of how scared we are these days.

> "These days, it is sometimes hard to know what to worry about more—the weak economy, the volatile stock market, the war, unemployment, or our usual concerns about families and friends. Such anxieties can lead to poor decision-making. The best defense: concentrate on what you can control."
> —Money Magazine

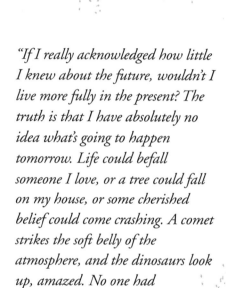

"If I really acknowledged how little I knew about the future, wouldn't I live more fully in the present? The truth is that I have absolutely no idea what's going to happen tomorrow. Life could befall someone I love, or a tree could fall on my house, or some cherished belief could come crashing. A comet strikes the soft belly of the atmosphere, and the dinosaurs look up, amazed. No one had mentioned this."

—*Sy Safransky*

It seems that facing these concerns gives us an opportunity to stop pretending that life is safe and predictable. If we leave before we stay, we lose our ability to try. Mark Nepo learned from first-hand experience with his fight to survive cancer what it meant to stay and try. He reminds us that we can allow these discomforts to awaken our ability to "love the world through our Spirit" or we can seek to control the worrisome concern.

"We get into all kinds of trouble by thinking that life can be measured, understood, and controlled solely through our conscious will...It is hard for us to admit that there is a great deal in life that is outside our control."

—Contentment, *by Robert A. Johnson and Jerry M. Ruhl*

When I take the time to really pay attention to my reality and how quickly things can change, I can respond in one of two ways: I can intensify my efforts to protect myself, or I can enter into the wonder of the gift of my life in the moment. In my encounter with my heart's propensity toward failure, I was finally able to appreciate the amazing gift of each beat. Entitlement separates me from that wonder; gratefulness reconnects me to it.

"Thank you terror
Thank you disillusionment
Thank you frailty
Thank you consequence...
How about me enjoying the moment for once?..."

—Thank U, *by Alanis Morrissette*

Take some time to complete the first Circuit Inspection worksheet for this Week. Pause to notice where the "shorts" are in your relationship with human frailty.

"You walk on, carrying on your shoulders a glass door to some house that's not been found. There's no handle. You can't insure it. Can't put it down."

—W.S. Merwin

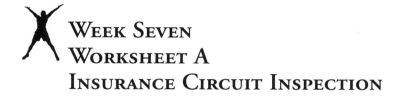

Week Seven
Worksheet A
Insurance Circuit Inspection

Life's Frailty and My Response

"We cannot escape fear. We can only transform it into a companion that accompanies us on all our exciting adventures. . . . Take a risk a day—one small or bold stroke that will make you feel great once you have done it."

—Susan Jeffers

Please begin by finding your My Documents binder and turning to Tabs 11-14. Use the documents and summary sheets you find there to complete the following table:

Type of Insurance	What Could We Lose?	What Do I Pay Each Year?
Example: Life	*A family member and their support.*	*$1,500*
Property: Auto		
Property: Home		
Property: Personal		
Renter's		
Health		
Accident		
Disability		
Long-term Care		
Liability—Business		
Liability—Personal		
Unemployment		
Life		

? What feelings surface as you list the risks you face, along with the insurance coverage you have purchased or might need to acquire?

❑ I don't feel that vulnerable. The chances of these things happening to me or my family are minimal. I'd like to reduce my insurance premiums. I see insurance as just a big rip-off.

❑ I shift into my "control mode" to avoid having to feel the reality that whatever is going on in the world could happen to me today. I wonder if I've made wise insurance decisions.

❑ I'm scared. I realize that no matter how much insurance I have, my family and I are vulnerable to the suffering that comes with each of those losses listed in that chart.

I suggest you "lean into the discomfort" of these vulnerabilities.

Close your eyes and try to visualize the risk you most fear. If you can, let the fear sink into your body before your mind turns toward a "fix." If you prefer, get up and walk to a quiet place. Read the remaining questions when you return.

? As you stayed with your feelings, what happened?

_____

_____

_____

_____

? Did you gain any insight into what would ease your suffering or that of your family?

_____

_____

_____

_____

? Did you experience a sense of gratitude growing from the soil of your frailty?

_____

_____

_____

_____

_____

Please turn to Week Four Worksheet A—Work and Identity Circuit Inspection.

? What did you calculate your hourly earnings to be? $_____ (a)

? What is the total of your annual insurance premiums that you calculated above?

$_____ (b)

? How many hours do you work in your household to pay these premiums?

(b ÷ a)_____ hrs.

? Does the time you spend working to pay for insurance reveal anything about your longing for security and protection?

_____

_____

_____

? Given the following categories of relating to risk and using insurance to manage those risks, where would you best fit?

❏ **Who needs insurance?**
Insurance just plays on fear. It can't prevent painful things from happening. I say its better to live in the present and set aside some money to pay for some emergencies myself than to send it off to an insurance company that will most likely deny my claim anyway. I think it's crazy to spend your whole life working just so you can pay for insurance you most likely will never use anyway.

❏ **I'm OK—I'll buy the insurance I have to but no more.**
Life is good! Why should I focus on all the things that could go wrong? No natural disasters have ravaged my neighborhood, my family is healthy, and my employer pays for workers' compensation insurance in case I get injured on the job. I carry the legal coverage on my cars and have enough fire insurance on my house that we could replace the home in that event. Why spend more money on something that I might use in 20 years, especially when cash flow is tight now?

❏ **Insurance is a good tool. I'll use it to help meet my responsibilities**.
I figure it's better to transfer these risks to an insurance company rather than self-insure. It takes a lot less cash. I feel it's selfish of me to not make adequate provisions for my family and loved ones in the event of my death, sickness, disability, and so on. Buying insurance also forces me to set aside money and generate cash value in some of my policies.

❑ **Purchasing insurance is an invitation for bad things to happen.**
I feel like buying insurance is inviting negativity into my life. Why not focus on the positive instead? Rather than spending $500 a month on health insurance, I'd prefer to have that money to care for my body so that I don't get sick in the first place. Insurance is based on reacting to tragedies instead of being more responsible for avoiding them in the first place.

? As you consider your response, especially in relation to the other options, what would you say is the underlying belief that influences your relationship to risk and insurance? (An example: *Who needs insurance? My parents were sold a life insurance policy when times were tough. They struggled to pay the premiums for several years and finally had to let the policy lapse. We needed that money and it was all lost to an agent and insurance company that profited at our expense. Maybe that's why I have such an aversion to buying insurance.*)

_____

_____

_____

_____

_____

_____

_____

_____

_____

 ## AN INSURANCE PHILOSOPHY

*"Be like the bird, pausing in his flight
On limb too slight,
Feels it give way, yet sings,
Knowing he has wings."*

—*Victor Hugo*

As I tried to stay with my discomfort around my inability to secure my health and my longevity, I experienced a strange sense of relief. Maybe the relief was due in part to this defeat of my illusion of "mind over matter," or "invincibility." A poem came to mind that expressed beautifully this deep inner struggle that we all have to face, eventually ending with an admission of defeat.

THE MAN WATCHING

I can tell by the way the trees beat, after
so many dull days, on my worried windowpanes
that a storm is coming,
and I hear the far-off fields say things
I can't bear without a friend,
I can't love without a sister.

The storm, the shifter of shapes, drives on
across the woods and across time,
and the world looks as if it had no age:
the landscape, like a line in the psalm book,
is seriousness and weight and eternity.

What we choose to fight is so tiny!
What fights with us is so great!
If only we would let ourselves be dominated
as things do by some immense storm,
we would become strong too, and not need names.

When we win it's with small things,
and the triumph itself makes us small.
What is extraordinary and eternal
does not want to be bent by us.

I mean the Angel who appeared
to the wrestlers of the Old Testament:
when the wrestlers' sinews
grew long like metal strings,
he felt them under his fingers
like chords of deep music.

Whoever was beaten by this Angel
(who often simply declined the fight)
went away proud and strengthened
and great from that harsh hand,
that kneaded him as if to change his shape.

Winning does not tempt that man.
this is how he grows: by being defeated, decisively,
by constantly greater beings.

—*Rainer Marie Rilke*

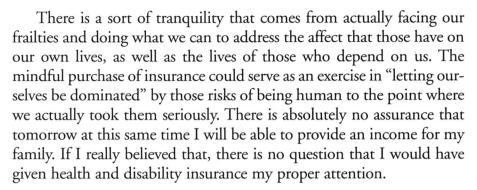

There is a sort of tranquility that comes from actually facing our frailties and doing what we can to address the affect that those have on our own lives, as well as the lives of those who depend on us. The mindful purchase of insurance could serve as an exercise in "letting ourselves be dominated" by those risks of being human to the point where we actually took them seriously. There is absolutely no assurance that tomorrow at this same time I will be able to provide an income for my family. If I really believed that, there is no question that I would have given health and disability insurance my proper attention.

> *"I used to think of my health, to the extent that I thought of it at all, as immutable. But mostly I gave it no more thought than the air I breathed. Certainly, I had no capacity to appreciate it as something that could be fundamentally altered in any way. It was only after my health departed—seemingly just flew off one day like some startled bird—that I began to understand that I had been mistaken."*
>
> *—Al Neipris, from an article in* The Sun Magazine

There needs to be a deeper reason for buying insurance than those that prompt many of us into reluctant action:

➤ *Alright already!* Just to appease a persistent agent that is adamant about what is more about his/her need than mine.

➤ *It's what a good parent/husband/wife should do.* Duty, guilt, and obligation to provide fiscally.

➤ *At least then I'll know everything will be OK.* Money seems to solve most every other problem, so it should work to solve these uncertainties.

➤ *It's what my advisor says I need. Just tell me what to do and I'll do it.* This seems like a good solution to having to deal with all these emotions and complicated insurance technicalities.

In his book, *Wealth Management Index,* Ross Levin suggests that everyone develop a philosophy of insurance. He suggests that four questions be answered with regard to each area of risk we face that can be addressed with insurance:

1. Whom do I want to protect from this particular risk?

2. What amount of money will this person need each month if this event occurred?

3. How long will this protection be needed?

4. Will the family (or person receiving these benefits) be able to cover this need without the help of insurance?

I would add another question that may be a bit more difficult to answer:

If I were to purchase this insurance, would it help me actually surrender to this "storm" and in so doing grow closer to my Authenticity?

Please take a few minutes and turn back to *Worksheet A* in this section. Sit quietly and think about the reality of these risks and the answer to this last question.

Before proceeding, turn to the Money Attention Page (MAP) section for Week Seven. Take the time to learn the basics about insurance as detailed below:

WEEK SEVEN MAP INDEX/OVERVIEW

MAP 7-1—Guide to Insurance Needs

A quick overview of the primary types of insurance you should consider. Use this information to supplement other MAP resources and your TEN WEEKS analysis.

MAP 7-2—Insurance Do's & Don'ts

Insurance policies come in a lot of sizes and shapes. Before you sign that policy, read here to avoid costly mistakes.

MAP 7-3—Who Should Be the Beneficiary of a Life Insurance Policy? Things to consider when choosing your beneficiary and potential tax consequences of those choices. Don't be overwhelmed by some of the technical terms. If you think a suggestion might apply to you, circle this and make a note to ask an advisor about it.

MAP 7-4—Types of Life Insurance Policies

Life insurance policies are often designed with expensive bells and whistles that primarily benefit the insurance salesperson. On this page, review the advantages and disadvantages of the different types of life insurance policies. Typically, the best and least expensive policy is term insurance.

MAP 7-5—Shopping for Insurance

Use this resource to supplement the work you will do in Quicken®. Let someone else do the legwork and provide you several quotes. The companies and websites listed on this page

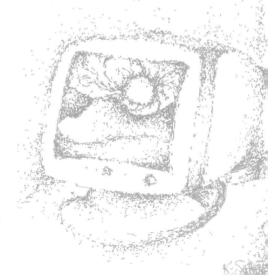

will search hundreds of policies for you (usually for free). Let them filter out the expensive policies and the poorly rated insurance companies.

MAP 7-6—Upgrade Insurance Policies with a Section 1035 Exchange.

If you already have a life insurance policy, you may be able to upgrade it to a newer policy without tax consequences or loss of insurability. This tax provision also applies to annuities, but be careful about the surrender fees that may still apply to your old contract.

MAP 7-7—Auto Insurance Buying Tips

A short "cheatsheet" to saving money on your auto insurance and to understanding the coverage.

MAP 7-8—Homeowner's Insurance Buying Tips

You home is possibly your largest financial investment. It's worth taking a few minutes to see that that you have adequate coverage at a reasonable premium cost.

MAP 7-9—Personal Umbrella Liability Policy

A lot of lawsuits are the result of accidents in our cars or on our property. An umbrella policy that increases your coverage to a million dollars typically costs a couple of hundred dollars a year. This is an inexpensive way to help protect your assets.

MAP 7-10—Health Insurance Basics

Let's face it, health insurance is complicated. This section will introduce you to the basic terminology and types of health insurance. By working through the referenced worksheets and checklists, you will gain an understanding of what policy is right for you. This MAP is a critical part of implementing your new insurance philosophy.

MAP 7-11—Long-term Care Insurance

A general overview of long-term care insurance. Answers to most of your questions: Tips on buying a long-term care policy, nursing home alternatives, Medicare/Medicaid benefits. Use this in conjunction with the other long-term care MAP resources.

MAP 7-12—Long-term Care Insurance—A Financial Analysis

A real-life example that illustrates the potential financial benefits of purchasing long-term care insurance rather than self-insuring this risk.

MAP 7-13—Long-term Care Insurance—Policy Comparison
Now that you've decided to get long-term care insurance, how are you going to shop for a policy? Use the chart on this page to compare the features of different policies.

MAP 7-14—Importance of Disability Insurance
A 35-year-old is far more likely to have a long-term disability before he/she reaches retirement age than he/she is to die before reaching retirement age. Most people have inadequate disability insurance. This page provides the rationale for obtaining disability insurance.

MAP 7-15—Disability Insurance 101
Learn about the different types of group and individual disability insurance. Find out how much coverage you should have, how you can reduce the cost of an individual policy, and learn the tax consequences of employer-paid policies vs. individual policies.

MAP 7-16—Disability Insurance Policy Checklist
Use these 15 questions to help evaluate different policies.

MAP 7-17—Disability Insurance Annual Premiums
So how expensive is disability insurance? The chart on this page provides sample rates for one insurer using a straightforward plan design.

MAP 7-18—Social Security Disability
Uncle Sam is already providing you with some disability insurance. The benefits to you and your dependents are outlined on this page. Be aware—in order to obtain Social Security Disability benefits, your disability must be severe.

MAP 7-19—Overview of Medicare
Medicare is health insurance provided by the government for people over age 65 or people that are disabled. This section outlines the benefits available and how to apply.

MAP 7-20—Standard Medigap Policies
For many people, the coverage provided by Medicare is inadequate. If you want to buy private health insurance to pay for those benefits that Medicare will not pay, then you can buy a "Medigap" policy. The standard Medigap policy features are outlined in this section.

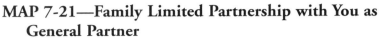

MAP 7-21—Family Limited Partnership with You as General Partner

A brief and clear description of a Family Limited Partnership and your potential role as both a General and Limited Partner. Note especially the problem a General Partner faces with liability exposure unless that interest is also owned by an LLC or corporation. A list of assets that should and should not be used to fund (transfer into) the partnership is also provided.

MAP 7-22—Advantages and Disadvantages of Family Partnerships

Things to consider prior to setting up a family partnership. It is extrememly important, speaking from experience, that there be a clear understanding among all family members of what has to be given up in order to gain the tax and liability protection benefits of a FP.

MAP 7-23—Entity Comparison Chart

What type of entity should you use to conduct your business? See MAP 8-30 for a practical example of the difference in tax from a Sole Proprietorship as compared to an S corporation. The entities examined in this chart are as follows; Partnership, Corporation, Limited Liability Company, S Corporation, Sole Proprietorship. The focus of this Week is the "Personal Liability" line on the chart.

MAP 7-24—Variable and Immediate Annuities

Variable annuities are often sold because of the high commissions they generate. Most investors can find more appropriate investments elsewhere. On this page, learn about the features of this tax-deferred insurance product. An immediate annuity is quite different from a variable annuity. Immediate annuities allow you to buy a lifetime income stream. Find out in this section if an immediate annuity is right for you.

MAP 7-25—Checklist of Factors Indicating a *Buy-Sell* Is Needed.

In brief, a buy-sell agreement facilitates the transfer of a closely-held business interest (one that is not publicly traded on a stock exchange) either upon death of the owner or another specified event. These agreements are often paid for (funded) through life insurance. Review this checklist carefully if you are a partner or shareholder in a company and don't want your heirs to have to deal with a nightmare when you are gone.

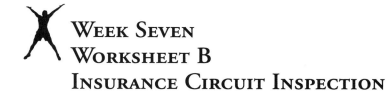

WEEK SEVEN
WORKSHEET B
INSURANCE CIRCUIT INSPECTION

My Insurance Philosophy

Start by loading Quicken® and inserting the Week Seven—TEN WEEKS CD. Complete the following chart with information you obtain from following the screen-by-screen instructions. Then, read Greg and Ginger's responses to this process to help you formulate your own insurance philosophy.

Greg and Ginger's Insurance Philosophy Chart

Cost	Risk	Beneficiary	$	Need for	Change?
	Greg Dies	Ginger and Gil	$500k	120 mo.	Yes (1)
	Ginger Dies	Greg and Gil	$500k	120 mo.	Yes (2)
	Auto crash	Family	Car Replacement until stop driving		Yes (3)
	Home Fire	Family	Home replacement until sell home		No (4)
	Health Loss	Self and Family	Costs > $5k per year for life		Yes (5)
	LT Care—Greg	Self and Family	120/day in real dollars for three yrs.		Yes (6)
	LT Care—Ginger	Self and Family	120/day in real dollars for three years.		Yes (6)
	Disability—Greg	Self and Family	2,500 per month until 65		Yes (7)
	Disability—Ginger	Self and Family	1,750 per month until 65		Yes (7)
	Liability	Family assets	Min. of $300k while own home		Yes (8)
	Rental Fire	Family	Rental replacement 'til sell rental		Yes (9)

Change? Greg and Ginger recorded their discoveries and the actions they needed to take to implement their new insurance philosophy:

1) *If the current life insurance policy is less expensive per $1,000 of insurance, we should call our agent to see if this policy can be extended or increased to satisfy the total insurance need for under $94/month. It is important that we DO NOT CAN-CEL THIS POLICY UNTIL ANY NEW COVERAGE IS IN EFFECT! We should consider the John Hancock policy, if appropriate, and apply online via* **www.quicken.com**

2) *Same as above for Ginger's existing policy.*

3) *Change insurance carriers as per Quicken® analysis when Greg purchases new truck in September. Update budget with new premiums at that time. See #4 on next page for new information from our existing agent that eliminated the need to change carriers.*

4) *Since the competing quote for home insurance was not much less than what we pay now we decided to keep our existing homeowner's policy. In the process of contacting our agent, we asked him for a comprehensive quote on all our vehicles, home, rental, and general liability. His new quote was cheaper than the combination of the other quotes we had obtained online.*

5) *After a detailed analysis of health insurance options, we decided it made more sense for us to privately insure and opt for different benefits from our employers. Neither of us had any preexisting health issues, nor were the quotes we received substantially less than what we will have to pay under new benefit packages at work next year. To implement this decision we need to: complete health insurance underwriting and convert policies once the group coverages can be dropped.*

   This action reduces our frustration that comes from seeing more and more take-home pay disappear because of increasing medical costs from the work force. At least shifting to an individual policy gives us a sense of responsibility for our choices with some hope of a reward for good health decisions. We were also able to shift from an HMO to a PPO plan that gives us more flexibility in seeing different doctors.

6) *Finish application process for long-term care policies as outlined in Scenario #9 update. This will integrate the likelihood that we will need some form of home or nursing home care before we die. It also honors our desire that Gil not be burdened with our care and that some of our estate be preserved for him.*

7) *Finish individual disability applications and purchase the related policies. This provides peace of mind that in the event of a sickness or injury away from work, the family's needs can be met and either one of us who is injured or sick can recuperate without any stress or worry of having to get back to work.*

8) *We noticed that our current net worth from the latest Quicken® Net Worth Statement was over $350,000. It sure doesn't feel like we're that rich. We contacted our home insurance agent and found out that it would only cost another $150 per year to purchase an extra $700,000 of liability protection. With all of the lawsuit madness in our society,, it seems that this is definitely a good use of those premiums. We'll authorize the agent to add that protection.*

9) *We never really understood how easy it was to limit our personal liability for unforeseen circumstances with our rental by simply transferring ownership of that property into a limited liability company. Our attorney indicated that this would not complicate our tax filing or the ownership of the property 50 percent by Greg and 50 percent by me. The action item here is to complete the LLC setup paperwork and the retitling of the property and mortgage.*

   The rental insurance policy review prevented us from making a potentially catastrophic mistake of having our insurance coverage invalidated due to the omission of the new wood-burning stove. Guess it really does make sense to pay attention to these financial details after all.

Record your own insurance philosophy in the following worksheet.

My Insurance Philosophy Chart

Risk	Beneficiary	$	Need for	Change?	Cost

Discoveries/Changes/Action Items:

_____

_____

_____

_____

_____

_____

_____

_____

_____

_____

Discoveries/Changes/Action Items—Continued:

_____

_____

_____

_____

_____

_____

_____

_____

_____

_____

_____

_____

_____

_____

_____

_____

_____

_____

_____

_____

_____

_____

_____

_____

WEEK SEVEN
WORKSHEET B-1

My Insurance Deductibles

Because a deductible is simply the amount of each loss or risk we choose to pay ourselves, it is a form of self-insurance. Whenever we have the option of lowering our insurance premium by assuming a higher deductible, it is tempting to take on more risk than we may, realistically, be able to pay.

This worksheet helps you take a realistic look at what deductibles are appropriate in your financial situation.

1. Summarize the required deductibles for your current insurance coverage: (See My Documents notebook, Tabs 10–13)

   Health—maximum family out-of-pocket per year   (a)$_____

   Auto Insurance—deductible per claim   (b)$_____

   Home Insurance—deductible per claim   (c)$_____

   Other risks which you currently are self-insuring: (d)$_____

   Disability—no coverage entails five months
   of a waiting period before Social Security benefits
   may begin: Monthly salary x 5   (e)$_____

   Total Current Self-insurance Exposure $_____ **a**

2. Emergency Fund Reserve:
   (See Week Six Worksheet F)

   Step 2 A Total $_____

   Step 2 B Total $_____

   Total Emergency Fund $_____ **b**

3. Remove duplication of salary loss included in step 2A:

   Less: Up to five months' salary
   loss included in Step 2A $_____ c

Equals Current Liquid Cash Requirements $_____ **d**

4. Current cash per most recent Net Worth stmt.   _____ e

5. Excess cash to pay for increased deductibles $_____ f*

*If the result of line "f" is negative, consider lowering your current deductibles. If "f" is a positive number, calculate your allowable deductible by dividing this number by 24 months. Allocate that increased deductible limit to the policy(ies) that result in the largest reduction in annual premium cost.

For example: If line "f" divided by 24 is $1,000, determine what your health insurance premiums would be if you allocated that deductible to that policy as compared to applying that same deductible to your auto insurance policy. Apply the deductible where you will receive the most "bang for your buck."

Policy	Premium Before Change in Deductible	Premium After Change

WEEK SEVEN
WORKSHEET B-2

My Home Insurance Summary

Current Home Insurance Premiums $_____

Comparable Coverage Quote Premium per *Quicken.com*   _____

Potential Savings $_____

Reasons for Premium Change:

Change in Deductible $_____

Change in Amount of Coverage $_____

Change in Risk—risk reduction measures implemented (i.e., Are there assumptions in the proposed policy that distort the policy comparison other than the two items listed here?) Other possible differences include the following.

Financial rating of the insurance company: _____

Coverage exclusions: _____

Changes in other coverage components if a blanket policy is proposed. (Are autos or other coverages altered to make this particular coverage cost look cheaper than it actually is?) _____

Revised quote from existing carrier based on
similar policy features $_____

Decision: Change to new carrier?** _____

**Never cancel any insurance coverage until you have proof of replacement coverage! Even one day of lapsed coverage can prove disastrous.

See MAP 7-8 For Homeowner's Insurance Buying Tips

WEEK SEVEN
WORKSHEET B-3
Do I Need to Consider
a New Health Insurance Policy?

STEP ONE—*Is switching health insurance an option for me?*

The answer will be most likely be *No* if the answer to the following questions are *Yes:*

Circle Yes or No

➤ Is our family covered by a work plan in which the
employer pays for the worker's coverage? . . . . .Yes   No

➤ Has a health condition developed since the existing
health insurance policy was purchased? . . . . .Yes   No

➤ Are you satisfied with your current coverage after
considering the following essential coverages? . . . . .Yes   No

▷ Your policy will pay for up to $1 million
in lifetime benefits. . . . . .Yes   No

▷ You are able to pay your co-insurance requirement
(out-of-pocket costs) in the event of a sickness or injury. . .Yes   No

▷ The policy provides for continuation of coverage for
your college-age children who attend school. . . . . .Yes   No

▷ Your policy is noncancelable and guaranteed renewable. . .Yes   No

▷ Your policies, assuming each partner is covered by his/her
employer, do not cover the same expenses.
If there is duplication of coverage, is the extra
cost minimal? . . . . .Yes   No

▷ You are over 65 and you have a Medigap policy.* . . . . . . .Yes   No

▷ Your coverage includes treatment in a foreign country,
if so required. . . . . .Yes   No

**If your answers were *Yes* to the previous questions, you can skip the Quicken®
Health insurance analysis.**

STEP TWO—*Insert the Week Seven TEN WEEKS CD and start the health insurance review section.*

➤ I recommend reviewing your Medigap policy after visiting
www.medicare.gov

➤ Once on that site select "Medigap Compare" for a step-by-step guide to
comparing different Medigap policies and insurers in your state.

➤ Also review MAP 7-20—Standard Medigap Policies.

WEEK SEVEN
WORKSHEET B-4

My Health Insurance Options Summary

Before completing this summary, return to **MAP 7-10 Health Insurance Basics**
and complete the *What's Most Important to You?* checklist and the *What is Your Best
Buy?* worksheet. Choose the best alternative health insurance plan and continue.
Three-hole punch your analysis and place those pages in your My Financial Education
binder, Week Seven—Insurance Resources.

Current Medical Insurance Premiums $_____

Comparable Coverage Quote Premium   <_____>

Potential Savings $_____

Reasons for Premium Change:

Change in Deductible $_____

Change in Coverage $_____

Change in Risk—risk reduction measures implemented:

_____

_____

Revised quote from existing carrier based on similar

policy features $_____

Decision: Change to new carrier?** _____

** IT IS CRITICAL THAT YOU CAREFULLY CONSIDER THE CONSEQUENCES OF CHANGING HEALTH
INSURANCE COMPANIES. PLEASE BE SURE YOU ANSWER ALL THE FOLLOWING QUESTIONS BEFORE
CANCELLING YOUR CURRENT COVERAGE.

1) _____ I AM FULLY AWARE OF CURRENT HEALTH CONDITIONS THAT MAY HAVE PREEXISTING-CONDITION LIMITATIONS UNDER MY NEW POLICY. I UNDERSTAND THAT I WILL BE FULLY RESPONSIBLE FOR PAYMENT FOR ANY MEDICAL TREATMENTS ON ACCOUNT OF SUCH EXCLUSIONS.

2) _____ I HAVE CONSIDERED THE FINANCIAL STABILITY OF THE COMPANY THAT IS OFFERING ME A BETTER QUOTE. I REALIZE THAT UNLESS THE NEW INSURANCE COMPANY CAN STAY IN BUSINESS, MY FUTURE CLAIMS MAY NOT BE PAID, MY INSURANCE PREMIUMS WOULD HAVE BEEN WASTED, AND MY FINANCIAL FUTURE WOULD BE JEOPARDIZED.

3) _____ I UNDERSTAND THE IMPORTANCE OF KEEPING MY INSURANCE COVERAGE IN FORCE CONTINUOUSLY. I WILL NOT ALLOW MY OLD POLICY TO LAPSE UNTIL I HAVE EVIDENCE THAT MY NEW POLICY IS IN FORCE. EVEN ONE DAY WITHOUT INSURANCE IS TAKING A RISK THAT COULD BE FINANCIALLY DEVASTATING.

WEEK SEVEN
WORKSHEET B-5

Liability Insurance

? Are your assets greater than your liability coverage under your current homeowner and auto insurance policies? Please refer to your most recent Quicken® Net Worth Report to determine your asset values. (Also see the second to last **?** for your current liability coverage.)

_____

_____

_____

_____

? Do you have a business (General Partnership, Sole Proprietorship—Schedule C, or rental property owned personally) that subjects your personal assets to liability?

_____

_____

_____

_____

_____

? Have you talked to an attorney or CPA about converting one of these businesses into either a Limited Liability Company or Sub Chapter S Corporation to help create a "veil" between your personal assets and your business activities?

_____

_____

_____

_____

_____

Please review the following MAP materials as it relates to entity usage to limit personal liability:

➤ MAP 7-21 Family Limited Partnership with You as General Partner

➤ MAP 7-22 Advantages and Disadvantages of Family Limited Partnerships

➤ MAP 7-23 Entity Comparison Chart—See the "Personal Liability" section of this chart to compare the differences between different types of business entities and their protection of personal assets from liability claims.

? Do you have liability insurance for your business activities?

_____

_____

_____

_____

_____

? If you are a professional, do you carry professional liability insurance?

_____

_____

_____

? Are you a co-owner of a business that would continue operating after your death? If the answer is yes, do you have a buy-sell agreement in place that would facilitate the sale of your interest should you die?

_____

_____

_____

➤ Please see MAP 7-25 Checklist of Factors that a Buy-Sell Is Needed.

? What liability coverage do you currently have through your homeowner's policy (see your My Documents binder Tab 11 for your policy):

Personal Liability Coverage $_____

Medical Payments to Others $_____

Additional Coverages $_____

Have you obtained a quote on an umbrella liability rider to your homeowner's policy? _____ If so, what is the additional annual premium and related increase in liability protection?

_____

_____

_____

_____

➤ Please refer to MAP 7-9 Personal Umbrella Liability Policy for details about this type of coverage.

? What change to your annual premiums results from any changes you have identified in this worksheet? $_____

WEEK SEVEN
WORKSHEET B-6

Property Insurance—Real Estate or Rentals

Refer to your My Documents binder Tab 9 to identify any real estate holdings that may require insurance. For each of these properties, complete the following information:

Description	Property Loss Coverage	Liability Coverage	LLC Ownership?*

Greg and Ginger's rental property was partially purchased with a mortgage loan that required that adequate rental insurance be purchased. The insurance premium is paid for by the mortgage company out of funds escrowed each month with the regular loan payment. A closer examination of the rental insurance policy indicated that the policy had not been updated to include a wood-burning stove that Greg had helped the new tenant install last month. Failure to notify the insurance company of this change could have invalidated the coverage and left Greg and Ginger responsible for paying off the mortgage had the property been destroyed by fire.

*In order to reduce the risk of liability to their personal assets, they considered transferring title of the rental property to a Limited Liability Company their attorney helped them establish. They felt the one-time legal and setup costs of $500 was a worthwhile investment to help segregate liability claims surrounding that property from their personal assets.

➤ See MAP 7-21, MAP 7-22, and MAP 7-23 for additional information about the use of business entities to limit personal liability.

WEEK SEVEN
WORKSHEET C

My Insurance Philosophy and My Life

Take a few minutes to enter the updated cost for each of the insurance policies listed in your My Insurance Philosophy chart.

Total Annual Insurance Premiums	$_____
Divided by 365 Days Per Year	divided by 365
= Average Daily Insurance Cost	$_____/day

? What effect do you think remembering this daily cost could have on your awareness?

_____

_____

_____

_____

_____

? Are you tempted to forget all those coverages—except, of course, the insurance that you would have to keep in order to drive your car? What do you think such a radical break from the "system" would provoke or engender?

_____

_____

_____

_____

? Do you know anyone who seemed to benefit or suffer from a certain insurance-related incident? From your impression of their experience, what do you learn that may help you with all of these insurance decisions?

_____

_____

_____

_____

A TRIP TO THE BREAKER BOX

Wally encouraged me to fight the urge to ditch Frailty 101. It felt to me like the class had been expanded into my "major" course of study after taking a long, hard look at all the risks of my humanity.

During our visit about insurance, I remember Wally saying something about the circuit breakers flipping at the most inopportune time. Now I understood how that tied back to what Wally had tried to explain to me with his electrical diagram:

Circuit Breakers
(Diagram Component #5)
*** a flashback***

"The circuit breaker box is the part of our homes we are forced to locate after everyone in the house decides to run his/her blow dryers at once."

"Oh, yes, when I had three teenage daughters at home, it always happened early in the morning when I was in the middle of a shower," I lamented.

"After the power is routed through a metering device so we can pay the utility company for bringing a usable form of power to our doorstep, the electrical wires enter the breaker box where all the different electrical circuits originate. Each circuit is fitted with a breaker that is sized to match the wire that will feed that section of the home's electrical system.

"If the electrical demand on that circuit exceeds the capacity of the wire, there is a heat-sensitive switch in the breaker to disconnect the power source from that circuit before a dangerous overheating occurs. We know that in order to restore power to that circuit of outlets in our home, we simply flip the breaker back on and everything works fine, unless there is a malfunction or short somewhere in the circuit.

"In my diagram I have a 5-amp breaker feeding 5-amp wire on the 6b circuit and a 12-amp breaker on the 6a circuit. I'll bet you know the wire size on that second circuit." I realized I'd better stay alert or the professor would catch me day-dreaming!

"As you can imagine, if I try and turn all three lights on at once in that first circuit, it won't be long until the breaker flips—just too much load for that small wire. If I'm persistent

and keep trying to turn on all three 60-watt lights, the breaker will flip more frequently each time. I'll finally have to accept the fact that only one or two lights will stay lit because the heat-sensitive switch is so easily triggered because of my continued excess demand. On the other hand, the 6a circuit would easily handle all three lights at once."

"So are you saying that the breaker flips when there's just more demand than the system can safely handle?"

"Exactly." My rudimentary understanding pleased Wally.

Insurance could serve in my life as a circuit breaker of sorts. Rather than constantly deny my frailty, I could enter into an appreciative relationship with those limitations. Not only could the insurance serve as a safety barrier to my tendency to overtax my life, but **it could remind me to "slow down" and appreciate the wonder of a life temporarily unencumbered by frailty and suffering.**

I can embrace or shun my frailty. Acceptance sees interruptions as gracious protection from destruction rather than as bothersome annoyances.

WEEK EIGHT

Your Tax Liabilities: More than Paying Uncle Sam

> *After your journey through this section, you will have made conscious choices about how you pay your "social dues." Through attentive tax planning, charitable giving, and active citizenship, what had been a necessary evil is transformed into an opportunity to speak out and make a positive difference in the world. The powerful financial impact of these changes is seen as your Authentic Money Guide is updated using Quicken®.*

AN "ELEVENTH HOUR" FILING

It was April 14th and I was relieved that I would be able to get a good night's sleep rather than spend half the night working on last-minute extensions for clients. It had been a little over a year from when I had sold my tax and accounting practice of 14 years and decided to devote my full-time attention to financial planning.

At 4:30 in the afternoon, I was about to call it a day and head home when the phone rang. I reluctantly picked up the phone and recognized the voice on the other end of the line as John, Jane's son. "Hello, Mr. Lemon, this is John from across the road. My mom suggested I call you and see if you could help me with my tax papers. I seem to have forgotten about them being due tomorrow. Would you mind if I came by?"

"Of course not, John," I said. "Bring your papers over and we'll see what we can do."

I hung up the phone and remembered that it was John's whole-hearted enthusiasm that had saved the day when lightning set fire to our property. The least I could do was help him file his tax return. I wondered if he had made enough to have to file. My busy little mind was already figuring out ways to get him a refund when he politely knocked on the office door.

"Come on in, John. How about a Coke?"

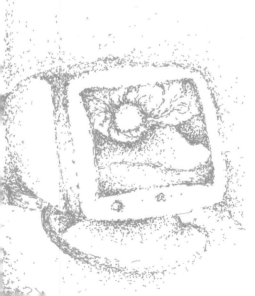

"No, thanks, Mr. Lemon. I'm sorry to have to bother you with this."

"Don't mention it. Please, just call me Paul. I think I'd even prefer 'Hey You!' to 'Mr. Lemon.' You probably know how sensitive we old geezers are to too much respect!"

"Yeah, I'll have to say that I can get under Wally's skin pretty easily ever since he turned 50."

"Well, that's good news," I joked. "I haven't been able to rattle him since we met. Do you think you could give me a few pieces of inside information before you leave today?"

"Sure!" exclaimed John. "If you can bail my butt out of this bind, I'd be happy to oblige."

I was glad to see John relax. Disclosing private financial records was about as comfortable as undressing at the doctor's office. A generous dose of good-hearted humor always seemed to be the most important service I could provide when it came to preparing someone's taxes for the first time.

"I just barely got my own returns in the mail, John. The thought of sending money to the IRS this year was more onerous than ever before. I put it off as long as I possibly could."

"I'm glad to hear you say that, Mr...I mean, Paul. I was beginning to think I was the only one who felt that way."

John and I headed for my conference table where we began to sort through his prior year's economic saga. It became clear that this was going to take some time as there were several large brown envelopes filled with crumpled receipts from John's landscape maintenance business. When I asked him for his check register that would show what income he had earned, John squirmed a bit and confessed. "Most folks are more than happy to pay me cash since the work I do for them is related to their houses and they can't deduct my fee anyway. Most of my friends who work with me don't even file a tax return."

I paused, prepared to give John my well-rehearsed "pay your fair share or the rest of us have to pay for you...you drive on these roads and benefit from the services of the government..." speech when I noticed a tear rolling down his cheek. We sat in awkward silence. Rather than giving my speech, I found myself offering solace, "I take it your reaction here today has something to do with some kind of reluctance to file your tax return?"

I waited and watched John slip below the surface of his relationship with money. Finally, he continued: "I know I benefit from things the government provides, but I also know that a large portion of the tax dollar goes to pay for things that I can't support. It may seem like my pittance is irrelevant in the overall federal budget, but I don't feel like I can, with a clear conscience, send any money in to the U.S. Treasury. I tried to explain this to Wally and Mom, but they just freak out thinking that I'll end up in some federal prison for tax evasion. I don't know what I can do to honor both my conscience and my obligations to the federal government."

I had to admit that in all my years of tax practice, I had never encountered a situation like this. I understood John's dilemma and recognized his anguish was genuine. What I was witnessing was vastly different from many clients' remorse of having to cough up more money than they wanted to for taxes. I summarized his deductions.

"Our own heart always exceeds us."

—Rainer Maria Rilke

"I don't envy your position, John. Usually, I am so relieved to get my return finished, I don't give a second thought to what I am funding with my taxes."

"I don't agree with our government's priorities," explained John. "Forty-seven percent of the federal budget is allocated to past and present military spending while human service organizations have lost their funding."

I was blown away by what John was saying. Not only was it obvious that he had done his homework, but what he said made me feel ashamed for not being more aware of the issues. I had to admit that the biggest dilemma I had with paying my taxes was that I would have that much less money to spend on myself.

"Try as I might, Paul, I either have to break the law or support government spending I don't approve of."

"I might have good news for you, John." I tallied up his cash income. "You've earned under the $7,800 that the tax laws allow before you have to pay any income taxes. You won't have to pay any money into the general fund, but only to the Social Security trust fund that is supposed to pay you a retirement benefit some day."

"Are you serious?!" piped John, clearly excited. "That's the best news I've had in weeks! I've made myself sick worrying over this, and now you're telling me it was all for nothing!"

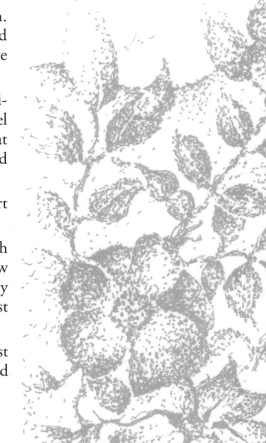

"Well, I wish I could tell you that our government didn't use your Social Security payments for their military expenditures," I said. "But technically they are borrowing your money to do that. It's not like you are directly authorizing the military payments."

John was so relieved that his moral dilemma had been solved that my technical rambling landed on deaf ears. We finished filling out his forms, and it ended up that he owed $565 in self-employment tax. John had the money in savings and would make the deadline.

"Thanks for hearing me out, Paul. You understand what I was up against. I appreciate that."

"Hey, John, could you send me the addresses of some of your research sites?"

"You bet, Paul." John grinned from ear to ear. "And thanks again."

I turned off the lights and headed up the driveway to the house, deep in thought. My stroll followed the same path of nine months earlier when I charged the scene of the lightning strike to battle that potentially destructive fire. John and his unselfish enthusiasm had saved that day. As I walked the path, I knew my conversation with John had tapped into something important within me that had the potential to smolder and burst into destructive flame unless I gave it some attention.

"What kept you so long? I thought you filed our tax returns early—as in yesterday." Katherine couldn't help but throw in a friendly jab.

"Oh, you know, I just love those tax returns so much I had to ask all the neighbors if they had any left over for me to do. Actually, John, brought his stuff over and I helped him get it filed. Is dinner ready?"

"You bet. Wash your dirty hands."

More Than I Really Wanted to Know

> ### *Request for Tolerance!*
> *This section is meant to illustrate one particular conversation with taxes and how they align with personal values. It conveys the author's own personal struggle and is not intended to suggest that this perspective is "absolute truth" or relevant for each reader. Please just bear in mind the real point: "Take the time to ground and examine how you pay your social dues."*

When I checked my email, there was one from John with 15 websites about government spending, current policy, and tax information. I jumped in.

> ➤ The most recent income tax return available for President Bush (2000) showed Adjusted Gross Income of $894,880. $610,782 of this total came from interest and dividends, $138,358 from investment capital gains, $75,000 from advance book royalties. The balance of $70,868 represented earned income. Federal income taxes paid for this year were $240,342, or 27 percent of total income.—*www.taxanalysts.com*

> ➤ The most recent income tax return available for Vice President Cheney (2000) showed Adjusted Gross Income of $36,086,635. Of this amount $5,139,832 was compensation from the Halliburton Company. This compensation does not include a $1,451,398 cash bonus paid January, 2001, from the same company. The bulk of the other 2000 income of $30,946,803 related to the sale of stock options that Cheney received from Halliburton. The total income taxes paid for 2000 were $14,295,058 or 39.61 percent of total income. *www.taxanalysts.com*

> ➤ "Democrats on Capitol Hill are criticizing what they say is an expanding role in Iraq for a subsidiary of the oil services company Halliburton...Back on March 24th (2003), the Bush administration announced that a contract worth up to $7 billion had been awarded to Kellogg, Brown, and Root, a subsidiary of

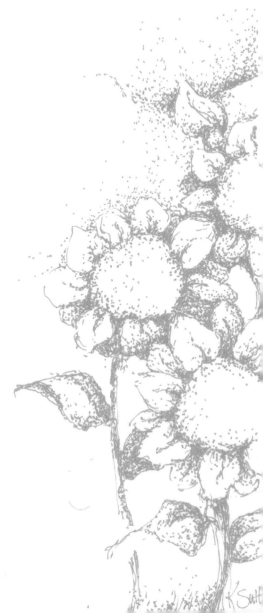

Halliburton…The KBR oil services contract also had a controversial beginning. It was awarded to the Halliburton subsidiary without competitive bidding. There should have been a competitive process, says Peter Singer, a military contracting specialist at The Brookings Institution." (NPR Transcript, May 7, 2003, "All Things Considered" report from John Ydstie)

➤ The Internal Revenue Code contains 7 million words. The Bible contains 700,000.—*www.howstuffworks.com*

➤ Tax Freedom Day in 2003 falls on April 19. This means the average U.S. citizen has to work until April 19th to pay their taxes. When differing state income tax rates are considered, workers in Connecticut have to work, on average, until May 9th, while Alaskans complete this social dues payment March 30.—*www.taxfoundation.org*

➤ In 2000, the average American worker worked 120 days, until April 30, to pay their taxes. The breakdown of those days by category of tax is as follows:

➢ 50 days to pay individual income tax

➢ 30 days to pay Social Security taxes

➢ 16 days to pay sales taxes

➢ 10 days to pay property taxes

➢ 12 days to pay corporate income taxes

➢ three days to pay business taxes

➢ two days to pay all other taxes—*www.taxfoundation.org*

➤ Consider how long Americans work to pay taxes in 2003 compared to major spending categories:

➢ 74 days—federal taxes

➢ 61 days—housing and household operations

➢ 46 days—all other expenses

➢ 44 days—medical care

➢ 35 days—state and local taxes

➢ 30 days—food

➢ 28 days—transportation

➢ 21 days—recreation

➢ 14 days—clothing and accessories

➢ 11 days—savings—*www.taxfoundation.org*

➤ The Fiscal Year 2004 Federal Budget spends $1,731,000,000,000 ($1,731 billion or $1.731 trillion) as follows:

➢ $593 billion to human resources—34 percent

➢ $459 billion to current military—27 percent

➢ $345 billion to past military—20 percent

➢ $235 billion to general government—13 percent

➢ $99 billion to physical resources—6 percent—*www.warresisters.org*

➤ The Peace Tax Fund Bill would allow those who conscientiously object to the use of their tax dollars for military purposes to pay their full tax obligation and have those funds used exclusively for nonmilitary purposes. The bill was first introduced in 1972 and is annually reintroduced in Congress. To date, it has failed to receive the support needed for passage even though no revenue loss from the bill would be sustained.—*www.peacetaxfund.org*

"I destroy my enemies when I make them my friends."

—Abraham Lincoln

I think what shocked me the most from these statistics was that the average American spent more time working to pay taxes than he/she did to pay for housing, food, and clothing combined.

It also bothered me to see the statistic that John had mentioned the day before, that nearly half of the federal budget was allocated to some form of military expenditure. When I thought about it in terms of days, I figured that I had to work 35 days a year to pay my share of those military costs. I was not comfortable with continuing that pattern but had no clue as to where to begin to change.

I was glad John had also sent along a selection of quotes about taxes that helped to lighten the heavy atmosphere I was feeling:

"Intaxication: euphoria at getting a refund from the IRS, which lasts until you realize it was your money to start with."

—Greg Oetjen

"I don't know of a single foreign product that enters this country untaxed, except the answer to prayer."

—Mark Twain

"Unofficial motto of the Internal Revenue Service: 'We have what it takes to take what you have.'"

—Anonymous

"Donors who are only interested in the tax benefits of their gifts may give philanthropy a bad name, but their money still helps."

—Mark Litzler

"Our entire tax system is threatened by the existence of tax avoidance techniques that are only available to the wealthy in our society."

—Barbara Kennelly

"Nothing makes a man and a wife feel closer, these days, than a joint tax return."

—Gil Stern

"I wouldn't mind paying taxes if I knew they were going to a friendly country."

—Dick Gregory

After all my years as a tax accountant, I felt like I should at least be able to respond to John's email with some originality so, after a moment of inspiration, I wrote:

TAXATION WITHOUT REPRESENTATION

I filed my 1040,
just like I'm supposed to do.
But it was the
"enclose what you owe"
that really made me blue.

It's up to me, a citizen
to pay my fair share.
But I don't remember anyone asking
what I felt was fair—
or how I'd care.

These days are so scary,
everyone wants to be heard—
but when the leaders won't acknowledge my messages,
my tax compliance seems so absurd.

109 days, a third of each year,
they tell me I'll toil—
all for access to the "Good Life,"
including unlimited oil.

I know it's not as simple
as "Uncle's bad" and "I'm good"—
I just wish I didn't feel
like a tax-paying hood.

My wife, smart and so pretty,
reminds me of Patriot Act Two,
"Just remember, I told you,
your taxes won't excuse you."

She's afraid that I'll end up
locked up in some jail
when life was so easy
pretending our system couldn't fail.

I was shocked what John had triggered in me. I still remembered the tear rolling down his cheek. How long had it been since I thought about the impact of my social choices. I knew it was easy for me to criticize the government, but a closer look revealed how I was willing to benefit from what I condemned.

"Oh, but you did buy that little diesel car that gets 50 miles per gallon in an effort to reduce your demand for oil at any price." My busy mind was at it again, telling me what I wanted to hear.

Once again, Wally's reminder seemed to apply: "Don't underestimate the importance of being grounded." I did not realize that pausing to think about taxes could reveal so much about the disparity between my stated values and actual behaviors. Maybe it was time I took a closer look at some of the suffering I invited into my life by not giving this aspect of money the attention it demanded.

"We are called to play the good Samaritan on life's roadside; but that will be only an initial act. One day, the whole Jericho road must be transformed so that men and women will not be beaten and robbed as they make their journey through life. True compassion is more than flinging a coin to a beggar; it understands that an edifice that produces beggars needs restructuring."

—Martin Luther King, Jr.

WEEK EIGHT
WORKSHEET A

Citizen Awareness & Involvement Circuit Inspection

*"We all know that community must be the center of our lives
because it is only in community that we can be citizens…it is only in community that we
can find care. It is only in community that we can hear people singing.
And if you listen carefully, you can hear the words:
'I care for you, because you are mine, and I am yours.'"*

—*John McKnight,* The Careless Society

The vast majority of Americans are "silent"—we live busy lives and find the political process both cumbersome and generally distasteful. In general, we live with the resolve that the less we have to deal with government, the better off we are.

The problem with this approach is that in the silence there is a vacuum filled with the voices of those who realize that "the squeaky wheel gets the most grease." Washington and each of our state capitals are filled with lobbyists who are sent by their respective special-interest groups to make sure our laws are friendly toward their particular agenda.

This is not new to us. We know that corporations and organizations spend lots of money to make sure their voices are heard. Over time, our laws have come to mirror the faces from whence these voices come.

The purpose of this exercise is to encourage you to reflect on your state of contentment with current governmental priorities. If you sense a level of discontent, what are some small steps you could take to make **your** voice heard?

"In these days of difficulty, we Americans everywhere must and shall choose the path of social justice, the path of faith, the path of hope, and the path of love."

—*Franklin Roosevelt*

? How would you describe your current political voice?

❑ loud and obnoxious

❑ calm and persistent

❑ timid but passionate

❑ silent

? What has had the greatest influence on your posture toward government and politics?

_____

_____

_____

? If you could write down one sentence (10 words or fewer) that conveyed your biggest social concern, what would it be?

_____

_____

? When you consider the following table, how do you feel about the taxes you have to pay?

_____

_____

Country	Corporate Taxes	Individual Taxes	Value-Added Taxes
USA	**15%–35%**	**10%–38.6%**	**sales; 0%–8%**
Canada	27%–43%	31%	7%
Finland	29%	5%–37%	22%
France	34%	10%–54%	20.6%
Germany	25%	0–48%	16%
Israel	36%	10%–50%	18%
Japan	30%	10–37%	0%
Mexico	34%	3%–35%	15%
Russia	24%	13%	20%
Vietnam	32%	0–60%	20%

(www.worldwide-tax.com)

Please respond to this statement:

"If you don't like the system here, go somewhere else to live."

❑ *That's exactly how I feel. Maybe then the complainers would get a little perspective about how lucky we really are to live in America.*

❑ *It's just a way to avoid having to do something to some of the problems we have. Taxes are just one issue. From the chart you can't get a fair comparison. In Canada, with nationalized health care and subsidized higher education, their citizens can afford to pay more tax because they don't have to pay for medical or college costs.*

❑ *I don't have the energy to go somewhere else. I am frustrated by how the system seems to benefit from my "hamster on a wheel" life. I'm so exhausted at the end of the day that the last thing on my mind is challenging the system. I'm too tired to really even care.*

If you had the choice of how you paid your social dues, how would you have paid your 2002 taxes?

Total Taxes Paid (From your latest tax return) $_____*

Income Taxes (**Just write the check**) $_____a

Service to Community—Donate time to local charities and churches—tax saved = $15/hour:
Hours donated ____ x $15/hr = tax savings $_____b

Charitable Donations—Lower income taxes by giving money to charity—save $1 for every $3 donated:
Cash donations ____x 33% = tax savings $_____c

Tax Planning—Invest 1 hour of study for every $100 saved in taxes:
 # Hours ____ x $100/hr. = tax savings $_____d

*a+b+c+d = Total Taxes Paid

? Write one sentence (15 words or fewer) that conveys your biggest social concern.

_____

_____

_____

_____

? What steps are you willing to take to help address this concern?

_____

_____

_____

_____

_____

"Ideally, one should have a great deal of courage and strength, but not boast or make a big show of it. Then, in times of need, one should rise to the occasion and fight bravely for what is right."

—*The Dalai Lama*

? Is there a local project that you can support (or establish) that could give you a sense of hope that you were helping to change things for the better?

_____

_____

_____

_____

_____

_____

Consider the following websites to:

➤ contact your U.S. Representative: *www.house.gov*

➤ contact your U.S. Senator: *www.senate.gov*

➤ track your Senators' and Representatives' support or opposition to different advocacy group positions: *www.vis.org* (Cost is $3.65/yr)

➤ see how one local group is addressing a particular social issue: *www.no-smoke.org*

PAYING OUR "SOCIAL DUES"

My encounter with John renewed my sense of empowerment. I didn't have to feel like I was a victim of the system. I could take some responsibility and start behaving like a good citizen by consciously choosing how I wanted to participate in making the world a better place.

But could I begin to see paying taxes as more than just a necessary evil? I knew that first I had to determine what share of my social dues I was willing to pay through income taxes. Then I needed to follow through to make my voice heard regarding how I felt my taxes should be used. It all boiled down to paying attention to what was going on in my community and the world and how I chose to engage in trying to help rather than harm. Maybe then I could actually see some good in paying my taxes.

Week Eight, Worksheet A helped you decide how much income tax you were willing to pay. It also provided some recommendations for alternatives to simply writing a check to the IRS to pay your social dues.

Let's explore some specific ways that you may free up social dues money that had previously been allocated to income taxes. As we address different tax-reduction strategies, refer to the Week Eight TEN WEEKS CD. Greg and Ginger's example will help you see how to update your Authentic Money Guide with the planning tools that appeal to you.

AWAKENED TAX PLANNING

"Anyone may arrange his affairs that his taxes shall be as low as possible; he is not bound to choose that pattern which will best pay the Treasury; there is not even a patriotic duty to increase one's taxes."

—*Learned Hand,* www.taxanalysts.com

Where You Currently Stand with Your Taxes

To know if you want to change your tax payments, you must first be able to know their current status.

Insert the Week Eight TEN WEEKS CD and follow it, screen by screen, to use the Tax Planner features of Quicken®. After setting up your Quicken® accounts properly, you will be able to estimate

"Why shouldn't the American people take half my money from me? I took all of it from them."

—*Edward A. Filene*

how much your taxes will be, as well as see how attentive financial decisions can significantly impact those tax liabilities. After calculating your current tax exposure, return here to read about the many tax-planning options that are at your disposal.

YOUR 401K AND IRA— KILLING TWO BIRDS WITH ONE STONE

The following Week Eight Money Attention Page (MAP) materials provide detailed information about IRA and retirement plan tax-saving benefits. Scan the materials to see which pages apply to your particular financial situation.

MAP 8-1—Pension Plan Comparison Chart: 2001 Tax Act Changes

The government has increased the amount you can put into different retirement plans—especially if you are over age 50. Review this chart to take advantage of the new contribution limits.

MAP 8-2—Traditional IRA Flowchart

This page provides a flowchart that describes the life cycle of a traditional IRA.

MAP 8-3—Overview of Roth IRAs

Roth IRAs are popular because any distributions are typically tax-free and because there is no required minimum distribution at age 70½. Just remember that you don't get a tax deduction for contributions made to a Roth like you do for a Contributory IRA.

MAP 8-4—Roth IRAs vs. Deductible IRAs

Assuming you are eligible to contribute to either a Roth or a Traditional IRA, which should you choose? This MAP lists factors to consider prior to making your choice. We'll also test this option in Quicken® during your use of the Week Eight TEN WEEKS CD.

MAP 8-5—Education IRA (Coverdell ESA) Flowchart

This diagram summarizes the restrictions on making contributions and distributions to an Education IRA. The limits have been increased from $500 to $2,000 and, unlike other Educational savings accounts, the money can be spent on elementary and seconday education expenses.

MAP 8-6—What Is a 401(k) Plan?*

This section outlines the necessary requirements to maintain a qualified plan and summarizes the advantages (to the employee) of having a 401(k). Some plans provide for an employer match, while others are completely funded by employee salary deferrals. No salary deferred (paid into) a 401(k) plan is taxed until that money is withdrawn.
*See also *www.howstuffworks.com/401k.htm.*

MAP 8-7—Qualified Retirement Plans

There are two primary types of Qualified Plans—(1) Defined Benefit plans wherein a formula is used to let the employees know how much money they will get each year when they retire and (2) Defined Contribution Plans wherein a formula is used to let employees know how much they can contribute each year.

Refer back to MAP 8-1 to review how Qualified Plans differ from IRAs in terms of contribution limits.

MAP 8-8—Comparison of SEPs and SIMPLE IRAs

Learn the advantages and disadvantages of SEPs and SIMPLE plans. The tremendous advantage of a SIMPLE over a SEP, not mentioned on this chart, is that a SIMPLE allows a 100 percent of net earnings contribution, whereas the SEP is limited to 25 percent of earnings. If a wife owns a business that can justify paying her husband $8,662* of salary in 2003, he could choose to contribute $8,000 to the company SIMPLE if one were established.

*$8,000 divided by .9235 (100 percent less employee share of Social Security tax of 7.65 percent).

The deadline for the initial establishment of a SIMPLE IRA is October 1 of the current tax year. If, by the time you read this, it is too late to establish a plan for 2003, plan on establishing one right after January, 2004. You can establish and contribute to a SEP by the due date of your 2003 tax return, including extensions.

MAP 8-9—Inherited Retirement Plan Decision Tree—Death Before Required Beginning Date.

The required beginning date is the date that a retirement plan participant is required to start taking distributions from his/her retirement plan. That date is not always the same for different retirement plans, but for IRAs that date is April 1st of the calendar year following the participant's 70½ birthday.

This flowchart clarifies how and when different classes of beneficiaries (spousal and nonspousal) should take distributions from a retirement account if death occurs before the participant had reached his/her RBD.

MAP 8-10—Inherited Retirement Plan Decision Tree—Death After Required Beginning Date.

This flowchart clarifies how and when the beneficiaries of a retirement plan or IRA should take distributions from an IRA or retirement plan if the participant died after their required beginning date. Please see the MAP 8-9 overview in the previous paragraph for an explanation of RBD.

Why all the fuss? Generally, it is desirable to leave money in an IRA as long as possible so the investments can continue to grow without being subject to income tax. You don't want to have to withdraw all the money out of a retirement plan in five years if you can figure out a way to take it out over your own life expectancy.

MAP 8-11—Rollovers and Transfers

Be careful when moving money between IRAs, as well as between retirement plans. It's better to take some time and read this if you plan to make a rollover or transfer than to be surprised with a hefty tax and penalty bill.

MAP 8-12—Withdrawals and Distributions

The IRS will generally penalize you 10 percent if you withdraw money out of your IRA or retirement plan before age 59½, but they insist that you begin taking withdrawals by April 1st of the year following your 70th birthday. Please note that there are exceptions for incurring the 10 percent penalty for early distributions, as long as you meet the criteria listed here. When it comes to finally getting their tax money, the government is dead serious: If you don't get your money out on time, the penalty is 50 percent of what you fail to distribute.

MAP 8-13—New Simplified Rules for Calculating Required Minimum Distributions

Many people want to minimize the amount of money that they withdraw from their IRA. These new rules simplify the process and actually let you take out less money than before.

MAP 8-14—Retirement Plan Contribution Summary

The new tax laws let you put more money into your IRAs, 401(k)s, 403(b)s, and SIMPLE IRA. Use this chart to plan your contributions for the next several years.

Making contributions to retirement savings accounts can help save income taxes now. A $3,000 tax-deductible contribution to a Traditional IRA can save a person in the 27 percent income tax bracket $810 of federal income taxes.

What is even more important than saving the $810 in taxes is that by saving $3,000 per year, the worker accumulates between $139,236 and $148,269—based on an 8 percent annualized investment return—over a period of 20 years. That's what I call "killing two birds with one stone."

MAP 8-14—provides a summary of allowable retirement contributions. Keep in mind a couple of points when using this resource:

➤ SEP IRAs are not listed in MAP 8-14 because most of the SEP plans in existence today do not allow for salary deferrals. The employer pays SEP contributions exclusively.

➤ The 401(k), 403(b), and Simple IRA plans allow for employees to designate a certain portion of their pay to be paid to the retirement account—they elect to "defer" or postpone the receipt of money they actually earned, and in so doing, postpone the taxation of those earnings. These latter three plans also allow for employer contributions.

Based on the plan, an employee can contribute up to $40,000 of his/her pay into a defined-contribution retirement plan without having to set up a complicated defined-benefit plan (see MAP 8-7 for an explanation of the difference). That contribution could save a taxpayer $16,000 in current federal and state income taxes.

Take a few minutes to explore changes in your retirement contributions as you follow along with the TEN WEEKS CD.

Charitable Giving—
Gaining More Than Just Tax Deductions

"As the light of the moon is 16 times greater than the light of all the stars, so is loving-kindness sixteen times more efficacious in liberating the heart than all other religious accomplishments together."

—*The Buddha*

The prospect of being able to write my social dues check to my favorite charity rather than the IRS got me excited. But my enthusiasm soon diminished as I remembered it wasn't an either/or proposition. If I were facing a $1,000 income tax bill, even if I did write out a $1,000 check to charity, it most likely would save me only between $250–$300 in federal and state income taxes. I would still have to send the IRS another $700. Did it really make much sense to spend $1,000 to save $300?

"Giving is the highest expression of potency."

—*Erich Fromm*

Economically, I was worse off. Instead of only being out the $1,000 of income taxes, my checking account is down $1,700 ($700 to the IRS and $1,000 to the charity). I paid dearly for the chance to redirect $300 of my tax bill.

But I sensed there was an opportunity in this economic decision to obtain much more than a $300 tax savings. The money in my checking account could serve as a tangible expression of my Authentic Self. At that level of being, I knew I could end up a very poor man indeed if my philanthropy was mainly about my money, rather than a deep need to connect to other human beings.

Wayne Muller, author and founder of Bread for the Journey, was my guest on "Money Matters" in the summer of 2001. Wayne has devoted his life to assisting people to connect with one another in such a way that each is enriched. I remember the distinction he made between capital and wealth that cuts to the core of how important true giving is in finding our Authenticity:

"It's important for us to make a distinction between capital and wealth. One of the things that I've learned in working with neighborhood philanthropy is that in point of fact, everyone in the community has some capital.

"Some people have kindness capital; some people have trust capital, in the sense that they have the trust of their neighbors and their communities; some people have financial capital. But if we stay separated from each other, then all we end up with is capital.

"When we bring all that to the table and marry the capital of wisdom and kindness and financial support, then it becomes wealth...and there's a very different emotional experience of having a lot of capital and having a lot of wealth."

—*Wayne Muller,* "Money Matters" Radio Show Interview

What struck me most was the phrase, "if we stay separated from each other."

I could stay just as separate and insulated from the needs of the world in my philanthropy as I did in my tax compliance. Giving to worthy causes was a good thing. The question is whether I would engage with that gift in such a way that I expressed my Authentic Self that longed for connection. I could no longer settle for one-sided philanthropy in which my needs were primary.

"The problem with the phrase 'giving back' is that it denies our true nature. It presumes that we perceive ourselves as standing on the outside of our community, feeling obligated to contribute because we're so privileged—as opposed to being deeply entrenched community participants...Our true nature calls us to connect deeply to our community and to find larger meaning in what we do there...In that way, making a contribution becomes a mutual exchange, rather than a one-way transaction."

—*Frances Moore Lappé,* Fast Company Magazine

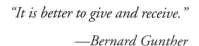

"It is better to give and receive."

—*Bernard Gunther*

WEEK EIGHT
WORKSHEET B

My Community Connection Circuit Inspection

"I don't know what your destiny will be, but one thing I know: the only ones among you who will be really happy are those who have sought and found how to serve."

—*Albert Schweitzer*

? Do you sense a need or desire to change the way you give?

_____

_____

_____

_____

_____

_____

? Recall a genuine act of kindness that just happened and that left you feeling good. (This can be an incident that you prompted or one that simply happened to you.)

_____

_____

_____

_____

"How can you reclaim your true nature? Find an exemplar. Seek out people who are emotionally intelligent and who are already acting on their deeper social nature. Call them, get on their boards, become friends with them. When you start associating with people who are living the way that you want to live, you start to become a different person."

—*Frances Moore Lappé,* Fast Company Magazine

? Who do you know that could be your "exemplar"?

_____

_____

? What do you notice about your sense of well-being as you take these steps?

_____

_____

_____

_____

_____

Take a few minutes to review your current charitable giving. From the Week Eight TEN WEEKS CD, go to the "My Charitable Giving" session and follow the instructions for printing a report about your current charitable giving.

Once you have this report, answer the following questions:

? What prompted you to give to these particular causes?

_____

_____

_____

_____

_____

? If you had $1,000 to give away right now, to whom are you inclined to give it and how much?

_____

_____

_____

_____

_____

"What does love look like? It has hands to help others. It has feet to hasten to the poor and needy. It has eyes to see misery and want. It has ears to hear the sighs and sorrows of men. That is what love looks like."

—St. Augustine

? Is an individual in need on your list?

_____

_____

_____

? Do you sense any obstacles that prevent your direct involvement with individuals or community grassroots organizations? Can you identify those obstacles?

_____

_____

_____

_____

_____

Take a minute to jot down on your Quicken® report any new insights or intentions. File that report in the *What I Want to Do* section of your Authentic Money Guide binder.

Keep in mind some tax information about charitable donations:

➤ You can deduct the mileage you drive for charitable purposes at the rate of 14 cents per mile—as compared to 36 cents per mile for business.

➤ If you give more than $250 at a time to a charity, you need to have a receipt from that organization in order to claim the deduction.

➤ Noncash donations—generally, you need written acknowledgement from the organization if the value of your donation is greater than $250. If you give more than $500 in a single tax year, you need to file Form 8283.

➤ If you give a charity property—like land, stocks, investments, etc.—generally, you can deduct the full value of that property on the date of the donation. The following example may be helpful in illustrating how this could create extra cash to both the donor and the charity:

> *Jerry called me recently and said that his great aunt had just given him 117 shares of IBM stock. He wondered what the tax ramifications would be if he sold the stock for $10,000 and gave some money to his favorite charity. I explained that if he sold the stock and gave the money to the charity he would only end up with $8,000 to give to the charity because federal and state taxes would snatch $2,000 from the sale. He would also end up with $3,040 in income tax savings on account of his gift.*
>
> *On the other hand, if he donated the stock directly to the charity, they would end up with the full $10,000 and he would save $3,800 in income taxes because of his gift. With a little careful planning, Jerry actually kept $760 extra in his pocket because of tax savings and the charity ended up with $2,000 more than if he had given them cash.*

Awakened tax planning really works.

Keep in mind that the donation of appreciated property to charity can only be used to offset 30 percent, rather than 50 percent, of current year income. The 50 percent limit can be used if the cost, rather than the fair market value, of the asset is used as the value of the gift.

➤ Certain types of property—business inventory, creative works, stocks held for less than one year, and business equipment—have to use their tax basis rather than fair market value as the value of the gift.

➤ To determine if an organization qualifies as tax-exempt, go to: *www.irs.ustreas.gov/charities/article.*

> *"One can give nothing whatever without giving oneself—that is to say, risking oneself. If one cannot risk oneself, then one is simply incapable of giving."*
>
> —James Baldwin

➤ To research a charity and review their financial information in order to determine percentage of administrative costs, etc. go to *www.give.org/reports*. Keep in mind that smaller charities will naturally have a higher percentage of overhead than national organizations. What you gain in fiscal efficiency may be lost in your ability to be more personally involved with a smaller local charity.

Return to the TEN WEEKS CD and update your Authentic Money Guide with one of your charitable intentions. This could be a small purchase that reminds you of your intention to follow through with your personal (time) involvement or a financial gift to a charity that you feel embodies your genuine concern.

COLLEGE FUNDING—USING TAX DOLLARS TO GET A DECENT EDUCATION

It may seem more like five years than five weeks, but Greg and Ginger gave us a taste of college planning in Week Three when they were setting up their budget using Quicken's planning features.

At that time, we calculated Greg and Ginger's contribution toward Gil's college expenses, and there was a question relating to estimated financial aid. We estimated a number and promised that in Week Eight there would be some guidance about the financial aid system. So here we are.

Before we dive into the numbers, let's take a minute to pause and reflect on some of the bigger picture issues with college.

WEEK EIGHT
WORKSHEET C

College Funding Philosophy

> *"We fail to teach our children that service to something greater than themselves is far more likely to lead to a joyful and satisfying life, not to mention one that is environmentally rich."*

> —*Carolyn Raffensperger,* "Before We Leap" *interview with Derrick Jensen,* The Sun, *November 2002*

Many parents struggle with how much they should pay of their children's college costs and how much their children should pay. The question allows for a deeper look at what may be driving some of the conflict. The dilemma intensifies as high school graduation looms.

Take a few minutes to answer these questions that probe at some of the emotions you may have about your children and college:

? Did you attend college?_____

? Who paid for your college expenses?_____

? Do you have any regrets about your college experience (or lack thereof)?

_____

_____

_____

_____

_____

? Are any of those regrets influencing how you are dealing with your child's college experience or how it is paid for?

_____

_____

_____

_____

_____

? Do you feel a person has to go to college to experience a full and rewarding life? Are there other experiences that could provide a breadth of perspective we have always looked to college to provide?

_____

_____

_____

_____

_____

_____

? How does your son/daughter feel about attending college?

_____

_____

_____

_____

? Have you determined how much college you can afford to pay, given your responsibilities to provide for your retirement, etc.?

_____

➤ If so, how much? _____

➤ If not, review your last Authentic Money Guide scenario to see how much money you have planned to pay for college costs.

_____

_____

? Have you talked with your son/daughter about how much money you can afford to pay and the options he/she has for paying the balance?
If so, what did he/she have to say?

_____

_____

_____

_____

? With your son/daughter, write out what each of you wants the college experience to provide and how you plan to pay for this privilege.

_____

_____

_____

_____

_____

_____

_____

_____

_____

COLLEGE PLANNING
A GREAT RETURN—A GREAT EXAMPLE

Take a minute and scan the following Money Attention Page (MAP) resources that relate to college planning:

MAP 8-15—Education Tax Incentives

The pain of paying for college can be eased a bit if you qualify for some tax savings through your payments. Use this chart to walk through the maze of programs designed to help ease the cost of higher education.

Please note that I've updated the chart for the only change from 2002 that is material. The Lifetime Learning Credit has been raised from $1,000 to $2,000 in 2003.

MAP 8-16—Steps in Applying for Financial Aid

Use these 6 steps to help ensure your child gets appropriate financial aid. The most important advice on this page is to apply to at least six colleges. You will be surprised at how badly colleges want your child as their student and what financial breaks they will offer you if you have completed the necessary application steps. So—start early and save a bundle of money that you can reallocate in accordance with your Authentic Money Guide.

MAP 8-17—Financial Aid Application

This provides a quick summary of the primary financial aid application forms and the information needed to complete them. File the FAFSA as soon in January as possible—even if you have to estimate a few items of income.

MAP 8-18—What Is a Qualified Tuition (Section 529) Program?

An easy-to-follow summary of the rules for this popular education savings vehicle is provided. Be careful about the prepaid plans, but seriously consider the benefits of the savings plans. Also visit *www.savingforcollege.com* to see if your contributions will garner you a state income tax deduction. This site also provides rankings for each of the 529 plans. (You don't have to invest money in a state plan located where you live or where your son/daughter plans to attend college—monies can be paid from the plan to any qualified educational institution.) Also exercise caution about taking too much investment risk with these funds. The age-based plans automatically adjust the risk of the investments as the child nears college age when the money will need to be withdrawn.

MAP 8-19—Summary of Federal Loan Programs

Need to borrow money for college? This chart highlights the differences between the three federal loan programs for higher education: Subsidized Federal Stafford Loans, Unsubsidized Federal Stafford Loans, and Federal PLUS Loans. Keep in mind that the interest you pay on education loans is tax deductible—see MAP 8-15 for details.

COLLEGE PLANNING—A TEAM EFFORT

I encourage you to include your son/daughter in the college financial aid planning process. Your willingness to pay proper attention to these financial details is one of the last lessons you can impart to your son/daughter before he/she leaves home. Many times, we parents do a disservice to our children in doing for them what they can either do on their own or with some respectful guidance.

Consider the following recommendations for discovering which colleges to consider and then how to pay for the costs:

I suggest you visit *www.howstuffworks.com/college-financial-aid.html/printable* and read the article. Click on the *Financial Aid Calculators* on the second page, where you will be directed to *www.collegeboard.com*. If the link from the first site doesn't connect you to the calculator page on the College Board site, select *Pay for College* and then *What You Need to Know—Financial Aid Calculators*. This calculator will take you, step by step, through how much you can expect to pay for your student's college experience.

Just remember, **the biggest mistake you can make when it comes to college financial aid is to assume you won't qualify for aid. You have to file need-based forms in order to walk through the doorway into merit-based aid.** You also need to remember that colleges are attempting to fill vacant chairs, and they will negotiate, especially if you are willing to apply to several institutions and have them compete for your child.

It is important for you to read the material and understand how college financial aid works. Consider this information:

➤ The percentage of parental income considered for college payment varies between 22–47 percent, after a living allowance and taxes are deducted.

➤ The percentage of the student's income considered is 50 percent.

➤ The percentage of parental assets considered for payment is 5.6 percent.

➤ The percentage of students' assets considered is 35 percent.

This information illustrates the critical nature of basic college financial aid planning. Let's assume Gil has $2,500 in his savings account before he fills out his financial aid forms. He needs a computer and other items for school. By paying for those items out of his account, rather than from his parents' money, he could obtain $735 more in financial aid—that's $735 for 30 minutes of reading and education. Not bad.

Section 529 Plans

In a nutshell, Section 529 plans provide an excellent way to save money for college. Most 529 plans offer both prepaid tuition and savings account programs. The prepaid tuition plans have not been as successful as the savings account plans.

The main advantages of a 529 account over the Coverdell ESAs are:

➤ The donor retains control over monies contributed to a 529 plan.

➤ Many states offer a tax deduction for amounts contributed to their 529 plan.

➤ Investment account options can be tailored to the age of the child and automatically adjusted as college approaches.

➤ Large sums of money can be transferred into a 529 plan ($240,000 in some states) vs. the smaller $2,000 per year limit for CESAs.

➤ The 529 account is not deemed to be the student's asset for financial aid purposes, but distributions from the account will reduce aid, dollar for dollar, in those years.

The main advantage of the Coverdell IRA over the 529 plan is that these accounts can pay for K–12 school expenses while the 529 plans are intended for college and graduate school expenses.

Review MAP 8-18 for more detailed information about 529 plans.

Once you have obtained an estimate of your expected family contribution from the work you have done, return to the Week Eight TEN WEEKS CD "College Planning Update" for guidance as to how to integrate this information in your most recent Authentic Money Guide scenario.

YOUR HOUSE—HOME SWEET TAX HAVEN!

"An Englishman's home is his tax haven."
—Economist Magazine

The American dream: home ownership. In fact, more than two out of three Americans own a home today. After achieving this dream, many of us have wondered who really owns whom? Gone are the days of calling the landlord when things start to fall apart.

While portfolio values have been dropping, home values have increased dramatically in most American cities. This increase in value has encouraged many homeowners to cash in on their equity by refinancing or borrowing on the increased value (equity) with a home equity line of credit.

Others have opted to trade up to nicer homes.

"Home ownership friendly" tax laws have encouraged all of this financial activity around our homes. The mortgage-interest deduction is usually the largest tax deduction Americans have. (Please refer to MAP 5-5 for detailed tax information about mortgage interest, as well as MAP 8-20 for information about buying vs. renting a home.)

In 2003, the standard deduction, or amount that a single person can deduct without having to itemize his/her deductions, is $4,750. Let's say that Gil finishes college in four years, gets a good job, and is able to save $25,000 over a five-year period. If Gil were to rent a home for $750 per month, he would pay $9,000 per year in rent, none of which would be tax deductible. If, on the other hand, he had purchased a $125,000 home with a 30-year $100,000 mortgage at 7 percent, his interest deduction for the first year would amount to $6,967. If Gil paid property taxes of $1,000/year and insurance of $400/year, his total monthly payment would amount to $781. By purchasing vs. renting, he would save approximately $72/month in taxes, bringing the true cost of his housing payment to $709. He was able to save $41/month by purchasing.

The only other cost of purchasing vs. renting is the lost interest that Gil would have earned on his $25,000 that he had paid down on the house. If Gil had been able to earn 5 percent on these savings, he would have had $76 extra in his pocket each month after paying his taxes on that income. If we subtract the $41 a month we calculated to be the savings from buying vs. renting from this $76/month of after-tax interest income, we see the true cost of Gil's home ownership was only $35/month. Now he could also benefit from any increase in value this home would most certainly give him.

And that's when the good news really begins.

What if Gil lives in the house for two years and then sells his home for $150,000, after paying all the sales expenses. The $25,000 profit is tax-free under current tax laws. If Gil had made $25,000 at work, his income and Social Security taxes would have amounted to approximately $10,000, leaving him only $15,000. If he had made $25,000 on land he had purchased and held for two years, his taxes would have approximated $5,000 (assuming a 5 percent state capital gains tax rate). But since he sold his "principal residence," he gets to keep every penny of the profit. After two years of payments, Gil's loan would have been paid down to $97,894, leaving him with $52,106 in tax-free cash. That's a great payback on his initial $25,000 investment.

Financially, it makes great sense to own vs. rent—especially when real estate prices just seem to continue their climb. Seduced by all those savings, it's easy to "let the tax tail wag the dog."

What would our lives look like, however, if we weren't enamored with bigger and more luxurious homes? What would it feel like not to be tied to a mortgage payment? What have we given up in terms of Authenticity, if anything? Would it be so difficult to explore new frontiers if we weren't so chained to our nice predictable lives with one of the strongest links—our home ownership?

"We finally get the last picture hung on the wall and everything is just the way we want it. And there's a knock at the door. It's those 'Three Strange Angels'. And you're out."

—David Whyte, Clear Mind, Wild Heart *tape series*

The sobering truth, however, is that we are not out. We are cemented in and there isn't a team of horses in the county strong enough to pull us out of our castle.

We know that David Whyte is not literally referring to our houses. He's speaking to our tendency to get things just the way we want them in our experience with life, and to becoming attached to things staying that way. Surely there won't come a day when we would have to literally pack up and move in order to stay true to our Inner Voice?

Some people seem to maintain their mobility and unattached mindset. But we all know that they are probably just as attached to their free-spirited lives as we are to our comfortable homes and pre-dictable lives. The challenge is not to polarize either way—"Being unencumbered is *good* and having responsibilities and commitments is *bad*." Either extreme seems to take a heavy toll on our Soul.

We have long since lost contact with the voice that warns of the price of becoming so completely identified with our homes. I wonder how many of us will regret spending so much time, energy, and money on our homes when there was so much more waiting at the threshold of our lives? Maybe it would be helpful for us to reconnect with the truth that we are really nothing more than pilgrims on a journey.

> *"I cannot believe that the purpose of life is to be 'happy.' I think the purpose of life is to be useful, to be responsible, to be honorable, to be compassionate. It is above all, to matter; to count, to stand for something, to have it make some difference that you lived at all."*
>
> —Leo Rosten

"We are meant to find our true home in God, and that means undergoing a series of new births. In a sense we never arrive. Never to arrive is a strange definition of 'home.' Home is the place we never reach... 'Home' becomes both a metaphor for our longings that will never be satisfied and the promise of being truly at home with ourselves in God even while we are on pilgrimage."

—Alan Jones, Passion for Pilgrimage

Despite how each of us defines "God," there seems to be a simul-taneous yearning within us to settle down and establish roots while maintaining an openness to rebirth and fresh beginnings.

Take a moment to reflect on your relationship with your home and how it relates to your Authenticity as you complete the next worksheet.

WEEK EIGHT
WORKSHEET D

My House…My Home

AT HOME

At home amidst
the bees
wandering
the garden
in the summer
light
the sky
a broad roof
for the house
of contentment
where I wish
to
live forever
in the eternity
of my own
fleeting
and momentary
happiness.

I walk toward
the kitchen
door as if walking
toward the
door of a recognized
heaven

and see the
simplicity
of shelves and
the blue dishes
and the
vaporing
steam rising
from the kettle
that called me in.

Not just this
aromatic cup
from which to drink
but the flavor
of a life made whole
and lovely
through the
imagination
seeking its way.

Not just this
house around me
but the arms
of a fierce
but healing world.

Not just this line
I write
but the
innocence
of an earned
forgiveness
flowing again
through hands
made new with
writing.

And a man
with no company
but his house,
his garden,
and his own
well-peopled solitude,

entering
the silences
and chambers
of the heart
to start again.

—*David Whyte,* House of Belonging

? In the previous poem, can you relate to Whyte's feelings about his home? How would you describe your feelings about your home?

_____

_____

_____

_____

_____

_____

? Have you ever wanted to go somewhere or do something that wasn't "practical" because of your commitments and responsibilities? If so, what did you want to experience?

_____

_____

_____

_____

_____

_____

Make a list of each of the components of your life—major possessions, important relationships, work commitments, hobbies, passions—write the items large enough so you can tear up your sheet so each item on your list has its own piece of paper. Now, go to the kitchen table and clear it off. Now go to the kitchen cabinet and gather several different sizes of plates, saucers, and bowls. Leave these plates, saucers, and bowls on the counter and return to the empty kitchen table.

Lay all those pieces of paper on the table. What pieces, after your journey thus far in the TEN WEEKS program, really are important to you? Which pieces aren't all that important to you? How much of the table top will you give to each of the pieces remaining? Place those individual pieces of paper in different sizes of containers to represent their relative importance to you until all the table top is filled.

? How do you feel about your life as you sit back and look at your table top?

_____

_____

_____

_____

_____

? What markers could you integrate into your Authentic Money Guide that would help keep your "chosen table top" aspirations alive, without calling for a radical "sell the house and move" approach?

_____

_____

_____

_____

_____

THE NUMBERS—YOUR HOUSE: FROM PURCHASE TO SALE

Please review the house information listed in the Week Eight MAP Section:

MAP 8-20—Buying a Home

This MAP provides an excellent discussion of the advantages and disadvantates of renting vs. buying a home. A thorough discussion of financing considerations, as well as what type of home to consider, is included. Remember to consider the nonfinancial aspects of your home decisions and what your housing cost will ask you to sacrifice.

Also see _www.freddiemac.com_ for an excellent "Route to Home Ownership."

MAP 8-21—Calculating the Principal Residence Gain Exclusion

As a continuation of the work you've done at Tab 9 of your My Documents binder, this worksheet provides a way of estimating how much, if any, tax might be due on the sale of your home.

Please insert the Week Eight TEN WEEKS CD to test the impact of selling your home and purchasing another or renting under "Home Option Planning."

BUSINESS BREAKS

"The ultimate purpose of business is not, or should not be, simply to make money. Nor is it merely a system of making and selling things. The promise of business is to increase the general well-being of humankind through service, a creative invention and ethical philosophy."

—*Paul Hawken,* The Ecology of Commerce

Business is tough these days. It's a challenge to hang out your shingle and expect folks to come flocking to your door.

This selection of recent quotes reveals some of the current sentiment among big and small business leaders:

"The tech industry faces a new reality of stiff competition, economic uncertainty, and global instability."

—Business Wire

"You simply have to make more than you are spending and deal head-on with hard issues like reducing overhead, lay-offs, not giving salary increases, and pushing suppliers to deliver more for less…it's essential for survival to make hard calls."

—Business Wire

"It seems like it's a struggle at times for businesses like mine because of taxes…That's the one thing that concerns me."

—*Deb Brewer,* Portsmouth Herald

There are economic and social challenges that face businesses today like never before. As always, there will be those who allow the pressure to mold them into something better and others who will see the difficulty as mandating playing hard ball.

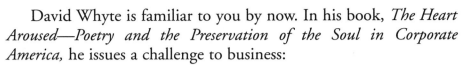

David Whyte is familiar to you by now. In his book, *The Heart Aroused—Poetry and the Preservation of the Soul in Corporate America,* he issues a challenge to business:

> *"Corporate America desperately needs the powers historically associated with the poetic imagination not only to see their way through the present whirligig of change, but also, because poetry asks for accountability to a human community, for rootedness and responsibility even as it changes.*
>
> *"The twenty-first century will be anything but business as usual. Institutions must now balance the need to make a living with a natural ability to change. They must also honor the souls of the individuals who work for them and the great soul of the natural world from which they take their resources."*

If Whyte is right, possibly the most critical payment of social dues comes through how businesses conduct themselves in the world. With over a million businesses starting up each year, there are certainly many of you who are self-employed or working in a business environment.

Whether or not we own our own business or work for a large corporation, there are things we can do that will ground us to a flow of energy that results in our current and future well-being.

WEEK EIGHT
WORKSHEET E

Mind Your Own Business

? What is the biggest financial challenge you face with your business or working as an employee of a business?

_____

_____

_____

_____

_____

? How do you cope with the pressure and stress of either owning or working in business?

_____

_____

_____

_____

_____

? If there were a way, would you prefer not having to make as much money as you do—either as an employee or business owner?

_____

_____

_____

_____

? How does your role/conduct in this business contribute to your own feeling of well-being?

_____

_____

_____

? Are there ways your involvement with the business drains you?

_____

_____

_____

_____

_____

? What role can your money and your Authentic Money Guide have in helping you make a small change at work?

_____

_____

_____

_____

_____

_____

_____

_____

THE NUMBERS—BUSINESS TAX

"A business is nothing more than a conduit for passing along costs to its customers. Taxes are a cost, so tax avoidance is part and parcel of competition to bring consumers better stuff at lower cost."

—Holman W. Jenkins, Jr.

Please review the Business section of the Week Eight MAP documents.

MAP 8-27—Top 10 Business Tax-Savings Ideas

➤ This list of 10 tax tips can save you thousands of dollars of tax. Several of the suggestions directly relate to making the world a better place as well.

MAP 8-28—"Being" in Business

➤ Despite what may seem to be far-out ideas for conducting business, pause to think how good it would be for the world and your Soul to at least try. Consider purchasing Hawken's book, *The Ecology of Commerce,* ©1993 by Paul Hawken, published by Harper-Collins Publishers.

MAP 8-30—How You Do Business Matters

➤ As this appendix illustrates, an S Corporation allows for savings with Social Security taxes because valid dividend payments are not subject to payroll taxes. In order for this tax-reduction strategy to work, a reasonable salary must be paid to the owner/employee, and there must be additional income generation sources in the business, such as equipment or employees. This strategy also has restricted application to professionals.

The MAP 7-23—Entity Comparison Chart gives a good synopsis of different business entities and their related advantages and disadvantages. Before making a final decision on the best entity for your business, I recommend consulting your CPA or TEN WEEKS financial advisor. See Section Four Appendix D for additional advisor selection information.

Insert the Week Eight TEN WEEKS CD and test one of the business tax reduction strategies on your Authentic Money Guide and watch how I do it for Ginger's business, Nurse Network.

THE NUMBERS—INDIVIDUAL TAX

Turn to the following Week Eight MAP section to learn ways to cut your individual tax bill:

MAP 8-22—Real Estate Comparison Chart

Is that a vacation property or a rental property? This table lets you identify the various types of real estate and how to take advantage of existing tax laws that pertain to each. Seriously consider the benefit of renting your home for two weeks each year—tax free. Read this chart for more details.

MAP 8-23—Like-kind Exchanges

If you don't want to pay capital gains on the sale of that investment property, think about trading it for another one.

Remember, real estate can be just as volatile as stock. Don't grow too complacent and attached to property that may be on the verge of declining in value. Pay attention to trends and use tax laws such as these to avoid paying tax on your trades.

Be careful, though. If you end up with some kind of cash benefit from the trade—even if it's a smaller mortgage—you'll end up paying some tax.

MAP 8-24—$25,000 Special Loss Allowance for Real Estate

Many rental property owners can deduct up to $25,000 of rental property losses on their tax return. See a short summary of the rules. Much of those losses are noncash in that depreciaton deductions make up a good portion of the loss. This is an area for which you may want to consult a qualified financial advisor before making any firm commitments.

MAP 8-25—Electric and Clean-burning Vehicles

Help the environment and get a tax credit. See which types of cars are eligible and what kinds of tax benefits to expect.

MAP 8-26—Top 10 Individual Income Tax Savings Ideas

Consider the benefit of saving thousands of dollars in tax, incorporating what you really want into your life, and making the world a better place—all this is available in this little MAP.

MAP 8-29—Jobs Growth and Tax Relief Reconciliation Act of 2003

See a summary of the provisions of this tax law signed into effect on May 28, 2003. The major provisions of the bill are as follows:

➤ An increase in the child tax credit from $600 to $1,000 with an automatic advanced payment of the credit.

➤ An increase in the married, filing joint standard deduction from $7,950 to $9,500.

➤ An expansion of the 10 percent income tax bracket.

➤ An acceleration of tax rate reductions enacted under prior legislation.

➤ An increase in the alternative minimum tax exemption from—

  ➢ $35,750 to $40,250 for singles

- ▷ $49,000 to $58,000 for marrieds and
- ▷ $24,500 to $29,000 for married filing separates
- ➤ Expansion of bonus depreciation on qualifying property purchases from 30 percent to 50 percent.
- ➤ Increase in the Section 179 equipment expensing election from $25,000 to $100,000.
- ➤ Capital gains taxes reduced as follows:
  - ▷ 5 percent for taxpayers in 10–15 percent bracket. (CG rate reduced from 10 percent)
  - ▷ 15 percent for taxpayers in brackets above 15 percent (CG rate reduced from 20 percent)

  These rates apply for sales after May 6, 2003.
- ➤ Dividend income tax rates reduced to equal the above capital gains rates. These dividend rates apply for all of 2003.

Most of these provisions are scheduled to expire within the next five years, unless extended by new legislation.

Insert the Week Eight TEN WEEKS CD and apply one of the individual tax saving ideas by creating a new What If scenario.

TAXES AND TRANSMISSION LINES

"Scatter joy."

—*Ralph Waldo Emerson*

I was amazed at how I had spent most of my professional career in the tax advisory business and had failed to see the many options that existed for connecting to others in society. Pausing to ground sure does change how things appear on the surface.

I had come to relate most of my insights about money groundedness back to Wally's Electrical Diagram. It seemed the part of the electrical system that best represented our need for a rewarding social connection was the transmission towers and high voltage lines, component #3:

Transmission Lines
(Diagram Component #3)
** a flashback **

"Generated power benefits no one unless that power is carried to where it is needed. I know you've seen those huge metal towers just over the hill from our homes. The reason those towers are so large is because the long distance to the power plant requires that extremely high voltages are used. In order to understand these terms, I need to write out a couple of formulas that really will help this all make sense."

Wally reached for another piece of drafting paper and wrote out the following equations, explaining as he went.

"The first equation explains the interdependence between current, voltage, and resistance and is called 'Ohms Law,' named after the scientist who supposedly first expressed it. That equation goes like this:

$E = IR$

Where E = Electromagnetic Force or EMF (measured in Volts)

I = Current (measured in Amperes)

R = Resistance (measured in ohms)

"Electricity makes more sense if you think of it in terms of a water system where there is a pump (E) providing the force to move the water, a meter (I) that tracks the usage of water, and the resistances (R) along the way that make it difficult to get the water where you want it (gravity, drag on the pipe, etc.)."

"So, if I'm following you correctly," I said, "the bigger the pump, the smaller the pipe needed to deliver the same volume of water. Is that why the transmission lines run at such high voltage so the power lines can be smaller?"

"Exactly, Paul. But there's another formula that we need," Wally continued, scratching on the draft paper. "It will actually help us measure the power that is being consumed."

$P = EI$

P = Power—measured in Watts

E = Voltage—measured in Volts

I = Current—measured in Amperes

"Using this formula, we can see that if you increase voltage 10 times, in order to deliver a constant supply of power, you can reduce the current 10-fold. Electrical engineers will tell you that there is less loss of power with low current than with high voltage."

"So, if I follow, that's why those transmission lines are sometimes known as 'high voltage' lines?"

"Yes, that high voltage provides the 'push' to get the electricity where it is really needed."

Those transmission towers and high voltage lines now remind me that power is useless unless it is distributed to those who need it. Taxes, the tip of my "social responsibility iceberg," help me remember to ask myself this question: "How am I transmitting benefit to others in the way that I choose to pay my social dues?"

I experience fulfillment in my life when I am present and engage fully with what is at hand. I have John to thank for reminding me of that important lesson, all over an "Eleventh Hour" tax filing.

"The luxury of doing good surpasses every other personal enjoyment."

—*John Gay*

When I make grounded social dues choices, I experience a fulfilling transmission of energy.

It feels good to connect with others and make the world a better place.

Week Nine

Your Retirement Dream: Is the Grass Really Greener?

> *Week Nine challenges you to take a serious look at your tendency to think "life will be better when…." Rather than looking ahead to your retirement party to really start enjoying your life, you will have found a way to access "true retirement" right now. Your Authentic Money Guide is updated with financial decisions that facilitate your focus on life's journey rather than an illusive destination. Quicken®'s planner allows you to identify the trade-offs you have for getting the retirement you want, starting today.*

"…You know we'll have a good time then…"

—*Harry and Sandy Chapin, from the song* "The Cat's in the Cradle"

It was finally Friday. Wally and I had migrated across the valley from his shop to my office deck for happy hour, our weekly ritual. A fall breeze drifting down from La Plata Peak took the edge off the hot afternoon sun.

"I'd sure love to hike into Crater Lake this weekend, Wally."

"What's stopping you?"

"The usual…Monday morning clients that I'm not prepared for."

"You seem to work pretty well under pressure, Paul. Not me." Unintentionally, my comment about my clients had hooked Wally into a discussion about time, something that had been on my mind a lot and something for which I appreciated Wally's insight.

"I know you've put in your *salt mine* time, Wally," I said. "But I am getting tired of this constant work grind. From my perspective, you have it made. I can hardly wait to retire."

"Before I retired, the 10-hour days were getting to me," explained Wally. "I'd come home so exhausted I could hardly finish dinner. And then, the company gave me what I wanted, early retirement. But it's not what it appears to be, Paul. I wasn't prepared for

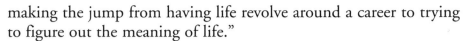

making the jump from having life revolve around a career to trying to figure out the meaning of life."

"Sorry, Wally, I didn't mean to stir up a painful subject," I said. "Actually, I've got a near perfect situation set up here."

Wally continued, "I need to be reminded that my life is a journey and not a destination. Sometimes I forget, though, so I think of this quotation to help remind me:

> *"Whether drifting through life on a boat*
> *or climbing toward old age leading a horse,*
> *each day is a journey and the journey itself is home."*
>
> *(From* Basho's Ghost, *by Sam Hamill, translator;*
> *copyright 1989 by Broken Moon Press)*

"I have trouble with the 'journey being home' concept," I admitted. "I know I find it difficult to appreciate whatever unfolds each day rather than fantasize about how good life will be when something special happens."

"That little saying seems to catch all of us," remarked Wally. "Whether we tend to be more laid back and drift, or we get off and lead our horse because he's not climbing fast enough, we all tend to be focused on something other than where we are right now."

Wally smiled and walked over to the edge of the deck, gazing back toward his cabin, tucked in the trees across the valley. "Just like I thought: My grass looks a lot greener from your place than it does from mine. I can't even see the dandelions."

LIFE RIGHT NOW—AS GOOD AS IT GETS

"As long as we have some definite idea about or some hope in the future, we cannot really be serious with the moment that exists right now."

—*Suzuki Roshi*

Wally's comment about the grass got me thinking about all the ways that my monkey mind tricked me into thinking that "the good life" was still ahead, waiting for me. My *fantasy du jour* happened to be retirement, but there were a host of other anticipations that frequently distracted me from the ordinariness of my daily existence.

When I paused to reflect on my life, I noticed that it seemed to be strung between the big events, sort of like cranberries threaded on a piece of string for the Christmas tree. Whether it was moving from junior high to high school, finally being able to drive, leaving home, getting married, making a name at work, being a dad, getting divorced, selling the business, moving to a new home, getting over my grief, finishing this book…there was always an event on the horizon that kept me moving on. "Won't life be grand, when…."

"Our destination is never a place, but rather a new way of looking at things."

—Henry Miller

In Week One we talked about our tendency to be "there" rather than "here." I labeled that mindset "Top of the Hill." We discussed the feelings of disappointment from working so hard to get to a summit only to realize that the summit wasn't what we had hoped for at all.

Years ago, I dragged two of my daughters and one of their unsuspecting friends on a backpacking adventure. Our goal was to hike 55 miles on the Continental Divide Trail over a period of seven days. If we stuck to our schedule the reward would be meeting Katherine at the end of our goal and getting a ride back home.

Our journey was, of course, full of surprises, including a life-threatening storm at 12,000-feet elevation that covered the trail with seven inches of hail. Somehow we managed to reach Lake El Dorado, where we had scheduled to spend the last night of the trip. The lake was nestled on a ridge overlooking a seemingly endless expanse of lime-green meadows that dissolved into a horizon of jagged mountain peaks and…the wonder of it all! The view overwhelmed me, and I wept.

The next day, our journey ended in the real world. However, I entered it inspired. I had begun to see that life was more than one event on the horizon after another. In an attempt to share my revelation with others, I penned these words to express to clients what I hoped the financial planning process could do for them:

LIFE AFTER...?
A MESSAGE FROM A FELLOW TRAVELER

At 13,000 feet on the Continental Divide Trail, rest captures my spirit. Gazing at the grandeur of the surrounding peaks from a field of wildflowers, I am overcome with the sense that I can simply "rest." Surely a Supreme Being that can orchestrate such beauty and order can manage to provide for me.

Yet, descending to my reality, the burdens of my financial obligations and those of my financial planning practice resettle with easy familiarity. The serenity that calms my fears and sees the beauty of the moment falls victim to a treadmill of false summits.

Each time I seek permission to relax and live, to have and be "enough," money issues loom large, and "enjoying life" falls just over the next hill. If money can't buy happiness, then why pay any attention to it?

The troubling issues are common to all of us: curbing our spending, enslavement to plastic cards, balancing our work with nurturing our children and friendships.... Surely, at the end of our quest for financial security we will find happiness and the permission to enjoy what we have worked so hard to obtain.

But there is nothing sure about it. Too often we see the scripts with empty plots and unhappy endings. The serenity that calms our fears and allows us to rest and experience the beauty of the moment eludes us in the frantic pace of the treadmill.

We want desperately to make wise financial decisions so the quality of life we covet can be obtained. But in running to the pace instead of the purpose of money, we choose to ignore crucial financial issues, justified by the certain knowledge that financial success (whatever that might mean) cannot guarantee happiness.

Is it possible that our lack of attentiveness to financial issues actually fetters us to the concept that money holds the key to true enjoyment of life?

In Money and The Meaning of Life, *Jacob Needleman writes, "...in order to obtain the most serious good of life it is necessary to give exactly the right amount of attention to the aspect of life represented by money. For, if we do not give sufficient attention to what is secondary in life, then sooner or later, what is secondary will take all our attention and leave us no energy or time to pursue what is most essential."*

As a CPA and CFP, I counsel my clients about money issues every day. I believe that paying proper attention to our money needs and issues allows us to focus on those aspects of life that truly offer meaning and joy.

This is not to say that completing a financial plan and implementing it will result in such. Rather, such attentiveness creates feasible space to pay attention to our own spirituality and the aspects of our lives that do indeed occupy "the top of the hill."

A financial plan zeroes in on reality, charts a course and sets the autopilot. Freed, our minds can center on the things we love, awake to the universe.

It is easy to love money—or at least the concept that money can solve all our problems. But I want more. I want to be mindful of the wonder of the sunrise, the gift of a smile, the lessons from the painful experiences.... I, as well as most of my clients, want to see more to life than an increasing net worth.

I am a slow learner, however. Despite my insight manifested from the wilderness, I, unknowingly, made the financial planning process a stepping-stone to something better. There was something more important out there—a *genuine* top of the hill. The process of paying close attention became just another means to an end of achieving that magical, illusive destination.

In categorizing life experience, I had perpetuated my obsession with finding my life somewhere other than in the ordinary, common, everyday details of existence. It is ingrained deeply within me that the day-to-day details are distractions, unwanted annoyances. The middle of life has become the target of my efficiency, but not my attention. The more tasks I can complete in an allotted amount of time, the sooner I can move on to something more important or pleasurable. I had forgotten the essence of what had happened on that ridge where I had stopped and entered into the moment and was touched to the core.

"We live extremely busy lives. Even though we do not have to do as much manual labor as people in former times, we never seem to have enough time for ourselves. I know people who say they do not have enough time to eat or breathe, and it appears to me to be true. What can we do about this? Can we take hold of time with both hands and slow it down?"

"First, let us light the torch of our awareness and learn again how to drink tea, eat, wash dishes, walk, sit, drive, and work in awareness. We do not have to be swept along by circumstances. We are not just a leaf or a log in a rushing river. With awareness, each of our daily acts takes on a new meaning, and we discover that we are more than machines, that our activities are not just mindless repetition. We find that life is a miracle, the universe is a miracle, and we too are a miracle."

—*Thich Nhat Hanh,* Ordinary Magic

Rather than scrambling for the top of the hill—whether that is retirement or not—what if we cultivated this kind of awareness of the wonder and sacredness of each detail? Buddhists, like Thich Nhat Hanh, are not the only ones who practice disciplines of noticing the miraculous.

"The Celtic Christians learned prayers to accompany getting up in the morning, for dressing, for starting the morning fire, for bathing or washing clothes or dishes, for 'smooring' the fire at days end, and for going to bed at night. One for starting the morning fire begins:"

'I will kindle my fire this morning
In the presence of the holy angels of heaven,
God, kindle Thou in my heart within
A flame of love to my neighbor,
To my foe, to my friend, to my kindred all,
To the brave, to the knave, to the thrall...'

—The Celtic Way of Evangelism, *by George G. Hunter III*

There are more hindrances to enjoying life one day at a time than just the Top of the Hill syndrome, however. Let's pause and take a look at the Retirement Expectation Circuit to see if there are other "shorts" preventing the free-flow of present-moment energy into our lives.

Week Nine
Worksheet A

Retirement Anticipation/Appreciation Circuit Worksheet
Turn to your Week One Money Reflection Inventory.

? Is there anything you would change to your response to The 'Top of the Hill' question in part one?

_____

_____

_____

_____

_____

? Sit quietly and recall an incident when you were completely attentive and present with an ordinary task of life. What do you remember about that experience?

_____

_____

_____

_____

_____

? If you want to cultivate this kind of awareness, what practices might help you integrate such an attitude into the whirlwind of your life?

_____

_____

_____

_____

_____

Consider the following statements and check those with which you identify:

❑ The problem with my life is: house / mate / job / weather / economy / city / government / neighbor / child(ren) or (_____)(_____)(_____). Once I'm free of this ball and chain, my life will be much better.

❑ Life is great. I mind my business and expect you to mind yours. The problems start when other people don't take responsibility for their lives. I know folks my age that are raising their grandkids because their kids are "basket cases." I'm not going to let anyone mess up my life. I've worked hard to get where I am. I'm going to enjoy it.

❑ The problem is not enough time. It all comes down to having too many things to do in a day. Retirement will give me back 40–50 hours of my life every week. Then I'll have time for the people and things that I really love.

❑ The day after we retire, we're loading up our RV and taking a trip across the country. We may be gone for a whole year, who knows. That's the kind of freedom I've been looking forward to for many years. We're going to have a good time then.

❑ Retirement is for old people. I plan to stay young at heart, so I'm going to work 25 hours a week until I'm 70. Who knows, I may not stop then. I love what I do, the people I work with, and I sure don't see any reason to throw all that away just to sit around on the porch and complain about my aches and pains.

❑ I'm excited about retirement because I'll be able to volunteer with my favorite charities. It seems like life is so hectic that we don't have time to give back to the community like my parents did during their working years. I think that will add a dimension to my life I feel is missing now.

❑ Retirement scares me to death. I've never learned what to do with leisure time. A week-long vacation and my family is ready to send me back to work. I guess I'm afraid I'll feel useless and unproductive and won't have much of an identity.

❑ With all the horror stories of retirees' economic woes, I don't plan to stop working until I've got $_____. The only thing worse than growing old is growing old in poverty.

❑ I'm already retired. It's definitely not what I expected. Some parts are much better, others a whole lot worse. I think one of the hardest parts is not really having any big life event to look forward to. I guess I'm just not into fantasizing about my death.

❑ Life is what you make it. They say if life hands you lemons, make lemonade. I've dealt with it as it has come my whole life, and things have worked out just fine. It seems like a pretty good game plan for the rest of the trip.

? Based on your responses to the options listed, write down what attitudes might "short circuit" your full enjoyment of life from now on.

_____

_____

_____

_____

_____

_____

_____

_____

_____

_____

Please turn back to the *What Is It I Really Want?* questionnaire in Week Three. Reread the "I would like to…" priorities.

? Does any of the options you checked above indicate a hesitation about taking action on those priorities? If so, which ones?

_____

_____

_____

_____

_____

"Go confidently in the direction of your dreams! Live the life you've imagined. As you simplify your life, the laws of the universe will be simpler."

—Henry David Thoreau

? What may be behind your reluctance to open to the life that you really want—"the direction of your dreams"—right now?

_____

_____

_____

_____

_____

_____

The "Golden Years" of Retirement

"I've long since retired, my son's moved away
I called him up just the other day
I said, 'I'd like to see you if you don't mind'
He said, 'I'd love to, Dad, if I can find the time.
You see my new job's a hassle and the kids have the flu;
But it's sure nice talking to you, Dad.'"

—song by Harry and Sandy Chapin, "The Cat's in the Cradle"

Retirement is our reward. It's the **Mother of All Carrots at the End of the Stick**. From the day we start working, we are programmed to start saving for the day when we stop working. And we're convinced the day that we can finally stop working will somehow be the best day of our entire lives.

We, as most societies, have our contradictions. We idolize thin, fit movie stars and supermodels yet half of the adults in the United States are overweight and one quarter are obese (*www.niddk.nih.gov/health*). We constantly read and fantasize about retirement, but overall we are woefully unprepared for it.

Consider a few statistics:

➤ Between 1989 and 1998 the percent of households headed by a person ages 47 to 64 that would be unable to maintain 50 percent of his/her pre-retirement income rose from 30 percent to 43 percent. (*www.prospect.org*)

➤ Approximately 52 percent of all males over 65 have annual incomes of less than $15,000. Eighty percent of women over 65 have incomes under $15,000. This includes Social Security income.

➤ For 64 percent of retirees, Social Security provides at least half of their retirement income, and 20 percent of retirees will have no other income in retirement. (*www.epinet.org*)

Just in case that last statistic didn't shock you, consider that the average retired worker's Social Security benefit for 2003 was $895/month. The average benefit for a worker and his/her spouse was $1,483/month. (Income Tax and Financial Planning Quickfinder handbook, *www.quickfinder.com*)

➤ Of households that were between the ages of 47 and 64 in 1998, almost one-fifth will fall below the poverty line by the time they retire.

In 2001, the poverty line was $8,494 of annual income for a single person over 65. If you were fortunate enough to be a single parent with two children that same year, you could make $14,128 without exceeding the poverty line.(*www.census.gov/hhes/poverty*)

➤ Only about half the workforce is covered by a pension, and the average pension wealth of households nearing retirement is only $108,300. This would provide a person who lives 20 years after retirement $5,400 per year. (*www.census.gov*)

➤ The average company annuity/pension income in 2000 for men was $14,232 and for women was $8,734. (*www.census.gov*)

Why beat a dead horse? It's obvious that many in America won't participate in the Golden Years without financial worry. Many retirees will be thankful for a job at a fast-food restaurant or Walmart, making minimum wage. But most of those folks, you say, aren't the types who would be reading TEN WEEKS, anyway.

There are a lot of people who are much better prepared for retirement, aren't there? Let's take a look at a few more statistics and see if we can uncover some good news.

➤ A 1998 study, "Baby Boomers Envision Their Retirement: An AARP Segmentation Analysis," revealed the following attitudes about retirement:

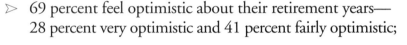

- 69 percent feel optimistic about their retirement years—28 percent very optimistic and 41 percent fairly optimistic;

- 76 percent say it is important to sacrifice and save now for the future, yet 47 percent say they find it hard to save;

- 55 percent say they have a very/somewhat favorable view of Social Security;

- Six in 10 feel confident in their ability to prepare for the future;

- Eight in 10 say they plan to work at least part-time in retirement—just 16 percent say they will not work at all;

- 35 percent expect that they will have to scale back their lifestyle in retirement; and

- 16 percent believe that they will have serious health problems. (*www.research.aarop.org*)

These generally optimistic responses were in the middle of a strong bull market that eventually peaked in March of 2000. Listed below are the annualized performance returns for the three years ending March 31, 2003:

- S&P 500 (U.S. Large Cap)   -16.09%
- Russell 2000 (U.S. Small Cap)   -11.00%
- Nasdaq Composite (U.S. Technology)   -33.35%
- MSCI EAFE (International Stocks)   -19.54%
- Lehman Brothers Agg. (Bonds)   9.81%
- Six-month Treasury (Short-Term Gov't.)   4.25%

Those respondents may have had some different opinions had they just lost 48 percent (three years times an annual loss of 16.09 percent) of their retirement account that was invested in an S&P 500 Index Fund.

Return to Week Eight, MAP 8-7 to review the differences between a defined benefit plan, in which the investment risk rests with the employer, and a defined contribution plan, in which the employee bears the risk of loss. Keep that in mind as you review the following information from the *Wall Street Journal*:

- Between March 2000 and Sept. 2002 more than $1.5 trillion evaporated from stock mutual funds.

- Stock funds assets declined to $2.8 trillion by July of 2002. That was the level of their assets in 1997.

➤ Just 74 percent of workers participated in their company's 401(k) plans in 2002—the lowest level since the early '90s.

➤ At least a dozen major employers have cut or suspended 401(k) contributions since January 2002.

Let's look elsewhere to see if we can uncover some good news:

➤ In 1975, of roughly half of employees who had any pension benefits on the job, 71 percent of those workers were covered by a defined-benefit plan. That dropped to 29 percent in 1999. (*www.prospect.org*)

➤ The average 401(k) balance was $45,000 in 1999. By 2001, it had fallen to $36,000 even though investors had made contributions between those times. (*Money Magazine*)

➤ The Enron debacle illustrated how top management could take advantage of elevated stock prices, bolstered by its own employee 401(k) stock purchases. The stock owned by employees was restricted—they couldn't sell it until they were 50 years old. Of course, the management's stock was not restricted in the same way, and they made millions before the company's failure, leaving the employees' 401(k)s filled with worthless stock. (*www.prospect.org*)

➤ Most financial advisors recommend using annual investment return values of 6–8 percent in determining how much people need to save for retirement. It is not uncommon to see clients who still think that the stock market can be expected to generate 10–15 percent annual returns. Consider the impact of such a gap in expectations:

▷ A $500,000 portfolio assumed to grow at 7 percent per year will return a monthly income stream of $3,326 for 30 years. Keep in mind, with inflation of 3 percent, the last month's income will only be worth $1,354 in real dollars.

▷ That same portfolio assumed to grow at 10 percent per year would generate a monthly income stream of $4,388. The present value of that last month's income would be $1,786.

▷ If the retiree insisted on spending $4,388 per month from the portfolio earning 7 percent rather than 10 percent, he/she would run out of money 15 years early.

Well, not too much luck in uncovering any great news on the asset side of things. What about taking a look at some of the expenses that retirees are likely to encounter?

➤ A couple retiring today at age 60 would need at least $200,000 in savings to cover their medical expenses during retirement. That does not include any long-term (home health or nursing home) care. (*Kiplinger's Retirement Report*)

➤ On average, Medicare covers roughly 55 percent of a beneficiary's medical costs during retirement, leaving a financial gap of approximately $7,000 per couple each year. (*Kiplinger's Retirement Report*)

➤ A 1999 study found that initial retirement spending was higher than preretirement spending, but that spending declines 20 percent between ages 65 and 75. (*Financial Planning Perspectives*)

➤ Increased costs in retirement for travel and recreational pursuits, along with a desire to assist with grandchildren's college funding, etc. may very well offset savings from lower debt balances, clothing, and life insurance premiums.

▷ To "ballpark" how your retirement expenses might look, go to *www.financecenter.com*, click on *Consumer Calculators*, then *Retirement Planning*, then *Retirement Planning as an Opportunity*, then *How Will Retirement Affect My Expenses?*

Facing the realities of lower-than-anticipated investment savings and higher-than-anticipated retirement expenses creates a dilemma. If retirement was the object of our hopes and dreams for finally experiencing the good life, what will we do with the disappointment of seeing that it might not turn out like we had hoped?

There are several options we have in responding to the financial dilemmas that threaten our retirement dreams:

1. **Concentrate on fixing the problem.**
   Now that you are comfortable with using the planning features of Quicken®, you are empowered to determine what combination of assets, savings levels, expenses before and after retirement, and longevity will optimize the possibility of you getting the retirement you have always wanted.

   The power of TEN WEEKS is that you finally have a way to give these financial issues your complete attention through the use of the Quicken® What if Event Scenario Planner. It's easy, though, to get carried away and end up using the Quicken® planner in a way that consumes your precious life energy.

   Remember my essay and how I fell into that trap, thinking that a financial plan would provide the missing link to what I really needed to be happy?

   You can easily be seduced into chasing a goal you may never reach, simply because life's events are beyond your control.

   Rather than using the retirement projections as a game plan to make sure you get what you want, let them teach you how flexible and adaptable you can be, no matter what comes along. By simply adjusting a few items in our lives, we deal with what comes—graciously, rather than frantically seeking to make things go exactly according to our plan.

   You may be surprised at how flexible you can be once we return to Quicken® and the TEN WEEKS CD.

2. **Redefine what retirement means and when you can have it.**
   A dictionary definition of ***retirement*** is: *withdrawal from one's occupation, business, or office; withdrawal into privacy or seclusion; a place of privacy or seclusion; a retreat;* (American Heritage Dictionary of the English Language, Fourth Edition) *withdrawal for prayer and study and meditation.* (WordNet 1.6, 1997, Princeton University)

   We have focused almost exclusively on the first definition of retirement—*Withdrawal from one's occupation, business, or office*—but we have not given much credence to other possibilities of meaning for this word and its relevance to our lives.

   What if we created a composite definition of retirement by integrating the elements that most of us imagine it to offer?

For example, in retirement, I plan to live a life of **leisure**, **vacation**, create opportunities for **recreation**, and possibly even take a **sabbatical** of sorts. What do each of those elements really mean and how might they inform a more holistic view of retirement?

Once again, let's see what the dictionaries have to say:

Leisure—*Freedom from time-consuming duties, responsibilities, or activities;* **to be permitted** (American Heritage Dictionary); *time at one's command, free from engagement; freedom to choose a pastime or enjoyable activity* (Webster's Revised Unabridged Dictionary)

Vacation—*A period of time devoted to pleasure, rest, or relaxation, especially one with pay granted to an employee;* **freedom from occupation** (American Heritage Dictionary); *a period of intermission; rest; leisure* (Webster's Revised Unabridged Dictionary).

Recreation—*Refreshment of one's mind or body after work through* **activity that amuses or stimulates**; *play; a forming anew* (Webster's Revised Unabridged Dictionary)

Sabbatical—*Relating or appropriate to the Sabbath as the day of rest; enjoying or bringing* **an intermission of labor** (Webster's Revised Unabridged Dictionary)

Sabbath—*A season or day of rest; one day in seven appointed for rest or worship;* **to cease**, *rest* (Webster's Revised Unabridged Dictionary)

Our expanded definition of retirement might read:

> *Permission to cease from labor and responsibility; freedom to do what one enjoys; engagement in that which provides refreshment, amusement, and stimulation.*

What is it that requires us to wait for the retirement party to experience this definition? Is not our fantasy with retirement fueled by the scarcity of these qualities in the routine of our lives?

No one seems to have captured the difficulty we have in giving ourselves permission to rest better than Wayne Muller, author of *Sabbath—Restoring the Sacred Rhythm of Rest*. While he was a guest on "Money Matters," I asked Wayne what he meant by creating a "Sabbath" or a "sanctuary in time" into our lives:

> *"Traditionally the Sabbath practice honors that there's a rhythm for every purpose under heaven. What that means is that there's a time to work and a time to rest, there's a time to produce and there's a time to enjoy. It's just like the heart that beats as the chambers open and close and the lungs expand and contract, the seasons move from summer to fall to winter to spring. This is the way of all life.*
>
> *"One of the things that puts us in synchronicity with being alive on the Earth is living in some kind of rhythm. If we're always at work; if we're always trying to make things happen; if we're always accumulating; if we're always, out of fear, trying to get more and more, we actually do great violence to the rhythm of the heartbeat of the world. Even when we're trying to do good in the world, we end up doing good badly.*
>
> *"…We want to be useful in the world, we want to be helpful, we want to feel like we're making a contribution. Where we get caught, of course, is the harder we work, we begin to imagine that it all depends on us. We say, 'When I get this project done…then I'll finally rest.' We can't wait until all our work is done. Sabbath is just a device to give ourselves permission to remember that if we wait until we're done, we might wait until we're dead."*

—*Wayne Muller, "Money Matters" Radio Show Interview*

It is impossible to listen to Wayne speak or to read his books without being drawn toward setting aside a time in the cycle of each week to truly stop. With nothing to accomplish or respond to (that means **no to-do list** of items to check off), there would be a set amount of time to practice our new definition of ***retirement.***

With all the things that can derail attainment of the Golden Years of Retirement—investment performance, job security, retirement expenses, personal or spousal health problems, Social Security reductions, international terrorism, etc.—why not take the time to truly rest, one day a week, right now?

If we had a weekly period of *retirement*, I believe there would be less of a compulsion to create a 30- to 40-year period in which we tried to "make up for lost time."

"Nothing has a stronger influence psychologically on their environment and especially on their children than the unlived life of the parent."

—*C. G. Jung*

There can be tremendous financial rewards from integrating rest into our lives in such a way that de-emphasizes the need to look forward to the age when we plan to stop working, retirement.

Insert the Week Nine TEN WEEKS CD and find the "Working in Retirement" section. Follow along with Greg and Ginger as you adjust your Authentic Money Guide with the impacts of working in retirement. Complete the Week Nine Worksheet B—*I'll Trade This for That" Retirement Option Worksheet*. For now, don't worry about the "Soc. Sec. %" column—we will get to that later in this section.

Greg and Ginger were able to retire two full years earlier because of their decision to earn $20,000 each per year until they were 70. What did your *postretirement earnings* allow you to achieve?

❑ An earlier retirement date?

❑ A reduction in current earnings?

❑ Increased living expenses in retirement?

❑ Ability to make a special purchase?

Don't forget to log your new scenario into the Week Three Appendix A summary, as well as to print out your planning reports for the "My Options" section of your Authentic Money Guide binder.

WEEK NINE
WORKSHEET B

"I'll Trade This for That"
Retirement Options Worksheet

Scenario #	Retirement Age	Preretirement Income	Postretirement Income	Expenses	Soc. Sec. % *	$ Until Yr.**

*Percentage of Calculated Maximum Social Security Benefit Utilized in the Scenario; 80 percent = "I assume I'll only receive 80 percent of my projected Social Security Retirement Benefit.

** Year that the "What If" plan runs out of money per the What If Scenario Graph.

But there is still another option we have in dealing with the disappointing prospects for our "Golden Years Retirement." It's awfully enticing.

3. Just pretend.
The other way of dealing with deflated savings, inflated retirement costs, and the likelihood of less than robust investment returns, is to believe that ***Time will heal all wounds.***

This approach would rely on investment balances and ongoing returns to rebound to levels we knew at the turn of the 21st Century, the government to take action that would save full Social Security benefits and curtail the escalation of health costs, and employers to show genuine concern for the long-term needs of their employees through the reestablishment of company pension plans rather than employee-funded 401(k) plans.

Before tackling just one of those issues, let me mention another way that we Just Pretend. "Present-only thinking" can be used as a way to escape from having to ground to the realities of life. Eckhart Tolle, author of the best-selling book *The Power of Now* exposes this misinterpretation of living in the present:

> *"Learn to use time in the practical aspects of your life— we may call this "clock time"—but immediately return to present-moment awareness when those practical matters have been dealt with. In this way, there will be no build-up of 'psychological time,' which is identification with the past and continuous compulsive projection into the future.*
>
> *"Clock time is not just making an appointment or planning a trip. It includes learning from the past so that we don't repeat the same mistakes over and over. Setting goals and working toward them. Predicting the future by means of patterns and laws, physical, mathematical, and so on, learned from the past and taking appropriate action on the basis of our predictions."*

Rather than pretending that "awakening" ushers you into a state of detachment from life's mundane details, give your full attention to the issues that present themselves to you. Your money and personal finances will ground you to the realities of the human condition and your particular dance with it—if you have granted such permission. It is then and only then that you

access the energy that flows when you have aligned your Authentic Self with your present life.

An example may help. One of the issues I mentioned that could devastate your Golden Retirement was rising healthcare costs. You have a choice in how to respond to this threat.

You can ignore the skyrocketing medical costs and hope that something will be done to alleviate any negative impact on your ability to provide responsibly for your physical needs.

You can also be compulsive about the threat and attempt to craft a "bullet-proof" financial strategy for protecting yourself.

The third option is to face how much your healthcare costs have actually risen in recent years, do some research on current trends, and integrate those findings into your planning. By taking these practical steps, you have done what Tolle suggests, "taking appropriate action on the basis of our predictions," and refused to shift out of the present by either ignoring or being compulsive about the future.

Now, let's return to the time will heal all wounds method of pretending. Without addressing each of the issues that could negatively impact your prospects for a prosperous retirement, let's just tackle one—the future outlook of Social Security.

Let's test your resolve to stop pretending by asking the million-dollar question: "Can I count on Social Security?"

"We can never insure 100 percent of the population against 100 percent of the hazards of life, but we have tried to frame a law which will give some measure of protection to the average citizen and to his family...against poverty-ridden old age..."

—*Franklin D. Roosevelt August 14, 1935*

From the inception of the Social Security system, we clearly see that it was never designed to entirely fund a comfortable retirement. Currently, the average Social Security benefit for a single retiree would leave the recipient just above the official poverty line. But will those basic benefits even be available to those retiring in the future?

Consider the following information obtained from *www.socialsecurity.gov*—"Frequently Asked Questions About Social Security's Future":

➤ *I'm 35 years old. If nothing is done to improve Social Security, what can I expect to receive in retirement benefits from the program?*

"Unless changes are made, at age 74 your scheduled benefits could be reduced by 27 percent and could continue to be reduced every year thereafter from presently scheduled benefits."

➤ *I'm 25 years old. If nothing is done to change Social Security, what can I expect to receive in retirement benefits from the program?*

"Unless changes are made, when you reach age 64 in 2042, benefits for all retirees could be cut by 27 percent and could continue to be reduced every year thereafter. If you lived to be 100 years old (which will be more common by then), your scheduled benefits could be reduced by 35 percent from today's scheduled benefits."

➤ *I hear Social Security has a big financial problem? Why?*

"Social Security's financing problems are long term and will not affect today's retirees and near retirees, but they are very large and serious. People are living longer, the first baby boomers are five years from retirement, and the birth rate is low. The result is that the worker-to-beneficiary ratio has fallen from 16-1 in 1950 to 3.3-1 today. Within 40 years, it will be 2-1. At this ratio there will not be enough workers to pay scheduled tax benefits at current tax rates."

➤ *Is there a Social Security trust fund?*

"Yes, presently, Social Security collects more in taxes than it pays in benefits. The excess is borrowed by the U.S. Treasury, which in turn issues special-issue Treasury bonds to Social Security. These bonds totaled $1.4 trillion at the beginning of 2003, and Social Security receives more than $80 billion annually in interest from them. However, Social Security is still basically a 'pay-as-you-go' system, as the $1.4 trillion is a small percent of benefit obligations."

➤ *What are the alternatives for modernization and reform?*

"The four basic alternatives that are being discussed—singularly or in combination with each other—are: 1) increasing payroll taxes, 2) decreasing benefits, 3) using general revenues, or 4) prefunding future benefits through either personal savings accounts or direct investments of the trust funds."

This careful look at the Social Security System leads me to the following conclusions and recommendations:

1) **Social Security will most likely not go bankrupt.**
Even though expenditures will exceed current inflows and the government has spent the excess money in the Trust Fund—and given an IOU in the form of U.S. Treasury Bonds to that fund—there is still a governmental obligation to pay. Because of the dramatic increases of seniors as a percentage of the total population, the percentage of our Gross Domestic Product that is dedicated to senior expenses will have to increase from the current 7 percent to approximately 12 percent. (*Social Security Under The Gun,* by Arthur Benavie) Taxes will have to be adjusted to cover these changes if benefits are not adjusted. Believe me, they will be.

2) **Until changes in the system are made, it makes good common sense to reduce projected benefits in your Authentic Money Guide by the percentages currently available.**
For workers currently 25–35, I would recommend reducing Social Security benefits by 25–27 percent in calculating financial projections. For those 35–45, 12–14 percent, and for those 45–55, 6–8 percent. For those workers currently over 55, I see no need to reduce projected benefits.

Please keep in mind that these percentage reductions are only estimates. They are based on current policies and do not consider future reforms. Once those reforms are instituted, these projections will need to be adjusted.

Please take a moment to return to the Week Nine TEN WEEKS CD and update your Authentic Money Guide, along with Week Nine Worksheet B ("I'll Trade This for That" Retirement Options worksheet) with any changes to your Social Security benefits in light of what you feel is realistic.

3) **Take responsibility for learning more about the issues and options for Social Security reform. Write your governmental representatives to voice your opinion.**

A good place to start is to purchase and read the book, *Social Security Under the Gun—What Every Informed Citizen Needs to Know About Pension Reform*, by Arthur Benavie. Consider Mr. Benavie's challenge:

> *"Beware of leaving this controversy to the politicians. Trite as it sounds, the right decisions won't be made unless you, the public, are informed and politically active…What kind of public pension system do you want? There is no higher authority here."*

RETIREMENT REPOSE

The Golden Years of Retirement do not exist. That may seem like bad news to those of us who have nibbled at that "carrot" for most of our working lives. The really good news is that we no longer have to subsist on a meager diet of carrot at the end of the stick. There is a banquet table of rest and delight waiting for us right now if we are willing to set aside our busy agendas and attend.

> *"In later life I care only for peace;*
> *Affairs of state are none of my concern.*
> *I know I have no plan to save the world,*
> *Only my old retreat here in this world.*
> *My girdle loosened to the cool pine wind,*
> *I play the lute beneath the mountain moon.*
> *You ask the laws of failure and success?*
> *The fishermen are singing in the cove…"*
>
> *—Chinese poem*

Start practicing this new way of living right now with the next Circuit Inspection Worksheet.

WEEK NINE
WORKSHEET C

True Retirement Circuit Inspection Worksheet

? After reading this Week's material, have any of your beliefs or expectations about retirement been affected? If so, in what ways?

_____

_____

_____

_____

_____

_____

_____

Remember Wally, Jane, Katherine, and me discussing in Week Five how the media encourages us to buy the "picture perfect life"? Wayne Muller, in *Sabbath—Restoring the Sacred Rhythm of Rest*, alludes to this idyllic scene with the beautiful couple, soft cotton clothes, Golden Retriever…

> *"Sabbath is a time to stop, to refrain from being seduced by our desires. To stop working, stop making money, stop spending money. See what you have. Look around. Listen to your life. Do you really need more than this? Spend a day with your family. Instead of buying the new coffee maker, make coffee in the old one and sit with your spouse on the couch, hang out—do what they do in the picture without paying for it. Just stop. That is, after all, what they are selling in the picture: people who have stopped. You cannot buy stopped. You simply have to stop.*

> *"Spend a day napping and eating what is left over in the refrigerator; play a game with your children, take a walk, have a cup of tea, make love, do nothing of any consequence or importance. Then, at the end of the day, where is the desperate need to consume, to shop, to buy what we do not need? It dissolves. Little by little, it falls away."*

? What resistance do you have in setting aside a block of time devoted to simple enjoyment of life without television, radio, phones, buying, going, doing—a time to experience *True Retirement—Permission to cease from labor and responsibility; freedom to do what one enjoys; engagement in that which provides refreshment, amusement and stimulation?*

_____

_____

_____

_____

_____

? What do you normally spend on one day of the week that could be set aside for your quiet enjoyment? Run another What If analysis in Quicken® to evaluate the results of that spending reduction in terms of giving you something that you value more. Record your results in Week Nine Worksheet B. What were you able to "buy" with that reduction in spending?

_____

_____

_____

_____

_____

? What are willing to trade from your existing Authentic Money Guide Scenario as you look at various retirement options after completing Worksheet B —*I'll Trade This for That Retirement Options Worksheet?*

_____

_____

_____

_____

_____

? What feelings do you have about the Social Security system and its viability to help you fund your retirement?

_____

_____

_____

_____

? What changes, if any, did you make to your Authentic Money Guide in terms of expected Social Security benefits as a percentage of your calculated monthly benefit? What impact, financially, did that have on your plan? (See Week Three Appendix A for the scenario that tested the change in Social Security benefits.)

_____

_____

_____

_____

OUT OF THE ASHES

*"As long as we see what has come to pass as
being unfair, we'll be a prisoner of
what might have been."*

—*Mark Nepo*

This Week's discussion may seem harsh and have a tone of "Just Deal With It!" In no measure is my intention to minimize the tremendous devastation many of you have experienced with regards to your retirement dreams.

You may be one of the many who has had to return to work after entering retirement because of losses in your investment accounts. If you are still working, you may see the need to work extra years in order to make up for similar investment losses or reductions in company benefits and retirement matching contributions. These are devastating setbacks to anybody who has worked hard and long to reap the rewards of retirement.

"Leonard Bentley was 25 when he first started dreaming about his retirement. He would quit work in his mid-50s, traveling for long stretches while still young enough to enjoy it.

"Those dreams came true two years ago, when Mr. Bentley, then 56, gave up his job as a supervisor for a California gas company. 'All of this was in the works for many years, and it actually worked,' said Mr. Bentley, of Santa Clarita, Calif.

"The stock market has taken the shine off these plans, leaving Mr. Bentley shaken and forcing him to cut back. A trip to Alaska is on hold, as are other travels once seen as a mainstay of his retirement. 'It's very scary,' he says. 'It has cost me sleep.'

"When he retired in 2000, Mr. Bentley had $725,000 from a lump-sum pension payout and an employee stock-purchase plan...But falling stocks and his withdrawals have whittled the account to about $570,000. Now, he worries he may run out of money.

"...He and his wife had bought a camper, expecting to travel for weeks at a time. Now it's just for short trips. 'We're kind of on a permanent vacation, but we're not going anyplace,' he says."

—Wall Street Journal, *"Stocks Relentless Slide Begins to Touch Many Investors' Lives"*

Mr. and Mrs. Bentley's dilemma may seem mild when compared to your particular situation. The point is that most of you can feel the pain of what has happened in the economy and financial markets over the past three years.

As painful as it may be, facing reality brings healing more quickly than any other course of action. If you were not convinced of this truth you would not be nine weeks into the TEN WEEKS program. But here you are, continuing to open to what life's lessons are revealing about the Real, Authentic You.

IT IS POSSIBLE

It is possible I am pushing through solid rock
in flintlike layers, as the ore lies, alone;
I am such a long way in I see no way through,
and no space: everything is close to my face,
and everything close to my face is stone.

I don't have much knowledge yet in grief—
so this massive darkness makes me feel small.
You be the master: make yourself fierce, break in:
then your great transforming will happen to me,
and my great grief cry will happen to you.

—*Rainer Marie Rilke*

This powerful poem reminds us that the moment of transformation occurs when we are willing to feel our intense grief, which usually happens when we come face to face with reality. Then, in that moment of despair, *it is possible* that we can experience a genuine shift in the way we interact with life that makes facing the pain and feeling the suffocating loss completely worthwhile.

WEEK NINE WORKSHEET D

Facing the Loss Circuit Inspection Worksheet

? Take a few minutes to still the noise and defenses you may feel when asked to honor a personal loss and sit with your grief. What is your "great grief cry" right now? It is not important if it relates to retirement.

_____

_____

_____

_____

_____

_____

_____

? What "great transforming" is waiting to break in to your life? Are you willing to exchange your "great grief cry" for this "great transforming"?

_____

_____

_____

_____

_____

_____

_____

? How can your Authentic Money Guide facilitate this transformation in the coming days, weeks, months, and years?

_____

_____

_____

_____

_____

_____

_____

RETIREMENT—IMPORTANT CONSIDERATIONS

"We think our life is going to end in a grand finale. No one else's has, but we think ours will. We believe these daily tasks and strivings are leading to something. They're like strings that someday will come together to form a rope we'll climb to an important and splendid platform. "What did I accomplish today?" we ask ourselves. "What steps did I take toward my goal?" But the true question is: What did we forgo doing? Did we withhold judgment? Did we decline to attack?"

—Hugh Prather

First, consider the following Week Nine MAP Material:

MAP 9-1—Quick Chart of Social Security Retirement Benefits
Review this chart to better understand the retirement benefits to which you are entitled under Social Security. Note the age at which you are eligible to retire with full benefits.

MAP 9-2—Quick Chart of Social Security Family, Survivor, and Disability Benefits
This chart is similar to MAP 9-1, except that it summarizes family, surivor, and disability Social Security benefits. Note that the waiting period for disability benefits is five months, if you are injured severely enough to qualify in the first place.

MAP 9-3—Social Security Benefits as a Percentage of PIA
This chart helps one see how your family's benefits are structured, as a percentage of your full retirement benefit. Note that your spouse can receive 50 percent of your retirement benefit, or his/her own benefit—whichever is higher, once he/she reaches at least 62.

MAP 9-4—Applying for Social Security Benefits
Here's what you'll need to apply for Social Security. Run a What If scenario to analyze the impact of retiring at 62 vs. 66—you might be surprised. (Also see MAP 9-6) Several months before those eligibility dates, gather these items and apply.

MAP 9-5—When Will My Principal Balance Equal Zero?
This little chart shows how important withdrawal rates are on your money lasting. If you have $100,000 that you want to last 23 years and you plan to make 7 percent per year interest, you can take the $7,000 (interest) + $8,000 of principal for a total of $15,000 per year. You can see that it is critical to be realistic about how much you can count on from your savings during retirement. By the way—the above numbers are pretty optimistic and don't take into consideration the risk you would have to take to earn 7 percent in today's market conditions.

MAP 9-6—Early Retirement Considerations
Should you retire early? When should you apply for Social Security benefits—at age 62 or 65/66? This MAP addresses some of these questions.

MAP 9-7—Fear of Transformation

This essay, written by an anonymous source, helps to capture what the terror and amazement we feel in the "in-between" places of our lives.

MAP 9-8—Pension Maximization

This material helps explain one option for maintaining the highest possible pension benefit when coverage for a surviving spouse is a concern. In order to see if buying permanent insurance is cost-effective you can return to the Week Seven TEN WEEKS CD and follow the steps to obtain another life insurance quote.

MAP 9-9—Top 10 Nonfinancial Retirement Issues

This list provides a reality check before big retirement moves are made. As Wally might say, "Don't underestimate the importance of…the nonfinancial retirement factors!"

Next, pause to ground about the realities of retirement and integrate what you discover into your Authentic Money Guide by completing Worksheet E.

"Finally you understand that the real motorcycle you're working on is yourself."

—*Robert M. Pirsig,* Zen and the Art of Motorcycle Maintenance

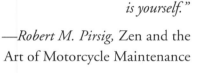

WEEK NINE
WORKSHEET E

Top 10 Ways to Prepare for Retirement

1) Consciously determine your definition of "retirement" and how it will look in your life, from this point forward.

2) Translate each of these phases of retirement into an estimate of financial costs. Consider the following phases and complete your own worksheet in Week Nine Worksheet F.

"I know a lot of men who are healthier at age 50 than they've ever been before, because a lot of their fear is gone."

—*Robert Bly*

Retirement Phase	Ages	Changes Affecting Budget
True Retirement	Now—Just Stop Once Each Week	Reduced weekly spending
Let's Practice	At Ages 62–65	1) Cut back to half time 2) Extra insurance costs 3) Extra travel costs
Full Go-Go	Ages 65–75	1) Work 500 hrs. per yr. 2) Travel even more 3) Qualify for Medicare 4) Medical out-of-pocket
Slow-Go	Ages 75–85	1) Stop working 2) One big trip each year 3) More medical 4) Gifts to family
No-Go	Ages 85–95	1) More medical 2) Stop driving 3) Home care 4) No big trips 5) Gifts to charity 6) Estate costs 7) Burial costs

3) Factor the above phases into your Authentic Money Guide, using the What If Scenario Analysis tool to test different options until the best mix is found. Follow along with Greg and Ginger's example on the Week Nine TEN WEEKS CD.

4) Find out about your Social Security benefits. Request a Personal Earnings and Benefit Estimate—See My Documents binder Tab 6.

5) Learn about your employer's pension and profit sharing plan or 401(k) and consciously determine your contributions.—See My Documents binder Tab 6.

6) If your employer doesn't have a retirement plan, or you are self-employed and have yet to start a retirement plan—pursue an establishment of a plan. See Week Eight, MAP 8-1 for Retirement Plan Options.

7) Contribute to an IRA. See Week MAP 8-2 through MAP 8-4 for detailed information about IRAs and Week Eight MAP 8-14 for contribution limits.

8) Invest your retirement savings wisely. Carefully choose a diversified portfolio of low-cost mutual funds as outlined in Week Six.

9) Build an Emergency Fund as outlined in Week Six and apply for a home equity line of credit to fund unexpected cash requirements, rather than withdrawing money from your retirement accounts.

10) Enjoy the Journey! Don't wait until you choose to completely stop working to enjoy the benefits of *true retirement*.

Week Nine
Worksheet F

Retirement Phase Worksheet

Refer to Week Nine, Worksheet E, for an example of how to complete this worksheet.

Retirement Phase	Ages	Change	Description	$ Amt.	To AMG*
True Retirement					
Let's Practice					
Full Go-Go					
Slow-Go					
No-Go					

*Create a new Authentic Money Guide scenario integrating these financial impacts. I recommend summarizing all items for each phase as a single entry. See Week Nine TEN WEEKS CD for guidance.

RETIREMENT CHOICES AND AN OUTLET BOX

(Diagram Component #9)
*** a flashback ***

"Wally, it seems like that electrical diagram you sketched for me the day you fixed my fan has become so imprinted in my brain that I am constantly trying to relate most everything in my life to one of those components of your system."

"That could pose quite a challenge. I didn't realize I was forming a new kind of philosophical framework." responded Wally as he walked from the deck railing to the wrought iron table where I sat.

"I tend to go overboard with my analogies, I'll have to admit—but it seems to help me to be more aware of the lessons that are trying to get my attention," I explained. "It seems to me that this whole idea of fantasizing about how great retirement will be, rather than enjoying the journey and the opportunities to rest along the way, comes back to 'plugging in' to an outlet box."

"You lost me, Paul. How do you equate this attitude toward retirement to an outlet receptacle?"

There just happened to be an outlet on the deck. Flipping up the protective cover, I pointed to the two outlets and began to explain. "I have a choice. Every day I can choose to 'plug in' and appreciate the ride or wait to 'plug in' by anticipating retirement. I think just noticing how foolish it is to wait, thinking that the energy will somehow have a better feel, will help me choose appreciation and happiness now rather than later."

"That's not so far-fetched after all," conceded Wally, eyes twinkling. "In fact, I think I'll also use it to remind me of my two options even if I am semiretired: Be Grateful and Filled with Wonder Now or Be Grumpy Waiting for the Good Life!"

We had a good laugh and then noticed that the sun had just lit up the Western sky, to a brilliant orange. What better time than now to plug in?

Why miss out on
happiness and rest now
by fantasizing
about retirement?

I'm ready to
"plug in" to
"true retirement"
now!

WEEK TEN

Will I...or Will I Not?
Your Mortality and Estate Plan

> *Week Ten focuses on death and its relevance to fully experiencing life. You will have had the opportunity to come face to face with your own relative acceptance or denial of death through an examination of your estate documents. You see what a generous gift you can give to your family, friends, and philanthropic organizations by organizing your financial affairs. The greatest gift of all, however, is the gift you give yourself and the world by living each day in alignment with your Authentic Self.*

THE DREADED PHONE CALL

"Paul, you have an urgent message," said Joanne, my office manager and receptionist. The sympathy and concern emanating from her voice, coupled with my intuition, told me what I was about to hear were the words I had been dreading for months. "We can't find Lollie!"

After 18 months of constant, excruciating back pain, untouched by surgery, medication, or treatment, Lollie, my mom, had finally given herself permission to end her suffering. The night before, Katherine and I had sat next to her where she lay on the couch, exhausted, fighting back her tears to avoid burdening us with her pain. This was not the ending to her story of self-reliance and giving to others she would have preferred. It was so very hard for her to feel worthy, to realize that her cries for help made us love her that much more. The fact that she needed to leave didn't buffer the intensity of the loss I felt those early days after her death.

NO CALL TODAY

"Did you get much snow today?
Remember feeding the cows with
Gomer and Bell…?"

"Not much here in town."
"…Sam dropped by—I
fed him a piece of apple pie—
"Fresh from the freezer!"

"Did you ever send anyone away
hungry, Mom?"

"My day?—Oh fine—
Busy—as Usual…
Working until 7 tonight…"
"Oh no—didn't get there 'til 7."
Now—
just the silence.

Oh, for some "small talk"
just a chance
to hear your voice.

Even if you never felt
like you deserved
more than two minutes—
maybe three.

If you only knew—
if I could have known, too,
the wonder of your voice—
expressing your love,
so soothingly.

All grown up—
a half century
to harden…
Mom—I didn't want
to break open—this way

Through your loss
leaving me longing
for your voice—
That three-minute call.
"We only got an inch
of snow today."

It had not gone according to plan. She was the one who would outlive all of us all—walking the ranch, at least five miles a day—as fit at 70 as most people at 35.

At age 14, she, along with her sister, dutifully shepherded her father's flock of sheep in the Colorado summer range, near timberline. Many nights the girls were awakened by the sounds of bear chasing their charges. Each time, they faced the bear attacks and prevailed. How could this woman's life end so broken, so completely disarmed by the body's frailty?

I, too, was not ready for what this loss would reveal about my own life. Mom's sudden death placed me face to face with what I had been able to avoid for 46 years. Who was this son for whom she had sacrificed so much of herself to bring into the world? Did I honor her by ignoring the voice of my Authentic Self?

WHO AM I?

The dingy white snow
reluctantly releases its grip
on the dark brown earth…
A bright yellow daffodil
bursts through.

This snow blanket—
Oh, cold and dark—but what
a protector from having to
break through to life's terror!

So many seeds
so much longing…
tiny ones carefully planted
in fertile soil at birth.

Breaking through, only to be
viciously choked by weeds
of deception—leafy and green,
adorned with beautiful crimson thorns.

Season after season—
perennials—these invaders—
Make this blanket of cold
seem like my best friend.

Oh, Great Sower—
Wise Discerner of True and False,
if I surrender and break through this cold blanket
into the Light—Save Me!

For my garden is almost lost—
and only You know my Name.

—Paul Lemon

I write the last pages of this book as the third anniversary of her death approaches. The agonizing days of grief will never completely vanish, but they have nurtured in me a journey toward something much more real than I had known before. My mother's death gave me an opportunity for rebirth. This book, I earnestly desire, is a very small gift back to her and to this world from that new beginning.

Mom's physical deterioration and suicide reminded me that death comes on its own terms, refusing to ask our opinion or cooperate with our sense of timing. Mom's pain consumed her. There were so many things she could have done to alleviate the suffering of her children after her death—but she didn't. The state of her estate resulted in broken relationships and unnecessary waste of money, time, and energy—so much damage that may never be repaired. I experienced, firsthand, the urgency to get our financial affairs in order, to establish an estate plan in alignment with our core values, before having to face the uninvited crises and answer the untimely knock of suffering and death on our door.

THE MOTHER OF ALL DELUSIONS

"Of all the world's wonders, what is the most wonderful?
That no man, though he sees others dying all around him,
Believes he himself will die."

—Bhagavad Gita

In Week Seven, the Insurance chapter, we took a look at the mind-set of a person who thought that buying insurance was an invitation for a dreaded occurrence to happen. It's possible that, even unconsciously, we have this attitude of *predictive avoidance* toward estate planning or getting our financial and legal affairs in order. "As soon as we finish our wills and durable powers of attorney we believe we are doomed to find out that we have cancer and three months to live.

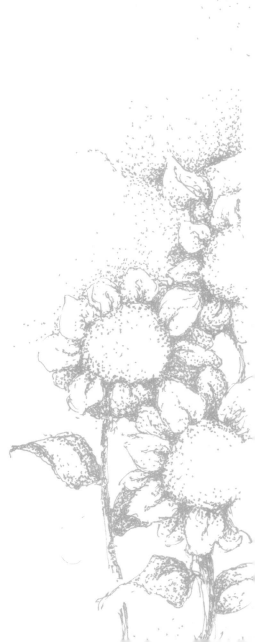

"What a wonderful life I've had! I only wish I'd realized it sooner."

—Colette

In a "Money Matters" program entitled, *Two Sure Things—Death and Taxes,* my guest was Steve Rickles, a practicing tax and estate-planning attorney in Denver, Colorado, with whom I have had the pleasure of working for more than 10 years. Steve offered this insight on clients who had faced their mortality by doing a thorough job of estate planning:

> *"These are not easy issues to deal with, and clients have a lot of fear to overcome before they can really address them. But I find that if they're not addressed, clients have a sense of unfinished business. When they do acknowledge mortality by talking about these issues, they really have a sense of relief and it can open up communication within the family and reduce some of the games that come with secrecy and money issues. Once that communication process is opened, people realize that this process is only partly about money, it's really more about relationships than anything else."*

Estate planning, then, is about honoring relationships by admitting that our death will have a tremendous impact on those we leave behind. We give a generous gift upon our death by allowing our loved ones to grieve rather than be distracted by the uncertainties of their financial situation. Financial uncertainty and lack of clarity about what the decedent really wanted can cause our survivors to languish in the decedent's business rather than move on with their lives in a wholesome way. If we could understand that putting our legal estate planning documents in order is a ticket to a healthy grieving process for our loved ones, we may be more motivated to give this part of our lives precise attention. Could you say this?

Because I grounded with my mortality and did what I could to conduct my affairs prior to my death, I have given my loved ones a ticket to:

➤ resist isolating;

➤ honor my loss without feeling the need to inflate or minimize my death;

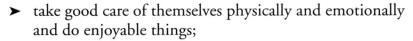

➤ take good care of themselves physically and emotionally and do enjoyable things;

➤ journal, read books about coping with grief, write poetry, paint, throw pottery, attend church, reach out with a helping hand to someone else who is suffering;

➤ plan events to look forward to like dinner with a friend, a weekend trip, etc.;

➤ plant something living as a memorial to memories that will never die;

➤ feel permission to change things and rearrange a room, or give some of my things away; and

➤ put off major decisions.

Hopefully my estate planning will make this possible.

"I don't want to get to the end of my life and find that I lived just the length of it. I want to have lived the width of it as well."

—Diane Ackerman

WEEK TEN
WORKSHEET A

The State of My Affairs? Circuit Inspection Worksheet

? Upon your death, do you feel your loved ones will have a ticket to process their grief with minimal distractions from your *financial residue?*

_____

_____

_____

_____

_____

_____

? If you could enclose the ticket we've discussed with a note to your immediate family and to your dearest friends, what would the note say?

_____

_____

_____

_____

_____

_____

_____

_____

_____

_____

? Steve Rickles said this process of facing mortality and getting documents in order "can open up communication within the family and reduce some of the games that come with secrecy and money issues." Are there points in what you just wrote that could help facilitate this kind of communication? How can you initiate a conversation with one or more of these people?

_____

_____

_____

_____

Complete the following chart as an initial inventory of where you stand with your personal estate planning. Refer to your My Documents binder Tab 15 for Estate Information. Monthly or quarterly account statements filed in the My Authentic Money Guide binder can be reviewed for ownership information requested in Steps 5–8.

➤ Numbers refer to steps to take in completing this table.

➤ Start by printing out a current Net Worth Report from Quicken® and titling it "Legal Ownership of Assets." Use this report to record information requested in steps 5–8:

Estate Document Inventory for_____

Document	I Don't Have It	I Have It	Dated*	Need to Change?**
Will (1)				
Durable Power of Attorney(2)				
Advanced Health Care Directive(3)				
My Documents Binder (4)			NA	
Joint AC List(5)			NA	
Beneficiary List (6)			NA	
Living Trust (7)				
Other Trusts (8)				

*Date legal document was signed

** Are you aware of any changes in your life that would require this document be updated? e.g. divorce, death of a spouse, marriage or remarriage, change in desired executors or trustees, birth of a child, adoption, relocation to a new state, inheritance, or other large influx of money.

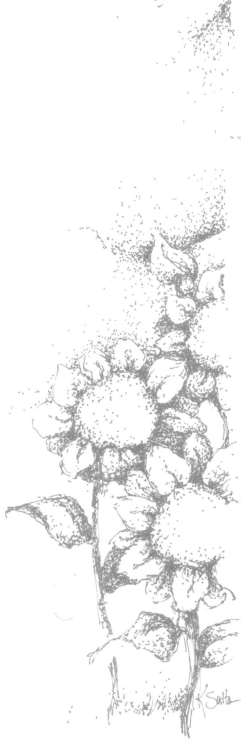

Step-by-Step Directions

1) See MAP 10-5 for a summary of the functions of a will.

2) See MAP 10-11 for an explanation of a durable power of attorney as well as documents that facilitate health care and personal decisions in the event of a coma or incompetence.

3) For information about the Five Wishes Document, contact *www.agingwithdignity.org* (or call 1-888-5-WISHES). This living will document is legally valid in all but 15 states: Alaska, Alabama, Oregon, Nevada, Utah, Kansas, Oklahoma, Texas, Wisconsin, Indiana, Ohio, Kentucky, South Carolina, Vermont, and New Hampshire. The Five Wishes Document costs $5, and it can effectively replace a 'living will' that communicates your end-of-life life care and support decisions in plain English. I highly recommend this document.

4) A complete My Documents binder organizes critical documents in one place, making it much easier for survivors to file for insurance claims, etc.

5) See MAP 10-12 and MAP 10-13 for explanations of joint tenancy. Accounts in joint tenancy are immediately available to the surviving joint tenant. Can you easily identify which assets on your most recent Quicken® Net Worth Report are titled in joint tenancy?

6) All assets with beneficiary designations pass directly to the surviving beneficiary. Can you indicate on your Net Worth Report who is the primary and contingent beneficiaries for all life insurance policies, IRAs, 401(k)s, annuities, pension plans, and other tax-deferred retirement accounts (403(b)s, 457s, etc.?

7) See MAP 10-17 and MAP 10-18 for explanations of revocable living trusts. It is critical that a revocable living trust be funded or that assets actually be titled in the trust name. Are all assets titled in the name of your revocable living trust identified as such on your Net Worth Report?

8) Trusts simply provide for directions to a trustee as to how assets in that trust are to be managed for the benefit of the trust beneficiary. Identify on your Net Worth Report any assets owned by another trust, separate from a revocable living trust mentioned in step 7.

What response below best describes your feelings at this point?

❑ *I haven't taken care of these things very well. It has nothing to do with my unwillingness to deal with my mortality. It is just one of those things that gets pushed to the side because life is so hectic.*

❑ *I admit it—I am very uncomfortable just looking at this list of documents and the decisions they ask of me. I don't like thinking about when I want someone to "flip the switch" and end my life if I've been in a coma for so many days. It's difficult talking about who will take responsibility for certain things when I'm gone. It just reminds me that my life is so "disposable" and that in a short period of time I'll be forgotten. I do resist this process.*

❑ *I have done the basics but see how important it is that I "clean house" and finish putting things in order. I just want to deal with this and get on with my life.*

❑ *There is a combination of things going on with me. There's no doubt that I have some reluctance to face my mortality, incompetence, and whatever else may come knocking on my door, but I think it's more that these decisions are so important and deserve some really serious thought. It's not something you can just knock out after dinner. Maybe the place to start is to start with MAP 10-2. If my partner and I can discuss this successfully, then maybe we can set aside a weekend or a Saturday to put some thought into what we really want, using the other MAP materials as a crash course in helping us understand our options.*

Take a moment to read this brief quote from Sy Safransky and jot down any thoughts that come to mind afterward.

"I'm dying. We're all dying. It's only the dead who are no longer dying, who have all the time in the world. Here among the living, the days never seem quite long enough. So we drink that extra cup of coffee, drive a little faster, skip the foreplay. There are only so many minutes in an hour, and it's the same no matter how important you are, even if you're the president, even if you think you're the president of your own little life."

—Sy Safransky

_____

_____

_____

_____

_____

_____

JUST WHAT YOU NEED—NO MORE, NO LESS

My dad always said, "If only one cow comes in to the feed ground, you don't unload the whole wagon of hay." In this section, I hope to provide just enough estate planning information for you to apply to what you need. I'll identify several "herds" of folks with similar estate planning needs. Hopefully, you'll feel right at home with one of those groups.

As you may have noticed, there's a pretty big load of "hay" on the wagon in the MAP section for this Week. Consider each of the MAP sections sections as a "bale" of estate planning that may or may not apply to you.

Our first step is to identify the bales and the second is to unload those bales based on your particular needs. In the final step, I will assist you in breaking apart those bales so they are easier for you to digest i.e. understand.

PART ONE—THE ESTATE PLANNING "BALES"

MAP 10-1—Quick Facts on Estate Planning

This resource gives you an overview of the estate planning process and the impact of estate tax laws on how detailed your planning needs to be. This MAP includes estate and gift tax tables to help you see the changes in the exemptions over the next few years. Just remember—estate planning is for everyone—no matter how much money you have.

MAP 10-2—Questions to Answer Before You See an Attorney

The "people" questions comprise the most significant component of the estate planning process. Who will be guardian for

your minor children, executor (personal representative) for your will, holder of your durable power of attorney? Who do you want to get what—and when?

MAP 10-3—Types of Wills

"If you've seen one will, you've seen them all," couldn't be further from the truth. Read this MAP to gain an understanding of what type of will best suits your needs at this point in your life.

MAP 10-4—What Happens Without a Will

If you want to complicate the lives of your family and loved ones unnecessarily after you die, don't bother drafting a will. Now that you know what can happen, you have the opportunity to prevent the involvement of the courts in their lives.

MAP 10-5—Functions of a Will

A nutshell summary of what your will should do.

MAP 10-6—What a Will Cannot Do

Just remember that your will has no power to direct assets that have a beneficiary designation (IRAs and other retirement accounts, and life insurance policies) or that are held in certain types of joint tenancy. See MAP 10-7 and MAP 10-13 for more detailed information.

MAP 10-7—Direct Transfers

This resource expands on what I mentioned earlier about IRAs and life insurance not being controlled by a will. If you understand this relationship between wills and direct transfers, you will have moved to the top 10 percent of your Estate Planning 101 class.

MAP 10-8—Tips on Handling a Will

We all wonder what to do with our estate planning documents and what happens when we move to another state. Here are some pointers.

MAP 10-9—Probate

You havel heard horror stories about how a person's estate was tied up in probate for years and left the survivors without the basic necessities of life. A good portion of those stories are told by estate planning attorneys that would like to sell you a living trust. Avoiding probate should not keep you awake at night— there are simplified procedures as long as you have a sound

will, durable power of attorney, and living will. Review this MAP to better understand the probate process and then read MAP 10-10.

MAP 10-10—Avoid Probate and Save?—Maybe Not

Before deciding to use a living trust or transfer assets to a non-spousal joint-tenant, read this MAP.

The comment about avoiding probate by transferring property into joint tenancy and incurring capital gains taxes simply means that if you leave a nonspouse property in your will, he/she gets a "stepped-up basis" for that asset. When he/she sells that asset, he/she can use its value at your date of death to determine whether or not he/she has a gain on the sale that would be subject to a 15 percent federal capital gains tax.

On the other hand, if you put his/her name on the deed as a joint tenant while you are living, you are supposed to file a gift tax return to document the transfer. When you die, he/she gets a "step up in basis" for the value of your half interest (even though the entire property value is included in your taxable estate). When the property is sold, there will be a capital gains tax due on the difference between the net sales price and the two components of the cost basis—the value of half of the property on the date of your death, and the actual cost of the property to the decedent (that's you).

As you can see, it is important that you don't get overly concerned with probate avoidance and make serious mistakes.

MAP 10-11—Planning for Illness and Disability

Important decisions still need to be made if you are suddenly incapacitated in an accident or from a disease. The types of powers of attorney are explained in this MAP, as well as documents that will communicate your wishes about life support and nourishment in the event you fall into a coma for a specified period of time. I highly recommend you use the Five Wishes Document to accomplish this latter goal (*www.aging-withdignity.org*) if this form is legal for use in your state (as outlined in this Week's text material).

MAP 10-12—Common Forms of Co-ownership

This summary is a great resource in evaluating how to hold property with a partner, spouse, or other co-owner. For estate tax minimization, remember the importance of avoiding joint-tenancy ownership since the decedent could easily end up wasting his/her estate tax exemption as explained earlier in this Week's text. See MAP 10-13 for further explanation.

MAP 10-13—Disadvantages to Joint Tenancies

Exercise caution before titling assets in joint tenancy. If you have assets (including life insurance) of less than $1 million, then joint tenancy ownership with a spouse is usually appropriate. Make sure to read this MAP, however, to understand the risks of this form of ownership.

MAP 10-14—Community Property and Asset Ownership

Congratulations if you live in one of the nine community property law states! You get to read this MAP to see the importance of asset ownership with yet another wrinkle—community property law. Don't pick up and move, however. It's simpler to read this MAP and take any necessary action.

MAP 10-14a—Basic Structure of Estate Plans for Married Couples

This is required reading for all married readers who have assets in excess of $1 million. You will gain a good understanding of how estate planning trusts can help you not only pay less estate tax, but administer assets in complex family structures. Refer to MAP 10-15 and MAP 10-16 when reading this MAP.

MAP 10-15—Flowchart of Basic A-B Trust Planning Structure

The A-B Trust arrangement allows the surviving spouse access to all the assets, without subjecting them to estate taxation at his/her death. Please keep in mind that the assets in the B Trust (which represent the value of the current estate tax exemption) cannot be distributed to the surviving spouse for needs other than health, education, support, and maintenance. This "ascertainable standard" rule is critical, and violation of it results in all the assets being included in the survivor's estate—invalidating the purpose of the 'B Trust'. Read this MAP in conjunction with MAP 10-14a.

MAP 10-16—Flowchart of Basic A-B-C Trust Planning Structure

The A-B-C Trust is commonly applied to those with children from a prior marriage. The C Trust provides for the surviving spouse for a certain period of time and then is distributed to the decedent's (i.e. person who died) heirs. Read this MAP in conjunction with MAP 10-14a.

MAP 10-17—Trusts

Trusts are nothing more than documents that instruct how a certain basket of assets are to be managed and distributed. This short primer will help you understand the people/parties involved in a trust.

MAP 10-18—Types of Estate Planning Trusts

It is important to understand the distinction between a testamentary trust and an inter-vivos (while living) trust. Many estate planning trusts are authorized in a person's will but not actually established until they die. The costs to administer these trusts are generally lower than the costs for a living trust.

MAP 10-19—Irrevocable Life Insurance Trusts

If you own large life insurance policies, you may want to consider an ILIT. Read this MAP to review the advantages and disadvantages and then weigh the likelihood of either an estate tax repeal or exemption increase—making such planning unnecessary. You also need to consider when your life insurance will expire, if you have purchased a term policy. If you still determine you need an ILIT, consider material earlier in this Week's text as to costs for establishment.

MAP 10-20—Comparison of Various Types of Transfers to Minors

Don't be too overwhelmed by the technicality of this chart—focus mainly on the "termination of guardian/fiduciary relationship" section. When transferring assets to minors, it is important to consider when they have the right to those assets. Beware of the distribution and tax limitations of each of your transfer options before making the transfer. Also consider MAP 10-21.

MAP 10-21—UGMA/UTMA Transfers

Please keep in mind that these accounts result in the minor receiving the money in the account at either age 18 or 21—depending on the laws of your state. Also consider the impact of these accounts on college financial aid. Generally, Section 529 Qualified Tuition Plans provide a better vehicle for funding college. See MAP 8-18 for more information on QTPs. Visit *www.savingforcollege.com* for specific 529 plan information on a state-by-state basis, including the possibility of converting UGMA/UTMA accounts to a 529 Plan.

MAP 10-22—Lifetime Gifts and Annual Exclusion

One easy way to avoid potential estate taxes is to give money away during your life. Just so people can't avoid all estate tax, there is a ceiling as to how much money you can transfer to one individual each year. Currently, that annual exclusion is $11,000. Direct payments of tuition and medical costs don't count toward this limit. Keep in mind that these rules do not apply to transfers of property between spouses—you can give all you want to one another, unless your spouse is not a full U.S. Citizen.

MAP 10-23—Transfers at Death vs. Lifetime Gifts

This MAP reminds you that there are advantages of not waiting until you die to give your money away to charity. It also makes sense to avoid the income tax to your heirs on retirement assets by leaving them to a charity that doesn't have to pay income tax. For example, if you leave a $100,000 IRA to your son, who is in a 30 percent tax bracket, he will only have $70,000 left after paying the income taxes. On the other hand, if you left that IRA to a charity, they would have use of the full $100,000. Just by choosing which asset goes to whom, you redirect $30,000 away from the U.S. Treasury!

MAP 10-24—Charitable Gifts and Bequests

Use this MAP if you need advanced estate planning tools and want to benefit charity, while at the same time helping your cash flow. By establishing a CRT, you can avoid a capital gains tax on a sale of property that you may need to fund your retirement by donating the remainder interest of that property to charity and retaining a life interest.

If I own a $100,000 piece of land that currently provides me no income, I could donate it to charity in exchange for a lifetime income stream. As long as I gift at least 10 percent of the value of the property, the IRS will give me some charitable deduction as well. By doing this, I avoided having to pay a $15,000 capital gains tax and am benefiting a charity I like.

Note especially the section here on conservation easements. Some states offer conservation easement credits against state income tax, making such donations even more attractive. See *www.landtrust.org* for more information. (Once on the site, select "protecting natural land" and then "conservation easement.")

MAP 10-25—Estate Tax Planning with Life Insurance

Review this MAP for ideas on how to save estate tax by transferring life insurance policies.

MAP 10-26—Unmarried Couples Should Consider Living-Together Documents

This is a critical MAP for those of you in this situation. I've found that dealing with these issues in an adult manner can take a lot of stress off the relationship, as difficult as the discussion may initially be.

MAP 10-27—Helpful Estate Planning Articles

Consider these articles that are written in plain English that will answer other important estate planning questions. Visit this section of *www.tenweeks.com* each month to see what new articles apply to your situation.

MAP 10-28—What Is the Federal Estate Tax?

This MAP provides a clear explanation of how the estate tax works. After reading this, you will understand what is included in your taxable estate, what deductions are allowed, and how the estate tax credit or applicable exclusion amount works.

MAP 10-29—What is the Federal Gift Tax?

The gift tax and estate tax are combined for certain calculations and differentiated for others. Please note that the estate tax deduction is currently scheduled to increase over the next six years (until 2009) to $3.5 million, whereas the gift tax exclusion is capped at $1 million. Failure to understand this distinction could result in serious tax consequences.

PART TWO—
IDENTIFY YOUR ESTATE-PLANNING "HERD" AND "BALES"

"Herd"	Life Characteristics	MAP Reference #("Bales") MAP 10-( )
1. Single (1)	No children or Partner Net Assets < $1 Million**	1–11
2. Married with Minor Children (1)	Children Under 21 Net Assets <$1 Million** No Community Property State	Same as Group 1 + 12, 13, 14a, 17, 20, 27
3. Single (2)	No Children or Partner Net Assets >$1 Million**	Same as Group 1 + 17, 18, 19, 22, 23, 24, 25, 28, 29
4. Married with Minor Children (2)	Children Under 21 Net Assets >$1 Million** No Community Property State	Same as Group 2 + 15, 16, 18, 19, 20 21, 22, 23, 24, 25 ,27, 28, 29
5. Single (3)	Have a Partner Net Assets >$1 Million**	Same as Group 3 + 12, 13, 26
6. Married Without Minor Children	No Minor Children Net Assets >$1 Million** No Community Property State	Same as Group 4 without 20, 21
7. Married Without Minor Children— Community Property	No Minor Children Net Assets > $1 Million** Live in Community Property State	Same as Group 6 + 10, 11, 12, 13, 14

Supplemental Information to the Above Chart—Critical Information for All Groups

1. ****'Net Assets'** for estate planning purposes can be calculated as follows:

   Fair Market Value of All Assets Owned $_____

   - Less: Outstanding Balance at Death of All Debts   <_____>

   + Add: Death Benefit of Life Insurance*   _____

   + Add: Gifts Made to Individuals in Excess of $10,000/Year
     ($11,000 if gift was made in 2003 or after)   _____

   Net Assets for Estate Planning $_____

*Please remember that the full face value of life insurance is taxable in your estate upon your death (MAP 10-25). If, for example, you own a $1 million term life insurance policy that currently does not show up on your Quicken® Net Worth Report because it has no cash value, that $1 million would have to be added to your Net Worth statement to calculate your estate tax liability upon death.

The exception to the above rule is when the insurance policy is owned in an irrevocable life insurance trust, as explained in MAP 10-19. There is a tricky three-year rule you need to understand about existing life insurance policies, so don't shortcut reading this MAP.

2. **Please Also Refer to the Federal Estate and Gift Tax Tables in MAP 10-1, MAP 10-28, and MAP 10-29.**

   You will note that under current law, the amount of net assets a person can own at his/her death without his/her heirs having to pay estate taxes reverts back to the 2002 exclusion amount— $1,000,000.

   Even though it is probable that the exclusion will remain higher than the $1 million level in 2011, there is no guarantee at this present time.

   Please note, however, that for deaths between 2004–2010, current law increases the exemption. In 2011, as noted in the preceding paragraph, the old 2002 exemption is reinstated.

   MAP Materials 10-15 through MAP 10-25 outline several techniques for minimizing estate tax liability.

   It is critical to remember that a married couple has an unlimited marital deduction" which simply means that even if they own $10 million in assets, there is no tax due when the first spouse dies. The problem with this unlimited deduction is that many times the first spouse to die fails to take advantage of the $1 million exemption.

   If, in the prior scenario, the husband died first and had no assets in his name at his death, there is a potential loss of estate tax exemption of the $1 million to which he was entitled. For this reason, it is important to put assets in each spouse's name. Please see MAP 10-14a for more explanation of how a "credit-shelter trust" is used to protect the $1 million from estate taxes—forever.

3. **Do you need to hire an attorney, or can you use a "do-it-yourself" will kit?**

   My advice is to hire an attorney to assist you in drafting accurate and thoughtful estate documents that will have no legal problems in the state in which you live.

   If, however, you want to try and prepare your own will and basic legal documents, there are several software programs that will guide you through the process. Start by testing your basic estate planning knowledge by taking the "Make a Will Quiz" at

www.msn.com, then click "Planning," then "Retirement and Estate," then from the Decision Centers Section, click on "Plan Your Estate," then "Make a Will Quiz."

If you pass the test with flying colors, then proceed on your own. You most likely can draft an accurate set of documents if you carefully follow all the instructions to a current legal forms software package that incorporates the laws of your state of residency.

Otherwise, if you would rather employ an attorney to prepare your estate planning documents consider the following ideas:

Talk to family and friends to see if they have an estate-planning attorney they can recommend. An attorney that works for a family member will have a conflict of interest in working for you, but at least she/he can refer you to another qualified attorney.

➢ Review MAP 10-2 for issues you will want to clarify before employing an attorney to draft your documents. Further reading can be found on at *www.tenweeks.com* referenced in MAP 10-27— Estate-Planning Articles, and at *www.msn.com*, "12 Easy Steps to Preparing Your Estate Plan" and "Not a Millionaire? You Still Need an Estate Plan."

➢ Contact a TEN WEEKS advisor™ by clicking on the Advisor Referral Link at *www.tenweeks.com*. Ask this person for a referral to an affordable, qualified estate-planning attorney near where you live.

If an attorney suggests you establish a revocable living trust, ask about the extra cost of that service over a will with contingent trust or a tax-saving will (See MAP 10-10 and MAP 10-11), coupled with a durable power of attorney.

Living trusts do not save estate taxes and can be an unnecessary complication. (See MAP 10-10) You can get help with making an informed decision by asking your attorney of the specific advantages there are for the additional costs. If you are still unsure, contact a TEN WEEKS Advisor™ for an opinion on the matter before any documents are drafted or fee agreements are signed.

PART THREE
ESTATE PLANNING—DIGESTING YOUR ESTATE PLANNING "BALES"

Find the *herd* with which you share most in common and use the narrative comments to help you understand the MAP materials that apply to your situation.

Group 1: Single, Without Children, Assets Under $1 Million

As for all groups, your main goal is to provide financially for your family after your death, but you also want to minimize financial and legal distractions so your survivors are free to grieve your death. Consider the following:

➤ Execute a simple will that will distribute your assets to those you want to benefit from them.

➤ Make sure your beneficiary designations on your IRAs, pension plans, other retirement accounts, and life insurance policies are reflective of to whom you want those assets to go.

➤ Discuss your intentions with these people. They may prefer that you will your assets to your favorite charity because of the high income taxes that become payable upon receipt of your assets. For example, a $10,000 IRA left to someone in a combined federal/state income tax bracket of 40 percent would leave them with $6,000 after tax. If that money were left to charity, the full $10,000 would be used to fund your intentions.

➤ Complete the Five Wishes booklet in place of a formal living will, unless you live in one of the 15 states outlined earlier. Order your copy from *www.agingwithdignity.org* for $5.

➤ Execute a durable power of attorney to grant someone you trust with the ability to conduct your financial affairs if you become incapacitated.

➤ Make sure your My Documents binder contains all your current documents. Also complete Week Ten Worksheet B, "Where to Find What in the Event of My Death or Incompetency."

Group 2—Married Couple with Minor Children —Net Assets Under $1 Million

➤ Start by completing all the steps outlined for Group 1 except the creation of a simple will.

➤ Review MAP 10-3—Most likely you will want a will with a contingent trust unless you have strong feelings about a living trust, then you will need a pour-over will.

➤ MAP 10-12 helps explain the importance of how you title your different assets. Section Two under the "Critical Information for All Groups" section above outlined the importance of each spouse owning assets to take full advantage of the estate tax exemption. With the uncertainty of estate tax law, protecting the use of the exemption is important.

Even when estate taxes are not an issue in planning, fairly sophisticated planning tools are often required to deal with mixed families and large variances in age between spouses.

Consider the following example:

If you title an asset "joint with rights of survivorship," when you die, the survivor who is listed on the title will own 100 percent of that asset, no matter what your will says. Compare that method of titling to the ownership of this asset as "50/50 tenants in common"—when you die, only 50 percent of the asset would be owned by the survivor, and your 50 percent share would be distributed under the terms of your will.

See MAP 10-12 and MAP 10-13 for a detailed explanation of co-ownership options. In order to deal with a situation in which there are children from a prior marriage that a spouse will want to help support after his/her death, consider a QTIP trust as illustrated in MAP 10-16. The QTIP is the C Trust in the illustration.

➤ MAP 10-20 and MAP 10-21 explain several ways of gifting assets to your children. Review Week Eight, MAP 8-15 and MAP 8-18 to review Qualified Tuition of Section 529 Plans. If gifting is done for college funding purposes, the 529 plans are preferable to the custodial account transfers described in MAP 10-21.

Even if your child decides not to go to college, the funds in the 529 Plan can be returned to the parent or other donor, providing income taxes and a 10 percent penalty tax are paid on any distributed earnings. The effect of the taxes and penalties are minimized the longer the funds are allowed to grow tax-free in the 529 Plan.

➤ If, after legal consultation, you decide to set up a revocable living trust (MAP 10-18), make sure you follow through and transfer assets into the trust. An "unfunded" trust is one that was established and signed but has never received any assets. It's as if the trust was never established if no assets are titled in the name of the trust.

➤ In the event you have a parent or child that is receiving public assistance in the form of Social Security Disability or Supplemental Security Income (SSI), a special needs trust may be a helpful tool. As long as certain guidelines are followed, distributions from such a trust will help improve the quality of the beneficiary's life without disqualifying him/her from public assistance.

Group 3—Single with No Children or Partner and Net Assets Greater than $1 million

➤ Start by completing the steps outlined for Group 1.

➤ Review the comments about Holding Title—MAP 10-12—under the Group 2 section.

➤ In the event you are concerned about management of your financial affairs in the event of death or incompetency, consider the advantages of a living trust as outlined in MAP 10-18.

➤ To minimize estate tax exposure consider the strategies outlined in MAP 10-22 through MAP 10-25. Weigh the advantages and disadvantages of implementing these techniques with the uncertainty of estate tax laws.

For example, if you make a large transfer to a CRT (MAP 10-24) in order to save estate taxes and the estate tax is repealed in 2011, you may regret your decision. Visit with your attorney, CPA, or TEN WEEKS advisor™ about these issues.

➤ If you are considering the purchase of a life insurance policy and already have a taxable estate, consider setting up an irrevocable life insurance trust and having the trustee of that trust purchase the policy. As is explained in MAP 10-19 you make a gift to the trust each year to pay the life insurance premium. Since you don't own the insurance directly, the death benefit is not included in your estate when you die.

A simple ILIT should not cost more than approximately $500–$750 to establish. Consider purchasing a term life insurance policy that can be converted to a permanent insurance product once estate tax laws become clearer. Often times, insurance is used to pay estate taxes so that more of the estate is available for intended heirs.

Group 4—Married Couple with Minor Children and Net Assets Greater than $1 Million

➤ Start by completing the steps outlined for Group 2.

➤ Review the effect of different planning tools in MAP 10-14a, MAP 10-15 and MAP 10-16. Remember that the credit shelter trust is what is referred to as a testamentary trust—or a trust created by your "last will and testament"—as compared to a revocable (changeable) living (created and funded while you are living) trust. A credit shelter trust can be created and then left inactivated until after you die. Because the estate tax credit varies from year to year under current tax law, no one will know how many assets to put into that trust until the credit amount is established at your date of death.

Two things must be done during your lifetime to make a credit shelter trust work upon your death:

1. Your will must use the language that activates this trust at death. This type of will is commonly called a tax-saving will.

2. You must have assets in your name at the time of death that can be funneled into the trust through your will. If all your assets are held in joint tenancy with right of

survivorship and you die first—before the other owner, or "tenant"—you will own no assets at death and your credit shelter trust will not work.

➤ Refer to the fourth bullet of Group 5 pertaining to lifetime gifts. Annual cash gifts that do not exceed the annual gift tax exclusion are the easiest way to reduce a person's taxable estate. Don't forget to consider the nonfinancial impacts of such gifts on the donees.

➤ Another area of estate planning utilizes estate freeze techniques. This is just a term that is used to describe planning efforts to remove appreciating assets from a person's estate so they do not accrue additional estate tax exposure.

The Family Limited Partnership (FLP) is commonly used to accomplish this goal. (Please see MAP 7-22 and 23 for FLP information.) Consider this illustration of how a FLP works:

If Greg and Ginger were facing an estate tax problem, they might decide to transfer their rental house into a family limited partnership. They could give Gil, their son, a portion of the value of the property each year in the form of a limited partnership interest, while maintaining control of the management of the partnership through retaining a general partnership interest. After several years of gifting, using the $11,000/year annual gift exclusion, they could help "freeze" their estate by transferring some of the property's appreciation to Gil. While Gil would own some of the rental, he would not have a say about how things were managed since he only owns a limited partnership interest.

When Greg and Ginger died, the rental house would not be valued at its full sale price less the outstanding balance of the mortgage. Because its ownership is in the form of a FLP, the IRS discounts the value of the asset by 20–40 percent, depending on what portion Greg and Ginger still owned at the time of their deaths. (These discounts are commonly referred to as lack of marketability and minority-interest discounts).

Be forewarned, however, that such arrangements can result in unpleasant family disputes if limited partnership rules are not clearly understood by all parties.

➤ Finally, refer to MAP 10-24. One-way charitable trusts work well if if you owned stock that had grown tremendously in value. If you sold that stock today, you would have to pay a large capital gains tax of 15–20 percent (depending on your state income tax rate) on the difference between the sales price and what you paid initially for the stock (your tax basis).

Rather than selling the stock, you could gift it to a charity in exchange for an annual income stream for the rest of your life or for a certain period of years. If you want a fixed payment each year, the arrangement is called a charitable remainder annuity trust (CRAT). If you want the payment to be a certain percentage of the value of the assets remaining in trust each year, the arrangement is called a charitable remainder unitrust (CRUT).

Not only do you avoid having to pay capital gains taxes on the sale of the stock, you get a charitable income tax deduction for the value of the "remainder interest" that you leave to the charity (see MAP 10-24 for a description of this split interest). The final advantage is no estate tax on this asset at death, unless the payments continue on to the heirs of the donor.

Group 5—Single Person with a Partner, Net Assets Over $1 Million

➤ Start by completing the steps outlined for Group 3.

➤ Refer to MAP 10-26—"Unmarried Couples Should Consider Living-Together Documents." After reading this, talk to your attorney about your wishes to determine whether he/she has experience drafting the documents you want.

➤ Read the third bullet-point for Group 2 regarding joint tenancy and asset titling. Decide if the use of joint tenancy makes sense in your particular situation.

➤ Refer to MAP 10-22. Gifts made to someone other than a spouse in excess of $11,000 reduce the donor's estate tax exemption.

To illustrate, consider the impact of a 2003 cash gift from Greg to Gil in the amount of $21,000. The $10,000 portion of this gift in excess of the allowable annual exclusion would have to be reported to the IRS using Form 709-A—Annual Gift Tax Return. No tax would be due the IRS when Greg files this return. The filing would simply notify the IRS that Greg's unified gift and estate tax exemption of $1,000,000 had just been reduced by $10,000 to $990,000. At Greg's death, assuming he were to die after Ginger, any net asset value in excess of the $990,000 would be subject to estate taxation

To avoid the reduction of his exemption, Greg could have simply given Gil $10,500 on December 31, 2003, and another $10,500 on January 1, 2004. Structuring the gift in this manner would have eliminated the need to even file a gift tax return.

(The full $21,000 could have been transferred to Gil in 2003 had Ginger elected to participate in the transfers. Please See MAP 10-22 for further information about married couple gifting.)

A question commonly asked is, "If I've been given a gift, do I have to report it on my income tax return?" The answer is no. In our example, Gil would not report the $21,000 on his income tax return.

Group 6—Married Couple Without Minor Children with Net Assets Greater than $1 Million

➤ Please follow the step-by-step instructions for Group 4.

➤ Information pertaining to MAP 10-21 may apply to gifts to grandchildren, even though they are excluded as pertinent on our Age/Stage/Asset Group Chart. Pay careful attention to the benefits of utilizing an IRC Section 529 Plan, as explained in the fourth bullet of Group 2.

Group 7—Married Couple Without Minor Children with Net Assets Greater than $1 Million Who Live in a Community Property State

➤ Please follow the instructions for Group 6.

➤ Read MAP 10-14. As you can see from the example, the manner in which title is held in a Community Property State (i.e. one of ten states detailed at the top of this MAP resource) can make a significant difference in capital gains taxes paid when a property is sold.

Find the Feelings

What a maze! But now you have given these critical issues your attention and have discovered that you had to shift into a very analytical mode in order to understand the legalese and how it all would apply to your particular situation.

In order to gradually reconnect with your feelings about your own death, complete the next worksheet. Try and focus more on your feelings rather than the actual information being requested as you complete what may be the most important document you leave for your family and loved ones.

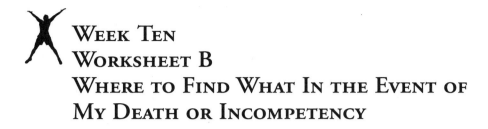

WEEK TEN
WORKSHEET B
WHERE TO FIND WHAT IN THE EVENT OF
MY DEATH OR INCOMPETENCY

Personal Information

My Legal Name: _____

My Social Security Number: _____

My Mother's Maiden Name: _____

My Father's Name: _____

My Service as a Veteran: _____

Child 1 Name: _____ Date of Birth: _____

Child 2 Name: _____ Date of Birth: _____

Child 3 Name: _____ Date of Birth: _____

Child 4 Name: _____ Date of Birth: _____

Child 5 Name: _____ Date of Birth: _____

Child 6 Name: _____ Date of Birth: _____

Child 7 Name: _____ Date of Birth: _____

Child 8 Name: _____ Date of Birth: _____

What and Where

See My Documents binder for a current listing of all documents that will summarize my financial affairs.

? This notebook is located:

_____

_____

_____

? A summary of my current financial condition is located in My Authentic Money Guide binder, which is located:

_____

_____

_____

? I do / do not (circle one) have a safety deposit box. If I do, it is located:

_____

_____

and the key to that box is:

_____

_____

_____

? My original will is located:

_____

_____

_____

? My passport is located:

_____

_____

_____

? My durable power of attorney is located

_____

_____

_____

? My Five Wishes Document/living will is located

_____

_____

_____

? The following people, with their phone numbers, have been given copies of my will, durable power of attorney, and/or living will:

Name	Telephone
Name	Telephone
Name	Telephone
Name	Telephone
Name	Telephone
Name	Telephone

The People I Want to Know About My Death

Please contact the following people. I have listed their phone numbers and email addresses, if they have one:

Name	Telephone	email
Name	Telephone	email
Name	Telephone	email

Name	Telephone	email
Name	Telephone	email
Name	Telephone	email
Name	Telephone	email
Name	Telephone	email
Name	Telephone	email
Name	Telephone	email
Name	Telephone	email
Name	Telephone	email
Name	Telephone	email
Name	Telephone	email

The People "In the Know" You May Need to Talk to

The doctor who took care of me:

_____

Name   Telephone

The attorney who drew up my will:

_____

Name   Telephone

My accountant and financial planner/advisor:

_____

Name   Telephone

My insurance agent(s)/type of insurance for each:

_____

Name   Telephone

_____

Name   Telephone

My investment manager or stock-broker:

_____

Name   Telephone

My banker:

_____

Name   Telephone

My minister or spiritual advisor:

_____

Name   Telephone

Other people with critical information:

_____

Name   Telephone

_____

Name   Telephone

_____

Name   Telephone

How I'd Like to Be Remembered

I would like my service to be held at:

_____

_____

_____

I would like for my body to:

_____

_____

_____

I would like the following to occur at my memorial service:

_____

_____

_____

_____

_____

_____

_____

_____

I would like to make sure the following people know these things:

_____

_____

_____

_____

_____

_____

_____

_____

_____

_____

_____

Final thoughts and wishes:

_____

_____

_____

_____

_____

_____

_____

_____

_____

_____

_____

ALL KINDS OF RICHES

Despite all the aches and pains, one day we'll finally comprehend how lucky we were to be living in these bodies on this Earth. Do you remember Nicholas Cage and Meg Ryan in the movie "City of Angels"? The angels, if capable of envy, long for the wonder of our ability to feel love and sorrow, pain, and pleasure. To feel a hand on our shoulder…

"Happy Birthday, Dad. It's been so many years since I've felt your hand on my shoulder. Maybe it's been there all along, guiding me. Here, among the living, we speculate endlessly about such things. Our pictures have all the subtlety of a point-by-numbers kit, but that's the best we can do. Is there anything you want to tell me about the city of the dead? Are you wiser now? Are you happier? Do you still get together with your friends on Friday nights to play pinochle, or did you leave all that behind, like your job, your wife, your daughter, your son? I'll leave it all behind, too, won't I? Everything that's so important to me now, everything I can't imagine living without. Just as, once, I couldn't imagine living without you."

—*Sy Safransky*

What will we leave behind when we die? Will we look back and treasure those precious moments of embrace as one of the greatest gifts of our mortal life?

What is it, if anything, that we can send ahead—not in the sense of accumulating something for ourselves or gaining some kind of special standing—but in using our money and awareness of our mortality to cultivate our Spirit Nature?

"Take care! Protect yourself against the least bit of greed. Life is not defined by what you have, even when you have a lot. Then he told them this story:

"The farm of a certain rich man produced a terrific crop. He talked to himself: 'What can I do? My barn isn't big enough for this harvest.'

"Then he said, 'Here's what I'll do: I'll tear down my barns and build bigger ones. Then I'll gather in all my grain and goods, and I'll say to myself, 'Self, you've done well! You've got it made and can now retire. Take it easy and have the time of your life!''

"Just then God showed up and said, 'Fool! Tonight you die. And your barnful of goods—who gets it?'

"That's what happens when you fill your barn with self and not with God...

"...Be generous. Give to the poor. Get yourselves a bank that can't go bankrupt, a bank in heaven far from bankrobbers, safe from embezzlers, a bank you can bank on.

"It's obvious, isn't it? The place where your treasure is, is the place you most want to be, and end up being."

—*Jesus, Luke 12,* The Message.

Part of giving money our complete attention allows us to see what it can and can't do. So far in TEN WEEKS, we've seen that it *can* teach us a great deal about our tendencies: how we pretend we don't need help, typically look to our bank accounts for feelings of adequacy and self-worth, deny our frailty, ignore our limits and capacities as well as our responsibility to others, deny our culpability for investing in companies that harm the world and its people, and—finally—assume we will get to use all our money before we die!

"Save your money, die rich."

—*American*

Money can do something else: it can facilitate finding the place where you are truly content—"the place you most want to be."

If I really believe these fleeting days of my life are not the end of the story, then wouldn't it make sense to use my money in a way that is consistent with that belief? Rather than translate our preoccupation with bank balances (protecting what is mine) to the life beyond, isn't the real point of this teaching that our relationship to money is possibly the most powerful tool in helping us realize and find "the place we most want to be"—right here and now. Using our money and finding that place will not only give us the happiness and meaning we want in this life, but will automatically prepare us for the unknown beyond our death.

WEEK TEN
WORKSHEET C

"I'll Leave It All Behind..."

? Can you recall a personal "near-death" experience? How did it impact your life then and how does it now?

_____

_____

_____

_____

_____

_____

_____

_____

? Reading Sy's writing, what riches of this human life have you failed to fully appreciate?

_____

_____

_____

_____

_____

? How do you want to be remembered?

_____

_____

_____

_____

_____

? In what ways can your money facilitate finding "the place you most want to be?"

_____

_____

_____

_____

? Are there ways your Authentic Money Guide can be adjusted to help you integrate these ideals into your day-to-day life?

_____

_____

_____

_____

AWAKENED BY DEATH

ENDGAME

> *Death pushed me to the edge.*
> *Nowhere to back off.*
> *And to the shame of my fears,*
> *I danced with abandon in his face.*
> *I never danced as free.*
>
> *And death backed off,*
> *the way dark backs off*
> *a sudden burst of flame.*
> *Now there's nothing left*
> *but to keep dancing.*
>
> *It is the way I would have chosen*
> *had I been born*
> *three times as brave.*
>
> —*Mark Nepo*

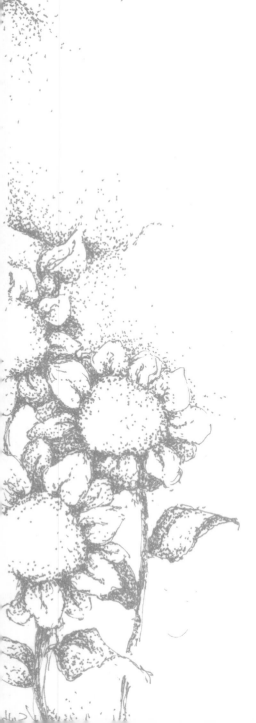

Intellectually, we know how brief our lives will be, but without going to the brink of death it is difficult to fully appreciate the significance of that fact.

One of my "Money Matters" radio shows, entitled "For Freedom We Are Here," explored mortality. After attentively facing the realities of our circumstances, we access a new-found energy and begin to experience freedom. Beneath the noise, compulsion, and worry manifested in our individual circumstances, our inner voice continues to speak to us. The clarity of that voice and how it resonates in our daily experience is amplified many-fold by a personal face-to-face encounter with death.

Mark Nepo was my guest on that show. Mark faced death by cancer twice and was allowed to return to life. I love how author Wayne Muller, Mark's lifetime friend, described Mark's journey in the foreward of Mark's book, *The Book of Awakening*:

> *"Mark had cancer, and it shook him awake. His descent into illness gave birth to an astonishing mindfulness. Now, he invites us to use his eyes and heart to see and feel how awake our being alive can be. Having survived his cancer, Mark brings with him the eyes of a caring person who is grateful simply to breathe. But more than gratefulness, he brings wisdom, clarity, kindness, and a passionate enthusiasm for sucking the marrow out of moments, out of the bones of time. If you ache to live this way, Mark is your guide."*

Those of us who have yet to experience the shivering touch of death desperately need guides to realize "how awake our being alive can be." I believe that with such teachers and simple daily disciplines, we can truly awaken to this quality of life. Rather than avoid those who suffer, we embrace the lessons of their experiences and, if we are mindful of those lessons, our perspective is altered.

Though used earlier in the book, I'll share one of Mark's poems again. We had an opportunity to talk about it on the radio show:

PRACTICING

As a man in his last breath
drops all he is carrying

each breath is a little death
that can set us free.

I asked Mark what he felt we tend to carry with us that gets in the way of our freedom. He responded, "We have the capacity, if we take the risk, and if we truly try to be present in this life, to start fresh every moment. It doesn't matter what mistakes we've made, it doesn't matter how we've misperceived things. We can, like that man, drop whatever it is that gets in our way.

"One of the biggest [obstacles to freedom] centers on our ego and our willfulness and our want to control life, which is not controllable. Another is our self-centeredness—seeing the world with us as the sun, as the center of the universe. Often, what happens is the rest of the world will simply not reveal itself to us. If you look in a lake it mirrors back everything until you wait long enough for it to get still enough so you can see through to the bottom. If we don't wait, then everything we look at in the world mirrors back us. We think, 'That's the world.'"

"The only important thing is liberation—people should not be attached to the means."

—Zen Master Yuanwu

By now, each of you has seen how this analogy applies to money. If we wait long enough, staring into the details of our finances, suddenly we see the truth rather than our distorted beliefs about money. We see the difference between our actual behavior and our Authentic Self.

"Like technology, money is used wrongly when it converts inner questions that should be lived into problems to be solved. Money fixes things, but not every difficulty in life should be fixed."

—Jacob Needleman, Money and the Meaning of Life

It's easy to spend $500–$2,000 on a thorough estate plan—pat yourself on the back—and continue to live as if you are immortal. There is definitely a huge benefit for your family in that they will not have a mess to deal with after you prove your mortality. You will have gifted them with the opportunity for a healthy grieving process and fulfilling life rather than a nightmarish financial fiasco. The tragedy, however, is that you could miss out on a splendid opportunity to drop what you are carrying and set yourself free. You could

use that estate-planning experience to access what Mark discovered—a spirit *suddenly awakened to how deep the life—how short its stay…* (Mark Nepo, *Inside the Miracle*)

Your Authentic Money Guide reflects your steps toward Awakening. The pattern you have set for yourself to regularly give money your attention and to see how it mirrors your interaction with life will have a great impact on your ability to live Authentically. But I believe you also need to nurture your spirit with a regular diet of Soul Food, not easily purchased in the marketplace. It's so easy to fall back into old patterns of trying to force money and people into making us happy, safe, and secure. We must continue to look for ways to nourish our "deep life" and to stay connected to the power source that empowers our efforts.

Author Bo Lozoff captures succinctly in words what might be our ultimate goal, as well as some critical elements that each of us needs in order to journey in alignment with that longing for a deep life:

> *"Rumi said that life is as if a king has sent you to a country to perform one special task. If you go there and accomplish a hundred other things, but not that one particular task, then it's as if you've accomplished nothing at all. What is the task?*
>
> *"All the sages tell us that we've come into this world to realize God. Buddhists, of course, would not say "God" but "Buddha nature." Or they might say that the task is to become fully awakened.*
>
> *"There are three fundamental rules that all the wisdom traditions say will help us accomplish our task, if we follow them.*
>
> *"The first is to be cautious about materialism—Don't want too much. Live modestly.*
>
> *"The second is to dedicate yourself to something you believe in, something you think is beautiful and important.*
>
> *"The third is to commit yourself to a personal spiritual practice that you can follow every day, even if just for a few minutes. Devote some part of your day to sitting in silence and saying, 'Here I am. Guide Me.'"*
>
> —Bo Lozoff, *interview in* The Sun *magazine*

The point of estate planning is not to prepare a whole stack of legal documents to exonerate yourself from feeling guilty for not fulfilling your responsibilities to your family. Neither is it the point of TEN WEEKS to create a meticulous financial management system so you can be free to cram something else in your life.

At least one part of our motivation for doing all this work is to direct our energy to Rumi's three fundamental rules, as stated above: be cautious about materialism, dedicate yourself to something you believe in, and commit yourself to a personal spiritual practice that you can follow every day. It is then we begin to live Authentically. After all, if we don't offer our unique gift to the world, it's as if we have "accomplished nothing at all."

TRANSFORMERS AND MORTALITY

Wally's diagram reminds me of the importance of my daily conversation with my mortality. He explained to me that the transformers "step" down power to safe levels for each particular distribution system:

Transformers
(Diagram Component #4)
*** a flashback ***

"The next stop along our electrical journey is the transformer," said Wally.

"Transformers are used to obtain the right voltage for the operation of a circuit or system. High voltage transmission lines are deadly unless the voltage is adapted to a safe and usable level. The high voltage is necessary to push the energy efficiently over long distances. Once the power, however, has arrived at its destination, a transformer must step down the voltage to a level manageable by local distribution lines. The local distribution lines are also then transformed to a safe voltage that can be used at our local businesses or homes."

"You mean that 'more is better' isn't always the case?" I asked.

"Well, Paul, plugging your shaver directly into a high voltage line might solve your need for a daily shave, but that's probably not what you had in mind!"

"No. I think I'd rather endure the daily agony of that electric shaver using 110V than a thousand-volt hair removal treatment!"

In my conversation with Mark Nepo, I caught a glimpse of how suddenly we can come face to face with death. As mortals in bodies of quivering protein, we struggle to remember that the essence of our Authentic Self is Spirit. I think of the transformers as a metaphor for the force that limits the level of energy that I am ready to receive.

The more I stop taking life for granted, I finally "get" this miracle of life. As I cultivate an appreciation of this ever-so-delicate combination of oxygen, nourishment, flesh, blood, bones, soul, and Spirit into a living being, I cannot help but sense that life is much more than a physical existence. The feelings I have as I remind myself daily that "today, I could die" helps me gauge my connection to the energy flow that transcends such physicality: Am I disconnected from the energy source, or am I limiting the flow through my attachment to my comfortable, predictable transformer?

Just as there are hundreds of sizes of transformers in an electrical system that match the energy level with the capacities of different delivery systems, I believe I restrict or expand my capacity for different levels of energy by the soulful choices I make. If I honor my depth through the practical alignment of my choices with my values, I experience an increased flow of energy. It's as if I hook up to a 220 volt-rather than a 110-volt transformer. The energy is boundless. My happiness and fulfillment is limited only by my openness to it.

"Here I am, still struggling with my passions, my fears. 'Lord,' Saint Francis prayed, 'make me an instrument of thy peace.' But do I need to become more tranquil to be 'an instrument of they peace?' Birth was a struggle; life is a struggle; dying will probably be a struggle, too. Maybe one way to be an instrument of peace is to honor the struggle, to recognize the dignity in the struggle. The sun is a never-ending source of light, yet it's burning."

—Sy Safransky

My task is not to regulate the energy that sustains my fragile life—

mine is to open fully to its precious gift one day at a time.

I'm more able to do that as I 'stay' vs. 'leave' with my mortality.

Section Four

The Process: Keep the Energy Flowing.
Grounded and Moving to Groundlessness:
Money and Happiness

Section Four lists each component of the TEN WEEKS program and its place in using money to reconnect to your Authentic Self. The conclusion explains the interrelationship between groundedness and groundlessness. Happiness and fulfillment can be found in cultivating both qualities into your daily experience through continued attentiveness to your Authentic Money Guide. A new pattern of living has been established, and the exciting journey has just begun.

Starry, Starry Night

"I want to know if you know how to melt into that fierce heat of living, falling toward the center of your longing."

—David Whyte, from Self Portrait

It was an unforgettable night. Jane, Wally, Katherine, and I sat in front of our backpacking tents staring up into the immense star-lit sky.

"Does being grounded lead to this?" I asked, lost in my longing for a sense of myself as I witnessed such vastness.

"I'm no authority, Paul, but I believe that when we surrender to the flow of energy by grounding, there is a transformation of consciousness into groundlessness. In that place, there is no separation, nothing to protect, simply the wonder of finally resting in our essential nature—Spirit."

"I can hear Paul already," Katherine responded. "Wally said, 'Don't forget the importance of groundlessness!'"

"Maybe it will at least provide a bit of relief from 'Don't forget the importance of being grounded,'" Jane jokingly added.

"There's no doubt in my mind that Katherine's destiny is to keep me grounded if it has anything to do with humility. I think I can really get into this groundlessness idea. It may mean that I can transcend reacting."

As I spoke those words, I glanced into Katherine's beautiful brown eyes and saw the reflection of the flickering fire. I was reminded how blessed I was to have such a companion. Despite the banter, I knew how meaningful these philosophical and psychospiritual explorations were to her as well. Even though we processed things differently, our final conclusions were similar.

In my momentary but precious connection with Katherine, I felt a wave of surrender come over me, in which I believe I experienced the meaning in Wally's answer to my question. "In that place there is no separation, nothing to protect, simply the wonder of finally resting in our essential nature—Spirit."

I realized that in that place of groundlessness, I could actually, all joking aside, find freedom from my reactions and methods of protecting myself. My separate identity needed those efforts, but my Authentic Self did not. In that moment of deep insight, I laughed.

"What's so funny, Paul," Jane asked. "I thought for a minute there you had checked out on us!"

"Inner peace is beyond victory or defeat."

—*Bhagavad-Gita*

"Oh, I just couldn't help but laugh when I thought how my journey of awakening began—cursing that little fan!"

"I'm glad that Gracey's chewing mania resulted in all of this, rather than your house catching fire," Wally replied.

At the sound of her name, Gracey walked over to Wally and placed her head in his lap. It was a picture-perfect ending to a beautiful day.

THE GROUNDING PARADOX

"When your life is filled with the desire to see the holiness in everyday life, something magical happens: ordinary life becomes extraordinary, and the very process of life begins to nourish your soul."

—*Rabbi Harold Kushner,* Handbook for the Soul

Wally started out reminding me of the importance of being grounded. His electrical diagram illustrated no energy could flow without a completed circuit. My pausing to notice was the equivalent of the ground wire communicating with the power source, the load on the system. Then, and only then, would the lights come on.

I had learned money groundedness involved engaging both with the "What?" and the "Why?" of each aspect of my finances to see how my behaviors aligned with my Authentic Self.

Grounding, pausing to notice what is really happening, is definitely not *conventional wisdom.* We have been told that "multitasking" is the way to cope with the dizzying pace of change in our lives: knock out a few phone calls on the cell phone while driving—eat fast food on the road—make sure you have a wireless connection so you can keep working, even on your vacation.

Who has the time to give precise, careful attention to mundane details such as

"No appointment, no disappointment."

—*Swami Satchidananda*

actual spending vs. budgeted spending, much less whether or not individual financial transactions align with personal Authenticity?

Stopping to ground—acknowledging what load exists by giving our attention to these details—is the key to not only a meaningful life, but to our ability to offer our unique gifts to the world.

Wally reminded me, paradoxically, that in slowing down to engage with the brick-and-mortar details of our lives, something else could happen. First, we were given the opportunity to embrace life full of uncertainty and surprises. Second, we could begin to experience this state of groundlessness in which outcome becomes insignificant compared to the paramount importance of our particular interaction with each moment of life: It's the journey, not the destination that really matters.

One of the outcomes we can easily become attached to is our belief systems.

We can become so certain that our perspective is right. In an effort to gain some sense of solidity, we forfeit the connection with the unknown that grows only out of our willingness to "melt into the fierce heat of living."

SELF-PORTRAIT

"It doesn't interest me if there is one God or many gods.

"I want to know if you belong or feel abandoned.

"If you know despair or can see it in others.

"I want to know if you are prepared to live in the world with its harsh need to change you. If you can look back with firm eyes saying this is where I stand.

"I want to know if you know how to melt into that fierce heat of living, falling toward the center of your longing.

"I want to know if you are willing to live, day by day, with the consequence of love and the bitter unwanted passion of sure defeat. I have been told, in that fierce embrace, even the gods speak of God."

—*David Whyte, from* Fire in the Earth

There is not much tolerance for this kind of "self-portrait" in today's world. One engaged in this "fierce embrace" of Authenticity pays little attention to the superficiality of the "you are what you consume" mantra. The system protests, "How dare you say, 'This is where I stand?—Don't you know you won't fit in and no one will like you…?'"

"We put our truths together in pieces, but you use nails, and I use glue. You mend with staples. I mend with screws. You stitch what I would bandage. Your truth may not look like mine, but that is not what matters. What mattes is this: you can look at a scar and see hurt or you can look at a scar and see healing. Try to understand."

—*Sheri Reynolds*

Cultivating this fierce embrace relationship with life is contrary to our tendency to build our castles and then wall out all the risks that threaten us. In the "Money Matters" interview, David Whyte described the exposed approach as a sea crossing;

> *"I think the image of a sea crossing for life is a very accurate one because you not only cannot tell where you are going to arrive on the horizon exactly, but as you look behind you, you cannot tell exactly where you've come from.*
>
> *"You see your glittering wake for a while, but then it disappears into the large formlessness of the vast ocean through which you've traveled. There's something about the way that your seamanship actually depends on the way you inhabit the vessel. It depends on your alertness and your sense of immediacy to the quite fierce elements that surround you at any one time."*

A Calculator and a Mirror—All in One!

At the beginning of the book, I said that financial planning can easily beget yet "another form of money suffering" unless our attention to money results in directed energy toward our Authenticity.

With a completed Authentic Money Guide, financial decision-making is not just achievable but somewhat enjoyable. Now you are equipped with a tool to evaluate the financial impacts of life choices, as well as having the experience of grounding with those choices long enough to see what it is you really want.

So, how could this financial planning lead to another form of money suffering? The answer is simple: this can happen when we only use our Authentic Money Guide's calculator functions and forget its mirror functions.

Let me explain:

Recall Gary Snyder's words quoted in the first video, *"You must first be on the path before you can turn and walk into the Wild."*

Each of you has done the amazing work of clearing a path. Your records are organized, budget balanced, insurance risks optimized, investment portfolio rebalanced, income taxes minimized, and estate documents executed. It feels good to have given each of these aspects of money your complete attention. In order to "be on the path," all this needed to be done. It would have been quite an impossible task had we not learned to use the calculator functions of your Authentic Money Guide as facilitated by your mastery of Quicken®.

But if you glance back through your TEN WEEKS TO FINANCIAL AWAKENING book, you will realize that more than half of your work has been in learning how to see the reflection of your Authentic Self in the money mirror. That's what all those Circuit Inspection worksheets helped you practice. That's why the margins are adorned with quotations and soulful artwork by Katherine Sutton. That's what that candle or small image next to your computer is all about—learning to use the money mirror to see your Soul.

You possess a new tool, your Authentic Money Guide, to ground the two critical pieces of your nature—mortal and immortal—into your everyday life experience. That tool comes with those two essential functions—calculator and mirror.

"Money is congealed energy, and releasing it releases life's possibilities."

—Joseph Campbell

Most all of us are blessed with two hands that we find extremely handy in our daily functioning. But very few of us are ambidextrous. Ask a "lefty" to throw a baseball from third to first base with his/her right hand and the game's score will soon be quite lop-sided. You get the point. We're much better using the calculator than the mirror.

The mirror function of your Authentic Money Guide reminds you that the point of finding the "path" is to periodically leave it, for the wild. Our energy must be directed toward our unfolding journey as Spirit-beings or we soon "trade one brand of money suffering for another." It's not enough to use the TEN WEEKS process to make efficient, savvy financial decisions. The program's intent is to help us all become more ambidextrous with money. Now you know how to look into the money mirror and see what is really happening in your life.

THE IN-BETWEEN STATE

What I have found to be a real challenge is to pay close attention to what crosses my life's path, interact with those people and experiences fully, and then forget about what it all means. It's easy for me to get side-tracked and try to find some solid ground, even if it involves thinking that I've figured out how to be free or Authentic. I'm not comfortable with just letting things be and settling into groundlessness.

Pema Chödrön captures the essence of groundlessness in her book, *The Places that Scare You—A Guide to Fearlessness in Difficult Times:*

> *"We are told about the pain of chasing after pleasure and the futility of running from pain. We hear also about the joy of awakening, of realizing our interconnectedness, of trusting the*

openness of our hearts and minds. But we aren't told all that much about this state of being in-between, no longer able to get our old comfort from the outside but not yet dwelling in a continual sense of equanimity and warmth…

Dwelling in the in-between state requires learning to contain the paradox of something's being both right and wrong, of someone's being strong and loving and also angry, uptight, and stingy…

Holding the paradox is not something any of us will suddenly be able to do. That's why we're encouraged to spend our whole lives training with uncertainty, ambiguity, insecurity…

It's important to hear about this in-between state. Otherwise, we think the warrior's journey is one way or the other; either we're all caught up or we're free. The fact is that we spend a long time in the middle. This juicy spot is a fruitful place to be. Resting here completely—steadfastly experiencing the clarity of the present moment—is called enlightenment.

My intention for writing this book was simple: show how money could help rather than hinder our longing to speak in our own true voice. I believe there is a way to experience fulfillment rather than suffering in our relationship to money by looking at it as a mirror to our Authenticity, rather than as a means to be safe, secure, and happy in the world.

Let's go back through TEN WEEKS and summarize each of the individual components of this program and how they combine to produce a functional and fulfilling relationship with money and further our quest for Authenticity.

MONEY AND "THE MIDDLE"— A PATHWAY TO HAPPINESS AND COMPASSION

➤ **Section One: "The Lesson from Electricity"—Wally's Electrical Diagram:**

Power is restored when I flip the ground wire switch on. I do this by "staying" with my discomforts rather than "leaving" with a financial fix.

I can pause to ask what need I am trying to fulfill by my actions rather than mindlessly chasing my wants and attempting to mask my discomfort with fixes. This practice includes honestly noticing when I resort to familiar patterns of "leaving."

"To laugh often and much; to win the respect of intelligent people and the affection of children; to earn the appreciation of honest criticism and endure the betrayal of false friends; to appreciate beauty and find the best in others; to leave the world a bit better whether by a healthy child, a garden patch, a redeemed social condition; to know even one life has breathed easier because you have lived—this is to have succeeded."

—Ralph Waldo Emerson

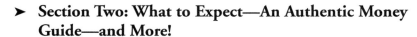

➤ **Section Two: What to Expect—An Authentic Money Guide—and More!**

I am building a new, grounded relationship with money. I know it means establishing an entirely new system, but it's worth the effort.

Taking the time to create a financial plan grounded to my genuine longings frees me from constantly being distracted by "money noise." This new framework for financial decision-making is built on the foundational premise that each aspect of my financial life can serve as a tool for expressing my Authentic Life.

> *"And as we let our own light shine, we unconsciously give other people permission to do the same. As we are liberated from our fears, our presence automatically liberates others."*
>
> —Marianne Williamson

Rather than clinging to my Authentic Money Guide as a source of security (i.e., using solely its calculator functions) I see this fluid document as a reminder of the dynamic nature of my journey. I know that happiness will come only as I pay close attention to life's lessons and integrate them into my financial decisions by pausing to look into my Authentic Money Guide mirror.

➤ **Weeks One and Two: Your Money Inventory—Notice & Get Involved**

An honest inventory, admitting my need, connects me to an abundant energy source.

Having the courage to face "what is" and ask myself how that aligns with what I say is important to me, helps me acknowledge how hard it is for me to reconcile the two. Admitting this helps me open up to my need for help, both from a Higher Power and from other people.

Financially, I choose to keep my Authentic Money Guide current so I am reminded of my need.

➤ **Week Three: Your Spending and Budget—What Is It You Really Want?**

Meaningful living is a process of aligning my daily choices with my Authentic Self.

I tap into real freedom when I can say *Yes* or *No* to my money desires based on an understanding of this key question. Rather than using spending as a way to escape, the Authentic Money Guide and its related budget becomes a vehicle of translating intent into action.

> *"The real function of a spiritual friend is to insult you."*
>
> —*Chogyam Trungpa Rinpoche, as quoted in* The Places That Scare You, *by Pema Chödrön*

Any teacher is to be welcomed on my journey toward awakening. It's so easy to deceive myself that a gentle, honest conversation with my Budget Buddy is extremely helpful in noticing when I return to seeking solid ground.

My financial budget keeps me from straying too far off-course from my Authentic Self. I need that kind of anchor.

➤ **Week Four: Your Work: Work Woes**

Authentic work rests comfortably on a three-legged stool.

Energy flows when I work Authentically, i.e. when I'm involved with my whole heart, cooperatevely participating with others, and working for meaning, not just money.

When I'm grounded, my work is meaningful; when I'm not, it's stressful.

As I begin to wean myself from the "I am what I do" identity trap, there is freedom to develop a more balanced relationship with work. The suffering I create by operating out of fixed concepts of self and then trying to maintain them, gradually becomes easier to notice.

When I cling too desperately to work, my Authentic Money Guide helps me see how many options I have in honoring the "one life I can call (my) own." (*All the True Vows*—David Whyte)

> ### Week Five: Your Credit Cards and Loans—Friends or Foes?

I am willing to acknowledge my limits as well as my capabilities. In doing so, I accept the full flow of power which I am currently capable of carrying—no more, no less.

Accepting my limits and living accordingly is presented as an option each time I pull out a credit card. Grounding in this aspect of money opens me up to the groundlessness of living in harmony with my Authentic Self, other human beings, and nature. I honestly face all the debts, which I can mindlessly incur.

I also have the chance to notice when I hoard money out of fear or an illusion that I can protect myself from pain and suffering with more money. My spending can then help me cultivate generosity and a groundless "non-clutching" relationship with money and my possessions.

> ### Week Six: Your Investments—Money Working You or Money Working for You

Aligning my investments with my Authenticity results in powerful returns. I'm no longer satisfied with economic performance alone.

An examination of how my investment management strategies have gradually become misaligned with my genuine values provides a practical way to reconnect with the power I've been missing.

Looking within for well-being rather than do the daily stock report is one indication I'm shifting toward groundless-ness. I see my willingness to moderate my expectations and not expect "something for nothing" as another indication that my TEN WEEKS work is helping me grow up.

Investment phobias provide an early warning detection system that I am no longer aligned with a genuine power source.

➤ **Week Seven: Your Insurance—Risky Business**

I can embrace or shun my human frailty. Acceptance sees interruptions as gracious protection from destruction rather than as bothersome annoyances.

The disruptions, inconveniences, and painful reminders of my human frailty that once caused me so much frustration can now be reminders that I desperately need "circuit protection." Forcing my agenda only burns me out. Groundlessness grows out of my willingness to smile at my impatience and sense of invincibility.

"Fearlessness is the first requisite of spirituality. Cowards can never be moral."

—*Mohandas Gandhi*

As insurance issues surface, I have the opportunity to ground and be grateful for each breath and blessing, fully aware that I carry no right to some kind of special immunity from the storms of life.

➤ **Week Eight: Your Tax Liabilities—More than Paying Uncle Sam**

When I make grounded "social dues" choices I experience a fulfilling transmission of energy. It feels good to connect with others and try to make the world a better place.

The responsibility I have as a citizen to society can be treated as a dreaded liability or an opportunity to reflect/act on how I would like to connect with others in making the world a better place. Active citizenship provides for a practical expression of groundlessness through the belief that no expression of genuine concern is ever wasted.

Tax planning can now be motivated by a new compassionate attitude: "My community/world awareness matters" and not just "More money for me matters."

"Kindness in words creates confidence. Kindness in thinking creates profoundness. Kindness in giving creates love."

—*Lao-tzu*

> **Week Nine: Your Retirement Dream—Is the Grass Really Greener?**
>
> *Why miss out on happiness and rest now by fantasizing about retirement? I'm ready to "plug in" to "true retirement" now.*

Cultivating contentment by staying grounded with the present and calling my busy mind back to the here and now gives me back my life, both now and through retirement. After doing what planning I can, I still realize the future is uncertain. I can choose to be grateful for each precious moment and proceed with happiness.

The losses I have experienced can embitter or transform my outlook on life. I realize that chronological age doesn't automatically translate into wisdom and happiness, so my responses really do matter.

> **Week Ten: Your Mortality and Estate Plan—Will or Will I Not?**
>
> *My task is not to regulate the energy that sustains my fragile life; mine is to open fully to its precious gift, one day at a time. I'm more able to do that as I stay vs. leave with my mortality.*

Fear of death is a major source of suffering for me. Cultivating more comfort with my mortality goes hand in hand with seeing my essential groundless or Spirit Nature.

Talking to my family and loved ones about my feelings and wishes—knowing I will die—gives me an opportunity to cultivate my Awakening to both compassion and whatever lies beyond this mortal veil.

"The Indians long ago knew that music was going on permanently and that hearing it was like looking out a window at a landscape which didn't stop when one turned away."

—*John Cage*

"Everything else can wait, but the search for God cannot wait. Love one another."

—*George Harrison, last words*

Just the Beginning

It may be 10 or 12 weeks, maybe even three years, from when you first purchased TEN WEEKS TO FINANCIAL AWAKENING and started this journey of honoring your own voice. Who ever thought that your money could be such a valuable ally in the most critical process of all?

By now, you have established a new pattern of thinking and living in the world. They say that an automatic physical response takes one thousand repetitions to establish. I know that you have practiced grounding at least 10,000 times if you've finished the work outlined in this program. I believe these repetitions of giving money your attention, rather than your energy, will facilitate you offering the gift that no one else can offer.

"Perhaps enlightenment is simply taking the hand of your love, the hand of your life in commitment, in a kind of faith. That you would rejoin with the frontier explorations, confrontations, conversations, encounters of your existence. And in that conversation, everything would make sense again, wherever you are on the trail."

—David Whyte, "Clear Mind, Wild Heart"

*"That which God said to the bloom
And caused it to laugh in full-blown beauty,
She said to my heart
And made it a hundred times
more beautiful."*

—Rumi

Your Authentic Money Guide mirrors the way you are "taking the hand of your life." The scenarios you explore tell you so much more than simply the financial ramifications of certain choices. Each what if analysis gives you the opportunity to ask what longing prompts the question. How will your decision, and its integration into your updated Authentic Money Guide, serve as a tangible expression of your willingness to open rather than close to your authenticity? How will your decision cultivate compassion rather than judgment? In what way does your decision enhance your intention to serve all creation rather than demand service?

Finally, money has taken its proper role in your life. Your Authentic Money Guide becomes your real-life journal of how you are seeking to align your actual behavior to your Authentic Self. Your financial decisions are tangible markers of the resolve you have to speak out in your own voice. All creation awaits in anticipation and delight to hear that completely unique sound. The echo you hear inside reminds you that this, indeed, is your greatest treasure.

THE STRIPPING OF OUR WILL

Like the silk that keeps the corn shiny,
all our delicate dreams
have served their purpose
once the heart pops up
like a kernel.

Now there is only to be sweet.

So dream as you will, plan
to build your version of the pyramids,
scheme to make and spend several fortunes.

For nothing matters but the sweetness,
the sweetness incubated
in our dreams and sufferings,
finally husked and
brought to air.

—Mark Nepo

Please take a moment to ground with Mark's poem and what you have accomplished over the last 10 (or 20…) weeks. You have acknowledged your dreams and sufferings and have husked away all the layers of protection that kept your sweetness hidden.

"Now there is only to be sweet."

Now there is only for you to continue this journey of awakening. I am so honored to have traveled thus far with you and send you my most heartfelt love as you go where your Soul leads. Thank you for sending back to me your intentions that I might stay true to my Soul's calling as well.

May we all remember Wally's words, "Don't underestimate the importance of being grounded."

Paul Lemon

September, 2003

Practicing groundedness with my money
Allows me to remember my true nature.
There I rest comfortably with groundlessness.

455

Final Appendix Materials

Please refer to the Section IV Appendix for critical guidance in the following areas:

Appendix A—Completion of Your Authentic Money Guide

Appendix B—Monitoring and Updating Your Authentic Money Guide

Appendix C—Resources and Support at *www.tenweeks.com*

Appendix D—Selecting a Financial Advisor—Who and When?

Section Four

APPENDIX A

*Completion of Your
Authentic Money Guide*

The TEN WEEKS CD will provide specific guidance in the use of Quicken® to complete your Authentic Money Guide. Please refer to the "Authentic Money Guide Completion" section of the Section Four CD.

Section Four

APPENDIX B

Monitoring and Updating Your Authentic Money Guide

AN ONGOING PROCESS

Your Authentic Money Guide should mirror the journey you are taking in your actual day-to-day life. It serves as a companion to help you evaluate different choices that constantly present themselves. There should be no need to schedule quarterly, semi-annual, or annual updates, as is typically the case in a traditional advisor-based comprehensive financial planning engagement.

Each time a new scenario is run, print out the What If Analysis Graph, and make a note of the change considered. If you choose not to include the change in your Current Authentic Money Guide, simply click on the Reset What If tab in the What If Event Scenarios tab of the Planning section of Quicken®.

Of course, if you choose to integrate that change, follow the standard procedures for updating Week Three Appendix A, printing out the reports for your Authentic Money Guide binder and logging the Action Items into the Action Steps section of your binder.

There should be only one Authentic Money Guide Plan Results Graph and related set of reports in the My Authentic Money Guide Tab of your Authentic Money Guide binder. The link between your Authentic Money Guide and your actual Quicken® reports is the Budget Report. Always print out a revised year-to-date Budget Report after every change to your Authentic Money Guide. These Budget Reports are filed as indicated on page 64 of this book.

QUARTERLY UPDATES

The ideal is to keep your Authentic Money Guide and related binder and monthly reports current on at least a monthly basis. There will be times, however, when you are unable to do this. We all know how time slips away.

In order to avoid time-consuming manual entries, Quicken® transactions should be downloaded at least quarterly.

Write on your calendar *AMG Update* the following dates:

January 15

April 15

July 15

October 15

When these dates occur, follow the instructions outlined in the Section Four TEN WEEKS CD—Quarterly Update Procedures. This will ensure that Quicken® is kept current and you have accurate financial information on which to make grounded financial and life decisions.

ANNUAL UPDATES

At minimum, annually you should take the following steps:

1. **Update Quicken® Deluxe and your TEN WEEKS CD.**
   Current tax tables and other financial information change each year. **Failure to keep your analysis accurate through these updates can result in distorted financial projections.**

   To order these annual updates, you can simply respond to the alerts Intuit will send, allowing you to update to the most recent version of Quicken®, or you can go directly to *www.intuit.com* and order any updates there.

   Once you have your updated Quicken® Deluxe, then order your updated TEN WEEKS CD and Annual Money Attention Page Update through *www.tenweeks.com.* You can sign up to be alerted of program updates automatically, either by returning the response card at the front of this book or registering at *www.tenweeks.com.*

2. **Follow the detailed, screen-by-screen instructions for** *Annual Update Procedures* **as outlined in the Section Four TEN WEEKS CD.**

3. **Consider a call or visit to a financial advisor** if any of the items in "Appendix D—Selecting a Financial Advisor—Who and When?" applies to you.

Section Four

APPENDIX C

Resources and Support at
www.tenweeks.com

TAKE ADVANTAGE OF THE FOLLOWING RESOURCES:

➤ Monthly TEN WEEKS TO FINANCIAL AWAKENING E-Newsletter

➤ Answers to Frequently Asked Questions About the Program

➤ Monthly Financial Article Postings

➤ Schedule for TEN WEEKS TO FINANCIAL AWAKENING Seminars

➤ Book and Software Orders

➤ Book and Software Updates

➤ Listing of TEN WEEKS Advisors™ Close to Where You Live.

Section Four

Appendix D

Selecting a Financial Advisor— Who and When?

The TEN WEEKS Program is built on the premise that every person who is willing to give money his/her complete, careful attention, given appropriate resources, can do his/her own core financial planning.

Now, more than ever, you appreciate the complexity of personal finance and understand why it is important to consult a certified financial planner under certain circumstances. Each CFP has passed a rigorous 10-hour exam, as well as has logged a minimum of three years of financial planning experience. Each CFP licensee must adhere to certain ethics requirements, as well as prove that he/she has satisfied continuing education requirements.

Financial planners can be grouped according to how they are compensated. It is critically important for you to understand exactly how your financial advisor will be paid. For that reason, I highly recommend you consider the following financial planner interview resources:

➤ *www.napfa.org*—"Consumer Services," "Consumer Brochures," "How to Choose a Financial Planner." (NAPFA stands for the National Association of Personal Financial Advisors. They are known for their strict "fee-only" standards for membership. No advisor who accepts commissions from the sale of financial products or referral fees can be a NAPFA-registered advisor.)

➤ *www.cfpboard.org*—"Request a Free Kit," (on the left-hand side of the page, select) "How to Choose a Planner," "Interviewing Checklist." The CFP Board is the Board of Standards for the Certified Financial Planner designation. This website offers helpful information about what it required to become a CFP licensee. There is also an excellent client questionnaire that helps people prepare for their first meeting with a planner.

Each of these websites also has a referral network that can link you to an advisor in your area. Any planner you interview should be happy to answer the questions on either of the interview checklists

recommended previously. In addition, please ask the following questions:

1. Are you familiar with Quicken® software's financial planning features?

2. Are you willing to honor the work I've done in compiling my Authentic Money Guide in the TEN WEEKS program in that you won't ask me to start over and use your particular financial planning system?

3. Will you review the work I have done with Quicken® and the TEN WEEKS TO FINANCIAL AWAKENING program and make constructive recommendations based on your analysis?

4. Will you work on an hourly fee basis to answer questions I have about my financial situation?

5. If you receive any compensation other than what I pay you, do you promise to disclose the specific amount of compensation you will receive for each financial product your recommend to me?

6. Will you support my intention to use money to help me express my Personal Authenticity?

I am in the process of training a network of CPA, CFP advisors who could answer each of those questions affirmatively. These TEN WEEKS Advisors™ will have completed the TEN WEEKS TO FINANCIAL AWAKENING program for their own personal finances, so they will be technically proficient with Quicken®'s features, as well as very supportive of your accomplishment, experiencing firsthand the hard work you have done in completing the program.

To see if there is a TEN WEEKS Advisor™ that can serve you, please check *www.tenweeks.com*, TEN WEEKS Advisors™.

When should you consult one of these professionals? I recommend paying for professional advice in the following situations:

1. **You've completed the program and want a professional familiar with Quicken®'s planning features** to review your input and ensure you haven't made some error that could distort your Authentic Money Guide's financial projections. If you have carefully followed the program and your records are clearly organized, the fee for this service should most likely be less than $500. That is a small price to pay for peace of mind that you didn't overlook something important.

2. **You've experienced a recent trauma that has significant financial ramifications,** such as—

   ➤ a divorce;

   ➤ the death of a family member;

   ➤ the loss of a job; and/or

   ➤ a property loss.

   Each of these and similar situations can leave you ill-equipped to make important financial decisions, many of which are very technical in nature. Always consult a CPA or CFP when faced with such trying times. He/she can help not only honor your loss, but review the financial ramifications of various choices through Authentic Money Guide Scenario Analysis.

3. **You are considering the purchase or sale of a business.**

   Even though the TEN WEEKS program has given you a basic understanding of business valuation and business entity considerations, there are many more issues you need to consider should you be faced with the sale or purchase of a business.

   It is important to ask potential advisors if they have experience in this area before engaging their services.

4. **You plan to buy investment real estate.**

   Several MAP resource sheets addressed the benefits and risks of owning real estate as an investment. It may be that you already own real estate that you would like to sell and reinvest. A qualified advisor, with experience in real-estate consulting, can review your situation and the advantages and disadvantages of such planning tools as a Section 1031 Like-Kind Exchange. This advisor should also help you integrate your choices into your Authentic Money Guide after reviewing the impacts of your alternatives with the What If Event Scenario feature of Quicken®.

5. **You want investment assistance in choosing alternatives to the traditional stock market "basket."**

   If you want help in structuring a Socially Responsible Investment portfolio, or in purchasing alternative investments, I recommend you hire a qualified advisor to assist you. Make sure you are clear what investments you don't want to buy before interviewing advisors, so they understand your expectations and whether or not they offer alternatives.

6. **You are faced with a large pension distribution** and have been presented with several payment options, or you have the option to purchase service credit in a public employee pension.

   The impact of poor pension choices can be avoided with quality financial advice. Don't be "penny wise and pound foolish" in this critical area.

7. **You are stuck at a certain point in the program and don't know how to get unstuck.**

   Maybe you have a spousal or partner conflict you can't seem to resolve, or you are overwhelmed with a certain aspect of the TEN WEEKS CD work, etc. It's much better to get some help to get back on track, than to go back to the old, familiar "money suffering" that prompted your trying TEN WEEKS in the first place. Honor your true voice and get the help you need to get over this obstacle.

   Even though this isn't a comprehensive list, it gives you an idea of when you really do need a professional. Keeping your Authentic Money Guide accurate will facilitate a life-long journey of Awakening, using money as one of your most valuable teachers. Don't pretend that money won't introduce you to some other helpful teachers as well.

MONEY ATTENTION PAGE (MAP) SECTION
Ten Weeks to Financial Awakening

The following worksheets are provided for your education about a wide range of financial topics. A critical step in giving money your attention, rather than your energy, is to take the time to understand essential financial concepts. Some material is rather technical in nature—don't worry about tax terminology—just focus on the "big picture" mentioned in the MAP synopsis in your text. Each MAP is referenced back to this synopsis in the book.

Some materials in this section were reprinted with the permission of Quickfinder, Incorporated, *www.quickfinder.com;* (800) 510-8997.

Some materials in this section were produced by Practitioners Publishing Company, *www.ppcnet.com;* (800)323-8724, and are used with permission.

Some materials in this section were reproduced with the permission of Kettley Publishing Company, 20271 SW Birch Street, Second Floor, Newport Beach, CA 92660, (800) 777-3162.

Some materials in this section were written by the author, Paul Lemon, CPA, CFP™.

The materials presented are based on financial information available as of June, 2003, including the Jobs and Growth Tax Relief Reconciliation Act of 2003 (MAP 8-29).

Because of the changing nature of tax laws and financial product offerings, it is important the reader update this material annually.

Updates are available at *www.tenweeks.com*.

Ten Weeks to Financial Awakening

MONEY ATTENTION PAGE (MAP)
TABLE OF CONTENTS

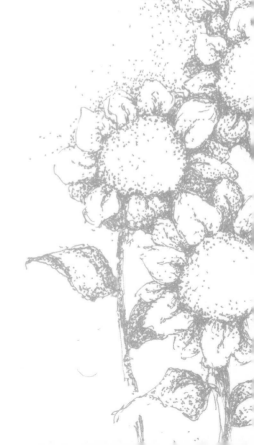

WEEK FIVE
MAP 5-1*
Some Debt Management Techniques
(refer to page 200)

Pay off all outstanding credit card balances. Consolidate credit card debt into one line of credit (either personal or home equity) through a bank or savings and loan. Many financial institutions now offer both personal and home equity lines of credit at rates significantly lower than credit card interest rates. You should be aware that some credit card issuers charge punitive interest rates of up to 10 percent over their standard credit card rate. Punitive rates may be charged if the cardholder is determined to be a high credit risk. This determination is based on an analysis of the cardholder's credit history or repayment activity.

Negotiate a lower interest rate on credit card balances. Many credit card companies will reduce their interest rates for customers who have good credit and payment histories. The companies, of course, do not advertise this, but may make the offer if the customer requests to have his account canceled or balance transferred to another card because of high rates. A listing of low-rate credit cards called CardTrak is available from RAM Research. The list is available via the Internet (at no cost) at *www.ramresearch.com*. Alternatively, it can be ordered by calling Ram Research at (800) 344-7714.

Discontinue the use of credit cards. Establish a definite amount to be paid monthly on outstanding credit card balances that exceed the minimum monthly payment required.

Lease or defer the purchase of a new car rather than purchase. The monthly payment on a leased automobile can be 25–35 percent lower than the monthly payment on a purchase. Also, the deposit required to lease a car may be significantly less than the down payment necessary to finance the purchase of the car. (Of course, your circumstances [e.g., high mileage] and the lease terms might be such that leasing would not be beneficial despite a smaller deposit and lower monthly payments.)

Develop strong banking relationships. You should not overlook the importance of a strong banking relationship. Establish such a relationship with an officer of your bank if you do not already have one. The relationship should be at the officer level since you will want to deal with someone who has knowledge of all the bank's services and products and who also has authority to act for the bank. Benefits of this relationship can include bank assistance in obtaining credit or resolving credit problems, assistance with the record keeping necessary in the PFP process, and complete information on any bank services or products that might be of value to you.

WEEK FIVE
MAP 5-2

Mortgage Planning Tips
(refer to page 200)

SECTION ONE:
Qualifying for a Home Mortgage

A common qualification test used by lenders for a fixed-rate mortgage with a 20 percent downpayment is the 28/38 ratio—28 percent of gross income to be spent on mortgage payments, property taxes and homeowner's insurance, and up to 38 percent on those costs plus other debts. The 38 percent could be increased with good credit rating.

See the Web site *www.homefair.com* for more information

Mortgage Qualification Worksheet

1) Monthly gross income x 0.28 = $ _____

2) Monthly real estate tax and homeowner's insurance payments.
   (Estimate—multiply home's value by .015 and divide by 12.) $ _____
   = Amount A: Subtract line 2 from line 1 $ _____

3) Monthly gross income x 0.38 = $ _____

4) Total of all monthly loan payments (all debts which will take 10 or more months to pay) + amount on line 2 $ _____
   = Amount B: Subtract line 4 from line 3 $ _____

Result: The lesser of amount A or B is the approximate monthly mortgage payment for which a person can qualify.

SECTION TWO:
When to Refinance

Before refinancing, homeowners need to consider up-front costs, how long the homeowner will live in the home, how much time is left on the current mortgage, and the income tax consequences.

An old rule of thumb advised refinancing an existing fixed-rate mortgage if it would save 2 percent or more on the annual percentage rate.

A homeowner who can obtain a lower interest rate at no cost or additional fees should refinance every time.

Payback Period Considerations

Number of months to recoup closing costs. Calculated by dividing total closing costs by the monthly savings.

Increase in tax liability. Due to a lower mortgage interest deduction, less tax benefit is generated by the lower interest rate (especially for taxpayers in high tax brackets or taxpayers with a small spread between interest rates).

Mortgage term. Compare the remaining number of payments of the current mortgage with the total payments of the refinanced mortgage. The term of the original mortgage must be decreased in order for substantial savings on refinancing to occur.

Points vs. Rates Trade-Off

Is a higher mortgage rate acceptable in return for lower up-front fees? It often depends on how long the home will be owned. Points push up the effective interest rate in the short run but wash out over time. The worksheet below calculates the real cost of a mortgage.

Compare:	Sample Mortgage	Actual Mortgage
1) Interest rate	7.0%	%
2) Plan to own home for	five years	
3) Multiply line 1 by line 2	35.0%	%
4) Mortgage points	2.0%	%
5) Add lines 3 and 4	37.0%	%
6) Divide line 5 by line 2 to get effective annual interest rate	7.4%	%

Section Three:
Pay Extra Principal on Mortgage

Several options are available that can significantly reduce interest charges over the life of a mortgage.

Example: A $100,000, 30-year mortgage at 8 percent has a monthly payment of $734. Early mortgage payments are applied mostly towards interest, with little going towards principal reduction. Assuming the mortgage is held the full 30 years, the taxpayer will pay a total of $264,240. The interest charge of $164,240 is over 160 percent the amount of money borrowed.

Options:

1) Refinance the mortgage at a lower interest rate. Make sure the savings more than cover closing costs, including any points charged for refinancing. See "Points vs. Rates Trade-off" above.

2) Switch mortgage term from 30 to 15 years. The monthly payment on a $100,000, 15-year mortgage at 8 percent is $956, or $222 more than on a 30-year mortgage. However, the total interest paid on the 15-year mortgage is reduced to $72,080. That is $92,160 less interest paid on a 15-year mortgage than on a 30-year mortgage.

3) Begin paying an extra amount toward principal each month or at regular or irregular intervals.

—Assumption: 30-year, $100,000 Mortgage— Amount of Interest Saved with Regular Prepayments

Monthly Prepayment	8%	9%	10%
$ 25	$ 23,337	$ 29,441	$ 36,664
$ 50	$ 39,906	$ 49,434	$ 60,332
$100	$ 62,456	$ 75,785	$ 90,508
$200	$ 88,260	$105,108	$ 123,176

Caution: Before prepaying a mortgage, consider investing the maximum possible in retirement plans—for example, 401(k); fully funding a regular or Roth IRA account, if eligible; paying off personal credit card debt; and accumulating an adequate amount of emergency funds. Consider the opportunity cost of the funds used to prepay on a mortgage and plans for long-term investing, insurance needs, tax and retirement planning, etc. The funds may do better in the U.S. stock market with historical returns at 10 percent or more. For a conservative investor buying bonds, money market funds, and CDs, making extra mortgage payments may be a smart move.

Tax analysis. Where to invest extra funds should be based on whether after-tax return on an investment is greater than the after-tax cost of the existing mortgage. Assume the taxpayer in the previous example will itemize deductions and has a combined federal and state marginal tax rate of 34 percent.

➤ Mortgage interest rate = 8.0%

➤ Less tax deduction (8% x 34%) = 2.72%

➤ Taxpayer's net after-tax cost = 5.28%

For every $1 paid in mortgage interest, there is 34¢ in tax savings and the taxpayer pays 66¢. Similarly, if the taxpayer has a taxable investment that earns $1, the taxpayer keeps 66¢. Unless an after-tax return on an investment is more than 5.28 percent, it is better to pay down the mortgage. Consider risk when investing compared with no risk when paying down a mortgage.

WEEK FIVE
MAP 5-3*

Types of Mortgages
(refer to page 201)

Type	Description	Considerations
Fixed rate mortgage	Fixed interest rate, usually long-term; equal monthly payments of principal and interest until debt is paid in full.	Offers stability and long-term tax advantages. Interest rates may be higher than other types of financing. New fixed rates are rarely assumable.
Fifteen-year mortgage	Fixed interest rate. Requires down payment or monthly payments higher than 30-year loan. Loan is fully repaid in 15 years.	Frequently offered at slightly reduced interest rate. Offers faster accumulation of equity than traditional fixed rate mortgage, but has higher monthly payments. Involves paying less interest, but this may result in fewer tax deductions.
Adjustable rate mortgage	Interest rate changes over the life of the loan, resulting in possible changes in your monthly payments, loan term and/or principal. Some plans have rate of interest caps.	Starting interest rate is slightly below market, but payments can increase sharply and frequently if index increases. Payment caps prevent wide fluctuations in payments but may cause negative amortization. Rate caps limit total amount debt can expand.
Renegotiable rate mortgage (rollover)	Interest rate and monthly payments are constant for several years; possible change thereafter. Long-term mortgage.	Less frequent changes in interest rate offer some stability.
Balloon mortgage	Monthly payments based on fixed interest rate; usually short-term; payments may cover interest only with principal due in full at term end.	Offers low monthly payments but possibly no equity until loan is fully paid. When due, loan must be paid off or refinanced. Refinancing poses high risk if rates climb.
Graduated payment mortgage	Lower monthly payments rise gradually (usually over 5-10 years), then level off for duration of term. With adjustable interest rate, additional payment changes possible if index changes.	Easier to qualify for. Buyer's income must be able to keep pace with scheduled payment increases. With an adjustable rate, payment increases beyond the graduated payments can result in additional negative amortization.
Shared appreciation mortgage	Below-market interest rate and lower monthly payments, in exchange for a share of profits when property is sold or on a specified date. Many variations.	If home appreciates greatly, total cost of loan jumps. If home fails to appreciate, projected increase in value may still be due, requiring refinancing at possible higher rates.
Assumable mortgage	Buyer takes over seller's original, below-market rate mortgage.	Lowers monthly payments. May be prohibited if a "due on sale" clause is in original mortgage. Not permitted on most new fixed rate mortgages.

Type	Description	Considerations
Seller take-back	Seller provides all or part of financing with a first or second mortgage.	May offer a below-market interest rate; may have a balloon payment requiring full payment in a few years or refinancing at market rates, which could sharply increase debt.
Wraparound	Seller keeps original low rate mortgage. Buyer makes payments to seller who forwards a portion to the lender holding original mortgage. Offers lower effective interest rate on total transaction.	Lender may call in old mortgage and require higher rate. If buyer defaults, seller must take legal action to collect debt.
Growing equity mortgage (rapid payoff mortgage)	Fixed interest rate but monthly payments may vary according to agreed-upon schedule or index.	Permits rapid payoff of debt because payment increases reduce principal. Buyerís income must be able to keep up with payment increases.
Land contract	Seller retains original mortgage. No transfer of title until loan is fully paid. Equal monthly payments based on below-market interest rate with unpaid principal due at loan end.	May offer no equity until loan is fully paid. Buyer has few protections if conflict arises during loan.
Buy-down	Developer (or other party) provides an interest subsidy which lowers monthly payments during the first few years of the loan. Can have fixed or adjustable interest rate.	Offers a break from higher payments during early years. Enables buyer with lower income to qualify. With adjustable rate mortgage, payments may jump substantially at end of subsidy. Developer may increase selling price.
Rent with option	Renter pays ì option feeî for right to purchase property at specified time and agreed upon price. Rent may or may not be applied to sales price.	Enables renter to buy time to obtain down payment and decide whether to purchase. Locks in price during inflationary times. Failure to take option means loss of option fee and rental payments.
Reverse annuity mortgage (equity conversion)	Borrower owns mortgage-free property and needs income. Lender makes monthly payments to borrower using property as collateral.	Can provide homeowners with needed cash. At end of term, borrower must have money available to avoid selling property or refinancing.

WEEK FIVE
MAP 5-4
The Bi-Weekly Mortgage
(refer to page 201)

By paying one-half of the typical monthly mortgage payment every two weeks rather than one full payment every month, a 30-year mortgage can be paid off in approximately 20 years. The 26 bi-weekly payments are the same as 13 monthly payments during the year; in other words, one extra monthly payment.

This extra monthly payment, along with the more frequent application of the payments against the loan balance, greatly speeds up the payoff of the loan.

Since the extra monthly payment is spread evenly throughout the year, it generally does not adversely affect the family budget.

Payments on the bi-weekly mortgage are generally made by automatic withdrawal from the homeowner's checking account every two weeks.

Payments on Various Size Loans and Total Interest Saved[1]

Interest Rate / Term in Months	$100,000		$150,000		$200,000	
	Bi-Weekly Payment Amount	Total Interest Savings	Bi-Weekly Payment Amount	Total Interest Savings	Bi-Weekly Payment Amount	Total Interest Savings
7.00% / 286	$333	$34,141	$499	$51,211	$665	$68,281
7.50% / 280	350	39,745	524	59,615	699	79,490
8.00% / 275	367	45,910	550	68,862	734	91,814
8.50% / 270	384	52,647	577	78,965	769	105,288
9.00% / 264	402	59,954	603	89,934	805	119,908
9.50% / 258	420	67,837	631	101,758	841	135,674
10.00% / 253	439	76,282	658	114,425	878	152,563
10.50% / 247	457	85,274	686	127,908	915	170,549
11.00% / 241	476	94,791	714	142,187	952	189,583

Note: All figures are approximate.

Week Five
MAP 5-5

*Mortgage Indebtedness—Tax Rules**
(See IRS Publication 936)

Mortgage Indebtedness (Three Kinds)

1) Acquisition Indebtedness—After October 13, 1987

➤ Debt incurred to acquire, construct, or substantially improve the taxpayer's main or second home. (Interest on a third home is nondeductible personal interest unless the home is a business or investment property not used personally by the taxpayer.)

➤ Debt must be secured by such home(s).

➤ Indebtedness is reduced as the debt is paid off and cannot be increased by refinancing.

➤ Indebtedness is limited to $1 million for purposes of determining deductible home interest ($500,000 MFS).

➤ Refinancing of an acquisition debt is considered acquisition debt to the extent it does not exceed the principal outstanding on the loan immediately before the refinancing.

➤ Additional amounts borrowed to make substantial improvements to the home increase acquisition indebtedness. Any debt above that amount is home equity indebtedness.

2) Home Equity Indebtedness—After October 13, 1987

➤ Debt secured by the home (main or second) which exceeds the acquisition indebtedness.

➤ Home equity debt is limited to the lesser of:

▷ FMV of the home minus total acquisition indebtedness on that home, or

▷ $100,000 ($50,000 MFS) for main and second homes combined.

Advantage: Home equity loans can be used for any purpose whatsoever, and the interest is fully deductible.

3) Mortgages Incurred—Before October 14, 1987

➤ All interest on debt secured by a main or second home is fully deductible, regardless of the purpose for which funds were used.

➤ Loans are treated as acquisition indebtedness and are not subject to the $1 million limit. However, pre-October 14, 1987, indebtedness reduces the amount of the $1 million limitation for additional debt after October 13, 1987.

➤ Refinancing pre-October 14, 1987, debt after October 13, 1987, is treated as acquisition indebtedness to the extent it does not exceed the outstanding principal immediately prior to the refinancing and the repayment period does not extend beyond a limited term.

The limited term is:

➢ The remaining term of the original debt, if the original debt was to be repaid over its; term, or

➢ If the original debt was not to be repaid over its term, the term of the first refinancing (but not more than 30 years after the first refinancing).

POINTS—MORTGAGES

Points (Rev. Proc. 94-27)

Points are deductible in full in the year paid if all of the following requirements are met:

1) The settlement statement must clearly identify the amount of points—often referred to as "loan origination fees," "maximum loan charges," "loan discount," "discount points" or "points."

2) The points must be computed as a percentage of the principal amount.

3) The amount paid as points must not exceed the normal rate charged in the area. Any additional amount paid must be amortized over the life of the loan.

4) The points must be paid on a loan to purchase or build a taxpayer's principal residence, and loan must be secured by the residence.

5) The points must be paid from the taxpayer's own funds, not from mortgage loan proceeds. Downpayments, escrow deposits, earnest money, seller-paid points, and other amounts paid at closing will satisfy these requirements as long as those amounts paid are at least as much as the points charged. Any points paid by the loan must be amortized over the life of the loan.

6) The taxpayer uses cash method of accounting. A taxpayer may choose to amortize points over the life of the loan even if points meet all requirements to be fully deductible in the year the home is purchased. Example: A first-time homebuyer purchasing a home late in the year may not have enough deductions to itemize. (Letter Rul. 9905033)

VA and FHA loans. "Loan origination fees" designated as such on VA and FHA loans qualify as deductible points if the requirements above are met.

Revenue Procedure 94-27 does not apply to:

➤ Points allocable to portion of a mortgage exceeding $1 million.

➤ Home improvement loans; see below.

➤ Loans to purchase or improve a second residence.

➤ Refinancing loans, home equity loans, or line–of–credit loans.

Home Improvement Loan Points

Although Revenue Procedure 94-27 does not apply to home improvement loans, points paid on a loan to purchase or improve the principal residence are fully deductible in the year paid. The loan must be secured by the residence, payment of points must be an established business practice in the area, and the number of points paid must not exceed the number generally charged in that area. [IRC §461(g)(2)]

Example: Ned takes out a home improvement loan for $20,000, but only $10,000 is actually used for home improvements. The other $10,000 is used to buy a car. If Ned pays a $200 loan origination fee, $100 is currently deductible as points, and the other $100 must be amortized over the life of the loan.

Seller-paid Points

Homebuyers are allowed to deduct seller-paid points as an itemized deduction. Points paid by the seller, including points charged to the seller, are treated as paid directly by the buyer from funds that have not been borrowed, provided the buyer subtracts the amount of seller-paid points from the purchase price of the residence in computing basis. (Rev. Proc. 94-27)

Example: Amy sells her home to Barb for $200,000. Barb makes a cash downpayment of $20,000 and borrows $180,000 from a mortgage company. Amy pays two points ($3,600) to the mortgage company to help Barb get the loan at a better rate of interest. Under Revenue Procedure 94-27, Barb is treated as having made a $3,600 payment of points directly to the mortgage company and a payment of only $196,400 to Amy for the purchase of the home.

Basis Calculation:

Seller: Reduce sales price of home by amount of seller-paid points.

Buyer: Reduce adjusted basis of home by seller-paid points.

Points Paid to Refinance

Taxpayers who refinance to obtain lower interest rates must amortize points over the life of the loan unless loan proceeds are used to substantially improve the main residence.

If only a portion of the loan is used to improve the home, only that portion is deductible in the year paid (remaining portion must be amortized). If the loan is paid off early, any remaining points may be deducted in full in the year the loan is paid in full. However, taxpayers who refinance a loan with the same lender must deduct the remaining points from the old loan over the life of the new loan.

Taxpayers who use short-term financing as a first step in securing a permanent mortgage may be entitled to deduct points on refinancing in the year paid.

Home Equity Line-of-Credit Points

Points paid initially for a line of credit secured by the home are deductible over the period of time until the credit line expires. However, if funds from a line of credit are used for home improvements, the points are fully deductible the first year.

---

* Material reprinted with the permission of Quickfinder Incorporated (*www.quickfinder.com*).

Business Property

Amortize the points over the life of the loan.

Vacation Second Home

Personal use only. Points are amortized as an interest expense over the entire loan period.

Business and personal use:

1) If personal use is not more than the greater of 14 days or 10 percent of the days the home is rented, the vacation second home is treated as a rental property. Amortize points over the life of the loan.

2) If personal use exceeds the 14-day-or-10-percent use rule, then divide the points proportionately, amortize one proportionate amount against the rental property, and amortize the balance as an interest expense over the entire loan period.

Investment Residential Property

Amortize the points over the life of the loan.

OTHER MORTGAGE INTEREST DEDUCTION RULES

Seller-financed Loans

A taxpayer claims a deduction on Schedule A for mortgage interest on a seller-financed loan, the seller's name, address, and TIN must be reported on Schedule A. The seller must also report the name, address and TIN of the buyer on Schedule B. A $50 penalty may be imposed on the buyer or seller for failure to provide the required information. (IRC §6723)

Late-payment Charges

Late-payment charges are generally deductible if they were not for a specific service such as a collection fee. If the late-payment fee is included in the Form 1098, there should be no problem. If not, attach a statement explaining why there is a discrepancy between the interest reported on the tax return and Form 1098.

Land Rent (Redeemable Ground Rent)

Annual or periodic lease payments made for the use of land (as opposed to a physical structure) can be deductible as mortgage interest. *To be deductible, all of the following must be true:*

1) The land lease term is more than 15 years, including renewal periods, and is freely assignable by the lessee;

2) The lessee has the right to terminate the lease and purchase the lessor's land by paying a specific amount; and

3) The lessor's interest in the land is a security interest to protect the entitlement to rental payment.

Construction Loans

Construction loans or loans to buy a building lot qualify as fully deductible mortgage interest if the following requirements are met:

1) A home under construction is treated as a qualifying home during a 24-month period provided that when ready for occupancy, the house is used as a main or second home.

2) If the construction period exceeds 24 months, only 24 months qualify. The interest for the remaining months is considered personal interest.

3) Loan proceeds must be directly traceable to home construction expenses, including the purchase of a lot.

4) Before construction begins, the loan does not qualify as acquisition debt, and interest incurred during that period generally is treated as personal interest.

5) Ninety day rule—A loan incurred within 90 days after construction is complete may also qualify, provided the debt is secured by the home. Construction expenses made within the period starting 24 months before completion of the house and ending on the date of the loan qualify.

Timeshares

Timeshares can be considered second homes for mortgage interest deductions. Depending on the type of timeshare, interest deductions for most timeshares are available under the mortgage interest rules.

In fee simple or deeded timeshares in which the taxpayer owns the property, deductions are allowed for timeshares used by the taxpayer less than 15 days when they are not rented at all. In right-to-use timeshares there is only a lease on the unit. Any interest on this will be consumer interest not eligible for the mortgage interest deduction.

Boats and Mobile Homes

Interest on a boat or mobile home used as a second home is deductible as home mortgage subject to mortgage interest rules.

Qualifications. The boat or mobile home must have basic living accommodations such as sleeping space and cooking and toilet facilities. Also, local law must allow for such use. For example, a houseboat moored at a marina which prohibits overnight sleeping would not qualify as a second home.)

Downpayment Loan Interest

If the funds used for the downpayment on a home need to be borrowed (for example, from a parent), the interest cannot be deducted as mortgage interest unless the loan is secured by the home itself. A contract for deed can be drawn up and recorded.

Legal Liability for Mortgage Debt

Generally, a homeowner must be legally liable for a home loan in order to deduct mortgage interest. However, the Tax Court has allowed an interest deduction for a married couple who did not actually hold title to the property and were not legally liable for the underlying mortgage.

The couple, having been through a bankruptcy, was unable to secure financing to purchase a home. To assist the couple, the husband's brother took legal title to the property the couple wished to purchase and obtained financing. The couple occupied the home, made all mortgage payments and provided all maintenance on the home. The court determined that the couple was obligated (to the brother) to make mortgage payments and allowed the mortgage interest deduction. (TC Memo 1997-551)

High Loan-to-Value (LTV) Mortgages

Under the home equity debt rules (see Page 5-7), interest deductions are not allowed for debt that exceeds the fair market value (FMV) of the home. Taxpayers obtaining high LTV mortgages (wherein the loan balance exceeds the property value) may only deduct interest on the portion of the loan (combined with all loans on the home) that does not exceed FMV.

Example: David has a home valued at $150,000 and acquisition mortgage debt of $120,000. He takes out a high LTV home equity loan of $40,000 in order to consolidate consumer debt. Deductible interest is limited to interest on $30,000 ($150,000 − $120,000) of the loan amount. Interest on the remaining $10,000 is considered nondeductible personal interest.

Prepaid Mortgage Interest

Mortgage interest prepaid in 2002 that fully accrues by January 15, 2003, may be included in Form 1098, box 1. This prepaid interest is not deductible in 2002; it should be deducted in 2003.

Note: Some lenders apply prepaid amounts to both interest and principal; others apply prepayments to principal only.

Reverse Mortgages

A reverse mortgage is used to convert home equity into cash. Payments can take the form of a line of credit, a lump sum, monthly payments for a specified number of years, or payments over the life of the borrower. Because the borrower is drawing from principal, the amount received is tax free and will not affect Social Security benefits. To qualify, all borrowers in the household must be at least age 62, and the home must be totally, or nearly, paid off.

When a reverse mortgage comes due, the lender recovers the amount owed from the borrower (or the heirs). If the amount owed is greater than the market value of the home, FHA insurance makes up the difference.

Mortgage interest deduction. Mortgage interest is added to the loan balance over the term of the loan but is not deducted until the loan is repaid.

WEEK FIVE
MAP 5-6[*]

Credit Cards
(refer to page 201)

The use of credit cards has become a widespread and accepted part of modern life. From modest beginnings in the early 1900s, credit card usage has grown to the point where 67.5% of American families have at least one general-purpose credit card, with a median credit balance outstanding of $1,900.[1]

Reasons to Use a Credit Card

There are many reasons individual consumers use a credit card.

- **Safety:** The use of credit cards allows a consumer to purchase goods and services without the need to carry large amounts of cash.

- **Opportunity:** A credit card allows a consumer to deal with short-term situations, such as Christmas or emergency auto repairs, when paying cash might not be possible.

- **Facilitate transactions:** Credit cards allow for payment of goods and services purchased via telephone or the Internet. Some transactions, such as renting a car, purchasing airline tickets or guaranteeing payment for late arrival at a hotel, would be impossible without the use of a credit card.

- **Leverage:** Paying with a credit card can provide a consumer with additional leverage, in case of disputes with merchants over defective or poor quality merchandise.

- **Identity:** In certain types of transactions, such as cashing a check, credit cards have become a means of personal identification.

Types of Credit Cards

Not all credit cards are alike. They will vary widely in terms of issuer, scope of use and contract terms.

- **Bankcards:** Are issued not only by banks, but also by other financial institutions such as savings and loans or credit unions. These general purpose credit cards can usually be used to purchase a wide range of goods and services. Credit is usually provided on a revolving basis, under which a borrower is granted a specific amount of credit. Typically, minimum monthly payments are required and any unpaid balance is subject to an interest charge. As borrowed amounts are repaid, the amount of available credit increases, up to the credit limit.

- **Charge cards:** Also known as travel and entertainment cards. Unlike bankcards, charge cards typically must be paid in full each month. Balances not paid are subject to heavy penalty fees. Like bankcards, charge cards are usually accepted widely.

---

[1] Taken from U. S. Statistical Abstract, 2001. See Report No. 1192 - Usage of General Purpose Credit Cards by Families: 1989 to 1998. Data is from 1998.

- **Retail credit cards:** Retail credit cards are issued by businesses such as department stores, airlines and gasoline companies. Credit is usually provided on a revolving basis and purchases are limited to the goods and services sold by the specific card issuer.

- **Secured credit cards:** Such cards are usually general-purpose bankcards, with a specified (typically lower) credit limit. The card is secured by a deposit in an account with the issuing institution. If a consumer defaults, the card issuer can use the deposited funds to cover the shortage. Such cards are useful for individuals who do not have an established credit history or for those rebuilding their credit rating.

- **Affinity cards:** Affinity cards are issued jointly by a lending institution such as a bank or savings and loan, and some other organization such as an airline, charity or college alumni group. Using an affinity card allows a cardholder to also achieve other goals such as earning frequent flyer miles or making charitable contributions.

Shopping for a Credit Card

When shopping for a credit card, a consumer should carefully compare the terms under which a card is offered:

- **Interest rate on unpaid balances:** The interest rate on unpaid balances can be either a fixed rate or a variable rate. Card issuers are required to state the interest rate as both an annual percentage rate (APR) and (for each billing cycle) as a periodic interest rate.

- **Unpaid balance computation:** The method by which a card issuer calculates the unpaid balance on an account. The unpaid balance, multiplied by the periodic interest rate, determines the finance charge.

Average Daily Balance	Previous Balance	Adjusted Balance
Each day the issuer subtracts any payments from, and adds new purchases to, the account balance. The daily balances for each day in a billing cycle are added together and then divided by the number of days in that cycle.	The issuer charges interest on the balance outstanding at the end of the previous billing cycle.	The issuer starts with the previous balance, subtracts any payments or credits, and charges interest on any remaining unpaid amount.

- **Fees:** Many card issuers will charge an annual fee, just to have the card. Fees may also be charged for such items as cash advances, late payments, charging over the established credit limit and lost card replacement.

- **Grace period:** The amount of time during which no interest is charged, if the entire amount is paid off.

- **Other benefits:** A card may provide other benefits such as cash advances, flight insurance, or discounts on travel or long-distance telephone charges.

- **Acceptance:** Some merchants may not accept a specific type of card.

Using a Credit Card

Many advisors recommend that consumers develop certain habits when using credit cards.

- Keep the number of open credit card accounts to a minimum.

- Understand the terms under which a card is issued.

- Sign all cards as soon as they are received.

- Pay credit card bills promptly to keep interest charges as low as possible and maintain a good credit rating.

- Keep detailed records of credit card account numbers, expiration dates and the telephone number of card issuers. The easiest way to do this is to photocopy the front and back of each card.

- Protect credit card information to avoid unauthorized use.

- Carefully review credit card statements each month. The customer copy of charge slips should be kept, to allow comparison with the monthly statement.

Lost or Stolen Credit Cards

Under federal law, a cardholder can be held liable for charges of up to $50.00 per card, even though the use was unauthorized. Such unauthorized credit card use is often the result of a card being lost, stolen or even counterfeited. If the loss of a card is reported to the issuer before the card is used, however, the issuer cannot hold the consumer liable for any unauthorized use.

- **Notify issuer:** A consumer should report the loss or theft of a credit card to the issuer as soon as possible. Many card issuers have toll-free, 24-hour telephone numbers for this purpose. Written notification should also be sent to the issuer.

- **Check monthly statement:** Review the monthly card statement to be sure that no unauthorized charges were made before it was noticed that the card was missing.

- **Registration service:** A consumer who carries more than one credit card may want to use a credit card registration service. For an annual fee, such services keep a record of all of a consumerís credit cards. In the event of a loss, the consumer makes one call, to the registration service. The registration service notifies all card issuers of the loss and, in many cases, arranges for replacement cards.

Week Five
Map 5-7

How Can I Get a Copy of My Credit Report?
(refer to page 201)

There are three major credit bureaus—Equifax, Trans Union, and Experian. It's best to order your report from all three. The federal Fair Credit Reporting Act (FCRA) entitles you to a copy of your credit report, and you can get one for free if:

➤ you've been denied credit because of information in your credit report, and you request a copy within 60 days of being denied credit;

➤ you're unemployed and looking for work;

➤ you receive public assistance; or

➤ you believe your file contains errors due to fraud.

In addition, you can get one free copy a year if you live in Colorado, Georgia, Maryland, Massachusetts, New Jersey, or Vermont.

The law says that if you don't qualify for a free report, you should pay no more than $8.50 to obtain a report from Equifax (P.O. Box 740241, Atlanta, GA 30374, (800) 685-1111, *http://www.equifax.com*), Trans Union (P.O. Box 1000, Chester, PA 19022, (800)888-4213, *http://www.tuc.com*) or Experian (P.O. Box 2002, Allen, TX 75013, (888) 397-3742, *http://www.experian.com*).

Provide the following information:

➤ your full name (including generations such as Jr., Sr., III),

➤ your birth date,

➤ your Social Security number,

➤ your spouse's name (if applicable),

➤ your telephone number, and

➤ your current address and addresses for the previous five years.

WEEK FIVE
MAP 5-8

What Should I Do if I Find Mistakes in My Credit Report? *(refer to page 201)*

As you read through your report, make a list of everything out-of-date. The credit bureaus should remove the following information from your credit report:

➤ Lawsuits, paid tax liens, accounts sent out for collection, criminal records (except criminal convictions, which may be reported indefinitely), late payments, and any other adverse information older than seven years.

➤ Bankruptcies older than 10 years from the discharge or dismissal. Credit bureaus often list Chapter 13 bankruptcies for only seven years, but they can stay for 10.

➤ Credit inquiries (requests by companies for a copy of your report) older than two years.

Next, look for incorrect or misleading information, such as:

➤ incorrect or incomplete name, address, phone number, Social Security number, or employment information;

➤ bankruptcies not identified by their specific chapter number;

➤ accounts not yours or lawsuits in which you were not involved;

➤ incorrect account histories–such as late payments when you paid on time;

➤ closed accounts listed as open–it may look as if you have too much open credit; and

➤ any account you closed that doesn't say "closed by consumer."

After reviewing your report, complete the "request for reinvestigation" form the credit bureau sent you, or send a letter listing each incorrect item and explain exactly what is wrong. Once the credit bureau receives your request, it must investigate the items you dispute and contact you within 30 days. Some states require bureaus to complete reinvestigations more quickly. If you don't hear back within 30 days, send a follow-up letter. If you let them know that you're trying to obtain a mortgage or car loan, they can do a rush investigation.

If you are right, or if the creditor who provided the information can no longer verify it, the credit bureau must remove the information from your report. Often, credit bureaus will remove an item on request without an investigation if rechecking the item is more bother than it's worth.

If the credit bureau insists that the information is correct, call the bureau to discuss the problem:

➤ Experian: (888) 397-3742

➤ Trans Union: (800) 888-4213

➤ Equifax: (800) 685-1111

If you don't get anywhere with the credit bureau, directly contact the creditor and ask that the information be removed. Write to the customer service department, vice president of marketing, and president or CEO. If the information was reported by a collection agency, send the agency a copy of your letter, too. Creditors are forbidden by law to report information they know is incorrect.

If you feel a credit bureau is wrongfully including information in your report, or you want to explain a particular entry, you have the right to put a brief statement in your report. The credit bureau must give a copy of your statement—or a summary thereof—to anyone who requests your report. Be clear and concise; use the fewest words possible.

Week Five
MAP 5-9*

Financing an Auto (refer to page 202)

Once a consumer decides to acquire an automobile, the next step is to decide how to pay for it. There are three methods of financing an auto:

- **Pay cash:** Using already accumulated funds.

- **Borrow the funds:** Taking out a loan and paying for the vehicle over time.

- **Lease:** Allows use of an auto for a specified period of time, in return for regular monthly payments.

The decision as to whether to pay cash, take out a loan, or lease a vehicle is usually made after considering a number of personal and financial issues.

Factors to Consider

The table below compares some of the factors to consider when considering how to finance an auto.

	Pay Cash	Borrow the Funds	Lease
Method of financing	Consumer uses cash to completely pay for the vehicle at the time of purchase.	Consumer borrows the funds to purchase the vehicle, and makes monthly payments to repay the loan.	Consumer obtains the right to use the vehicle for a specified period of time, in return for monthly payments.
Out-of-pocket costs	Entire purchase price.	Down payment and/or trade-in. Special offers may allow zero down.	Down payment and/or trade-in. Often less than for an auto loan. Special offers may allow zero down.
Monthly payments	None	Payments cover repayment of loan amount, plus interest.	Payments cover estimated depreciation during the lease period, and other costs. Typically less than for an auto loan.
Vehicle ownership	Consumer is the owner.	Consumer is the owner, subject to a lien held by lender. Once loan is repaid, consumer takes title free and clear. Lender may repossess vehicle if payments not made as scheduled.	Leasing firm retains ownership. Consumer usually has the right to purchase the vehicle at the end of the lease.

	Pay Cash	Borrow the Funds	Lease
Excess mileage charges	None	None	Typical lease limits consumer to no more than 10,000 ñ 15,000 miles per year. Miles in excess of lease limits subject to a per-mile charge.
Excess wear and tear	No additional charges. Excess wear and tear, or high mileage, can reduce a vehicleís resale value.	No additional charges. Excess wear and tear, or high mileage, can reduce a vehicleís resale value.	Additional charges for excess wear and tear usually apply.
Risk of future vehicle resale value	Risk remains with the consumer.	Risk remains with the consumer.	With a closed-end lease, risk of future vehicle resale value remains with leasing firm. With an open-end lease, consumer may be responsible for substantial additional charges.
Early disposal of vehicle	Consumer is free to sell vehicle at any time.	Consumer is free to sell vehicle at any time, subject to repayment of loan balance to lender. Early loan termination fees may apply.	Additional fees for early lease termination normally apply.
Tax issues	Deduction available for business use of vehicle.[1]	Deduction available for business use of vehicle.[1]	Deduction available for business use of vehicle. In certain situations, leasing may provide a larger deduction for business use than an owned vehicle.[1]
Lifestyle issues	Limits consumer to vehicle that he or she can currently afford. Consumer avoids additional debt burden.	Usually allows consumer to purchase more expensive vehicle than if full cash payment is required.	Consumer typically has use of more expensive vehicle than with other financing options. May also allow consumer to drive a new car more frequently. No equity at end of lease.

---

[1] Based on federal law. State law may vary.

Comparing the Dollar Costs

The following table provides a hypothetical comparison of the costs involved in the three options for financing an auto:

- **Pay cash:** Purchase price of $22,500, sales tax of $1,631, registration and fees of $350. Total purchase price of $24,481.

- **Borrow the funds:** Total purchase price of $24,481, less down payment of $2,250. Financed over a 48-month period at 9.5% annual interest.

- **Lease:** 48-month closed-end lease, with same costs and interest rate as under the ìloanî option. $500 down payment, and an assumed resale value at the end of the lease of $12,000.

	Pay Cash	Borrow the Funds	Lease
Up-front cash	$24,481	$2,250	$500
Monthly payment	$0	$554	$388
Total payments over 48 months	$0	$26,592	$18,624
Opportunity costs[1]	$3,117	$286	$64
Total costs after 48 months	**$27,598**	**$29,128**	**$19,188**
Value of vehicle after 48 months	($12,000)	($12,000)	$0
Total	**$15,598**	**$17,128**	**$19,188**

---

[1] The amount of interest the ìup-front cashî shown for each option would have earned over the 48 month period, at an assumed 3.0% annual after-tax rate of return.

WEEK SIX
MAP 6-1

*The Natural Investment Services, Inc., Social Rating**
(refer to page 237)

Natural Investment Services Inc. (NIS) has developed a system of analyzing the social screens used by each fund. The number of screens, importance of each screen and application of each screen have been weighted and scored. Participation in shareholder activism and community investing is also evaluated. Financial performance is not a part of the rating*. The resultant scores are then arranged into five 20th percentiles. A rating of ♥ indicates a limited number of social issues are considered by the fund. A ♥♥♥♥♥ rating indicates that the fund is comprehensively screened.

NIS SOCIAL RATING℠
UPDATED 1/22/03

FUND NAME	SYMBOL	RATING
American Trust Allegiance	ATAFX	♥
Aquinas		
Equity	AQEGX	♥♥♥
Fixed-income	AQFIX	♥♥♥
Small-cap	AQBLX	♥♥♥
Value	AQEIX	♥♥♥
Ariel		
Appreciation	CAAPX	♥♥♥
Growth	ARGFX	♥♥♥
Calvert		
Capital Accumulation	CCAFX	♥♥♥♥
New Vision	CNVAX	♥♥♥
Social Balanced	CSIFX	♥♥♥♥♥
Social Bond	CSIBX	♥♥♥♥♥
Social Enhanced Equity	CMIFX	♥♥♥♥♥
Social Equity	CSIEX	♥♥♥♥♥

* For individual fund performance, please visit the Social Investment Forum's Socially Responsible Mutual Fund guide.
Copyright NIS 2003—used by permission.

FUND NAME	SYMBOL	RATING
Social Index	CSSAX	♥♥♥♥♥
Social Large-cap	CLGAX	♥♥♥♥♥
World Values International Eq.	CWVGX	♥♥♥♥
Citizens Funds		
Citizens Core Growth	WAIDX	♥♥♥♥♥
Citizens Emerging Growth	WAEGX	♥♥♥♥♥
Citizens Global	WAGEX	♥♥♥♥
Citizens Income	WAIMX	♥♥♥♥
Citizens International Growth	N/A	♥♥♥♥♥
Citizens Small-cap Index	CSCSX	♥♥♥♥♥
Citizens Value Fund	MYPVX	♥♥♥♥♥
Concert Social Awareness	SSAIX	♥♥♥
DEM Equity	DEMEX	♥
Delaware Social Awareness	DEQAX	♥♥
Domini		
Social Equity	DSEFX	♥♥♥♥♥
Social Bond	DSBFX	♥♥♥♥♥
Dreyfus Third Century	DRTHX	♥♥♥♥
Eclipse Ultra-short	ECUIX	♥♥♥
Enterprise Global Socially Responsive	EGSAX	♥♥♥♥♥
Flex Fund		
Total Return Utility	FLRUX	♥♥♥♥
Utilities Growth	FPBAX	♥♥♥♥
Green Century		
Balanced	GCBLX	♥♥♥♥
Equity	GCEQX	♥♥♥♥♥
IPS		
Millenium	IPSMX	♥♥
New Frontier	IPFSX	♥♥

FUND NAME	SYMBOL	RATING
MMA Praxis		
Core Stock	MMPGX	♥♥♥♥♥
Intermediate Income	MMPIX	♥♥♥♥
International	MMPNX	♥♥♥♥♥
Value Index	MVIAX	♥♥♥♥♥
Neuberger & Berman Socially Responsive	NBSRX	♥♥♥♥
New Alternatives	NALFX	♥♥♥♥
New Covenant		
Balanced Growth	NCBGX	♥♥
Balanced Income	NCBIX	♥♥
Growth	NCGFX	♥♥
Income	NCICX	♥♥
Parnassus		
California Tax-free	PRCLX	♥♥♥♥
Equity Income	PRBLX	♥♥♥♥♥
Fixed-income	PRFIX	♥♥♥♥♥
Fund	PARNX	♥♥♥♥♥
Pax World		
Fund	PAXWX	♥♥♥♥
Growth	PXWGX	♥♥♥♥
High-yield	PAXHX	♥♥♥♥
Portfolio 21	PORTX	♥♥♥♥♥
Rightime Social Awareness	RTAWX	♥♥♥♥
Security Social Awareness	SWAAX	♥♥♥
Sierra Club		
Sierra Club Balanced	N/A	♥♥♥
Sierra Club Stock	SCFSX	♥♥♥
TIAA-CREF Social Choice	TCSCX	♥
USAA First Start	USSGX	♥
Vanguard Calvert Social Index	VCSIX	♥♥♥♥
Victory Lakefront	VLFRT	♥

FUND NAME	SYMBOL	RATING
Walden/BBT		
International Social Index	WISIX	♥♥♥♥♥
Domestic Index	WDSIX	♥♥♥♥♥
Walden Social		
Balanced	WSBFX	♥♥♥♥♥
Equity	WSEFX	♥♥♥♥
Winslow Green Growth	WGGFX	♥♥
Womens Equity	FEMMX	♥♥♥♥

Week Six
MAP 6-2

Socially Responsible Investing Resources
(refer to page 237)

1. To review an SRI portfolio based on your answers to several questions about your investment risk, time horizon, and SRI preferences:

   ➤ Go to *www.calvertgroup.com.*

   ➤ Select Tools.

   ➤ Select Asset Allocator.

   ➤ Verify that the recommended allocation to stocks and bonds is consistent with your Authentic Money Guide assumptions.

   ➤ Research recommended fund performance by typing in the fund name at the Morningstar Analyzer in Quicken®.

      ▷ Go to Quicken® Home

      ▷ Click on Investing

      ▷ Select Investing Activities

      ▷ Click on Investment Research

      ▷ Look Up Ticker Symbol

      ▷ Type in Name and Select Mutual Fund

      ▷ Compare the Fund to a Competitor if You Like

2. Evaluate your current portfolio for various socially-responsible screens.

   ➤ Go to *www.calvertgroup.com.*

   ➤ Select Tools.

   ➤ Select Know What You Own Service.

   ➤ Select the fund family of your mutual fund using the alphabet tab or by typing in the fund name.

   ➤ Choose from the drop-down menu of screens.

   ➤ Print out your report.

   ➤ Decide if owning this investment is in alignment with your Authentic Self.

3. Research other SRI funds or topics of interest using the index at *www.naturalinvesting.com.* Before implementing or taking action on any investment, ensure that the asset allocation guidelines match those determined with the Week Six procedures.

WEEK SIX
MAP 6-3

*Index of the Indexes**
(refer to page 262)

Dow Jones industrial average. The oldest and most well-known benchmark, the Dow represents only 30 companies. It reflects the market moves in a given day, but only represents 20 percent of the market (which is comprised of some 6,500 companies). Since Dow companies are weighted by stock price instead of capitalization, it can assign equal value to companies of vastly different sizes.

Standard & Poor's 500. The S&P represents 500 companies—almost all large-capitalization stocks traded on the New York Stock Exchange and NASDAQ that make up the majority of the market's overall value. A committee periodically adds or subtracts companies from the list based on which ones are dominant in various industry sectors. The S&P 400, despite its billing as a mid-cap index, also tends to be skewed toward bigger companies.

Russell 3000. Russell includes 3,000 stocks representing 98 percent of the total equity market capitalization. The top 1,000 form a large-cap index (Russell 1000), and the bottom 2,000 form the widely used Russell 2000 for small-cap stocks. Because the Russell indexes are calculated purely by size rather than committees, some argue they are truer reflections of given segments.

NASDAQ composite. Lists all the companies in the National Market System—stocks that are traded only over–the–counter and not on an exchange.

Wilshire 5000. This index truly represents all 6,500 stocks traded in the U.S. for which price data is available (there were only 5,000 when it started). Wilshire breaks these down into large-cap (Wilshire 750), mid-cap (Wilshire Next 1750) and small-cap indexes.

* Material reprinted with the permission of Quickfinder Incorpora ted *(www.quickfinder.com).*

Many Faces of Risk*
(refer to page 262)

Market risk. An investor's portfolio can lose money because of economic or other swings in the stock market as a whole, and not as a result of a specific security's decline.

Inflation risk. Due to increases in consumer prices (inflation), an investor's money will not be worth as much in the future as it is now. Inflation affects bonds much more than stocks. Inflation may wipe out any return for an investor solely invested in so-called "safe" investment vehicles, such as treasury bills.

Liquidity risk. Such investments as small-cap stocks, munis, and corporate bonds tend to be illiquid, or harder to resell in a pinch.

Credit risk. Companies can go under or fail to repay the bond principal and interest they owe an investor.

Interest-rate risk. The value of bonds and sometimes stocks moves in inverse relation to interest rates.

Reinvestment risk. As rates drop, companies refinance by paying off bonds before maturity, forcing investors to reinvest at lower rates.

Prepayment risk. This risk for mortgage-backed securities is similar to reinvestment risk. When rates drop, people refinance their mortgages.

Currency risk. If an investor is heavily invested in foreign stocks, his/her portfolio can lose value if the dollar becomes stronger.

Structural risk. Risky derivatives, such as futures and options, can create losses in the underlying investment.

* Material reprinted with the permission of Quickfinder Incorporated *(www.quickfinder.com)*.

COMPOUND ANNUAL RATES OF RETURN BY DECADE*

Time Period:	1920s	1930s	1940s	1950s	1960s	1970s	1980s	1990s
Large Company	19.2%	<0.1>%	9.2%	19.4%	7.8%	5.9%	17.5%	18.2%
Small Company	<4.5>%	1.4%	20.7%	16.9%	15.5%	11.5%	15.8%	15.1%
Long-Term Corporate Bonds	5.2%	6.9%	2.7%	1.0%	1.7%	6.2%	13.0%	8.4%
Long-Term Government Bonds	5.0%	4.9%	3.2%	<0.1>%	1.4%	5.5%	12.6%	8.8%
Intermediate-Term Government Bonds	4.2%	4.6%	1.8%	1.3%	3.5%	7.0%	11.9%	7.2%
Treasury Bills	3.7%	0.6%	0.4%	1.9%	3.9%	6.3%	8.9%	4.9%
Inflation	<1.1>%	<2.0>%	5.4%	2.2%	2.5%	7.4%	5.1%	2.9%

* Material reprinted with the permission of Quickfinder Incorporated *(www.quickfinder.com)*.

WEEK SIX
MAP 6-5

*Mutual Fund Investing**
(refer to page 262)

TYPES OF MUTUAL FUNDS

Aggressive Growth. Invest in new companies and industries, or those in financial trouble or out-of-favor with the market. Sometimes referred to as capital appreciation funds, they usually have above-average increase in price with little or no current income and very high risk.

Balanced. Generally invest in common stocks, preferred stocks and bonds. Balanced funds provide an opportunity for share price appreciation with added income and price stability from the bonds in the fund. Conservative investors seeking share price appreciation and some dividend income may choose a balanced fund.

Global Bond. Invest primarily in the bonds of governments and companies all over the world, including the United States. These funds seek to provide income and global diversity. An investor wanting international exposure or diversification for an income portfolio would consider this type of fund. Currency fluctuations and political developments add to the price instability of this type of fund.

Growth. Invest in common stock of well-established companies. The primary goal is to produce an increase in the value of the investment. Investors in a growth fund are more interested in the rise of the fund's share price than in receiving income from dividends.

Growth and Income. Invest in companies that consistently pay good dividends and also have a strong growth potential with moderate risk.

High-grade Corporate Bond. Invest primarily in high-grade corporate bonds. These funds seek to provide a higher level of monthly income than U.S. government funds and therefore carry slightly more risk. Investors seeking monthly income may choose this type of fund.

High-yield Bond. Invest primarily in lower quality corporate bonds. These funds provide higher income potential than other bond funds but also entail credit risk. Investors seeking maximum monthly income—and willing to tolerate more share price fluctuation— may invest in this type of fund.

Index. Invest in stocks in the companies included in a specific market average or index like Standard & Poor's 500-stock average of large companies or the Wilshire 4,500 index of smaller companies. Fund mirrors the movements of the market. Stock funds usually lag behind market averages because they incur expenses (management fees, trading costs) and because they typically hold at least some cash which acts as a drag on performance in a rising stock market.

International. Invest in common stocks of companies located outside the United States. These funds provide a way to access opportunities in overseas markets. Investors seeking

* Material reprinted with the permission of Quickfinder Incorporated *(www.quickfinder.com)*.

diversification and share price appreciation may put a portion of their assets in an international fund. Currency fluctuations and political developments add to the price instability of this type of fund.

Money Market. Seek to provide income while maintaining a stable $1-per-share price. These funds invest in short-term, high-grade securities such as Treasury bills, bank certificates of deposit, and commercial paper (short-term IOUs from large, well known, high-quality corporations), but are not guaranteed or insured by the U.S. government. Conservative investors wanting to earn income while preserving principal may choose a money market fund.

Tax-free Income. Invest in bonds issued by towns, cities, counties, and states to finance public projects. These funds provide income that is free from federal and, in some instances, state or local income taxes. High tax bracket investors wanting monthly income but not wanting to increase tax burden may choose a tax-free income fund.

Potential pitfalls:

1) Tax-exempt interest must be included when computing taxable Social Security benefits.

2) Tax-exempt interest from private activity bonds must be included for alternative minimum tax purposes.

U.S. Government Income. Invest primarily in a portfolio of income-producing securities issued or guaranteed by the U.S. government, its agencies, or instrumentalities. The fund's shares, however, are not guaranteed. These funds usually provide monthly dividend income. A conservative investor seeking a monthly income check may choose this type of fund.

Factors to Consider Before Investing

➤ Check fund's track record. Has it performed consistently well?

➤ Compare fund's performance with other funds with similar investment objectives.

➤ Make sure fund's investment objective and risk level are in line with the investor's goals.

➤ Compare fund's fees and expenses with that of similar funds.

➤ Is the manager responsible for the fund's performance record still around?

➤ Realize that past performance is a good starting point when picking a fund, but there are no guarantees for the future.

Note: Before investing in a new mutual fund or purchasing additional shares in a fund already owned, investors should call the fund company to verify the amount of any possible capital gains distribution. The investor can then wait until after the distribution to purchase the shares.

By law, mutual funds must pay substantially all dividends, interest, and net capital gains realized by the fund to their shareholders annually. Capital gains distributions are the net long-term capital gains realized from the sale of securities held by the fund and are included in the price of the fund's shares.

Example:

Ezra purchases 1,000 shares of Fund X in November for $10 per share. Fund X declares a capital gains distribution of $1 per share in December, giving the investor $1,000 of taxable capital gain. The fund's net asset value drops to $9 per share after the distribution. Ezra could have avoided the unfair capital gains tax by purchasing the fund shares after the record date at $9 per share.

Week Six
MAP 6-6

*Bonds**
(refer to page 263)

Types of Bonds

Corporate Bonds. Most corporate bonds are long-term, callable debt obligations issued by large corporations at a price close to par value. They typically pay interest semiannually. You should determine whether the bonds are secured by corporate assets or not at all, as is the case with debentures. Generally, higher coupon rates indicate higher risk. Lower coupon rates indicate better security.

Convertible Corporate Bonds. Convertible corporate bonds are corporate debt issues that can be converted to shares of common stock. They are hybrid securities with investment characteristics similar to a combination portfolio of common stocks and nonconvertible corporate bonds. They provide fixed income from the guaranteed interest payments and maturity dates.

State and Local Government Debt (Municipal Bond). Municipal bonds are debt obligations issued by a variety of entities including states, counties, cities, tax districts, schools, hospitals, street and highway departments, and port authorities. Generally, interest on municipal bonds is not subject to federal income tax. The interest on certain issues is taxable to investors, however, because interest income on certain municipal bonds is subject to the alternative minimum tax.

Treasury Notes and Bonds. Treasury notes are U.S. government securities maturing in two–10 years. Treasury bonds have a maturity range of from 10-30 years. U.S. securities are safe from default. As a consequence, yields are lower than for high-quality corporate bonds. Unlike Treasury bills, Treasury notes and bonds are sold at face value. The minimum denomination for a Treasury note maturing in two or three years is $5,000 and $1,000 with a maturity longer than three years. Minimum investment is $1,000. Interest is paid semi-annually.

Treasury Inflation-Protection Securities. The U.S. Treasury Department sells 10-year Treasury bonds that are indexed to inflation. This bond, known as a Treasury Inflation-Protection Security (TIP) is sold in $1,000 denominations and provides investors with a guaranteed hedge against inflation. Interest on a TIP is paid semiannually at a fixed rate.

U.S. Savings Bonds. Three types of U.S. savings bonds are currently available (with no commission charge):

1. Series EE Bonds are non-interest-bearing; have a 17-year original maturity and 30-year final maturity. They are sold at a discount, and interest accrues and is paid

at redemption (rather than periodically). They are available in denominations ranging from $50 to $10,000. Maximum purchase is $15,000 ($30,000 face amount) per individual per calendar year. Series EE bonds cannot be redeemed until they have been held six months from issue.

2. Series HH Bonds offer the investor the opportunity to continue to defer reporting interest on Series E and EE bonds beyond their maturity date. They can be purchased only in exchange for Series E or EE bonds or U.S. savings notes that are at least six months old and have not passed final maturity by more than one year or in exchange for matured Series H bonds. A minimum of $500 in eligible bonds is necessary to make an exchange. Like EE bonds, Series HH bonds cannot be redeemed until they have been held six months from issue.

3. Series I bonds became available September 1,1998. They are sold at face value and grow with inflation-indexed earnings for up to 30 years. Interest earnings are added to the bond each month, and interest is compounded semiannually. I bonds are sold in denominations of $50, $75, $100, $200, $500, $1,000, $5,000, and $10,000. A single owner can buy up to $30,000 of I bonds in each calendar year.

U.S. Savings Bond Characteristics

Series	Value at Issue Date	Interest Paid	Status	Method of Purchase	Purchase Limit (per person per year)	Final Maturity[a]
E[b]	Discount	At redemption	No longer issued. (Issued through June 1980)	N/A	N/A	
Issued before December 1965						40 yrs.
Issued after November 1965						30 yrs.
H[b]	Face Value	Semiannually	No longer issued	N/A	N/A	
Issued June 1952—January 1957						29 yrs., 8 mos.
Issued February 1957 and later						30 yrs.
EE[c]	Discount	At redemption	Available	Cash	$15,000 ($30,000 face amount)[d]	30 yrs.
HH	Face Value	Semiannually	Available	Only in exchange for E or EE bonds[e]	No limit if obtained in exchange for E or EE bonds	20 yrs.

Notes:

a   Maximum life of bond.

b   Bonds will not earn interest after the final maturity date, and all accrued but unrecognized interest is generally taxable in that year. (There is an exception for Series HH bond exchanges.)

c   Bonds will not earn interest after the final maturity date, and the accrued interest is generally taxable in that year. (There is an exception for Series HH bond exchanges.)

d   If bonds are held by two persons, ownership can be attributed to either co-owner or apportioned between them to a combined maximum of $60,000.

e   If the redemption value is an uneven amount, the bondholder may add cash to the redemption value or accept cash to round to the nearest multiple of $500.

Zero-Coupon Bonds. Zero-Coupon bonds do not pay periodic interest. Instead, they are purchased at a deep discount, and the investor receives the face value, which represents principal and interest when the bond is redeemed at maturity. Zero-Coupon bonds basically have two advantages over coupon-bearing bonds:

1. A relatively small investment is required to purchase Zero-Coupon bonds.

2. The investor is assured of a specific yield throughout the term of the investment (i.e., if the obligation is held to maturity).

Four Types of Zero-Coupon Bonds

1. *Zero-Coupon Treasury Bonds.* These are U.S. Treasury bonds or notes that have been stripped of their coupons by the Treasury or by a brokerage house. A broker, bank, or other custodian then markets the stripped bonds at a discount, and the purchaser receives the face amount at maturity.

2. *Zero-Coupon Certificates of Deposit.* These are issued by banks and are insured up to $100,000 by the FDIC. Zero-Coupon CDs are offered at a larger discount than are zero coupon Treasury bonds, thereby providing the investor with greater return on investment.

3. *Zero-Coupon Corporate Bonds.* These are issued by corporations and provide a greater rate of return than stripped Treasury bonds or Zero-Coupon CDs because the investor assumes more risk. They are not insured against the issuer defaulting at maturity.

4. *Zero-Coupon Municipal Bonds.* These are Zero-Coupon bonds that provide interest income that is not subject to federal, and, in many cases, state taxation. They alleviate the problem of the investor having to report interest income that has not been received.

WEEK SIX
MAP 6-7

*Treasury Inflation-Protection Securities**
(refer to page 263)

All bond investors face the risk of inflation. Long-term bond investors in particular can lose a substantial portion of the purchasing power of their invested funds due to a gradual increase in prices. Treasury inflation-protection securities (TIPS) are one answer to the inflation risk problem.

How It Works

TIPS are marketable, book-entry debt securities issued by the U.S. Treasury. TIPS are sold by the government at a quarterly auction, in minimum amounts of $1,000. They carry a fixed annual interest rate, and pay interest twice a year. The inflation protection is provided by adjusting the principal amount of the security according to changes in the inflation rate.[1] The semiannual interest payment is then calculated based on the adjusted principal amount. The inflation-adjusted principal amount is paid at maturity.

Example: An investor purchases a $1,000 TIPS bond, paying 3.0% annual interest, in January. By July, when the first interest payment is due, inflation has increased 1.0%. The adjusted principal amount of the bond is now $1,010. The interest payable at that time is $15.15, calculated as ($1,010 x 3.0%) ÷ 2. If by January of the following year, when the second interest payment becomes due, inflation had run at a 3.0% level for the whole year, the principal amount of the bond would be $1,030. The second interest payment would be $15.45, calculated as ($1,030 x 3.0%) ÷ 2.

If deflation becomes a problem, and the adjusted principal amount of the bond at maturity is less than the principal amount at issue, an additional sum will be paid to return to the investor at least the original principal amount.

Income Tax Issues[2]

Interest income from Treasury Inflation-Protection Securities is treated in the same manner as interest income from other ì direct obligationsî of the federal government. The interest is taxable by the federal government, but is generally exempt from state and local tax.

A unique characteristic of TIPS is that any adjustment of the principal amount is considered to be currently taxable interest income. Thus, in our example above, the investor would have $25.15 of taxable interest income from the bond for the first year; $15.15 of interest actually received as cash, and $10.00 in the form of inflation adjustment to the principal amount.

---

[1] As measured by the change in the inflation rate between the date the bond is issued and the current interest payment date. The index used is the non-seasonally adjusted, U.S. City Average All Items Consumer Price Index for Urban Consumers, the CPI-U. The CPI-U is published every month by the Bureau of Labor Statistics.

[2] See Treasury Decision 8830, IRB 1999—38, and Treasury Decision 8709, IRB 1997—9, for a more detailed discussion of the tax treatment of Treasury Inflation-Protection Securities.

TIPS - Market Prices and Interest Rates

Although Treasury inflation-protection securities are guaranteed against default by the U.S. government, they are also marketable securities, which means they can be bought and sold in the open market. If an investor buys a TIPS and holds it to maturity, the government is obligated to repay at least the original principal amount. If a bond is sold before it matures, however, the investor may receive more, or less, than originally paid, due to fluctuations in market value. TIPS prices in the open market can move up and down, most often in response to changes in the general level of interest rates. In general, if rates rise, the price of existing bonds will fall; if interest rates decline, the market value of existing bonds will increase.

Investment Uses

Treasury inflation-protection securities can serve as a source of periodic income, for investors seeking to meet current expenses. The inflation adjustment feature of these bonds is expected to be a prime attraction for many fixed-income investors. The currently taxable nature of the inflation adjusted principal amount may be a drawback for some. TIPS can be a useful investment in a tax-deferred IRA or other qualified retirement plan.

How to Invest

- **Direct ownership:** Investors can own TIPS directly, in their own names.

- **Indirect ownership:** Open-end investment companies, known as mutual funds, are an indirect method of owning treasury inflation-protection securities.[1] Mutual funds pool the resources of many individuals, and offer an investor access to a diversified, professionally managed portfolio.

Possible Risks

- **Market risk:** If a bond is sold before maturity, an investor may receive more or less than originally paid.

---

[1] The Securities and Exchange Commission requires that all prospective mutual fund investors be given a prospectus. The prospectus contains valuable information concerning how an investment works, its goals and risks, and any expenses and charges involved.

WEEK SIX
MAP 6-8*

Bonds 101
(refer to page 264)

SHIFTS IN BOND PRICES

As interest rates rise or fall, new bonds issued in the marketplace offer yields that reflect these changing interest rates. Since existing bonds offer fixed yields, they have no way to compensate for interest rate changes except by changing in price.

Prices move in opposite direction of interest rates. As interest rates go up, bond prices are pushed down; as rates move down, bond prices rise.

Example: If an investor is selling a $1,000 bond yielding 6 percent ($60 per year) in a marketplace wherein newly issued $1,000 bonds have a 7 percent yield ($70 per year), the bond will be less attractive to potential buyers. To compete with higher-yielding new issues, the investor will have to sell the bond at a discount so the $60 return the buyer receives on the bond will approximate a yield of 7 percent of the amount paid. When a bond purchased at a discount is eventually sold, the part of the gain due to the discounted price must be treated as ordinary income [IRC §1276(a)(1)]. The Revenue Reconciliation Act of 1993 extended this rule to all tax-exempt bonds and to all market discount bonds purchased after April 30, 1993, regardless of when the bonds were originally issued. Prior to this rule, bonds issued on or before July 18, 1984, were excluded from Section 1276 ordinary income treatment. Bonds issued on or before July 18, 1984, and purchased before May 1, 1993, will still receive capital gain treatment.

BONDS AND CHANGING MARKET CONDITIONS

Quality. Generally, the higher a bond's quality, the less volatile its price will be as interest rates rise or fall.

Maturity. Bonds with longer maturities are more likely to fluctuate in price.

The longer an investor's money is tied up at a certain rate, the greater the likelihood that interest rates—and therefore bond yields—will change before the bond matures.

WEEK SIX
MAP 6-9[*]

Bond Maturity and Duration *
(refer to page 264)

A bond's maturity is a measure of its economic lifetime stated strictly in terms of the timing of repayment of principal at the bond's maturity date.

Duration, however, measures a bond's lifetime but considers the present value of all cash flow of the bond over its life. It reflects how long an investor must hold a bond bought at face value to realize the stated yield, regardless of how the market performs. Duration is expressed in years, but it also serves as an indication of the bond's performance as interest rates change (i.e., it measures volatility).

Example: Difference between bond maturity and duration.

> Ralph paid face value for two newly issued 20-year bonds. One has a coupon rate of 9 percent and the other 12 percent. The maturity of both bonds is 20 years, i.e., the period that will elapse before Ralph will receive repayment of the principal of the debt.
>
> The duration (economic life) of the 9 percent bond is longer than the 12 percent bond's duration because the interest payments on the 9 percent bond are smaller. Ralph will recover his investment in the 9 percent bond over a longer period than he will in the 12 percent bond.

The following graphs compare the maturity and duration of a 9 percent and 12 percent coupon bond. Both bonds have a maturity of 20 years as indicated in the first graph. However, in the second graph, the duration of both bonds is less than 20 years. In addition, the duration of the 12 percent bond is less than that of the 9 percent bond due to the higher yield and resultant cash flow.

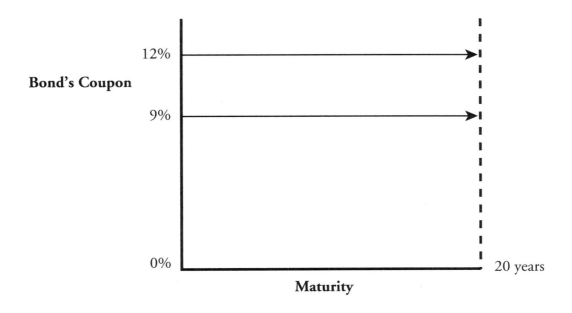

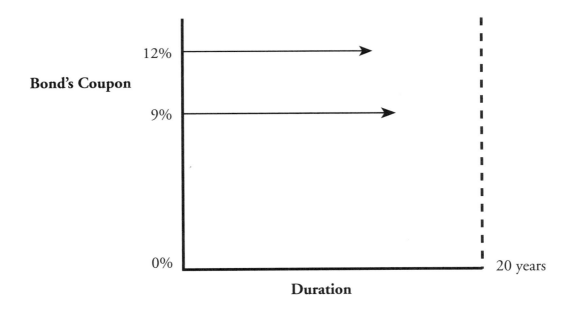

Summary. Duration tells a bond investor that shorter-duration bonds (and bond portfolios) have less risk associated with them. Greater volatility is associated with bonds of longer duration. Duration also affects total return by affecting the price of a bond.

Week Six
MAP 6-10*

*Categories of Equity Investments**
(refer to page 264)

Equity investments are categorized differently by various members of the investment community. The following table provides categories of equity investments and highlights distinguishing characteristics of each category.

Category	Features	Example
Blue chip stocks	• Large, highest quality, and well-established companies with proven earnings capabilities • Consistent dividends • Lower volatility	Dow Jones Industrial Average companies
Income stocks	• Higher-than-average dividend yields	Utility stocks
Growth stocks	• Profits tend to increase faster than average market • Held by investors for capital appreciation • Volatile • Little or no income paid to shareholders because profits are reinvested • High P/E ratio	High-tech and research and development companies
Cyclical stocks	• Performance and stock price depend on their business cycle (i.e., performance and price are strong when the economic factors influencing their business are strong, and poor when the economic factors are weak)	Housing and steel industries
Speculative stocks	• High-risk, bigger gamble to a non-expert investor than other stock issues because they are typically new issues or in an unpredictable business • High volatility and high P/E ratios	New issues and glamour stocks

WEEK SIX
MAP 6-11

Advantages and Disadvantages of Investing in Real Estate*
(refer to page 265)

Advantages	Disadvantages
Preservation and growth of capital through carefully structured purchase and sale of appreciated property (inflation hedge).	Real estate is illiquid because: 1. It has no established market; and 2. A buyer must be found who wants to buy a particular property (with unique traits) at a particular price and who can obtain the cash or financing to buy it.
Tax benefits such as depreciation write-offs, limited passive loss deductibility for certain rental real estate, and preferential capital gain rates on certain gains from disposition.	It usually takes greater resources to invest in real estate than other investments, such as stock and fixed-income securities.
Opportunities for investments highly leveraged with non recourse debt because of real estate's value as security for loans.	Real estate usually requires management.
	High costs are usually incurred on real estate transactions.
	It is difficult to project return on investment.
	Tax benefits cannot be relied upon.
	Real estate has significant liability exposure compared to stocks, bonds, and most other assets (e.g., environmental hazards, personal injury, and other tort liability).

WEEK SIX
MAP 6-12
Real Estate Investment Trust (REIT) *
(refer to page 265)

A method to invest indirectly in real estate is to purchase shares in an REIT, which is essentially a publicly traded closed-end investment company that invests in a managed, diversified portfolio of real estate or real estate mortgages, rather than in financial securities such as stocks and bonds. As long as an REIT derives 75 percent of its income from real estate (for example, interest on mortgage loans and rents) and distributes at least 95 percent of the income as cash dividends, the trust is exempt from federal income tax. Thus REITs, like mutual funds and other closed-end investment companies, are conduits through which earnings pass to the shareholders.

The ease of marketability differentiates REITs from other types of real estate investments since shares of REITs are readily sold on the New York and American stock exchanges. REITs allow an investment in real estate without a large capital investment. It may be desirable for an investor to purchase a portfolio of three to five REITs in order to limit his/her dependence on a single property or geographic location.

* Material reprinted with the permission of Quickfinder Incorporated *(www.quickfinder.com)*.

WEEK SIX
MAP 6-13*

The Key to Investing–Invest!
(refer to page 265)

PRICE OF PROCRASTINATION

Amount to be invested each month to accumulate $250,000 (assuming 12 equal payments to a savings program per year, earning 8 percent compounded monthly) is shown below for different time periods.

Time Period	Investment	Savings Goal
5 Years	$3,402 per month	$250,000
10 Years	$1,367 per month	$250,000
20 Years	$424 per month	$250,000
30 Years	$168 per month	$250,000

Early Saver Wins—Time Is the Key

Investors with modest lifetime annual incomes can retire in comfort if a retirement plan is started early. The example below shows that a late saver will never catch up with an early saver due to compounding interest.

Early Saver: Saves $1,000 per year at 8 percent for 10 years.

Late Saver: Saves nothing for 10 years and then begins a $1,000 per year savings program for 40 years.

Early Saver Year Deposits $1,000/year at 8 percent	Late Saver Deposits nothing
1 .... $1,083	$0
5 .... $6,397	$0
10 .... $15,939	$0

Deposits nothing, builds at 8 percent	Deposits $1,000/year at 8 percent
11........ $ 17,267	$ 1,083
20........ $ 35,471	$ 15,939
30........ $ 78,934	$ 51,939
40....... $175,656	$130,344
50...... $390,895	$306,000

* Material reprinted with the permission of Quickfinder Incorporated (*www.quickfinder.com*).

LET'S SAVE MONEY!

A modest amount of monthly savings can add up to big dollars. If a kindergartner (age six) starts a monthly savings plan, how much money can be accumulated assuming an 8 percent return?

Monthly Savings	$5	$10	$15	$20
Through high school	$1,373	$2,747	$4,121	$5,495
Through college	$2,173	$4,347	$6,520	$8,694
Through age 40	$10,603	$21,206	$31,809	$42,413
Through age 65	$82,616	$165,232	$247,848	$330,463
	.16¢/day	.33¢/day	.50¢/day	.66¢/day

If a seventh grader (age 12) starts a monthly savings plan, how much money can be accumulated assuming an 8 percent return?

Monthly Savings	$20	$30	$40	$50
Through high school	$ 1,853	$ 2,779	$ 3,705	$ 4,632
Through college	$ 3,683	$ 5,525	$ 7,367	$ 9,208
Through age 40	$ 25,137	$ 37,707	$ 50,276	$ 62,844
Through age 65	$ 203,663	$ 305,494	$ 407,326	$ 509,157
	66¢/day	$1/day	$1.33/day	$1.66/day

*What Are Mutual Fund Sales Charges or Loads?**
(refer to page 266)

The first portion of the fee table found in a mutual fund's prospectus discloses shareholder transaction expenses. These expenses typically include sales commissions, also known as loads, to purchase fund shares (front-end sales loads). Other types of sales charges are deferred sales commissions (known as back-end or deferred sales loads), sales commissions to reinvest dividends, fees to redeem fund shares, and fees to exchange fund shares.

Mutual funds that charge sales loads usually do so to pay for commissions to registered representatives of broker-dealers who sell the fund's shares to the investor. It is important to understand that sales loads do not buy performance. In fact, funds charging sales loads (load funds) do not perform better on average (absent the load) than funds that do not charge sales loads (no-load funds).

Only load mutual funds charge sales commissions. No-load funds do not charge sales commissions.

Classes of Shares

Many mutual fund companies have different classes of shares. The letters A, B, or C usually label shares with sales loads.

Class A shares have front-end sales loads. Class B and C shares have deferred sales loads. It is important to understand that regardless of the class of share, the investor is getting the same fund and the same fund manager. The only substantive difference between the classes is the way the mutual fund company is charging the investor to own the shares.

WEEK SIX
MAP 6-15*

What Are Mutual Fund Annual Operating Expenses? *
(refer to page 266)

The second portion of the fee table found in a mutual fund's prospectus discloses the annual operating expenses paid by the fund as a percentage of the fund's assets, usually for the most recent fiscal year. These expenses typically include management fees, 12b-1 fees, and other expenses.

The total annual fund operating expenses disclosed in the prospectus is known as the expense ratio for the fund. A higher expense ratio of one fund over another means that the fund is paying a higher percentage of fund assets out as expenses than the fund with the lower expense ratio and has a greater relative impact on the shareholder's net asset value.

Both load and no-load mutual funds charge annual operating expenses.

Management Fees

Management fees are charges to administer the investment-management operations of the fund. These fees typically include salaries and other administrative costs. Every mutual fund charges a management fee. The amount of the fee varies from fund to fund. In some cases, the management fee is waived to attract new investors and enhance fund performance.

12b-1 Fees

Some mutual funds charge an annual fee known as a 12b-1 fee. The term "12b-1" refers to the Securities and Exchange Commission (SEC) rule that permits a mutual fund to charge marketing and distribution expenses directly against fund assets. Thus, 12b-1 fees are marketing-and distribution-related expenses.

Other Fees

The expense catagory includes transfer agent fees, custodian fees, legal fees, director fees, and other similar administrative costs of running the fund.

Fund Expense Ratio

A mutual fund's expense ratio is the sum of its annual operating expenses (management fees, 12b-1 fees, and other fees) expressed as a percentage of the fund's average net assets. Expense ratios vary from fund to fund, with a typical range from around 0.20 percent (or $2 per $1,000 of assets) to around 2 percent ($20 per $1,000 of assets).

The expense ratio is helpful in determining the fund's overall efficiency. Of course, a lower expense ratio is preferable because it means higher total returns for the investor.

Week Six
MAP 6-16*

*Comparing Index Funds and Actively Managed Funds** (refer to page 266)*

The debate about whether passive investing (i.e., using index funds that mimic stock and bond indexes) is a superior long-term strategy has grown in intensity in recent years, as index funds have consistently outperformed the majority of actively managed funds.

Passive Management Defined

Passive management refers to the strategy of holding every security in a predefined market, with each represented in exactly the same proportions as in the market. For example, a "market" could be defined as the 500 stocks tracked by Standard & Poors and published as their S&P 500 Index, or it could be the 5,000 stocks tracked by Wilshire to represent the broad market.

Regardless of how the market is defined, the passive investor would hold all of the securities in that market, thus replicating the returns for that specific market or index. The fund only buys and sells securities to keep the fund's composition consistent with the index it is mimicking.

Because passive management attempts to replicate an index, it is also known as "indexing."

Active Management Defined

Active management is whatever is not passive. Active managers believe they can identify investments that are underpriced or offer growth potential. Unlike a passive investment in a fixed basket of securities, active managers tend to trade investments more frequently, thus earning the name "active."

Indexing as a Strategy

There are many reasons to consider a passive investment approach, including:

➤ low costs,

➤ good performance, and

➤ the ability to accurately position a portion of a portfolio within a targeted asset subclass.

There are several reasons for the better performance by index funds, but the most likely are:

➤ substantially lower operating expenses and trading costs, and

➤ lower management fees.

Diversifying with Index Funds

Index funds are especially effective for asset allocation because they remain consistently invested in the intended asset class.

Index funds allow advisors to allocate their client's assets to particular asset categories with precision. Actively managed funds, on the other hand, are imprecise because they tend to drift into other asset categories when the fund manager believes it is necessary to improve the fund's performance.

WEEK SIX
MAP 6-17*

*Comparing Variable Annuities and Mutual Funds**
(refer to page 266)

Because mutual funds are so popular, insurance companies tout the resemblance of a variable annuity contract to a family of mutual funds as an advantage. However, there are actually major differences—some good and some bad.

1. Variable annuities include a life insurance feature, called a "death benefit" by insurance companies. If the investor dies, his/her heir will receive at least as much as the investor paid into the contract. This provides limited protection against market value declines. The death benefit feature has been used as a major selling point in distinguishing variable annuities from mutual funds.

    The problems with the death benefit concept are:

    a. it only applies when the investor dies,

    b. it is irrelevant if the market keeps rising, and

    c. insurance companies charge a fee which is usually buried in the "mortality and expense risk" charge. These annual charges typically run about 1.25 percent percent of the asset value of the contract.

2. There is a major difference between variable annuities and mutual funds under the tax rules. Unlike mutual fund investments, variable annuities are tax-deferred. The investor owes no federal income tax until money is withdrawn from the contract. While the tax deferral benefit is nice, the income will all be taxed at ordinary rates. Most withdrawals before age 59½ will be subject to the 10 percent penalty tax. In contrast, a good part of most mutual fund dividends will be taxed at long-term capital gains rates, and so will gains on the sale of appreciated shares held over one year. With a capital gains rate of 15 percent, this advantage of mutual funds over variable annuities should be given additional weight. While mutual fund investors may face immediate recognition of taxable gain when they transfer money from one fund to another, they can also deduct losses (subject to the capital loss restrictions). Variable annuity fund investors pay no current tax when they move money among subaccounts, but losses are deferred as well. In addition, when an investor dies, the heir(s) get no basis step-up for a variable annuity and thus will owe income tax as money is withdrawn from the contract. In contrast, mutual fund shares (as well as bonds and stock shares in general) are stepped up to FMV on the date of death. This step-up generally insulates the heir(s) from any capital gains tax when appreciated shares are sold.

3. Variable annuities may charge higher fees (beyond the death benefit expense) than mutual funds. There may be a fixed annual administrative charge and additional fees for management and transactions such as transfers among subaccounts. Combined administrative, management, and death benefit charges can run as high as 3 percent or more annually. When the stock market is booming, this is hardly noticeable. But if the market declines, fees this high will stand out. Variable annuities also will usually impose a hefty "surrender charge" if the investor liquidates the contract in the first five to 10 years. The bottom line is it may take 10 or more years of aggressive and successful investing for the tax-deferral advantage of variable annuities to overcome the disadvantages of higher fees and income taxed at ordinary rates.

Week Six
MAP 6-18

Dollar-Cost Averaging & DRIPS*
(refer to page 267)

Dollar-cost Averaging

With dollar-cost averaging, an investor invests a fixed amount of money in an individual stock or a mutual fund at regular intervals. The investment buys more shares when the price is low, fewer shares when the price is high.

Like diversification, dollar-cost averaging is an effective way of reducing an investment program's risk. By spreading share purchases over both high and low price periods, an investor can usually accumulate more shares at a lower average cost than if purchased all at once. In addition, dollar-cost averaging provides a mechanical strategy which does not require investor decision-making.

Month	Monthly Investment	Share Price	Number of Shares Purchased
January	$100	$10	10.0
February	$100	$8	12.5
March	$100	$5	20.0
April	$100	$8	12.5
May	$100	$11	9.1
Totals	$500		64.1

Average cost: ($500 ÷ 64.1 shares) = $7.80 per share

Note: If the total $500 had been invested in January, the average per share cost would have been $10.00 vs. $7.80 using the dollar-cost averaging strategy.

Dividend Reinvestment Plans (DRIPs)

DRIPs allow shareholders to reinvest dividends for more stock instead of receiving a cash dividend payment. DRIPs are an effective way to dollar-cost average.

Information. *Directory of Companies Offering Dividend Reinvestment Plans.* Directory includes over 800 companies offering DRIPs.

Contact: Evergreen Enterprises, PO Box 763, Laurel, MD 20725. Phone: (301) 549-3939. website: *www1.netstockdirect.com*

* Material reprinted with the permission of Quickfinder Incorporated *(www.quickfinder.com)*.

12b-1 fees. These mutual fund fees are often referred to as hidden loads, i.e., sales or distribution costs (marketing costs, such as advertising and commissions). They are charged every year based on a percentage of the account's assets; therefore, the higher the balance, the higher the fee.

Alpha. A measure of a portfolio's return in excess of the market return after adjusting for risk. Measures the manager's contribution to performance.

Antifraud provisions of the Investment Advisers Act of 1940 (IAA). Section 206 of the IAA, which makes it unlawful to enter into any conduct or transaction that directly or indirectly defrauds, deceives, or manipulates any client or prospective client. Section 206 imposes a fiduciary duty on investment advisors. The provisions apply to those who are "investment advisors" under the IAA, even those who are exempt from registration. Those who are excluded from the definition are not subject to these provisions.

Asset allocation. The spreading of assets over a variety of asset classes and subclasses to achieve a desired balance between expected return and risk. A method of diversification across broad asset classes to reduce nonsystematic risk.

Asset manager. A financial professional who typically manages client investment funds using portfolios composed of multiple asset classes rather than focusing on one type of individual security (e.g., growth equities or high-yield bonds).

Balanced fund. A fund that combines equities and bonds in an effort to obtain the highest return consistent with a low-risk strategy. Typically offers a higher yield than a pure stock fund and performs better than a pure stock fund when stocks are declining.

Banker's acceptances. Short-term drafts drawn on a bank. The bank agrees to pay a specific sum on a future date. They are negotiable, normally sold at a discount from face value. They are sold in denominations of at least $100,000.

Beta. The measure of the relative variability of a security versus the market as a whole (i.e., its systematic risk). It represents the change that can be expected for a stock compared with the market. The market as a whole has a beta of 1.0. The covariance of each security is then compared with the market to derive its unique beta coefficient. A stock with a beta of 1.2, for example, would be 20 percent more volatile than the market. If the market rose (or declined) by 10 percent, a stock with a beta of 1.2 should be expected to rise (or fall) by 12 percent.

Broker-Dealer. A financial firm that serves two roles—broker and dealer. In its role as a broker, it acts as an agent for the customer, such as in executing the purchase of securities. For its services, it receives a commission. In its dealer role, the BD buys and sells securities for its own account. The customer who sells to or buys from the dealer is charged a markdown or markup, respectively.

Business risk. The risk associated with the specific industry or market in which a company operates.

Call risk. The risk that a bond issuer will exercise its right under the bond contract (indenture) to retire all or a portion of the bond before maturity. A bond is more likely to be called in an environment of declining interest rates, and the investor can usually count on a bond not being called while the market interest rate is higher than the bond's coupon rate. A call allows the issuer to retire outstanding bonds with relatively higher interest rates to enable it to issue new bonds with lower (more-favorable-to-the-issuer) interest rates.

Capitalization. The total market value of a company (number of shares outstanding x stock price).

Certified Financial Planner Board of Standards, Inc. (CFP Board). An independent nonprofit corporation established to ensure that CFP designees practice in accordance with recognized standards of conduct and to further ensure that they perform their work effectively, ethically, and in the best interests of their clients and the public.

CFA (Chartered Financial Analyst). The professional designation offered by the Association for Investment Management and Research.

CFP (Certified Financial Planner). A designation granted by the Certified Financial Planner Board of Standards.

Chartered Financial Analyst. (See CFA.)

ChFC (Chartered Financial Consultant). A program and professional designation offered by the American College in Bryn Mawr, PA. This program concentrates on the comprehensive financial planning process. It is generally targeted to insurance professionals who provide financial and investment planning services.

College for Financial Planning. The nation's first financial planning education program. The College offers coursework and continuing education in insurance, investment, retirement, income tax, and estate planning.

Commercial paper. Unsecured, short-term promissory notes, which are usually sold at a discount by financially strong companies. Denominations begin at $100,000.

Contrarian. Contrarian managers evaluate the current trends or prevailing "wisdom" and usually invest in contrast. The opposite of a contrarian is the manager who invests in stocks currently in favor.

Convertible corporate bonds. Corporate debt issues that can be converted to shares of common stock. They are hybrid securities having investment characteristics similar to a combination portfolio of common stocks and nonconvertible corporate bonds. They provide fixed-income via the bond's guaranteed interest payments and maturity dates. In addition, convertible bonds offer potential appreciation through participation in future price increases of the underlying common stock.

Convertible preferred stock. Convertible preferred stock gives the shareholder the option of exchanging preferred shares for common shares at a given ratio (e.g., one convertible preferred share of XYZ Corporation stock for four shares of XYZ common stock). In doing so, the shareholder is exchanging his/her preferred position for earnings and liquidation proceeds for an opportunity to share in any appreciation of the value of the company. Normally, the fixed dividend rate on convertible preferred stock is slightly less than on nonconvertible preferred because of the conversion feature. Also, the convertible preferred is usually subordinate to other preferred stock.

Correlation coefficient. A measurement of the degree to which the movements of different investments are related. The perfectly positive correlation is described by a correlation of +1.0. The perfectly negative correlation is described by a correlation of -1.0. Patterns of return unrelated to one another have correlations near 0.

Covariance. A measure of the mutual variation between two assets. A positive covariance means that assets move together. A negative covariance means that assets move in opposite directions.

Credit analysis. The fixed-income manager makes portfolio decisions based on the ratings and projected ratings of the issuers and specific issues.

Custody. Directly or indirectly holding client assets, having the authority to obtain possession of them, or having the ability to appropriate them. The power to direct or cause the direction of the management or policies of a company, whether through ownership of securities, by contract, or otherwise.

Day order. A broker is directed to make a trade before the close of the trading day or it expires.

Default (or credit) risk. The risk that a bond issuer will not be able to make interest payments or pay the principal to the investor at the bond's maturity.

Discretionary authority. The shared or individual authority to make decisions about what assets to buy or sell on a client's behalf.

Diversification. The process of spreading a portfolio over many different investments to minimize or avoid excessive exposure to any one source of risk. Diversification occurs both within and among asset categories or classes. Within an asset class, diversification reduces or eliminates the risks specific to one issue. In the stock market, diversification is used to reduce unnecessary exposure to one company or industry.

Diversity of maturities. The fixed-income manager uses short-term, intermediate-term, and long-term bonds in the management of the portfolio.

Dividend yield. The current annualized dividend paid on a share of stock, stated as a percentage of the stock's current market price.

Dollar-cost averaging. Dollar-cost averaging (DCA) is an approach to periodic investing that involves making equal investments at regular intervals. DCA is a strategy to avoid making large investments just as the markets are reaching temporary highs. If share prices continue to advance, at least a portion of the client's assets have been invested and benefit from the advance. If, on the other hand, share prices begin to decline, the client can buy more shares with the same fixed investment amount.

Dow Jones Industrial Average. A composite of 30 major industrial companies. The index is a price-weighted average.

Duration. A measure of a bond's lifetime based on the present value of all of the bond's cash flow over its life. Duration reflects how long an investor must hold a bond bought at face value to realize the stated yield, regardless of how the market performs. Duration also serves as an indication of the bond's performance as interest rates change. For every interest rate change of 1 percent, the bond will change by an amount (or multiple) equal to the duration.

Earnings per share. A firm's earnings divided by the number of outstanding shares of common stock, calculated after paying taxes, bondholders, and preferred shareholders.

Efficient frontier. The graph representing a set of efficient portfolios (i.e., portfolios which offer the highest expected return for a given level of risk).

Efficient market theory (EMT). The theory that a security's market price reflects its true value because market prices reflect all available information. The weak form of the EMT assumes that stock prices are independent of each other, with all historical data about the stock already reflected in the current price. The semistrong form of EMT holds that all historical data and all new public information will be immediately reflected in the security's price. The strong form of the EMT holds that not only is all historical data and all new public information reflected in the price of the stock, but all nonpublic information (e.g., insider information) is also reflected in the current stock price.

Efficient portfolio. In accordance with modern portfolio theory, a portfolio that achieves the greatest expected return for a given level of risk. Alternatively, an efficient portfolio is one that achieves the least amount of risk for a given level of expected return.

Emerging markets. Markets in emerging second and third world countries.

Employee pension plan. Any plan that provides retirement income to employees or results in a deferral of income by employees for periods extending to the termination of covered employment or beyond. Thus, for ERISA, a pension plan includes both defined benefit and defined contribution plans, such as profit sharing, 401(k) plans, and stock bonus plans.

Employee welfare benefit plan. An ERISA plan that provides, through the purchase of insurance or otherwise, benefits such as (1) medical, hospital, sickness, accident, disability, death, or unemployment benefits; (2) vacation benefits; (3) apprenticeship or other training programs; (4) daycare; (5) scholarship funds; or (6) prepaid legal services. Certain severance pay plans are also welfare benefit plans.

Eurodollars. Generally, short-term time deposits or certificates of deposit (CDs) denominated in dollars and held in foreign banks or U.S. banks located abroad. The yield normally exceeds money market yields.

Fiduciary. One who has power or discretion over someone else's interests. The fiduciary has an obligation to put the interests of the client, retirement plan, and beneficiary first. For purposes of ERISA, a person becomes a fiduciary by being named in the plan document or by being selected through procedures specified in the plan document. The persons named in the plan are "named fiduciaries." A person can become a fiduciary by performing any fiduciary function regardless of title.

Fill-or-kill order. A broker is directed to execute the transaction immediately, otherwise the order expires.

Form ADV. The application for registration with the SEC (Services and Exchange Commission) and is used by most states as the basis for their applications.

Fundamental analysis. A system for making investment decisions that uses economic and company-specific information to value securities. Earnings, sales growth, dividends, market share, interest rates, and numerous other factors could be considered in attempting to formulate a fair value for a company's stock using fundamental analysis.

Government intervention risk. This is risk that a foreign government may nationalize a company or regulate a company in such a way that investors' returns will be diminished.

Growth and income manager. The equity manager looks for either companies with exceptional payout records or bonds that are convertible into stock. The emphasis is on income as well as appreciation.

Growth investing. Growth investing assumes that the markets are efficient and securities are fairly priced. A growth investment style emphasizes earnings growth as the primary criterion for selecting stocks. Companies with rapidly growing revenues and earnings are identified and purchased on the belief that the fundamental determinant of stock prices is earnings.

Growth manager. The equity manager looks for companies whose earnings are expected to grow at a faster rate than the rest of the market.

Hedge. A risk-reducing strategy typically involving short-selling and similar strategies.

Index fund. A passively managed fund designed to mimic the performance of a specific market index.

Index manager. This equity or fixed-income manager invests in index mutual funds or constructs portfolios that mimic the index. This is also known as passive management.

Inflation risk. The risk of the loss of the invested asset's purchasing power due to rising price levels.

Interest rate risk. The risk of reduction of return on invested assets due to changes in market interest rates.

Investment policy. The specific selection of acceptable investment strategies. Investment policy differs from a simple statement of investment strategy because it includes procedures to guide and determine present and future investment decisions.

Investment policy statement (IPS). A formal, detailed, written statement of the investment strategy to be followed by the investment advisor and/or money manager for a client. It is a roadmap or blueprint of the investment plan the client and advisor(s) have agreed to. It should document the client's goals, investment objectives, investment preferences and constraints, time horizon, risk profile, asset allocation plan, risk parameters, and performance expectations and benchmarks. It can also include investment procedures and other specifics. The client and advisor(s) should sign it.

Investment strategy. For an advisor working with individual clients, investment strategy is the global plan of investing designed to meet the client's needs and goals. It is distinct from investment policy or investment implementation.

Junk bonds. Debt securities with less-than-investment-grade ratings.

Large capitalization manager. The equity manager invests heavily or exclusively in large-cap stocks.

Limit order. A broker is directed to buy or sell at a specific price.

Liquidity. The ease by which a financial asset can be converted into cash. The ability to sell an asset quickly without having to make a substantial price concession.

Liquidity risk (or illiquidity risk). The risk of being unable to sell an asset quickly without conceding the price desired.

Load. The percentage commission or sales charge on a mutual fund or other investment.

Market order. A broker is directed to buy or sell immediately, at the current market price.

Market risk. The systematic risk common to all securities in an asset class. Stocks can be dramatically affected by market risk, which is related to the fluctuations in the overall market or economy.

Market timer. The manager attempts to time the high and low points in the price of stocks to optimize the timing of purchases and sales.

Maturity. A bond's maturity is the date it is scheduled to have principal returned at full face value. While maturity is meaningful in terms of when cash flows are expected to occur, it is not a particularly useful fact in assessing risk.

Maturity (yield-curve) risk. The risk related to the maturity (term) of a bond. The longer the period to maturity, the greater the risk simply because the future is unpredictable.

Modern Portfolio Theory (MPT). An approach for making investment decisions based upon quantification of expected risk and return for a given portfolio of assets. MPT provides a framework for choosing the most efficient portfolio (i.e., highest expected return for a given level of risk).

Money manager (or separate account manager). A financial professional whose single goal is to make investment selection decisions involving individual stocks and bonds. The money manager typically adheres to a single investment philosophy when making individual securities selections.

Money market. The money market consists of marketable, low-risk, short-term debt securities that generate interest income (often referred to as "cash equivalents"). Examples include Treasury bills, commercial paper, Eurodollars, negotiable certificates of deposit, banker's acceptances, and repurchase agreements.

Money market securities. Short-term, highly liquid, low-risk debt instruments offered by financial institutions, government entities, and corporations.

Mortgage-backed security (MBS). A security backed by a pool of mortgages assembled by an entity that services them (e.g., collection of mortgage payments). Investors share in the principal and interest payments received on the mortgages.

Municipal bonds. Debt obligations issued by a variety of entities including states, counties, cities, tax districts, schools, hospitals, street and highway departments, and port authorities. Generally, interest on municipal bonds is not subject to federal income tax. The interest on certain issues is taxable to investors, however, because interest income on certain municipal bonds is subject to the alternative minimum tax (AMT). Normally, municipal bond interest is not taxed by the state in which the bonds are issued.

Mutual fund. Professionally managed investment company consisting of assets from multiple investors combined to create a diversified portfolio of securities.

NASD. (National Association of Securities Dealers) A membership organization whose members are securities firms. It was created by an amendment to the Securities Exchange Act of 1934 to promote fair trade in the securities industry.

Negotiable certificates of deposit. Similar to short-term CDs except they are negotiable. A secondary market exists for these instruments. The minimum deposit is $100,000.

Net asset value (NAV). The market value of a mutual fund's portfolio divided by the number of shares outstanding.

Nonsystematic risk. The risk attributable to the variability in a security's return associated with factors that relate to that specific security (e.g., business risk, liquidity risk, and financial risk). Nonsystematic risk can be reduced through diversification.

Open order. A customer's order to buy or sell that has not yet been executed.

Passive management of investments. Passive management involves holding every security in a predefined market, with each represented in exactly the same proportions as in the market. Because passive management attempts to replicate an index, it is also known as "indexing."

Passive manager. The fixed income or equity manager selects a diversified portfolio of securities that closely resembles (i.e., it imitates) an asset class's overall performance (i.e., the market index for that class).

Payout ratio. The portion of earnings over a 12-month period that is paid out as dividends. Equal to ex-dividends per share divided by fully diluted earnings per share, excluding extraordinary items and discontinued operations.

Preferred stock. Preferred stock represents an equity interest in a corporation, but an interest with a claim to the company's assets and earnings that falls between the claims of bondholders and common shareholders. Preferred stock is often held by an investor as a fixed-income security because it has fixed-income characteristics (i.e., the dividends paid are of a known fixed amount). Dividends are not automatic, but instead have to be approved by the corporation's board of directors. If the stock is cumulative, the board does not have to approve payment of a dividend in a given period, but any dividends in arrears must be paid before common stock dividends. If the stock is not cumulative, dividends in arrears never have to be paid.

Price-earnings ratio. A measure of value equal to the firm's current stock price divided by its earnings per share.

Price-to-book. A measure of value equal to the market value of all the shares of common stock divided by the book value of the company.

Prudent Man Rule. Required fiduciaries to focus on probable income and safety of capital. Many states have adopted the Uniform Prudent Investor Act (or a similar provision) as the standard fiduciaries are held to instead of the prudent man rule.

Qualified investment managers. An ERISA plan may allow a "named fiduciary" to appoint a qualified investment manager to manage the plan's investments. If properly appointed, qualified investment managers are fiduciaries with respect to investments so managed. They also relieve the named fiduciary of certain responsibilities.

Real estate investment trusts (REITs). A REIT pools funds raised from shareholders to invest in a diversified portfolio of real estate assets, much the way a mutual fund pools shareholders' money to invest in stocks. Shares of beneficial interest in the trusts are traded like stocks, and most are listed on the major stock exchanges or traded over the counter.

Real estate mortgage investment conduit (REMIC). The REMIC was created by the Tax Reform Act of 1986 to clear up uncertainties surrounding the income tax treatment of mortgage-backed securities (MBSs). The investor in a REMIC avoids the prepayment risk associated with direct investments in MBSs. A REMIC is a straight mortgage-backed bond. It is distinguishable, however, by the requirement that in case of default, the collateral mortgages will be sold to raise the money to redeem the obligations.

Reinvestment risk. The risk that the cash flows from a bond must be reinvested at a lower rate of return than was received on the investment generating the cash flows.

Repurchase agreements. A lender (an institution in most cases) contracts with a buyer (the investor) to sell him/her government securities and to repurchase them at a contracted price on a contracted date. These are typically very short-term securities (overnight or for a number of days) and are in denominations of at least $100,000.

Residual risk. The unsystematic (i.e., firm-specific or diversifiable) risk of a security or portfolio.

Return on equity. A measure of a company's profitability equal to income divided by total common equity. An indicator of profits derived from the equity investment in the firm.

R-Squared. The coefficient of determination. A measure of the explanatory power of a statistical relationship. The higher the number, the more confidence users can have in the estimation.

Secondary market. The securities market consisting of securities exchanges, the over-the-counter market, and transactions between two parties.

Sector analysis. The manager attempts to find the sectors or industries that are ready to advance, and targets markets and companies within those sectors. The focus of this style of management is on the sector weightings rather than on the selection of individual securities.

Separate account manager. (See Money manager.)

Sharpe ratio. A measure of risk-adjusted return calculated by subtracting the risk-free return from the portfolio return and dividing the result (i.e., the excess return) by the portfolio's total standard deviation (a measure of risk).

Short-seller. The manager uses short-selling on a regular or consistent basis. (When securities are sold "short," the securities sold are not owned by the seller—they are borrowed, probably from the broker. The manager looks for companies whose stock price appears to be at a peak and is expected to decline. He/she then sells the borrowed shares and later buys shares (hopefully at a lower price than the sale price) to replace the borrowed shares. The difference in the selling price and the purchase price of the replacement shares is the short seller's profit.)

Short-term certificates of deposit (CD). A savings certificate issued by a bank or other financial institution. They are offered with varying maturities and interest rates.

Small capitalization manager. The equity manager invests heavily or exclusively in small-cap stocks as defined by the manager.

Socially responsible manager. The equity manager invests primarily in companies that exhibit some degree of social responsibility. For instance, he/she will not invest in companies that are known polluters or are involved with tobacco products.

Solicited. Notation used by brokers to indicate that a transaction was their idea, as opposed to the client's idea. Often abbreviated as "SOL."

Specialists. Persons who make a market in the stock of one or more companies, which may entail buying and selling stocks from their own inventory and acting as a broker to execute orders placed by other brokers. Specialists might act as dealers and buy or sell for their own portfolios or take the other side of trades.

Standard deviation. The measurement of an investment's total risk. Specifically, the measure of the variability of possible returns around its expected returns (i.e., its arithmetic mean). The greater the variance of possible returns from the arithmetic mean, the higher the standard deviation. The higher the standard deviation, the greater the risk associated with that asset class or individual asset.

Stop-loss order. A broker is directed to sell if the price of a security falls below a specific amount (e.g., "Sell if the price drops below $30").

Systematic risk. The risk attributable to the variability in a security's returns caused by factors that exist in the overall market, such as market risk, interest rate risk, and inflation risk. Systematic risk cannot be reduced by diversification.

Technical analysis. A system for making investment decisions based on the identification of historical patterns in the movement of prices.

Term-to-maturity. The time remaining until a bond reaches its maturity date.

Time-weighted rate of return. A measure of portfolio return calculated by measuring changes in a portfolio's value over time, taking into account the timing of additions to, and withdrawals from, the portfolio. This is the preferred method of performance measurement because it is not distorted by additions and withdrawals, as is the dollar-weighted method.

Treasury bills. Liquid, short-term debt instruments of the U.S. Treasury. Treasury bills are sold at a discount from face value at auction in denominations ranging from $10,000 to $1 million. They are also traded in the secondary market. Maturities are typically 13, 26, or 52 weeks.

Treasury bonds. U.S. debt securities with maturities over 10 years and up to 30 years that can be purchased at auction or from the Federal Reserve Bank, commercial banks, or brokerage firms. They are sold at face value. The minimum investment in a Treasury bond is $1,000. Interest is paid semiannually.

Treasury inflation-protection securities. Five- and 10-year Treasury notes indexed to inflation. The notes are sold in $1,000 denominations. Interest is paid semiannually at a fixed rate. The bond's principal for computing interest is adjusted semiannually for economic inflation or deflation (based on the CPI-U [the nonseasonally adjusted consumer price index for all urban consumers]). The investor is guaranteed the face value at maturity. Holders are taxed on interest payments received or accrued (depending on the holder's accounting method) each year and on any increases in principal resulting from the inflation adjustment, even though such adjustment is not received until maturity.

Treasury notes. U.S. debt securities with maturities of two–10 years that can be purchased at auction or from the Federal Reserve Bank, commercial banks, or brokerage firms. They are sold at face value. The minimum denomination for a Treasury note is $5,000 for two- or three-year maturities, and $1,000 for maturities longer than three years.

Treynor ratio. A measure of the excess return per unit of systematic market risk in a portfolio. The ratio is equal to the excess return of the portfolio divided by the beta of the portfolio.

Turnover. Turnover is the percentage of the assets in a portfolio that are replaced every year. For example, if a $100,000 portfolio has sales of $25,000 during the year, the turnover rate is 25 percent. Expenses are generally higher as turnover increases because the transaction costs increase as additional sales and purchases are made. As turnover increases, recognized gains also increase proportionately, resulting in higher tax liabilities.

Uniform Prudent Investor Act. Uniform Act approved in 1994 by the National Conference of Uniform Law Commissioners (also known as the Prudent Investor Rule). It is based on the Restatement (Third) of Trusts and specifically applies to trustees. The Uniform Act, like the Restatement (Third) of Trusts requires the fiduciary to use (or engage a qualified investment professional to use) a process based on modern portfolio theory.

Unit investment trust. An entity organized by a financial institution to carry out a specific investment objective, such as dependable tax-exempt income. Units are sold to investors in $1,000 increments through brokerage and investment firms and financial professionals. They are redeemable and represent undivided interests in the trust's assets. All assets in a trust are similar as to type (e.g., tax-exempt, corporate, and international bonds; CDs; Ginnie Maes; and equities), quality, and maturity date. Once the trust assets are selected, they are seldom traded, if at all. Therefore, the fund does not require active management, but it is monitored. The trust terminates when the securities mature.

Unsolicited. A notation used by brokers to indicate that a transaction was the client's idea, which is often abbreviated as "UNSOL."

Value averaging (VA). Value averaging is a variation of the dollar-cost averaging (DCA) strategy. Unlike DCA, which uses a fixed dollar amount invested at regular intervals, VA uses a fixed increase in the value of the investment as the target for each new investment. During periods when the price of the fund declines, more shares need to be purchased to bring the value back up to the desired level. Similarly, when the price of the fund increases during any given period, fewer shares need to be bought to reach the desired value.

Value investing. Value investors believe that security prices do not always reflect actual intrinsic worth. Value investors purchase underpriced securities on the belief that the market will eventually recognize the inaccuracy of the pricing and the security will increase in value.

Value manager. The equity manager looks for stocks that are currently undervalued, but whose worth eventually may be recognized by the market.

Variable annuities. Mutual funds with an insurance wrapper that shelters gains from current taxation. A typical variable annuity allows the investor to put funds in stock, bond, and money market portfolios (called "subaccounts"). The investment is limited only by the flexibility of the insurance company. In many cases, these subaccounts are managed by some of the largest mutual fund companies in the country.

Wash sale rules. Under IRC Sec. 1091, a loss due to the sale or disposition of stock or securities (including stock in a mutual fund) is not deductible if, within a period beginning 30 days before the date of the sale and ending 30 days after the date of the sale, the taxpayer acquires substantially identical stock or securities. In addition, the rules apply if the taxpayer sells stock and his/her spouse or a corporation he/she controls buys substantially identical stock. The wash sale rules apply only to losses; gains resulting from wash sales are taxable in the year of sale.

Wrap-Fee program. A program under which investment advisory and brokerage execution services are provided for a single "wrapped" fee that is not based on the transactions in a client's account.

Zero-Coupon bonds. Zero-Coupon bonds do not pay periodic interest. Instead, they are purchased at a discount, and the investor receives the face value (which represents principal and interest) when the bond is redeemed at maturity.

WEEK SEVEN
MAP 7-1

Guide to Insurance Needs*
(refer to page 291)

Life. The protection needed depends on the number of people dependent upon the insured person for support. A family of four with two young children needs approximately five times their annual income. Those who can probably do without life insurance coverage are single people, non-income-producing spouses with no anticipated dependents, and retirees without dependents living off investment or retirement income whose estates are not large enough to be subject to estate taxes. Life insurance has the primary purpose of protecting a family against loss of income, but it is also used to build cash reserves for a future event, such as retirement, college tuition or estate taxes.

Health. A medical policy should cover 80 percent of all medical costs in excess of the deductible and provide a minimum lifetime benefit of $1,000,000.

Disability. A disability policy should pay 60–70 percent of an insured's income should he/she become disabled and unable to work at his/her own occupation. For reduced premiums, elect a long waiting period of 90 days or more if the insured has an adequate emergency fund.

Auto. A policy is needed that provides a minimum of $100,000 for a single injury, $300,000 for all injuries and $100,000 for property damage. Drop collision coverage when the premium is equal to 10 percent or more of the auto's value. Avoid duplicate medical coverage. Insured may qualify for one or more discounts the insurance company offers—ask the insurance agent.

Homeowner. Insure a minimum of 80 percent of the home's replacement cost (excluding land) and at least $300,000 against liability suits. *Caution:* If a taxpayer runs a business out of the home, an insurance rider to the current homeowner's policy or a separate insurance policy should be considered.

Umbrella liability policy. Personal liability coverage is included with both auto and homeowner insurance and may be adequate for most people. However, if an insured has substantial assets, he/she should purchase an umbrella liability policy. A $1 million policy may cost less than $250 per year.

*Material reprinted with the permission of Quickfinder Incorporated *(www.quickfinder.com).*

WEEK SEVEN
MAP 7-2

*Insurance Do's and Don'ts**
(refer to page 291)

Do:

Buy the maximum deductible affordable. *Example:* Increasing the deductible on a car's collision insurance from $100 to $500 could reduce the premium cost by 25 percent.

Ask the agent/company about qualifications for discounts.

Consider term life insurance. Term policies are usually 10–20 percent cheaper than whole life contracts.

Try to get health insurance through a group policy (almost always cheaper than an individual policy) or from an employer, professional association, or union. If over age 50, check with the American Association of Retired Persons, (800) 424-3410, *www.aarp.com.*

Don't:

Buy policies with narrowly defined coverage, such as credit, travel or cancer insurance. These policies frequently duplicate other coverage.

Confuse the guaranteed rate with the projected rate used to forecast the future cash value of a policy. Most insurers guarantee a return of only 4—5%.

Switch among cash-value life insurance policies. Fees and agent commissions often outweigh a slightly higher return.

Buy life insurance as an investment. The primary goal should be the best insurance coverage. *Exceptions:* Single-premium life and variable insurance can be used as tax-deferred investments.

Insurance companies operate under state regulations which are usually unable to cope with the complexities of an insurance company's financial operations. In the event of a failure of an insurance company, an individual policyholder cannot obtain federal assistance. Most states have some type of a guarantee plan to pay policyholders of failed firms. For information on the solvency of a life insurer doing business in a particular state, call or write to the state's department of insurance.

Insure the Parent, Not the Child

In order to protect a child, a parent needs insurance on his/her life and not on the child's life. If a parent dies, the child will receive the funds needed for such things as a college education. An insurance agent may argue that a child's premium is very low and that the insurance policy will protect the insurability of the child should the child become chronically ill.

Material reprinted with the permission of Quickfinder Incorporated (www.quickfinder.com).

Who Should Be the Beneficiary of the Life Insurance Policy?
(refer to page 291)

Carefully structuring beneficiary designations is an important part of insurance planning. For example, beneficiary designations can be structured to minimize the estate taxes paid on insurance proceeds. Also, you can avoid conflicts by carefully naming beneficiaries. Furthermore, naming an immature beneficiary could result in mismanagement and wasting of insurance proceeds.

Nontax Considerations

The obvious purpose of a beneficiary designation in a life insurance policy is for you to specifically name the person(s) who are to receive the insurance proceeds when you die. The beneficiary designation within the policy rather than your will is controlling. However, if your estate is the named beneficiary in the policy, the proceeds are payable to your estate and must be distributed in accordance with your will (or the intestacy laws if there is no will).

Immature Beneficiaries. If the intended beneficiary is too young (from a legal or maturation standpoint) or is otherwise unable to manage insurance proceeds, the beneficiary of the proceeds could be a trust established for that person's benefit. The trust instrument would specify your wishes regarding distributions by the trustee to the beneficiary.

Disabled Beneficiaries. Where in insurance is intended to provide for a disabled person, it should be payable to a special needs trust to avoid jeopardizing government aid.

Naming Intended Beneficiaries in the Policy. If you know whom you want to benefit from the policy, it is best to name him/her/them in the policy rather than naming your estate as beneficiary. If named in the policy, the beneficiaries will receive the proceeds directly from the insurance company after your death. If you name your estate as the beneficiary, your will controls who receives the insurance proceeds. Also, distribution of the proceeds may be delayed because the proceeds become part of your probate estate.

Incidents of Ownership. The insurance policy proceeds are included in your estate if you possessed any incidents of ownership within three years of your death, even if your estate neither receives nor benefits from the proceeds. Examples of incidents of ownership are your ability to change the policy beneficiary, surrender or cancel the policy, assign the policy, revoke an assignment, pledge the policy for a loan, or obtain a loan against the policy from the insurer.

Beneficiary Designations Should Be Clear and Specific. Conflicts and legal problems can arise if the designations are ambiguous.

Revocable Beneficiaries. As the owner of the policy, you have the right to designate the beneficiary, as well as the right to change the beneficiary throughout the term of the policy. This type of beneficiary is referred to as a revocable beneficiary. The revocable beneficiary does not have a legal interest in the policy until you die. Therefore, the beneficiary has no voice with respect to loans against the policy's cash value, the surrender of the policy, assignments, or exchanges.

Tax Considerations

Determining the intended beneficiary of a life insurance policy frequently begins with nontax considerations (e.g., the surviving spouse's need for an income source). Invariably, though, the decision must include a review of the tax implications of the choice.

The Surviving Spouse May Not Be the Best Choice. The surviving spouse is a common choice and one that usually shelters the insurance proceeds from estate taxes on the death of the insured. (This is because assets can pass to the spouse free of estate taxes due to the unlimited marital deduction.) However, if the estate of the surviving spouse (inherited from the spouse who dies first) is likely to exceed the applicable exclusion amount ($1 million for 2003), this choice rarely is the best one.

Decedent's Estate Is Another Option. Instead of naming your spouse as beneficiary, your estate could be named. However, you would be treated as owning the policy and thus, the insurance proceeds would be included in your estate. In some states, this would subject otherwise exempt insurance proceeds to inheritance tax.

Naming an Irrevocable Trust as Both Owner and Beneficiary. An irrevocable trust is often a better choice for beneficiary than either your spouse or your estate. By properly structuring the trust, the proceeds of a life insurance policy owned by and payable to the trust can completely escape estate tax on the death of both spouses.

Term Insurance

Term insurance is pure protection against financial loss resulting from death during a specified period of time. Term insurance is usually the best buy for a person needing insurance for a relatively short period of time—less than 10 years. Term insurance offers the most coverage for the least amount of premium. It is not designed to meet a permanent need.

Advantages:

➤ Usually 10–20 percent cheaper than whole life contracts.

➤ Pure protection.

➤ Can be renewed or converted.

Disadvantages:

➤ No savings element.

➤ No benefit if insured outlives specified period.

Three types of term insurance:

1) **Annual renewable term (ART).** Offers level coverage with increasing yearly premiums that automatically renews each policy year when premiums are paid. Suited for the individual who desires coverage for five years or less.

2) **Level term (LT).** Premiums and coverage remain level for the specified period of time stated in the policy (usually 10, 15, 20 years). After the level premium period ends, re-entry is available for the next period of time. Designed to provide guaranteed current premiums for longer periods of time and is suited for individuals needing coverage 15 years or more. Over an extended period of time, LT plans are generally more cost-effective than ART policies.

3) **Decreasing term (DT or mortgage insurance).** Coverage decreases annually by a specified percentage for a predetermined period of time while the premiums remain the same. Generally the most expensive. Coverage ends when the policy face amount decreases to zero.

WHOLE LIFE INSURANCE

Whole life insurance provides insurance protection at a level premium for the entire lifetime of the insured—"straight life policy." This classic policy still makes sense for those who can afford the premium, need the discipline of enforced savings and will not need to cash in the policy for at least 15 years.

Advantages:

➤ Protects insured for lifetime.

➤ Cash value on savings element accumulates tax free.

➤ Provides loan values which may be borrowed at low rates.

Disadvantages:

➤ More costly than term insurance.

➤ Rate of return not disclosed.

UNIVERSAL LIFE INSURANCE

Universal life insurance combines pure life protection (term) with a cash value fund that accumulates tax free as long as the policy remains in force. Unlike deferred annuities or single-premium life, universal life is purchased chiefly for insurance. The insurance company deducts certain expenses and the first month's pure insurance protection from the initial premium paid. The balance of the premium earns market-rate interest in a cash-value fund which is normally a high-yielding government securities fund. Each month thereafter, the cost of an additional month's pure insurance plus expenses is deducted from the cash value fund.

Advantages:

➤ Policy earns tax-free interest at current market rates.

➤ Flexible premium payments. Policyholder can choose to pay for its cost with one single payment, payments for five or 10 years, or any other payment schedule desired. Premiums may even be made at different intervals of time or stopped temporarily, as long as the next month's policy reserve covers the cost of next month's pure insurance protection.

➤ Adjustable benefits so a policyholder can increase or decrease the policy face value according to needs.

➤ Policy loans are generally at a 6–8 percent interest rate.

➤ Investment, expense, and mortality elements are separately defined.

Disadvantages:

➤ Policyholder ends up with neither the most competitive insurance coverage nor the most competitive savings vehicle.

➤ Future yield potential is uncertain due to inflation.

JOINT AND SURVIVOR LIFE POLICIES (SECOND-TO-DIE INSURANCE)

Unlike conventional life insurance, joint and survivor (second-to-die) insurance covers two lives and pays off only after the second death. The policy is usually confined to husband-wife, parent-child, or business co-owners, including key employees. It is designed to solve the common problems of not having the needed or desired cash available upon the death of a second insured person to cover tax bills, provide for the needs of heirs, make charitable contributions, or provide a cash infusion into a business in the event of the death of a second of two key persons. The premium cost for a joint and survivor policy is usually less than for separate policies on two lives because premiums are based on a hypothetical "joint equal age" and the insurer's administrative expenses are less.

This type of policy can be used to lessen the federal estate tax burden for a couple who has elected to take maximum advantage of the marital deduction. In addition, if the policy is owned by an irrevocable life insurance trust, the proceeds escape estate taxation. The policy can provide the heirs with cash to pay estate taxes so the heirs can inherit an intact estate. The estate tax savings could be substantial for a couple with an already taxable estate exceeding $2 million.

ADJUSTABLE LIFE INSURANCE

Adjustable life insurance offers flexibility and the ability to keep pace with inflation. The policyholder can adjust various components of the policy in order to meet ever-changing needs for protection and the ability to pay.

At issuance. Policy may provide either cash value coverage (whole life) or noncash value coverage (term) depending on the face amount of coverage and the amount of premium payment the insured wishes to pay.

After issue. Premium and face amount may be adjusted at any monthly policy anniversary. The policy can be changed from whole life to term or vice versa (unlike universal and variable life policies).

Advantage:

Flexibility. Policyholders may change their policy as their needs change with just one policy and one insurance company. When the premiums exceed the cost of protection, the policy cash value increases; when the cost of protection exceeds the premiums paid, the cash value decreases.

* Material reprinted with the permission of Quickfinder Incorporated *(www.quickfinder.com).*

Disadvantage:

Cost. Adjustable life is more expensive than term or whole life due to the numerous administrative complexities. The minimum term for an adjustable life policy is 10 years.

Variable Life Insurance

Variable life insurance combines the traditional tax-deferred savings functions of life insurance with the growth potential of equities. Like traditional life insurance, variable policies have fixed premiums and a guaranteed minimum death benefit. However, the cash value is not guaranteed and will fluctuate with the performance of the portfolio invested by the insurer.

The policyholder can allocate (and switch) his/her investment choices—for example, growth stocks, aggressive growth stocks, money market funds, bonds, real estate securities, etc. Variable life may be appropriate for policyholders who prefer to combine some insurance coverage with a long-term investment (10 years or more) that can provide additional income for retirement or other needs. Taxpayers should consider variable life only after maximum deductible contributions have been made to retirement plans. Variable products are also attractive to upper-income taxpayers who can benefit from tax-deferred compounding.

Advantages:

➤ Earnings compound, tax-deferred, within the policy.

➤ Life insurance death benefits are income-tax-free to beneficiaries.

➤ Several investment options with tax-free exchanges are within the product.

➤ Professional asset management.

➤ Third-party ownership may result in death proceeds being exempt from estate tax.

➤ Possible inflation hedge; loans and withdrawals are tax free if policy remains in force until death of insured.

Disadvantages:

➤ Inherent risk. Death benefit and cash value are not guaranteed; they increase or decrease based upon investment performance of underlying assets.

➤ Tends to be more expensive than other types of cash-value insurance, and the high returns that equities may provide are needed to justify those costs over time.

Week Seven
MAP 7-5

Shopping for Insurance*
(refer to page 291)

Shopping for Insurance

A simple and economical way to shop for term insurance without an insurance agent is to use insurance-quote firms that provide computerized analyses listing the four or five lowest-cost policies in their databases. These firms deal most often with insurance companies with the highest ratings.

National services include:

➤ Insurance Information, 23 Route 134, South Dennis, MA 02660, (800) 472-5800. Operational in all states; does not sell insurance.

➤ Insurance Quote, 3200 N. Dobson Road, Building C, Chandler, AZ 85224, (800) 972-1104.

➤ Select Quote, 595 Market St., Fifth Floor, San Francisco, CA 94105, (800) 343-1985. Licensed in all states but Hawaii and South Dakota.

➤ Term Quote Services, Inc., 6768 Loop Road, Centerville, OH 45459-2161, (800) 444-8376.

➤ Quotesmith Corp: (800) 556-9393. Searches database of insurance companies for the cheapest term insurance rates.

Websites:

➤ Quotesmith: www.quotesmith.com

➤ InsureMarket: www.insuremarket.com

➤ QuickQuote: www.quickquote.com

Consumer Federation of America. (202) 387-0087. Charges $40 to analyze whether it is cost-effective to drop/replace an existing policy.

Caution: The cheapest policy is not always the best value. Use the information provided above as a research tool to select a few policies that appear to offer the best rates and value, then check with an independent insurance agent who carries policies from a wide assortment of insurers to see if the agent can beat the quotes.

Check Life Insurers				
Rating Service	Top Two Grades	Fourth Grade	Telephone Number	Web Sites
A.M. Best*	A+, Contingent A+	Contingent A	908.439.2200	www.ambest .com
Fitch IBCA, Duff and Phelps	AAA, AA+	AA–	212.908.0500	www.fitchibca .com
Moody's Investors Service	Aaa, Aa1	Aa3	212.553.1658	www.moodys .com
Standard & Poor's	AAA, AA+	AA–	212.438.7760	www.standard poor.com
*A.M. Best charges for a rating by phone				

10-Day Free Look

Most people are not aware that they have up to 10 days after an insurance policy arrives to cancel it and receive a full refund.

Week Seven
MAP 7-6

Upgrade Insurance Policies with a Section 1035 Exchange*
(refer to page 292)

Many insurance companies have designed tax-free exchange programs that allow policyholders to trade in outdated policies for newer, more economical policies. A policyholder could be uninsurable and still be able to exchange the old policy for a new policy. Also, the exchange can occur with either the insured's present insurance company or any other insurance company. Single-premium annuities can also be exchanged for a higher-paying annuity with another insurance company. However, most companies charge a surrender fee of 1–6 percent if an annuity is cashed in or transferred before a specified date, generally five to eight years after it was purchased.

*Material reprinted with the permission of Quickfinder Incorporated (*www.quickfinder.com*).

Week Seven
MAP 7-7

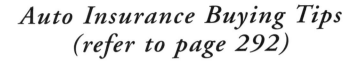

Auto Insurance Buying Tips
(refer to page 292)

Basic Coverages:

Collision—pays for damage to your car resulting from a collision or accident.

Comprehensive—coverage for most everything other than collision or accident, such as wind or hail damage, broken windshield, and theft.

Bodily Injury Liability—covers you and any other designated driver if you cause injury to another person. The Insurance Information Institute recommends you have $100,000 of bodily injury protection per person and $300,000 per accident.

Property Damage Liability—covers damages that you may cause to someone else's property, i.e., vehicle, fence, landscape, etc.

Medical Payments or Personal Injury Protection (PIP)—pays for medical payments and possibly lost wages of someone injured in an auto accident.

Uninsured and Underinsured Motorist Coverage—reimburses you if accident is caused by an uninsured or underinsured driver.

Ways to Reduce Costs of Auto Insurance:

Shop Around for competitive quotes. *www.insure.com www.quicken.com/insurance*

Increase Your Deductibles for Collision and Comprehensive coverages. According to the Insurance Information Institute, increasing your deductible from $200 to $500 could reduce your collision and comprehensive coverage cost by 15 percent to 30 percent. Going to a $1,000 deductible can save you 40 percent or more.

Maintain a Clean Driving Record.

Purchase Auto and Homeowners Coverage Through the Same Company; Inquire About Discounts.

For more tips on auto insurance visit *www.iii.org/individuals/auto*. Adapted with permission from the Insurance Information Institute.

WEEK SEVEN
MAP 7-8

Homeowners Insurance Buying Tips
(refer to page 292)

BASIC COVERAGES:

COVERAGE FOR THE STRUCTURE OF YOUR HOME—pays to repair or rebuild your home if it is damaged or destroyed by fire, hurricane, wind, hail, lightning, or other disaster listed in your policy. Separate coverage must be obtained for flood and earthquake protection. Be sure to obtain "full replacement cost" coverage for your home. Note: you do not need to insure the land, only the physical structures and contents. Most policies also cover "detached" structures, (i.e., garage or shed) up to 10 percent of the coverage on the structure. Additional coverage can be purchased.

COVERAGE FOR YOUR PERSONAL PROPERTY—pays to replace the contents of your home if items are stolen, damaged, or destroyed by a covered risk. Most policies cover up to 70 percent of the amount of your coverage on the structure. If you have specialty items (jewelry, electronics, antiques) or collectibles (stamps, coins, figurines) you may need a separate "rider" for those items. Consult with your homeowners' insurance agent to confirm that your coverage is adequate. Consider videotaping and/or completing a detailed inventory listing of the contents of your home. Keep this documentation off premises, such as in a safe deposit box.

LIABILITY PROTECTION—covers you against lawsuits for bodily injury or property damage that you, family members, or your pets cause to other people. Liability limits generally start at $100,000. We recommend at least $300,000 of liability protection. You can purchase an umbrella liability policy, which provides coverage above and beyond your auto and homeowners liability protection. This coverage costs about $150 to $250 per year for a $1,000,000 policy.

WAYS TO REDUCE COSTS OF HOMEOWNERS INSURANCE:

SHOP AROUND for competitive quotes. (*www.insure.com*) (*www.quicken.com/insurance*). Check the financial health of insurance companies with rating companies such as A.M. Best (*www.ambest.com*) and Standard & Poor's (*www.standardandpoors.com/ratings*).

INCREASE YOUR DEDUCTIBLES—We recommend deductibles of at least $500. If you can afford to raise it to $1,000, you may save as much as 25 percent according to the Insurance Information Institute.

PURCHASE AUTO, HOMEOWNERS, AND UMBRELLA LIABILITY COVERAGES THROUGH THE SAME COMPANY; INQUIRE ABOUT DISCOUNTS.

For more tips on homeowners insurance, visit *www.iii.org/individuals/homei*. Adapted with permission from the Insurance Information Institute.

Week Seven
Map 7-9*
Personal Umbrella Liability Policy
(refer to page 292)

Umbrella liability policies are designed to protect individuals and families from large personal liability claims. Umbrella coverage supplements your underlying liability coverage, and in fact, the existence of an underlying basic liability policy is a prerequisite for obtaining and maintaining umbrella coverage. Umbrella policies cover losses up to the maximum amount of the policy in excess of the amount covered by the underlying basic policy. Umbrella coverage usually begins at $1 million and is relatively inexpensive ($100–$500 per $1 million of coverage).

Basic coverage under an umbrella policy is broad. Generally, umbrella policies cover property damage, bodily injury, mental anguish, shock, sickness, disease, disability, false arrest, false imprisonment, wrongful entry, wrongful eviction, malicious prosecution, discrimination, humiliation, libel, slander, defamation of character, and invasion of privacy. Umbrella policies can be tailored to cover other types of claims, depending upon the needs of the insured. However, keep in mind that if a loss occurs, the claims adjuster (not the agent who sold the policy) will be the one who decides whether the loss is covered.

Example: *Interplay between basic liability policy and umbrella liability policy.*

The Smith's carry $300,000 of liability insurance under their homeowners' policy. The homeowners' coverage is supplemented by an umbrella policy with a $1 million limit. A child is injured on the Smith's front lawn, and the child's parents win a $1.5 million judgment against the Smiths. The Smith's homeowners' policy will pay $300,000 of the claim and their umbrella policy will pay $1,000,000 ($1.5 million less the coverage limit of the underlying homeowners' policy up to the $1 million limit) of the claim. The remaining $200,000 must be paid by the Smiths.

Umbrella policies often exclude coverage for the following: (1) the insured's obligation for worker's compensation, unemployment compensation, or disability benefits; (2) property owned by the insured; (3) business pursuits; (4) owned or leased aircraft and certain watercraft; and (5) professional services (unless covered by the underlying policy).

Due to policy exclusions and the possibility of insurer default, umbrella liability coverage, like any other form of insurance, does not provide complete asset protection. However, its relatively low cost and broad coverage make it an essential part of most asset-protection plans.

Week Seven
Map 7-10

Health Insurance Basics
(refer to page 292)

This Week Seven MAP outlines essential information you must understand about health insurance. It is not intended to serve as a comprehensive treatment of the subject but only to introduce basic concepts. The checklists and worksheets referred to in this section will need be completed after obtaining alternative health insurance quotes. This step takes place in the completion of Week Seven's Insurance Circuit Inspection Worksheet B.

Medical insurance is available individually or part of a group plan. Individual plans can be expensive and hard to obtain since your individual health history is considered. Any preexisting conditions such as heart disease, diabetes, and even pregnancy can make it difficult to obtain a policy and, if you do, the premiums may be outrageous.

Check with your state insurance commissioner to see if they require insurance providers licensed to sell insurance in your state to offer everyone a *guaranteed issue* plan. You can locate your state commissioner by selecting *State Information* on the *www.insure.com* website.

On this same site, you can click on *Health Plans for College Students* on affordable health insurance options when a parent's policy refuses coverage.

Group plans allow everyone to obtain coverage, regardless of his/her medical history. As you can imagine, claims are usually higher within group plans than individual plans. If you make a conscious effort to avoid medical costs through preventive care, you may still be forced to pay higher premiums because of the performance of the entire group of which you are a part. Group premiums can increase in double-digit percentiles each year to allow insurance companies to cover claims.

In certain instances employers, offer their employees the option of selecting benefits from a cafeteria plan. This type of plan might allow you to choose alternative benefits and pay for your own private health insurance policy if your health history would qualify you for much lower rates than your employer is paying in the group plan.

Consider the following website that provides this general summary:
www.ehealthinsurance.com

➤ Select Health Insurance Basics at the bottom of the page.

Then

➤ Select Checkup on Health Insurance Choices.

➤ Print out the 15-page article and insert it in you're My Education binder under Insurance (Tab 7).

Take the time to interact with this excellent article. I have quoted key information, but you will benefit greatly by taking the time to read the article.

After reading **What Are Your Choices?**, you'll discover you have three types of insurance plan options:

➤ Fee for Service—also known as Point of Service or Indemnity Plans

➤ HMOs—Health Maintenance Organizations

➤ PPOs—Preferred Provider Organizations

Which Type Is Right for You? gives you practical examples of how to trade off your preference for medical service choice with controlling your costs. Fee-for-service plans tend to be more expensive than the other two plans but may be more suitable to your needs. Answer the questions in this section to determine which best fits you.

Fee for Service:

➤ Not all health expenses you have count toward your deductible. Only those covered by the policy do. You need to check the insurance policy to find out which ones are covered.

➤ Most fee-for-service plans have, "cap", or the most you will have to pay for medical bills in any one year. The cap does not include what you pay for your monthly premium.

➤ Check your policy to make sure you have both kinds (basic and major medical) kinds of protection. This is sometimes called a comprehensive plan.

➤ **Before buying a fee-for-service plan, ask yourself the** *Questions to Ask About Fee-for Service Insurance.*

What Is a Customary Fee?

➤ Most insurance plans will pay only what they call a reasonable and customary fee for a particular service; you will be billed for the difference. This is in addition to the deductible and coinsurance you would be expected to pay.

Health Maintenance Organizations (HMOs):

➤ HMOs are prepaid health plans—as an HMO member, you pay a monthly premium.

➤ Your total medical costs will likely be lower and more predictable in an HMO than with fee-for-service insurance.

➤ Many people like HMOs because they do not require claim forms for office visits or hospital stays. However, you may have to wait longer for an appointment.

➤ You cannot see a specialist without a referral from your primary care doctor, who is expected to manage the care you receive.

➤ Before purchasing an HMO plan, ask yourself the ***Questions to Ask About an HMO.***

Preferred Provider Organizations (PPOs):

➤ The preferred provider organization is a combination of traditional fee-for-service and an HMO.

➤ In a PPO, you can use doctors who are not part of the plan and still receive some coverage. At these times, you will pay a larger portion of the bill yourself (and also fill out the claims forms).

➤ Before purchasing a PPO plan, ask yourself the ***Questions to Ask About a PPO.***

Checklist: "What's Most Important to You?"

➤ Complete this checklist as part of Your Week Seven Worksheet B completion.

➤ Before choosing a plan, decide what is most important to you.

➤ Take the time to complete this checklist when considering different health insurance plans.

Worksheet: "What Is Your Best Buy?"

➤ Complete this worksheet as part of your Week Seven Worksheet B Completion.

➤ Look at your medical and insurance records from last year as a guide to what services you might use this year. Add up the actual costs to you, including premiums. Do not enter this historical information in this worksheet—rather, use it as a guide for estimating future costs.

➤ Estimate what you might spend on your health care in terms of deductibles, coinsurance and or co/payments, and services that are not covered.

➤ Now look at the checklist of services that are important to you. Is your best buy the same policy that gives you the most services you need?

Other Types of Insurance:

➤ Medicare is the federal health insurance program for Americans age 65 and older. Medicare has two parts: hospital insurance, known as Part A, and supplementary medical insurance, known as Part B, which provides payments for doctors and related services and supplies.

➤ If you are eligible for Medicare, Part A is free, but you must pay a premium for Part B. In 2003, Part B premiums are $58.70 per month.

➤ Per the Social Security Administration, the following out-of-pocket costs apply to Part A Hospital Insurance;

  ▷ First 60 days in the hospital - . . . . $840.

  ▷ 61–90 days in the hospital - . . . .$210 per day.

  ▷ 90–150 days in the hospital . . . .$420 per day.

  ▷ First 20 days in skilled nursing facility . . . .$0.

  ▷ 21st–100 days in skilled nursing facility . . . .$105/day.

➤ For 2003, Part B the Medical Insurance deductible is $100 per year.

➤ After the deductible, Part B pays for 80 percent of covered services.

➤ Medigap policies cover Medicare's deductibles, and some pay for health services not covered by Medicare. There are 10 standard plans from which you can choose.

➤ You may get another free booklet, *"Guide to Health Insurance for People with Medicare."* Write to: Health Care Financing Administration, Publications, N!-26-27, 7500 Security Blvd., Baltimore, MD 21244-1850.

Understanding Health Insurance Terms:

➤ Read this page to make sure you understand the terms you will encounter in your analysis of your health insurance alternatives.

Week Seven
Map 7-11

*Long-Term Care Insurance** *(refer to page 292)*

Nursing Home Cost

Nursing home costs are currently averaging approximately $153 per day ($55,845 per year), depending on the region of the country. High spot: New York City at $295 per day. Low spot: Hibbing, Minnesota, at $90 per day.

Website: *www.efmoody.com.*

Long-Term Care Insurance Cost

Newer policies broaden the scope of coverage to include such things as adult day care, have more triggers for the insurance to kick in, and offer more options, such as inflation protection. Coverage has become less expensive in recent years, but it remains costly. The average annual premium for a 65-year-old ranges between $1,000 and $2,000, depending upon the deductible period, years of coverage, inflation protection, and other coverage options.

Tips on buying long-term care insurance:

➤ Consider a policy that pays for both nursing home stays and home care. Choose home care benefits that cover a wide range of services.

➤ Beware of the lowest-priced policy. It may offer inferior coverage and the premiums may increase when the insured is least able to afford them.

➤ Beware of the potential for unaffordable price increases. Do not buy an "attained age" policy—one with initial low premiums that rise rapidly with the policyholder's age.

➤ Avoid policies that require a hospital stay of at least three days before the company will pay nursing home benefits. Many people go straight from home to a nursing home.

➤ If purchasing coverage through an employer, be assured of continued coverage if there is a job change or if the employer terminates the plan.

➤ Inflation protection is important. Choose a company that charges a level premium for protection.

➤ If purchasing a home care policy, buy one that covers aides who primarily help patients with personal or custodial care, rather than one that pays only for skilled care.

* Material reprinted with the permission of Quickfinder Incorporated (*www.quickfinder.com*).

➤ Beware of policies requiring that care be medically necessary for sickness or injury. Look for updated policies that use a disability standard. It takes into consideration medical necessity, cognitive impairment, and ability to perform activities of daily living. The policy should cover Alzheimer's disease.

➤ Obtain outlines of the major aspects of the policy to be purchased. Make sure that the form numbers on the brochures and policy match.

➤ Look for a policy containing a nonforfeiture clause. These policies are more expensive, but they are worth it. This option typically allows an individual to collect some reduced benefit if, for any reason, the individual stops premium payments after a number of years.

➤ Don't buy long-term insurance if the high premiums pose more of a financial burden than an extended nursing home stay. *General rule:* Do not spend more than five to seven percent of income on long-term care insurance.

Long-Term Care Insurance Purchase

Many planners recommend long-term care insurance for people between the ages of 55—72 with a net worth between $150,000–$1,000,000, excluding house and car. Individuals with a low net worth probably do not have enough to make the high cost of premiums worthwhile. Wealthy individuals may be able to fund long-term care through personal wealth, but they should not dismiss insurance, as long-term care costs are skyrocketing and could quickly wipe out a personal fortune.

Medicare/Medicaid

Medicare. Provides health insurance, not life insurance. Medicare provides limited assistance for recuperative care in nursing homes but does not pay for long-term custodial care. Custodial care is designed primarily to assist in meeting personal needs, such as walking, bathing, eating, and related activities.

Medicaid. Represents the only public program available that covers the cost of long-term care. It is administered by states under guidelines established by the federal government. However, an individual has to be basically impoverished in order to qualify for medicaid.

Week Seven
Map 7-12

Long-term Care Insurance—
A Financial Analysis
(refer to page 292)

Assumptions:

➤ Greg is 53 and will live until age 95. He needs three years of care beginning at 92.

➤ Ginger is 53 and has the same longevity and long-term care needs as Greg.

➤ Nursing home costs in Colorado average $125/day. They are increasing at a 5 percent per-year rate.

➤ If Greg and Ginger wanted to pay for long-term care insurance from savings, they could earn a 5 percent rate of return on that account.

➤ Long term care insurance premiums will increase at an average rate of 1 percent per year.

Scenario 1—Greg and Ginger don't buy long-term care insurance.

➤ Thirty-nine years from now the daily cost of care will be $838 per day, assuming a continued 5 percent annual growth rate. Three years of coverage would cost $917,610. This cost would apply to both Greg and Ginger for a total cost of $1,835,522.

➤ Assuming a 5 percent earnings rate, Greg and Ginger would need to set aside $16,088 per year to cover this need.

Scenario 2—Greg and Ginger purchase long-term care insurance.

➤ Greg's monthly premium is $71/month, and Ginger's is $77/month.

➤ Each policy has a 100-day elimination period that is waived if they use home health care before nursing home care. We assume they will not be eligible for the waiver and will have to pay for the first 100 days of their care.

➤ If Greg and Ginger can set aside a lump sum to cover both the annual premiums and the 100-day elimination period, assuming a 5 percent return, they would need $55,443. The average annual cost using this method would amount to $1,422.

➤ If Greg and Ginger were to save for their elimination costs, they would need to contribute $1,469/year. If a fund is not established and premiums are paid out of cash flow, the annual cost of the premiums is currently $1,776. The total of these costs is $3,245.

Results:

➤ Greg and Ginger would save an average of $14,666 per year if they could set aside $55,443 today to fund their long-term care costs using insurance, instead of paying for all those projected costs themselves. Over 39 years, this amounts to $571,974.

➤ If Greg and Ginger pay for their long-term care premiums and elimination costs out of annual cash flows, they save an average of $12,843 per year over paying for the long-term care costs themselves when these are incurred. Over the 39 year period before needing these services, the total savings amounts to $500,877.

➤ If Greg and Ginger do not use their long-term care coverage, they would have lost only the monthly premiums paid. The total payments, in today's dollars, amounts to $30,446. Any savings set aside for the elimination period would be retained as part of their financial net worth.

If you would like additional information about long-term care, please go to *www.insiderisc.com* and under the About Us section on the home page, select Understanding LTC. This will provide detailed financial calculations about costs in your particular state, as well as premium changes for different ages.

Long-Term Care Insurance Policy Comparison
(refer to page 293)

	John Hancock Life Insurance Co.	GE Capital Assurance	Ryan's Comments
Policy Name	Custom Care LTC-02 TQ	LTC Choice TQ	
Insurance Company Ratings & Rank			
A.M. Best Rating	A++	A+	
Weiss Rating	A-	B	
Comdex Rating	95%	90%	This is percentile rank of financial strength compared to all other companies.
Renewal Provisions			
Is policy non-cancelable and guaranteed renewable for life?	Yes	Yes	Company must renew policy as long as premiums are paid.
Are premiums guaranteed for life?	No	No	In fact, I expect a 50% rate increase over the life of the policy.
Is policy tax qualified?	Yes	Yes	This means premiums may be deductible and benefit received are tax-free. Normally, premiums are tax deductible when they, together with other un-reimbursed medical expenses, exceeds 7.5% of your adjusted gross income for the year.
Benefit Eligibility			
How do I qualify for benefits?			If the insured is unable to perform at least two activities of daily living (ADL) for a period expected to last at least 90 days, or If the insured suffers from a cognitive impairment such as Alzheimer's disease or senile dementia and require supervision. ADL's include bathing, continence, dressing, eating, toileting, transferring.
Are benefits paid if my physician determines I qualify?	No	No	"Medical necessity" alone is not enough to trigger benefits. Your personal physician recommendation must also be confirmed by an independent health care professional. (second opinion)

	John Hancock Life Insurance Co.	GE Capital Assurance	Ryan's Comments
ADL's needed for benefit payment (bathing, continence, dressing, eating, toileting, transferring)	2/6	2/6	The loss of at least two of six ADL's must occur for benefit eligibility.
Is care outside US covered?	Anywhere–paid up to 75% DB	Territories/ Possessions	
Benefits Payable			

Prepared By: John Ryan, CFP™ (800) 796-0909
Date: 5/19/2003

Where can services be rendered?	Nursing Home; Assisted Living; Home Care; Adult Day Care and similar facilities designed for 24 hr medical care for those who qualify for benefits		
Assisted Living, Home Health Care, and Nursing Home (NH) benefit payment model	Reimbursement	Reimbursement	Most policies are reimbursement model, meaning if you incur an eligible expense, you will be reimbursed. Indemnity model policies, however, will pay the flat daily benefit regardless of expenses, while on claim. Indemnity models are said to simplify the claim process by reducing paperwork
Percent of benefit paid	100%	100%	
Homemaker covered?	Yes	Yes	Homemakers can assist with cleaning, meal prep, errands, etc.
	John Hancock Life Insurance Co.	**GE Capital Assurance**	**Ryan's Comments**
Is care by friends covered?	No	No	
Is care by family members covered?	No	No	
Is care by spouse covered?	No	No	
Alternate Plan of Care (APC). Included in policy	Yes	Yes	This provision makes coverage possible for care or services that may be developed years from now but are not specifically referred to in your policy today.
Must be on claim for APC?	Yes	Yes	
Other home care benefits	Under Stay at Home Benefit (a built-in feature), expenses paid for home modifications, durable medical equipment, caregiver training, home safety checks, provider care checks and medical alert systems. The amount paid is equal to 30X DB on a lifetime basis. The benefit is not subject to the elim period and does not reduce policy limit.	In-home safety devices; home delivered meals; rental of emergency medical response devices.	
Waiting Period			
Accumulation period	Lifetime	Lifetime	Lifetime means you have your whole lifetime to satisfy the elimination period without ever having to start over again. Otherwise, you have a set number of days (3x elim period for Unum) to satisfy your elimination period with days of care..
Additional Options			
Types of inflation adjustments	Simple, Compound or GPO	Simple, Compound	Inflation adjusters will increase your maximum daily benefit for as long as you own your policy, even while on claim.
Inflate original or remaining	Remaining	Original	Compounding the original pool of money can create more benefits. This is only an advantage if a claim exhausts your initial pool of money.
Other than automatic, can simple and compound inflation increase coverage later without evidence of	Guaranteed Purchase Option - Before age 91, every 3rd anniversary, can	No	Elective cost of living adjusts like the Guaranteed Purchase Option (GPO) or Consumer Price Index adjustment (CPI) can lower your initial cost of insurance when compared to automatic adjustments (compound or simple). But analysis

Prepared By: John Ryan, CFP™ (800) 796-0909
Date: 5/19/2003

	John Hancock Life Insurance Co.	GE Capital Assurance	Ryan's Comments
insurability?	increase DB. Insured not eligible if benefits paid in preceding 2 years.		shows these elective options may ultimately (within 12-15 years) cost considerable more than the automatic adjustments over time.
Surviving spouse paid up	Available by Rider	**Automatically included in some states,** rider in others	If one spouse dies, the other spouse's policy is paid up for life, guaranteed. Certain restrictions apply
Yrs held for paid up	10 yrs	10 yrs	Most policies must be in-force for 10 years
Restricted if claims	Yes, if claim within 10 yrs	Yes, if claim within 10 yrs	Most policies require no claims within the first 10 years for survivorship policy to be paid up.
Shared benefit with spouse	Rider to Share benefits	Available by Rider	Policies can be structured so that spouses can share between each other's policy or separate pool of money in case a claim exhausts their own pool. Adds 8-12% to cost of plan with 6 yr benefit period.
Nonforfeitures benefits	Shortened benefit period after 3 years	Shortened benefit period after 3 years	Non-forfeiture benefit means if you stop paying premiums for your policy, you can elect a paid-up policy with reduced benefits equally the total of all premiums paid thus far. Usually your maximum daily benefit can be paid out for a future claim, but for a fewer number of days, and until your reduced pool of money (premiums paid) is exhausted. This is a rider that must be purchased. Additional cost is usually between 20% and 30%.
Restoration of benefits	Available by Rider	Available by Rider	If you exhaust some (not all) of your pool of money, and completely recover from your illness or injury for more than 6 months, your pool of money is fully restored for a future claim in necessary. (add 5% to premium)
Other riders	Additional Cash Benefit Rider – provides a separate pool of money equal to 15% of monthly benefit or 4.5 x DB to assist you in stay at home while receiving HHC. Can be spent any way you chose (i.e. prescription drugs). Benefit paid does not reduce policy maximum.	N/A	JH waiver of elim period for HHC adds 6% to cost of policy. JH cash benefit rider adds 10% to cost of policy.
Premium Waiver			
Are policy premiums waived while on claim?	Yes	Yes	No premiums are payable while on claim.
Other Benefits and Features			
Bed reservation	60 days	50 days	If you must leave the nursing home and go to a hospital, your bed will be reserved at the NH for when you return.
Bed reservations conditions	Any reason	Any reason	
Respite care days per year	21 @ 100%	21 days	
Hospice care %	100%	100%	

Prepared By: John Ryan, CFP™ (800) 796-0909
Date: 5/19/2003

	John Hancock Life Insurance Co.	GE Capital Assurance	Ryan's Comments
Equipment amount	30X Daily Benefit (DB) lifetime max*	50X Daily Benefit max	
Drugs/med amount	No	No	
Caregiver training	30X DB lifetime max*	5X DB lifetime max	Family/friends can be trained to assist you.
Paid from care benefit pool	No	Yes	
Paid-up options	10 yr, to age 65	None	You can elect to pay a higher premium for a shorter period of time and received a policy that is fully paid up after 1 yr, 10 yrs or by age 65. 10-pay premium about 2x regular premium.
Exclusions			
Mental illness covered?	Not excluded	Not excluded	
Are pre-existing medical conditions covered immediately if fully disclosed on the application?	Yes	Yes	
Exclusions (See Sample Policy for specific exclusions)			

This is not intended to be a complete comparison of all policy provisions. Due to limited space, some policy provisions have not been included based on subjective judgment as to the importance of those provisions. See an actual or specimen policy for the exact wording of all contract provisions.

Prepared By: John Ryan, CFP™ (800) 796-0909
Date: 5/19/2003

WEEK SEVEN
MAP 7-14

*Importance of Disability Insurance**
(refer to page 293)

Insurance experts agree that disability insurance is the one kind of insurance wherein most people have inadequate coverage. The leading cause of home foreclosures is disability, yet fewer than 20 percent of adults have disability insurance. Disability insurance replaces wages that are lost when the insured person is sick or injured and cannot work for a long time. The biggest asset most people have is their ability to work.

Statistics reveal that nearly three in 10 workers between the ages of 35 and 65 become disabled and are unable to work for periods of 90 days or more at some time during their working lives. Yet surveys show a strong it-can't-happen-to-me attitude among most workers. Although Social Security provides disability benefits, the benefits cannot replace a disabled worker's wages. Social Security has a strict definition of disability and has a five-month waiting period. Few people can afford to live for five months without any income, especially with the medical costs associated with disability. Therefore, Social Security disability benefits should only be used to supplement an individual disability income policy.

* Material reprinted with the permission of Quickfinder Incorporated *(www.quickfinder.com)*.

WEEK SEVEN
MAP 7-15

*Disability Insurance 101**
(refer to page 293)

Definitions of Disability

Own occupation. Best definition of disability. Under this definition, the insured is considered totally disabled if unable to engage in any and every duty of his/her own occupation. Note: Typical policy limits own-occupation coverage to two to five years.

Any occupation. The most strict definition of disability. Under this definition, the insured is considered totally disabled when unable to perform any and every duty of a job for which he/she is suitably fit by training and/or experience.

Split definition. Insurance companies use a combination of the two definitions stated above for disability.

Recommended Coverage

Insurance experts recommend that disability insurance equal 60–70 percent of before-tax earnings, with benefits starting 90 days after becoming disabled. Although a longer elimination period reduces premiums, the significant factor is the length of time the insured can manage without an income. If the insured will have adequate pension and Social Security benefits at age 65, the policy should terminate disability benefits at that time. Ultimate goal of disability insurance is to replace as much income as possible under affordable terms. It requires in-depth analysis of financial obligations and of sources of income.

Features of Good Disability Plans

➤ Noncancellable and guaranteed renewable policies.

➤ Monthly benefits to replace 60–70 percent of the insured's predisability income until age 65.

➤ Cost-of-living adjustment rider. Protects benefits from inflation.

➤ Future insurability option to increase insurance as income rises, regardless of health.

➤ Elimination of premium payments while the insured is disabled.

➤ Residual-benefits clause. Allows partial payouts for partial disabilities.

➤ Waiting period to begin receiving benefits—norm is 90 days.

➤ Rehabilitation clause. Pay for treatment necessary to get back to work.

* Material reprinted with the permission of Quickfinder Incorporated *(www.quickfinder.com).*

Reduce Annual Cost on Individual Policy

➤ By electing a 90-day waiting period, an insured can save up to 20 percent in premium cost. Electing a one-year waiting period could trim the premiums by another 10 percent.

➤ Employer-sponsored coverage is usually 20–35 percent cheaper than comparable individual plans.

➤ Have monthly benefit payments stop after a certain amount of time. People with adequate savings to supplement Social Security do not generally need disability benefits past age 65.

➤ Settle for a smaller monthly benefit.

Women More Likely to Become Disabled

Many insurance carriers charge higher premiums to women (average of 25 percent more), depending on age, because women are more likely to become disabled.

TAX CONSEQUENCES OF DISABILITY INSURANCE

Disability insurance through employer:

➤ Group plans typically cover no more than 60 percent of salary.

➤ Disability benefits are taxable if the employer paid the premiums and the premiums were not taxable income.

➤ Disability benefits are not taxable if reimbursement is for medical expenses, permanent loss, or loss of use of part of the body or disfigurement.

Disability insurance paid by individual:

➤ Benefits are not taxable.

WEEK SEVEN
MAP 7-16

Disability Insurance Policy Checklist
(refer to page 293)

Date:_____

Circle Yes or No

1. Does my company have a Comdex rating of at least 80? *Yes   No*

2. Is my policy noncancelable? *Yes   No*

3. Are the premiums guaranteed? *Yes   No*

4. Does the definition of total disability protect me in my occupation? *Yes   No*

5. Are part-time and full-time return-to-work income-replacement benefits included and payable to age 65? *Yes   No*

6. Can I receive benefits without being totally disabled first? *Yes   No*

7. Does my policy use the "earned and received" method of accounting during my residual (partial) disability? *Yes   No*

8. Can my earnings loss be averaged to generate a greater benefit? *Yes   No*

9. When I am on claim, are my policy benefits adjusted for inflation? *Yes   No*

10. Can I increase my monthly benefits even if I am uninsurable? *Yes   No*

11. Can these increases be made (and are they payable) during an existing claim? *Yes   No*

12. Does my policy pay benefits for my lifetime if I am totally disabled? *Yes   No*

13. Do I have a policy (Business Overhead Expense Disability Plan) to cover my business expenses if I am disabled? *Yes   No*

14. Do I have a policy (Reducing-term Disability Plan) to cover my business loan payments? *Yes   No*

15. Do I have maximum benefits based on my current income and fixed business expenses? *Yes   No*

Note: It is advisable to review your disability insurance policies once a year with a qualified specialist.

WEEK SEVEN
MAP 7-17

Disability Insurance Annual Premiums
(refer to page 293)

Plan Design: 90-Day Elimination Period

$1,000 per month benefit

Benefit Period to Age 65

Benefit Update Rider

Cost of Living Adjustment Rider

Residual Benefit Rider

5A Occupation Class:

This class includes persons in professional, managerial, and technical occupations within select business and professional sectors of the economy. These occupations require extensive education, training, and experience. All work is performed in an office setting with less than 20 percent of the person's time spent out of the office and no direct supervision of persons with manual duties. Annual premiums per $1,000 per month of benefit are;

Age	Male	Female
30	$370	$540
35	$420	$640
40	$550	$780
45	$670	$900
50	$840	$1,070

4A Occupation Class:

This class consists primarily of those professional, managerial, and technical occupations which are not generally eligible for our most favorable classes. Work may involve more than 20 percent of the person's time being spent outside of the establishment. Occupational duties involve no direct supervision of persons with manual duties. Annual premiums per $1,000 per month of benefit are;

Age	Male	Female
30	$390	$620
35	$450	$670
40	$580	$820
45	$710	$950
50	$900	$1,120

Reprinted with permission of John Ryan, Ryan Insurance Strategy Consultants, 8301 E. Prentice Ave., Suite 310, Greenwood Village, CO 80111.

Week Seven
MAP 7-18

Social Security Disability
(refer to page 293)

Social Security disability requires that a worker have a physical or mental condition which;

➤ prevents him/her from doing any substantial gainful work for which he/she is suited, and

➤ the disability is either expected to last for at least 12 months or expected to result in death.

Workers' compensation or certain other government disability benefits may reduce Social Security disability benefits, or Social Security disability benefits may reduce other disability payments. The sum of all Social Security disability benefits paid to the worker and to his/her family cannot exceed 80 percent of the worker's earnings averaged over a period of time shortly before the disability.

Family benefits may also be payable for disability under the following conditions:

➤ The spouse of the worker is 62 or older and he/she does not collect a Social Security benefit that is higher than the disability award.

➤ The spouse of the worker at any age if he/she is caring for the worker's child who is under the age of 16 or is disabled and is receiving Social Security benefits.

➤ The worker's children if they are unmarried and:

  ▷ under the age of 18,

  ▷ under 19 but in elementary or secondary school as a full-time student, or

  ▷ age 18 or older and severely disabled (the disability must have started before age 22).

➤ An ex-spouse (even if the worker is remarried) if:

  ▷ he/she was married to the worker for at least 10 years,

  ▷ is at least 62 and unmarried, and/or

  ▷ is not eligible for an equal or higher benefit on his/her own or someone else's record.

In 2003, the average disabled worker benefits were $833 per month. That same year, the average benefits for a disabled worker, his/her spouse, and children was $1,395.

There is a full five-month waiting period after the disability before payments can begin for all Social Security disability payments.

Go to *www.socialsecurity.gov* and select Do You Qualify? under the Disability and SSI section. Next select Calculators to estimate actual benefits.

WEEK SEVEN
MAP 7-19

*Overview of Medicare**
(refer to page 293)

Medicare is a national health insurance program for:

➤ persons age 65 and older,

➤ certain disabled persons, and/or

➤ persons of any age with permanent kidney failure.

Medicare is two programs:

➤ **Part A: Hospital insurance.** Helps pay for inpatient hospital care, skilled-nursing facility care following a hospital stay, home health care, hospice care, and blood after the first three pints.

➤ **Part B: Medical insurance.** Helps pay for physicians' services; outpatient hospital care; home health care; diagnostic X-ray, laboratory, and other tests; necessary ambulance services; and other medical services and supplies.

Medicare does not cover routine physicals, most dental care, dentures, routine foot care, hearing aids, and most prescription drugs. Eyeglasses are only covered if corrective lenses are needed after a cataract operation. Exclusions are not limited to the ones listed above.

Premiums for Medicare:

➤ *Part A.* For most Medicare beneficiaries, there is no premium for Medicare Part A.

➤ *Part B.* Monthly premium of $58.70 for 2003.

Medicare premium break. If a Medicare recipient has limited income and assets, there are two programs available to help pay medical costs. State rules vary. Contact state or local Medicaid, public welfare, or social services office.

1) **Qualified Medicare Beneficiary (QMB) Program.**
Pays Medicare premiums, deductibles, and coinsurance for certain elderly and disabled persons entitled to Medicare Part A. Income must be at or below national poverty level, and savings and other assets cannot exceed $4,000 for one person or $6,000 for a couple.

2) **Specified Low-income Medicare Beneficiary (SLMB) Program.**
Pays the medical insurance (Part B) premium for persons with incomes slightly higher than the national poverty level.

* Material reprinted with the permission of Quickfinder Incorporated *(www.quickfinder.com).*

Applying for Medicare Benefits

➤ Individuals receiving Social Security retirement, disability, or railroad retirement benefits are contacted by Social Security a few months prior to eligibility.

➤ Anyone not receiving Social Security retirement, disability, or railroad retirement benefits should contact Social Security three months before turning age 65.

➤ Individuals who must contact Social Security for Medicare:

▷ disabled widow(er) age 50 to 65 who have not applied for disability benefits because he/she is getting another kind of Social Security benefit;

▷ government employee disabled before age 65;

▷ individual, or his/her spouse or dependent child, with permanent kidney failure;

▷ individual who had Medicare Part B in the past but dropped coverage; and/or

▷ individual who turned down Medicare Part B when he/she became entitled for Medicare Part A.

Note: The sign-up period for Medicare Part B lasts seven months. It begins three months before the 65th birthday, includes the birthday month, and ends three months after the 65th birthday. If not enrolled during initial enrollment, another opportunity is given each year from January 1 through March 31, with coverage beginning the following July. Anyone not enrolling in Medicare Part B when eligible pays a penalty to enroll later. The penalty is an increase in premium of 10 percent for each year eligible and not enrolled.

Eligibility for Hospital Insurance (Part A)

Age 65 and older. A person is eligible for Medicare Part A if he/she:

1) is receiving Social Security or railroad retirement benefits,

2) is not receiving Social Security or railroad retirement benefits, but has worked long enough to be eligible for them,

3) is entitled to Social Security benefits based on his/her spouse's (or divorced spouse's) work record, and that spouse is at least age 62 (the spouse does not have to apply for benefits in order for the person to be eligible based on the spouse's work), or

4) has worked long enough in federal, state, or local government to be insured for Medicare.

Under age 65. A person is eligible for Medicare Part A if he/she:

1) is entitled to disability benefits for at least 24 months, or

2) has worked long enough in a federal, state, or local government job and meets the requirements of the Social Security disability program.

Family members:

1) Under certain conditions, a spouse, divorced spouse, widow(er), or dependent parents may be eligible for hospital insurance at age 65.

2) Disabled widow(er) under age 65, disabled divorced widow(er) under age 65, or disabled children may be eligible, usually after a 24-month qualifying period.

Kidney failure:

1) A person at any age is eligible for Medicare Part A is he or she requires maintenance dialysis or a kidney transplant and:

   a) is insured or is getting monthly Social Security or railroad retirement benefits, or

   b) has worked long enough in government employment to be insured for Medicare.

2) A spouse or child may be eligible if he/she receives continuous dialysis for permanent kidney failure or had a kidney transplant. Only the family member who has permanent kidney failure is eligible.

Certain age or disabled.

Certain persons not eligible under the above rules may be able to enroll by paying the full cost of coverage ($316 per month for 2003). Coverage is reduced to $174 per month in 2003 for individuals and their spouses with 30 or more quarters of coverage. Certain state and local government retirees are no longer required to pay the premium for hospital insurance benefits.

Eligibility for Medical Insurance (Part B)

1) A person age 65 or older, or a person entitled to hospital insurance benefits, can enroll in the medical insurance plan by paying a monthly premium. No Social Security or government work quarters of coverage are needed. The cost is $58.70 per month for 2003.

2) Aliens age 65 or older not eligible for hospital insurance must be lawfully admitted, permanent residents and live in the U.S. for five years before they can enroll in Medicare Part B.

Medicare Options

Medicare beneficiaries can choose fee-for-service or coordinated care to receive all Medicare benefits.

1) **Fee-for-service.** Medicare pays a set percentage of hospital, doctor, and other health care expenses, and the beneficiary is responsible for certain deductibles and coinsurance payments. Beneficiaries can choose any licensed physician and use the services of any hospital, health care provider, or facility approved by Medicare. Note: A Medigap policy is usually needed to supplement fee-for-service coverage.

2) **Coordinated care.** Health maintenance organizations (HMOs) and competitive medical plans (CMPs) have contracts with the Medicare program and provide all hospital and medical benefits covered by Medicare. Services must be obtained from their network unless for an emergency inside/outside the service area. The HMO or CMP receives a monthly payment from Medicare, and the beneficiary must be enrolled in and pay the monthly premium for Medicare Part B. A monthly premium and a small co-payment is charged each time a service is used. In addition, some benefits beyond Medicare are provided, including preventive care, prescription drugs, dental care, hearing aids, and eyeglasses.

Note: A Medigap policy is usually not needed with coordinated care coverage.

* Material reprinted with the permission of Quickfinder Incorporated *(www.quickfinder.com).*

*Standard Medigap Policies**
(refer to page 293)

Medicare supplemental insurance policies (Medigap) are private insurance policies designed to cover all or part of the deductible and coinsurance amounts not covered by Medicare. Government reforms under the Omnibus Budget Reform Act of 1990 (OBRA) narrowed the options to the offering of 10 standard policies (labeled A–J).

They all must contain the core package. See the chart below.

Coverage	Ten Plans Insurance Companies Offer									
	A	B	C	D	E	F	G	H	I	J
Core Benefits	Yes	Yes	Yes	Yes	Yes	Yes	Yes	Yes	Yes	Yes
Hospital deductible (Part A)	No	Yes	Yes	Yes	Yes	Yes	Yes	Yes	Yes	Yes
Doctor deductible (Part B)	No	No	Yes	No	No	Yes	No	No	No	Yes
Skilled nursing facility co-insurance	No	No	Yes	Yes	Yes	Yes	Yes	Yes	Yes	Yes
Doctor charges beyond Medicare	0%	0%	0%	0%	0%	100%	80%	0%	100%	100%
Foreign country emergency care	No	No	Yes	Yes	Yes	Yes	Yes	Yes	Yes	Yes
At-home recovery	No	No	No	Yes	No	No	Yes	No	Yes	Yes
Outpatient prescription drugs	No	No	No	No	No	No	No	Yes*	Yes*	Yes**
Preventive care	No	No	No	No	Yes	No	No	No	No	Yes

*$1,250 maximum benefits; $250 deductible/calendar year; 50% co-insurance
**$3,000 maximum benefits; $250 deductible/calendar year; 50% co-insurance

Enrollment. After the effective date of Medicare Part B, there is a six-month open enrollment period for Medigap policies. During this period, a person age 65 or older cannot be denied or charged a higher premium due to poor health.

Preexisting conditions. Policies may exclude coverage for preexisting conditions during the first six months the policy is in effect. Preexisting conditions are conditions diagnosed or treated during the six-month period before the effective date of the Medigap policy.

Standard Medigap Policies
All 10 plans must cover the basic (core) package:

➤ Hospital insurance (Part A) coinsurance (days 61–90).

➤ Hospital insurance co-insurance (days 91–150).

➤ Hospital insurance expenses for extra 365 days in hospital.

➤ Parts A and B deductible for cost of first three pints of blood.

➤ Medical insurance (Part B) coinsurance—20 percent of allowable charges.

For additional information on Medigap policies, call the Health Insurance Association of America (HIAA), (202) 824-1600, for the "Guide to Medicare Supplement Insurance."

WEEK SEVEN
MAP 7-21
Family Limited Partnership Flowchart
(with You as General Partner)
(refer to page 294)

Description: Legally, family partnerships can be structured as general partnerships (GPs) or limited partnerships (LPs). When asset protection, retained control, and valuation discounts are important goals, the limited partnership form of entity will be necessary.

The limited partnership form is often useful in family partnership situations. A Family Limited Partnership (FLP) is a legal entity formed under state law, wherein the partners are family members. An FLP must have at least one general partner (which can be an individual, trust, or corporation) and one limited partner. The general partner must own at least 1 percent of the partnership. Typically, the parent is the general partner and the children are limited partners. The general partner can also own a limited partnership interest, which can be used to generate cash flow for that partner.

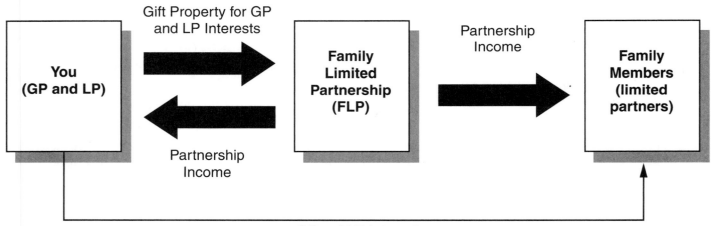

Description: From an operational standpoint, the general partner controls the FLP by making investment, business, and management decisions. This includes determining when (or if) cash distributions will be made to the limited partners (typically, you and your children). The general partner should charge a reasonable management fee for these services. However, the general partner is exposed to unlimited liability from partnership activities. This unlimited liability issue can be mitigated by using a corporate (or Limited Liability Corporation) general partner. In this way, no individual is exposed to unlimited liability from the FLP's activities.

Funding the Partnership—

Assets that should be used:

- Marketable securities
- Real estate
- Closely held stock
- Business assets
- Life insurance

Assets that should not be used:

- S Corporation stock
- Stock in a professional corporation
- Personal assets
- Retirement plan accounts
- Encumbered property
- Passive activities

Week Seven
MAP 7-22

Advantages and Disadvantages of Family Partnerships
(refer to page 294)

Advantages:

- Income tax and transfer-tax savings

- Estate freeze (divert future appreciation)

- Valuation adjustments

- Control over assets

- Facilitate family gifting

- Management flexibility

- Avoiding probate

- Greater certainty of tax treatment

- Protection from Creditors

- Control over family members' access to wealth and income

- Economies/diversification of investment opportunities

- Keep assets within family

- Flexibility to adapt

- Dispute management

- Avoidance of guardianship

- Family communication and harmony

Disadvantages:

- Administration expenses

- Potential family disharmony

- IRS scrutiny

- Reduced fringe benefits

- Restrictive income tax rules

- Difficult trust administration

- Loss of basis step-up

- Underfunded marital deduction

- Liquidity concerns

- S Corporation incompatibility

- Investment company rules

- Potential business purpose attack by IRS

WEEK SEVEN
MAP 7-23
*Entity Comparison Chart**
(refer to page 294)

M-2

2003 Edition — Small Business Quickfinder® Handbook

ENTITY COMPARISON CHART

	Sole Proprietorship—Tab F	Partnership—Tab B	Corporation—Tab C	S Corporation—Tab D	Limited Liability Company—Tab F
IRS Pub.	334	541	542	589	541
IRS Form	Sch. C, Form 1040	Form 1065	Form 1120	Form 1120S	Form 1065
Entity Description	A sole proprietorship consists of one individual who carries on an unincorporated trade or business. (If a husband and wife carry on a business together as partners, they should file Form 1065, *U.S. Return of Partnership Income*.)	A partnership is an association having two or more owners that functions as a trade or business. A joint undertaking merely to share expenses or share ownership of property does not necessarily constitute a partnership. An LLC with two or more members is generally classified as a partnership for tax purposes. A partnership can make the election to be taxed as a corporation.	A corporation is a business entity that carries its own legal status, separate and distinct from its owners. An entity formed as a legal corporation cannot elect out of corporate taxation. See "Check the Box Rules" in Tab F.	A corporation can elect to be taxed as an S corporation by filing Form 2553. Only domestic corporations with one class of stock are eligible. A corporation is limited to 75 shareholders, and may not have another corporation as a shareholder. (An exception exists for qualified subchapter S subsidiaries.) Other restrictions apply.	An LLC is a hybrid entity, generally formed under state law, that combines the pass-through attributes of a partnership with the limited liability of a corporation. An LLC can elect to be taxed as a C corporation. For purposes of this chart, the LLC is assumed to have not made such an election and is therefore subject to taxation as a partnership.
Taxation	Net profit is computed on Schedule C and is reported as income on the owner's Form 1040.	Partnership income and expenses flow through to the individual partners. Income is taxed to the partner whether or not it is actually distributed. Pass-through items retain the same character in the hands of the partner as they had in the hands of the partnership.	A C corporation pays tax on its profits. When the owners (shareholders) take profits from the corporation, the distributions take the form of taxable dividends (double taxation). Personal service corporations are taxed at a higher rate.	A corporation is taxed in the same manner as a partnership. Income and expenses flow through to shareholders. Pass-through items retain the same character in the hands of the share-holder as they had in the hands of the corporation.	An LLC is taxed as a partnership. Income and expenses flow through to members.
Wages and SE Tax	The owner is subject to SE tax of 15.3% of net earnings. SE tax is computed on Schedule SE and is reported as "Other Taxes" on Form 1040.	A general partner's share of business income (including guaranteed payments) is subject to SE tax. A limited partner's share of business income is not subject to SE tax unless the partner performs services for the partnership. Other items, such as interest and dividends, retain their character and are passed through to the partner's individual income tax return.	Shareholders who perform services for a corporation, including officers, are treated as employees. Wages of corporate employees are subject to payroll tax and withholding. Wages paid to employee-shareholders must be reasonable. Dividend distributions are not subject to SE tax.	An employee-shareholder of an S corporation receives wages for services rendered. Wages paid to employee-shareholders must be reasonable. Additional profits are passed through to the shareholder and are taxable for income tax purposes but not for SE tax purposes. Double taxation of profits is avoided.	Profits are subject to income tax in the same way as a partnership. Members' business income (including guaranteed payments) may be subject to SE tax. See Tab F for exceptions.
Losses	Business losses can offset other income such as interest, capital gains, or a spouse's wages if filing a joint return. Subject to "Hobby Loss" rules under IRC §183.	Losses flow through to partners. Recognition of loss by a partner is limited by the partner's basis, at-risk rules and passive activity rules. Subject to "Hobby Loss" rules under IRC §183.	Capital losses are allowed only to the extent of capital gains. NOL of a corporation may be carried over against corporate income, but is not directly passed through to shareholders.	Losses flow through to shareholders. Recognition of loss is limited by the shareholder's basis, at-risk rules and passive activity rules. Subject to "Hobby Loss" rules under IRC §183.	Losses flow through to members. Recognition of loss by members is limited by the member's basis, at-risk rules, and passive activity rules. Subject to "Hobby Loss" rules under IRC §183.
Fringe Benefits (See Tab K)	Only the amount paid on behalf of employees is deductible. Amounts paid on behalf of the sole proprietor are not deductible. *Exception:* A sole proprietor can deduct medical insurance premiums and medical reimbursement costs under an accident and health plan that covers all employees. If the sole proprietor's spouse is covered under a plan that also covers the owner as part of the family, the deduction is still allowed.	Generally not tax free to partner. Must be included in partner's income.	Owner-employees are entitled to the same tax-free fringe benefits as other employees (subject to discrimination rules).	Restricted for employee-shareholders that own more than 2% of the corporation. Must generally be included in wages.	Subject to the same rules as a partnership.
Personal Liability	The sole proprietor is liable for all business debts and actions.	A general partner is personally liable for all partnership debt. A limited partner's liability is usually limited to the partner's investment in the partnership.	Shareholders are not liable for debts incurred by the corporation. Liability is generally limited to the amount invested.*	Shareholders have limited liability, just as with a C corporation.*	The degree of liability protection for LLC members varies from state to state.

*Caution: The courts may disregard the so-called "corporate liability shield" in the case of single shareholder corporations.

Material reprinted with the permission of Quickfinder Incorporated (www.quickfinder.com).

ENTITY COMPARISON CHART

	Sole Proprietorship—Tab F	Partnership—Tab B	Corporation—Tab C	S Corporation—Tab D	Limited Liability Company—Tab F
IRS Pub.	334	541	542	589	541
IRS Form	Sch. C, Form 1040	Form 1065	Form 1120	Form 1120S	Form 1065
Organization and Administration	A sole proprietorship is the easiest business to organize. Complete intermingling of business and personal funds is allowed (although this is not recommended). A business return is filed along with the owner's individual income tax return.	A partnership is easy to organize. A written partnership agreement is recommended, but not required. The partnership agreement determines how income and losses are allocated to the partners. If a partnership agreement does not exist, partnership items pass through based on the partners' ownership interest.	A corporation is difficult and expensive to organize. Corporations must hold periodic board meetings and keep minutes. Corporations must comply with federal and state regulations.	An S corporation is set up as a regular corporation. S corporations must make election to be treated as an S corporation. Certain events will cause automatic termination of S status.	An existing partnership can generally register for LLC status in the state in which it conducts business. Registration is generally less complicated than forming a corporation.
Bookkeeping and Accounting	There are fewer requirements on what type of bookkeeping system or accounting method is used in sole proprietorships. The system must be consistent, clearly show income and expenses, and allow the taxpayer to file an accurate return. The sole proprietorship must follow the same tax year as the owner.	Depending on income and assets, the partnership may be required to include a balance sheet with its income tax return. Therefore, the partnership should use the double-entry method for bookkeeping purposes. If a partner exchanges property other than cash in exchange for an interest in a partnership, special accounting rules apply. See "Contributed Property" in Tab B.	The balance sheet on the corporation's tax return must agree with the corporate books. The corporation must use a double-entry bookkeeping system. The corporation must file all necessary employment tax returns.	The S corporation must use double-entry bookkeeping. The S corporation must file all required payroll tax and reporting forms.	Same as a partnership.
Owner Control and Flexibility	The owner is free to make all business decisions.	Control of the business operations is divided among partners.	Shareholders have control over the corporation to the extent that they own voting stock.	Shareholders have control over the corporation to the extent that they own voting stock.	Control is divided among members.
Transfer of Ownership	A sole proprietorship is not a separate entity from its owner. "Sale" of a sole proprietorship is actually a sale of assets.	The partnership agreement may restrict the sale of a partnership interest, and may control the terms of the sale.	Ownership is easily transferred by selling shares of stock. The corporate charter may place certain restrictions on the sale of stock by shareholders.	Ownership is easily transferred by selling shares of stock. The corporate charter may place certain restrictions on the sale of stock by shareholders.	The operating agreement may restrict transfer of ownership interest.
Advantages and Disadvantages	Advantages: – Minimum legal restrictions. – Easy to discontinue. Disadvantages: – Unlimited liability. – May not bring in new owners or outside capital contributions. – Income tax cannot be deferred by retaining profits.	Advantages: – A partnership can be a good way to combine the skills and/or financial abilities of several people. Disadvantages: – A partnership is often easier to get into than out of. – General partners are liable for actions of other partners.	Advantages: – Limited liability. – Perpetual life. – Ability to raise capital through issuance of stock. – Ease of transfer of ownership. Disadvantages: – Double taxation of profits. – Corporate charter restricts types of business activities. – Subject to various state and federal controls.	Advantages: – Limited liability. – Avoids double taxation of profits. – Profits passed through are not subject to SE tax as in a partnership. Disadvantages: – Shareholders pay tax on earnings even if undistributed. – Less flexibility in choosing a tax year. – Contribution limits to a qualified retirement plan are based on employee-shareholder's wages, not overall profits such as a sole proprietor.	Advantages: – Avoids certain S corporation restrictions. – Avoids double taxation of profits. Disadvantages: – Inconsistent treatment state to state. – Must have at least two owners if it wants to be taxed as a partnership for federal tax purposes. – Relatively new business entity with little regulatory or case law to follow.

Business Insurance: The limited liability characteristics of certain business entities should not be considered a substitute for proper insurance coverage. The business owner should consider coverage to protect against fire and theft, business interruption, errors and omissions, employment practices, employee benefit plans and employee dishonesty. General liability coverage, including umbrella policies for personal injury and property damage, should also be considered. See information about workers' compensation insurance on Page M-10.

*Caution: The courts may disregard the so-called "corporate liability shield" in the case of single shareholder corporations.

WEEK SEVEN
MAP 7-24

*Variable and Immediate Annuities**
(refer to page 294)

Variable Annuities

A variable annuity bundles a collection of mutual funds into a tax-deferred wrapper that functions much like an IRA. Investors can switch money among funds without triggering taxes, and earnings, grow tax-deferred, until withdrawn when regular income tax rates of up to 38.6 percent apply. The insurance component of the investment is a guaranteed death benefit. The insurance benefit is a guarantee to pay the value of the retirement account either at death or when the payment period starts, whichever is sooner. Most annuities pay at least the principal amount the customer invested over the years, even if the stock market wipes out the account entirely.

Because of cost and illiquidity, variable annuities are best suited for investors who have maxed out contributions they can make to IRAs and company retirement plans, who have established an adequate liquidity fund, who fully intend to leave their money intact for at least a decade, and who are willing to accept more risk in return for potentially higher returns.

While all annuities are tax deferred, the eventual tax treatment is less favorable than mutual funds because all the earnings on the funds are subject to income tax at ordinary rates. The long-term gains earned on mutual fund holdings are taxed at the oftenlower capital-gains tax rate. (Currently, a 15 percent top capital gains tax rate is applied for investments held over 12 months.) Also, variable annuities involve insurance expenses, provide no step-up in basis at death, and generally impose early withdrawal penalties.

Immediate Annuities

An immediate annuity is one that begins to pay a monthly income immediately. The insured deposits a specified sum of money with an insurance company who agrees to pay a monthly income for life or for a certain number of years, depending on the annuity option selected.

Single-premium immediate annuities make good investments for those with good health and long-lived ancestors. Since monthly payments are based on average life expectancy, an immediate annuity is a wise choice if one lives longer than actuarially expected. Immediate annuities offer a convenient way of providing for the income needs of another person, such as an aged parent or a handicapped child.

Immediate annuities can provide a continuing tax shelter for a lump-sum payment received from a pension or profit-sharing plan upon retirement. If the funds are rolled over into an immediate annuity, taxes will not have to be paid on the funds—only on the payments as they are received monthly.

* Material reprinted with the permission of Quickfinder Incorporated *(www.quickfinder.com)*.

While no one should put all his/her money in an immediate annuity, individuals with cash to spare might consider this option for steady income. In general, the size of the monthly check will depend upon age, gender, amount invested, and whether payments cease at death or continue for a specified number of years. A major drawback of immediate annuities is that monthly payments do not keep pace with inflation.

Comparative shopping is a must since the immediate annuity market is very fluid and rates can fluctuate widely. A particular insurance company may post attractive payouts one month but not the next; it may be competitive at some ages but unattractive at others.

* Material reprinted with the permission of Quickfinder Incorporated *(www.quickfinder.com)*.

WEEK SEVEN
MAP 7-25*

Checklist of Factors Indicating that a Buy/Sell Agreement Is Needed
(refer to page 294)

❏ **Liquidity of Ownership Interests Is Desired.** If the owners want to ensure a ready market for their ownership interests (in the event of death, disability, retirement, etc.), a buy/sell agreement is advisable.

❏ **Owners Want to Eliminate Uncertainty about Ownership Transfers.** Co-owners may be comfortable with a fellow owner's plans to transfer ownership—for example, to a well-regarded child in the event of death or disability. However, a buy/sell agreement between the parent and the child (with an option on the part of the remaining owners to buy the interest if the child does not) removes the uncertainty that exists if a will or other document is being relied upon to effectuate the transfer. Wills can be changed at the last minute or challenged by heirs or potential heirs. A binding buy/sell agreement can nail down the rights and obligations of the various parties.

❏ **Future Ownership Conflicts Can Be Foreseen.** If it is anticipated that the remaining owner (or owners) would have difficulties coexisting with the family of a deceased or withdrawing co-owner (such as a spouse or child who would inherit an interest), a buy/sell agreement can ensure that the remaining owners gain control over the interest of the deceased or withdrawing owner. Note that owners should not overlook the possibility that a former spouse could wind up with an ownership interest pursuant to a divorce settlement.

❏ **Ownership by Outsiders Is Undesirable.** This factor is most commonly present in closely held family businesses, but it can arise in any closely held business when the existing owners are a tight-knit group. For example, in the event of insolvency of an owner, a creditor may become a member of the ownership group. A buy/sell agreement ensures that ownership interests cannot fall outside the existing group without the group's approval.

❏ **Owners' Heirs Have No Interest in Ownership.** This factor can arise because the heirs feel the business is too risky for their tastes or because they have no desire to participate.

❏ **Valuation for Estate Tax Purposes Is Desired.** When owners are interested in establishing the value of their ownership interests for federal and state estate tax purposes, a buy/sell agreement can be used if certain requirements are met.

Week Eight
MAP 8-1
*Pension Plan Comparison Chart**
(refer to page 326)

Pension Plan Comparison Chart—2001 Tax Act Changes						
Maximum Contributions Allowed for:	**2001**	**2002**	**2003**	**2004**	**2005**	**2006**
Traditional and Roth IRAs—under age 50	Lesser of $2,000 or earned income.	Lesser of $3,000 or earned income.			Lesser of $4,000 or earned income.	
Traditional and Roth IRAs—age 50 or older	Lesser of $2,000 or earned income.	Lesser of $3,500 or earned income.			Lesser of $4,500 or earned income.	Lesser of $5,000 or earned income.
SEP	15% of wages up to $25,500 (13.0435% of net SE income after SE tax deduction for self-employed) = $170,000.	25% of wages up to $40,000 (20% of net SE income after SE tax deduction for self-employed). Compensation limit = $200,000.				
SIMPLE— under age 50	Employee elective deferrals = lesser of $6,500 or earned income. Employer must match up to 3% of wage.	Employee elective deferrals = lesser of $7,000 or earned income. Employer must match up to 3% of wage.	Employee elective deferrals = lesser of $8,000 or earned income. Employer must match up to 3% of wage.	Employee elective deferrals = lesser of $9,000 or earned income. Employer must match up to 3% of wage.	Employee elective deferrals = lesser of $10,000 or earned income. Employer must match up to 3% of wage.	Employee elective deferrals = lesser of $10,000 or earned income. Employer must match up to 3% of wage.
SIMPLE— age 50 or older	Employee elective deferrals = lesser of $6,500 or earned income. Employer must match up to 3% of wage.	Employee elective deferrals = lesser of $7,500 or earned income. Employer must match up to 3% of wage.	Employee elective deferrals = lesser of $9,000 or earned income. Employer must match up to 3% of wage.	Employee elective deferrals = lesser of $10,500 or earned income. Employer must match up to 3% of wage.	Employee elective deferrals = lesser of $12,000 or earned income. Employer must match up to 3% of wage.	Employee elective deferrals = lesser of $12,500 or earned income. Employer must match up to 3% of wage.
Money-Purchase Defined-Contribution Plan	25% of wages up to $35,000 (20% of net SE income after SE tax deduction for self-employed). Compensation limit = $170,000.	Contributions per participant up to lesser of 100% of compensation or $40,000. Compensation limit = $200,000. Employer deduction limited to 25% of aggregate compensation for all participants (20% of net SE income after SE tax deduction for self-employed).				
Profit-Sharing Defined-Contribution Plan	15% of wages up to $25,500 (13.0435% of net SE income after SE tax deduction for self-employed). Compensation limit = $170,000.	Contributions per participant up to lesser of 100% of compensation or $40,000. Compensation limit = $200,000. Employer deduction limited to 25% of aggregate compensation for all participants (20% of net SE income after SE tax deduction for self-employed).				
401(k)	Employee elective deferrals limited to $10,500. Employer deduction limited to 15% of combined wages of all employees (elective deferrals must reduce wages for purposes of the 15% limit). Combined employer contributions and employee elective deferrals per employee limited to 25% of wage up to $35,000.	Employee elective deferrals limited to $11,000 ($12,000 for employees age 50 or older). Employer deduction limited to 25% of combined wages of all employees (elective deferrals do not reduce wages for purposes of the 25% limit). Combined employer contributions and employee elective deferrals per employee limited to 100% of wage up to $40,000.	Employee elective deferrals limited to $12,000 ($14,000 for employees age 50 or older). Employer deduction limited to 25% of combined wages of all employees (elective deferrals do not reduce wages for purposes of the 25% limit). Combined employer contributions and employee elective deferrals per employee limited to 100% of wage up to $40,000.	Employee elective deferrals limited to $13,000 ($16,000 for employees age 50 or older). Employer deduction limited to 25% of combined wages of all employees (elective deferrals do not reduce wages for purposes of the 25% limit). Combined employer contributions and employee elective deferrals per employee limited to 100% of wage up to $40,000.	Employee elective deferrals limited to $14,000 ($18,000 for employees age 50 or older). Employer deduction limited to 25% of combined wages of all employees (elective deferrals do not reduce wages for purposes of the 25% limit). Combined employer contributions and employee elective deferrals per employee limited to 100% of wage up to $40,000.	Employee elective deferrals limited to $15,000 ($20,000 for employees age 50 or older). Employer deduction limited to 25% of combined wages of all employees (elective deferrals do not reduce wages for purposes of the 25% limit). Combined employer contributions and employee elective deferrals per employee limited to 100% of wage up to $40,000.
403(b)— under age 50	Employee elective deferral portion only = $10,500.	Employee elective deferral portion only = $11,000.	Employee elective deferral portion only = $12,000.	Employee elective deferral portion only = $13,000.	Employee elective deferral portion only = $14,000.	Employee elective deferral portion only = $15,000.
403(b)— age 50 or older	Employee elective deferral portion only = $10,500.	Employee elective deferral portion only = $12,000.	Employee elective deferral portion only = $14,000.	Employee elective deferral portion only = $16,000.	Employee elective deferral portion only = $18,000.	Employee elective deferral portion only = $20,000
Employer Qualified Defined-Benefit Plan	Actuarially determined contribution. Limit on benefits received equals 100% of average compensation for highest three years not to exceed $140,000. Compensation limit = $170,000.	Actuarially determined contribution. Limit on benefits received equals 100% of average compensation for highest three years not to exceed $160,000. Compensation limit = $200,000.				

Note: Dollar limits are also indexed for inflation for various items on this chart depending on the year in question. This chart is not intended to present all of the exceptions to the rule. IRA limits increase to $5,000 in tax year 2008 and beyond with the age 50 or older limit increasing to $6,000. The age 50 or older increase in elective deferrals for 401(k) plans also applies to SARSEPs.

* Material reprinted with the permission of Quickfinder Incorporated *(www.quickfinder.com)*.

Week Eight
MAP 8-2

Traditional IRA Flowchart
(refer to page 326)

An IRA is your own personal savings plan for your retirement. Technically, it is a trust created for the exclusive benefit of an individual or the individual's beneficiaries.

You

Annual contribution generally limited to lesser of $3,000[a] or 100% of earned income ($6,000[a] if you are married, however, no more than $3,000[a] can be contributed per spouse).[a]

Up to $3,000[a] can be contributed to a " Spousal IRA" for a non-working spouse.

Note: The annual combined contributions to a traditional IRA and a Roth IRA cannot exceed these limitations. Thus, you cannot contribute $3,000[a] to a traditional IRA and another $3,000[a] to a Roth IRA.

Contributions may be tax deductible depending on your participation in an employer-sponsored retirement plan, your income level and your filing status.

Contributions

IRA

Contributions can be made and the IRA opened beginning with the first day of the tax year through April 15 of the year following the tax year.

Earnings are not taxable until distributed to you. Thus, your money grows on a tax-deferred basis.

No part of the IRA may be invested in life insurance contracts or certain collectables. The IRA may, however, be invested in annuity contracts.

You control the investment in the IRA (i.e. the amount invested in each specific investment vehicle).

Generally, the IRA funds may not be commingled with other accounts.

Distributions

Death

The value of your IRA is included in the value of your estate for estate tax purposes.

Surviving spouse can roll over the inherited IRA. Other heirs cannot roll over the inherited IRA.

Surviving spouse can elect to treat the decedent's IRA as being his or her own IRA; thus deferring the required minimum distributions until the year after reaching age 70 $1/2$. Other heirs cannot make this election.

Retirement

Distributions must start by April 1 of the year after the year you reach age 70$1/2$.

There is a minimum amount you must withdraw each year starting the year after reaching 70 $1/2$ (known as the minimum required distribution).

Distributions of earnings and previously deducted contributions are taxed as ordinary income when received.

There is generally a 10% penalty if distributions are received before age 59 $1/2$. Exceptions exist and may apply.

Note: [a]$3,500 for individuals who turn 50 by the end of 2003 and $7,000 if both individuals turn 50 by the end of 2003.

What Is a Roth IRA?

A Roth Individual Retirement Account (IRA) is a retirement vehicle that allows for the tax-deferred buildup of investment earnings on nondeductible contributions made to the Roth IRA. Certain tax laws and limits must be met that are discussed later.

How Much Can Be Contributed to a Roth IRA?

For 2003, annual contributions are generally limited to the lesser of $3,000 ($3,500 if age 50 or older) or 100 percent of earned income. However, unlike traditional IRAs, Roth contributions can be made beyond age 70½. Contributions to Roth IRAs are not deductible for income tax purposes.

The annual limit applies to the combined contributions to traditional IRAs (see "Traditional IRAs") and Roth IRAs. Thus, during 2003 you can't contribute to a Roth IRA and another $3,000 to a traditional IRA.

If your spouse doesn't work (i.e., has no earned income) during 2003, up to $3,000 ($3,500 if age 50 or older) can still be contributed to your nonworking spouse's Roth IRA provided your earned income is greater than the total of both spouses' IRA contributions.

Contributions to a Roth IRA are not deductible. In addition, the maximum contribution to a Roth IRA is phased out ratably over a range of adjusted gross income (AGI) with certain modifications, as follows:

Filing Status	AGI Phaseout Range
Joint returns	$150,000–$160,000
Single or head of household	$95,000–$110,000
Married filing separate return	$0–$15,000

What Is the Deadline for making Roth IRA Contributions?

Contributions can be made and the Roth IRA opened from January 1 to April 15 of the year following your tax year. Thus, for the tax year 2003, you have from January 1, 2002 to April 15, 2004 to make Roth IRA contributions.

How Is My Money Invested?

You control the investments in the Roth IRA. You cannot invest IRA funds in life insurance contracts or certain collectibles. However, you can invest Roth IRA funds in annuity contracts. Generally, Roth IRA funds cannot be commingled with non-IRA funds. Roth IRA earnings are not taxable when distributed to you. Thus, your money can grow on a tax-free basis.

What Are My Distribution Options?

Distributions due to retirement. Distributions from a Roth IRA are not taxable and not subject to the early distribution tax if they meet certain requirements. All such qualified distributions must have been received after the five-year tax period beginning with the first year for which a contribution was made to a Roth IRA and is:

1. made after you reach age 59½;

2. made to your designated beneficiary or estate after your death.

3. attributable to your being disabled; and/or

4. made for first-time home purchase expenses up to $10,000.

Distributions to the extent attributable to earnings that do not meet these requirements are subject to regular income tax, plus a 10 percent penalty unless an exception applies. Exceptions to the early distribution penalty include the following:

1. distributions made on account of death or disability;

2. distributions used to pay medical expenses;

3. payments structured as a series of substantially equal payments;

4. IRA distributions used for first-time home purchases (up to $10,000); and/or

5. IRA distributions used to pay for higher education expenses.

No portion of a distribution from a Roth IRA is taxable until the cumulative distributions from all of your Roth IRA accounts exceed the total amount of contributions. Thus, contributions to a Roth IRA can be withdrawn tax-free and penalty-free at any time. This is true even if the five-year waiting period has not expired and you are not yet age 59½.

Example: Tax-free withdrawal of principal from a Roth IRA.

George is age 50 when he sets up two Roth IRA accounts in 2000. He contributes $1,000 to each account that year and $1,000 to each in 2001 and 2002, so he has made total contributions to each account of $3,000. On July 10, 2003, he has $4,500 in Account One and $4,000 in Account Two. He withdraws all $4,500 from Account One. The distribution is not a qualified distribution because George is not yet age 59½ and the five-year waiting period has not expired. But even though the distribution is composed of $3,000 principal and $1,500 earnings from Account One, the withdrawal is considered to come first from George's $6,000 of total Roth IRA contributions, so the entire withdrawal is tax free and penalty free.

Unlike traditional IRAs, which are subject to the minimum distribution rules, there is no minimum amount you must withdraw each year, and there is no age requirement as to when you must begin distributions.

Distributions due to death. Once the Roth IRA owner dies, the rules for inherited IRAs apply to the beneficiary(ies) as though the Roth IRA owner died before his/her required beginning date. For example, distributions from a Roth IRA made to a surviving spouse can be treated as the surviving spouse's own Roth IRA or rolled over into her own Roth IRA. This enables the surviving spouse to delay distribution until his/her death, if desired.

A nonspouse beneficiary must receive the entire balance of the Roth IRA within five years of the owner's date of death, or if so elected, over the beneficiary's life expectancy.

For estate tax purposes, the value of your Roth IRA is included in the value of your estate.

WEEK EIGHT
MAP 8-4

*Roth IRAs vs. Deductible IRAs**
(refer to page 326)

Roth IRA advantages:

➤ Roth IRAs provide tax-free growth. Traditional IRAs provide tax-deferred growth. Roth IRAs are more attractive the longer they have to grow.

➤ Roth IRAs are more flexible than traditional IRAs. Roth IRAs have no age requirements for when a taxpayer must start taking withdrawals or stop making contributions.

➤ Income phaseout limits are higher for Roth IRAs than for traditional IRAs.

➤ Accumulations of earnings in a Roth IRA can be transferred to beneficiaries income tax free. Beneficiaries pay tax on inherited traditional IRAs.

➤ Roth IRAs have more flexibility regarding withdrawals since contributions are withdrawn tax-and penalty free before earnings. Nondeductible contributions to traditional IRAs have to be withdrawn in proportion to taxable earnings.

➤ Roth IRAs favor younger taxpayers who have a longer period before retirement. They also favor taxpayers who expect to be in a significantly higher tax bracket when distributions begin.

Traditional IRA advantages. A deductible IRA is generally the better choice for taxpayers expecting to be in a significantly lower marginal tax bracket when funds are withdrawn. The deductible IRA may also be the choice for a taxpayer who is close to retirement and needs to withdraw funds in a few years.

Uncertain about the future. A traditional IRA follows conventional financial planning wisdom in that there is an immediate benefit for making tax-deductible contributions. Roth IRAs realize a benefit in the future. For people who are uncertain about future tax laws, receiving an immediate benefit may be better than a future benefit, even if the future benefit turns out to be greater. The Roth IRA has a certain degree of risk involved with the decision process. In many cases, it may take at least 15–20 years before the benefits of a Roth IRA overtake the benefits of a traditional IRA. Of course, for those who do not qualify for traditional IRA contributions, the uncertain risk of a Roth IRA is removed.

* Material reprinted with the permission of Quickfinder Incorporated *(www.quickfinder.com).*

WEEK EIGHT
MAP 8-5

Coverdell ESA Flowchart
(refer to page 326)

Contributions

Donor

Up to $2,000 of aggregate contributions can be made annually to an ESA set up for a designated beneficiary. The contribution limit is per beneficiary. Thus no more than $2,000 in aggregate from one or more persons may be contributed to a given beneficiary's ESA.

Contributions are not tax deductible.

The maximum contribution may be phased out depending on your income level and filing status.

Contributions must be made in cash and cannot be made after the beneficiary attains the age of 18.

No limitations exist on who can contribute to an ESA on behalf of a designated beneficiary. Thus, any friend, relative, or even the beneficiary himself could establish and contribute to an ESA.

Similarly, the same people can set up as many ESAs for as many different beneficiaries as they choose, provided the beneficiaries are under age 18 and no more than a total of $2,000 is contributed to a beneficiary's account.

Coverdell ESA

Contributions can be made and the ESA opened beginning with the first day of the tax year through the original due date of tax return (generally, April 15).

Tax-free accumulation of earnings.

The beneficiary can be changed or the funds may be rolled over to a new ESA for a new beneficiary if the new beneficiary is a member of the prior beneficiary's family.

Distributions

Education Expenses

Distributions are excluded from the beneficiary's taxable income as long as they do not exceed qualified education expenses.

If distributions during a tax year exceed the beneficiary's qualified education expenses, the earnings portion (previous tax-free build-up) of the distribution not used to pay the education expenses is included in the beneficiary's taxable income. An additional 10% penalty tax generally also applies.

Qualified education expenses generally include tuition, fees, books, supplies, equipment, and room and board.

Week Eight
MAP 8-6

What Is a 401(k) Plan?
(refer to page 327)

A 401(k) plan is a type of profit-sharing or stock bonus plan that allows employees to elect to have their employers make pretax contributions (e.g., salary deferrals) on the employees' behalf in lieu of paying an equivalent amount in currently taxable cash wages. These plans are sometimes called "cash or deferred arrangements" (CODAs).

Advantages to Employees

Contributions accumulate in the plan, along with investment gains, and are taxed when distributed to the plan participant from the plan. One potential benefit to the participant of deferring taxation on contributions and earnings until retirement is that he/she may be in a lower tax bracket than during the period when he/she accumulated the assets in his/her 401(k).

Because the 401(k) plan is part of a profit-sharing plan, employers still have the advantage of flexibility in making discretionary contributions. Even if an employer cannot afford to make discretionary contributions, a 401(k) plan is still an attractive benefit for employees who wish to contribute on their own.

Requirements for 401(k) Plans

Nondiscrimination requirements. Contributions made to 401(k) plans must meet certain tests to ensure they are not discriminatory in favor of highly compensated employees. Salary deferral contributions must satisfy one of two nondiscrimination tests that apply only to 401(k) plans. Each of these tests relates the salary deferrals made by highly compensated employees to the salary deferrals made by nonhighly compensated employees. This may present a problem because lower-paid employees often elect to receive cash in lieu of deferring salary. To encourage their participation, employers can offer to "match" salary deferrals under a formula stated in the plan. For example, an employer may match 50 cents of each dollar deferred by employees. The employer can also set a cap on the maximum amount they will match. For example, the employer may match 50 cents of each dollar, up to a maximum of 6 percent of compensation (resulting in a maximum match amount of 3 percent of compensation). Matching contributions may also be discretionary (i.e., decided at year-end), but they must be made according to the terms of the plan document.

Defer only future compensation. Employees must elect to defer only future compensation. In other words, only compensation that has not yet been earned or that the employee does not have the right to receive is eligible for salary deferrals.

Internal Revenue Code requirements. To qualify as a 401(k) plan, the plan must satisfy all the requirements of Internal Revenue Code Section 401(k). These include the following:

1. Limits on plan distributions. These limits restrict an employee from receiving a distribution before completing a stated number of years of service or the passing of a fixed number of years.

2. An employee's salary deferral contributions must be nonforfeitable (i.e., the employee is always 100 percent vested in his/her contributions and the related earnings).

3. Generally, an employee cannot be required to have more than one year of service to participate in a salary deferral feature.

4. Benefits (other than matching contributions)—(e.g., employer discretionary contributions) must not be contingent on the employee's election to make salary deferrals.

5. Employees eligible to participate in the salary deferral feature (regardless of whether they elect to contribute) must satisfy the coverage tests (see "What Are the Minimum Coverage Rules"). Under the coverage tests, the plan must meet either the ratio percentage test or the average benefit test.

6. Limitations on the maximum salary deferrals. The limit is $12,000 for 2003. In addition, a participant can elect to contribute up to an additional $2,000 in 2003 if he/she is age 50 by year-end. (This is the maximum amount of compensation the employee can elect to defer in a given year. It does not include employer contributions, earnings on contributions, or plan forfeitures that are credited to the employees' account).

Example: Using a 401(k) plan.

John Nagel, D.D.S., Inc., maintains a 401(k) plan that allows employer contributions to be made on a discretionary basis. The employer does not match any elective contributions made by employees to the 401(k) plan. Employer contributions are based on the participants' compensation in relation to total qualified compensation. In the current year, the corporation authorizes a contribution equal to 10 percent of compensation. The employees' elective deferrals are shown in the following table, as well as the allocation of the employer's contribution.

Participant	Compensation	10% Employer Contribution	Employee 401(k) Deferrals	Total Annual Additions (Allocations)
John Nagel	$170,000	$17,000	$4,000	$21,000
Betsy Smith	40,000	4,000	2,000	6,000
Jane Davis	25,000	2,500	1,000	3,500
Alisia Barker	28,000	2,800	1,120	3,920
Totals	**$263,000**	**$26,300**	**$8,120**	**$34,420**

WEEK EIGHT
MAP 8-7

Qualified Retirement Plans*
(refer to page 327)

A qualified retirement plan complies with special requirements imposed by Internal Revenue Code and Regulations. A qualified plan has tax advantages such as deducting funding costs of the plan.

Characteristics of a qualified plan include:

➤ Contributions can be made by both employer and employee.

➤ The plan cannot discriminate among certain employees.

➤ It must be for exclusive benefit of employees or beneficiaries.

➤ It must be permanent, not temporary.

➤ It must satisfy the minimum vesting standards.

Some advantages of a qualified plan included:

➤ Employer contributions are deductible.

➤ Employer contributions are tax deferred.

➤ Plan earnings are tax deferred.

Two Types of Qualified Plans

1) **Defined-benefit plan.** The employer decides how each participant's monthly payments will be determined after retirement, based on the employee's final earnings and years of service. The employer contributes an amount that will enable the plan to reach the required payout level. A problem with this type of plan is that inflation can make this fixed-income pension inadequate in later years.

2) **Defined-contribution plan.** Instead of determining benefit levels in advance, the employer makes defined contributions on behalf of the employee each year.

   a) *Money-purchase pension plan.* Contributions are fixed and are usually calculated as a percentage of income.

   b) *Profit-sharing pension plan.* Contributions by the employer may vary from year to year.

In both types of defined-contribution plans, benefits at retirement are based on the plan's investment performance. If markets are down when the employee retires, or if the plan's managers make poor investment decisions, the benefits could be inadequate at retirement.

* Material reprinted with the permission of Quickfinder Incorporated (*www.quickfinder.com*).

WEEK EIGHT
MAP 8-8

Comparison of SEPs and SIMPLE IRA Plans
(refer to page 327)

Provisions	SIMPLE IRA	SEP[a]
Eligible employers	Generally 100 or fewer employees earning at least $5,000 in the preceding year and having no other retirement plan. Tax-exempts and governmental employers allowed.	Any size employer. Governmental and tax-exempt employers allowed; plus it is OK for employer to also sponsor a qualified retirement plan.
Eligible employees	Employees who earned at least $5,000 from the employer in any two prior years and who are expected to earn that much or more in the current year. Employers can have less restrictive requirements. Exclusion allowed for collectively bargained and nonresident alien employees.	Employees who are at least 21, worked for the employer three or more years in the last five, and received at least $450 of compensation in the current year. Employer can have less restrictive requirements. Exclusion allowed for collectively bargained and nonresident alien employees.
Employee deferral limit	$8,000 ($9,000 for those 50 and over).	No deferrals allowed.
Required employer contributions	Choice of a 2 percent of compensation contribution for all eligible employees (regardless of whether they defer any compensation) or a 3 percent of compensation matching contribution (that can go as low as 1 percent in two out of five years).	None—completely discretionary.
Maximum employer contribution per employee	$8,000 ($9,000 for those 50 and over).	$40,000, unless integrated with Social Security.
Compensation limit	No limit for elective deferral or employer match. Limit of $200,000 on 2 percent nonelective contribution.	$200,000.

Provisions	SIMPLE IRA	SEP[a]
Employee access to funds	Immediate, although income tax (and early withdrawal penalty) may apply. Early withdrawal penalty is 25 percent for first two years after participation starts and 10 percent thereafter.	Immediate, although income tax (and potentially a 10 percent early withdrawal penalty) will apply.
Plan contribution subject to income or payroll taxes?	Employer-matching or nonelective contributions are not currently taxable. Employee elective deferrals are subject to payroll taxes currently and income taxes at distribution.	No.
Plan counts as an employer-sponsored pension plan for purposes of the regular IRA deduction?	Yes.	Yes.
Vesting	100 percent immediately.	100 percent immediately.
Filing requirement with the IRS?	No (although certain W-2 reporting is required).	No (although certain W-2 reporting is required).
Deadline for setting up plan	October 1. (Companies established after October 1st generally have until December 31 to establish a plan.)	Due date (including extensions) of employer's return for the year the plan is being established.
Compensation that may be taken into account in first plan year	Only compensation earned after plan is established is eligible to be deferred. (However, with a self-employed, calendar-year individual, this is not a problem because all compensation for the year is deemed earned on last day of the year.) All compensation for the year considered on employer-matching or nonelective contribution.	Compensation for the entire plan year, even if plan is not established until after year-end.

Provisions	SIMPLE IRA	SEP[a]
Plan year	Must be calendar year.	Calendar year (or the employer's fiscal year, if nonmodel plan is used.)
Hardship withdrawals or loans allowed?	No.	No.

Note:

[a]Excluding salary- reduction SEPs.

WEEK EIGHT
MAP 8-9*

Inherited Retirement Plan Decision Tree—Death Before Required Beginning Date[1] (refer to page 327)

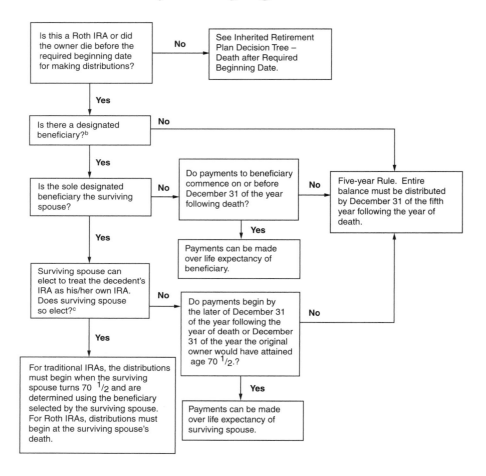

Notes:

[a] For minimum distribution purposes, only individuals and certain trusts are treated as designated beneficiaries.

[b] A surviving spouse will be deemed to have made an election to treat the IRA as his/her own if any of the MRDs required due to the death of the owner are not made, or the surviving spouse makes any contributions to the IRA. A surviving spouse can also roll over distributions to his own IRA.

[c] Surviving spouse can still roll over distributions to his/her own IRA.

[1] These rules apply to both traditional and Roth IRAs.

WEEK EIGHT
MAP 8-10

Inherited Retirement Plan Decision Tree—Death After Required Beginning Date[a] (refer to page 328)

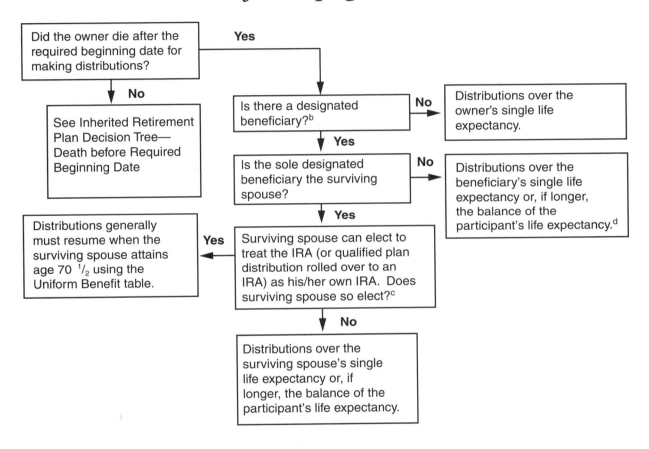

Notes:

[a] This table applies to distributions made after 2002.

[b] For minimum distribution purposes, only individuals and certain trusts are treated as designated beneficiaries. The designated beneficiary is determined on September 30 of the year following the year of owner's death.

[c] A surviving spouse will be deemed to have made an election to treat the IRA as his/her own if any of the MRDs required due to the death of the owner are not made, or the surviving spouse makes any contributions to the IRA. A surviving spouse can also roll over distributions to his/her own IRA.

[d] Distributions to the surviving spouse can be rolled over to the surviving spouse's IRA.

Week Eight
MAP 8-11

Rollovers and Transfers (refer to page 328)*

Qualifying Rollovers

From one IRA into another IRA. All or a portion of the funds in an IRA are withdrawn, and the custodian makes the check payable to the taxpayer. The taxpayer then contributes the funds into another IRA within 60 days. Funds contributed back into the same IRA will also qualify as a rollover, (Letter Rul. 9010007) Each IRA can be rolled over no more than once every 12 months.

From an employer's plan into an IRA. All or a portion of the funds from an employer's qualified pension, profit-sharing, stock bonus, annuity, or tax-sheltered annuity plan are distributed to the taxpayer. The taxpayer then contributes the funds into an IRA within 60 days of receiving the distribution. The 60-day requirement applies even if the distribution was a mistake and the taxpayer did not want the funds distributed. (Letter Rul. 9826036)

From one employer's plan into another employer's plan. An employee can roll over funds from one qualified retirement plan into another qualified retirement plan. The funds can also be rolled first into a new IRA and later rolled over into a new employer's qualified retirement plan.

From a traditional IRA to a qualified retirement plan. An eligible rollover distribution from a traditional IRA may be rolled over into a qualified employer plan, 403(b) tax-sheltered annuity or Section 457 deferred-compensation plan. Nondeductible after-tax contributions made to IRAs are not eligible to be rolled over into an employer plan. They can, however, be rolled over into another IRA.

From a SIMPLE-IRA to a qualified retirement plan. A SIMPLE IRA distribution is treated like a traditional IRA distribution once the employee has participated in the SIMPLE plan for two years. As a traditional IRA, it can be rolled over into an employer plan. If the employee has not participated for two years, the SIMPLE IRA can only be rolled over into another SIMPLE IRA.

From a Section 457 plan to a qualified retirement plan. A Section 457 plan can be rolled over into another 457 plan, IRA, 401(k), 403(b), or other qualified plan. In addition, eligible rollover distributions from qualified plans and IRAs can be rolled over, tax free, into 457 plans [IRC §402 (c)(8)(B)(v)]. This does not apply to Section 457 plans maintained by nongovernmental, tax-exempt organizations.

* Material reprinted with the permission of Quickfinder Incorporated *(www.quickfinder.com).*

From a 403(b) annuity plan to a qualified retirement plan. Eligible rollover distributions from 403(b) annuity plans (plans for employees of public schools and certain tax-exempt organizations) can be rolled over into other qualified plans such as 401(k) or 457 plans. In addition, eligible rollover distributions from other qualified plans can be rolled over, tax free, into 403(b) annuity plans.

From a deceased spouse's qualified plan to the surviving spouse's qualified plan. Eligible rollover distributions from the decedent's qualified plan can be rolled, tax free, into a qualified plan of the surviving spouse.

Rollover of after-tax contributions. Taxpayers can roll over the entire distribution from qualified plans, including the portion representing after-tax contributions, into another qualified plan or an IRA. Rollovers of after-tax contributions are allowed provided a direct trustee-to-trustee transfer is made, the qualified plan is a defined-contribution plan, and the qualified plan separately tracks the after-tax contributions and related earnings.

After-tax contributions rolled into IRAs do not need to be separately tracked by the IRA trustee. However, the taxpayer will need to keep track of basis on Form 8606. IRA-to-IRA rollovers of nondeductible after-tax contributions are permitted. However, nondeductible after-tax contributions made to IRAs are not eligible to be rolled over into an employer's qualified plan.

Notes:

> A Roth IRA can be rolled over into another Roth IRA, but a Roth IRA cannot be rolled over into a traditional IRA.

> A traditional IRA can be converted into a Roth IRA by direct transfer or rollover. However, the terms transfer and rollover do not carry the same meaning because the transaction is a taxable event (as opposed to continued tax-deferred status for traditional transfers and rollovers).

> A rollover from an employer plan to an IRA may subsequently be converted to a Roth IRA.

> Although the 2001 Tax Act liberalizes the rules for rollovers, employer-sponsored retirement plans are not required to accept rollovers from other plans.

> The capital gain and lump-sum averaging provision available to participants born before 1936 is not available for any distributions from a qualified plan [including 403(b) and 457 plans] which has accepted rollover contributions under any of the 2001 Tax Act provisions. The House Committee Report (H.R. Rep. No. 107-51) says that in order to preserve capital gain and lump-sum averaging treatment, rollovers must be made to a conduit IRA and then back into a qualified plan.

▷ Qualified plan administrators are required to provide written explanations of the restrictions and potential tax consequences of rollover distributions to recipients of eligible rollover distributions.

TRANSFERS

A transfer is like a rollover—all or part of an IRA or pension is moved to a different IRA or pension. Unlike a rollover, the funds are never in the taxpayer's hands. One custodian makes out the check to the next custodian or trustee and forwards the funds.

➤ Because the funds are always held by a custodian or trustee, the IRS does not require custodians to report IRA transfers on Form 1099-R.

➤ Transfers are not subject to the rule that requires rollovers to be made at least one year apart.

➤ There is no limit on the number or timing of transfers.

➤ A transfer from a qualified plan to an IRA is considered a distribution and a subsequent rollover by plan participant. Employers must report the direct rollover on Form 1099-R.

Generally, it is sound advice for employees leaving a job to roll over funds from a 401(k) or profit-sharing plan. However, if the qualified plan includes employer company stock that has significantly appreciated, it may be advantageous to receive a distribution of the employer's stock and roll the remaining funds into an IRA or other qualified plan. (IRC §402)

Example: *Assume 100 shares of stock currently valued at $80 per share were valued at $20 per share when they were contributed to Joan's 401(k) plan 10 years ago. If Joan leaves her job, she may take a distribution of the 100 shares and pay income tax plus a 10 percent penalty on $2,000 (value of the shares when they were added to her account) instead of rolling the shares into an IRA. When Joan sells the shares, it will be necessary to pay tax on the appreciation, but it will be applied at long-term capital gains rates rather than regular income tax rates. If the stock is eventually passed on to her beneficiaries, they will only pay tax on the appreciation that occurred before the shares were taken out of the plan.*

Caution: This strategy may not be wise in every case. If a major portion of a taxpayer's investment portfolio is invested in the employer's stock, an IRA rollover may be advised wherein diversification of the investment can be achieved.

* Material reprinted with the permission of Quickfinder Incorporated *(www.quickfinder.com)*.

WEEK EIGHT
MAP 8-12

*Withdrawals and Distributions**
(refer to page 328)

DISTRIBUTION RULES BY AGE

Before age 59½.

Distributions from an IRA or qualified pension plan are taxable as ordinary income (except for the portion that represents a return of nondeductible contributions) and are also subject to a 10 percent penalty for early withdrawal.

SIMPLE plans have a 25 percent early withdrawal penalty if the withdrawal is less than two years from when the taxpayer first participated in the plan.

Age 59½–70½.

Distributions are taxable as ordinary income (except for the portion that represents a return of nondeductible contributions). There is no early withdrawal penalty or minimum distribution requirement. The plan participant has total flexibility on the amount and timing of distributions, if any.

Age 70½ and later:

➤ For non-Roth IRAs, distributions must begin by age 70½. Distributions are taxable as ordinary income (except for the portion that represents a return of nondeductible contributions).

Distributions can be in the form of a lump sum or periodic distributions that will deplete the account over the life expectancy of the plan participant. Distributions can be any amount that is at least as much as the required minimum distribution for each year. The required minimum distribution can come from any, all, or only one account.

➤ For participants in qualified pension plans other than 5 percent owners, the required minimum distribution rules do not apply until the employee reaches age 70½ or retires, whichever is later. If the employee chooses to delay distributions after age 70½, the employee's accrued benefit must be actuarially increased to reflect the value of benefits that the employee would have received if distributions had begun at age 70½. The actuarial adjustment does not apply to defined contribution plans.

* Material reprinted with the permission of Quickfinder Incorporated *(www.quickfinder.com).*

Annuity Payout Exception to 10 percent Penalty

When a taxpayer is under age 59½, the 10 percent early withdrawal penalty can be avoided if distributions from an IRA or qualified plan are distributed as part of a scheduled series of substantially equal periodic payments made over the life expectancy of the participant and the beneficiary. Once the annuity form of payment is elected, it cannot be switched until five years have elapsed or until age 59½, whichever is longer.

There are three methods for satisfying the "substantially equal periodic payment" exception to the 10 percent penalty mentioned in IRS Notice 89-25. Two of these methods result in a fixed amount required to be distributed each year. With the recent decline in the stock market, many who began their payout schedule prior to the decline saw a larger portion of their investment being distributed with a risk of depleting their funds sooner than expected. In response to this situation, the IRS has released Revenue Ruling 2002-62. If a series of payments began prior to January 1, 2003, the method of calculating the payments in the series is permitted to be changed from a method under which the amount is fixed to a method that changes from year to year based on the value in the account from which distributions are made. The Revenue Ruling also allows for the use of the new Uniform Lifetime table, which can be found in the June 2002 supplement to IRS Publication 590.

Required Minimum Distributions

Annual IRA minimum distributions must begin by age 70½. A taxpayer can choose to delay receipt of the first distribution until April 1 of the year following the calendar year in which he or she turns age 70½. Thereafter, the required minimum distribution for each year must be made by December 31. If the first distribution is delayed until April 1 of the following year, the next distribution must be made by December 31 of that same year.

Excess accumulation penalty (Form 5329). An excess accumulation is any amount of a required minimum distribution that is not distributed in a timely fashion. The required minimum distribution is recomputed each year. Any excess accumulation in a tax year is subject to a 50 percent penalty.

The penalty may be waived under the following situations:

➤ Erroneous advice from a plan advisor.

➤ Good faith effort to apply required withdrawal formula produced a miscalculation or misunderstanding of the formula.

To have the penalty waived, file Form 5329 and pay the penalty. Attach a letter to the return requesting the IRS to waive the penalty under Section 4974. Include in the letter the reason for the error and steps that are being taken to eliminate the excess accumulation.

Note: Required minimum distribution rules do not apply to Roth IRAs. Distributions from Roth IRAs are required only after the death of the participant.

---

* Material reprinted with the permission of Quickfinder Incorporated *(www.quickfinder.com)*.

WEEK EIGHT
MAP 8-13

New Simplified Rules for Calculating Required Minimum Distributions*
(refer to page 328)

The IRS issued final regulations in April, 2002, for computing RMD's from qualified retirement plans and IRAs. With a few minor changes, the new regulations finalize the simplifications made by the 2001 proposed regulations. The final regulations also include the new life expectancy tables mandated by the 2001 Tax Act. The new tables are based on longer life expectancies, producing smaller required distributions. RMDs for 2002 can be calculated using the final regulations, the 2001 proposed regulations, or the 1987 proposed regulations. The final regulations must be used in 2003 and later years.

RMD Calculation—Lifetime Distributions

The RMD for each calendar year is the account balance on December 31 of the preceding year divided by the distribution period from the "Uniform Lifetime Table," above, for the owner's age at the end of the distribution year.

Exception: If the owner's sole beneficiary at all times during the year is a spouse more than 10 years younger than the owner, use the distribution period from the Joint and Last Survivor Table from IRS Publication 590 for a smaller RMD. *New Rule*: Marital status is determined on January 1 of the distribution year. The owner does not fail to have a spouse as beneficiary because of death or divorce later in the year unless the owner changes beneficiaries before the end of the year (or before the spouse's death). [Reg. §1.401(a)(9)-5, Q&A 4(b)]

Uniform Lifetime Table					
Age	Distribution Period	Age	Distribution Period	Age	Distribution Period
70	27.4	86	14.1	101	5.9
71	26.5	87	13.4	102	5.5
72	25.6	88	12.7	103	5.2
73	24.7	89	12.0	104	4.9
74	23.8	90	11.4	105	4.5
75	22.9	91	10.8	106	4.2
76	22.0	92	10.2	107	3.9
77	21.2	93	9.6	108	3.7
78	20.3	94	9.1	109	3.4
79	19.5	95	8.6	110	3.1
80	18.7	96	8.1	111	2.9
81	17.9	97	7.6	112	2.6
82	17.1	98	7.1	113	2.4
83	16.3	99	6.7	114	2.1
84	15.5	100	6.3	115+	1.9
85	14.8				

Example: Tim and Ann each have an IRA valued at $90,000 on December 31, 2002. Tim was born on September 5, 1932. Ann was born on March 5, 1933. Both reach age 70½ in 2003. Tim will be 71 at the end of 2003: Ann will be 70. Their minimum distributions for 2003 are:

Tim . . . .$90,000 ÷ 26.5 = $3,396
Ann . . . .$90,000 ÷ 27.4 = $3,285

WEEK EIGHT
MAP 8-14

Retirement Plan Contribution Summary
Based on Tax Law as of August 1, 2003
(refer to page 329)

IRA Allowable Contributions

Year	Base Contribution	Catch up Contribution*
2003	$3,000	$500
2004	$3,000	$500
2005	$4,000	$500
2006-2007	$4,000	$1,000
2008	$5,000	$1,000

*Additional contribution allowed for those over 50.

401(k) & 403(b) Allowable Contributions

Year	Base Employee Deferral**	Catch up Contribution*
2003	$12,000	$2,000
2004	$13,000	$3,000
2005	$14,000	$4,000
2006	$15,000	$5,000

*Additional contribution allowed for those over 50.
**Not to exceed 100 percent of compensation.

SIMPLE IRA Allowable Contributions

Year	Base Employee Deferral**	Catch up Contribution*
2003	$8,000	$1,000
2004	$9,000	$1,500
2005	$10,000	$2,000

*Additional contribution allowed for those over 50.
**Not to exceed 100 percent of compensation.

Education Tax Incentives*
(refer to page 339)

Education Tax Incentives Comparison Chart for 2002

	Hope Credit	Lifetime Learning Credit	Coverdell ESA (1)	Withdrawal from Traditional and Roth IRAs (1)	Student Loan Interest	Qualified Tuition Programs	U.S. Gov't Savings Bond Exclusion (1)	Educational Assistance Program (1)	Tuition and Fees Deduction
Tax Benefit (2)	Nonrefundable Tax Credit	Nonrefundable Tax Credit	Withdrawals are tax free	No 10% early withdrawal penalty	AGI Deduction	Prepay future tuition or tax-free withdrawals	Interest is excludable from income	Employer benefits are excludible from income	AGI Deduction
2002/2003 Annual Limits	Credit up to $1,500 per student; 100% of first $1,000 and 50% of next $1,000	Credit up to $2,000 per family; 20% of up to $10,000 of expenses	$2,000 contribution per child under age 18 and any age special-needs child	Amount of qualifying expenses	Interest paid deduction of up to $2,500	Amount considered necessary to cover qualified expenses	Amount of qualifying expenses	Exclude up to $5,250 of benefits	Deduction of up to $3,000
Qualifying Expenses Besides Tuition and Required Enrollment Fees (2)	None	None	Books, supplies and equipment; room and board if at least half-time attendance; payments to QTP	Books, supplies and equipment; room and board if at least half-time attendance	Books, supplies and equipment; room and board, transportation, other necessary expenses	Books, supplies and equipment; room and board if at least half-time attendance	Payment to QTP; payment to Coverdell ESAs	Books, supplies and equipment	None
Qualifying Education	First two years of Undergraduate	All Undergraduate and Graduate Levels	Elementary, Secondary, Undergraduate and Graduate Levels	All Undergraduate and Graduate Levels	All Undergraduate and Graduate Levels	All Undergraduate and Graduate Levels	All Undergraduate and Graduate Levels	Undergraduate Level	All Undergraduate and Graduate Levels
Other Requirements	Can be claimed only for two years; must be enrolled at least half-time in a degree program	Available for unlimited number of years for both degree and non-degree programs	Contributions are not deductible and must be made by the return due date; may also contribute to QTP	See Tab 14 for requirements	Must be enrolled at least half-time in a degree program		Applies only to qualified Series EE bonds issued after 1989 or Series I bonds	Cannot also claim as education credit	Not allowed if expense is allowable under another provision
2002 AGI Phase-Out MFJ .... All Others .... MFS	$82,000 – $102,000 $41,000 – $51,000 $0	$82,000 – $102,000 $41,000 – $51,000 $0	$190,000 – $220,000 $95,000 – $110,000 $95,000 – $110,000	N/A	$100,000 – $130,000 $50,000 – $65,000 $0	N/A	$86,400 – $116,400 $57,600 – $72,600 $0	N/A	Not allowed if AGI exceeds: MFJ $130,000 MFS $0 All Others $65,000

(1) Any nontaxable withdrawal is limited to the amount of qualifying educational expenses.
(2) Qualifying educational expenses must be reduced by any tax-free income. The same educational expenses cannot be used for figuring more than one benefit.

* Material reprinted with the permission of Quickfinder Incorporated (*www.quickfinder.com*).

WEEK EIGHT
MAP 8-16

Steps in Applying for Financial Aid
(refer to page 339)

Prospective students should apply to and be accepted by at least six colleges. This allows them to compare and negotiate the financial awards of several colleges. If not accepted, the college will not give financial aid. Failure to submit sufficient applications will limit chances for receiving the best financial aid offer. Think of applying to college as shopping for a car; when you shop for a car, you look at and negotiate the price of several cars, not just one.

There are six basic steps in applying for financial aid:

➤ Step 1: The student applies to and is accepted at several colleges. This allows the student the freedom to choose among several financial aid offers and appeal the offers that are financially unsatisfactory.

➤ Step 2: The student may have to fill out as many as three financial aid application forms—one form for federal and state funds and one or two additional forms (depending on the college) for the college's own funds.

➤ Step 3: After the student files the financial aid application form, the Student Aid Report (SAR) is received. He/she reviews this report, makes any corrections, and refiles (if corrections are made) with the Department of Education is processing center.

➤ Step 4: If the information on the Student Aid Report is picked for verification, copies of tax returns to support the student's application (i.e., the parents' and/or student's tax returns) must be furnished, along with any other requested information, to the colleges who request it.

➤ Step 5: The student receives financial aid award offers from the colleges where he/she is accepted for admission. The family reviews and compares the various financial aid awards.

➤ Step 6: If the family that the awards are financially unacceptable or that special family financial circumstances need to be brought to the attention of the college financial aid administrator, an appeal for increased financial aid may be made.

WEEK EIGHT
MAP 8-17*

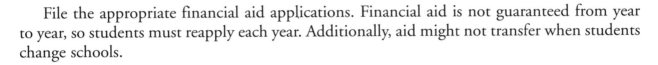

Financial Aid Application
(refer to page 339)

File the appropriate financial aid applications. Financial aid is not guaranteed from year to year, so students must reapply each year. Additionally, aid might not transfer when students change schools.

Basic Application Forms

Free Application for Federal Student Aid (FAFSA) This application form is used by all colleges to calculate the expected family contribution (EFC) using the federal methodology formula and is available at high school guidance offices or at college financial aid offices, as well as online at *www.fafsa.org*. The earliest date the form can be filed is January 1; the federally imposed deadline is June 30. However, colleges may (and often do) have an earlier deadline. The deadline may be used to distribute all the financial aid funds that can be distributed at the college's discretion. Consequently, it is important not to miss the individual college's deadline. As the Pell Grant and Stafford Loan are federal entitlements, the federally imposed date is applicable to awards of those funds.

Financial Aid Profile (PROFILE). This application form is used by some private colleges to calculate the EFC using the institutional methodology formula. As with the FAFSA, each college may have its individual deadline for filing the form, which is available at high school guidance offices or at college financial aid offices.

While many college-imposed financial aid filing deadlines are as early as February 15, few families have their tax returns completed by this date. Because much financial aid is based on a first-come, first-served basis, the chances to receive financial aid will increase by estimating the tax information and reporting the actual figures as corrections to the Student Aid Report (SAR).

Information Necessary to Complete the FAFSA or PROFILE

The following records and information pertaining to the financial aid applicant and his/her parents are needed to plan and apply for financial aid:

➤ current and previous years' federal and state income tax returns;

➤ records of income earned in the most recent tax year; e.g., W-2s and 1099s;

➤ list of assets and corresponding debt;

➤ business and farm records;

➤ current bank statements;

➤ details of nontaxable income and benefits such as Social Security income and 401(k) contributions;

➤ current mortgage information; and

➤ student's driver's license and Social Security numbers.

Since college deadlines for filing the application forms are important, the student may want to have proof of mailing these forms. The application forms should not be sent by certified or registered mail as this may slow down the application process when someone must personally sign for it. The preferred mailing procedure is called "Certificate of Mailing." The receipt from this mailing procedure often will be enough proof to the college that the student has filed his/her financial aid application on time.

Week Eight
MAP 8-18*

What Are Qualified Tuition Programs (QTPs)?
(refer to page 340)

QTPs (also called "Section 529 programs" after the tax law that created them) are tuition programs that permit tax-free buildup and distributions, provided certain requirements are met. A QTP is not "financial aid." It is a program established and maintained by a state, state agency, or eligible educational institution under which you can:

1. purchase tuition credits or certificates on behalf of a "designated beneficiary" (e.g., your child or grandchild) entitling him/her to a waiver or payment of "qualified higher education expenses," or

2. make contributions to an account established to fund the designated beneficiary's qualified higher education expenses.

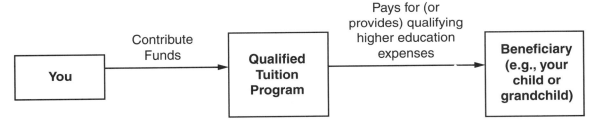

Most QTPs are offered in conjunction with professionally managed investment companies. These plans offer market returns on many different investment options and generally can be used at any U.S. college or university. In addition, some states offer programs that allow contributions to be deductible for state income tax purposes.

Perhaps the most unique attribute of QTPs is that there are no income limits on who can contribute. Thus, for example, QTPs are available to high-earning individuals who are not eligible for the other well-publicized education tax breaks (like the education credits, write-offs for college loan interest, Coverdell education savings accounts, and tax-free redemptions of U.S. Savings Bonds).

DEFINITIONS

Designated Beneficiary. A designated beneficiary generally is the individual designated as the beneficiary of the QTP when contributions are first made to the program. You can only change the designated beneficiary without tax consequences to a member of the original beneficiary's family. A member of the family for these purposes includes the individual's spouse, ancestor or his/her spouse, lineal descendant or his/her spouse, legally adopted children, and first cousins. However, once a plan for a particular beneficiary is established, most permit contributions from nearly any source, regardless of relationship. Thus, a grandparent can establish (and be the "owner" of) a plan for a grandchild, but the parents or any other person may contribute to it.

Qualified Higher Education Expenses. Most QTPs cover room and board costs in addition to tuition, fees, books, supplies, and equipment. Qualified expenses also include expenses of special needs services for special needs beneficiaries. Qualifying room and board expenses are limited to the amount the institution uses when computing its cost of attendance or, for students living on campus, the actual amount charged, if greater. In addition, for room and board expenses to qualify, the student must carry at least a half-time load during the academic period in question.

Note: Both undergraduate and graduate school costs meet the definition of qualifying higher education expenses, and virtually all accredited public, private, and proprietary post-secondary institutions are included.

TYPES OF QTPs

QTPs are subject to Internal Revenue Code qualification requirements but are operated by the various states and institutions under varying policies defined by them. QTPs come in two basic flavors: (1) prepaid plans and (2) savings plans.

A prepaid plan is best thought of as a way to lock in the price of covered educational services at today's prices, thus ensuring against college cost inflation. The tax benefits are a nice bonus. In contrast, a savings plan is best thought of as a tax-advantaged way to build up a college fund. Savings plans do *not* lock in the cost of covered educational services. For both types of plans, the federal tax advantages are identical.

Prepaid Plans. Prepaid tuition plans allow individuals (generally parents or grandparents) to prepay the education costs of a designated beneficiary (generally a child or grandchild) at specified institutions and thereby lock in the price. The prepayments are invested by the QTP. In effect, the investment return is guaranteed to keep pace with inflation in the cost of the covered educational services—nothing more; nothing less. If it does not actually turn out that way, there is no obligation to make further payments; the plan makes up the difference if investment returns fall short. However, if the QTP earns more than enough to finance the cost of the covered educational services, the plan gets to keep the excess. In either case, once college time arrives, the covered costs of the designated beneficiary will either be waived or paid for by the QTP.

Some prepaid plans are sometimes referred to as contract plans because they effectively sell contracts to deliver one or more year's worth of future educational services.

Other prepaid plans sell future educational services in much smaller chunks—for example, "units" representing 1 percent of a four-year college education. These arrangements are sometimes referred to as unit plans.

In addition, some prepaid plans allow account balances to be transferred in full to in-state private schools or eligible out-of-state colleges. The balance can then be applied to the cost of attending those schools. However, there's no guarantee the balance will be enough to fully cover the cost.

Savings Plans. Unlike prepaid plans, QTP savings plans make no promises that contributions will cover a given amount of future college education. As their name implies, savings plans simply provide tax-favored savings accounts for higher education expenses.

The bad news is savings plans are not a surefire hedge against college cost inflation, and the account owner assumes the risk that the accounts might decline in value. The good news is they allow upside potential. If the savings plan's investment return exceeds the rate of inflation for college costs, less money is needed to fund the account. Basically, you decide how much to contribute to the savings plan and then hope for the best. At college time, the account is drawn down to pay some or all of the designated beneficiary's eligible expenses.

Many states have engaged some of the well-known mutual fund companies to handle the investment aspects of the QTP savings plan. Although the account owner has limited ability to direct the investments, the age-based investment plans used by the QTPs may be somewhat similar to what the owner would have chosen if the college funds were invested outside the plan.

For example, the Iowa College Savings Plan offers four different savings tracks that invest in stock and bond index funds managed by the Vanguard Group. As the account beneficiary ages, the investment strategy automatically shifts to less aggressive, smaller percentage-of-stock investments.

Another good example of a savings plan is New Hampshire's Unique College Investing Plan, which is administered by Fidelity Investments. The plan invests in a variety of Fidelity equity and fixed-income mutual fund offerings. As the designated beneficiary approaches college age, his/her account is weighted towards more conservative fixed-income funds. Plan distributions can be used to attend any school on a long list of out-of-state institutions. Up to $250,000 can be contributed to the New Hampshire plan. New York has a similar savings plan. The New York College Savings Program allows pay-ins of up to $100,000 and attendance at any accredited school of higher education in the country. New York taxpayers get state income tax deductions for their contributions (deduction are limited to $5,000 annually or $10,000 for a married couple) and are not penalized when it comes to eligibility for state financial aid. The plan's investments are age-based portfolios managed by TIAA-CREF, renowned for excellent results in running retirement programs for public school teachers.

The law prohibits the owner or beneficiary from directing the investments within the account. However, while the rules for particular state plans may vary, the IRS permits investments in an account to be changed once annually and upon the change in the designated beneficiary.

WEEK EIGHT
MAP 8-19

Summary of Federal Loan Programs
(refer to page 340)

	Subsidized Federal Stafford Loans	Unsubsidized Federal Stafford Loans	Federal PLUS Loans
Who Can Borrow?	Undergraduate or graduate/professional school students enrolled at least half time in a degree or certificate program.	Undergraduate or graduate/professional school students enrolled at least half time in a degree or certificate program.	Parents of dependent undergraduate students who are enrolled at least half time in a degree or certificate program.
Eligibility?	➤ U.S. citizen or permanent resident alien ➤ Demonstrate financial need ➤ Undergraduates must first apply for a Pell Grant	➤ U.S. citizen or permanent resident alien ➤ Must first apply for a Pell Grant and a Subsidized Federal Stafford Loan	➤ U.S. citizen or permanent resident alien ➤ No negative credit history
Maximum?	Undergraduate: $2,625 for year one; $3,500 for year two; $5,500 per year for years three, four, and five; Total of $23,000.	Undergraduate: Maximum depends on student's dependency status and/or whether parents are able to borrow under Federal PLUS Program.	Total cost of education (tuition, fees, housing, etc.) minus the total of any financial aid awarded, including a subsidized Federal Stafford Loan. No dollar limit.
Maximum?	Graduate/professional: $8,500 per year. Total of $65,500 in undergraduate plus graduate loans.	If student is dependent and parents qualify for a PLUS loan: $2,625 for year one; $3,500 for year two; $5,500 per year for years three, four, and five; Total of $23,000. If student is independent or if student is dependent but parents cannot borrow under Federal PLUS:	

616

	Subsidized Federal Stafford Loans	**Unsubsidized Federal Stafford Loans**	**Federal PLUS Loans**
Maximum?		$6,625 for year one; $7,500 for year two; $10,500 per year for years three, four, and five; Total of $46,000. Graduate/professional: $18,500 per year. Total of $138,500 in undergraduate plus graduate loans (including both subsidized and unsubsidized)	
Minimum?	Usually $250 (may vary by guarantor).	Usually $250 (may vary by guarantor).	Usually $250 (may vary by guarantor).
Interest Rate?	Variable, based on 91-day T-bill plus 3.10percent. Capped at 8.25percent. Federal government pays interest during enrollment.	Variable, based on 91-day T-bill plus 3.10 percent. Capped at 8.25 percent.	Variable, based on 52-week T-bill plus 3.10 percent. Capped at 9.00 percent. Federal government pays interest during enrollment.
Repayment?	Begins six months after student graduates, leaves school, or drops below half-time status.	Begin monthly or quarterly payments of interest when loan is disbursed or capitalize interest until loan goes into repayment six months after student graduates, leaves school, or drops below half-time status.	Begin monthly or quarterly payments of principal and interest within 60 days of loan disbursement, or make monthly or quarterly interest-only payments and defer repayment of principal until student graduates, leaves school, or drops below half-time status.
Term?	Up to 10 years. Term may be extended based on special needs.	Up to 10 years. Term may be extended based on special needs.	Up to 10 years. Term may be extended based on special needs.
Fees?	3 percent origination fee and 1 percent guarantee fee, deducted from amount of loan.	3 percent origination fee and 1% guarantee fee, deducted from amount of loan.	3 perecnt origination fee and 1 percent guarantee fee, deducted from amount of loan.
Paid How?	Checks copayable to student and school; mailed directly to school.	Checks copayable to student and school; mailed directly to school.	Checks copayable to student and school; mailed directly to school.

WEEK EIGHT
MAP 8-20*

Buying a Home
(refer to page 348)

Owning a home has long been a part of the American dream. Itís a goal that many Americans have already achieved. According to recent statistics from the U. S. Census Bureau, 67.4% of all households in the United States live in owner occupied housing.[1]

Although the process of buying a home is often complex and confusing, it can be made more understandable by dividing it into several parts:

Renting vs. Home Ownership

There are advantages and disadvantages to both renting and buying a home:

	Advantages	Disadvantages
Renting	**Mobility** - Renter can move without having to worry about selling the home or the homeís market value at time of sale. **Initial cost** - No need for large down payment. **Monthly cost** - Monthly rent usually less than mortgage payment; in some areas rents are controlled; other opportunities may provide greater investment return. **Maintenance** - Few or no maintenance responsibilities.	**Monthly cost** - Rents can increase over time. **Equity** - Renter builds no equity in home. **Space** - Often less floor space. **Personalization** - Less freedom to decorate the home. **Taxes**[2] - No deduction for rent payments.
Buying	**Monthly cost** - With a fixed rate mortgage, monthly payments remain level; with a variable rate mortgage, monthly payments can increase or decrease. **Equity** - Homeowner can build substantial equity over time. **Space** - Typically larger floor space than with a rented home. **Personalization** - Can usually decorate to make home reflect ownerís tastes. **Taxes**[2] - Interest and property taxes are usually deductible.	**Mobility** - Ownership limits ability to move; homeowner must be concerned with selling the home as well as the homeís market value at time of sale. **Initial cost** - Substantial cash usually needed for down payment and closing costs. **Monthly cost** - Monthly mortgage payment typically higher than monthly rent; other opportunities may provide greater investment return. **Maintenance** - Homeowner is usually responsible for all maintenance and repairs.

---

[1] Taken from Statistical Abstract of the United States: 2001. See Report No. 957 - Homeownership Rates, by State: 1985 to 2000. Data is for 2000.
[2] Based on federal law. State law may vary.

Financing a Home

- **Size of mortgage:** One of the key issues a prospective homebuyer confronts is determining what size mortgage can be obtained. As a first step to answering this question, many lenders use two guidelines[1] to determine how much of a monthly payment a borrower can safely manage:
    - The monthly housing payment[2] should be no more than 28% of a consumer's gross monthly income.
    - The monthly housing payment, plus the monthly payments for any other debt, should not exceed more than 36% of a consumer's gross monthly income.

Example: Assume a couple has a total, gross monthly income of $4,000. Under the 28% rule, their total monthly housing payment should be no more than $1,120 ($4,000 x .28). Under the 36% rule, their monthly housing payment plus any other debt should not exceed $1,440 ($4,000 x .36).

Given a specified monthly payment, the next step is to determine what size mortgage that monthly payment will allow. The answer to this depends primarily on the number of years to repay, and the interest rate. The table below illustrates the approximate total monthly payment[3] under various assumptions.

Loan Amount	6% Annual Interest Monthly Payment		7.0% Annual Interest Monthly Payment		8.0% Annual Interest Monthly Payment	
	15 Years	30 Years	15 Years	30 Years	15 Years	30 Years
$100,000	$956.36	$712.05	$1,011.33	$777.80	$1,068.15	$846.26
$150,000	$1,434.54	$1,068.08	$1,516.99	$1,166.70	$1,602.23	$1,269.40
$200,000	$1,912.71	$1,424.10	$2,022.66	$1,555.60	$2,136.30	$1,692.53
$250,000	$2,390.89	$1,780.13	$2,528.32	$1,944.51	$2,670.38	$2,115.66

- **Down payment and closing costs:** Lenders ordinarily require a homebuyer to pay a certain portion of the home price in cash. Depending on the lender, this down payment usually ranges from 5% to 20% of the purchase price. With down payments of less than 20%, the lender may require the borrower to apply for private mortgage insurance, which protects the lender in case the buyer defaults. Under some government programs, a buyer may be allowed to purchase a home with no down payment. A buyer will also be required to pay certain ì closing costsî, fees and charges associated with processing the sale. Closing costs can be 3% to 6% of the purchase price.

---

[1] These guidelines have been developed by the Federal National Mortgage Association (FNMA). Some lending institutions may have different guidelines.

[2] Payment includes principal, interest, property taxes, insurance and any monthly condominium or co-op fees.

[3] Payment includes principal, interest, and estimated taxes and insurance. Monthly repayment figures for principal and interest taken from Barron's Financial Tables for Better Money Management - Mortgage Payments; 2nd Edition, 1992. Property taxes and insurance estimated at 1.35% of loan amount.

- **Tax deductibility of interest and property taxes:** Prospective homebuyers will also want to consider the ì after-taxî cost of home ownership. Taxpayers who itemize deductions, and whose adjusted gross income is less than certain limits, can usually deduct mortgage interest and property taxes from taxable income[1]. For example, assuming a taxpayer pays $10,000 in deductible mortgage interest and property taxes during a year, and is in a 28% marginal tax bracket, the after-tax cost of these expenses is $7,200 ($10,000 x .28 = $2,800; $10,000 - $2,800 = $7,200).

Finding a Home

What type of home? There are three basic forms of home ownership:

	Property Owned	Sell or Rent	Maintenance	Owner Payments	Other Issues
Single-Family Home	The structure and the land	Owner can decide to rent or sell home.	Owner responsible for all repairs and maintenance.	Mortgage, insurance, and real estate taxes. Loan secured by home.	Greater freedom to personalize the home. Generally more responsibility.
Condo	Individual living space. Homeowner's association owns building, land and common areas.	Owner can decide to sell. Restrictions on renting will vary.	Homeowner's association pays for most building maintenance and repair.	Mortgage, insurance, and taxes on individual unit; monthly fee to homeowner's association; mortgage secured by individual unit	Can be more restrictive with regard to issues such as children, pets, outside decoration. Fewer maintenance concerns. May have extra amenities such as swimming pools, tennis courts. Owners may be responsible for additional expenses or charges.

---

[1] Based on federal law. State law may vary.

	Property Owned	Sell or Rent	Maintenance	Owner Payments	Other Issues
Co-op	Shares in a corporation which owns building. Individual lease with corporation grants exclusive right to use apartment.	Owner can decide to sell. New buyer subject to approval by co-op board. May have restrictions on renting.	Co-op pays for most building maintenance and repair.	Monthly payments to co-op cover insurance, taxes, mortgage on building and operating costs. Loan payments to repay purchase of shares in co-op. Loan secured by shares in co-op.	Can be more restrictive on issues such as children and pets. Fewer maintenance concerns. May have extra amenities (pools, tennis courts, etc.). Owners may be responsible for additional expenses or charges.

Other Factors to Consider

- **Neighborhood:** Real estate agents will often refer to this as ì location.î In general, the relative attractiveness of an area will usually be reflected in the level of prices in the neighborhood. Personal issues such as good schools, easy access to public transportation, or proximity to features such as shopping, recreation, or work, are important factors in determining what is a ì goodî location.

- **Home features and characteristics:** Specific home features such as a minimum square footage, number of bedrooms or bathrooms, or a swimming pool. Many shoppers will list the most attractive features in priority order, in case an offered home lacks some of the desirable features. Keeping in mind that the home will one day be sold, many individuals look for features that are attractive and useful both to themselves and to others.

Searching for a Home

- **Real estate agents:** Real estate agents can be quite helpful in locating a home, particularly those who have access to a computerized multiple listings service. A good agent will have extensive real estate experience, as well as detailed knowledge of a specific area or neighborhood.

- **New home developments:** New homes tend to be more expensive than existing homes. New homes also tend to have fewer problems, and often have builder warranties.

- **Classified ads:** Classified ads in newspapers (both in print and via the Internet) can be useful sources of information. Such ads can provide a sense of general price levels. They can also provide leads to homes which are being sold directly by their owners, and not through an agent.

WEEK EIGHT
MAP 8-21

Calculating the Principal Residence Gain Exclusion (refer to page 348)

It most instances, the gain on the sale of a principal residence is not taxed.

In the completion of your My Documents binder Tab 9, "Purchase Documents for your Home," you calculated the tax cost of your current home. It is important to distinguish between *purchase price* and *tax cost or tax basis* since these two pieces of information about your home could differ.

Complete the following worksheet to determine if any portion of your house sale would be taxed:

Potential Sales Price After Sales Exp.	$_____	a
My Home's Tax Cost (Tab 9)	$_____	b
Gain on Sale (a-b)	$_____	c
Exclusion	$_____	d
Taxable Gain (d-e)	$_____	e

The sale of a principal residence is generally not reported on your tax return unless a portion of the gain is taxable. All gain is excludable if:

➤ The gain (net sales price less tax cost) does not exceed $250,000. If a married couple sells a home, the exclusion is increased to $500,000.

➤ The individual(s) must have owned and used the home as a principal residence for at least two out of the five years prior to the sale. The two years do not have to be consecutive.

➤ There has only one principal residence exclusion used in a two year period.

A portion of the gain will be taxable in the following circumstances:

➤ Part of the home was used for business or rental purposes. In this instance, any depreciation that was claimed on the property at May 7, 1997, would have to be reported as income and taxed at a rate of 25 percent (federal).

➤ The gain exceeds the $250,000/$500,000 limits.

➤ The taxpayer elected to use pre-May 7, 1997 rules.

➤ The taxpayer had to sell the home early due to job location, health, or unforeseen circumstances. The exclusion is prorated by calculating the number of days that the people lived in the home as a percentage of the required two-year period. This result is then multiplied by the maximum exclusion to arrive at the gain that is excludable. The difference will be taxed.

If Greg and Ginger were forced to relocate because of Greg's job and they had only lived in their home for one year, their exclusion would be calculated as follows:

> Number of days lived in home 365
>
> Divided by # days in 2 yrs. 730
>
> Percentage of exclusion available . . . . 50 percent
>
> Total exclusion for couple $500,000
>
> Gain to be excluded $250,000

Other Factors:

➤ The exclusion does not apply to Limited Partnership or LLC ownership of residences.

➤ A grantor-trust (living trust) can own the home and still qualify for the exclusion.

➤ A portion of the exclusion will be lost if owned by an irrevocable trust.

➤ Temporary absences for vacation, even if rented, will count as part of the two year occupancy requirement.

➤ In a divorce, no gain is recognized if one spouse buys the other out. The tax cost of the home to the purchaser is the same as it was for both spouses before the divorce.

Real Estate Comparison Chart				
Description of Property	**Taxable Income**	**Deductible Expenses**	**Gain on Sale**	**Loss on Sale**
Principal Residence				
Rented less than 15 days per year. Only one principal residence allowed.	None	• Interest secured by residence. See Page 5-7 for limitations. • Property taxes. • Casualty losses.	Reportable as capital gain. *Exceptions:* • Exclusion of $250,000 ($500,000 MFJ) of gain if two out of five year ownership and use test are met. (IRC §121) • Gain attributable to depreciation after May 6, 1997, cannot be excluded. *Example:* Rental converted to principal residence.	None allowed
Principal Residence				
Rented 15 days or more per year. *Example:* Portion of residence is rented to tenants.	All rental income is reportable	• Must be treated as if two properties. • Interest, taxes and casualty losses attributable to the personal-use portion are deducted on Schedule A. • Rental portion of interest and taxes, and any expenses totally attributable to the rental activity, are deducted from rental income. • Depreciation is based on the rental portion of basis only. • Losses from the rental activity are deductible to the extent allowed by passive loss limitations.	Must be treated as if two properties. • Gain from the rental portion is part ordinary and part capital gain income. Sections 1231, 1245 and 1250 apply. • Depreciation allowed or allowable decreases the rental portion of basis. • Up to $250,000 exclusion ($500,000 MFJ) of gain available on personal-use portion.	None allowed on the personal-use portion. Loss on rental activity is allowed. Report on Form 4797. Loss on temporary rental not allowed.
Second Home				
Rented less than 15 days per year. Can be a house, co-op, condo, mobile home, house trailer, boat, houseboat or similar property. (Must have sleeping, cooking and toilet facilities.)	None	• Interest (with limitations). • Property taxes. • Casualty losses.	Reportable as capital gain. (Portfolio income) (IRC §1221) No exclusion allowed as with a principal residence.	None allowed
Second Home/Vacation Home				
Rented 15 days or more per year and personal use exceeds the greater of 14 days per year or 10% of days rented. Vacation home rules apply.	All rental income is reportable	• Interest (with limitations). • Property taxes. • Casualty losses. Other expenses that are deductible only to the extent of income that exceeds interest and tax are, in this order: 1) Insurance, repairs and utilities. 2) Depreciation.	• Must be treated as if two properties. • Gain attributable to the personal-use portion is reportable as a capital gain. (Portfolio income) (IRC §1221) • No exclusion allowed as with a principal residence. • Gain attributable to the rental portion is part ordinary and part capital gain under Sections 1231, 1245 and 1250. • Depreciation allowed or allowable decreases the rental portion of basis.	None allowed on the personal-use portion. Loss on rental portion is an ordinary loss. Loss on temporary rental and timeshare losses are not allowed.

* Material reprinted with the permission of Quickfinder Incorporated *(www.quickfinder.com)*.

Real Estate Comparison Chart*
(continued)

		Real Estate Comparison Chart		
Description of Property	**Taxable Income**	**Deductible Expenses**	**Gain on Sale**	**Loss on Sale**
Section 1221 Asset				
Held for investment. Not used personally or in a trade or business. Includes inherited house not used as a personal residence by the beneficiary.	None	• Interest limited to net investment income. • Property taxes. • Casualty losses. • Other expenses are treated as investment expenses subject to the 2% AGI limitation.	Reportable as capital gain. (IRC §1221) Gain or loss on inherited property is always long term. • For decedents dying before January 1, 2010: Basis of inherited house equals FMV at the time of decedent's death. • For decedents dying after December 31, 2009: Rules for determining basis of inherited property change.	Capital loss limited to $3,000 per year. [IRC §1211(b)]
Rental Home				
Not meeting the vacation home personal-use test. *Note:* See Tab 8 for passive activity rules on real property rentals.	All rental income is reportable	• All ordinary and necessary expenses are deductible. • Losses are deductible to the extent allowed by passive loss limitations. See Tab 8. • Unallowed losses are carried forward to future years.	Part ordinary and part capital gain income. (IRC §1231, §1245 and §1250)	All losses are deductible, inc. unallowed passive losses from prior years. (Ordinary loss)
Section 1231 Asset				
Not rented out, but used in a trade or business. (Commercial RE)	None	All ordinary and necessary expenses are deductible.	Section 1231, 1245 and 1250 gains.	Ordinary loss (IRC §1231)
Note: Transitional rules and grandfathering provisions are not within the scope of this chart.				

* Material reprinted with the permission of Quickfinder Incorporated *(www.quickfinder.com).*

WEEK EIGHT
MAP 8-23

*Like-kind Exchanges**
(refer to page 353)

No gain or loss is recognized if property held for productive use in trade or business or for investment is exchanged solely for property of a like kind to be held either for productive use in trade or business, or for investment.

Definition. Like-kind property means property of the same nature or character, not necessarily of the same grade or quality. *Example:* Improved real estate can be exchanged for unimproved real estate.

Exchanges can thus include business for business, business for investment, investment for business, or investment for investment property. Property held for personal use, inventory, and securities do not qualify under the like-kind exchange provisions.

Requirements. Nonrecognition treatment for like-kind exchanges is mandatory rather than elective. A taxpayer who wants to recognize a realized gain or loss must structure the transaction around the statutory requirements for a like-kind exchange.

To qualify as a tax-deferred, like-kind exchange, all six of the following conditions must be met:

1) Both the property traded and the property received must be held by the taxpayer for business or investment purposes.

2) The property must not be held for sale to customers, such as inventory or merchandise.

3) There must be an exchange of like property. In general, any kind of real estate is treated as of like kind with other real estate. By contrast, different kinds of personal property (for example, equipment and vehicles) are not treated as like kind. Tangible and depreciable personal property may be either *like kind* (based on individual facts and circumstances) or *like class* (an objective test).

4) Exchanges of intangible personal property depend on the nature or character of the rights involved. Stocks, bonds, notes, and other securities do not qualify for a like-kind exchange. The "goodwill" of any business will not qualify in a like-kind exchange.

5) The property to be received in an exchange must be identified in a written agreement within 45 days after the transferred property is surrendered.

* Material reprinted with the permission of Quickfinder Incorporated *(www.quickfinder.com).*

6) The property in the exchange must be received on or before the earlier of:

 ➤ 180 days after the transfer of the property given up, or

 ➤ the due date (including extensions) for the tax return year in which the transfer of the property given up occurs.

Liabilities

All liabilities transferred to the other party in an exchange are netted against all liabilities transferred to the taxpayer. The taxpayer is treated as receiving boot or taxable not-like-kind property, only if relieved of greater liabilities than those assumed.

Boot

Property that is not like-kind property (including cash) is known as "boot." If the transferee either assumes a liability or takes property subject to a liability, the amount of the liability is treated as boot received by the transferor.

The receipt of boot will cause a realized gain on an exchange to be recognized. Gain is realized if the FMV of the property received exceeds the tax basis of the property given. The amount of gain to recognize is the lesser of the boot received or the realized gain. The realized gain is the maximum gain that can be recognized in an exchange.

WEEK EIGHT
MAP 8-24

*$25,000 Special Loss Allowance for Real Estate**
(refer to page 354)

Rental of real estate is generally a passive activity. However, up to $25,000 in passive losses from rental real estate can be deducted each tax year against income from nonpassive sources, such as wages or portfolio income.

The following rules apply:

1) The taxpayer must actively participate in the rental activity. Active participation standards are met if the taxpayer owns at least 10 percent of the rental property and has substantial involvement in managing the rental. *Note:* Active participation is a lower standard of involvement than material participation under passive activity rules.

2) A limited partner cannot meet the active participation test.

3) The amount of loss eligible for the $25,000 allowance is determined by netting income and losses from all of the taxpayer's rental real estate activities in which the taxpayer actively participates.

AGI Phaseout

The $25,000 special loss allowance is phased out by 50 percent of the amount by which the taxpayer's modified AGI exceeds $100,000 ($50,000 MFS). Thus, the allowance is reduced to zero when modified AGI reaches $150,000. The phaseout is computed and reported on Form 8582, Part II.

* Material reprinted with the permission of Quickfinder Incorporated (*www.quickfinder.com*).

WEEK EIGHT
MAP 8-25

*Electric and Clean-burning Vehicles**
(refer to page 354)

Qualified Electric Vehicle Credit (IRC §30)

Taxpayer purchasing a qualified electric vehicle (QEV) can claim a credit of 10 percent of the cost up to $4,000 on Form 8834.

A QEV is:

1) manufactured for use on public roads and has at least four wheels,

2) powered primarily by an electric motor,

3) originally used by the taxpayer, and

4) acquired for use and not for resale. The QEV credit is scheduled to be phased out beginning in 2004. The credit will be reduced-by:

   ➢ 25 percent for vehicles placed in service in 2004.

   ➢ 50 percent for vehicles placed in service in 2005.

   ➢ 75 percent for vehicles placed in service in 2006.

   The credit will be phased out completely by 2007.

Clean-fuel Vehicle Deduction (IRC §179A)

Taxpayer purchasing a qualified clean-fuel vehicle can claim the following, depending on the gross vehicle weight as follows:

   ➢ Deduction is $2,000, if gross vehicle weight is not more than 10,000 pounds.

   ➢ Deduction is $5,000, if gross vehicle weight is over 10,000 pounds and not more than 26,000 pounds.

   ➢ Deduction is $50,000, if gross vehicle weight is over 26,000 pounds.

Qualified clean fuels include natural gas, liquefied petroleum gas, hydrogen, electricity and any fuel at least 85 percent alcohol or ether. The clean-fuel vehicle deduction is scheduled to be phased out beginning in 2004. The credit will be reduced by:

   ➢ 25 percent for vehicles placed in service in 2004.

   ➢ 50 percent for vehicles placed in service in 2005.

   ➢ 75 percent for vehicles placed in service in 2006.

The credit will be phased out completely by 2007.

* Material reprinted with the permission of Quickfinder Incorporated *(www.quickfinder.com).*

Where to claim deduction:

> ➢ Form 1040, line 34, if claimed by individuals for nonbusiness use or employees for partial or full business use. On dotted line next to line 34, write "Clean Fuel."

> ➢ Schedule C or F for sole proprietors.

Note: The clean-fuel vehicle deduction cannot be claimed on vehicles that qualify for the QEV credit.

WEEK EIGHT
MAP 8-26

Top 10 Individual Income-tax-saving Ideas (refer to page 354)

1. Contribute to a Roth or Regular IRA and maximize contributions to a 401(k) or other retirement account. See MAP 8-14 for limits.

2. Contribute to a Section 529 College Savings Plan. See MAP 8-18.

3. Consider a Coverdell IRA if you plan to pay for elementary or secondary school. Earnings grow, tax free, if used for education. See MAP 8-5 and MAP 8-15.

4. Rent your home, tax free, for up to 14 days per year. (IRC Sec. 280A(g))—See MAP 8-22.

5. Maximize use of Flexible Spending Accounts and Accountable Reimbursement Plans at work. [IRC Sec. 125 and Sec. 62(a)(2)(A)].

6. Maximize use of employer-reimbursed educational expenses—up to $5,250 is tax free. (IRC Sec. 127).

7. Encourage parents with potential estate problems to consider gifting. Up to $11,000 per year is tax free to the donee and excludable from the estate of the donor. (IRC Sec. 102)

8. Reduce income through charitable gifts. See MAP 10-23.

9. Consider working less. Run a Quicken® scenario with reduced income and associated expenses, and you may be in for a surprise.

10. Purchase a qualified electric vehicle and take a tax credit. The credit limit is $4,000 for 2003, $3,000 for 2004, $2,000 for 2005, and $1,000 for 2006. (IRC Sec. 30) See MAP 8-25.

WEEK EIGHT
MAP 8-27

*Top 10 Business-tax-saving Ideas
(refer to page 352)*

1. Consider an S Corporation if you make more profit than a reasonable payment for your services in salary. See MAP 8-30 for details.

2. Establish a retirement plan. See MAP 8-1 through MAP 8-8.

3. Qualify for a 50 percent credit of eligible retirement plan startup costs, up to $500, for a maximum of three years. (IRC Sec. 45E – Form 8881)

4. Investigate establishing a Health Reimbursement Plan (IRC Sec. 105). Under the proper circumstances, all family medical expenses can be deducted as a legitimate business expense. Consider a call to BASE at (888) 386-9680 for further information, or visit their website *www.base105.com.*

5. Employ children in your business. For substantiated work performed, children can earn up to $4,750, tax free, and the business can take the deduction. Unincorporated businesses do not incur FICA or Medicare on salaries paid to the owner's children under 18.

6. Take full advantage of equipment depreciation and expense allowances. Up to $100,000 of equipment costs may be eligible for immediate write-off in the first year of acquisition (IRC Sec. 179). For property purchased after Sept. 10, 2001 and before Sept. 11, 2004, an additional 50 percent first-year special depreciation deduction may apply. See the provisions of the new 2003 Tax Act at MAP 8-29.

7. Set up an Employer-Provided Child Care Program. Tax credits range from 10–25 percent, and the maximum allowable credit is $150,000/year. (IRC Sec. 45(f)—Form 8882).

8. Hire targeted employees and receive up to a 40 percent credit on the first $6,000 of wages paid. (IRC Sec. 51, Form 5884)

9. Participate in the Welfare to Work program and receive a 35 percent credit on $10,000 of first year wages and a 50 percent credit on up to $10,000 of second-year wages. (IRC Sec. 51A, Form 8861).

10. Defer any gain on the sale of real estate through a like-kind exchange. As long as you receive no cash or are relieved of any debt, no tax will be due on the exchange. (IRC Sec. 1031(a)(1). See MAP 8-23.

Use *www.irs.gov* to locate additional information about topics that may apply to your particular situation. Type in the topic in the "Search Forms and Publications For_____" section on the home page.

Week Eight
Map 8-28

"Being" in Business
(refer to page 353)

"We must design a system where…doing good is like falling off a log, where the natural, everyday acts of work and life accumulate into a better world as a matter of course, not a matter of conscious altruism."
—*Paul Hawken*

Hawken lists eight objectives that will contribute to a new sustainable business model—not simply for the environment but for everyone. What is one way that you can begin taking a tiny step in that direction with your business or in your workplace in each of these eight areas?

1. **Reduce absolute consumption of energy and natural resources in the North by 80 percent in the next half century.** ("About 1.1 billion people currently metabolize 82.7 percent of the world's resources, leaving the balance of 17.3 percent of the resources for the remaining 4.5 billion.")

2. **Provide secure, stable, and meaningful employment for people everywhere.** ("Asking people to reduce consumption without increasing employment will create a world as destructive as the one they would replace.")

3. **Be self-actuating as opposed to regulated or morally mandated.** ("Government has a critical role to play, but that role must coincide with the natural impulses in society. Humans want to flourish and prosper, and they will eventually reject any system of conservation that interferes with these desires.")

4. **Honor market principles.** ("We can't just ask people to pay more to save the planet. They won't do it in some cases—and can't in most.")

5. **Be more rewarding than our present way of life.** ("Present-day limits need to become opportunities.")

6. **Exceed sustainability by restoring degraded habitats and ecosystems to their fullest biological capacity.** ("The dirty secret in environmentalism is that there is no such thing as sustainability… Any viable economic program must turn back the resource clock and devote itself actively to restoring damaged and deteriorating systems—restoration is far more compelling than the algebra of sustainability.")

7. **Rely on current income.** ("This doesn't mean being cold and hungry in winter, but redesigning all industrial, residential, and transportation systems so that everything we use springs easily from the Earth and returns back to it.")

8. **Be fun and engaging, and strive for an aesthetic outcome.** ("Some think humans are predatory by nature. I cast my vote with those who feel humans take the shape of their culture and that shifts in culture can occur in rare moment with remarkable speed and vigor.")

Jobs and Growth Tax Relief Reconcilliation Act of 2003 (JGTRRA)[1]
(refer to page 353)

FPA Executive Summary

Note: All provisions of JGTRRA of 2003 will expire after December 31, 2010, similar to provisions under the Economic Growth and Tax Relief Reconciliation Act of 2001 (EGTRRA). (Congress may choose to extend these provisions at a later date.) In general, JGTRRA accelerates previously enacted tax rate reductions retroactively to January 1, 2003, and provides for a maximum 15 percent rate on dividends and long-term capital gains.

2003 Income Tax Provisions

➤ Effective January 1, 2003, new tax rates applicable to individuals and married couples will be as follows: 10, 15, 25, 28, 33, and 35 percent, (previous rates were 10, 15, 27, 30, 35, and 38.6 percent).

➤ The standard deduction for married couples is increased to twice the amount of the standard deduction for single taxpayers only in 2003 and 2004 ($9,500). The standard deduction for single taxpayers remains at $4,750.

➤ The taxable income levels for those in the 10 percent bracket increases from $6,000 to $7,000. For married couples, the income threshold increases from $12,000 to $14,000.

➤ The 15 percent tax bracket for joint filers is expanded to twice the width of the same bracket for single filers for 2003 and 2004.

2003 Revised Tax Rate Structure:

	Single	Joint	HoH	MFS
10% bracket	$0–7,000	$0–14,000	$0–10,000	$0–7,000
15% bracket	7,001	14,001	10,001	7,001
25% bracket	28,401	56,801	38,051	28,401
28% bracket	68,801	114,651	98,251	57,326
33% bracket	143,501	174,701	159,101	87,35l
35% bracket	311,951	311,951	311,951	155,976
Standard deduction	4,750	9,500	7,000	4,750

Note: The 10 percent bracket is expanded for all except heads of households.

---

[1] This executive summary is solely for general informational purposes and does not represent legal advice from the FPA concerning United States tax law. If legal advice or other expert assistance is required the user should consult a professional. The information contained in this executive summary is offered in good faith and was obtained from federal sources deemed to be reliable; however, the information is offered without warranties, express or implied, as to its merchantability, fitness for a particular purpose, or any other matter.

*reprinted with the permission of the Financial Planning Association www.fpanet.org

Child Tax Benefits

➤ The amount of the child tax credit is increased from $600 to $1,000 in 2003 and 2004. In 2003, the increased amount of the child tax credit will be paid in advance beginning in July 2003 on the basis of information on the 2002 tax return of taxpayers who claimed the credit. *Taxpayers will not have to take any action to receive this advance payment, as the Treasury and the IRS will make the necessary calculations and automatically mail checks to eligible taxpayers.* Anyone born before 1987 would qualify for the credit.

Capital Gains and Dividend Relief

➤ The maximum tax rates on dividends paid by corporations to individuals and on individual capital gains is reduced to 15 percent in 2003 through 2008. For taxpayers in the 10 percent and 15 percent ordinary income tax brackets, the rate on dividends and capital gains is reduced to 5 percent in 2003 through 2007 and to zero in 2008. The lower capital gains rates do not apply to corporate taxpayers or to gains from collectibles (taxed at 28 percent) and certain gains from depreciable real estate (taxed at 25 percent).

➤ The new rates apply to capital gains realized on or after May 6, 2003, and to dividends received in 2003 and thereafter.

➤ The reduced dividend rate applies to dividends received by individual taxpayers from domestic corporations and from qualified foreign corporations. The term "qualified foreign corporation" includes a foreign corporation whose stock (or American Depository Receipts [ADRs] with respect to such stock) is tradable on an established securities market in the United States. A qualified foreign corporation also includes a foreign corporation that is eligible for the benefits of a comprehensive income tax treaty with the United States which the Treasury Department determines to be satisfactory for purposes of this provision and which includes an exchange of information program. Until further guidance is issued, a foreign corporation will be treated as eligible if substantially all of its income in the taxable year in which the dividend is paid would qualify for the benefits of a tax treaty with the United States. The test for qualified foreign corporation is an either/or test in which the foreign corporation can qualify for the reduced dividend rate if it meets either: 1) stock (or ADRs) traded in U.S. market, or 2) eligible for a tax treaty.

*Dividends paid to tax-deferred accounts will not receive the reduced rate (i.e., a dividend paid to an Individual Retirement Account [IRA], while not taxable on receipt, would be subject to the reduced tax rate upon ultimate distribution from the IRA to the holder.)

➤ Dividends are not eligible for the reduced rates unless received by the shareholder who has held the stock more than 60 days during the 120-day period, beginning 60 days before the ex-dividend date. For preferred stock, the relevant holding period is 90 days during the 180-day period, beginning 90 days before the ex-dividend date.

*reprinted with the permission of the Financial Planning Association *www.fpanet.org**

➤ Dividends generated by Regulated Investment Companies (RICs) will be eligible for the reduced tax rates to the extent they are attributable to qualifying dividends received by the RIC. Mutual funds, which are normally taxed as regulated investment companies, are able to distribute their long-term capital gains to shareholders as capital gains dividends. Such capital gains dividends will qualify for the lower 15 percent rate on long-term capital gains to the extent that the distribution is attributable to long-term gains on or after May 6, 2003. Long-term gains on the sale of shares in a regulated investment company on or after May 6, 2003 will also qualify for the lower capital gains rates.

➤ Generally, ordinary dividends received from a Real Estate Investment Trust (REIT) will not enjoy the favorable tax rate on dividends, although long-term capital gains dividend distributions will.

Alternative Minimum Tax

➤ The exemption for single taxpayers rises to $40,250 for 2003 and 2004 and reverts to the 2002 tax level the following year and thereafter. The exemption for married couples rises to $58,000 in 2003 and 2004 and reverts to the 2002 level in 2005.

Small Business Expensing

➤ The amount of investment (other than real estate) in depreciable tangible personal property and off-the-shelf software that may be immediately deducted by small businesses is increased from $25,000 to $100,000 beginning in 2003. The amount of investment qualifying for this deduction begins to phase out for small businesses that place more than $400,000 of such property into service during the year. These changes are effective for taxable years beginning in 2003, 2004, and 2005.

Bonus Depreciation

➤ Bonus depreciation rises to 50 percent for tangible personal property, other property depreciable over a period of less than 20 years, and computer software acquired after May 5, 2003 but before January 2, 2005. Property does not qualify for 50 percent bonus depreciation if a binding, written contract was in effect before May 6, 2003. The enhanced bonus depreciation continues to apply on top of regular depreciation in the first year only. The maximum business vehicle depreciation for new vehicles purchased on or after May 6, 2003 is $10,710.

2004 Income Tax Provisions

➤ The 10 percent bracket will be indexed for inflation.

2005 Income Tax Provisions

➤ The income threshold for those in the 10 percent bracket reverts to $6,000 for single filers and $12,000 for married filers.

*reprinted with the permission of the Financial Planning Association *www.fpanet.org**

➤ The 15 percent tax bracket falls to 180 percent of the maximum taxable income in the same bracket for unmarried individuals (adjusted for inflation).

➤ The standard deduction for married taxpayers will fall to 174 percent of the standard deduction for single taxpayers and gradually rise to double the amount in 2009.

Child Tax Benefits

➤ The child tax credit is lowered to $700.

2006 Income Tax Provisions

➤ The 15 percent deduction and the standard deduction for married couples continues to phase up under the 2001 Act already in place.

Child Tax Benefits

➤ The child tax credit is $700.

2007 Child Tax Benefits

➤ The child tax credit is $700.

2008 Income Tax Provisions

➤ The income threshold for those in the 10 percent bracket is raised to $7,000 for single filers and $14,000 for married filers, indexed for inflation in subsequent years.

Child Tax Benefits

➤ The Child Tax Credit is $700.

Capital Gains

➤ The 5 percent rate on capital gains for low-income taxpayers drops to zero for one year only.

2009 Child Tax Benefits

➤ The child tax credit is raised to $800.

2010 Child Tax Benefits

➤ The child tax credit is raised to $1,000.

2011 Income Tax Provisions

➤ All tax rate cuts revert to 15, 28, 31, 36 and 39.6 percent

Week Eight
Map 8-30

How You Do Business Matters
(refer to page 353)

Income Type	Sole Proprietorship	S Corporation	C Corporation	LLC
Wage	None	$40,000	$70,000	None
SE Taxable Earnings	$75,000	None	None	$75,000
Benefits	None	None	<$5,000>	None
Dividend	None	$35,000	None	None
Total Income	**$75,000**	**$75,000**	**$70,000**	**$75,000**
Expense Type				
FICA Tax—Employer	None	<$6,120>	<$10,710>	None
SE Tax	<$11,195>	None	None	<$11,195>
Income Tax	<$24,750>	<$24,750>	<$23,100>	<$24,750>
Deduction Type	**Sole Proprietorship**	**S Corporation**	**C Corporation**	**LLC**
SE Health Ins. Savings	$1,000	$1,000	None	$1,000
Medical Costs	<$5,000>	<$5,000>	None	<$5,000>
Extra Costs	None	<$500>	<$500>	<$500>
Tax Saved on Extra Costs	None	$165	$165	$165
Unemployment Insurance	None	<$200>	<$200>	None
Tax Saved on Unempl.	None	$66	$66	None
After Tax Income	**$35,055**	**$39,661**	**$35,721**	**$34,720**

Assumptions:

1. $75,000 profit from each entity. C Corporation nets $70,000 because $5,000 extra payroll tax costs.

2. $40,000 reasonable salary for S Corporation owner based on duties performed and invested capital

3. $3,000 health insurance premiums for owner

4. $2,000 health insurance out of pocket costs for owner

5. Income tax brackets—federal 27 percent, State 6 percent = 33 percent

6. Extra Costs = tax filing and initial legal fees

7. Unemployment insurance—estimate of state unemployment for salaried officer

Week Nine
MAP 9-1

*Quickchart of Social Security Retirement Benefits**
(refer to page 389)

Quick Chart of Social Security—Retirement Benefits

	Early Retirement (Permanently Reduced Benefits)	Full Retirement (Full Benefits)	Delayed Retirement (Permanently Increased Benefits)
Eligibility for Benefits	A worker is eligible for early retirement benefits at age 62. *Note:* If poor health forces a person to retire early, he or she should apply for Social Security disability benefits. The amount of disability benefits is generally the same as full retirement benefits.	Full retirement age is when a worker can retire and collect full retirement benefits (assuming sufficient work credits). For a person born in 1937 or earlier, the full retirement age is 65. Full retirement age will increase in gradual steps until it reaches age 66 in 2009, and age 67 in 2027.	Delayed retirement is available for a worker over the full retirement age. At age 70, the worker automatically receives benefits. *Note:* The worker should remember to sign up for Medicare at age 65 regardless of when he or she retires.
Age and Benefit Payments	Early retirement permanently reduces monthly benefits, even after full retirement age. A permanent benefit reduction of ⅝ of 1% is imposed for every full month benefits are received prior to full retirement age. The reduction will increase as full retirement age increases. When the phase-in to a full retirement of age 67 in the year 2027 is complete, early retirement at age 62 will yield 70% of the full benefit a person is entitled to at full retirement age.	Maximum monthly benefit if retiring at age 65: $1,536 in 2001, $1,660 in 2002 and $1,741 in March of 2003 (age 65 and two months).	Benefits are increased by a monthly percentage if the worker delays retirement. Also, each additional year a person works adds another year of earnings to the Social Security record, possibly resulting in higher lifetime earnings and a higher benefit amount.

Age and Benefit Payments (continued)

Worker born:	% of full benefits received if retired at age 62:	Worker born:	% of full benefits received if retired at age 62:	Worker born:	Retire and collect full benefits at:	Worker born:	Retire and collect full benefits at:	Worker born:	Percent increase each year:	Worker born:	Percent increase each year:
1937 and earlier	80.000%	1955	74.167%	1937 and earlier	65 yrs, 0 months	1955	66 yrs, 2 months	1917 – 1924	3.0%	1935 – 1936	6.0%
1938	79.167%	1956	73.333%	1938	65 yrs, 2 months	1956	66 yrs, 4 months	1925 – 1926	3.5%	1937 – 1938	6.5%
1939	78.333%	1957	72.500%	1939	65 yrs, 4 months	1957	66 yrs, 6 months	1927 – 1928	4.0%	1939 – 1940	7.0%
1940	77.500%	1958	71.667%	1940	65 yrs, 6 months	1958	66 yrs, 8 months	1929 – 1930	4.5%	1941 – 1942	7.5%
1941	76.667%	1959	70.833%	1941	65 yrs, 8 months	1959	66 yrs, 10 months	1931 – 1932	5.0%	1943 and later	8.0%
1942	75.833%	1960 and later	70.000%	1942	65 yrs, 10 months	1960 and later	67 yrs, 0 months	1933 – 1934	5.5%		
1943 – 1954	75.000%			1943 – 1954	66 yrs, 0 months						

Quarters of Coverage Needed for Benefits *(Used to determine eligibility benefits)* See Page 14-24 for how to earn a quarter of coverage	The same quarters of coverage are needed as for full retirement. See the next column.		The same quarters of coverage are needed as for full retirement. See the previous column.

Worker born:	Minimum quarters of coverage needed:	Nonprofit Employees Age on Dec. 1, 1984:	Minimum quarters of coverage needed:
1929 or later	40	60 or over	6
1928	39	59	8
1927	38	58	12
1926	37	57	16
1925	36	55 or 56	20
1924	35		

Earning Limits/ Reduction of Benefits	**Under age 65:** 2003: Benefits reduced by $1 for each $2 earned over $11,520. 2002: Benefits reduced by $1 for each each $2 earned over $11,280. 2001: Benefits reduced by $1 for each $2 earned over $10,680.	**Full retirement age:** *(65 in 2002, 65 and two months in 2003)* 2003: Exempt from earnings limits beginning the month the individual attains full retirement age. For months in the year prior to the individual attaining full retirement age, benefits are reduced by $1 for each $3 earned above $30,720. 2002: Exempt from earnings limits beginning the month the individual attains full retirement age. For months in the year prior to the individual attaining full retirement age, benefits are reduced by $1 for each $3 earned above $30,000. 2001: Exempt from earnings limits beginning the month the individual attains full retirement age. For months in the year prior to the individual attaining full retirement age, benefits are reduced by $1 for each $3 earned above $25,000.	
Average 2003 Social Security Benefit		Retired worker: $895. Retired worker and spouse: $1,483.	
Medicare Insurance	The worker is not eligible for Medicare until he/she is age 65, is disabled or has permanent kidney failure.	**Part A:** *Medicare hospital insurance.* Helps pay for inpatient hospital care, care in a skilled nursing facility following a hospital stay, home health care and blood. See the chart on Page 14-28 for more information. **Part B:** *Medicare medical insurance.* Helps pay for doctors' services and a wide range of medical services and supplies. See the chart on Page 14-28 for more information.	

639

Week Nine
MAP 9-2

Quickchart of Social Security—
*Family, Survivor, Disability Benefits**
(refer to page 389)

Quick Chart of Social Security—Family, Survivor, Disability Benefits

	Family Benefits (Worker Living)	Survivor Benefits (Worker Deceased)	Disability Benefits (Worker Disabled)

Eligibility for Benefits	When a worker begins collecting Social Security retirement benefits, the other family members who may also be eligible for benefits are:
	• The spouse of the worker if he or she is age 62 or older (unless he or she collects a higher Social Security benefit on his or her own record).
	• The spouse of the worker at any age if he or she is caring for the worker's child (the child must be under age 16 or disabled and receiving Social Security benefits).
	• The worker's children, if they are unmarried and:
	  – Under age 18,
	  – Under age 19 but in elementary or secondary school as a full-time student, or
	  – Age 18 or older and severely disabled (the disability must have started before age 22).
		Family members of a deceased worker who may collect benefits if the worker earned enough credits while working:
		• Widow(er) age 60 or older.
		• Widow(er) age 50 or older and disabled.
		• Widow(er) at any age if he or she is caring for the worker's child under age 16 or a disabled child who is receiving Social Security benefits.
		• Children if they are unmarried and:
		  – Under age 18,
		  – Under age 19 but in an elementary or secondary school as a full-time student, or
		  – Age 18 or older and severely disabled (the disability must have started before age 22).
		• Dependent parents at age 62 or older.
			Disability benefits are paid to a worker at any age. At full retirement age, if a worker is receiving disability benefits, they become retirement benefits, although the amount remains the same.
			Family members who may also be eligible for benefits:
			• A spouse of the worker if he or she is age 62 or older (unless he or she collects a higher Social Security benefit on his or her own record).
			• A spouse of the worker at any age if he or she is caring for the worker's child (the child must be under age 16 or disabled and receiving Social Security benefits).
			• The worker's children, if they are unmarried and:
			  – Under age 18,
			  – Under age 19 but in elementary or secondary school as a full-time student, or
			  – Age 18 or older and severely disabled (the disability must have started before age 22).

Ex-Spouse (Divorced) Benefits	An ex-spouse (even if the worker is remarried) is entitled to benefits (at times even if the worker is not receiving benefits) if he or she: • Was married to the worker for at least 10 years, • Is at least age 62 and unmarried, and • Has been divorced at least two years. **Note:** The amount of benefits an ex-spouse receives does not affect the amount of benefits the worker's family receives.	An ex-spouse (even if the worker remarried) is entitled to benefits if he or she is: • At least age 60 (or age 50 if disabled) and was married to the worker for at least 10 years, • Any age and caring for a child who is eligible for benefits on the worker's record, • Not eligible for equal or higher amount on his/her own record, or • Not currently married, unless the remarriage occurred after age 60 (after age 50 if disabled). **Note:** The amount of benefits an ex-spouse receives does not affect the amount of benefits the worker's family receives.	An ex-spouse (even if the worker is remarried) is entitled to benefits (at times even if the worker is not receiving benefits) if he or she: • Was married to the worker for at least 10 years, • Is at least age 62 and unmarried, and • Is not eligible for an equal or higher benefit on his or her own record or on someone else's record. **Note:** The amount of benefits an ex-spouse receives does not affect the amount of benefits the worker's family receives.
Quarters of Coverage Needed for Benefits	The same number of quarters of coverage needed for a worker to receive his or her retirement benefits is needed by the worker in order for his or her family to receive family benefits. See Page 14-22.	**Worker Born:** *Minimum quarters of coverage needed:* 1929 or earlier ... One quarter of coverage needed for each year after 1950, up to the year of death. 1930 or later ...... One quarter of coverage needed for each year after 1921, up to the year of death. *Special rule for worker who dies without enough quarters of coverage:* Social Security survivor benefits can be paid to the worker's children, and the worker's spouse who is caring for the children, if the worker has six quarters of coverage in the three years just before his or her death.	*Disabled at age:* *Minimum quarters of coverage needed:* Before age 24 ... Six quarters of coverage earned in the three-year period ending when the disability began. 24 – 30 ... Quarters of coverage for working half the time between age 21 and the time of disability. *Example:* A worker disabled at age 27 needs three years of work (12 quarters of coverage) out of past six years (between age 21 and age 27). 31 or older ... Number of quarters of coverage needed dependent on age, and the worker must have earned 20 quarters of coverage in the 10 years immediately before the disability began (unless the worker is blind). See the chart below for quarters of coverage needed if disabled at age 31 or older.
Amount of Payment	• The amount of payment to each qualified person is a percentage of the worker's primary insurance amount (PIA). See the PIA chart on Page 14-32. • The total amount payable to the family is limited to family maximum benefit (equal to about 150 – 180% of the retiree's benefit). • The total amount payable does not include the amount payable to an ex-spouse.	• The amount of payment to each qualified person is a percentage of the worker's PIA. See the PIA chart on Page 14-32. • The total amount payable to survivors is limited to the family maximum benefit (equal to about 150 – 180% of the decedent's benefit.) • The total amount payable does not include the amount payable to an ex-spouse.	The waiting period for disability benefits (a full five months) begins with the first full month after the date the disability is determined to have begun. Benefits begin in the sixth full month. • The amount of payment to each qualified person is a percentage of the worker's PIA. See the PIA Chart on Page 14-32. • The total amount payable to the family is limited to the family maximum benefit (equal to about 150 – 180% of the disabled's benefit) and does not include the amount payable to an ex-spouse. • The amount is the same as the amount of the retirement benefit at age 65. • If disabled, benefits may be reduced if eligible for other disability benefits. See Page 14-25.
Average 2003 Benefits	• Retired worker: $895. • Retired worker and spouse: $1,483.	• Widow(er) of worker: $862. • Widow(er) of worker with two children: $1,838. • A one-time death benefit of $255 is payable to the widow(er) or to minor children.	• Disabled worker: $833. • Disabled worker, spouse, children: $1,395.

Quarters of coverage needed if disabled at age 31 or older:

Born after 1929, disabled at age:	Quarters of coverage needed to collect disability benefits:	Born after 1929, disabled at age:	Quarters of coverage needed to collect disability benefits:
31 – 42	20	54	32
44	22	56	34
46	24	58	36
48	26	60	38
50	28	62 or older	40
52	30		

WEEK NINE
MAP 9-3

Social Security Benefits as a Percentage of PIA*
(refer to page 389)

Social Security Benefits as a Percentage of PIA		
PIA is the monthly amount a worker can expect to receive when Social Security benefits begin at full retirement age. See Page 14-31 for computation of PIA using the Social Security benefit computation worksheet.		
Retirement Benefit	Full retirement age, per year of birth	PIA
	Age 62 or above, but below full retirement age, per year of birth	PIA reduced
Disability Benefit		PIA
Spouse's Benefit	Caring for a child who is under age 16 or disabled	50% of PIA
(Spouse of retired or disabled worker)	Full retirement age, per year of birth	50% of PIA
	Age 62 or above, but below full retirement age, per year of birth	50% of PIA reduced
Child's Benefit	Child of retired or disabled worker	50% of PIA
	Child of deceased worker	75% of PIA
Mother's or Father's Benefit [Widow(er) caring for child under age 16 or disabled]		75% of PIA
Widow(er)'s Benefit	Full retirement age, per year of birth	100% of PIA
(Not caring for child)	Age 60 or above, but below full retirement age, per year of birth	100% of PIA reduced
Disabled Widow(er)'s Benefit	Beginning at age 50 to 60	71.5% of PIA
Parent's Benefit	One dependent parent	82.5% of PIA
(Dependent parent of deceased worker)	Two dependent parents	75% of PIA for each parent

WEEK NINE
MAP 9-4

*Applying for Social Security Benefits**
(refer to page 389)

Contact Social Security the year before the planned retirement year to determine the most beneficial retirement date. The retirement month can affect the amount of benefits payable to the worker and his/her family.

Provide the following:

➤ Social Security card/number

➤ Certified copy of birth certificate

➤ Spouse's Social Security number and birth certificate if he/she is applying for benefits; and children's Social Security numbers and birth certificates if they are applying for benefits

➤ Marriage certificate if applying under a spouse's record

➤ Divorce decree if applying as an ex-spouse

➤ Death certificate if applying as a widow(er)

➤ W-2 forms for the last two years

➤ Tax returns for the last two years if self-employed

➤ Military service records for 1951—1956 and discharge papers

➤ Bank account numbers for direct deposit

Notes:

➤ If a worker stops working before age 62, he/she misses the opportunity to increase the retirement benefit amount by replacing low-earning years with higher-earning years.

➤ If poor health causes someone to retire early (before full retirement age), he/she should apply for Social Security disability benefits. The amount of Social Security disability benefits is the same as unreduced Social Security retirement benefits.

* Material reprinted with the permission of Quickfinder Incorporated *(www.quickfinder.com)*.

WEEK NINE
MAP 9-5

When Will Principal Balance Equal Zero?
(refer to page 389)

When Will Principal Balance Equal Zero?						
		Return Earned Per Year on Balance				
		6%	**7%**	**8%**	**9%**	**10%**
Percentage of Principal Withdrawn Per Year	**7%**	33	–	–	–	–
	8%	23	30	–	–	–
	9%	18	22	28	–	–
	10%	15	17	20	26	–
	11%	13	14	16	19	25
	12%	11	12	14	16	18
	13%	10	11	12	13	15
	14%	9	10	10	11	13
	15%	8	9	9	10	11
		Number of Years Principal Will Last				

WEEK NINE
MAP 9-6

*Early Retirement**
(refer to page 389)

To begin building an early retirement program, look at what will be given up by retiring early. Money earned while working between ages 62 and 65 or later could be several times the amount received from Social Security over the same period. Working longer could mean qualifying for higher Social Security benefits and a bigger payout from a pension or profit-sharing plan.

If a person born before 1938 retires at age 62, Social Security benefits are 20 percent lower than waiting until age 65 to retire. People born after 1937 who contemplate early retirement face a steeper bite. As the normal Social Security retirement age rises to age 67 between 2003 and 2027, the penalty for retiring at age 62 will grow to 30 percent.

Consider: Assuming everything remains unchanged, a person who waits until age 65 to apply for retirement benefits will be 77 years old before he/she reaches the break-even point.

If a person at age 62 saves the money received in early retirement benefits for the three-year early retirement period and invests it at money market rates or better, the interest will more than offset the amount of benefits he/she lost due to drawing the early retirement benefits. The age 65 retiree will never catch up.

Note: If early retirement is being considered, find out how other entitlements would be affected.

* Material reprinted with the permission of Quickfinder Incorporated *(www.quickfinder.com)*.

WEEK NINE
MAP 9-7

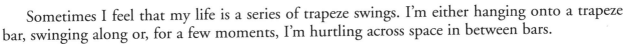

Fear of Transformation
(refer to page 390)

Sometimes I feel that my life is a series of trapeze swings. I'm either hanging onto a trapeze bar, swinging along or, for a few moments, I'm hurtling across space in between bars.

Most of the time I'm hanging on for dear life to my trapeze bar of the moment. It carries me along at a certain steady rate of swing, and I have the feeling that I'm in control of my life. I know most of the right questions and even some of the right answers. But once in awhile as I'm merrily swinging along, I look ahead of me into the distance and I see another bar swinging towards me. It's empty and I know, in that place in me that *knows*, that this new trapeze bar has *my* name on it. It is my next step, my growth, my aliveness coming to get me. In my heart-of-hearts, I know that for me to grow, I must release my grip on the present, well-known bar to move to the new one.

Each time it happens, I hope and pray I won't have to grab the new trapeze bar. But in my *knowing place* I realize I must totally release my grasp on my old bar and, for some time, I must hurtle across space before I can grab onto the new bar. Each time, I am filled with terror. It doesn't matter that in all my previous hurtles across the void of unknowing, I have always made it. Each time I am afraid I will miss—that I will be crushed on unseen rocks in the bottomless chasm between the bars. But I do it anyway. Perhaps this is the essence of what the mystics call the faith experience. No guarantees, no net, no insurance policy, but you do it anyway because somehow, to keep hanging onto that old bar is no longer an alternative. And so for an eternity that can last a microsecond or a thousand lifetimes, I soar across the dark void of "the past is gone, the future is not yet here." It is called transition. I have come to believe it is the only place that real change occurs.

I have noticed in our culture this transition zone is looked upon as a nothing—a no-place between places. Surely the old trapeze bar was real and that new one coming towards me, I hope that's real, too. But the void in-between? That's just a scary, confusing, disorienting, "nowhere" that must be gotten through as fast and as unconsciously as possible. What a waste! I have a sneaking suspicion that the transition zone is the only real thing, and that the bars are illusions we dream up to avoid the void where the real change, the real growth, occurs for us. Whether or not my hunch is true, it remains that the transition zones in our lives are incredibly rich places. They should be honored—even savored. Even with all the pain and fear and feelings of being out-of-control that can accompany transitions, they are still the most alive, most growth-filled, most passionate, most expansive moments in our lives.

And so, transformation of fear may have nothing to do with making fear go away, but rather with giving ourselves permission to "hang out" in the transition between trapeze bars. Transforming our need to grab that new bar… any bar… is allowing ourselves to dwell in the only place where change really happens. It can be terrifying. It can also be enlightening, in the true sense of the word. Hurtling through the void—we just may learn how to fly.

—Anonymous

WEEK NINE
MAP 9-8

Pension Maximization

Or Avoiding Pension Survivorship Income Costs
(refer to page 390)

The Problem

At retirement, married pension plan participants are required to make a choice. They can:

- Take the maximum monthly income for the life of the retiring employee only (e.g., $1,000 per month); or

- Take a substantially reduced pension for the lifetime of both the retiring employee and his/her spouse (e.g., $800 per month).

In the absence of any planned alternatives, most employees and their spouses feel compelled to take the reduced life income at retirement. Unfortunately, once this option is selected it may not be changed.

Consider the Potential Costs

- If spouse lives but a short time, the surviving retiree faces a lifetime of reduced pension benefits.

- If both live a full life and die within a year or so of each other, little benefit is ever realized after 20 years or more of reduced pension.

- In no case do children or other heirs inherit any benefits.

Conclusion

Pension survivorship options equate to very expensive term life insurance which may never pay a benefit.

A Solution

Purchase permanent life insurance prior to or at retirement in an amount that would provide the survivor or other heirs with a similar monthly income benefit. Then still take the maximum monthly pension benefit.

Caution: In some cases, eligibility for continuing surviving spouseís group health care is dependent on survivor option election.

The following examples illustrate the potential cost of the survivorship benefit over the life expectancy of the retiree and his or her spouse.

Example 1 - Full Survivorship Benefit on Pension Plan

	With No Survivorship	With 100% Survivorship
Anticipated monthly income at retirement (age 65)	$1,000	$800
Cost of survivorship election	$200 per month for both spousesí remaining lifetimes	
Joint life expectancy[1] at 65	25 years x $2,400 = $60,000 total potential cost	

Example 2 - 55% Survivorship Benefit on Pension Plan

	With No Survivorship	With 55% Survivorship	
		Retiree	**Spouse**
Anticipated monthly income at retirement (age 65)	$1,000	$900	$495
Cost of survivorship election	$100 per month for both spousesí remaining lifetimes		
Joint life expectancy[1] at 65	25 years x $1,200 = $30,000 total potential cost		

Alternative Funding

Purchase a permanent life insurance policy in an amount that will provide a death benefit for the spouse to replace the income that might have been received with the survivorship option. For example, to provide $800 per month for 25 years (assuming an 8% growth rate on the remaining balance) would require an initial sum of approximately $104,000 ($64,500 for 55% survivorship benefit) of death benefit. Of course, the 8% return is not guaranteed, so, if desired, a guaranteed lifetime payout available from the insurance company could be used.

---

[1] Based on IRS Annuity Table VI - Ordinary Joint and Last Survivor.

Advantages to Alternative Funding

- Premiums can be paid when income is higher, before retirement, from discretionary income.

- The monthly premium may be more or less than the difference in the monthly retirement benefit, depending on the insured's age and health at the time a life insurance policy is issued. However, in general, the overall cost of the life insurance will be less than the total potential cost of lower pension benefits if the insured lives to normal life expectancy.

- A large part of the death benefit proceeds payable in monthly installments will be income tax free. Normally, pension income is fully taxable.

- If the retiree and spouse die simultaneously or if the spouse dies first, their children or other heirs may receive the insurance death benefits. Typically, no additional benefits would be payable from the pension plan. If the spouse dies first and the retiree does not have any other beneficiaries deserving of the proceeds, the retiree can surrender the policy for its cash surrender value.

Week Nine
MAP 9-9

Top 10 Nonfinancial Retirement Issues
(refer to page 390)

1. **Couple communication.** If you are married or share your life with a partner, talk to one another about what each of you expects from retirement. How can each of your needs be honored? What are you willing to accommodate in order to integrate your partner's wishes? What is he/she willing to accommodate in order to integrate your wishes?

2. **Fear of transformation.** Read MAP 9-7. If you have a spouse/partner, ask him/her to read it as well. How can you honor the terror and excitement of the transitions in your life? Can you give yourself permission to "hang out" in the transition between the trapeze bars?

3. **Boredom.** If you are retiring early, this may especially be a problem. As great as golf is, it can get pretty old eight hours a day, seven days a week. Have you practiced retirement to see if doing all those things you've dreamed of really floats your boat?

4. **Change in stress.** If you've grown accustomed to the high-energy work world at a 120 mph, how will you deal with a 35-mph life?

5. **Loss of social contact.** You've grown accustomed to seeing people and interacting with them, if only on a superficial business level, multiple times a day. If your friends are still working, how will you meet this need?

6. **Different retirement dates.** Retirement may not look so great if one spouse/partner isn't free to "play" or travel. The retiree may be ready to move to a different climate, while the working spouse wants to stay put with the job he/she loves. It's much better to face these issues before one of you retires.

7. **More than a great severance package.** If your company offers you an incentive to take early retirement, think about the factors outlined above. There's more to life than more money in your bank account, and you may want to turn them down.

8. **Comfortable understanding current finances and analyzing future options.** Practice with TEN WEEKS and Quicken® until you are easily able to take an accurate understanding of your finances and look at various alternatives with the What If Scenario tool. Give these options your attention—not your energy that is inevitable with worry.

9. **Relocation.** Have you considered the following?

➤ "Wherever you go, there you are?"

➤ Keep your current home and rent in the new location for six months–one year to make sure it's what you really want.

➤ Visit the new city in all seasons.

➤ Subscribe to the new location's local newspaper.

➤ Check out opportunities to do what you enjoy in terms of recreation, charitable volunteerism, the arts, worship, etc.

➤ How easy it is for you (and your partner) to meet new people.

➤ How the new location will impact your contact with relatives and existing friends.

➤ Job opportunities if there is a possibility that you may need to work part-time after retirement.

➤ Health care facilities and related cost of care with your existing health coverage.

➤ General cost of living, including income, property, and sales tax rates compared to where you currently live.

10. **Loss of identity.** Are you practiced in seeing yourself and liking yourself apart from your work? Can you naturally leave your work and accomplishments out of a social conversation?

Week Ten
MAP 10-1

*Quick Facts on Estate Planning** *
(refer to page 405)

Basic Steps in Estate Planning

1) Make a complete and accurate inventory of all assets and their value.

2) Determine the form of ownership of each asset and understand its effect on transfer of property at death.

3) Verify beneficiary designations on life insurance and retirement assets.

4) Estimate the size of the estate to determine whether estate tax planning is needed.

5) Decide whether certain family members or assets need special protection (i.e. minor children, adults with special needs, family business).

6) Select beneficiaries and determine what provisions should be made for each.

7) Determine how financial and health care decisions will be made in the case of illness or disability.

8) Determine how health care will be funded.

9) Estimate the cost of alternative estate planning methods that will meet the goals.

10) Select and implement the estate plan.

11) Laws and family circumstances change. Review plan regularly.

Special Considerations

Individuals or couples with minor children. Individuals with minor children should nominate a guardian to care for their children. Guardian nominations must be made in a will. Even individuals with trust-based estate plans should have wills nominating guardians for their minor children.

Anyone with minor heirs or beneficiaries. If a minor is given property by will or as the direct beneficiary of an insurance policy or other asset, the minor receives the property when he/she reaches adulthood, usually age 18. Most people do not want large sums of money placed unconditionally in the hands of 18-year-olds. A contingent family trust can be included in a will to delay the receipt of an inheritance. Anyone leaving a sizable amount to a minor child should consider this alternative. Many states have statutory custodial arrangements to delay receipt of specific assets until age 21.

* Material reprinted with the permission of Quickfinder Incorporated *(www.quickfinder.com).*

Married couples with estates over $1 million. Each spouse has a separate estate tax credit ($1 million in 2003). When both credits are used, the couple can shield $2 million from estate tax. Couples who own all property jointly or whose wills leave all property to the survivor may miss the opportunity to use the tax credit of the first spouse to die. See "Bypass Trusts," for estate planning to solve this problem. Couples who already have bypass trust provisions in a will or trust agreement written before 2001 should review the funding provisions. Typical provisions pass an amount equal to the estate tax exemption to a bypass trust with the remainder going to the surviving spouse. The surviving spouse's share under such provisions will decrease substantially as the exemption amount increases from $1 million in 2003 to $3.5 million in 2009.

Family businesses and farms. Specialized estate planning is essential for taxpayers who own businesses they hope to transfer to their heirs as going concerns. The valuation of family-owned-business interests is generally a contentious issue between the heirs and the IRS. Planning prior to death may help fix the value of the business interests or allow part of the business to be transferred before death at an estate tax savings. Estate tax breaks designed to help heirs avoid a forced sale of family business property are also available if family business interests are a significant part of a decedent's estate. The business must meet rules for family participation and ownership both before and after death to qualify. Again, planning prior to the owner's death may help the heirs take advantage of these estate tax breaks.

Estate Planning and the 2001 Tax Act

Estate tax exemption increase and repeal. Estate tax is repealed in 2010. The estate tax exemption increases to $1.5 million in 2004, $2 million in 2006 and $3.5 million in 2009.

Gifts. Gift tax is not repealed. The exemption increased to $1 million in 2002 and will remain at that level indefinitely. It is not indexed for inflation.

Rates. The top rate for estate and gift tax will decrease gradually from 55–45 percent between 2002 and 2007. The top gift tax rate after repeal will be 35 percent.

Basis rules. Stepped-up basis for inherited property will be replaced by carryover basis in 2010. Estate executors will be able to increase the carryover basis of a decedent's assets by $1.3 million (with an additional $3 million increase for qualifying property passing to a spouse). The value of any specific asset cannot increase above FMV at the decedent's death. Basis increase does not apply to IRAs and other tax-deferred assets.

Keep basis records. Those inheriting from a decedent who has less than $1.3 million at death will see little change under the new rules—basis of all qualifying assets can be increased to FMV. Executors of estates with assets over $1.3 million will need to know the decedent's basis in all assets in order to allocate the basis increase. There is no fresh start under the new rules to wipe away a decedent's poor record keeping. Taxpayers who want to do their heirs and representatives a favor should organize their basis records.

State laws. Changes to the estate tax and its eventual repeal could cost states billions. Several states have already decided not to follow the federal changes. Change of some kind is likely in most states before 2005.

Sunset. Perhaps the biggest planning problem is the uncertainty of estate tax repeal. The estate tax changes, like all other provisions of the 2001 Tax Act, will sunset in 2011. If Congress does nothing, the 2001 rules will be reinstated in 2011. Since Congress must act to extend the changes, it seems as likely that a future Congress will modify the plan before 2010.

Estate Tax Exclusion and Credit		
Year	Exclusion	Credit
2000 – 2001	$ 675,000	$ 220,550
2002 – 2003	$1,000,000	$ 345,800
2004 – 2005	$1,500,000	$ 555,800
2006 – 2008	$2,000,000	$ 780,800
2009	$3,500,000	$1,455,800
2010	No tax	No tax

Maximum family-owned business deduction = $675,000. Estate tax exclusion when maximum business deduction is claimed = $625,000. Family-owned business deduction repealed for decedents dying after December 31, 2003.

Gift Tax Exclusion and Credit		
Year	Exclusion	Credit
2000 – 2001	$ 675,000	$ 220,550
2002 – 2009	$1,000,000	$ 345,800
2010	$1,000,000	$ 330,800

Week Ten
MAP 10-2

Questions to Answer Before You See an Attorney—
"People Decisions" of Estate Planning
(refer to page 406)

Who Will Care for Our Minor Children?

A guardian, the one responsible for caring for your children until they reach 18 (or 21 in some states), must be named in your will. Consider some of the following factors in choosing a guardian:

➤ Who is prepared to deal with children of your offsprings' ages? Grandparents may not be up to the task.

➤ Do the candidates have children of their own that may impact how they care for your children?

➤ How healthy are the candidates?

➤ Who could serve as an alternative if your first candidates decline?

➤ What happens if one partner dies—would you want the surviving candidate to serve as sole guardian?

➤ Whom would you like to serve as guardian if the candidates divorce?

➤ How do the candidates manage their financial affairs? Would they be good stewards of monies entrusted to their oversight by your personal represenative or trustee?

Who Will Administer Our Estate?

If you own assets that are not held in joint-tenancy or through a retirement plan or life insurance policy, you most likely will need someone to distribute your assets and pay your liabilities in accordance with your will. This person has historically been known as the executor but is now more commonly referred to as the personal representative.

It's always good to name a backup, or successor person, to serve in the event the primary personal representative is incapacitated in some way.

Please refer to MAP 10-27 and locate the April, 2000 article at *www.tenweeks.org* entitled, "Choosing an Executor for Your Estate Is a Critical Task."

Who Will Serve as Trustee of our Trusts?

After reading MAP 10-17, decide if you want to establish a living trust or another type of trust. In the event you do, you will need to choose a trustee, as well as a successor trustee, to administer the trust. They typically manage investments or hire someone to do this job, make distributions, pay taxes, and ensure that your wishes, as outlined in the prior trust document, are followed.

Consider similar factors that are outlined in the article mentioned in the prior section as you select these trustees.

In certain instances, it makes sense to hire a corporate trustee. Unless there are more than $250,000 of assets in the trust, the costs of such management is generally not cost-effective. It is also advisable to consider a trust company that does not provide investment management services, but focuses on trust administration. Two companies that provide such services are Capital Trust Company of Delaware (*www.ctcdelaware.com*) and Santa Fe Trust (*www.santafetrust.com*).

Who Will Get What—When?

A major purpose of estate planning is to ensure that the people you want (Who), get the things you want (What), when you want (When).

Discuss when you want your assets distributed to your children. Some people distribute a portion of the trust assets to their children at different ages, in addition to providing for certain expenses such as college education, medical insurance, etc. In order to hold assets after a child has reached majority, you will need to establish a trust as part of your estate planning process.

Discuss whom you want to receive your assets in the event your children or partner predeceases you. Would you like to leave something to a favorite charity or long-lost relative?

Are there specific assets (family heirlooms, photographs, etc.) that you want to leave to specific individuals? A personal property memorandum, easily updated without having to change your entire will, accomplishes this.

What About Uncle Sam?

There are several postdeath estate planning tactics that can be utilized to minimize estate taxes, as long as the people in charge of your affairs are aware that it is important to you to do everything possible to minimize estate taxes. Discuss how aggressive you would like to be in this area.

All These Questions Need to Be Considered Before Consulting an Estate-Planning Attorney or Attempting to Draft Your Own Will.

WEEK TEN
MAP 10-3

Types of Wills
(refer to page 406)

While your will is tailored to your needs, most wills generally fall into one of four categories. The categories are divided based upon the ages of the family members and the value of the estate. The four principal types of wills are:

➤ a simple will;

➤ a will containing a contingent trust for the benefit of minor children;

➤ a will designed to provide optimal use of the marital deduction (marital deduction will); or

Simple Will

Frequently, each spouse will desire to make an outright disposition of his/her entire estate to the surviving spouse to provide the survivor with complete freedom and control of total ownership of the combined marital estate. Leaving the entire estate to the surviving spouse via the marital deduction is a common provision of a simple will.

A simple will is appropriate when you have no minor children and your total estate is less than the applicable exclusion amount ($1 million for 2002 and 2003). You may also decide to use a simple will if you are not married and your total estate is greater than the applicable exclusion amount. This type of will is referred to as a "simple" will because no trusts are created in the instrument. However, the terms of the will may be even more complex than in other types of wills, depending upon what your specific requirements are.

Contingent Trust for the Benefit of Minor Children

This form of will is used in nontaxable estates ($1 million or less in 2002 and 2003). You would consider using it if there is a possibility that your property will pass to minor beneficiaries. Typically, you designate (via a specific bequest) who will receive your residence and tangible personal property. Everything else goes to your surviving spouse. However, if your spouse does not survive you, the will establishes a trust for the benefit of your minor children. A guardian should also be designated for the minor children.

656

Marital Deduction Will

A marital deduction will is used when you are married and the combined value of your estates approaches or exceeds the applicable exclusion amount ($1 million in 2002 and 2003). A typical marital deduction will works as follows:

➤ Specific bequests are made to your spouse or others.

➤ A pecuniary formula bequest to your surviving spouse (e.g., gift to a marital deduction trust equal to the smallest amount that can be given without causing your estate to pay estate tax) is included.

➤ Residuary bequest is made to a bypass trust (also known as a credit shelter trust, family trust, or exemption equivalent trust). Typically, this is the amount of the applicable exclusion amount ($1 million for 2002 and 2003) plus administration expenses, debts, and taxes to be paid from your residuary estate. However, this amount will be reduced by any specific bequest you make to someone other than your surviving spouse, as well as property passing to persons other than your spouse outside the will, such as life insurance proceeds and joint tenancy accounts.

WEEK TEN
MAP 10-4

*What Happens Without a Will?**
(refer to page 406)

Distribution of property. When a person dies without a will, his/her nonprobate assets transfer automatically to the new owners. Nonprobate assets include such things as joint tenancies, assets with named beneficiaries, and assets held in trust.

All other assets are subject to probate and are distributed according to state intestacy laws. Most intestacy laws rank heirs in the order listed below and give property to heirs in a lower ranking only when there are no living heirs in the preceding ranks.

1) Spouse, children, and other descendants

2) Parents

3) Siblings and children of deceased siblings

4) Other kin

5) The state

In most states, a surviving spouse inherits all property if neither spouse has children from another relationship. If either spouse has children from another relationship, the decedent's children may be entitled to a share of the probate estate. When other heirs inherit, most intestacy laws provide for equal division among heirs of the same rank. Most intestacy laws also include per stirpes rules, which allow the children of a deceased heir to represent their parent and split his/her share.

Estate administrators and guardians. Without a will, state law determines who will be the administrator, usually giving preference to closer-related heirs. When more than one heir is entitled to preference, those heirs must agree on who will act. The courts determine in case of disagreement. With or without a will, courts in most states play a role in the appointment of guardians for minors. Nomination of a guardian in a will carries great weight but does not always determine the final appointment.

Minor beneficiaries. When a minor inherits under intestacy laws, the property is generally held in a restricted account or controlled by a court-appointed fiduciary until the minor reaches the state's legal age. A separate court proceeding may be required to make these arrangements, increasing probate costs.

* Material reprinted with the permission of Quickfinder Incorporated *(www.quickfinder.com).*

WEEK TEN
MAP 10-5

*Functions of a Will**
(refer to page 406)

1) Leave property to someone who would not inherit under the state's intestacy laws (domestic partners, stepchildren, inlaws, friends, charities, pets, etc.).

2) Prevent a person who would inherit under the state's intestacy laws from inheriting.

3) Leave property to heirs in unequal shares or in amounts different from those in the intestacy law.

4) Name a personal representative for the estate.

5) Nominate a guardian for minor children.

6) Name a custodian to hold and manage assets passing to minors until the minors reach majority age.

7) Establish trusts to take effect at death, including:

  ➤ Bypass and marital trusts to minimize estate tax for married couples.

  ➤ Trusts which delay receipt of an inheritance by minor children beyond the state's majority age.

  ➤ Special-needs trusts which make funds available for disabled adults without disqualifying them from government benefits.

  ➤ Trusts which give a beneficiary the right to use property for a limited time.

* Material reprinted with the permission of Quickfinder Incorporated *(www.quickfinder.com)*.

Week Ten
MAP 10-6

What a Will Cannot Do*
(refer to page 406)

Distribute nonprobate assets. Wills have no effect on the transfer of most nonprobate assets. Wills do not override beneficiary designations or determine who receives property owned by joint tenants. If a married couple owns all property in joint tenancy, the will of the first spouse to die will have no effect. There are no probate assets to be distributed under the will.

Avoid probate. A will does nothing to avoid probate.

Change statutory rights. In many states, a surviving spouse by law is entitled to a share of the estate. A will generally cannot be used to disinherit a spouse, unless the spouse consents. In virtually all states, a will can be used to disinherit adult children and other heirs.

WEEK TEN
MAP 10-7

*Direct Transfers**
(refer to page 406)

Assets subject to direct transfer pass automatically at death without probate. Terms of a will generally do not determine who will receive these assets.

Beneficiary designations. Some assets can be transferred by filing a beneficiary designation with the insurance company or sponsoring organization (insurance policies, annuities, profitsharing and pension plan accounts, Keoghs, deferred-compensation plans, and IRAs).

Payable-on-death (POD) accounts allow the owner of an account to name payees to receive the account assets at the owner's death. POD accounts are generally available at banks, savings and loans, and credit unions. POD designations do not give the payees any rights in the account during the lifetime of the owner, and designated payees can be changed by the owner at any time.

Transfer-on-death (TOD) registration allows the owner of securities or security accounts to name beneficiaries to receive these assets at the owner's death. Availability of TOD accounts depends on state law. Taxpayers interested in this designation should seek information from their brokers. TOD registration avoids probate of the asset while giving the beneficiaries no rights over the accounts during the lifetime of the owner.

* Material reprinted with the permission of Quickfinder Incorporated (*www.quickfinder.com*).

Week Ten
MAP 10-8

*Tips on Handling a Will**
(refer to page 406)

➤ Consult an attorney. Although wills written without legal advice are generally valid, an attorney can help ensure that the will actually accomplishes the testator's objectives and that the language does not invite a probate battle.

➤ If a lawyer is not used, know the requirements for witnessing and executing valid wills in the state. Follow them precisely. A will is more likely to be invalidated for mistakes in execution than for mistakes in writing.

➤ Store the original will in a secure place, such as a safe deposit box, home safe, or with an attorney or county probate court. Inform a few trusted friends or family members of the location of the will so it can be found when needed.

➤ Review the will periodically. Do not write changes on an existing will or it may be invalidated. To make small changes, sign a formal codicil following the state's rules for witnessing and executing wills. To make substantial changes, execute a new will.

➤ If the testator moves from one state to another, have the will reviewed by an attorney in the new state.

➤ Include provisions for alternate dispositions of property in the event the primary beneficiary does not survive or a couple dies simultaneously.

* Material reprinted with the permission of Quickfinder Incorporated *(www.quickfinder.com)*.

Week Ten
MAP 10-9

Probate*
(refer to page 406)

The term *probate* generally refers to the court procedures for validating a will and passing ownership of property from a decedent to others. Most states have some form of simplified probate, allowing many estates to be probated informally with minimal court supervision.

Informal probate can be reduced to the following steps:

1) One of the heirs or the personal representative (PR) nominated in the will submits a written probate application.

2) If the application is acceptable, the court appoints the PR.

3) Court or PR publishes notice of probate.

4) PR notifies heirs, beneficiaries, and decedent's creditors of probate.

5) Court issues a document authorizing the PR to act (usually Letters Testamentary or Letters of Administration).

6) PR verifies the deadlines for probate filings and for tax returns and determines who will do the work (PR, attorney or tax preparer).

7) PR lists, values, and collects decedent's property and may sell the decedent's home or other assets.

8) PR files tax returns and pays tax and other debts of the decedent and estate.

9) PR makes a full accounting to the beneficiaries and distributes the remaining property according to the will or, if none, according to state law.

10) PR notifies the court that probate is complete. In most states, probate takes a minimum of four months. During that time, creditors have the right to assert claims for payment.

Probate costs depend on the complexity of the estate and the amount of professional assistance required. In some states, attorneys and PRs are allowed to charge a percentage of the estate; in other states, they are limited to flat or hourly rates. Factors that complicate probate include minor beneficiaries, disputes among heirs, insolvency, and other circumstances requiring formal procedures.

* Material reprinted with the permission of Quickfinder Incorporated *(www.quickfinder.com).*

Probate and Nonprobate Assets

Nonprobate assets transfer automatically to the new owners at death. A state court must authorize transfer of probate assets.

Probate Assets	Nonprobate Assets
• Assets owned individually by decedent • Decedent's share of assets owned as tenant in common • Life insurance, annuities and retirement assets without beneficiary designations • Life insurance, annuities and retirement assets if the estate is the named beneficiary or if the estate receives the asset because the named beneficiaries are deceased	• Assets owned jointly with right of survivorship • Life insurance, annuities and retirement assets with valid beneficiary designations other than the estate • Bank accounts and other assets with "pay on death" or trust designations • Securities or security accounts to be "transferred on death" • Assets in trust if instrument includes a plan for distribution after death

When Probate Is Required

In most states, probate is required when a decedent's probate assets exceed a threshold amount, generally $20,000–$100,000. Estates that have probate assets under the state's threshold do not need to be probated. Even if an estate is worth millions, a probate is not required if probate assets do not exceed the threshold. When probate is required, nonprobate assets are not included in the probate proceeding. A probate may be required regardless of the size of the estate if the decedent had sole guardianship or custody of a minor child.

If there is a will, is probate required? Yes, if the probate assets exceed the threshold amount. Making a will does not avoid probate. A will allows the decedent to name the representative of the estate, nominate a guardian for minor children, and determine who will receive property. In the absence of a will, these decisions are made according to state law.

If there is a surviving spouse, is probate required? Yes, if the probate assets exceed the threshold amount. Commonly, the estate of the first spouse to die does not require probate because the couple owned all assets jointly and there are few, if any, probate assets.

Small estates—collection of property by affidavit. Although estates under a state's threshold do not need to be probated, ownership of the probate assets will not pass automatically. Many states allow these assets to be claimed by affidavit. Commonly, the successors (those entitled to property either by will or, if none, under the state's intestacy laws) prepare a sworn statement that the estate is under the filing threshold and that they are entitled to the property. Third parties are generally allowed to transfer assets to the successors without verifying that the facts in the affidavit are true. Legal title passes directly from the decedent to the successors.

WEEK TEN
MAP 10-10

*Avoid Probate and Save?—Maybe Not**
(refer to page 407)

An estate planning tip is "avoid probate at all costs." For many estates, avoiding probate is a reasonable goal. For others, the costs of probate are less than the costs of alternatives.

Examples:

➤ **Revocable living trusts.** Revocable living trusts have many advantages and generally do avoid probate, but they are not for everyone. Costs of a living trust (setting up and transferring assets to a revocable living trust and transferring property from the living trust at death) can be higher than the costs of probate.

Clients who choose revocable living trusts solely to avoid probate costs should estimate the costs of probate and a simple estate plan in their locality and compare that with the cost of a revocable living trust. Attorney fees and other costs for setting up a revocable living trust must be paid up front. Probate costs are paid by the estate after death. If financial security during retirement is a concern, spending money now to avoid probate later may not be wise.

➤ **Joint tenancies.** Joint tenancies are easy and inexpensive. Placing noncash property in a joint tenancy in order to avoid probate can result in a capital gains tax in excess of the cost of probate.

* Material reprinted with the permission of Quickfinder Incorporated (*www.quickfinder.com*).

WEEK TEN
MAP 10-11
*Planning for Illness and Disability**
(refer to page 407)

Financial Affairs

When a person becomes too ill to manage his/her affairs, family members may be able to transact some business for the incapacitated person through the use of joint accounts and other banking arrangements. However, family members may be unable to deposit income checks, liquidate assets to pay bills, or agree to pay for hospital or nursing home care on behalf of the incapacitated person. If the person cannot communicate, the family members may be forced to apply to the court for appointment of a guardian or conservator to solve these problems. Guardianship/conservatorship procedures are expensive and frequently require the guardian/conservator to make annual accountings to the court. Two arrangements made in advance of incapacity are commonly used to avoid the need for a court-appointed guardian/conservator.

1) **Power of attorney.** Legal document allowing one person (the principal) to authorize another person (the agent) to act on the first person's behalf.

   a) **A power of attorney is general or special.**
   General. Grants the agent authority to perform nearly every transaction the grantor can perform.
   Special. Authorizes the agent to act only in matters specified in the document.

   b) **A power of attorney is durable or nondurable.**
   Durable. Effective when signed. It continues to be effective even if the principal becomes incapacitated or incompetent. The power expires at death. Some states also authorize a "springing" power of attorney, which becomes effective only when the principal becomes incapacitated. The usefulness of springing powers is limited by the need for satisfactory proof of incompetence before it will be accepted by third parties.
   Nondurable. Effective when signed. It expires if the principal becomes incompetent. If the principal never becomes incompetent, the power lasts until death. A nondurable power can also be drafted so that it expires on a date specified by the principal.

A general and durable power of attorney is the most commonly used form for disability planning since it gives the agent broad authority and continue to be effective during incapacity. The usefulness of a power of attorney depends on whether it is acceptable to third parties. Many states have laws to facilitate acceptance of powers of attorney. These states generally authorize a specific form of power of attorney (statutory form) and either protect third par-

* Material reprinted with the permission of Quickfinder Incorporated (*www.quickfinder.com*).

ties who accept the authorized form or penalize third parties who reject it. These laws generally require that the statutory language be used word-for-word in order for the protections or penalties to apply. Use of a state's statutory form is not required for a valid power of attorney. However, using the statutory form decreases the risk that the form will be rejected. **Caution:** Preprinted power of attorney forms are available in most states and can be executed without legal advice. Because the power of attorney gives broad authority to the agent, advise clients to choose agents they trust completely. Although the principal has the right to revoke the power at any time, once the document is signed and in the physical possession of the agent, it is difficult to revoke. Third parties who rely on the power of attorney generally are not liable to the principal for acts by the agent authorized in the document. A client being pressured to sign a power of attorney or who has doubts should consult with a lawyer of his/her own choosing before signing. Powers can be drafted to require two or more agents to act jointly or to limit agents' ability to transfer property to themselves.

2) **Living trusts.** Trust agreements establishing living trusts generally allow a successor trustee to step in and manage the trust property when the grantor becomes disabled. Because a living trust is considerably more expensive than a durable power of attorney, living trusts are generally not used solely for disability planning unless the grantor expects an extended period of disability or wants professional management of his/her assets during disability.

Health Care and Personal Decisions

When a person becomes unable to make decisions regarding his/her own care, a court-appointed guardian of the person may be required. Two documents, available in most states, can help avoid this possibility and also avoid conflict among family members regarding medical care.

1) **Health care power of attorney, or proxy.** Document that allows a person to appoint an agent to make health care decisions when he/she is unable to make or communicate such decisions. Unlike a living will, a person does not need to be in a terminal condition for the health care power of attorney to be effective.

2) **Living will.** Written statement of a person's wishes and instructions about the kind of medical treatment he/she wants if terminally ill. Although most people use living wills to instruct that no extraordinary measures be used to extend life, living wills are not limited to statements concerning withholding of life-sustaining treatment. A living will can be used to make any instruction about care, including that a person wants all available medical treatment.

Most states authorize some form of these documents, but state laws vary widely. A principal should sign forms accepted in all states where he/she expects to receive medical care, following the specific requirements of each state.

WEEK TEN
MAP 10-12

Common Forms of Co-Ownership*
(refer to page 408)

Joint tenancy. Property is owned equally by two or more persons who have rights of survivorship (i.e. when one joint tenant dies, the property passes automatically to the surviving tenants).

Tenancy in common. Similar to sole ownership. Tenants in common do not have rights of survivorship. At death, an owner's share passes to his/her estate and requires probate. Tenants in common may own unequal shares in proportion to their contributions.

Tenancy by the entirety. Exists only between spouses and is generally used for real property. It includes a right of survivorship. Neither spouse can encumber or dispose of the property without the other's permission. Dissolution creates a tenancy in common. Tenancies by the entirety are not recognized in all states.

Community property. Certain property acquired by a married couple while domiciled in a community property state (AZ, CA, ID, LA, NV, NM, TX, WA, and WI). Each spouse is considered to own one-half of community property. There is no right of survivorship in community property (when one spouse dies, the other spouse does not automatically inherit the deceased spouse's share). The earnings of both spouses and the property purchased with those earnings are generally community property. Property owned by one spouse prior to marriage and gifts or inheritances received by one spouse during the marriage are generally that spouse's separate property.

Life estates and remainder interests. A life estate is the right to use property or receive its income until death. A remainder interest is the right to receive whatever is left when all life estates end. Both life estates and remainder interests can be sold but are usually not marketable unless all interests are sold together. A life estate ends at the death of the original holder regardless of a sale. An owner of property can give or sell the remainder interest and retain the life estate.

Week Ten
MAP 10-13

Disadvantages to Joint Tenancies*
(refer to page 408)

Sales of joint tenancy gifts prior to death. Joint tenancies are commonly created to avoid probate or to qualify the owner for government assistance for nursing home care. This strategy may not be appropriate for a principal residence. If the home must be sold prior to death, a portion of the capital gains may be taxable to the other joint tenants if the home is not their principal residence. Even if the home is given back to the original owner, the exclusion may not be available if the house is sold within two years.

Between spouses. A spouse who inherits solely owned property from a spouse receives a stepped-up basis on the entire value of property, while a joint owner receives a stepped-up basis on half.

Spouses with assets over $1 million. Joint ownership can defeat estate tax planning. Married couples can shield a combined total of $2 million (in 2003) from estate tax. In order to do so, some assets must be owned individually by the first spouse to die and must pass to a trust or a person other than the surviving spouse. If all the couple's property passes to the surviving spouse as joint tenant, all property will be taxed to the survivor's estate.

Rights after death. People often place bank accounts in joint tenancy to allow another person to assist them with their financial affairs. A surviving joint tenant may receive the remaining assets at death even though this was not the owner's intention. Conversely, because so many people use joint accounts only for convenience, a joint tenant who is actually the intended beneficiary may be challenged by other heirs if there is no clear proof of the decedent's intention to make the gift. Many banks offer alternatives to allow another person access to the account during the owner's life without granting a right of survivorship.

Rights during life. Joint tenancies usually give the joint owners access to the assets even when the sole purpose of creating the joint tenancy is to pass property at death. Joint tenancies may also subject the assets to claims of the creditors and divorced spouses of all joint tenants.

Example: Donald wants his niece June to have his property when he dies. He changes the ownership of his bank accounts to make June a joint tenant and executes a deed for his house, making himself and June joint tenants. A few weeks later, June withdraws Donald's money from the bank and disappears. Donald's only recourse is to find June. He has no claims against the bank for releasing the funds. Donald also now needs June's written consent to sell his house.

* Material reprinted with the permission of Quickfinder Incorporated (*www.quickfinder.com*).

Week Ten
MAP 10-14

Community Property and Asset Ownership
(refer to page 408)

For those living in AZ, CA, ID, LA, NV, NM, TX, WA, and WI

General Rule: Community Property is qualified for a full step-up in basis on the death of one of the owners, whereas only the decedent's share receives this step-up if the property is held jointly.

Planning Point: By dissolving joint tenancy ownership in community property states on certain assets, significant taxes can be saved.

Example:

Say Greg and Ginger lived in Arizona instead of Colorado and they purchased an unimproved lot for $40,000. If the value of that lot in 20 years were $200,000 and they chose to sell the property, they would pay a 15–20 percent capital gains tax rate on the gain of $160,000 ($32,000 tax), leaving them with approximately $168,000.

If, they owned this property jointly and Greg died, Ginger would be treated as the sole owner. If she, the following year, decided to sell the property for the same $200,000, she would end up owing capital gains tax on the gain of $200,000 less $20,000 (Ginger's share of the purchase price) less $100,000 (Greg's half-interest valued at his date of death), for a gain of $80,000 and a capital gains tax of $16,000. Ginger would end up with $184,000.

On the other hand, if Greg and Ginger held the property as community property, Ginger would also receive a step-up in basis in her half ownership of the property to the value of the property on the date of Greg's death. If Ginger sold the property shortly after Greg's death when the value was the same, she would have no gain. She would walk away from the sale with the full $200,000 in her pocket.

A little planning saved Ginger as much as $32,000 in tax on a $200,000 sale.

Please keep in mind that these basis rules will change in 2010 if Congress decides to repeal the estate tax.

WEEK TEN
MAP 10-14a

Basic Structure of Estate Plan for Married Couples (refer to page 408)

A common estate plan for married couples whose combined net worth exceeds the applicable exclusion amount ($1 million for 2002 and 2003) is the use of the marital deduction in conjunction with the family-owned-business deduction and a credit-shelter (bypass) trust. Assets worth $1 million are used to fund the bypass trust, and the family-owned-business deduction and the marital deduction shelter the other assets from estate tax.

The assets sheltered by the marital deduction may also be placed in a trust, generally referred to as a marital trust. When two trusts are used, the arrangement is often referred to as an A-B Trust. Nontax reasons generally drive a decision to use a trust to hold assets that do not pass outright to a surviving spouse.

The estate and generation-skipping transfer taxes are repealed for decedents dying after December 31, 2009. However, under current law, they will be reinstated in 2011. The applicable exclusion amount for estate tax purposes will gradually increase to a maximum of $3.5 million. (The GST exemption remains at $1,000,000, adjusted for inflation, until 2004 when it becomes the same as the estate tax applicable exclusion amount.)

In the case of an A-B Trust estate plan, the increase in the applicable exclusion amount to $3.5 million will shift substantially more wealth to the bypass trust. Thus, planners should confirm that this shift in wealth is consistent with the client's and surviving spouse's estate planning goals. In many instances, the client may want to cap the bequest to the bypass trust at an amount less than the applicable exclusion amount.

Bypass Trust

This trust gets its name from the fact that the trust assets bypass (i.e., are not included in) your surviving spouse's gross estate. To make this work, the assets cannot qualify for the marital deduction in your estate. However, your surviving spouse is given as much access to and control over the assets as possible.

A bypass trust is usually funded with assets equal in value to the applicable exclusion amount ($1 million for 2002 and 2003). However, if you used part of the applicable exclusion amount for gifts made during your life, you would reduce the amount of assets transferred to the bypass trust by this amount. This amount is used because it is the maximum value of assets that you can transfer to someone (other than your spouse or charity) free of estate tax.

To accomplish this, your surviving spouse can be given certain rights and control over the assets but not absolute ownership. Your surviving spouse may be entitled to the following interests and rights without causing the marital deduction to apply:

➤ an income interest for life;

➤ certain limited powers of appointment;

➤ the right to receive distributions at the trustee's discretion or to invade corpus for health, education, support, and maintenance; and

➤ a noncumulative power to withdraw corpus annually, limited to the greater of $5,000 or 5 percent of the value of the trust corpus at the time such power is exercisable.

Your spouse's possession of only these limited rights will ensure the trust assets are not included in your spouse's estate, thus escaping estate tax entirely.

Typically, assets that will appreciate in value (e.g., growth stocks and appreciating real estate) are best suited for the bypass trust, since their appreciation will also escape inclusion in your surviving spouse's estate. In many cases, however, this may not be possible.

Marital Trust

In the A-B Trust structure, two trusts are established. Assets to be sheltered by your applicable exclusion amount (i.e., $1 million for 2002 and 2003) are used to fund the bypass trust. A marital trust is used to hold property from your estate for the benefit of your surviving spouse (as opposed to your spouse being the direct beneficiary). A marital trust receives the decedent's property that is held for the benefit of the surviving spouse. The marital trust must meet certain formalities to qualify for the marital deduction.

1. All trust accounting income is payable to the surviving spouse at least annually.

2. The surviving spouse has a general power of appointment either during lifetime, by will, or both, over trust assets (i.e., the unlimited power of the surviving spouse or his/her estate to determine who will receive the assets at some future time).

3. Generally, the trust may hold unproductive assets (i.e. assets that do not generate current income) only if the trust document requires, or permits the surviving spouse to require the trustee to either make the property productive or convert it to productive property within a reasonable time. However, if the surviving spouse has unlimited lifetime general power of appointment over the trust, the trust property does not have to be productive.

An advantage to using this type of marital trust is that it allows the surviving spouse additional time to determine who will ultimately receive the remainder interest in the decedent's property when perhaps more facts and circumstances are known. Factors such as divorce, financial hardships, and longer life expectancies create the need for flexibility, even after one's own death.

A disadvantage to this trust is that unless the surviving spouse has an unlimited general power of appointment, it generally requires trust assets to produce income. The trustee may be forced (by either the surviving spouse or the trust document) to dispose of a nonproductive asset that the decedent may have wanted to have remain in the family (such as undeveloped real estate).

Another possible disadvantage to the general power of appointment trust is that it gives the surviving spouse ultimate control of disposition of the trust property. Thus, the spouse may pass the trust assets to a beneficiary of whom the decedent does not approve (e.g., children of a subsequent marriage). Additionally, state law may allow the surviving spouse's or the estate's creditors to reach trust assets.

Estate Trust. This trust must meet the following requirements:

1. Trust income, or corpus, may be paid to the surviving spouse at the trustee's discretion.

2. Upon the death of the surviving spouse, the remaining trust property and undistributed income must pass to the estate of the surviving spouse.

Under these requirements, an estate trust does not have to provide the surviving spouse with trust income for life as long as the remaining trust property passes to the surviving spouse's estate upon his/her death. If someone other than the surviving spouse is the income beneficiary, the marital deduction is the present value of the remainder payable to the estate of the surviving spouse.

Estate trusts do not have to produce income. If unproductive assets are used to fund a general power of appointment trust or a QTIP trust, the trustee generally must be directed (through the trust document or the surviving spouse) to convert them to productive assets. The decedent may not wish to convey such a power for fear that it would not be exercised judiciously.

One possible disadvantage to the estate trust is that it gives the surviving spouse complete control of disposition of the trust property at death. Such power may be a concern to a decedent with children from a former marriage. Another potential disadvantage is exposure of assets included in the spouse's estate to the claims of creditors. Finally, since the ultimate disposition of the assets will be controlled by the surviving spouse's will, the property will be subject to probate at the surviving spouse's death. Another disadvantage is the income tax rate structure for trusts, which effectively penalizes trusts that accumulate income. Thus, the estate trust is rarely used as the marital trust.

Qualified Terminable Interest Property Trust. A qualified terminable interest property (QTIP) trust (also called a marital-deduction trust) allows a transfer of property that would not otherwise be eligible (because of the terminable interest rule) to qualify for the marital deduction. An interest in property is a terminable interest if it will terminate or fail because of the passage of time or because of the occurrence or nonoccurrence of an event or contingency (such as the death or remarriage of the surviving spouse). Thus, for example, life estates, terms for years, and annuities, are terminable interests because they will terminate at some designated point in time.

The QTIP trust provides a surviving spouse with an income interest for life and enables an estate owner to control the disposition of the remainder interest in the trust after the surviving spouse's death. The ability of the decedent to direct who will be the ultimate beneficiary of the QTIP trust assets is a primary consideration in choosing to use a QTIP trust.

However, the property does not escape estate tax entirely. The fair market value of the property at the date of the surviving spouse's death is included in the surviving spouse's estate. A QTIP trust must meet the following requirements:

1. All trust accounting income is payable to the surviving spouse, at least annually.

2. No one, including the surviving spouse, has a power to appoint or distribute the assets of the trust during the life of the surviving spouse to any person other than the surviving spouse. However, the surviving spouse can be permitted to appoint the property at his/her death via his/her will, although one of the principal reasons for using a QTIP trust is to allow the first spouse to die to designate who will receive the property at the surviving spouse's death. But, the surviving spouse may be given a special power of appointment exercisable at death to change the allocation of assets among family members.

3. The trust may hold unproductive assets (i.e. ones not generating current income) only if the trust document requires, or permits the surviving spouse to require, the trustee to either make the property productive or convert it to productive property within a reasonable time. However, there are certain exceptions for residential property or tangible assets held for use by the surviving spouse.

The executor of the decedent's estate must elect on a timely filed estate tax return to have some or all of the trust property qualify for the marital deduction.

WEEK TEN
MAP 10-15[*]

Flowchart of Basic A-B Trust Planning Structure
(refer to page 408)

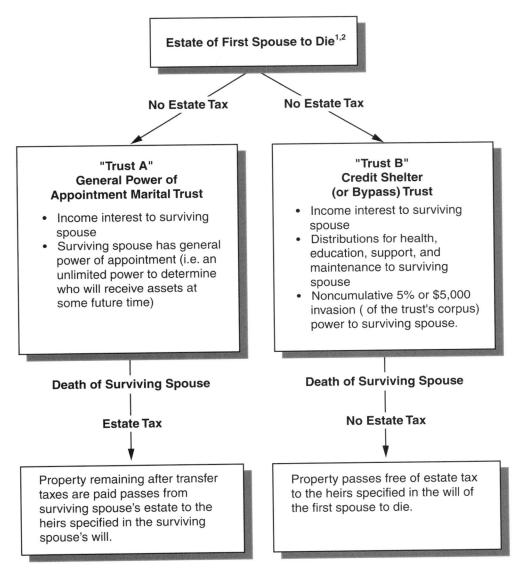

Estate of First Spouse to Die[1,2]

No Estate Tax — No Estate Tax

"Trust A"
General Power of
Appointment Marital Trust

- Income interest to surviving spouse
- Surviving spouse has general power of appointment (i.e. an unlimited power to determine who will receive assets at some future time)

"Trust B"
Credit Shelter
(or Bypass) Trust

- Income interest to surviving spouse
- Distributions for health, education, support, and maintenance to surviving spouse
- Noncumulative 5% or $5,000 invasion (of the trust's corpus) power to surviving spouse.

Death of Surviving Spouse

Estate Tax

Property remaining after transfer taxes are paid passes from surviving spouse's estate to the heirs specified in the surviving spouse's will.

Death of Surviving Spouse

No Estate Tax

Property passes free of estate tax to the heirs specified in the will of the first spouse to die.

Notes:

[1] If applicable, the family-owned-business deduction is to be considered when using the basic A-B Trust planning structure.

[2] It is common for each spouse's will to include this structure.

WEEK TEN
MAP 10-16[*]

Flowchart of Basic A-B-C Trust Planning Structure
(refer to page 409)

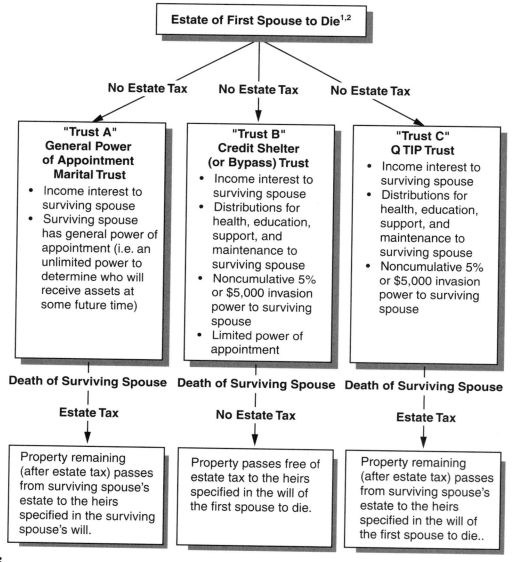

Notes:

[1] If applicable, the family-owned-business deduction is to be considered when using the basic A-B-C Trust planning structure.

[2] Each spouse's will can include this structure, and it is common for this to be the case since they don't typically know who will die first.

WEEK TEN
MAP 10-17

*Trusts**
(refer to page 409)

A trust is a legal entity in which title to property is held by one person for the benefit of another. The terms and conditions of a trust are set out in the written instrument that creates the trust, usually a will or trust agreement. Every trust is also governed by the laws of the state or other local jurisdiction in which it is established. The governing state law is usually designated in the written instrument. The laws of that state govern the trust if a term is not addressed by the written instrument or if a dispute arises.

Trusts are used in estate planning to postpone receipt of a gift or inheritance and to provide management of assets for beneficiaries who are unable to personally manage them.

Parties to a trust:

1) **Grantor.** Creates the trust, determining its terms and conditions and generally gives assets to the trust.

2) **Trustee.** Holds legal title to the assets, manages the property, and makes distributions from the trust. A trustee is appointed by the grantor in the trust instrument and must follow its terms and conditions.

3) **Beneficiaries.** Persons selected by the grantor to benefit from the trust. Trusts commonly have different types of beneficiaries. Income beneficiaries have a right to receive income earned by the trust, generally paid annually. An income right can end at the beneficiary's death, on the happening of a specific event, or at a set time. Remainder beneficiaries have the right to receive the remaining assets when the trust ends.

A trust instrument may also allow distributions of principal prior to the termination of the trust, even though such distributions reduce the value of the remainder interest.

* Material reprinted with the permission of Quickfinder Incorporated *(www.quickfinder.com)*.

Types of Estate Planning Trusts*
(refer to page 409)

Testamentary trust. Terms creating and governing a testamentary trust are included in a will. The trust comes into existence only at the grantor's death, at which time it is irrevocable. The grantor can change the trust terms any time prior to death by revoking or amending the will. Testamentary trusts can be contingent. If the contingency is not met at the time of the grantor's death, the trust is not created.

Living trust (inter-vivos trust). Established during the grantor's life when he/she executes a trust agreement and transfers property to the trustee. A living trust can expire at the grantor's death or continue to exist after that time. Property held in a living trust is generally distributed to the ultimate beneficiaries under the terms of the trust agreement and not by the will.

Two types of living trusts:

1) **Revocable.** Allows the grantor to cancel or change provisions of the trust.

2) **Irrevocable.** Takes assets completely out of the control of the grantor.

Irrevocable Life Insurance Trusts
(refer to page 409)

One of the best methods of keeping life insurance proceeds out of your estate and ensuring that your estate has the necessary amount of liquidity is to create an irrevocable life insurance trust. Such a trust can have the following advantages and disadvantages:

Advantages:

➤ The trust can remove the insurance proceeds from the estates of both you and your spouse, while at the same time making those proceeds available to both your surviving spouse and your estate.

➤ You can select the trustee who will manage the insurance proceeds and specify how such proceeds should be invested. (This advantage also applies to a revocable trust, but a revocable trust does not keep insurance proceeds out of your estate.)

➤ You can determine (via the trust instrument) when beneficiaries receive the proceeds. Alternatively, you can provide the trustee with the discretion to decide the amount and timing of distributions to beneficiaries, depending upon their special needs.

➤ Assets in the trust, whether a life insurance policy or otherwise, are not subject to probate. Thus, insurance proceeds can generally be made available to the trust's beneficiaries more quickly than if the proceeds passed through your estate first.

➤ Trust assets can be protected from creditor claims.

Disadvantages:

➤ You generally lose the ability to completely control the trust's assets.

➤ Compared to holding a life insurance policy outright, an irrevocable life insurance trust causes you to incur legal (and perhaps accounting, tax preparation, and trustee) expenses that would not otherwise be incurred.

➤ Holding a policy through a trust is more complex than holding it outright.

➤ The trust must have special (e.g., Crummey) provisions in order for gifts to the trust to qualify for the annual gift tax exclusion ($11,000 for 2003).

➤ If an existing life insurance policy is transferred to an irrevocable trust, and you are married and die within three years of the transfer, the estate tax could be more than if the trust were never formed. This result would occur because if the policy were not held in the trust, the policy proceeds included in your estate would presumably qualify for the marital deduction, which would eliminate any estate tax. If the insurance policy is held in the trust and included in your estate, the proceeds might not qualify for the marital deduction. This problem can be avoided by having the trust purchase life insurance directly or by including a provision in the trust instrument that has the effect of qualifying the proceeds for the marital deduction (or some other deductible provision) in the event the proceeds are included in your gross estate.

WEEK TEN
MAP 10-20

Comparison of Various Types of Transfers to Minors
(refer to page 409)

	Outright Gift	Guardianship	UGMA/UTMA	Crummey Trust	Section 2503(b) Trust	Section 2503(c) Trust
Description/ requirements of transfer	Property vests in the minor at date of transfer.	Property vests in the minor at the date of transfer.	Property vests in the minor at the date of transfer. Assets must be distributed by age 18, 21, or other age, as stipulated by state law.	Beneficiaries must have an unrestricted power to invade the trust and remove the assets. Notice must be given to beneficiaries of any additions to the trust subject to invasion. Beneficiary must be given a reasonable time to exercise the power to invade.	Income must be distributed to the beneficiary at least annually. Corpus can be retained by the trust. (There is no requirement that the trust terminate when the beneficiary turns age 21.)	Trustee must have the power to use property and/or income for the benefit of the donee until age 21. The donee must receive all accumulated income and corpus at age 21. If donee dies before age 21, all accumulated income and corpus must pass to the donee's estate or as the donee appoints.
Amount of gift	Fair market value (FMV).	FMV.	FMV.	FMV.	Generally FMV.	Generally FMV.
Amount of current year transfer qualifying for annual exclusion	Entire FMV up to the annual exclusion amount ($11,000 for 2003).	Entire FMV up to the annual exclusion amount ($11,000 for 2003).	Entire FMV up to the annual exclusion amount ($11,000 for 2003).	FMV of property subject to the withdrawal power [up to the annual exclusion amount ($11,000 for 2003)].	FMV of income interest [up to the annual exclusion amount ($11,000 for 2003)].	Generally FMV [up to the annual exclusion amount ($11,000 for 2003)].
Fiduciary/ custodian selection option	N/A	Court appoints.	Donor selects.	Donor/Settlor (person who funds the trust) selects.	Donor/Settlor (person who funds the trust) selects.	Donor/Settlor (person who funds the trust) selects.
Consequences of donor also being custodian/ fiduciary	N/A	Included in donor's estate if guardian at the time of death.	Included in donor's estate if custodian at the time of death.	If donor has the discretionary power to distribute income and corpus, then included in donor's estate.	If donor has the discretionary power to distribute corpus, then included in donor's estate.	If donor has the discretionary power to distribute income and corpus, then included in the donor's estate.
Income distribution	Donee/minor has the right to all income.	May be used to benefit the donee/minor.	May accumulate in account or be distributed to or for the benefit of the minor/donee.	Trustee must follow trust instrument. May accumulate income in trust or be distributed to beneficiary.	Must be distributed to beneficiary at least annually.	Trustee must follow trust instrument. May accumulate income in trust or be distributed to the beneficiary.
Taxation of income	To minor/ donee. If under age 14, taxed at parents' marginal rates (i.e., kiddie tax rules).	To minor/ donee. If under age 14, taxed at parents' marginal rates (i.e., kiddie tax rules).	To minor/ donee. If under age 14, taxed at parents' marginal rates. If income is used to satisfy the donor/ grantor's legal obligation to support, that portion of income is taxed	Generally, taxed at trust level unless distributed. IRS may consider donee to be the owner of any portion subject to withdrawal power. If distributed.	Donee/beneficiary is taxed on income since it is required to be distributed. If income is used to satisfy the donor/ grantor's legal obligation to support, then that portion of income is taxed to the	Taxed at trust level unless distributed. If distributed, taxed to beneficiary. If any of the income is used to satisfy the donor/ grantor's legal obligation to support, that portion of income is taxed to the donor/grantor.

	Outright Gift	Guardianship	UGMA/UTMA	Crummey Trust	Section 2503(b) Trust	Section 2503(c) Trust
			to the donor/grantor.	taxed to beneficiary. If income is used to satisfy the donor/grantor's legal obligation to support, that portion of income is taxed to the donor/grantor.	donor/grantor.	
Accounting or income tax return requirements	Donee files Form 1040 (or possibly included on parents' return).	A formal accounting required by the court. Donee files Form 1040 (or possibly included on parents' return).	Donee files Form 1040 (or possibly included on parents' return).	Trust files Form 1041 with Schedule K-1 reporting income to beneficiary if distributions are made. Trust may be a grantor trust to extent of portion subject to beneficiary withdrawal power.	Trust files Form 1041 with Schedule K-1 reporting income to beneficiary. Beneficiary files Form 1040.	Trust files Form 1041 with Schedule K-1 reporting income to beneficiary if distributions are made. Beneficiary files Form 1040.
Fiduciary responsibility regarding management of property	N/A	Typically, limitations are placed on guardian with court approval necessary for transactions outside of these limitations.	State statute may limit the type of investments but there are no formal approvals necessary.	Generally, "prudent man" or "prudent investor" standard although instrument may provide limitations and/or discretion.	Generally, "prudent man" or "prudent investor" standard although instrument may provide limitations and/or discretion.	Generally, "prudent man" or "prudent investor" standard although instrument may provide limitations and/or discretion.
Termination of guardian/ fiduciary relationship	N/A	Age of majority as determined under state law.	Determined under state law.	Trust instrument determines termination.	Trust instrument determines termination.	Age 21.
What happens if donee/ beneficiary dies before property is distributed?	Property passes to donee's estate and will generally pass to heirs under state law. Typically, the parents receive the property because minors usually cannot make a valid will under state law.	Property passes to donee's estate and will generally pass to heirs under state law. Typically, the parents receive the property because minors usually cannot make a valid will under state law.	Property passes to donee's estate and will generally pass to heirs under state law. Typically, the parents receive the property because minors usually cannot make a valid will under state law.	Property distributed per the terms of the trust instrument.	Property distributed per the terms of the trust instrument.	Property passes to the donee's estate or can be directed by donee's appointee (under general power of appointment).
Included in gross estate of donee/ beneficiary	Yes.	Yes.	Yes.	Yes-if instrument provides for distribution to estate. No if trust is distributed to others.	No-unless trust instrument requires payment to donee's estate or the donee has a general power of appointment over the trust property.	Yes-because instrument requires distribution to donee's estate or to donee's appointee under a general power of appointment.

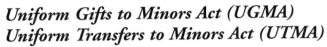

*UGMA/UTMA Transfers**
(refer to page 409)

Uniform Gifts to Minors Act (UGMA)
Uniform Transfers to Minors Act (UTMA)

Generally, minors are not legally allowed to own money or property.

For this reason, each state has a uniform gifts to minors act or a uniform transfers to minors act either of which is used to facilitate ownership of assets by children. A custodial account created under a state's UGMA is similar to a trust, except terms are set in statute instead of requiring a separate trust document.

Most banks, brokers, and other financial institutions will set up UGMA accounts for minor beneficiaries.

Under a state's UGMA, legal title to money or property is held in a custodial account. The custodian, often a parent, has a fiduciary responsibility to manage the account in a prudent manner for benefit of the child. When the child reaches the age of majority, usually 18, control of the account transfers to the child. Some states allow the custodian to retain control until the child reaches age 21.

Income tax. A UGMA account is set up using the child's Social Security number and income is taxed to the child. *Exception:* Income used by the parent to pay for support of the minor child is taxable to the parent if the parent has a legal obligation to make such payments.

Gift/estate tax. A gift in trust generally does not qualify for the $11,000 annual gift exclusion because the gift represents a future interest. However, gifts made to UGMA accounts are considered gifts of present interest and therefore qualify for the $11,000 annual gift exclusion.

Caution: It may be a good planning technique to appoint someone other than the donor as custodian of the child's account. If the donor is also the custodian, the donor continues to exercise substantial control over the assets. The value of the gift is therefore includable in the gross estate of the donor for federal estate tax purposes. This effectively eliminates the benefits of the $11,000 annual gift exclusion.

* Material reprinted with the permission of Quickfinder Incorporated *(www.quickfinder.com)*.

*Lifetime Gifts and Annual Exclusion** *(refer to page 410)*

Annual Gift Tax Exclusion

A taxpayer can give $11,000 per person to any number of recipients in a calendar year without paying federal estate and gift tax. An unlimited amount can be given each year, as long as no recipient receives more than $11,000. Gifts that qualify for this annual exclusion are never taxed—no gift tax is owed when the gift is made, and the gift is not taxed at death. If a gift is over $11,000, only the excess is a taxable gift. The annual exclusion is indexed for inflation. It increased from $10,000 to $11,000 in 2002 and will change again when cost-of-living adjustments reach the next $1,000 multiple.

Present interest required. In order to qualify for the annual exclusion, a gift must be a present interest—the recipient must have all immediate rights to the use, possession, enjoyment, and income of the property. The annual exclusion does not apply to a future interest—the recipient's rights to benefit from the property begin at some future date. Most gifts to trusts do not qualify for the exclusion because they are gifts of future interests. Exceptions include gifts to a minor's trust.

Gifts from married couples. Each spouse has an annual exclusion. Couples can therefore transfer a combined total of $22,000 to a single recipient each year.

Gift splitting. If a gift in excess of $11,000 is made by only one spouse, the couple can use both annual exclusions by filing gift tax returns electing to split gifts. A gift-splitting election applies to all gifts made by the couple in a calendar year and attributes one-half of each gift to each spouse.

Qualified Transfers

Tuition and Medical Care. Direct payment of medical expenses or tuition for another person is not a gift for gift tax purposes [IRC §2503(e)]. Payment must be made to the medical provider or school and not to the beneficiary. Qualified transfers are not reported on Form 709. Payments for books, supplies, dormitory fees, and board do not qualify. Medical payments can cover any type of expense deductible for income tax purposes, including payment of insurance premiums. Tuition for part-time students qualifies. The beneficiary of a qualified transfer does not need to be related to the taxpayer. An annual exclusion gift can also be made to the beneficiary of a qualified transfer.

Political transfers. A transfer to a political organization as defined in Section 527(e)(1) for use by the organization is not a taxable gift and does not need to be reported on a gift tax return.

Week Ten
MAP 10-23

Charitable Gifts—Transfers at Death vs. Lifetime Gifts*
(refer to page 410)

Most transfers for charitable and public purposes are fully deductible on gift tax returns as well as on the estate tax return.

Transfers at Death vs. Lifetime Gifts

Although gifts made to charity at a taxpayer's death can be deducted on the estate tax return, the value of the donated property is generally not allowed as an income-tax deduction. Most lifetime gifts, on the other hand, are deductible in full on the gift-tax return and also allowed as income-tax deductions. Taxpayers who have decided to include charitable gifts in their estate plans can often increase the value of their after-tax estates by making charitable gifts before death or during high-income years when they can take full advantage of the income-tax deductions. Unlike gifts to family members, there is no capital gains tax incentive to postpone charitable gifts of appreciated property until death.

Gifts of Tax-deferred Assets

Tax-deferred assets are subject to income tax even though they are received on the death of the owner. In order to minimize income tax, tax-deferred savings may be given to the beneficiary with the lowest income tax rate. Making a qualified charity the beneficiary of tax-deferred assets rather than other assets can increase the after-tax value of the estate.

* Material reprinted with the permission of Quickfinder Incorporated (*www.quickfinder.com*).

WEEK TEN
MAP 10-24

*Charitable Gifts and Bequests—Partial Interests** *
(refer to page 410)

Partial Interests (Split Interests)

When a transfer of property has both charitable and noncharitable beneficiaries, the value of the interest passing to charity is deductible only if the transfer is one of the following:

1) **Residence or farm remainder:** [IRC §170(f)(3)(B)]. A taxpayer can transfer a remainder interest in a personal residence or farm by signing and recording a deed. The transfer gives the charity the right to receive the property at the taxpayer's death. The owner retains a life estate, which is the right to own and use the property until death as if the transfer of the remainder had not occurred. The transfer of a remainder is a completed gift and is irrevocable—the taxpayer generally cannot sell the property unless the charitable recipient agrees to sell its remainder interest. The taxpayer can claim both an income-tax and a gift-tax deduction for the value of the remainder transferred to the charity. The deductions apply only to a home or farm; furnishings in the home are not included. Remainder interests in other types of property must be given in trust to be deductible.

2) **Qualified conservation contributions.** The value of an interest given to a government agency or nonprofit holding company strictly for conservation purposes is deductible for both income, estate, and gift-tax purposes. The interest may be an outright gift, a remainder, or a permanent restriction on the use of the land (qualified conservation easement). Conservation purposes include protection of wildlife, open spaces, and public recreation lands, as well as protection of historically important lands or structures [IRC §170(h), IRC §2055(f)]. The Tax Relief Act of 1997 added an additional estate-tax exclusion of up to 40 percent of the value of land subject to a qualified easement. Values are determined as of the date of contribution.

3) **Charitable remainder trusts.** (IRC §664). Charitable remainder trusts (CRTs) are generally used by taxpayers who would otherwise make a charitable gift at death. A CRT allows the taxpayer to receive income from donated property until death and claim an income tax deduction that would not be available on a transfer at death.

The maker of a CRT transfers some type of income-producing property into trust. The maker, or other beneficiaries designated by the maker, receives annual payments from the trust for life or for a specified number of years. When the last beneficiary dies, the charities selected by the maker receive the trust assets. The transfer of the asset to the trust is a completed gift which must be reported on a gift-tax return. The maker of the

* Material reprinted with the permission of Quickfinder Incorporated (*www.quickfinder.com*).

trust receives a gift-tax deduction for the current value of the charity's remainder interest. The maker also can generally claim an income-tax deduction in the same amount in the year of transfer. Trust income is generally taxable to the noncharitable beneficiaries who receive Schedule K-1 from the trust annually.

A taxpayer may be able to increase the income stream from an asset by donating it to a CRT. The trust can sell a poorly performing, low-basis asset without paying capital gains tax [IRC §664(c)] and reinvest the funds to produce higher returns.

WEEK TEN
MAP 10-25

*Estate Planning with Life Insurance**
(refer to page 411)

The tax value of an insurance policy during the insured's life is usually considerably less than the insurance proceeds payable at death. Because of the difference in these values, a taxpayer can reduce estate tax by transferring insurance policies to other owners prior to death. The policy is subject to gift tax at the time of transfer, but the proceeds are not subject to estate tax if the insured lives more than three years after transferring the policy. The gift tax value is generally the cost of the policy (new policy), the cost of the unexpired premium (term insurance), or the cost of a comparable policy on a person of the insured's age (single premium policy). The owner should request that the insurer prepare Form 712, *Life Insurance Statement,* to value the asset. See Section 25.2512-6 for more information on valuation.

Example: *Howard owns a policy on his life with a face value of $200,000. His children are the beneficiaries. He transfers ownership to his children in 1995. The transfer is a completed gift, which Howard reports on his 1995 gift tax return. The insurer values the gift at $44,000—the amount the insurer would charge in 1995 for a similar contract on the life of a person Howard's age. When Howard dies in 2002, the $200,000 proceeds paid to his children are not subject to estate tax.*

A taxpayer can also gift funds that are used by others to purchase insurance on the taxpayer's life. Although the funds are subject to gift tax, the proceeds are not taxed at the insured's death even if the insured dies within three years of making the gift. The three-year rule does not apply to gifts of cash even if used to purchase insurance.

WEEK TEN
MAP 10-26

Unmarried Couples Should Consider Living-Together Documents (refer to page 411)

Many unmarried couples living together should have several written legal documents to serve as a proxy in place of a marriage contract and to help minimize potential financial disputes or complications in the event of a breakup or death, say Certified Financial Planner™ professionals.

Unmarried couples face many of the same financial issues as married couples but without benefit of marital laws: property rights, inheritances, employee benefits, and division of income and debts, for example. Unmarried couples should consider signing these legal documents when one or both bring substantial assets or debts to the relationship, they plan to stay together a long time, children are involved, or they plan to buy a home or move together into one of their respective homes.

The first key document is a nonmarital agreement, commonly called a "living together" or "domestic partner" agreement. This agreement is similar to a prenuptial agreement that a couple with accumulated assets might sign before they marry.

The agreement can be as specific or as broad as you wish to make it. Typically, the agreement will spell out how assets and income will be divvied up during a relationship or after a relationship, should it end. For example, it might spell out what portion each will contribute to the monthly bills. Will paychecks be pooled or kept separate? Will assets each person brings to the relationship be pooled or kept separate? What about assets inherited by one person during the relationship? Will he/she share employee benefits if the employer allows it? Will ownership of property bought during the relationship be based on who actually buys the property, kept proportional to the income each party earns, or split down the middle? How will existing or future debts be handled? (It's often best to avoid jointly titled credit cards). How will property be divided at separation or death?

A living-together agreement is especially important when the purchase of a major asset is involved, such as a home. How will ownership be titled? Who pays what portion of the downpayment and monthly mortgage, and how will any gains from the sale of the house be split up?

The agreement also might spell out a method for resolving future financial disagreements, such as using third-party mediation before resorting to the courts. Some agreements even go so far as to delineate who will cook and wash dishes and take out the trash, though some legal experts recommend a separate agreement be drafted for nonfinancial issues.

While there is little in the way of state statutes, most courts recognize living-together agreements—even oral agreements in some cases. But interpretations vary, so you'll want to hire an attorney (perhaps one for each party) to draft the agreement based on your specific needs and local court rulings.

A living-together agreement is only a start, however. Unmarried couples also should have a will, living will, and powers of attorney—legal documents even married couples should have. A power of attorney allows the partner to step in financially should the other become incapacitated. You can rescind such a power as long as you're mentally competent, so don't feel you're stuck with it.

A living will spells out what life-sustaining medical treatment you wish or don't wish should you become incapacitated, and the medical power of attorney grants your partner or other appointed agent, such as a relative, the legal authority to make medical decisions on your behalf, usually based on what you spell out in your living will. While married couples should have such documents, they are especially important to unmarried couples because relatives would otherwise likely supercede such decisions.

The same goes for a will. While married couples should have wills, state statute will typically—though not always—distribute property to the surviving spouse where there is no will. For an unmarried couple without a will, however, it's unlikely property or custody of a child will go to the surviving partner.

All these agreements may sound unromantic, but many relationships, unmarried ones as well as married ones, can end in bitter feuds. Written agreements not only can minimize such feuds, they can actually promote a healthier relationship by focusing attention on financial issues central to all relationships.

April 2003—This column is produced by the Financial Planning Association, the membership organization for the financial planning community, and is provided by Paul Lemon, CFP™, CPA, a local member in good standing of the FPA.

Week Ten
MAP 10-27

Helpful Estate Planning Articles on
www.tenweeks.com
(refer to page 411)

Article Title	Date of Article
"Should You Name a Trust as Beneficiary of Your Retirement Plan?"	July, 2003
"Children Not Prepared for Financial World"	July, 2003
"13 Estate Planning Terms You Should Know"	May, 2003
"The Benefits of Planned Charitable Giving"	July, 2002
"Eight Estate Planning Strategies You Should Know"	April, 2002
"Keys to a Comprehensive Will"	February, 2002
"Prepare Now for 'New' 2010 Tax on Inherited Property"	August, 2001
"Estate Tax Changes Require Careful Planning"	July, 2001
"Keeping the Peace Among Your Heirs"	February, 2001
"How Much Money Should You Pass on to Your Kids?"	August, 2000
"Stop: Look Before Rolling Over Company Stock Into an IRA"	May, 2000
"Choosing an Executor for Your Estate—a Critical Task"	April, 2000

WEEK TEN
MAP 10-28

What Is the Federal Estate Tax?
(refer to page 411)

The federal estate tax is imposed on property transfers at your death. The tax is calculated by applying the unified tax rates (which are the same rates used in computing the gift tax) to the value of the property transferred. Generally, your property is valued at the date of your death, or, if elected, six months after your date of death. Your estate is primarily liable for paying any tax due—generally within nine months after your date of death. However, in certain situations, your estate can elect to pay the tax in installments.

The estate and generation-skipping transfer (GST) taxes are gradually phased-out, resulting in total repeal beginning in 2010. But under current law, the taxes are to be reinstated. After repeal and before reinstatement of the taxes, assets received from a decedent will have a carryover basis (i.e., the current stepped-up basis is eliminated). However, the decedent's estate can increase the basis of appreciated assets transferred up to a total of $1.3 million. An additional $3 million step-up is allowed for appreciated property transferred to the surviving spouse. Although the estate and GST taxes are scheduled to be repealed, the gift tax remains (with an increased applicable exclusion amount of $1 million).

Unified Gift and Estate Tax Rates

A unified rate structure was enacted in 1976, creating a table of uniform transfer tax rates that applies to cumulative lifetime (gift) and death (estate) transfers. (Before 1977, separate gift and estate tax systems existed.) The rates are applied to the sum of your adjusted taxable lifetime gifts made after 1976 and your gross estate less deductions. The federal gift or estate tax computed from the table is reduced by:

1. an applicable credit amount,

2. previously paid gift taxes on post-1976 gifts, and

3. a state death tax credit.

The Taxable Federal Estate

    Gross Estate

−   Allowable Deductions

=   **Federal Taxable Estate**

Gross Estate. This includes all property in which you own a beneficial interest when you die. The more obvious examples include cash, stocks, bonds (including tax-exempts), notes, real estate, business interests, artwork, and personal effects.

Allowable Deductions. Your gross estate is then reduced by the following items:

➤ Funeral expenses

➤ Administration expenses

➤ Claims against the estate

➤ Indebtedness associated with property included in the gross estate

➤ Casualty and theft losses incurred during administration

➤ Transfers to the surviving spouse

➤ Charitable contributions

➤ Family-owned-business deduction

Applicable Credit Amount

One of the credits deductible against the gross estate tax is the applicable credit amount. The amount for 2003 is $345,800, which will completely shelter $1 million (i.e., the applicable exclusion amount) from estate tax. Therefore, a taxable estate of $1 million or less will not pay any federal estate taxes (unless the applicable credit amount was previously used to shelter lifetime gifts). However, your estate may be subject to state inheritance taxes.

The applicable credit amount is allowed against cumulative taxes imposed on lifetime transfers and transfers at death. Thus, for example, in 2003, you could potentially make gifts totaling $1 million and not pay any gift taxes, or use the amount to shelter the transfer of assets at your death from estate taxes.

The estate and generation-skipping transfer taxes are scheduled to be repealed for decedents dying after December 31, 2009. However, under current law, the taxes are to be reinstated in 2011. The applicable exclusion amount for estate tax purposes gradually increases to a maximum of $3.5 million in 2009. (The GST exemption remains at $1,000,000, adjusted for inflation, until 2004, when it becomes the same as the estate tax applicable exclusion amount.)

WEEK TEN
MAP 10-29

What Is the Federal Gift Tax?
(refer to page 411)

Giving away your property during your lifetime is a powerful way to accomplish many of your wealth-transfer-planning goals and objectives. In addition, significant transfer and income tax savings can be generated from a properly structured lifetime giving program.

The federal gift tax is an excise tax imposed on gifts you make during your life. The gift may be direct (e.g., cash gift to your child) or indirect (e.g., cash gifted to a trust for the benefit of your child). The amount of the gift is the fair market value of the property at the date of the gift.

The Annual Gift Tax Exclusion

The gift tax is imposed on taxable gifts, which includes the total amount of gifts you make during the year less certain deductions. However, the total amount of taxable gifts you make during the year generally does not include the first $11,000 (for 2003) of qualified gifts you make to any (and there can be more than one) individual. This allowance is commonly referred to as the annual-gift-tax exclusion.

Gifts for Educational and Medical Purposes

You can pay unlimited amounts to educational or medical providers for certain tuition and medical expenses without having to pay any gift or generation-skipping transfer taxes on these amounts. These exclusions are in addition to the annual-gift-tax exclusion and represent an excellent (but often overlooked) opportunity for you to transfer property to benefit your children or grandchildren, and even parents and grandparents, with no gift tax effects.

Cumulative Nature of Gift Tax

The gift tax is computed on a cumulative basis that takes into account taxable gifts that you made in prior years. Generally, transfers that were taxable gifts under the applicable gift-tax laws at the time you made the gifts, net of exemptions and deductions applicable for those years, are added to your current year-taxable gifts to arrive at total taxable gifts. The tax is calculated on this amount but is offset by the items listed in "Unified Gift and Estate Tax Rates," below.

Unified Gift and Estate Tax Rates

A unified rate structure was enacted in 1976, creating a table of uniform transfer tax rates that apply to cumulative lifetime (gift) and death (estate) transfers. (Before 1977, separate gift and estate tax systems existed.) The rates are applied to both (1) the gifts you make during life, and, at your death, and (2) all gifts you made during your life plus the net assets included in your estate. The federal gift or estate tax computed from the table is reduced by:

1. an applicable credit amount,

2. previously paid gift taxes on post-1976 gifts, and

3. a state death-tax credit.

The estate and generation-skipping transfer taxes are scheduled to be repealed for decedents dying after December 31, 2009. However, under current law, the taxes are to be reinstated in 2011. The applicable exclusion amount for estate tax purposes gradually increases to a maximum of $3.5 million in 2009. (The GST exemption remains at $1,000,000, adjusted for inflation, until 2004 when it becomes the same as the estate tax applicable exclusion amount.)

Although estate and GST taxes are repealed beginning in 2010, the gift tax remains. For 2003, the applicable exclusion amount for gift-tax purposes is $1 million. However, unlike the estate and GST tax applicable exclusion amount, which gradually increases to $3.5 million, the amount for gift-tax purposes remains at $1 million.

Applicable Credit Amount

One of the credits deductible against the gift tax is the applicable credit amount. The applicable credit amount is simply the tax computed on a certain amount of assets (called the applicable exclusion amount) that the law allows you to exclude for purposes of calculating gift and estate tax. For example, the applicable credit amount for 2003 is $345,800. This credit, which offsets the calculated gift or estate tax, is calculated by applying the graduated gift and estate tax rates to the first $1 million of assets a person transfers during life or at death. The following shows you how the $345,800 applicable credit is calculated:

Tax on the first $1 million transferred based on the Unified Rate Schedule = $345,800 = Applicable Credit Amount (i.e., tax on $1 million of transfers).

The amount for 2003 is $345,800, which completely shelters $1 million (i.e., the applicable exclusion amount) from gift tax. For 2003, the applicable exclusion amount is $1 million. Therefore, if you make gifts totaling $1 million or less, you will not pay any federal gift taxes. However, the $1 million is for cumulative gifts. Thus, for example, if in prior years you used your applicable credit amount to shelter $500,000 of gifts from gift tax, in 2003 you can only shelter an additional $500,000 from gift tax.

Remember, the $11,000 annual exclusion and qualifying educational and medical gifts do not count towards this limit. Thus, for example, in 2003 you could make gifts of $11,000 each to 20 (or whatever number) different people without having to use any of your $1 million applicable exclusion amount.

ACKNOWLEDGMENTS

I am most grateful to Kathy, my partner and spouse, for believing in me and for making the sacrifices that accompanied 30 months of a first-time author's "book-birthing." I would have quit many times had it not been for her constant support and encouragement.

This book would look much different had it not been for the patient and persistent insistence of my writing coach, Michael Thunder, to find my own voice. Thank you, Michael.

Jerry Muth, my good friend, faithfully read each installment of the book and gave me encouragement to keep writing. His feedback was invaluable in merging the philosophical with the practical.

I am so thankful that good fortune brought Jan Nesset, project manager, along the path of this book. His diligent and untiring efforts to obtain permissions and review countless manuscript drafts played a critical role in this book's formation.

I am indebted to Kathy Sutton for her sensitive artistic renditions of each section of this book. Her soulful engagement provides a container in which to carry the principles of money groundedness into our day-to-day lives. Kathy's address is PO Box 267, Mancos, CO 81328 if you like her artwork.

Wes (Wink Winkler) and Lynn (Lisa Pedolsky), my real-life clients who shared their stories in the book are such an inspiration to me. They demonstrate that it is possible to live authentically and use money as a help rather than a hindrance in that journey.

I appreciate Bill Smith of *E7 Systems.com* who coordinated the CD production associated with this book. Bill's unselfish efforts and concern that the program be as user-friendly as possible were a great help to me.

Milt Adams and Judith Palmateer at *Beaver's Pond Press* were the bridge between concept and reality for this book. They pointed me in the right direction and gave me hope that publication was, in fact, possible!

Jay Monroe and Jack Caravella at *Mori Studio* in Saint Anthony, MN were invaluable in designing the book. None of my ideas or changes were ever met with anything but support and encouragement from Jay and Jack.

Paul Douglas of *Personal Producer* was instrumental in the final production of the TEN WEEKS CD. Without his tireless efforts, the hundreds of hours of recording would have been fruitless.

Many people at *Intuit, Inc.* made this dream of making the personal financial planning process accessible to anyone willing to invest his/her time a reality. Many thanks to Michael Zupa, Lisa Warshauer, and Jonathan Seckler in particular.

Bill Birza, my engineer friend, had the courage to fill Wally's shoes and sketch out his Electrical Diagram. I'm sure Wally would approve of Bill's rendition.

Without Lisa Schneiderman of *Schneiderman Public Relations*, I would have been lost as to how to deliver the book and related TEN WEEKS program to those who could benefit from it. Her soulful support and belief in the book were critical in my willingness to risk sharing the work in a broad context.

I am so thankful for each of my guests on the 2001 "Money Matters" a Radio Show series. The interviews with each of the following people has had a profound influence on the formation of this book: Karen Ramsey, Sheryl Garrett, Wynn Berven, Bill Bernstein, Jack Brill, Jerrold Mundis, Deborah Knuckey, Steve Rickles, David Heitmiller, Jacqueline Blix, Bill Plotkin, David Whyte, Mark Nepo, and Wayne Muller.

I am deeply indebted to each of the 11 families who were willing to participate in the TEN WEEKS INITIAL PROGRAM. It is their testimonials that confirm the hope that money and happiness can coexist in our practical, day-to-day lives.

CONTRIBUTIONS TO MORE THAN ONE BOOK SECTION

Julia Cameron

Many margin quotes used in my book were found in *The Artist's Way* (©1992 by Julia Cameron and published by G.P. Putnam's Sons) and are used here under the guidelines of "fair use."

Pema Chödrön

The excerpts (in Weeks Six & Seven) from *Comfortable with Uncertainty* by Pema Chödrön ©2002 are reprinted by arrangement with Shambhala Publications, Inc., Boston, *www.shambhala.com.*

The excerpt (in Section Four) from *The Places That Scare You* by Pema Chödrön ©2001 is reprinted by arrangement with Shambhala Publications, Inc., Boston, *www.shambhala.com.*

Bo Lozoff

Excerpts and quotes from *It's a Meaningful Life—It Just Takes Practice* by Bo Lozoff Copyright ©2000 Bo Lozoff, used with permission from Lark Productions.

The excerpt in Week Ten from an interview with Mr. Lozoff and *The Sun* magazine was used with permission from Bo Lozoff and *The Sun.*

Other works written by Mr. Lozoff can be accessed via *www.humankindness.org.*

Wayne Muller

Excerpts from *Sabbath—Restoring the Sacred Rhythm of Rest,* ©1999 by Wayne Muller, is used by permission of Bantam Books, a division of Random House, Inc.

I highly recommend all of Rev. Muller's books, including; *Legacy of the Heart—How, Then, Shall We Live?—Learning to Pray: How We Find Heaven on Earth*

For more information about these works, please contact *www.breadforthejourney.org*

Jerrold Mundis

Many of the margin quotations in this book were drawn from Jerrold Mundis's own fine book *Making Peace with Money.* I am grateful to him for his permission to use his work this way in my own. I highly recommend all three of his books on money; *Earn What You Deserve: How to Stop Underearning & Start Thriving.* New York: Bantam Books, 1995. *How to Get Out of Debt, Stay Out of Debt & Live Prosperously.* Revised edition. New York: Bantam Books, 2003. *Making Peace with Money.* Kansas City, MO: Andrews McMeel, 1999.

Jerrold may be reached through his website at *www.mundismoney.com.*

Jacob Needleman

The excerpts (Ten Week's Introduction and Week One/Two) from *Money and the Meaning of Life*, ©1991 by Jacob Needleman, are used with permission of Doubleday, a division of Random House, Inc.

The excerpt from Jacob Needleman's book *Money and the Meaning of Life* (©1991) in Week Ten is used with permission of Random House, Inc. under the provisions of Fair Use.

Mark Nepo

Excerpts from *The Book of Awakening* by Mark Nepo are reprinted with permission from Conari Press, an imprint of Red Wheel/Weiser. To order *The Book of Awakening*, please call 1(800) 423-7087.

Excerpts from *Acre of Light* by Mark Nepo are reprinted with permission of Greenfield Review Press. To order *Acre of Light*, please call (518) 584-1728. *Acre of Light* is also available as an audiotape under the title, *Inside the Miracle*, from Parabola Audio Library. Please call 1 (800) 560-MYTH.

I am deeply grateful to Mark Nepo for his generous contribution to this work through the following poems: "Look Around," "Practicing," "Endgame," and "Stripping of Our Will." In addition to *The Book of Awakening*, Mark has written the following fine books: *Acre of Light; Fire Without Witness; God, the Maker of the Bed and the Painter;* and *The Exquisite Risk*, due out from Harmony Books (Spring 2004)

The Sun magazine—Sy Safransky, editor

I would like to thank *The Sun* magazine for allowing me to draw a sizeable number of margin quotations from material published in its works. *The Sun* can be reached at *www.thesunmagazine.org*.

Eckhart Tolle

Excerpts from *The Power of Now* ©1999 by Eckhart Tolle are used with permission from New World Library, Novato, CA 94949, *www.newworldlibrary.com*.

David Whyte

I acknowledge the generous contribution of David Whyte for the permission to use the following poems:

"Self Portrait" from *Fire in the Earth* © 1992 by David Whyte. Used with permission from Many Rivers Press, Langley, Washington.

"All the True Vows" from *The House of Belonging* ©1997 by David Whyte. Many Rivers Press. Used with permission from Many Rivers Press, Langley, Washington.

"The Well of Grief" from *Where Many Rivers Meet* ©1990 by David Whyte. Used with permission from Many Rivers Press, Langley, Washington.

"It Is Not Enough" from *Where Many Rivers Meet* ©1990 by David Whyte. Used with permission from Many Rivers Press, Langley, Washington.

"Sweet Darkness" from *The House of Belonging* ©1997 by David Whyte. Used with permission from Many Rivers Press, Langley, Washington.

"The Opening of Eyes" from *Songs for Coming Home* ©1989 by David Whyte. Used with permission from Many Rivers Press, Langley, Washington.

"The Sun" excerpt from *The House of Belonging* ©1997 by David Whyte. Used with permission from Many Rivers Press, Langley, Washington.

"The Journey" from *The House of Belonging* ©1997 by David Whyte. Used with permission from Many Rivers Press, Langley, Washington.

"Loaves and Fishes" from *The House of Belonging* ©1997 by David Whyte. Used with permission from Many Rivers Press, Langley, Washington.

"At Home" from *The House of Belonging* ©1997 by David Whyte. Used with permission from Many Rivers Press, Langley, Washington.

I also am grateful for the use of an excerpt from *The Heart Aroused* by David Whyte reprinted with the permission of the publisher Currency Doubleday ©1994.

Other excerpts, as noted, were taken from *Crossing the Unknown Sea*, ©2001 by David Whyte. Used by permission of Riverhead Books, an imprint of Penguin Group (USA), Inc.

A complete listing of David's works is available at *www.davidwhyte.com*.

OTHER CONTRIBUTORS—LISTED BY WEEK

Section Two

Scripture taken from *THE MESSAGE.* ©1993, 1994, 1995, by Eugene H. Peterson. Used by permission of NavPress Publishing Group.

Weeks One & Two

The poem "Lost" is from *Traveling Light: Collected and New Poems*, ©1999 by David Wagoner. Used with permission of the poet and the University of Illinois Press.

The song, "When I Lost My Faith" by John Gorka is from his album *The Company You Keep*, produced by Red House Records.

Week Three

The Rainer Marie Rilke quote was cited from *Rilke on Love and Other Difficulties*, ©1975 by John J.L. Mood. Used by permission of W. W. Norton & Company.

The first Robert Johnson quote is a brief passage on page 12 in *Contentment: A Way to True Happiness,* ©1999 by Robert A. Johnson and Jerry M. Ruhl. Reprinted by permission of HarperCollins Publishers, Inc.

The second Robert Johnson quote is a brief passage on page 80 from *He: Understanding Masculine Psychology,* Revised Edition, ©1989 by Robert A. Johnson. Reprinted by permission of HarperCollins Publishers, Inc.

Scripture taken from *THE MESSAGE.* ©1993, 1994, 1995, by Eugene H. Peterson. Used by permission of NavPress Publishing Group.

The quote by Charles Gray was taken from *Toward a Nonviolent Economics* ©1994, by Charles Gray. Used with permission from the author.

Week Four

The writings of 'Wes' and 'Lynn' are used by permission of Waldemar (Wink) Winkler, and Lisa Pedolsky.

Week Five

Don't Worry, Be Happy, lyrics by Bobby McFerrin used by permission by the artist and ProbNoblem Music/BMI.

Bad Moon Rising ©1969 lyrics by John Fogerty used by permission. Jondora Music (BMI). Courtesy of Fantasy, Inc. All Rights Reserved.

The quote by John Welwood is from *Ordinary Magic* ©1992, by John Welwood. Reprinted by arrangement with Shambhala Publications, Inc., Boston, *www.shambhala.com.*

The excerpted passage from Rose Wild is from an article entitled "Readers Write" published in *The Sun* Magazine. Reprinted with permission from Rose Wild.

Nickel and Dimed: On Not Getting by in America ©2001, by Barbara Ehrenreich. Reprinted by permission of Henry Holt and Company, LLC.

The passage from *Let the Mountains Talk, Let the Rivers Run* ©2000, by David Brower. Reprinted with permission from New Society Publishers.

I gratefully acknowledge Dr. Bill Plotkin and the staff of Animas Valley Institute in Durango, Colorado (*www.animas.org*) for facilitating my own Vision Quest experience. I highly recommend Dr. Plotkin's book, *Soulcraft: Crossing into the Mysteries of Nature and Psyche,* released September, 2003 by New World Library.

The Consumer's Guide to Effective Environmental Choices by Dr. Michael Brower and Dr. Warren Leon. ©1999, Union of Concered Scientists, Three Rivers Press

Week Six

The lyrics from "Life Is Just a Bowl of Cherries," performed by Fosse, are reprinted with the permission of Warner Chappell Music, Inc.

The lyrics from "Face Yourself," by Michael Hedges are from the album *Watching My Life Go By*, published by Windham Hill.

The excerpts from *Investing with Your Values* ©1999, by Hal Brill, Jack A. Brill, and Cliff Feigenbaum. Bloomberg Press, are used by permission of the authors.

The excerpts from *The Four Pillars of Investing* ©2002 and *The Intelligent Asset Allocator* ©2001 by William J. Bernstein, are reprinted with the permissin of McGraw-Hill Companies, Inc.

The excerpt from "East Coker" in *Four Quartets* ©1940 by T.S. Eliot and renewed 1968 by Esme Valerie Eliot, is reprinted by permission of Harcourt, Inc.

Week Seven

The lyrics from "Thank U" by Alanis Morrissette are produced under the Maverick label.

"The Man Watching" is from *Selected Poems of Rainer Maria Rilke*, ©1981 edited and translated by Robert Bly. Reprinted by permission of HarperCollins Publishers, Inc.

The quote from Al Neipris appeared in the May, 2003 issue (# 329) of *The Sun* magazine and is used with the permission of the author and publisher.

The Wealth Management Index, ©1997, by Ross Levin, is published by Times Mirror Higher Education Group.

Week Eight

Many of the quotations regarding taxes are from *www.taxanlysts.com*

The excerpt from, *The Careless Society*, by John Knight, is published by Basic Books (Perseus), reprinted May, 1996.

The quote from the Buddha in Week Eight was taken from *How Then Shall We Live?* ©1996 by Wayne Muller. Reprinted by permission of Random House, Inc.

The excerpts from the interview with Frances Moore Lappé are from issue 41 of the *Fast Company* magazine, *www.fastcompany.com*

Excerpt from *Passion for Pilgrimage* ©1989, by Alan Jones is used with acknowledgement from Morehouse Publishing.

The quote by Paul Hawken, as well as the material in MAP 8-28, are excerpts from *The Ecology of Commerce* by Paul Hawken ©1993 by Paul Hawken. Reprinted by permission of HarperCollins Publishers, Inc.

The quote by Deb Brewer is excerpted from an article by Christine Gillette and reprinted here with permission from the *Portsmouth Herald*.

Week Nine

The lyrics from "Cat's in the Cradle," written by Harry & Sandy Chapin, are reprinted with the permission of Warner Chappell Music, Inc.

The quote by Thich Hhat Hanh is from *Ordinary Magic* ©1992, by John Welwood. Reprinted by arrangement with Shambhala Publications, Inc., Boston, *www.shambhala.com*.

Excerpts from *The Celtic Way of Evangelism* © 2002, by George G. Hunter III. (February 2000) Used by permission of Abingdon Press.

The excerpt is from the book *Social Security Under the Gun* ©2003, by Arthur Benavie, was published by Palgrave Macmillan™.

"It's Possible" is from *Selected Poems of Rainer Maria Rilke*, ©1981 edited and translated by Robert Bly. Reprinted by permission of HarperCollins Publishers, Inc.

Week Ten

Scripture taken from *THE MESSAGE*. ©1993, 1994, 1995, by Eugene H. Peterson. Used by permission of NavPress Publishing Group.

Section Four

The quote by Rabbi Harold Kushner was taken from *Handbook for the Soul*, ©1995, edited by Richard Carlson and Benjamin Shield, and published by Little, Brown, and Company.

Money Attention Pages

A significant portion of material in the Money Attention Page (MAP) section of this publication was used with permission of Quickfinder, Inc. of Minnetonka, MN (*www.quickfinder.com* & (800) 510-8997).

Some materials in the Money Attention Page (MAP) section of this publication was used with permission of Practitioner's Publishing Company. *www.ppcnet.com* and (800) 323-8724.

Some materials in the Money Attention Page (MAP) section of this publication were reproduced with the permission of Kettley Publishing Company, 20271 S.W. Birch Street, Second Floor, Newport Beach, CA 92660 (800) 777-3162.

Material from *Nolo* ©2003, reprinted with permission from the publisher, Nolo, *http://www.nolo.com*.

Ten Weeks CD's

The Quicken® screen shots were used with permission of Intuit, Inc. Quicken 2004 Deluxe screen shots © 2003 Intuit, Inc. All rights reserved. Quicken is a registered trademark of Intuit, Inc.

FINAL NOTE

An intensive effort has been made to clear all reprint permissions for this book. This process has been complicated; if any required acknowledgments have been omitted, it is unintentional. If notified, the author will be pleased to rectify any omission in future editions.